THE PROVINCE OF PROSE

THE PROVINCE
OF PROSE

SECOND EDITION

Edited by
WILLIAM R. KEAST
Cornell University

and
ROBERT E. STREETER
University of Chicago

New York
HARPER & BROTHERS, PUBLISHERS

Contents

CONTENTS

PART TWO. *Writers at Large*

SUPPLEMENTS

CONTENTS

Preface

THE ESSAYS collected in this book are intended to provide varied and interesting materials for reading, discussion, and writing. Although we regard these activities as correlative, we have arranged the essays to give special prominence to problems of writing in Part One and to problems for analysis and discussion in Part Two. Topics for written assignments arise throughout. The essays in Part One illustrate or discuss four problems that every writer (and, by implication, every careful reader) has to face: defining his subject, fixing his point of view toward it, finding an appropriate procedure for treating it, and expressing his views clearly and responsibly. The emphasis in Part Two is on content rather than on procedures: in some of the sections the essays are grouped under a common theme or interest ("The American Experience," "Man in a Diversity of Cultures"), in others under a common structure or form ("Biography," "History").

Our intention in these groupings is to set the essays in meaningful contexts and to stimulate discussion by displaying significant similarities and contrasts in content or approach. We have sought, however, to make the headings loose enough so that the selections can easily be used in other arrangements and combinations. Many cross connections, in addition to those obvious within each section, will be found among the essays. Thus, although the selections from Hawthorne and Twain in the opening section illustrate the problem of defining the writer's subject, they may equally well be used in conjunction with the essays in the second section to get at the problem of point of view. The selections from Hawthorne and from the three American travelers in the opening section are relevant to the problems treated by the essayists in the section on "The American Experience," and the essays on Thoreau's *Walden* in Part One may be considered under this heading too. The essays by Hawthorne, Howells, Twain, and James from the opening section might be combined with the essays by Rebecca West, Trollope, Alistair Cooke, and Tocqueville from later sections to form a group on the attitudes of the foreign observer. Possibilities for recombinations of this sort are numerous, and a special effort has been made in the questions to suggest a number of them. All of the essays in Part Two, of course, illustrate the writing problems treated in Part One, for those who wish to deal with these problems more fully. Most of the essays in Part One, in turn, can easily be ranged under one or more of the rubrics in Part Two.

We have chosen each essay for its intrinsic values, and not merely for its suitability to the various divisions of the book. We have tried to make a fresh selection, avoiding essays that have become hackneyed through repeated appearance in anthologies, and bringing in writers who have something different to say and vigorous or individual ways of saying it. Although most of the essays are modern, we have not aimed at the merely contemporary, and we have represented some of the characteristic styles, attitudes, and problems of earlier writers. The essays range considerably in length and difficulty, as well as in subject, procedure, and style, so that there should be something here for many tastes and interests. By concentrating on essays based on direct observation, we hope to provide materials well within the range of the student's own experience or imagination; but we have included several examples of more abstract discussion, to round out the student's introduction to the major modes of statement, and to help him extend his interests and sensibilities.

Each essay is followed by two groups of questions. The first group, "Understanding the Text," is addressed to matters of purpose, structure, style, and the like. The second group, "Topics for Discussion and Writing," is designed to raise broader questions for comment or criticism, to suggest topics for writing, and to link the essay to other selections in the book. We have probably supplied more questions than any instructor will have time or inclination to use, but we have aimed at giving a varied choice, realizing that where questions are concerned, one instructor's meat may be another's poison.

The first two supplements are a special feature of this book. Supplement 1, "Writing, Reading, and Reasoning," deals with problems of logic, and Supplement 2, "Taking Another Look," with the question of revision. Neither is offered as a definitive treatment of its subject; but both, we believe, will provide valuable materials for a realistic treatment of these two important topics, which are too frequently presented in abstract terms.

For generous and useful advice in the preparation of this book we are grateful to several colleagues, particularly to Ferris Cronkhite, Wilma Ebbit, Norman F. Maclean, and William M. Sale, Jr. For their welcome assistance in getting the manuscript ready for the press we are indebted to Winston Hannesson, Janet Hunter, and Mary Alice Keast.

W. R. K.
R. E. S.

Preface to the Second Edition

IN THIS edition we have retained, with a few modifications, the general plan and organization of our book. But we have taken the opportunity of a revision to delete a number of essays that seemed, whatever their other merits, to offer least scope for student and instructor in freshman writing courses, to introduce some twenty-two new essays that we hope will prove interesting and useful, and to regroup some of the essays retained from the first edition.

We wish to express our gratitude to the many friends and colleagues whose interest in the book has led them to make suggestions for its improvement. And we want to record our indebtedness to Nancy West for her skillful help with the manuscript.

W. R. K.
R. E. S.

PART ONE

The Writer's Problems

Introduction

———⌣———

IF WE ask ourselves what a writer must do in any job of writing—whether he is describing an object, narrating a sequence of events, setting forth a definition, or trying to persuade an audience to a particular view —we can distinguish four fundamental problems with which he must deal:

1. He must define his subject and assemble his materials in relation to a specific purpose.

2. He must fix his point of view toward his subject.

3. He must find an appropriate method of procedure for treating his material.

4. He must choose the right language for what he has to say.

These four problems, while they are stated here as the problems of the writer, are no less important for the reader, though the reader faces them in different forms. The writer must assemble his materials; the reader must ask whether the right materials have been assembled. The writer must limit and fix the subject; the reader must locate the true subject of the text he is reading in order to understand it. The writer must fix his point of view and adopt a consistent approach to his subject; the reader must isolate the assumptions made by the writer in order to judge the nature and value of his statements. The writer has to find the best method of organizing and treating his material; the reader must understand the method he has chosen and come to some judgment about its utility and value. The writer must find the right words and sentences; the reader must be conscious of the contribution which diction and style make to the text. It is not always true that excellence in reading means excellence in writing, because among other things the writer has to find or invent his material and contrive good sentences, while the reader does not have to do these things. But the problems of the writer and the reader have so

3

much in common that practice in one usually produces improvement in the other. The kind of reading in which you try to think through the reasons which led a writer to proceed as he did is certain to increase your own power, when writing, to deal with similar problems.

These four problems, therefore, are central both to the task of writing and to the task of critical reading. Although it is convenient and helpful to consider these matters separately, it is necessary to remember that, in actual practice, the writer deals with no one of them in isolation from the others. For the writer's final task, which is broader than any of these specific categories of problems, is to arrange the entire composition so that the parts will be in proper balance with the whole, and so that the whole will fit the subject and the purpose. To meet this objective, the writer must ask himself a series of important questions: Is the scale on which the different parts are treated the right scale, considering their intrinsic interest or difficulty and their contribution to the whole? Is the order among the several parts the best order? Are the transitions from one part to the next clear? Are there signposts from time to time to inform the reader where he is going? Is the subject being continuously treated, or is there deadwood that can be pruned out? Are the tone, the level of approach, the attitude toward the audience, and the point of view consistent throughout? Most important of all, does the piece really say what it was intended to say—or does the reader have to do most of his own work in extracting the meaning?

Similarly, although the four fundamental problems of the writer have been listed here in a numerical order, they must not be thought of as invariable stages in the sequence of writing. Naturally the writer must decide on his subject before he starts to write; that problem has to be solved before he begins to worry about the procedure he is going to follow. But although you think you have your subject pretty well defined and limited, you will frequently discover your real subject—the precise point on which you want to focus your attention—only after you have begun to write. Again, the writer usually decides on his method of procedure before he writes many sentences. But the act of composition often suggests changes in the basic plan of attack, and in any case the plan remains only a plan until it is realized in sentences. Writing always involves (unless one is a natural genius or wonderfully lucky, neither of which we can count on) a great deal of backing and filling, of drafting and redrafting, of writing down and tearing up and throwing away. Probably the sequence is never the same for any two writers, or for the same writer on any two occasions. So we must think of these as distinct though related problems with which the writer—and as we have said, the reader too in his way—has to deal, in whatever order the given subject and his own preferred method of work suggest.

The four sections in Part One of this book bring together essays designed to help you understand these fundamental problems in reading and writing. The introductions to the sections are intended to suggest the more important features of each problem. The questions and exercises call for careful analysis of the essays and give opportunities for discussion of the larger implications of each problem and for written assignments. Close study of the essays and questions should help you see how careful writers have worked with these problems; they should help you face them more skillfully and confidently in your own writing. You will notice that the essays illustrate the inseparability of the problems. Each essay is a unified whole, which means that the writer has embodied solutions to all these problems in his writing. The essay may illustrate the use of a particular method of procedure or a powerful handling of language, but you will want to see the writer's method or style in relation to the other aspects of the writing process. The various elements must finally be viewed in their composition—organically, instead of as lifeless parts—if we are to come to a full understanding of the writer's problems.

1. The Writer and His Subject

Nathaniel Hawthorne Describes Two Weddings in Manchester Cathedral

From *The English Note-Books*
From *Our Old Home*

Mark Twain Describes the Dawn on the Mississippi River

From *The Adventures of Tom Sawyer*
From *Life on the Mississippi*
From *The Adventures of Huckleberry Finn*

Three American Travelers Describe Venice

WILLIAM DEAN HOWELLS, from *Venetian Life*
MARK TWAIN, from *The Innocents Abroad*
HENRY JAMES, from *Portraits of Places*

THE FIRST of the writer's problems is the problem of the subject. The subject is the thing we worry about first as we pace the floor trying to get ready to write tomorrow's theme. Once chosen, the subject in large measure determines everything else the writer does, for a piece of writing is a treatment of a subject. The subject is no less crucial for the reader. It is to the subject that the reader first attends; and what he finally judges is the interest, cogency, persuasiveness, or penetration with which the subject has been treated. What can we say about the "problem of the subject" that will be generally useful, that will apply to writings of the many different kinds you will be called upon to do?

Probably no two people find the same subjects interesting or the same subjects dull. Your classic may be my trash and vice versa. But we have

6

all surely had the experience of reading something of absorbing interest on a subject we had always found dull before. And we have all had the experience of being bored stiff by something on a subject that we are usually interested in. What makes the difference? Isn't it the ability of the writer to see interest or significance in a subject, however unpromising it may seem to the superficial eye, and to set what he sees before us in so compelling a way as to change our customary attitudes toward the subject? We may grant that certain subjects may offer more to the attentive eye; we may admit that one has to be gifted with a special quality of mind to find much of anything in certain subjects. But even if we make these concessions, we will be left with the central fact: Given a subject of whatever inherent quality you like, differences in the effect of what is said about it will depend not so much on the subject itself as on the interest, curiosity, commitment, or power of the mind that deals with it.

We all know people to whom interesting things always seem to happen—people who are always ready with a new and fascinating account of their experiences. These people don't have to be mountain climbers or hot-rod drivers, either. As often as not they live normal and predictable lives just like the rest of us. But whereas nothing very remarkable seems to happen to most of us, these lucky ones lead lives of rich or hilarious adventure. If we look more closely, we will usually discover that the same things that happen to them also happen to us. The difference is that they are always alert to the ridiculous, the laughable, the paradoxical, the poignant, the outrageous. Things fall into place for them in interesting patterns because they are ready to receive them in such patterns. Some people, as we have heard, are accident-prone. These people, we might say, are perception-prone. They see things the rest of us miss, even when we have the same chance to observe them. It is this perceptiveness, this habit of making something out of the materials of experience, this ability to see in a subject what isn't there until it is seen—it is this quality of mind that underlies all really good writing. It is this quality of mind that we must cultivate if we are to improve as writers.

This notion carries with it an important corollary for the writer. There is really no such thing as a "subject" until it has been conceived in the writer's mind. To conceive of anything is to have ideas about it, to set limits to it, to fix it in the mind, to reduce it to a structure of ideas. Most of us, as we get ready to write, haven't really *conceived* of our subject. We entertain a vague notion of writing about college education, let us say, or freedom of speech or vitamins or the Brooklyn Bridge. These are not subjects. We have no real conception of them—not the kind of conception we have, no doubt, of our last date before leaving for college—vivid, clear, and meaningful. Suppose, in wrestling with the problem of a subject, we decide on "The Building of the Brooklyn Bridge." Now we are beginning to get somewhere, but only beginning; we have the glimmer of an idea, but so far it is little more than a principle of exclusion: it suggests some of the things we can leave out, but it scarcely tells us what to put in. And above all, it doesn't have any center, any focus, any point at which we are going to try to concentrate our own thoughts and get the reader to concentrate his. So we think some more and come up with the notion that what really interests us about the building of the Brooklyn Bridge is not primarily how long it took, or how many workers were killed, or how much stone and steel was used, or how original the design was, but how ironic that Roebling, the designer, should have died before his great work was completed. We are still quite a way from a paper, but we have our point. A dead body of material has begun to come to life in our minds. We have ceased to be passive to the random play of thoughts and impressions and have begun to exert our own authority over our material. We have a direction for our reading or our observation. As we go on, each decision we make in collecting material, planning the arrangement, and setting down sentences will be controlled by our conception of the subject. At the same time, our conception of the subject will become sharper and fuller—and perhaps it will even be modified in important ways by what we do. But the writer has now established himself at the center; the subject is no longer something outside him; it is truly *his* subject.

Making the subject his own enables the writer to define his role: to identify the quality of his relationship to his subject and to his audience. He can decide whether he is to approach his material and his reader as, say, the Expert, the Informed Layman, or (like James Thurber in so many of his essays) the Lost Innocent or Bewildered Victim. He knows whether his approach is to be that of the Witness, the Recorder, the Informant, the Teacher, the Critic, or the Judge; whether he will address his reader as Friend or Stranger, Petitioner or Advocate. His conception of his role will of course grow out of his purpose; it will be affected by the occasion for writing and by the kind and amount of his knowledge about the subject. His conception of his role will affect the tone the writer uses in dealing with his material, and it will be conditioned by his mode of access to the subject—whether through direct observation and participation, or indirectly through reading or reflection, or both.

Having a clear conception of his subject, and having chosen the role in which he is going to approach it, the writer is prepared to deal with a further range of problems. He can now make sound decisions on such questions as *relevance, completeness, scale,* and *level of treatment.* He will know more clearly what topics have to be covered and what can be omitted; he will have a basis on which to eliminate everything that cannot justify itself by its direct contribution. Having a clear notion of the view of the subject he wishes to communicate to his reader, he will know when he is finished; he will be less likely to run on beyond the useful limit of statement or to leave too much for the reader to fill in for himself. Given the set limits within which he is to write (whether a 1000- or a 5000-word paper, say), he will be able to control the scale on which he develops each part of his subject so that each will be able to make its proper contribution and the whole will emerge as he conceives of it. And his view of the subject and of his own role in relation to it and to his reader will enable the writer to fix the appropriate level at which to treat it: whether as a personal account or as an objective one, as a statement about specific objects or actions or as a more generalized statement about groups or classes, and so forth.

We have distinguished between the external subject matter of a piece of writing and the true subject, between the material and what the writer finds or sees in it. This implies a distinction between two kinds of unity: between the kind of unity which comes from the fact that all the statements relate somehow to the general topic and the kind of unity which arises from their dependence on a single controlling conception. But here we must introduce a word of caution. The subject in writing is what the writer conceives it to be; the more sharply, the more fully, the more perceptively he conceives it, the more truly it is his subject. But we do not mean to imply that the subject becomes true or interesting or important merely because it is *his* conception. We are not advocating self-expression as an end in itself. The point is not that your writing acquires interest or value simply because it is *your* writing, or that anything goes so long as you can say, "This is the way I see it." That is not the point at all. What is silly or inaccurate or simple-minded or fatuous doesn't become mature, true, or perceptive merely because it is ours. Our views have to establish themselves in terms of the common criteria of truth, adequacy, maturity, and interest. The point of importance is not that writing puts a premium on our personal views but that writing requires us to have views which we can present.

The three groups of essays in this section have been chosen to show the relation between the subject matter and the true subject of a piece of writing. In the first group Nathaniel Hawthorne "works up" observations that he had previously recorded in his notebooks. In the second group Mark Twain describes the same subject on three different occasions, and in three very different ways. In the third group a single subject is variously handled by three different writers. Taken together, these essays should help make clear the essential distinction between the subject as that which exists in its own right outside the writer and the subject as conceived and "made" by him, between the subject as something that might be treated by anyone and the writer's subject as his own.

Nathaniel Hawthorne Describes Two Weddings in Manchester Cathedral

NATHANIEL HAWTHORNE, like a number of other American authors of the nineteenth century, combined periods of government service with his career as a writer. He was for a time customs officer in Salem, Massachusetts; readers of *The Scarlet Letter* find that experience reflected in the long introductory chapter on "The Custom House." In 1853, famous as the author of *The Scarlet Letter*, *The House of the Seven Gables*, and other books, Hawthorne was appointed American consul at Liverpool, a post he held for four years. During his stay in England, Hawthorne traveled widely and observed acutely the country and society from which America had sprung, recording his observations in "seven closely written volumes of journal." When he returned to the United States Hawthorne quarried from these English notebooks the material for a series of articles on "English scenery, life, and character," published in the *Atlantic* between 1860 and 1863. In 1863 they were gathered together in a volume called *Our Old Home*.

In the selections that follow we can watch Hawthorne making his on-the-spot observations and subsequently reshaping the same material for his articles on England. On two visits to Manchester in 1857, Hawthorne chanced to see weddings performed in Manchester Cathedral; he recorded each occasion in his journal. Stimulated no doubt by the social contrast implicit in the two events, he brought the materials in these two notebook entries together as part of the chapter called "Some Glimpses of English Poverty" in *Our Old Home*.

From The English Note-Books

NATHANIEL HAWTHORNE

I

WE TOOK the train for Manchester, over pretty much the same route that I travelled last year. Many of the higher hills in Yorkshire were white with snow, which, in our lower region, softened into rain; but as we approached Manchester, the western sky reddened, and gave promise of better weather. We arrived at nearly eight o'clock, and put up at the Palatine Hotel. In the evening I scrawled away at my journal till past ten o'clock; for I have really made it a matter of conscience to keep a tolerably full record of my travels, though conscious that everything good escapes in the process. In the morning we went out and visited the Manchester Cathedral, a particularly black and grimy edifice, containing some genuine old wood-carvings within the choir. We stayed a good while, in order to see some people married. One couple, with their groomsman and bride's-maid, were sitting within the choir; but when the clergyman was robed and ready, there entered five other couples, each attended by groomsman and bride's-maid. They were all of the lower orders; one or two respectably dressed, but most of them poverty-stricken,—the men in their ordinary loafer's or laborer's attire, the women with their poor, shabby shawls drawn closely about them; faded untimely, wrinkled with penury and care; nothing fresh, virgin-like, or hopeful about them; joining themselves to their mates with the idea of making their own misery less intolerable by adding another's to it. All the six couples stood up in a row before the altar, with the groomsmen and bride's-maids in a row behind them; and the clergyman proceeded to marry them in such a way that it almost seemed to make every man and woman the husband and wife of every other. However, there were some small portions of the service directed towards each separate couple; and they appeared to assort themselves in their own fashion afterwards, each one saluting his bride with a kiss. The clergyman, the sexton, and the clerk all seemed to find something funny in this affair; and the woman who admitted us into the church smiled too, when she told us that a wedding-party was waiting to be married. But I think it was the saddest thing we have seen since leaving home; though funny enough if one likes to look at it from a ludicrous point of view. This mob of poor marriages was caused by the fact that no marriage fee is paid during Easter. (April, 1857)

II

Passing by the gateway of the Manchester Cathedral the other morning, on my way to the station, I found a crowd collected, and, high overhead, the bells were chiming for a wedding. These chimes of bells are exceedingly impressive, so broadly gladsome as they are, filling the whole air, and every nook of one's heart, with sympathy. They are good for a people to rejoice with, and good also for a marriage, because through all their joy there is something solemn,—a tone of that voice which we have heard so often at funerals. It is good to see how everybody, up to this old age of the world, takes an interest in weddings, and seems to have a faith that now, at last, a couple have come together to make each other happy. The high, black, rough old cathedral tower sent out its chime of bells as earnestly as for any bridegroom and bride that came to be married five hundred years ago. I went into the churchyard, but there was such a throng of people on its pavement of flat tombstones, and especially such a cluster along the pathway by which the bride was to depart, that I could only see a white dress waving along, and really do not know whether she was a beauty or a fright. The happy pair got into a post-chaise that was waiting at the gate, and immediately drew some crimson curtains, and so vanished into their Paradise. There were two other post-chaises and pairs, and all three had postilions in scarlet. This is the same cathedral where, last May, I saw a dozen couples married in the lump. (August, 1857)

From "Glimpses of English Poverty," in Our Old Home (1863)

NATHANIEL HAWTHORNE

I WAS once present at the wedding of some poor English people, and was deeply impressed by the spectacle, though by no means with such proud and delightful emotions as seem to have affected all England on the recent occasion of the marriage of its Prince. It was in the Cathedral at Manchester, a particularly black and grim old structure, into which I had stepped to examine some ancient and curious wood-carvings within the choir. The woman in attendance greeted me with a smile (which always glimmers forth on the feminine visage, I know not why, when a wedding is in question), and asked me to take a seat in the nave till some poor parties were married, it being the Easter holidays, and a good time for them to marry, because no fees would be demanded by the clergyman. I sat down accordingly, and soon the parson and his clerk appeared at the altar, and a considerable crowd of people made their entrance at a side-door, and ranged themselves in a long, huddled line across the chancel. They were my acquaintances of the poor streets, or persons in a precisely similar condition of life, and were now come to their marriage ceremony in just such garbs as I had always seen them wear: the men in their loafer's coats, out at elbows, or their laborer's jackets, defaced with grimy toil; the women drawing their shabby shawls tighter about their shoulders, to hide the raggedness beneath; all of them unbrushed, unshaven, unwashed, uncombed, and wrinkled with penury and care; nothing virgin-like in the brides, nor hopeful or energetic in the bridegrooms;—they were, in short, the mere rags and tatters of the human race, whom some east-wind of evil omen, howling along the streets, had chanced to sweep together into an unfragrant heap. Each and all of them, conscious of his

14

or her individual misery, had blundered into the strange miscalculation
of supposing that they could lessen the sum of it by multiplying it into
the misery of another person. All the couples (and it was difficult, in such
a confused crowd, to compute exactly their number) stood up at once,
and had execution done upon them in the lump, the clergyman addressing only small parts of the service to each individual pair, but so man-
aging the larger portion as to include the whole company without the
trouble of repetition. By this compendious contrivance, one would apprehend, he came dangerously near making every man and woman the husband or wife of every other; nor, perhaps, would he have perpetrated
much additional mischief by the mistake; but, after receiving a benedic-
tion in common, they assorted themselves in their own fashion, as they
only knew how, and departed to the garrets, or the cellars, or the un-
sheltered street-corners, where their honeymoon and subsequent lives
were to be spent. The parson smiled decorously, the clerk and the sexton
grinned broadly, the female attendant tittered almost aloud, and even the
married parties seemed to see something exceedingly funny in the affair;
but for my part, though generally apt enough to be tickled by a joke,
I laid it away in my memory as one of the saddest sights I ever looked
upon.

   Not very long afterwards, I happened to be passing the same venerable
cathedral, and heard a clang of joyful bells, and beheld a bridal party
coming down the steps towards a carriage and four horses, with a portly
coachman and two postilions, that waited at the gate. One parson and one
service had amalgamated the wretchedness of a score of paupers; a Bishop
and three or four clergymen had combined their spiritual might to forge
the golden links of this other marriage-bond. The bridegroom's mien had
a sort of careless and kindly English pride; the bride floated along in her
white drapery, a creature so nice and delicate that it was a luxury to see
her, and a pity that her silk slippers should touch anything so grimy as
the old stones of the churchyard avenue. The crowd of ragged people,
who always cluster to witness what they may of an aristocratic wedding,
broke into audible admiration of the bride's beauty and the bridegroom's
manliness, and uttered prayers and ejaculations (possibly paid for in
alms) for the happiness of both. If the most favorable of earthly conditions could make them happy, they had every prospect of it. They were
going to live on their abundance in one of those stately and delightful
English homes, such as no other people ever created or inherited, a hall
set far and safe within its own private grounds, and surrounded with

venerable trees, shaven lawns, rich shrubbery, and trimmest pathways, the whole so artfully contrived and tended that summer rendered it a paradise, and even winter would hardly disrobe it of its beauty; and all this fair property seemed more exclusively and inalienably their own, because of its descent through many forefathers, each of whom had added an improvement or a charm, and thus transmitted it with a stronger stamp of rightful possession to his heir. And is it possible, after all, that there may be a flaw in the title-deeds? Is, or is not, the system wrong that gives one married pair so immense a superfluity of luxurious home, and shuts out a million others from any home whatever? One day or another, safe as they deem themselves, and safe as the hereditary temper of the people really tends to make them, the gentlemen of England will be compelled to face this question.

UNDERSTANDING THE TEXT

1. State as precisely as you can the new purpose to which Hawthorne puts the material from the notebooks in *Our Old Home*. Do the notebook entries give any hint of this later purpose?
2. Does Hawthorne include any details about the two weddings in the passage from *Our Old Home* that he did not give in the notebook entries? If so, specify what they are, consider where Hawthorne got them when he came to write the book, and discuss his reasons for including them.
3. What does Hawthorne gain by the addition of each of the following comments in *Our Old Home?*
   a. "they were, in short, the mere rags and tatters of the human race, whom some east-wind of evil omen, howling along the streets, had chanced to sweep together into an unfragrant heap." (To what are the people being compared in this sentence?)
   b. "had execution done upon them in the lump."
   c. "nor, perhaps, would he have perpetrated much additional mischief by the mistake."
   d. "even the married parties seemed to see something exceedingly funny in the affair."
4. Which of the two marriages is most altered in the description given in *Our Old Home*, as compared to the notebook original? Why?
5. Account for each of the following changes, in relation to your theory of the differences between Hawthorne's two conceptions of his subject:
   a. All references to the "groomsmen" and "bride's-maids" are omitted from the account of the "poor" wedding in *Our Old Home*.
   b. In the notebooks there are six couples in the first wedding; in *Our Old Home* Hawthorne says it is difficult to compute the number exactly.

c. "The throng of people" who watch the second wedding in the notebooks becomes a "crowd of ragged people" in *Our Old Home*.

d. Most of the details about the sound of the church bells are omitted in *Our Old Home*.

e. The detail about the married couple drawing crimson curtains in the post-chaise and vanishing into their Paradise is omitted in *Our Old Home*.

6. Compare the ways in which Hawthorne describes the clergyman's pronouncement of the marriage service in the two accounts of the "poor" wedding. Why do you think he made these changes?

TOPICS FOR DISCUSSION AND WRITING

7. Using the material provided in Hawthorne's notebook entries, write a short paper which embodies a different conception of the subject from the one in *Our Old Home*. Notice the effect of your different intention on your selection, ordering, and treatment of the material.

8. As if you were keeping a notebook, write a separate paragraph on two related subjects which you have recently had an opportunity to observe—two of your teachers or classmates, two college buildings, the pattern of two days, or the like. Then write a paper in which you compare the two from a new point of view.

Mark Twain Describes the Dawn
on the Mississippi

THE WORKS of Samuel L. Clemens (1835–1910), who wrote under the pseudonym of Mark Twain, contain many notable evocations of both the natural scene and village life in the Mississippi Valley, where the author grew up in the days before the Civil War. In the three passages which follow, Mark Twain treats, in significantly different ways, a single event: the breaking of day as it appears to a particular observer in a specific context. The first passage is the beginning of Chapter XIV, "Happy Camp of the Free-Booters," in *The Adventures of Tom Sawyer;* at this point in the story, Tom Sawyer, Huck Finn, and Joe Harper, as a crew of make-believe pirates running away from home, have spent the night camping out on Jackson's Island in the Mississippi River. The second excerpt is taken from *Life on the Mississippi*, a volume of reminiscences about Mark Twain's experiences as a river-boat pilot; the passage appears in Chapter XXX, "Sketches by the Way," in that part of the book which describes how Mark Twain, as an established author, revisits the scenes of his piloting days. The third passage, from Chapter XIX of *The Adventures of Huckleberry Finn*, tells how Huck Finn views the dawn as he and the runaway slave Jim float down the Mississippi on a raft; the description immediately follows a chapter dealing with a bloody feud between two families, the Grangerfords and the Shepherdsons.

For an interesting interpretation of these passages in relationship to the development of Mark Twain's literary style, the reader may consult an article by Leo Marx entitled "The Pilot and the Passenger: Landscape Conventions and the Style of *Huckleberry Finn*," which appeared in *American Literature* in May, 1956.

From The Adventures of Tom Sawyer (*1876*)

MARK TWAIN

WHEN Tom awoke in the morning, he wondered where he was. He sat up and rubbed his eyes and looked around. Then he comprehended. It was the cool gray dawn, and there was a delicious sense of repose and peace in the deep pervading calm and silence of the woods. Not a leaf stirred; not a sound obtruded upon great Nature's meditation. Beaded dewdrops stood upon the leaves and grasses. A white layer of ashes covered the fire, and a thin blue breath of smoke rose straight into the air. Joe and Huck still slept.

Now, far away in the woods a bird called; another answered; presently the hammering of a woodpecker was heard. Gradually the cool dim gray of the morning whitened, and as gradually sounds multiplied and life manifested itself. The marvel of Nature shaking off sleep and going to work unfolded itself to the musing boy. A little green worm came crawling over a dewy leaf, lifting two-thirds of his body into the air from time to time and "sniffing around," then proceeding again—for he was measuring, Tom said; and when the worm approached him, of its own accord, he sat as still as a stone, with his hopes rising and falling, by turns, as the creature still came toward him or seemed inclined to go elsewhere; and when at last it considered a painful moment with its curved body in the air and then came decisively down upon Tom's leg and began a journey over him, his whole heart was glad—for that meant that he was going to have a new suit of clothes—without the shadow of a doubt a gaudy piratical uniform. Now a procession of ants appeared, from nowhere in particular, and went about their labors; one struggled manfully by with a dead spider five times as big as itself in its arms, and lugged it straight up a tree-trunk. A brown spotted lady-bug climbed the dizzy

Reprinted by permission of the publishers, Harper & Brothers.

height of a grass-blade, and Tom bent down close to it and said, "Lady-bug, lady-bug, fly away home, your house is on fire, your children's alone," and she took wing and went off to see about it—which did not surprise the boy, for he knew of old that this insect was credulous about conflagrations, and he had practised upon its simplicity more than once. A tumblebug came next, heaving sturdily at its ball, and Tom touched the creature, to see it shut its legs against its body and pretend to be dead. The birds were fairly rioting by this time. A catbird, the Northern mocker, lit in a tree over Tom's head, and trilled out her imitations of her neighbors in a rapture of enjoyment; then a shrill jay swept down, a flash of blue flame, and stopped on a twig almost within the boy's reach, cocked his head to one side and eyed the strangers with a consuming curiosity; a gray squirrel and a big fellow of the "fox" kind came scurry-ing along, sitting up at intervals to inspect and chatter at the boys, for the wild things had probably never seen a human being before and scarcely knew whether to be afraid or not. All Nature was wide awake and stirring, now; long lances of sunlight pierced down through the dense foliage far and near, and a few butterflies came fluttering upon the scene.

From Life on the Mississippi (*1883*)

MARK TWAIN

I HAD myself called with the four-o'clock watch, mornings, for one cannot see too many summer sunrises on the Mississippi. They are enchanting. First, there is the eloquence of silence; for a deep hush broods everywhere. Next, there is the haunting sense of loneliness, isolation, remoteness from the worry and bustle of the world. The dawn creeps in stealthily; the solid walls of black forest soften to gray, and vast stretches of the river open up and reveal themselves; the water is glass-smooth, gives off spectral little wreaths of white mist, there is not the faintest breath of wind, nor stir of leaf; the tranquillity is profound and infinitely satisfying. Then a bird pipes up, another follows, and soon the pipings develop into a jubilant riot of music. You see none of the birds; you simply move through an atmosphere of song which seems to sing itself. When the light has become a little stronger, you have one of the fairest and softest pictures imaginable. You have the intense green of the massed and crowded foliage near by; you see it paling shade by shade in front of you; upon the next projecting cape, a mile off or more, the tint has lightened to the tender young green of spring; the cape beyond that one has almost lost color, and the furthest one, miles away under the horizon, sleeps upon the water a mere dim vapor, and hardly separable from the sky above it and about it. And all this stretch of river is a mirror, and you have the shadowy reflections of the leafage and the curving shores and the receding capes pictured in it. Well, that is all beautiful; soft and rich and beautiful; and when the sun gets well up, and distributes a pink flush here and a powder of gold yonder and a purple haze where it will yield the best effect, you grant that you have seen something that is worth remembering.

Reprinted by permission of the publishers, Harper & Brothers.

From The Adventures of Huckleberry Finn (*1885*)

MARK TWAIN

TWO OR three days and nights went by; I reckon I might say they swum by, they slid along so quiet and smooth and lovely. Here is the way we put in the time. It was a monstrous big river down there—sometimes a mile and a half wide; we run nights, and laid up and hid daytimes; soon as night was most gone we stopped navigating and tied up—nearly always in the dead water under a towhead; and then cut young cottonwoods and willows, and hid the raft with them. Then we set out the lines. Next we slid into the river and had a swim, so as to freshen up and cool off; then we set down on the sandy bottom where the water was about knee-deep, and watched the daylight come. Not a sound anywheres—perfectly still—just like the whole world was asleep, only sometimes the bullfrogs a-cluttering, maybe. The first thing to see, looking away over the water, was a kind of dull line—that was the woods on t'other side; you couldn't make nothing else out; then a pale place in the sky; then more paleness spreading around; then the river softened up away off, and warn't black any more, but gray; you could see little dark spots drifting along ever so far away—trading-scows, and such things; and long black streaks—rafts; sometimes you could hear a sweep screaking; or jumbled-up voices, it was so still, and sounds come so far; and by and by you could see a streak on the water which you know by the look of the streak that there's a snag there in a swift current which breaks on it and makes that streak look that way; and you see the mist curl up off of the water, and the east reddens up, and the river, and you make out a log cabin in the edge of the woods, away on the bank on t'other side of the river, being a wood-yard, likely, and piled by them cheats so you can

Reprinted by permission of the publishers, Harper & Brothers.

throw a dog through it anywhere; then the nice breeze springs up, and comes fanning you from over there, so cool and fresh and sweet to smell on account of the woods and the flowers; but sometimes not that way, because they've left dead fish laying around, gars and such, and they do get pretty rank; and next you've got the full day, and everything smiling in the sun, and the song-birds just going it!

A little smoke couldn't be noticed now, so we would take some fish off of the lines and cook up a hot breakfast. And afterwards we would watch the lonesomeness of the river, and kind of lazy along, and by and by lazy off to sleep. Wake up by and by, and look to see what done it, and maybe see a steamboat coughing along up-stream, so far off towards the other side you couldn't tell nothing about her only whether she was a stern-wheel or side-wheel; then for about an hour there wouldn't be nothing to hear nor nothing to see—just solid lonesomeness. . . .

Sometimes we'd have that whole river all to ourselves for the longest time. Yonder was the banks and the islands, across the water; and maybe a spark—which was a candle in a cabin window; and sometimes on the water you could see a spark or two—on a raft or a scow, you know; and maybe you could hear a fiddle or a song coming over from one of them crafts. It's lovely to live on a raft. We had the sky up there, all speckled with stars, and we used to lay on our backs and look up at them, and discuss about whether they was made or only just happened. Jim he allowed they was made, but I allowed they happened; I judged it would have took too long to *make* so many. Jim said the moon could 'a' *laid* them; well, that looked kind of reasonable, so I didn't say nothing against it, because I've seen a frog lay most as many, so of course it could be done. We used to watch the stars that fell, too, and see them streak down. Jim allowed they'd got spoiled and was hove out of the nest.

UNDERSTANDING THE TEXT

1. Precisely what is the scene being described in each of these selections? Where is the observer? Does he remain in one place or does he move? How much time elapses in each description?

2. How many of the differences in the specific details included in the three descriptions can be accounted for by these differences in the scene and the observer?

3. Classify the descriptions as they range from the most impersonal to the most personal, from the most sharply focused on the scene itself to the most sharply focused on the reactions of the observer.

4. At what points in the excerpts from *The Adventures of Tom Sawyer* does Mark Twain try to convey what Tom Sawyer was thinking and feeling? How sharply is the focus kept on Tom? Which details does it seem Tom took in, and which details seem to be included because the narrator, but not Tom, is aware of them?

5. In the excerpts from *The Adventures of Tom Sawyer* and *Life on the Mississippi* there are a good many generalized statements interpreting or commenting on the quality of the scene, or its significance. For example, "there was a delicious sense of repose and peace in the deep pervading calm and silence of the woods"; "the marvel of Nature shaking off sleep and going to work unfolded itself"; "there is the eloquence of silence." Trace the way such generalized comments are integrated with the concrete detail of the descriptions. Are they always well integrated?

6. The excerpt from *Huckleberry Finn* contains almost none of this kind of comment; it is all observed particulars. Why would such general comment be inappropriate? By what devices does Twain manage to suggest a typical day on the river rather than a single, unique experience? How does he manage to convey an interpretation of Huck's experience? Does that experience seem more or less vivid and meaningful than the experience recorded in the first two descriptions?

7. The diction and sentence structure of Huck's description are of course designed to suggest the thought and speech of a sensitive and shrewd but uneducated boy. Point to some of the chief ways Twain gets these effects.

8. Of course Huck's speech is a literary invention, and a very remarkable one at that. For it is much clearer and more vivid than the actual speech of an uneducated person would be. It is very difficult to write good sentences like this one on p. 22: "by and by you could see a streak on the water which you know by the look of the streak that there's a snag there in a swift current which breaks on it and makes that streak look that way." To convince yourself that this is hard to do, try rewriting, in Huck's style, the sentence in the first description beginning "A little green worm came crawling over a dewy leaf . . ." (p. 19).

9. Why do you think details such as the little green worm, the ants, the ladybug, and the tumblebug, noticed by Tom in the first description, are omitted in the other two descriptions? Is the reason the same in both cases?

TOPICS FOR DISCUSSION AND WRITING

10. Rewrite the excerpt from *The Adventures of Tom Sawyer* keeping the focus sharply and consistently on Tom's thoughts, senses, and feelings. Include all the details you can, but be sure to handle them appropriately, that is, with reference to Tom as the observer.

11. Write a paragraph comparing the kinds and numbers of descriptive adjectives in the three passages, and drawing conclusions from your comparison.
12. Write two paragraphs comparing Tom and Huck on the basis of the sorts of things they notice and the way they seem to appraise their experience in the first and third descriptions.

Three American Travelers Describe Venice

DOWN through the years probably no other European city has held greater fascination for American travelers, especially writers, than Venice. Their responses have ranged from the sensitive aesthetic appreciation of Henry James to the remark, attributed to virtually every American humorist who visited Italy, that Venice would be a fine place if the civic authorities could only solve the problem of street drainage. When writers have attempted to capture the subject matter that lies in Venice, they have necessarily had to say something about the gondola and the gondolier, just as the contemporary European writer, chronicling a visit to the United States, is likely to find the New York taxicab driver an inevitable part of his subject.

The descriptions of Venice which follow were written by three American novelists; as it happens, all three accounts were produced during the earlier stages of their authors' long and distinguished careers. The passages all deal with Venice during the same era, roughly the years between 1860 and 1880. William Dean Howells (1837–1920) was appointed American consul at Venice in 1861 and lived there until 1865. After returning to the United States, Howells was active in literature for half a century, as magazine editor, critic, and novelist; the best known of his novels is *The Rise of Silas Lapham* (1885). Samuel L. Clemens (1835–1910), or Mark Twain, visited Venice a year or two after Howells had left the city. Mark Twain came to Venice while on a sightseeing tour of Europe and the Holy Land which he described in *The Innocents Abroad*, the book which earned him his reputation as a popular humorist. Unlike Howells and Mark Twain, Henry James (1843–1916) was familiar with Europe during his boyhood and youth. From 1877 until the end of his life, James lived most of the time in England and made frequent visits to the Continent. Many of his most successful works of fiction are concerned with the reactions of Americans to European scenes and manners.

From Venetian Life (*1866*)

WILLIAM DEAN HOWELLS

I THINK it does not matter just when I first came to Venice. Yesterday and to-day are the same here. I arrived one winter morning about five o'clock, and was not so full of Soul as I might have been in warmer weather. Yet I was resolved not to go to my hotel in the omnibus (the large, many-seated boat so called), but to have a gondola solely for my-self and my luggage. The porter who seized my valise in the station, inferred from some very polyglottic Italian of mine the nature of my wish, and ran out and threw that slender piece of luggage into a gondola. I followed, lighted to my seat by a beggar in picturesque and desultory costume. He was one of a class of mendicants whom I came, for my sins, to know better in Venice, and whom I dare say every traveler recol-lects,—the merciless tribe who hold your gondola to shore, and affect to do you a service and not a displeasure, and pretend not to be abandoned swindlers. The Venetians call them *gransieri*, or crab-catchers; but as yet I did not know the name or the purpose of this *poverino*[1] at the station, but merely saw that he had the Venetian eye for color: in the distribu-tion and arrangement of his fragments of dress he had produced some miraculous effects of red, and he was altogether as infamous a figure as any friend of brigands would like to meet in a lonely place. He did not offer to stab me and sink my body in the Grand Canal, as, in all Venetian keeping, I felt that he ought to have done; but he implored an alms, and I hardly know now whether to exult or regret that I did not understand him, and left him empty-handed. I suppose that he withdrew again the blessings which he had advanced me, as we pushed out into the canal; but I heard nothing, for the wonder of the city was already upon me. All my

[1] *Poverino* is the compassionate generic for all unhappy persons who work for a living in Venice, as well as many who decline to do so.

nether-spirit, so to speak, was dulled and jaded by the long, cold, railway journey from Vienna, while every surface-sense was taken and tangled in the bewildering brilliancy and novelty of Venice. For I think there can be nothing else in the world so full of glittering and exquisite surprise, as that first glimpse of Venice which the traveler catches as he issues from the railway station by night, and looks upon her peerless strangeness. There is something in the blessed breath of Italy (how quickly, coming south, you know it, and how bland it is, after the harsh, transalpine air!) which prepares you for your nocturnal advent into the place; and O you! whoever you are, that journey toward this enchanted city for the first time, let me tell you how happy I count you! There lies before you for your pleasure, the spectacle of such singular beauty as no picture can ever show you nor book tell you,—beauty which you shall feel perfectly but once, and regret forever.

For my own part, as the gondola slipped away from the blaze and bustle of the station down the gloom and silence of the broad canal, I forgot that I had been freezing two days and nights; that I was at that moment very cold and a little homesick. I could at first feel nothing but that beautiful silence, broken only by the star-silvered dip of the oars. Then on either hand I saw stately palaces rise gray and lofty from the dark waters, holding here and there a lamp against their faces, which brought balconies, and columns, and carven arches into momentary relief, and threw long streams of crimson into the canal. I could see by that uncertain glimmer how fair was all, but not how sad and old; and so, unhaunted by any pang for the decay that afterward saddened me amid the forlorn beauty of Venice, I glided on. I have no doubt it was a proper time to think all the fantastic things in the world, and I thought them; but they passed vaguely through my mind, without at all interrupting the sensations of sight and sound. Indeed, the past and present mixed there, and the moral and material were blent in the sentiment of utter novelty and surprise. The quick boat slid through old troubles of mine, and unlooked-for events gave it the impulse that carried it beyond, and safely around sharp corners of life. And all the while I knew that this was a progress through narrow and crooked canals, and past marble angles of palaces. But I did not know then that this fine confusion of sense and spirit was the first faint impression of the charm of life in Venice.

Dark, funereal barges like my own had flitted by, and the gondoliers had warned each other at every turning with hoarse, lugubrious cries; the lines of balconied palaces had never ended;—here and there at their doors larger craft were moored, with dim figures of men moving uncertainly about on them. At last we had passed abruptly out of the Grand Canal into one of the smaller channels, and from comparative light into a darkness only remotely affected by some far-streaming corner lamp. But always the pallid, stately palaces; always the dark heaven with its trembling stars above, and the dark water with its trembling stars below; but now innumerable bridges, and an utter lonesomeness, and ceaseless sudden turns and windings. One could not resist a vague feeling of anxiety, in these strait and solitary passages, which was part of the strange enjoyment of the time, and which was referable to the novelty, the hush, the darkness, and the piratical appearance and unaccountable pauses of the gondoliers. Was not this Venice, and is not Venice forever associated with bravoes and unexpected dagger-thrusts? That valise of mine might represent fabulous wealth to the uncultivated imagination. Who, if I made an outcry, could understand the Facts of the Situation—(as we say in the journals)? To move on was relief; to pause was regret for past transgressions mingled with good resolutions for the future. But I felt the liveliest mixture of all these emotions, when, slipping from the cover of a bridge, the gondola suddenly rested at the foot of a stairway before a closely-barred door. The gondoliers rang and rang again, while their passenger

"Divided the swift mind,"
in the wonder whether a door so grimly bolted and austerely barred could possibly open into a hotel, with cheerful overcharges for candles and service. But as soon as the door opened, and he beheld the honest swindling countenance of a hotel *portier*, he felt secure against every thing but imposture, and all wild absurdities of doubt and conjecture at once faded from his thought, when the *portier* suffered the gondoliers to make him pay a florin too much.

So, I had arrived in Venice, and I had felt the influence of that complex spell which she lays upon the stranger. I had caught the most alluring glimpses of the beauty which cannot wholly perish while any fragment of her sculptured walls nods to its shadow in the canal; I had been penetrated by a deep sense of the mystery of the place, and I had been touched already by the anomaly of modern life amid scenes where its presence offers, according to the humor in which it is studied, constant occasion for annoyance or delight, enthusiasm or sadness.

From The Innocents Abroad (*1869*)

MARK TWAIN

WE REACHED Venice at eight in the evening, and entered a hearse belonging to the Grand Hotel d'Europe. At any rate, it was more like a hearse than anything else, though, to speak by the card, it was a gondola. And this was the storied gondola of Venice!—the fairy boat in which the princely cavaliers of the olden time were wont to cleave the waters of the moonlit canals and look the eloquence of love into the soft eyes of patrician beauties, while the gay gondolier in silken doublet touched his guitar and sang as only gondoliers can sing! This the famed gondola and this the gorgeous gondolier!—the one an inky, rusty old canoe with a sable hearse-body clapped on to the middle of it, and the other a mangy, barefooted gutter-snipe with a portion of his raiment on exhibition which should have been sacred from public scrutiny. Presently, as he turned a corner and shot his hearse into a dismal ditch between two long rows of towering, untenanted buildings, the gay gondolier began to sing, true to the traditions of his race. I stood it a little while. Then I said:

"Now, here, Roderigo Gonzales Michael Angelo, I'm a pilgrim, and I'm a stranger, but I am not going to have my feelings lacerated by any such caterwauling as that. If that goes on, one of us has got to take water. It is enough that my cherished dreams of Venice have been blighted forever as to the romantic gondola and the gorgeous gondolier; this system of destruction shall go no farther; I will accept the hearse, under protest, and you may fly your flag of truce in peace, but here I register a dark and bloody oath that you shan't sing. Another yelp, and overboard you go."

I began to feel that the old Venice of song and story had departed forever. But I was too hasty. In a few minutes we swept gracefully out into the Grand Canal, and under the mellow moonlight the Venice of poetry and romance stood revealed. Right from the water's edge rose long lines of stately palaces of marble; gondolas were gliding swiftly hither and thither and disappearing suddenly through unsuspected gates and alleys; ponderous stone bridges threw their shadows athwart the glittering waves. There was life and motion everywhere, and yet everywhere there was a hush, a stealthy sort of stillness, that was suggestive of secret enterprises of bravoes and of lovers; and, clad half in moonbeams and half in mysterious shadows, the grim old mansions of the Republic seemed to have an expression about them of having an eye out for just such enterprises as these at that same moment. Music came floating over the waters—Venice was complete.

It was a beautiful picture—very soft and dreamy and beautiful. But what was this Venice to compare with the Venice of midnight? Nothing. There was a fête—a grand fête in honor of some saint who had been instrumental in checking the cholera three hundred years ago, and all Venice was abroad on the water. It was no common affair, for the Venetians did not know how soon they might need the saint's services again, now that the cholera was spreading everywhere. So in one vast space— say a third of a mile wide and two miles long—were collected two thousand gondolas, and every one of them had from two to ten, twenty, and even thirty colored lanterns suspended about it, and from four to a dozen occupants. Just as far as the eye could reach, these painted lights were massed together—like a vast garden of many-colored flowers, except that these blossoms were never still; they were ceaselessly gliding in and out, and mingling together, and seducing you into bewildering attempts to follow their mazy evolutions. Here and there a strong red, green, or blue glare from a rocket that was struggling to get away splendidly illuminated all the boats around it. Every gondola that swam by us, with its crescents and pyramids and circles of colored lamps hung aloft, and lighting up the faces of the young and the sweet-scented and lovely below, was a picture; and the reflections of those lights, so long, so slender, so numberless, so many-colored and so distorted and wrinkled by the waves, was a picture likewise, and one that was enchantingly beautiful. Many and many a party of young ladies and gentlemen had their state gondolas handsomely decorated, and ate supper on board, bringing their swallow-tailed, white-cravated varlets to wait upon them, and having their tables tricked out as if for a bridal supper. They had brought along the costly globe lamps from their drawing-rooms, and the lace and silken curtains from the same places, I suppose. And they had also brought pianos and guitars, and they played and sang operas, while the plebeian paper-lanterned gondolas from the suburbs and the back alleys crowded around to stare and listen.

There was music everywhere—choruses, string bands, brass bands, flutes, everything. I was so surrounded, walled in with music, magnificence, and loveliness, that I became inspired with the spirit of the scene, and sang one tune myself. However, when I observed that the other gondolas had sailed away, and my gondolier was preparing to go overboard, I stopped.

The fête was magnificent. They kept it up the whole night long, and I never enjoyed myself better than I did while it lasted.

What a funny old city this Queen of the Adriatic is! Narrow streets, vast, gloomy marble palaces, black with the corroding damps of centuries, and all partly submerged; no dry land visible anywhere, and no sidewalks worth mentioning; if you want to go to church, to the theater, or to the restaurant, you must call a gondola. It must be a paradise for cripples, for verily a man has no use for legs here.

For a day or two the place looked so like an overflowed Arkansas town, because of its currentless waters laving the very doorsteps of all the houses, and the cluster of boats made fast under the windows, or skimming in and out of the alleys and byways, that I could not get rid of the impression that there was nothing the matter here but a spring freshet, and that the river would fall in a few weeks and leave a dirty high-water mark on the houses, and the streets full of mud and rubbish.

In the glare of day, there is little poetry about Venice, but under the charitable moon her stained palaces are white again, their battered sculptures are hidden in shadows, and the old city seems crowned once more with the grandeur that was hers five hundred years ago. It is easy, then, in fancy, to people these silent canals with plumed gallants and fair ladies —with Shylocks in gaberdine and sandals, venturing loans upon the rich argosies of Venetian commerce—with Othellos and Desdemonas, with Iagos and Roderigos—with noble fleets and victorious legions returning from the wars. In the treacherous sunlight we see Venice decayed, forlorn, poverty-stricken, and commerceless—forgotten and utterly insignificant. But in the moonlight, her fourteen centuries of greatness fling their glories about her, and once more is she the princeliest among the nations of the earth.

From Portraits of Places (*1883*)

HENRY JAMES

THERE are certain little mental pictures that rise before the sentimental tourist at the simple mention, written or spoken, of the places he has loved. When I hear, when I see, the magical name I have written above these pages, it is not of the great Square that I think, with its strange basilica and its high arcades, nor of the wide mouth of the Grand Canal, with the stately steps and the well-poised dome of the Salute; it is not of the low lagoon, nor the sweet Piazzetta, nor the dark chambers of St. Mark's. I simply see a narrow canal in the heart of the city—a patch of green water and a surface of pink wall. The gondola moves slowly; it gives a great, smooth swerve, passes under a bridge, and the gondolier's cry, carried over the quiet water, makes a kind of splash in the stillness. A girl is passing over the little bridge, which has an arch like a camel's back, with an old shawl on her head, which makes her look charming; you see her against the sky as you float beneath. The pink of the old wall seems to fill the whole place; it sinks even into the opaque water. Behind the wall is a garden, out of which the long arm of a white June rose—the roses of Venice are splendid—has flung itself by way of spontaneous ornament. On the other side of this small water-way is a great shabby façade of Gothic windows and balconies—balconies on which dirty clothes are hung and under which a cavernous-looking doorway opens from a low flight of slimy water-steps. It is very hot and still, the canal has a queer smell, and the whole place is enchanting.

It is poor work, however, talking about the colour of things in Venice. The sentimental tourist is perpetually looking at it from his window, when he is not floating about with that delightful sense of being for the moment a part of it, which any gentleman in a gondola is free to entertain. Venetian windows and balconies are a dreadful lure, and while you rest your elbows on these cushioned ledges the precious hours fly away. But, in truth, Venice is not, in fair weather, a place for concentration of mind. The effort required for sitting down to a writing-table is heroic, and the brightest page of MS. looks dull beside the brilliancy of your *milieu*. All nature beckons you forth, and murmurs to you sophistically that such hours should be devoted to collecting impressions. Afterward, in ugly places, at unprivileged times, you can convert your impressions into prose. Fortunately for the present proser, the weather was not always fine; the first month was wet and windy, and it was better to look at the lagoon from an open casement than to respond to the advances of persuasive gondoliers. Even then, however, there was a constant entertainment in the view. It was all cold colour, and the steel-gray floor of the lagoon was stroked the wrong way by the wind. Then there were charming cool intervals, when the churches, the houses, the anchored fishing-boats, the whole gently-curving line of the Riva, seemed to be washed with a pearly white. Later it all turned warm—warm to the eye as well as to other senses. After the middle of May the whole place was in a glow. The sea took on a thousand shades, but they were only infinite variations of blue, and those rosy walls I just spoke of began to flush in the thick sunshine. Every patch of colour, every yard of weather-stained stucco, every glimpse of nestling garden or daub of sky above a *calle*, began to shine and sparkle—began, as the painters say, to "compose." The lagoon was streaked with odd currents, which played across it like huge, smooth finger-marks. The gondolas multiplied and spotted it all over; every gondola and every gondolier looking, at a distance, precisely like every other.

There is something strange and fascinating in this mysterious impersonality of the gondola. It has an identity when you are in it, but, thanks to their all being of the same size, shape, and colour, and of the same deportment and gait, it has none, or as little as possible, as you see it pass before you. From my windows on the Riva there was always the same silhouette—the long, black, slender skiff, lifting its head and throwing it back a little, moving yet seeming not to move, with the grotesquely-graceful figure on the poop. This figure inclines, as may be, more to the graceful or to the grotesque—standing in the "second position" of the dancing-master, but indulging, from the waist upward, in a freedom of movement which that functionary would deprecate. One may say, as a general thing, that there is something rather awkward in the movement of even the most graceful gondolier, and something graceful in the movement of the most awkward. In the graceful men of course the grace predominates, and nothing can be finer than the large firm way in which, from their point of vantage, they throw themselves over their tremendous oar. It has the boldness of a plunging bird, and the regularity of a pendulum. Sometimes, as you see this movement in profile, in a gondola that passes you—see, as you recline on your own low cushions, the arching body of the gondolier lifted up against the sky—it has a kind of nobleness which suggests an image on a Greek frieze. The gondolier at Venice is your very good friend—if you choose him happily—and on the quality of the personage depends a good deal that of your impressions. He is a part of your daily life, your double, your shadow, your complement. Most people, I think, either like their gondolier or hate him; and if they like him, like him very much. In this case they take an interest in him after his departure; wish him to be sure of employment, speak of him as the gem of gondoliers, and tell their friends to be certain to "secure" him. There is usually no difficulty in securing him; there is nothing elusive or reluctant about a gondolier. They are, for the most part, excellent fellows, and the sentimental tourist must always have a kindness for them. More than the rest of the population, of course, they are the children of Venice; they are associated with its idiosyncrasy, with its essence, with its silence, with its melancholy.

When I say they are associated with its silence, I should immediately add that they are associated also with its sound. Among themselves they are an extraordinarily talkative company. They chatter at the *traghetti*, where they always have some sharp point under discussion; they bawl across the canals; they bespeak your commands as you approach; they defy each other from afar. If you happen to have a *traghetto* under your window, you are well aware that they are a vocal race. I should go even farther than I went just now, and say that the voice of the gondolier is, in fact, the sound of Venice. There is scarcely any other, and that, indeed, is part of the interest of the place. There is no noise there save distinctly human noise; no rumbling, no vague uproar, nor rattle of wheels and hoofs. It is all articulate, personal sound. One may say, indeed, that Venice is, emphatically, the city of conversation; people talk all over the place, because there is nothing to interfere with their being heard. Among the populace it is a kind of family party. The still water carries the voice, and good Venetians exchange confidences at a distance of half a mile. It saves a world of trouble, and they don't like trouble. Their delightful garrulous language helps them to make Venetian life a long *conversazione*.

This language, with its soft elisions, its odd transpositions, its kindly contempt for consonants and other disagreeables, has in it something peculiarly human and accommodating. If your gondolier had no other merit, he would have the merit that he speaks Venetian. This may rank as a merit, even—some people perhaps would say especially—when you don't understand what he says. But he adds to it other graces which make him an agreeable feature in your life. The price he sets on his services is touchingly small, and he has a happy art of being obsequious, without being, or, at least, without seeming, abject. For occasional liberalities he evinces an almost lyrical gratitude. In short, he has delightfully good manners, a merit which he shares, for the most part, with Venetians at large. One grows very fond of these people, and the reason of one's fondness is the frankness and sweetness of their address. That of the Italian people, in general, has much to recommend it; but in the Venetian manner there is something peculiarly ingratiating. One feels that the race is old, that it has a long and rich civilisation in its blood, and that if it has not been blessed by fortune, it has at least been polished by time. It has not a genius for morality, and indeed makes few pretensions in that direction. It scruples not to represent the false as the true, and is liable to confusion in the attribution of property. It is peculiarly susceptible to the tender sentiment, which it cultivates with a graceful disregard of the more rigid formalities. I am not sure that it is very brave, and was not struck with its being very industrious. But it has an unfailing sense of the amenities of life; the poorest Venetian is a natural man of the world. He is better company than persons of his class are apt to be among the nations of industry and virtue—where people are also, sometimes, perceived to lie and steal. He has a great desire to please and to be pleased.

UNDERSTANDING THE TEXT

1. Make a list of the specific aspects of the Venetian scene which each of these authors takes up. Which aspects are noted by all three observers? Which are mentioned by only one of the writers?
2. State in a brief paragraph what you believe to be the essential *subject* of each writer. Show how his selection and presentation of details reflect his definition of the subject.
3. Which of the writers attempts to evoke a sense of the danger and intrigue traditionally associated with Venice? By what means does he try to convey this sense? How seriously do you think he intends the suggestion of menace to be taken?

4. Both Howells and Mark Twain refer to the contrast between the present and the past in Venice. How, in his choice of details and language, does each of the writers develop this contrast? What is the relationship between this central contrast and the comparison Mark Twain makes between Venice by day and Venice by night?

5. Study the James essay carefully, and see how many passages you can find in which the writer makes use of terms drawn from the vocabulary of the pictorial artist. What light does this habit throw on the way James has conceived his subject?

6. James begins by describing a scene which he regards as representative of the meaning the "sentimental tourist" finds in Venice. Examine closely the details presented in this scene. Are they in accord with the characteristics he develops later in the essay? Are all the elements of this first picture conventionally beautiful?

7. In some parts of his sketch Mark Twain uses a humorous and colloquial style, while in others he employs a more conventional "literary" style. See if you detect the passages characterized by each of these styles. What is the connection between this variation in style and Mark Twain's view of his subject?

8. In the next to last paragraph of his essay, Howells refers to "the honest swindling countenance of a hotel *portier*." In the particular context, what is the point of this turn of phrase?

9. In which of the three essays does the personal viewpoint of the writer seem most strongly marked? What are the ways in which the writer's opinions emerge?

TOPICS FOR DISCUSSION AND WRITING

10. What are some of the ways in which a writer, while describing the physical appearance of a place, can also suggest some of the characteristics of the people who live there? Look through these essays and see if you can discover instances of the writers' hinting at human qualities in the way they handle physical description.

11. Write a descriptive essay about a place you know well—your home town, a section of a city, a college campus. Keep your essay from becoming a drab recital of details by developing one or two salient points which, on the basis of your long familiarity, seem to you important in understanding the place.

12. Using the same basic material as in the preceding question, write an essay describing the place as it would appear to a person seeing it briefly and for the first time, much as Mark Twain saw Venice.

13. All of us have had the experience of visiting a place which seemed familiar to us beforehand from our reading or other sources—perhaps a big city, or a

historical shrine, or a scenic landmark. Write an essay which develops a comparison between your preconception of such a place and what you actually observed.

14. Write a brief paper comparing the Howells, Mark Twain, and James passages with specific respect to the way each writer describes the gondolier and interprets his position in the Venetian scene.

15. Choose a typical American urban figure—the taxicab driver, the newspaper vender, the bus driver, and the like—and develop a descriptive essay which (a) tells what he is like, not as an individual but as a type, and (b) attempts to relate the type to the city life of which it is a part.

2. The Approach to the Subject:
Point of View, Assumptions, and Premises

WE HAVE seen that the writer's subject achieves its meaning, not from any special inner quality of the subject itself, but from the way the writer conceives it. In developing and interpreting his subject, the writer is inescapably influenced by whatever general ideas he may have on a variety of topics: morality, religion, science, politics, psychology, and so on. These general ideas are what we mean when we speak of *assumptions* or *premises*. If as you read you are to grasp the full meaning which the author intends to convey, you will need to be alert to the assumptions underlying the way he presents his subject. If as a writer you are to be clear and persuasive, you must be aware of the premises of your own statements.

Even an extremely simple and concrete statement will often be found to spring from a complex web of general ideas about, for example, the way human beings behave. Thus, a busy executive may say to a departing visitor, "Please leave the door open." On the surface this seems to be a matter-of-fact request, but perhaps if we interrogated the executive at this point, we might discover that, as unspoken reason for the simple request, he has a rather interesting cluster of ideas: People working together on the same project like to feel a sense of joint participation. They like to feel that the boss is interested in their work, and is accessible to them. One way of symbolizing this spirit is for the boss to work with his office door open.

In ordinary life, then, the way we act and the way we speak are affected by the ideas which give shape and sense to our human experiences. When a woman says, "I'll take *this* hat instead of that one," probably she is making her decision on the basis of a premise which she may or may not put into words. It may be an aesthetic premise—"That kind of hat does nothing for a short, stocky figure"—or it may be an economic premise—"No one should pay that much for a hat."

In writing, the role of assumptions and premises is equally important. Every well-wrought piece of prose bears the stamp of the way the writer looks upon the world, or at least upon that portion of it which he has placed under inspection. Let us suppose that three students write essays about teachers whom they admire. One student may describe a teacher who lectures clearly and fully and who, as the student puts it, "lays the subject out cold, so that you really feel you have it under control." Another student may write about a teacher who proceeds less systematically, who concentrates on stirring up discussion, and who, in the student's words, "really makes you think." Still a third essayist may praise a teacher for creating an atmosphere of folksy comradeship in the classroom. Obviously, these three essays are different, not merely because they are written about different teachers, but also because the three authors have radically different ideas—assumptions and premises—about what education is.

Assumptions and premises are important in writing, not only because they are inevitable, but because, properly understood and properly used, they enable the writer to see and realize his subject, and to set it apart, for himself and for his reader, from all that is *not* his subject. Our general ideas give order, sequence, and meaning to the flux of human existence; they serve the same purpose in conferring form and significance upon the things we write about. On his assumptions and premises the writer builds the vantage point from which he surveys, describes, and evaluates the people and things that interest him. For example, in one of the selections that follow, Benjamin Franklin knew he had a subject—his opposition to paying salaries to government officials—because he believed that ambition and avarice, combined, are dangerously powerful motives in human life. Similarly, the four writers who in this section render varying verdicts on one unusual man, Henry Thoreau, do so because they are working from different ideas of "nature," individualism, and the individual's relationship to society. On the basis of what each writer thinks important about life—on the basis, that is, of assumptions and premises—he has found something significant to say about Thoreau and his work.

Ideas which influence the way the writer conceives his subject may be either explicit or implicit. In Franklin's protest against government salaries, his essential premises about human nature are fully stated, enter directly into the discourse, and in fact serve to get the argument under way. In the Declaration of Independence, the political theory justifying the break with Great Britain is explicitly developed; the assumption that "all men are created equal" is directly stated, and consequences are drawn from it. Often, however, ideas which are very important to an understanding of what the writer is attempting to accomplish may never be directly presented to the reader. Such implicit assumptions and premises preside over, and control, the writer's work; in a sense, they are so central and ever present that they do not need to be written down. When we read a history, for example, we may never encounter an out-and-out statement of what the author considers important in the life of men and nations; nevertheless, by close attention to the events he chooses to emphasize, and to the way he presents them, we can generally discover what the writer's view of history is. An example of a general conception so widespread and influential that people were affected by it almost without knowing it is the idea of progress, which is discussed by Carl Becker in a later essay in this book. Becker's essay is an analysis of the way certain generally accepted assumptions about the nature and destiny of mankind have originated and have come to dominate the thinking of individual men. As you read Becker's brilliant dissection of other people's implicit assumptions, you may wish to inquire whether the analyst himself is operating on the basis of any silent premises. What does he assume to be the relationship between outward events and men's ideas? Do ideas shape events, or is it generally the other way around?

In the Franklin speech, too, although the main premise is given explicitly, you may note other assumptions which, though important to the argument, are not stated. Observe how Franklin assumes that something which is true of a compact, homogeneous group like the Quakers will also be true of a large, heterogeneous body like the political state.

So far, in referring to the ideas which guide the writer in treating his subject, we have used the words "assumption" and "premise" interchangeably. In ordinary usage, however, "premise" is the broader term, since it is employed to describe any general idea which enters into the writer's thought, while the term "assumption" is frequently reserved for the kind of idea which the writer, in a sense, takes for granted, and thus either does not include or states very briefly. For even when a writer decides to put down his fundamental premises directly, he may do so with more or less fullness. The degree of thoroughness with which he supports or "proves" his premises will depend pretty much on whether these ideas are likely to strike his audience as sound or as debatable. Speaking to a group of eighteenth-century politicians, Franklin saw no need to labor the point that men are moved by ambition and avarice. On the other hand, if in a speech before a convention of police officials you were to introduce the idea that all men are inherently virtuous, you would probably be well advised to develop this notion in persuasive detail.

It should be clear that all writing, from straightforward exposition through complex argument, rests on a framework, either expressed or understood, of assumptions and premises. Since his general views are inevitably reflected in what he writes, it is the writer's task to see to it that these premises operate in a way that clarifies and vivifies his subject. He should, for one thing, either work consistently from the same set of assumptions throughout a piece of writing or, if he decides that it is necessary to switch to a different viewpoint, make it clear to the reader what is happening and why the change is occurring. In *Life on the Mississippi*, Mark Twain describes a river town before, during, and after the arrival of the daily steamboat. Before the boat arrives, he writes, the town was "glorious with expectancy." Then two or three sentences later he launches into an effective description of the absolute quiet and somnolence of the town in the hour before the steamboat appears; in Mark Twain's account, there is nothing even remotely "expectant" in the attitude of the town's inhabitants. Since the earlier phrase, "glorious with expectancy," was clearly not intended to be ironic, it is evident that Mark Twain suddenly changed the view he was taking toward his material, and that the abrupt switch weakens the force of an otherwise remarkably evocative passage.

In addition to maintaining consistency of viewpoint, the skillful writer is economical in deploying his premises. That is, he works within a structure of ideas which is appropriate in range to the dimensions of the specific problem facing him. If he is writing about the cultivation of radishes, he sees no need to prove that the planet Mars is inhabited. If he is writing about juvenile delinquency in a modern American city, he will not ordinarily expound John Locke and the natural-rights theory of government. The United States Supreme Court's general rule is never to make pronouncements on broad constitutional issues when particular cases can be settled on more specific grounds. Similarly, the good writer's rule is never to make assumptions more sweeping than the particular problem of writing requires. When the rule is violated, digression and irrelevance are frequently the results.

Finally, as has already been suggested, the careful writer realizes that he cannot take for granted premises which will seem to his readers to be highly controversial or even arguable. (Let us note here, as an obvious exception, the kind of ironic piece—see Swift's *A Modest Proposal*, pp. 224–231—in which the author works out the implications of a clearly unacceptable assumption.) This is not to say that the writer must prudently confine himself to presenting ideas which will be tame and acceptable to his readers. It means, rather, that when the writer wishes to convey to the reader his conception of a thing, a person, a place, or an institution, he cannot do so by main force, by flat assertion. He can achieve his purpose only if the reader realizes that the writer sees his subject in a way which, however different from the reader's own vision, is consistent and intelligible. If the writer wishes to look upon his fellow men and society from a special vantage point, as Thoreau does in *Walden*, he has the responsibility, which Thoreau accepts, of developing fully the meaning of his individual set of values.[1]

---

[1] Supplement 1 (pp. 617–629), "Writing, Reading, and Reasoning," gives an introduction to the problems of logic in writing.

Point of View

BERGEN EVANS AND
CORNELIA EVANS

JEREMY BENTHAM once made a list of motives, naming each motive in three columns, according as it was approved by the speaker, tolerated, or disapproved of. Thus "love of the social board" appeared in one column and "gluttony" in its opposite.

This is an interesting exercise for the writer because he must be aware of the manner in which our values, prejudices and passions reveal themselves in our choice of words. He must be aware, for example, that the woman whom others regard as "skinny" may regard herself as "slender," that one who considers himself "broad-minded" may be considered "unprincipled" by others, that "tact" and "hypocrisy," "fluency" and "glibness," and "frankness" and "brutality" may describe the same actions to different people. It may be that the only difference between a man's having "initiative" and being "a trouble maker" is whether or not we happen to approve of his ends. The proverb of the early bird is strictly for the birds; it offers no incentive for early rising to worms.

Point of view is inherent in almost every statement that passes a judgment and is often found in words and phrases that seem, superficially, to be purely descriptive. Thus in our references to China and Japan as "the East" we unconsciously reveal the fact that our world-outlook is European. And, still more striking, Japan, in her emblem of the Rising Sun, may reveal the same point of view. What an extraordinary comment on the insincerity of some of our democratic pretensions lies in our use of the word "exclusive" as a term of the highest commendation!

The writer must not only "see people as they are"—that is, as they seem to him—but he must see them as other people see them as they are! And he must accept the fact that under different circumstances different points of view can all be valid. To Hamlet Polonius is a "wretched, rash, intruding fool," a pompous, subservient dotard with weak hams and a weaker wit. To Ophelia he is a stern but loving father. To King Claudius he is a trusted counselor and to Queen Gertrude "the good old man." So completely does Shakespeare lead us to sympathize with Macbeth that we are startled, and almost offended, when after Macbeth and Lady Macbeth are dead Malcolm refers to them as "this dead butcher and his fiend-like Queen." We don't believe in "anthropophagi and men whose heads do grow beneath their shoulders," but we are shocked when Iago says that Othello won Desdemona's love "by bragging and telling her fantastical lies."

The ability to imagine a wholly different point of view is one of the surest indications of high intelligence and often serves in itself to make a book. The secret of H. G. Wells's *The War of the Worlds* is not that he had the power to create, in his Martians, something before unconceived, but that under disguise of the Martians he presented the white man much as he must have seemed to savages on their first disastrous contact with him. Virginia Woolf in *Flush* makes a much more successful attempt, one feels, to present life as a dog would experience it than does, say, Jack London in *White Fang* or *The Call of the Wild*.

One of the advantages of wit and paradox is that by shifting the viewpoint they force us to look at life from unaccustomed points of view and so enlarge the boundaries of truth.

A new point of view always comes as a shock to us. We don't regard our own point of view as a point of view at all; rather it seems to us the obvious, the only way of looking at the situation. We rarely say "This is the way it seems to one with my limitations and predilections," but rather "This is the way it is," "Anyone with an ounce of sense can see," etc. And when someone does *not* see it that way, we are taken aback. Ivor Brown says that he once asked an attendant at Highgate Cemetery how to find Karl Marx's grave. The attendant gave him the necessary instructions and then, to make sure, added, "Look for the name of Scrimmage. It's behind that."

UNDERSTANDING THE TEXT

1. In this brief discussion of how the writer's point of view influences everything he does, how have the Evanses organized their treatment of the subject? What different ways in which point of view is reflected in writing have they chosen to take up? What principle of progression governs the authors' movement from point to point in the analysis?

2. Study the reference to Jeremy Bentham in the opening paragraph and the anecdote about Karl Marx's grave in the final paragraph. As they are placed in the essay, what function does each of these have? Would the story about Marx's grave have been equally satisfactory as the opening of the essay?

3. What meaning do the authors give to the term "point of view" in this essay? Is this meaning implicit, or is it explicitly stated?

4. Throughout this essay are the Evanses talking about a single kind of writing, or are some of their remarks more applicable than others to the kind of expository and argumentative writing most of us are likely to engage in?

5. Examine closely the examples which the authors offer to support their general statements in the second, third, fourth, and fifth paragraphs. Which examples strike you as especially good? How do you account for their effectiveness?

6. This passage appears in a volume entitled *A Dictionary of Contemporary American Usage*. How would you characterize the general tone of the passage? What does this tone suggest concerning the writers' purpose—concerning, let us say, their own point of view on the question of advising people on word usage and literary art?

TOPICS FOR DISCUSSION AND WRITING

7. In this entry for a dictionary the Evanses have necessarily treated their subject succinctly. Can you think of ways other than those the authors have mentioned in which a piece of writing may reflect the writer's point of view?

8. As an exercise see how many sets of "good" and "bad" words you can add to the list of paired terms which the Evanses give in the second paragraph.

9. Most of the attention in this essay is directed toward the use of words which reflect either an affirmative or a negative position on the person or thing under discussion. Sometimes, however, a person's usage indicates a desperate attempt to be noncommittal, to avoid taking a stand. For example, someone may say, "Well, of course, it was an *interesting* play." Make a list of words which often suggest neutrality or uncertainty in point of view.

10. Write an essay in which you expand, with different and more numerous examples, the authors' statement that "point of view . . . is often found in words and phrases that seem, superficially, to be purely descriptive."

11. Do you believe the Evanses would advocate that all assertions of opinion should be preceded by some such remark as "It seems to me that . . ." or "As I see the situation . . ."?

12. Choose a play or novel with which you are familiar, and write a paper indicating the different points of view which several of the characters adopt toward either a central episode or an important character. Make clear whether any of these viewpoints seems to represent the author's personal opinion concerning the episode or character.

13. From your personal experience write a narrative account of an incident— a quarrel among friends, a school election, or the like—which has been seen according to different lights by different people. Your essay should present your own view of the incident, and should also take into account the differing interpretations held by other persons who were involved in it or knew about it.

Speech in the Constitutional Convention
on the Subject of Salaries
2 June 1787

BENJAMIN FRANKLIN

~

SIR,

It is with reluctance that I rise to express a disapprobation of any one article of the plan, for which we are so much obliged to the honorable gentleman who laid it before us. From its first reading, I have borne a good will to it, and, in general, wished it success. In this particular of salaries to the executive branch, I happen to differ; and, as my opinion may appear new and chimerical, it is only from a persuasion that it is right, and from a sense of duty, that I hazard it. The Committee will judge of my reasons when they have heard them, and their judgment may possibly change mine. I think I see inconveniences in the appointment of salaries; I see none in refusing them, but on the contrary great advantages.

Sir, there are two passions which have a powerful influence in the affairs of men. These are *ambition* and *avarice;* the love of power and the love of money. Separately, each of these has great force in prompting men to action; but when united in view of the same object, they have in many minds the most violent effects. Place before the eyes of such men a post of *honor*, that shall at the same time be a place of *profit*, and they will move heaven and earth to obtain it. The vast number of such places it is that renders the British government so tempestuous. The struggles for them are the true source of all those factions which are perpetually dividing the nation, distracting its councils, hurrying it sometimes into fruitless and mischievous wars, and often compelling a submission to dishonorable terms of peace.

And of what kind are the men that will strive for this profitable pre-eminence, through all the bustle of cabal, the heat of contention, the infinite mutual abuse of parties, tearing to pieces the best of characters? It will not be the wise and moderate, the lovers of peace and good order, the men fittest for the trust. It will be the bold and the violent, the men of strong passions and indefatigable activity in their selfish pursuits. These will thrust themselves into your government, and be your rulers. And these, too, will be mistaken in the expected happiness of their situation; for their vanquished competitors, of the same spirit, and from the same motives, will perpetually be endeavoring to distress their administration, thwart their measures, and render them odious to the people.

Besides these evils, sir, though we may set out in the beginning with moderate salaries, we shall find that such will not be of long continuance. Reasons will never be wanting for proposed augmentations, and there will always be a party for giving more to the rulers, that the rulers may be able in return to give more to them. Hence, as all history informs us, there has been in every state and kingdom a constant kind of warfare between the governing and the governed; the one striving to obtain more for its support, and the other to pay less. And this has alone occasioned great convulsions, actual civil wars, ending either in dethroning of the princes or enslaving of the people. Generally, indeed, the ruling power carries its point, and we see the revenues of princes constantly increasing, and we see that they are never satisfied, but always in want of more. The more the people are discontented with the oppression of taxes, the greater need the prince has of money to distribute among his partisans, and pay the troops that are to suppress all resistance and enable him to plunder at pleasure. There is scarce a king in a hundred, who would not, if he could, follow the example of Pharaoh,—get first all the people's money, then all their lands, and then make them and their children servants for ever. It will be said that we do not propose to establish kings. I know it. But there is a natural inclination in mankind to kingly government. It sometimes relieves them from aristocratic domination. They had rather have one tyrant than 500. It gives more of the appearance of equality among citizens; and that they like. I am apprehensive, therefore—perhaps too apprehensive—that the government of these states may in future times end in a monarchy. But this catastrophe, I think, may be long delayed, if in our proposed system we do not sow the seeds of contention, faction, and tumult, by making our posts of honor places of profit. If we do, I fear, that, though we employ at first a number and not a single person, the number will in time be set aside; it will only nourish the foetus of a king (as the honorable gentleman from Virginia very aptly expressed it), and a king will the sooner be set over us.

It may be imagined by some, that this is an utopian idea, and that we can never find men to serve us in the executive department, without paying them well for their services. I conceive this to be a mistake. Some existing facts present themselves to me, which incline me to a contrary opinion. The High Sheriff of a county in England is an honorable office, but it is not a profitable one. It is rather expensive, and therefore not sought for. But yet it is executed, and well executed, and usually by some of the principal gentlemen of the county. In France, the office of Counsellor, or member of their judiciary parliaments, is more honorable. It is therefore purchased at a high price; there are indeed fees on the law proceedings, which are divided among them, but these fees do not amount to more than three per cent on the sum paid for the place. Therefore, as legal interest is there at five per cent, they in fact pay two per cent for being allowed to do the judiciary business of the nation, which is at the same time entirely exempt from the burden of paying them any salaries for their services. I do not, however, mean to recommend this as an eligible mode for our judiciary department. I only bring the instance to show, that the pleasure of doing good and serving their country, and the respect such conduct entitles them to, are sufficient motives with some minds, to give up a great portion of their time to the public, without the mean inducement of pecuniary satisfaction.

Another instance is that of a respectable society, who have made the experiment, and practised it with success, now more than a hundred years. I mean the Quakers. It is an established rule with them that they are not to go to law, but in their controversies they must apply to their monthly, quarterly, and yearly meetings. Committees of these sit with patience to hear the parties, and spend much time in composing their differences. In doing this, they are supported by a sense of duty, and the respect paid to usefulness. It is honorable to be so employed, but it was never made profitable by salaries, fees, or perquisites. And indeed, in all cases of public service, the less the profit the greater the honor.

To bring the matter nearer home, have we not seen the greatest and most important of our offices, that of General of our Armies, executed for eight years together, without the smallest salary, by a patriot whom I will not now offend by any other praise; and this, through fatigues and distresses, in common with the other brave men, his military friends and companions, and the constant anxieties peculiar to his station? And shall we doubt finding three or four men in all the United States, with public spirit enough to bear sitting in peaceful council, for perhaps an equal term, merely to preside over our civil concerns, and see that our laws are duly executed? Sir, I have a better opinion of our country. I think we shall never be without a sufficient number of wise and good men to undertake, and execute well and faithfully, the office in question.

Sir, the saving of the salaries, that may at first be proposed, is not an object with me. The subsequent mischiefs of proposing them are what I apprehend. And therefore it is that I move the amendment. If it is not seconded or accepted, I must be contented with the satisfaction of having delivered my opinion frankly, and done my duty.

UNDERSTANDING THE TEXT

1. What is the chief reason developed by Franklin for refusing salaries to the executive branch of the government?
2. Why do you suppose he refrains from setting forth other possible reasons, such as the saving of money which would result from the course he proposes?
3. In building up his argument, what use does he make of his premise concerning the "two passions which have a powerful influence in the affairs of men"?
4. Is this premise consistent with his later reference to "the wise and moderate, the lovers of peace and good order, the men fittest for the trust"?
5. In Franklin's opinion, what is the chief thing wrong with the British government? How is this criticism of the British government related to his argument?
6. What does Franklin assume will be the attitude of honest and moderate men toward a government in which executive salaries are paid?
7. When Franklin predicts a growing tendency to make salaries larger, what kind of relationship between those who govern and those who are governed does he seem to take for granted?
8. On what grounds does Franklin rest his belief that "there is a natural inclination in mankind to kingly government"?
9. How does the speaker connect his fear of a possible American monarchy to his argument against paying salaries?
10. Evaluate the effectiveness of the four examples of officers who serve without salaries. Is there any point to the particular order in which the examples are cited?

TOPICS FOR DISCUSSION AND WRITING

11. How would you go about writing a refutation of Franklin's argument—demonstrating, that is, that salaries *should* be paid to executive officers of government? Could you do this while accepting Franklin's view of the fundamental motives which influence human behavior? If you were to substitute another interpretation of men's conduct, what form would it take?

12. Some years before making this speech, Franklin defended the conduct of American agents in France who were accused of having appropriated for their personal use some of the money intended for supplies. He is reported to have said, "Muzzle not the ox that treads the grain"—in other words, do not object if those who are doing work for you make some money at the job. Is this attitude necessarily inconsistent with the views expressed in the speech?

13. Does it follow from Franklin's argument that *all* executive employees of the government should serve without pay? If not, what kinds of officials might be paid?

14. Write a paragraph, using present-day examples and your own ideas, developing this sentence: "And indeed, in all cases of public service, the less the profit the greater the honor."

15. Do you believe the government should employ "dollar-a-year men"—temporary officials who serve in time of emergency for nominal salaries? On what grounds would you defend, or oppose, this practice?

Home by Gruda

REBECCA WEST

OUR CHAUFFEUR was the son of a Swabian, which is to say a German belonging to one of those families which were settled by Maria Theresa on the lands round the Danube between Budapest and Belgrade, because they had gone out of cultivation during the Turkish occupation and had to be recolonized. His father had come to Dubrovnik before he was born, and he can never have known any other people but Slavs, yet quite obviously Slavs struck him as odd and given to carrying on about life to an excessive degree. He himself, particularly when he spoke in English, attempted to correct the balance by under-statement. Hence, when we approached the village of Gruda, on our way from Dubrovnik to Kotor, he turned his head and said, "Nice people." He meant, it proved, that the men and women of this district were undistinguishable in appearance from gods and goddesses. This was one of those strange pockets one finds scattered here and there at vast intervals in the universe, where beauty is the common lot.

"But why," the chauffeur was asking himself, "make a fuss about that?" He put the question to himself with a kind of stolid passion, when we passed through the village again on our way home to Dubrovnik, and a group of three young girls, lovely as primroses in a wood, came towards us, laughing and stretching out their hands and crying out, "Pennies, pennies," as if they were not only begging but were ridiculing the ideas of beggary and benevolence alike. Since we were on the return journey we knew we had time to waste, and hammered on the glass and made the chauffeur stop. He slowed up under protest. "They will beg," he said. "Why not?" said my husband. They were, indeed, most prettily prepared to do so, for each of them carried a little bouquet of flowers for an excuse.

"Pennies, pennies!" they cried, laughing, while we stared at them and adored them. This was no case of a racial tendency imposing itself on the mass, each germ-cell had made an individual effort at beauty. One was black, one was chestnut, one was ash-blonde; they were alike only in their golden skins, their fine eyebrows, their full yet neat mouths, the straightness of their bodies within their heavy black woollen gowns. "Have you any pennies, my dear? I have none," said my husband, full of charitable concern. "Not one," I answered, and I turned to the chauffeur. "Give me three tenpenny pieces," I said. "Three tenpenny pieces!" he exclaimed very slowly. "But you must not give them three tenpenny pieces. Three tenpenny pieces! It is very wrong. They should not beg at all. Begging is disgraceful. And even if it were excusable, three tenpenny pieces is far too much."

There was much to be said for his point of view. Indeed, he was entirely right and we were wrong. But they were so beautiful, and in spite of their beauty they would be poor all their lives long, and that is an injustice I never can bear. It is the flat violation of a promise. Women are told from the day they are born that they must be beautiful, and if they are ugly everything is withheld from them, and the reason scarcely disguised. It follows therefore that women who are beautiful should want for nothing. "Please, I would like to give it to them," I besought the chauffeur, "just three tenpenny pieces; it's not much for us English with the exchange as it is."

He did not answer me at once. His nature, which was so profoundly respectful of all social institutions, made him hate to refuse anything to an employer. At last he said, "I have only one tenpenny piece on me." As I took it we both knew that we both knew that he lied. Glumly he started the engine again, while the lovely girls stood and laughed and waved good-bye to us, a light rain falling on them, the wet road shining at their feet, the creamy foam of the tamarisk on the bank behind them lighter in the dusk than it is in the day, but the yellow broom darker. "I wonder how old those girls were," said my husband, a few miles further on. "Let's ask the chauffeur. Since he's a native he ought to know." The chauffeur answered, "They were perhaps fifteen or sixteen. And if they are encouraged to be impudent when they are so young, what will they be like when they are old?"

UNDERSTANDING THE TEXT

1. Summarize the meaning of the incident narrated in this passage. Does Miss West indicate directly the significance she finds in the incident? In general, what means does she use to convey to the reader the meaning of the episode?

2. What is the function of the explanation, in the first paragraph, of the chauffeur's family and its historical origins?

3. Study carefully the way Miss West selects details in her characterization of the chauffeur. What specific words does she use in describing his actions? How does she present his speech? Does she confine herself to what he does and says, or does she attempt to set forth what is going on in his mind?

4. How full an account does the author give of the three girls? How much effort does she make to differentiate among the three? In your opinion, why has she chosen to describe the girls at this level of generality?

5. Many persons, including the chauffeur, regard beggars as squalid and unpleasant. How does Miss West's choice of language make it clear, from the beginning of the episode, that she and her husband do not share this reaction?

6. In the fourth paragraph Miss West presents a brief argument justifying her desire to give money to the girls. What is the function of this argument in the passage? How seriously do you think Miss West intends it to be taken?

TOPICS FOR DISCUSSION AND WRITING

7. Using the central facts of the incident narrated by Miss West, write a paper which retells the story without making use of the contrast in point of view between the chauffeur and his employers. You may wish to supply another interpretation of the event, or you may narrate the incident in as neutral and objective a manner as possible.

8. Choose an event which is likely to impress different kinds of people in different ways—perhaps a sports contest or a theatrical performance—and write a descriptive essay which brings out this difference in reaction.

9. Examine closely the structure of the sentence in the final paragraph which begins, "Glumly he started the engine again. . . ." What is noteworthy about the way this sentence is put together? What effect do you think Miss West is trying to gain by this sentence structure?

10. After listening to a conversation between two of your friends, attempt to set down a detailed transcript of what they have said. Then examine the transcript and decide which remarks are most important, and which remarks contribute little, in characterizing the point of view of each speaker.

11. Prepare an outline for an essay comparing two teachers you have known—one of a subject in which you are vitally interested, and the other of a subject in which you have little interest. After you have finished the outline, study it to see whether your difference in attitude toward the two subjects has affected the way you view the teachers.

12. All of us have had, while traveling, encounters similar to the one narrated by Miss West. Write a brief objective account of such an encounter; then see if you can expand the account by discovering meaning in the event—by developing, that is, a point of view toward the incident.

13. Select for study a newspaper "human interest" story—an article, that is, which deals, not with conventional news events, but with a down-to-earth crisis involving ordinary human beings. Has the newspaper writer taken a point of view toward his material? What are the signs of this point of view? From the standpoint of your own interest in the incident, has the writer exercised good judgment in his choice of detail?

Thinking Like a Mountain

ALDO LEOPOLD

A DEEP chesty bawl echoes from rimrock to rimrock, rolls down the mountain, and fades into the far blackness of the night. It is an outburst of wild defiant sorrow, and of contempt for all the adversities of the world.

Every living thing (and perhaps many a dead one as well) pays heed to that call. To the deer it is a reminder of the way of all flesh, to the pine a forecast of midnight scuffles and of blood upon the snow, to the coyote a promise of gleanings to come, to the cowman a threat of red ink at the bank, to the hunter a challenge of fang against bullet. Yet behind these obvious and immediate hopes and fears there lies a deeper meaning, known only to the mountain itself. Only the mountain has lived long enough to listen objectively to the howl of a wolf.

Those unable to decipher the hidden meaning know nevertheless that it is there, for it is felt in all wolf country, and distinguishes that country from all other land. It tingles in the spine of all who hear wolves by night, or who scan their tracks by day. Even without sight or sound of wolf, it is implicit in a hundred small events: the midnight whinny of a pack horse, the rattle of rolling rocks, the bound of a fleeing deer, the way shadows lie under the spruces. Only the ineducable tyro can fail to sense the presence or absence of wolves, or the fact that mountains have a secret opinion about them.

My own conviction on this score dates from the day I saw a wolf die. We were eating lunch on a high rimrock, at the foot of which a turbulent river elbowed its way. We saw what we thought was a doe fording the torrent, her breast awash in white water. When she climbed the bank toward us and shook out her tail, we realized our error: it was a wolf. A half-dozen others, evidently grown pups, sprang from the willows and all joined in a welcoming mêlée of wagging tails and playful maulings. What was literally a pile of wolves writhed and tumbled in the center of an open flat at the foot of our rimrock.

In those days we had never heard of passing up a chance to kill a wolf. In a second we were pumping lead into the pack, but with more excitement than accuracy: how to aim a steep downhill shot is always confusing. When our rifles were empty, the old wolf was down, and a pup was dragging a leg into impassable slide-rocks.

We reached the old wolf in time to watch a fierce green fire dying in her eyes. I realized then, and have known ever since, that there was something new to me in those eyes—something known only to her and to the mountain. I was young then, and full of trigger-itch; I thought that because fewer wolves meant more deer, that no wolves would mean hunters' paradise. But after seeing the green fire die, I sensed that neither the wolf nor the mountain agreed with such a view.

*   *   *

Since then I have lived to see state after state extirpate its wolves. I have watched the face of many a newly wolfless mountain, and seen the south-facing slopes wrinkle with a maze of new deer trails. I have seen every edible bush and seedling browsed, first to anaemic desuetude, and then to death. I have seen every edible tree defoliated to the height of a saddlehorn. Such a mountain looks as if someone had given God a new pruning shears, and forbidden Him all other exercise. In the end the starved bones of the hoped-for deer herd, dead of its own too-much, bleach with the bones of the dead sage, or molder under the high-lined junipers.

I now suspect that just as a deer herd lives in mortal fear of its wolves, so does a mountain live in mortal fear of its deer. And perhaps with better cause, for while a buck pulled down by wolves can be replaced in two or three years, a range pulled down by too many deer may fail of replacement in as many decades.

So also with cows. The cowman who cleans his range of wolves does not realize that he is taking over the wolf's job of trimming the herd to fit the range. He has not learned to think like a mountain. Hence we have dustbowls, and rivers washing the future into the sea.

*   *   *

We all strive for safety, prosperity, comfort, long life, and dullness. The deer strives with his supple legs, the cowman with trap and poison, the statesman with pen, the most of us with machines, votes, and dollars, but it all comes to the same thing: peace in our time. A measure of success in this is all well enough, and perhaps is a requisite to objective thinking, but too much safety seems to yield only danger in the long run. Perhaps this is behind Thoreau's dictum: In wildness is the salvation of the world. Perhaps this is the hidden meaning in the howl of the wolf, long known among mountains, but seldom perceived among men.

UNDERSTANDING THE TEXT

1. For Leopold what is "the hidden meaning in the howl of the wolf"? Does he find a single significance in the howl, or does he detect different layers of meaning?

2. At what point in the essay does the reader begin to understand the nature of the meaning Leopold attaches to the howl of the wolf? How has he prepared, in the opening paragraphs of the essay, for the kind of statement which comes later?

3. What does Leopold really mean when he says that the deeper significance of the howl is "known only to the mountain itself"? What effect does he achieve by interpreting this phenomenon from, as it were, the point of view of the mountain? How would the effect have been altered if he had said explicitly, "Let's consider this phenomenon from the viewpoint of those of us who are interested in preserving wild life"?

4. Describe the assumptions concerning nature, and the proper relationship between nature and man, which underlie this essay.

5. Not until the end of the second paragraph does Leopold tell the reader plainly that he is writing about the howl of a wolf. In view of his purpose in the essay, can you account for his decision to describe the howl, and to enumerate some of its more specific meanings, before definitely identifying it?

6. How would you characterize the diction and sentence structure which Leopold uses in this essay? Do such phrases as "the ineducable tyro," in

the third paragraph, and "anaemic desuetude," in the seventh paragraph, strike you as consistent with the diction elsewhere in the essay?

7. In the fourth, fifth, and sixth paragraphs Leopold tells what happened when he first saw a wolf die. Indicate how, through selection of detail and choice of words, he adapts this stretch of narrative to the larger purpose of the essay.

TOPICS FOR DISCUSSION AND WRITING

8. Try your hand at recasting the central argument of this essay in the form of a paraphrase. After reflecting on your summary, see if you can think of other concrete approaches, similar to Leopold's, for conveying this cluster of meanings.

9. In the second sentence of the second paragraph, Leopold suggests, through a series of poetic phrases, what the wolf call means to the deer, to the pine, to the coyote, to the cowman, and to the hunter. As an exercise rewrite this sentence in more literal language.

10. Write an essay in which you support or attack the idea presented in the following statement: "Since man is part of nature, and since competition is the rule of nature, it is surely sentimental to criticize man for using his superior wit to extirpate worthless or dangerous wild creatures."

11. Take a sound which occurs either in nature or in settled society and develop an essay in which you point out the various meanings which this sound may carry for different kinds of people.

12. Do you feel that, in his essay, Leopold has covered all the obvious significances which the wolf call may suggest? If you can think of other possible meanings, why do you suppose Leopold decided not to mention them?

13. Are Leopold's ideas relevant primarily to the question of conserving natural resources, or does he intend them to have broader implications? Write a paper commenting upon the dictum, adapted from Thoreau, "In wildness is the salvation of the world."

14. Read the essay "Thoreau," by James Russell Lowell, and compare Lowell's views on the relationship between nature and man with those of Leopold.

15. Would Leopold's essay have been as persuasive, in your judgment, if he had chosen some other animal as his symbol for wildness—a grizzly bear, perhaps, or a moose?

Where I Lived, and What I Lived For

HENRY DAVID THOREAU

AT A certain season of our life we are accustomed to consider every spot as the possible site of a house. I have thus surveyed the country on every side within a dozen miles of where I live. In imagination I have bought all the farms in succession, for all were to be bought, and I knew their price. I walked over each farmer's premises, tasted his wild apples, discoursed on husbandry with him, took his farm at his price, at any price, mortgaging it to him in my mind; even put a higher price on it,— took every thing but a deed of it,—took his word for his deed, for I dearly love to talk,—cultivated it, and him too to some extent, I trust, and withdrew when I had enjoyed it long enough, leaving him to carry it on. This experience entitled me to be regarded as a sort of real-estate broker by my friends. Wherever I sat, there I might live, and the landscape radiated from me accordingly. What is a house but a *sedes*, a seat? —better if a country seat. I discovered many a site for a house not likely to be soon improved, which some might have thought too far from the village, but to my eyes the village was too far from it. Well, there I might live, I said; and there I did live, for an hour, a summer and a winter life; saw how I could let the years run off, buffet the winter through, and see the spring come in. The future inhabitants of this region, wherever they may place their houses, may be sure that they have been anticipated. An afternoon sufficed to lay out the land into orchard, woodlot, and pasture, and to decide what fine oaks or pines should be left to stand before the door, and whence each blasted tree could be seen to the best advantage; and then I let it lie, fallow perchance, for a man is rich in proportion to the number of things which he can afford to let alone.

My imagination carried me so far that I even had the refusal of several

Reprinted from *Walden* (1854).

farms,—the refusal was all I wanted,—but I never got my fingers burned by actual possession. The nearest that I came to actual possession was when I bought the Hollowell place, and had begun to sort my seeds, and collected materials with which to make a wheelbarrow to carry it on or off with; but before the owner gave me a deed of it, his wife—every man has such a wife—changed her mind and wished to keep it, and he offered me ten dollars to release him. Now, to speak the truth, I had but ten cents in the world, and it surpassed my arithmetic to tell, if I was that man who had ten cents, or who had a farm, or ten dollars, or all together. However, I let him keep the ten dollars and the farm too, for I had carried it far enough; or rather, to be generous, I sold him the farm for just what I gave for it, and, as he was not a rich man, made him a present of ten dollars, and still had my ten cents, and seeds, and materials for a wheelbarrow left. I found thus that I had been a rich man without any damage to my poverty. But I retained the landscape, and I have since annually carried off what it yielded without a wheelbarrow. With respect to landscapes,—

> I am monarch of all I *survey*,
> My right there is none to dispute.

I have frequently seen a poet withdraw, having enjoyed the most valuable part of a farm, while the crusty farmer supposed that he had got a few wild apples only. Why, the owner does not know it for many years when a poet has put his farm in rhyme, the most admirable kind of invisible fence, has fairly impounded it, milked it, skimmed it, and got all the cream, and left the farmer only the skimmed milk.

The real attractions of the Hollowell farm, to me, were: its complete retirement, being about two miles from the village, half a mile from the nearest neighbor, and separated from the highway by a broad field; its bounding on the river, which the owner said protected it by its fogs from frosts in the spring, though that was nothing to me; the gray color and ruinous state of the house and barn, and the dilapidated fences, which put such an interval between me and the last occupant; the hollow and lichen-covered apple trees, gnawed by rabbits, showing what kind of neighbors I should have; but above all, the recollection I had of it from my earliest voyages up the river, when the house was concealed behind a dense grove of red maples, through which I heard the house-dog bark. I was in haste to buy it, before the proprietor finished getting out some rocks, cutting down the hollow apple trees, and grubbing up some young birches which had sprung up in the pasture, or, in short, had made any more of his improvements. To enjoy these advantages I was ready to carry it on; like Atlas, to take the world on my shoulders,—I never heard what compensation he received for that,—and do all those things which had no other motive or excuse but that I might pay for it and be unmolested in my possession of it; for I knew all the while that it would yield the most abundant crop of the kind I wanted if I could only afford to let it alone. But it turned out as I have said.

All that I could say, then, with respect to farming on a large scale (I have always cultivated a garden) was, that I had had my seeds ready. Many think that seeds improve with age. I have no doubt that time discriminates between the good and the bad; and when at last I shall plant, I shall be less likely to be disappointed. But I would say to my fellows, once for all, As long as possible live free and uncommitted. It makes but little difference whether you are committed to a farm or the county jail.

Old Cato, whose "De Re Rusticâ" is my "Cultivator," says,—and the only translation I have seen makes sheer nonsense of the passage,—"When you think of getting a farm, turn it thus in your mind, not to buy greedily; nor spare your pains to look at it, and do not think it enough to go round it once. The oftener you go there the more it will please you, if it is good." I think I shall not buy greedily, but go round and round it as long as I live, and be buried in it first, that it may please me the more at last.

The present was my next experiment of this kind, which I purpose to describe more at length, for convenience, putting the experience of two years into one. As I have said, I do not propose to write an ode to dejection, but to brag as lustily as chanticleer in the morning, standing on his roost, if only to wake my neighbors up.

When first I took up my abode in the woods, that is, began to spend my nights as well as days there, which, by accident, was on Independence day, or the fourth of July, 1845, my house was not finished for winter, but was merely a defence against the rain, without plastering or chimney, the walls being of rough, weather-stained boards, with wide chinks, which made it cool at night. The upright white hewn studs and freshly planed door and window casings gave it a clean and airy look, especially in the morning, when its timbers were saturated with dew, so that I fancied that by noon some sweet gum would exude from them. To my imagination it retained throughout the day more or less of this auroral character, reminding me of a certain house on a mountain which I had visited the year before. This was an airy and unplastered cabin, fit to entertain a travelling god, and where a goddess might trail her garments. The winds which passed over my dwelling were such as sweep over the ridges of mountains, bearing the broken strains, or celestial parts only, of terrestrial music. The morning wind forever blows, the poem of creation is uninterrupted; but few are the ears that hear it. Olympus is but the outside of the earth everywhere.

The only house I had been the owner of before, if I except a boat, was a tent, which I used occasionally when making excursions in the summer, and this is still rolled up in my garret; but the boat, after passing from hand to hand, has gone down the stream of time. With this more substantial shelter about me, I had made some progress toward settling in the world. This frame, so slightly clad, was a sort of crystallization around me, and reacted on the builder. It was suggestive somewhat as a picture in outlines. I did not need to go out-doors to take the air, for the atmosphere within had lost none of its freshness. It was not so much within-doors as behind a door where I sat, even in the rainiest weather. The Harivansa says, "An abode without birds is like a meat without seasoning." Such was not my abode, for I found myself suddenly neighbor to the birds; not by having imprisoned one, but having caged myself near them. I was not only nearer to some of those which commonly frequent the garden and the orchard, but to those wilder and more thrilling songsters of the forest which never, or rarely, serenade a villager,—the wood-thrush, the veery, the scarlet tanager, the field-sparrow, the whippoorwill, and many others.

I was seated by the shore of a small pond, about a mile and a half south of the village of Concord and somewhat higher than it, in the midst of an extensive wood between that town and Lincoln, and about two miles south of that our only field known to fame, Concord Battle Ground; but I was so low in the woods that the opposite shore, half a mile off, like the rest, covered with wood, was my most distant horizon. For the first week, whenever I looked out on the pond it impressed me like a tarn high up on the side of a mountain, its bottom far above the surface of other lakes, and, as the sun arose, I saw it throwing off its nightly clothing of mist, and here and there, by degrees, its soft ripples or its smooth reflecting surface was revealed, while the mists, like ghosts, were stealthily withdrawing in every direction into the woods, as at the breaking up of some nocturnal conventicle. The very dew seemed to hang upon the trees later into the day than usual, as on the sides of mountains.

This small lake was of most value as a neighbor in the intervals of a gentle rain storm in August, when, both air and water being perfectly still, but the sky overcast, mid-afternoon had all the serenity of evening, and the wood-thrush sang around, and was heard from shore to shore. A lake like this is never smoother than at such a time; and the clear portion of the air above it being shallow and darkened by clouds, the water, full of light and reflections, becomes a lower heaven itself so much the more important. From a hill top near by, where the wood had been recently cut off, there was a pleasing vista southward across the pond, through a wide indentation in the hills which form the shore there, where their opposite sides sloping toward each other suggested a stream flowing out in that direction through a wooded valley, but stream there was none. That way I looked between and over the near green hills to some distant and higher ones in the horizon, tinged with blue. Indeed, by standing on tip-toe I could catch a glimpse of some of the peaks of the still bluer and more distant mountain ranges in the north-west, those true-blue coins from heaven's own mint, and also of some portion of the village. But in other directions, even from this point, I could not see over or beyond the woods which surrounded me. It is well to have some water in your neighborhood, to give buoyancy to and float the earth. One value even of the smallest well is, that when you look into it you see that earth is not continent but insular. This is as important as that it keeps butter cool. When I looked across the pond from this peak toward the Sudbury meadows, which in time of flood I distinguished elevated perhaps by a mirage in their seething valley, like a coin in a basin, all the earth beyond the pond appeared like a thin crust insulated and floated even by this small sheet of intervening water, and I was reminded that this on which I dwelt was but *dry land*.

Though the view from my door was still more contracted, I did not feel crowded or confined in the least. There was pasture enough for my imagination. The low shrub-oak plateau to which the opposite shore arose, stretched away toward the prairies of the West and the steppes of Tartary, affording ample room for all the roving families of men. "There are none happy in the world but beings who enjoy freely a vast horizon," —said Damodara, when his herds required new and larger pastures.

Both place and time were changed, and I dwelt nearer to those parts of the universe and to those eras in history which had most attracted me. Where I lived was as far off as many a region viewed nightly by astronomers. We are wont to imagine rare and delectable places in some remote

and more celestial corner of the system, behind the constellation of Cassio-
peia's Chair, far from noise and disturbance. I discovered that my house
actually had its site in such a withdrawn, but forever new and unpro-
faned, part of the universe. If it were worth the while to settle in those
parts near to the Pleiades or the Hyades, to Aldebaran or Altair, then I
was really there, or at an equal remoteness from the life which I had left
behind, dwindled and twinkling with as fine a ray to my nearest neighbor, and to be seen only in moonless nights by him. Such was that part of
creation where I had squatted;—

> There was a shepherd that did live,
>   And held his thoughts as high
> As were the mounts whereon his flocks
>   Did hourly feed him by.

What should we think of the shepherd's life if his flocks always wandered
to higher pastures than his thoughts?

Every morning was a cheerful invitation to make my life of equal simplicity, and I may say innocence, with Nature herself. I have been as sincere a worshipper of Aurora as the Greeks. I got up early and bathed in
the pond; that was a religious exercise, and one of the best things which I
did. They say that characters were engraven on the bathing tub of king
Tching-thang to this effect: "Renew thyself completely each day; do it
again, and again, and forever again." I can understand that. Morning
brings back the heroic ages. I was as much affected by the faint hum of a
mosquito making its invisible and unimaginable tour through my apart-
ment at earliest dawn, when I was sitting with door and windows open, as
I could be by any trumpet that ever sang of fame. It was Homer's re-
quiem; itself an Iliad and Odyssey in the air, singing its own wrath and
wanderings. There was something cosmical about it; a standing advertisement, till forbidden, of the everlasting vigor and fertility of the world.
The morning, which is the most memorable season of the day, is the
awakening hour. Then there is least somnolence in us; and for an hour, at
least, some part of us awakes which slumbers all the rest of the day and
night. Little is to be expected of that day, if it can be called a day, to
which we are not awakened by our Genius, but by the mechanical nudg-
ings of some servitor, are not awakened by our own newly-acquired force
and aspirations from within, accompanied by the undulations of celestial
music, instead of factory bells, and a fragrance filling the air—to a higher
life than we fell asleep from; and thus the darkness bear its fruit, and

prove itself to be good, no less than the light. That man who does not believe that each day contains an earlier, more sacred, and auroral hour than he has yet profaned, has despaired of life, and is pursuing a descending and darkening way. After a partial cessation of his sensuous life, the soul of man, or its organs rather, are reinvigorated each day, and his Genius tries again what noble life it can make. All memorable events, I should say, transpire in morning time and in a morning atmosphere. The Vedas say, "All intelligences awake with the morning." Poetry and art, and the fairest and most memorable of the actions of men, date from such an hour. All poets and heroes, like Memnon, are the children of Aurora, and emit their music at sunrise. To him whose elastic and vigorous thought keeps pace with the sun, the day is a perpetual morning. It matters not what the clocks say or the attitudes and labors of men. Morning is when I am awake and there is a dawn in me. Moral reform is the effort to throw off sleep. Why is it that men give so poor an account of their day if they have not been slumbering? They are not such poor calculators. If they had not been overcome with drowsiness they would have performed something. The millions are awake enough for physical labor; but only one in a million is awake enough for effective intellectual exertion, only one in a hundred millions to a poetic or divine life. To be awake is to be alive. I have never yet met a man who was quite awake. How could I have looked him in the face?

We must learn to reawaken and keep ourselves awake, not by mechanical aids, but by an infinite expectation of the dawn, which does not forsake us in our soundest sleep. I know of no more encouraging fact than the unquestionable ability of man to elevate his life by a conscious endeavor. It is something to be able to paint a particular picture, or to carve a statue, and so to make a few objects beautiful; but it is far more glorious to carve and paint the very atmosphere and medium through which we look, which morally we can do. To affect the quality of the day, that is the highest of arts. Every man is tasked to make his life, even in its details, worthy of the contemplation of his most elevated and critical hour. If we refused, or rather used up, such paltry information as we get, the oracles would distinctly inform us how this might be done.

I went to the woods because I wished to live deliberately, to front only the essential facts of life, and see if I could not learn what it had to teach, and not, when I came to die, discover that I had not lived. I did not wish to live what was not life, living is so dear; nor did I wish to practise resignation, unless it was quite necessary. I wanted to live deep and suck out all the marrow of life, to live so sturdily and Spartan-like as to put to rout all that was not life, to cut a broad swath and shave close, to drive life into a corner, and reduce it to its lowest terms, and, if it proved to be mean, why then to get the whole and genuine meanness of it, and publish its meanness to the world; or if it were sublime, to know it by experience, and be able to give a true account of it in my next excursion. For most men, it appears to me, are in a strange uncertainty about it, whether it is of the devil or of God, and have *somewhat hastily* concluded that it is the chief end of man here to "glorify God and enjoy him forever."

Still we live meanly, like ants; though the fable tells us that we were long ago changed into men; like pygmies we fight with cranes; it is error upon error, and clout upon clout, and our best virtue has for its occasion a superfluous and evitable wretchedness. Our life is frittered away by detail. An honest man has hardly need to count more than his ten fingers, or in extreme cases he may add his ten toes, and lump the rest. Simplicity, simplicity, simplicity! I say, let your affairs be as two or three, and not a hundred or a thousand; instead of a million count half a dozen, and keep your accounts on your thumb nail. In the midst of this chopping sea of civilized life, such are the clouds and storms and quicksands and thousand-and-one items to be allowed for, that a man has to live, if he would not founder and go to the bottom and not make his port at all, by dead reckoning, and he must be a great calculator indeed who succeeds. Simplify, simplify. Instead of three meals a day, if it be necessary eat but one; instead of a hundred dishes, five; and reduce other things in proportion. Our life is like a German Confederacy, made up of petty states, with its boundary forever fluctuating, so that even a German cannot tell you how it is bounded at any moment. The nation itself, with all its so-called internal improvements, which, by the way, are all external and superficial, is just such an unwieldy and overgrown establishment, cluttered with furniture and tripped up by its own traps, ruined by luxury and heedless expense, by want of calculation and a worthy aim, as the million households in the land; and the only cure for it as for them is in a rigid economy, a stern and more than Spartan simplicity of life and elevation of purpose. It lives too fast. Men think that it is essential that the *Nation* have commerce, and export ice, and talk through a telegraph, and ride thirty miles an hour, without a doubt, whether *they* do or not; but whether we should live like baboons or like men, is a little uncertain. If we do not get our sleepers, and forge rails, and devote days and nights to the work, but go to tinkering upon our *lives* to improve *them*, who will build railroads? And if railroads are not built, how shall we get to heaven in season? But if we stay at home and mind our business, who will want railroads? We do not ride on the railroad; it rides upon us. Did you ever think what those sleepers are that underlie the railroad? Each one is a man, an Irishman, or a Yankee man. The rails are laid on them, and they are covered with sand, and the cars run smoothly over them. They are sound sleepers, I assure you. And every few years a new lot is laid down and run over; so that, if some have the pleasure of riding on a rail, others have the misfortune to be ridden upon. And when they run over a man that is walking in his sleep, a supernumerary sleeper in the wrong position, and wake him up, they suddenly stop the cars, and make a hue and cry about it, as if this were an exception. I am glad to know that it takes a gang of men for every five miles to keep the sleepers down and level in their beds as it is, for this is a sign that they may sometime get up again.

Why should we live with such hurry and waste of life? We are determined to be starved before we are hungry. Men say that a stitch in time saves nine, and so they take a thousand stitches to-day to save nine to-morrow. As for *work*, we haven't any of any consequence. We have the Saint Vitus' dance, and cannot possibly keep our heads still. If I should only give a few pulls at the parish bell-rope, as for a fire, that is, without setting the bell, there is hardly a man on his farm in the outskirts of Concord, notwithstanding that press of engagements which was his excuse so many times this morning, nor a boy, nor a woman, I might almost say, but would forsake all and follow that sound, not mainly to save property from the flames, but, if we will confess the truth, much more to see it burn, since burn it must, and we, be it known, did not set it on fire,—or to see it put out, and have a hand in it, if that is done as handsomely; yes, even if it were the parish church itself. Hardly a man takes a half hour's nap after dinner, but when he wakes he holds up his head and asks, "What's the news?" as if the rest of mankind had stood his sentinels. Some give directions to be waked every half hour, doubtless for no other purpose; and then, to pay for it, they tell what they have dreamed. After a night's sleep the news is as indispensable as the breakfast. "Pray tell me any thing new that has happened to a man anywhere on this globe,"— and he reads it over his coffee and rolls, that a man has had his eyes gouged out this morning on the Wachito River; never dreaming the while that he lives in the dark unfathomed mammoth cave of this world, and has but the rudiment of an eye himself.

For my part, I could easily do without the post-office. I think that there are very few important communications made through it. To speak critically, I never received more than one or two letters in my life—I wrote this some years ago—that were worth the postage. The penny-post is, commonly, an institution through which you seriously offer a man that penny for his thoughts which is so often safely offered in jest. And I am sure that I never read any memorable news in a newspaper. If we read of one man robbed, or murdered, or killed by accident, or one house burned, or one vessel wrecked, or one steamboat blown up, or one cow run over on the Western Railroad, or one mad dog killed, or one lot of grass-hoppers in the winter,—we never need read of another. One is enough. If you are acquainted with the principle, what do you care for a myriad instances and applications? To a philosopher all *news*, as it is called, is gossip, and they who edit and read it are old women over their tea. Yet not a few are greedy after this gossip. There was such a rush, as I hear, the other day at one of the offices to learn the foreign news by the last arrival, that several large squares of plate glass belonging to the establish-ment were broken by the pressure,—news which I seriously think a ready wit might write a twelve-month or twelve years beforehand with suf-ficient accuracy. As for Spain, for instance, if you know how to throw in Don Carlos and the Infanta, and Don Pedro and Seville and Granada, from time to time in the right proportions,—they may have changed the names a little since I saw the papers,—and serve up a bull-fight when other entertainments fail, it will be true to the letter, and give us as good an idea of the exact state or ruin of things in Spain as the most succinct and lucid reports under this head in the newspapers: and as for England, almost the last significant scrap of news from that quarter was the revolu-tion of 1649; and if you have learned the history of her crops for an average year, you never need attend to that thing again, unless your spec-ulations are of a merely pecuniary character. If one may judge who rarely looks into the newspapers, nothing new does ever happen in for-eign parts, a French revolution not excepted.

What news! how much more important to know what that is which was never old! "Kieou-he-yu (great dignitary of the state of Wei) sent a man to Khoung-tseu to know his news. Khoung-tseu caused the mes-senger to be seated near him, and questioned him in these terms: What is your master doing? The messenger answered with respect: My master desires to diminish the number of his faults, but he cannot come to the end of them. The messenger being gone, the philosopher remarked: What a worthy messenger! What a worthy messenger!" The preacher, instead of vexing the ears of drowsy farmers on their day of rest at the end of the week,—for Sunday is the fit conclusion of an ill-spent week, and not the fresh and brave beginning of a new one,—with this one other draggle-tail of a sermon, should shout with thundering voice,—"Pause! Avast! Why so seeming fast, but deadly slow?"

Shams and delusions are esteemed for soundest truths, while reality is fabulous. If men would steadily observe realities only, and not allow themselves to be deluded, life, to compare it with such things as we know, would be like a fairy tale and the Arabian Nights' Entertainments. If we respected only what is inevitable and has a right to be, music and poetry would resound along the streets. When we are unhurried and wise, we perceive that only great and worthy things have any permanent and ab-solute existence,—that petty fears and petty pleasures are but the shadow of the reality. This is always exhilarating and sublime. By closing the eyes and slumbering, and consenting to be deceived by shows, men estab-lish and confirm their daily life of routine and habit everywhere, which still is built on purely illusory foundations. Children, who play life, dis-cern its true law and relations more clearly than men, who fail to live it worthily, but who think that they are wiser by experience, that is, by failure. I have read in a Hindoo book, that "there was a king's son, who, being expelled in infancy from his native city, was brought up by a forester, and, growing up to maturity in that state, imagined himself to belong to the barbarous race with which he lived. One of his father's ministers having discovered him, revealed to him what he was, and the misconception of his character was removed, and he knew himself to be a prince. So soul," continues the Hindoo philosopher, "from the circum-stances in which it is placed, mistakes its own character, until the truth is revealed to it by some holy teacher, and then it knows itself to be *Brahme*." I perceive that we inhabitants of New England live this mean life that we do because our vision does not penetrate the surface of things. We think that that *is* which *appears* to be. If a man should walk through this town and see only the reality, where, think you, would the "Mill-dam" go to? If he should give us an account of the realities he beheld there, we should not recognize the place in his description. Look at a meeting-house, or a court-house, or a jail, or a shop, or a dwelling-house, and say what that thing really is before a true gaze, and they would all go to pieces in your account of them. Men esteem truth re-mote, in the outskirts of the system, behind the farthest star, before

Adam and after the last man. In eternity there is indeed something true and sublime. But all these times and places and occasions are now and here. God himself culminates in the present moment, and will never be more divine in the lapse of all the ages. And we are enabled to apprehend at all what is sublime and noble only by the perpetual instilling and drenching of the reality that surrounds us. The universe constantly and obediently answers to our conceptions; whether we travel fast or slow, the track is laid for us. Let us spend our lives in conceiving then. The poet or the artist never yet had so fair and noble a design but some of his posterity at least could accomplish it.

Let us spend one day as deliberately as Nature, and not be thrown off the track by every nutshell and mosquito's wing that falls on the rails. Let us rise early and fast, or break fast, gently and without perturbation; let company come and let company go, let the bells ring and the children cry,—determined to make a day of it. Why should we knock under and go with the stream? Let us not be upset and overwhelmed in that terrible rapid and whirlpool called a dinner, situated in the meridian shallows. Weather this danger and you are safe, for the rest of the way is down hill. With unrelaxed nerves, with morning vigor, sail by it, looking another way, tied to the mast like Ulysses. If the engine whistles, let it whistle till it is hoarse for its pains. If the bell rings, why should we run? We will consider what kind of music they are like. Let us settle ourselves, and work and wedge our feet downward through the mud and slush of opinion, and prejudice, and tradition, and delusion, and appearance, that alluvion which covers the globe, through Paris and London, through New York and Boston and Concord, through church and state, through poetry and philosophy and religion, till we come to a hard bottom and rocks in place, which we can call *reality*, and say, This is, and no mistake; and then begin, having a *point d'appui*, below freshet and frost and fire, a place where you might found a wall or a state, or set a lamp-post safely, or perhaps a gauge, not a Nilometer, but a Realometer, that future ages might know how deep a freshet of shams and appearances had gathered from time to time. If you stand right fronting and face to face to a fact, you will see the sun glimmer on both its surfaces, as if it were a cimeter, and feel its sweet edge dividing you through the heart and marrow, and so you will happily conclude your mortal career. Be it life or death, we crave only reality. If we are really dying, let us hear the rattle in our throats and feel cold in the extremities; if we are alive, let us go about our business.

Time is but the stream I go a-fishing in. I drink at it; but while I drink I see the sandy bottom and detect how shallow it is. Its thin current slides away, but eternity remains. I would drink deeper; fish in the sky, whose bottom is pebbly with stars. I cannot count one. I know not the first letter of the alphabet. I have always been regretting that I was not as wise as the day I was born. The intellect is a cleaver; it discerns and rifts its way into the secret of things. I do not wish to be any more busy with my hands than is necessary. My head is hands and feet. I feel all my best faculties concentrated in it. My instinct tells me that my head is an organ for burrowing, as some creatures use their snout and fore-paws, and with it I would mine and burrow my way through these hills. I think that the richest vein is somewhere hereabouts; so by the divining rod and thin rising vapors I judge; and here I will begin to mine.

UNDERSTANDING THE TEXT

1. The title of this essay suggests that Thoreau has two concerns: to describe his home at Walden Pond and to explain why he lived there. Which parts of the essay deal primarily with the first concern and which are devoted especially to discussing the second point? How distinct and separate does Thoreau keep his remarks on the two questions? Which of the two does he seem to consider more important?

2. What reasons does Thoreau give for his residence at Walden? How early in the essay does he first suggest the nature of these reasons?

3. What does Thoreau find wrong with the ordinary life of his times? Why will living at Walden provide a corrective for these evils? What assumptions about the nature of man, and the meaning of life, underlie these opinions?

4. Thoreau writes, "Shams and delusions are esteemed for soundest truths, while reality is fabulous." In his framework of general ideas, what does he mean by "reality" and what does he consider "sham" or "appearance"?

5. Does Thoreau believe that man is able, through conscious effort, to improve himself, to make himself a better man? How is his position on this question related to the central point of the essay?

6. Sometimes a writer represents his ideas by using concrete things or physical acts as symbols. In this essay, study the way Thoreau gives a general moral meaning to morning and the act of waking up. How many different examples of this procedure can you find elsewhere in the essay?

7. In view of the central purpose of the essay, why do you think Thoreau begins with the whimsical narrative of his adventures in "farm-buying"? Why does he list the "real attractions" of the Hollowell farm in the way he does?

8. What details does he choose to mention in his description of Walden Pond? Why does he single out these aspects?

TOPICS FOR DISCUSSION AND WRITING

9. In his criticism of ordinary life, Thoreau chides his fellow men for their reliance on newspapers and the post office. If he were writing today, and wished to make the same point, would he be likely to mention these same institutions, or are there others to which he might refer?

10. Thoreau once refused to pay taxes because he believed the state was not acting according to right principles. Was this act consistent with the general views on the relationship of the individual to society which are expressed or implied in this selection from *Walden?*

11. Describe a place that has a special meaning for you, choosing and developing the details in such a way as to bring out this particular significance.

12. Thoreau says that he went to the woods because he wished "to front only the essential facts of life." Write a paragraph setting forth what you believe Thoreau means by "the essential facts of life."

13. Write a commentary on this metaphorical passage: "Time is but the stream I go a-fishing in. I drink at it; but while I drink I see the sandy bottom and detect how shallow it is. Its thin current slides away, but eternity remains." What does the passage mean, and how is it related to the general drift of the essay?

Thoreau

JAMES RUSSELL LOWELL

I HAVE just been renewing my recollection of Mr. Thoreau's writings, and have read through his six volumes in the order of their production. I shall try to give an adequate report of their impression upon me both as critic and as mere reader. He seems to me to have been a man with so high a conceit of himself that he accepted without questioning, and insisted on our accepting, his defects and weaknesses of character as virtues and powers peculiar to himself. Was he indolent, he finds none of the activities which attract or employ the rest of mankind worthy of him. Was he wanting in the qualities that make success, it is success that is contemptible, and not himself that lacks persistency and purpose. Was he poor, money was an unmixed evil. Did his life seem a selfish one, he condemns doing good as one of the weakest of superstitions. To be of use was with him the most killing bait of the wily tempter Uselessness. He had no faculty of generalization from outside of himself, or at least no experience which would supply the material of such, and he makes his own whim the law, his own range the horizon of the universe. He condemns a world, the hollowness of whose satisfactions he had never had the means of testing, and we recognize Apemantus behind the mask of Timon. He had little active imagination; of the receptive he had much. His appreciation is of the highest quality; his critical power, from want of continuity of mind, very limited and inadequate. He somewhere cites a simile from Ossian, as an example of the superiority of the old poetry to the new, though, even were the historic evidence less convincing, the sentimental melancholy of those poems should be conclusive of their modernness. He had none of the artistic mastery which controls a great

Reprinted from *My Study Windows* (1871). Originally published in *North American Review*, October, 1865.

work to the serene balance of completeness, but exquisite mechanical skill in the shaping of sentences and paragraphs, or (more rarely) short bits of verse for the expression of a detached thought, sentiment, or image. His works give one the feeling of a sky full of stars—something impressive and exhilarating certainly, something high overhead and freckled thickly with spots of isolated brightness; but whether these have any mutual relation with each other, or have any concern with our mundane matters, is for the most part matter of conjecture—astrology as yet, and not astronomy.

It is curious, considering what Thoreau afterwards became, that he was not by nature an observer. He only saw the things he looked for, and was less poet than naturalist. Till he built his Walden shanty, he did not know that the hickory grew in Concord. Till he went to Maine, he had never seen phosphorescent wood, a phenomenon early familiar to most country boys. At forty he speaks of the seeding of the pine as a new discovery, though one should have thought that its gold dust of blowing pollen might have earlier drawn his eye. Neither his attention nor his genius was of the spontaneous kind. He discovered nothing. He thought everything a discovery of his own, from moonlight to the planting of acorns and nuts by squirrels. This is a defect in his character, but one of his chief charms as a writer. Everything grows fresh under his hand. He delved in his mind and nature; he planted them with all manner of native and foreign seeds, and reaped assiduously. He was not merely solitary, he would be isolated, and succeeded at last in almost persuading himself that he was autochthonous. He valued everything in proportion as he fancied it to be exclusively his own. He complains in *Walden* that there is no one in Concord with whom he could talk of Oriental literature, though the man was living within two miles of his hut who had introduced him to it. This intellectual selfishness becomes sometimes almost painful in reading him. He lacked that generosity of "communication" which Johnson admired in Burke. De Quincey tells us that Wordsworth was impatient when anyone else spoke of mountains, as if he had a peculiar property in them. And we can readily understand why it should be so: no one is satisfied with another's appreciation of his mistress. But Thoreau seems to have prized a lofty way of thinking (often we should be inclined to call it a remote one) not so much because it was good in itself as because he wished few to share it with him. It seems now and then as if he did not seek to lure others up "above our lower region of turmoil," but to leave his own name cut on the mountain peak as the first climber. This itch of originality infects his thought and style. To be misty is not to be mystic. He turns commonplaces end for end, and fancies it makes something new of them. As we walk down Park Street, our eye is caught by Dr. Winship's dumbbells, one of which bears an inscription testifying that it is the heaviest ever put up at arm's length by any athlete; and in reading Mr. Thoreau's books we cannot help feeling as if he sometimes invited our attention to a particular sophism or paradox as the biggest yet maintained by any single writer. He seeks, at all risks, for perversity of thought, and revives the age of *concetti* while he fancies himself going back to a pre-classical nature. "A day," he says, "passed in the society of those Greek sages, such as described in the Banquet of Xenophon, would not be comparable with the dry wit of decayed cranberry vines and the fresh Attic salt of the moss beds." It is not so much the True that he loves as the Out-of-the-Way. As the Brazen Age shows itself in other men by exaggeration of phrase, so in him by extravagance of statement. He wishes always to trump your suit and to *ruff* when you least expect it. Do you love Nature because she is beautiful? He will find a better argument in her ugliness. Are you tired of the artificial man? He instantly dresses you up an ideal in a Penobscot Indian, and attributes to this creature of his otherwise-mindedness as peculiarities things that are common to all woodsmen, white or red, and this simply because he has not studied the pale-faced variety.

This notion of an absolute originality, as if one could have a patent right in it, is an absurdity. A man cannot escape in thought, any more than he can in language, from the past and the present. As no one ever invents a word, and yet language somehow grows by general contribution and necessity, so it is with thought. Mr. Thoreau seems to me to insist in public on going back to flint and steel when there is a matchbox in his pocket which he knows very well how to use at a pinch. Originality consists in power of digesting and assimilating thought, so that they become part of our life and substance. Montaigne, for example, is one of the most original of authors, though he helped himself to ideas in every direction. But they turn to blood and coloring in his style, and give a freshness of complexion that is forever charming. In Thoreau much seems yet to be foreign and unassimilated, showing itself in symptoms of indigestion. A preacher-up of Nature, we now and then detect under the surly and stoic garb something of the sophist and the sentimentalizer. I am far from implying that this was conscious on his part. But it is much easier for a man to impose on himself when he measures only with himself. A greater familiarity with ordinary men would have done Thoreau good, by showing him how many fine qualities are common to the race. The radical vice of his theory of life was that he confounded physical with spiritual remoteness from men. A man is far enough withdrawn from his fellows if he keep himself clear of their weaknesses. He is not so truly withdrawn as exiled, if he refuse to share in their strength. "Solitude," says Cowley, "can be well fitted and set right but upon a very few persons. They must have enough knowledge of the world to see the vanity of it, and enough virtue to despise all vanity." It is a morbid self-consciousness that pronounces the world of men empty and worthless before trying it, the instinctive evasion of one who is sensible of some innate weakness, and retorts the accusation of it before any has made it but himself. To a healthy mind, the world is a constant challenge of opportunity. Mr. Thoreau had not a healthy mind, or he would not have been so fond of prescribing. His whole life was a search for the doctor. The old mystics had a wiser sense of what the world was worth. They ordained a severe apprenticeship to law, and even ceremonial, in order to the gaining of freedom and mastery over these. Seven years of service for Rachel were to be rewarded at last with Leah. Seven other years of faithfulness with her were to win them at last the true bride of their souls. Active Life was with them the only path to the Contemplative.

Thoreau had no humor, and this implies that he was a sorry logician. Himself an artist in rhetoric, he confounds thought with style when he undertakes to speak of the latter. He was forever talking of getting away from the world, but he must be always near enough to it, nay, to the Concord corner of it, to feel the impression he makes there. He verifies the shrewd remark of Sainte-Beuve, "*On touche encore à son temps et très-fort, même quand on le repousse.*"[1] This egotism of his is a Stylites pillar after all, a seclusion which keeps him in the public eye. The dignity of man is an excellent thing, but therefore to hold one's self too sacred and precious is the reverse of excellent. There is something delightfully absurd in six volumes addressed to a world of such "vulgar fellows" as Thoreau affirmed his fellow men to be. I once had a glimpse of a genuine solitary who spent his winters one hundred and fifty miles beyond all human communication, and there dwelt with his rifle as his only confidant. Compared with this, the shanty on Walden Pond has something the air, it must be confessed, of the Hermitage of La Chevrette. I do not believe that the way to a true cosmopolitanism carries one into the woods

[1] We are still very much a part of our time, even when we reject it.

or the society of musquashes. Perhaps the narrowest provincialism is that of Self; that of Kleinwinkel is nothing to it. The natural man, like the singing birds, comes out of the forest as inevitably as the natural bear and the wildcat stick there. To seek to be natural implies a consciousness that forbids all naturalness forever. It is as easy—and no easier—to be natural in a *salon* as in a swamp, if one do not aim at it, for what we call unnaturalness always has its spring in a man's thinking too much about himself. "It is impossible," said Turgot, "for a vulgar man to be simple."

I look upon a great deal of the modern sentimentalism about Nature as a mark of disease. It is one more symptom of the general liver complaint. To a man of wholesome constitution the wilderness is well enough for a mood or a vacation, but not for a habit of life. Those who have most loudly advertised their passion for seclusion and their intimacy with nature, from Petrarch down, have been mostly sentimentalists, unreal men, misanthropes on the spindle side, solacing an uneasy suspicion of themselves by professing contempt for their kind. They make demands on the world in advance proportioned to their inward measure of their own merit, and are angry that the world pays only by the visible measure of performance. It is true of Rousseau, the modern founder of the sect, true of Saint Pierre, his intellectual child, and of Chateaubriand, his grandchild, the inventor, we might almost say, of the primitive forest, and who first was touched by the solemn falling of a tree from natural decay in the windless silence of the woods. It is a very shallow view that affirms trees and rocks to be healthy, and cannot see that men in communities are just as true to the laws of their organization and destiny; that can tolerate the puffin and the fox, but not the fool and the knave; that would shun politics because of its demagogues, and snuff up the stench of the obscene fungus. The divine life of Nature is more wonderful, more various, more sublime in man than in any other of her works, and the wisdom that is gained by commerce with men, as Montaigne and Shakespeare gained it, or with one's own soul among men, as Dante, is the most delightful, as it is the most precious, of all. In outward nature it is still man that interests us, and we care far less for the things seen than the way in which they are seen by poetic eyes like Wordsworth's or Thoreau's, and the reflections they cast there. To hear the to-do that is often made over the simple fact that a man sees the image of himself in the outward world, one is reminded of a savage when he for the first time catches a glimpse of himself in a looking glass. "Venerable child of Nature," we are tempted to say, "to whose science in the invention of the tobacco pipe, to whose art in the tattooing of thine undegenerate hide not yet enslaved by tailors, we are slowly striving to climb back, the miracle thou beholdest is sold in my unhappy country for a shilling!" If matters go on as they have done, and everybody must needs blab of all the favors that have been done him by roadside and river brink and woodland walk, as if to kiss and tell were no longer treachery, it will be a positive refreshment to meet a man who is as superbly indifferent to Nature as she is to him. By and by we shall have John Smith, of No. -12-12th Street, advertising that he is not the J. S. who saw a cow lily on Thursday last, as he never saw one in his life, would not see one if he could, and is prepared to prove an alibi on the day in question.

Solitary communion with Nature does not seem to have been sanitary or sweetening in its influence on Thoreau's character. On the contrary, his letters show him more cynical as he grew older. While he studied with respectful attention the minks and woodchucks, his neighbors, he looked with utter contempt on the august drama of destiny of which his country was the scene, and on which the curtain had already risen. He was converting us back to a state of nature "so eloquently," as Voltaire said of Rousseau, "that he almost persuaded us to go on all fours," while the wiser fates were making it possible for us to walk erect for the first time. Had he conversed more with his fellows, his sympathies would have widened with the assurance that his peculiar genius had more appreciation, and his writings a larger circle of readers, or at least a warmer one, than he dreamed of. We have the highest testimony[2] to the natural sweetness, sincerity, and nobleness of his temper, and in his books an equally irrefragable one to the rare quality of his mind. He was not a strong thinker, but a sensitive feeler. Yet his mind strikes us as cold and wintry in its purity. A light snow has fallen everywhere in which he seems to come on the track of the shyer sensations that would elsewhere leave no trace. We think greater compression would have done more for his fame. A feeling of sameness comes over us as we read so much. Trifles are recorded with an over-minute punctuality and conscientiousness of detail. He registers the state of his personal thermometer thirteen times a day. We cannot help thinking sometimes of the man who

> Watches, starves, freezes, and sweats
> To learn but catechisms and alphabets
> Of unconcerning things, matters of fact,

[2] Mr. Emerson, in the Biographical Sketch prefixed to the *Excursions*.

and sometimes of the saying of the Persian poet, that "when the owl would boast, he boasts of catching mice at the edge of a hole." We could readily part with some of his affectations. It was well enough for Pythagoras to say, once for all, "When I was Euphorbus at the siege of Troy"; not so well for Thoreau to travesty it into "When I was a shepherd on the plains of Assyria." A naïve thing said over again is anything but naïve. But with every exception, there is no writing comparable with Thoreau's in kind, that is comparable with it in degree where it is best; where it disengages itself, that is, from the tangled roots and dead leaves of a secondhand Orientalism, and runs limpid and smooth and broadening as it runs, a mirror for whatever is grand and lovely in both worlds.

George Sand says neatly that "Art is not a study of positive reality" (*actuality* were the fitter word), "but a seeking after ideal truth." It would be doing very inadequate justice to Thoreau if we left it to be inferred that this ideal element did not exist in him, and that, too, in larger proportion, if less obtrusive, than his nature worship. He took nature as the mountain path to an ideal world. If the path wind a good deal, if he record too faithfully every trip over a root, if he botanize somewhat wearisomely, he gives us now and then superb outlooks from some jutting crag, and brings us out at last into an illimitable ether, where the breathing is not difficult for those who have any true touch of the climbing spirit. His shanty life was a mere impossibility, so far as his own conception of it goes, as an entire independency of mankind. The tub of Diogenes had a sounder bottom. Thoreau's experiment actually presupposed all that complicated civilization which it theoretically abjured. He squatted on another man's land; he borrows an ax; his boards, his nails, his bricks, his mortar, his books, his lamp, his fishhooks, his plow, his hoe, all turn state's evidence against him as an accomplice in the sin of that artificial civilization which rendered it possible that such a person as Henry D. Thoreau should exist at all. *Magnis tamen excidit ausis.*[3] His aim was a noble and a useful one, in the direction of "plain living and high thinking." It was a practical sermon on Emerson's text that "things are in the saddle and ride mankind," an attempt to solve Carlyle's problem (condensed from Johnson) of "lessening your denominator." His whole life was a rebuke of the waste and aimlessness of our American luxury, which is an abject enslavement to tawdry upholstery. He had "fine translunary things" in him. His better style as a writer is in keeping with the simplicity and purity of his life. We have said that his range was

[3] "He fell, however, in a great attempt" (Ovid).

narrow, but to be a master is to be a master. He had caught his English at its living source, among the poets and prose writers of its best days; his literature was extensive and recondite; his quotations are always nuggets of the purest ore: there are sentences of his as perfect as anything in the language, and thoughts as clearly crystallized; his metaphors and images are always fresh from the soil; he had watched Nature like a detective who is to go upon the stand; as we read him, it seems as if all out-of-doors had kept a diary and become its own Montaigne; we look at the landscape as in a Claude Lorraine glass; compared with his, all other books of similar aim, even White's *Selborne*, seem dry as a country clergyman's meteorological journal in an old almanac. He belongs with Donne and Browne and Novalis; if not with the originally creative men, with the scarcely smaller class who are peculiar, and whose leaves shed their invisible thought-seed like ferns.

UNDERSTANDING THE TEXT

1. In this interpretation, what does Lowell consider to be the central aspect of Thoreau's character? How early in the essay does he mention this trait?
2. Lowell asserts that, for a naturalist, Thoreau had surprisingly little precise knowledge of nature. How does the critic relate this circumstance to his general view of Thoreau's character?
3. What premises concerning the proper relationship of man and society does Lowell work from in this essay? How do these premises differ from Thoreau's on the same subject?
4. In referring to Thoreau's "itch of originality," and in developing this criticism, what ideas and attitudes are implied by the tone of Lowell's remarks? How does Lowell define true originality?
5. On what grounds does Lowell attack "the modern sentimentalism about Nature"? Are these grounds consistent with the premises he uses elsewhere in the essay?
6. Lowell says that Thoreau "had none of the artistic mastery which controls a great work to the serene balance of completeness." Is this judgment contradicted when, near the end of the essay, Lowell finds a number of things to praise in Thoreau's writing?
7. Look up the following and establish their meaning in the contexts where they occur: Apemantus, Timon, Ossian, Rachel and Leah, a Stylites pillar, the Hermitage of La Chevrette, the tub of Diogenes.

TOPICS FOR DISCUSSION AND WRITING

8. Do you agree with Lowell that "Thoreau had no humor"?
9. Lowell believes that it is as easy "to be natural in a *salon* as in a swamp."

Do you agree? In an essay support or criticize the idea that one can lead a natural life regardless of environment. Make clear what you mean by "natural." If you disagree with Lowell, you may wish to describe the kind of environment which seems to you to encourage naturalness.

10. According to Lowell, Thoreau tried to solve the problem of "lessening your denominator." In a brief essay, explain the meaning of this figure of speech, and suggest how, in the contemporary world, a student might attempt to "lessen his denominator."

11. At the end of the first paragraph, Lowell sums up his impression of Thoreau's works by terming them "astrology as yet, and not astronomy." Write an explanation of what Lowell means by this remark.

The Meaning of Thoreau's Walden

HENRY SIEDEL CANBY

THE DOMINANT idea of *Walden*, which is simple, has been abundantly misunderstood. Thoreau's problem is the poor student's (or artist's or scientist's) who wishes to study, investigate, create, in a society which will not pay him enough for the proceeds of his labor, and is not interested in his brand of happiness. His solution is self-reliance, simplification of living, willingness to labor with the hands if necessary, resignation of everything not essential to his particular temperament, and a shrewd study of how he can provide for his sustenance with the least waste of time. Thoreau's own estimate of time needed was a month to six weeks out of a year.

This solution is worthless, however, unless it brings with it an expansion of every taste, interest, vocation, and avocation which is possible to the experimenter, wished for by him, and practicable in a life of disciplined simplicity. *Walden* calls for more life, not less. Nor is Thoreau's particular solution prescribed, like a reformer's panacea, to everyone, but only to the discontented who live lives of quiet desperation. "Strong and valiant natures, who . . . spend more lavishly than the richest, without ever impoverishing themselves . . . those who are well employed," can take care of themselves. He writes for that "most terribly impoverished class of all, who have accumulated dross, but know not how to use it," and "the mass of men [alas, how much more numerous!] who are discontented, and idly complaining of . . . their lot or of the times, when they might improve them." "I desire that there may be as many different persons in the world as possible; but I would have each one be very careful to find out and pursue *his own* way, and not his father's or his mother's or his neighbor's instead." The book is the story of how he, a poor scholar, and discontented, found *his* way, and how he enjoyed it.

The idea that *Walden* is a study in asceticism is quite wrong. If Thoreau was an ascetic (though not always) in his eating, if he was an ascetic in physical love, nevertheless he was passionate in most of his pursuits, an epicure in many of the delights of the senses, and a propagandist for life that tingles from the brain to the toe-tips. He was unmarried and childless, which made his problem easier to solve economically, but no less a problem. Marriage—in a cabin with a bean or corn field—was raising poor whites all along the frontier, even as Thoreau wrote, and such simplicity solved no problems. If you wish to get married, if you love good wine, if you must live in a library, or go to Europe, or belong to a country club—these are merely the terms of your problem. The principle is the same—simplify in what is not necessary for your content. And if your needs are spiritual and intellectual, do not starve them in order to feed less durable pleasures. Learn in any case what *you* can do in order to live the life you really desire while earning what you have to earn. Industrialism has made the problem of the man with a soul as well as a stomach more acute because it sells only for money, which must somehow be had. Thoreau's solution was to reduce his wants, grow beans for cash, build his house with his own hands, and be willing to be solitary as long and as much as solitude did him good. What is yours?

UNDERSTANDING THE TEXT

1. What misunderstandings of Thoreau's ideas is Canby trying to remove in this essay?
2. How does he go about correcting the misunderstandings?
3. In view of this purpose, why, in the first sentence of the second paragraph, does Canby refer to Thoreau, or a person who follows him, as "the experimenter"?
4. Observe the way Canby, in the second paragraph, uses quotations from Thoreau to support his point that *Walden* was not intended as a universal prescription. Why are the quotations arranged in this particular order?

TOPICS FOR DISCUSSION AND WRITING

5. Do you believe that Thoreau's problem, as defined by Canby, is still an important one in the present-day world? Has it been made irrelevant by the shortening of working hours and the corresponding expansion of leisure time?

6. Do you agree with Canby that industrialism has made more acute the problem of finding opportunity to do what is of first importance to a person? How would the problem be different in an agricultural or handicraft economy?

7. Would Thoreau be likely to accept Canby's opinion that one possible meaning of *Walden* is that even the out-and-out materialist should so arrange his life that he can enjoy the material or social satisfactions which he desires?

8. How would you answer the question which concludes the essay?

Walden

E. B. WHITE

MISS NIMS, take a letter to Henry David Thoreau. Dear Henry: I thought of you the other afternoon as I was approaching Concord doing fifty on Route 62. That is a high speed at which to hold a philosopher in one's mind, but in this century we are a nimble bunch.

On one of the lawns in the outskirts of the village a woman was cutting the grass with a motorized lawn mower. What made me think of you was that the machine had rather got away from her, although she was game enough, and in the brief glimpse I had of the scene it appeared to me that the lawn was mowing the lady. She kept a tight grip on the handles, which throbbed violently with every explosion of the one-cylinder motor, and as she sheered around bushes and lurched along at a reluctant trot behind her impetuous servant, she looked like a puppy who had grabbed something that was too much for him. Concord hasn't changed much, Henry; the farm implements and the animals still have the upper hand.

I may as well admit that I was journeying to Concord with the deliberate intention of visiting your woods; for although I have never knelt at the grave of a philosopher nor placed wreaths on moldy poets, and have often gone a mile out of my way to avoid some place of historical interest, I have always wanted to see Walden Pond. The account which you left of your sojourn there is, you will be amused to learn, a document of increasing pertinence; each year it seems to gain a little headway, as the world loses ground. We may all be transcendental yet, whether we like it or not. As our common complexities increase, any tale of individual simplicity (and yours is the best written and the cockiest) acquires a new fascination; as our goods accumulate, but not our well-being, your report of an existence without material adornment takes on a certain awkward credibility.

My purpose in going to Walden Pond, like yours, was not to live cheaply or to live dearly there, but to transact some private business with the fewest obstacles. Approaching Concord, doing forty, doing forty-five, doing fifty, the steering wheel held snug in my palms, the highway held grimly in my vision, the crown of the road now serving me (on the right-hand curves), now defeating me (on the lefthand curves), I began to rouse myself from the stupefaction which a day's motor journey induces. It was a delicious evening, Henry, when the whole body is one sense, and imbibes delight through every pore, if I may coin a phrase. Fields were richly brown where the harrow, drawn by the stripped Ford, had lately sunk its teeth; pastures were green; and overhead the sky had that same everlasting great look which you will find on Page 144 of the Oxford pocket edition. I could feel the road entering me, through tire, wheel, spring, and cushion; shall I not have intelligence with earth too? Am I not partly leaves and vegetable mold myself?—a man of infinite horsepower, yet partly leaves.

Stay with me on 62 and it will take you into Concord. As I say, it was a delicious evening. The snake had come forth to die in a bloody S on the highway, the wheel upon its head, its bowels flat now and exposed. The turtle had come up too to cross the road and die in the attempt, its hard shell smashed under the rubber blow, its intestinal yearning (for the other side of the road) forever squashed. There was a sign by the wayside which announced that the road had a "cotton surface." You wouldn't know what that is, but neither, for that matter, did I. There is a cryptic ingredient in many of our modern improvements—we are awed and pleased without knowing quite what we are enjoying. It is something to be traveling on a road with a cotton surface.

The civilization round Concord today is an odd distillation of city, village, farm, and manor. The houses, yards, fields look not quite suburban, not quite rural. Under the bronze beech and the blue spruce of the departed baron grazes the milch goat of the heirs. Under the porte-cochère stands the reconditioned station wagon; under the grape arbor sit the puppies for sale. (But why do men degenerate ever? What makes families run out?)

It was June and everywhere June was publishing her immemorial stanza; in the lilacs, in the syringa, in the freshly edged paths and the sweetness of moist beloved gardens, and the little wire wickets that preserve the tulips' front. Farmers were already moving the fruits of their toil into their yards, arranging the rhubarb, the asparagus, the strictly fresh eggs on the painted stands under the little shed roofs with the patent shingles. And though it was almost a hundred years since you had taken your ax and started cutting out your home on Walden Pond, I was interested to observe that the philosophical spirit was still alive in Massachusetts; in the center of a vacant lot some boys were assembling the framework of a rude shelter, their whole mind and skill concentrated in the rather inauspicious helter-skeleton of studs and rafters. They too were escaping from town, to live naturally, in a rich blend of savagery and philosophy.

That evening, after supper at the inn, I strolled out into the twilight to dream my shapeless transcendental dreams and see that the car was locked up for the night (first open the right front door, then reach over, straining, and pull up the handles of the left rear and the left front till you hear the click, then the handle of the right rear, then shut the right front but open it again, remembering that the key is still in the ignition switch, remove the key, shut the right front again with a bang, push the tiny keyhole cover to one side, insert key, turn, and withdraw). It is what we all do, Henry. It is called locking the car. It is said to confuse thieves and keep them from making off with the laprobe. Four doors to lock behind one robe. The driver himself never uses a laprobe, the free movement of his legs being vital to the operation of the vehicle; so that when he locks the car it is a pure and unselfish act. I have in my life gained very little essential heat from laprobes, yet I have ever been at pains to lock them up.

The evening was full of sounds, some of which would have stirred your memory. The robins still love the elms of New England villages at sundown. There is enough of the thrush in them to make song inevitable at the end of day, and enough of the tramp to make them hang round the dwellings of men. A robin, like many another American, dearly loves a white house with green blinds. Concord is still full of them.

Your fellow-townsmen were stirring abroad—not many afoot, most of them in their cars; and the sound which they made in Concord at evening was a rustling and a whispering. The sound lacks steadfastness and is wholly unlike that of a train. A train, as you know who lived so near the Fitchburg line, whistles once or twice sadly and is gone, trailing a memory in smoke, soothing to ear and mind. Automobiles, skirting a village green, are like flies that have gained the inner ear—they buzz, cease, pause, start, shift, stop, halt, brake, and the whole effect is a nervous polytone curiously disturbing.

As I wandered along, the toc toc of ping pong balls drifted from an attic window. In front of the Reuben Brown house a Buick was drawn up. At the wheel, motionless, his hat upon his head, a man sat, listening to Amos and Andy on the radio (it is a drama of many scenes and without an end). The deep voice of Andrew Brown, emerging from the car, although it originated more than two hundred miles away, was unstrained by distance. When you used to sit on the shore of your pond on Sunday morning, listening to the church bells of Acton and Concord, you were aware of the excellent filter of the intervening atmosphere. Science has attended to that, and sound now maintains its intensity without regard for distance. Properly sponsored, it goes on forever.

A fire engine, out for a trial spin, roared past Emerson's house, hot with readiness for public duty. Over the barn roofs the martins dipped and chittered. A swarthy daughter of an asparagus grower, in culottes, shirt, and bandanna, pedalled past on her bicycle. It was indeed a delicious evening, and I returned to the inn (I believe it was your house once) to rock with the old ladies on the concrete veranda.

Next morning early I started afoot for Walden, out Main Street and down Thoreau, past the depot and the Minuteman Chevrolet Company. The morning was fresh, and in a bean field along the way I flushed an agriculturalist, quietly studying his beans. Thoreau Street soon joined Number 126, an artery of the State. We number our highways nowadays, our speed being so great we can remember little of their quality or character and are lucky to remember their number. (Men have an indistinct notion that if they keep up this activity long enough all will at length ride somewhere, in next to no time.) Your pond is on 126.

I knew I must be nearing your woodland retreat when the Golden Pheasant lunchroom came into view—Sealtest ice cream, toasted sandwiches, hot frankfurters, waffles, tonics, and lunches. Were I the proprietor, I should add rice, Indian meal, and molasses—just for old time's sake. The Pheasant, incidentally, is for sale: a chance for some nature lover who wishes to set himself up beside a pond in the Concord atmosphere and live deliberately, fronting only the essential facts of life on Number 126. Beyond the Pheasant was a place called Walden Breezes, an oasis whose porch pillars were made of old green shutters sawed into lengths. On the porch was a distorting mirror, to give the traveler a comical image of himself, who had miraculously learned to gaze in an ordinary glass without smiling. Behind the Breezes, in a sun-parched clearing, dwelt your philosophical descendants in their trailers, each trailer the size of your hut, but all grouped together for the sake of congeniality. Trailer people leave the city, as you did, to discover solitude and in any weather, at any hour of the day or night, to improve the nick of time; but they soon collect in villages and get bogged deeper in the mud than ever. The camp behind Walden Breezes was just rousing itself to the morning. The ground was packed hard under the heel, and the sun came through the clearing to bake the soil and enlarge the wry smell of cramped housekeeping. Cushman's bakery truck had stopped to deliver an early basket of rolls. A camp dog, seeing me in the road, barked petulantly. A man emerged from one of the trailers and set forth with a bucket to draw water from some forest tap.

Leaving the highway I turned off into the woods toward the pond, which was apparent through the foliage. The floor of the forest was strewn with dried old oak leaves and *Transcripts*. From beneath the flattened popcorn wrapper (*granum explosum*) peeped the frail violet. I followed a footpath and descended to the water's edge. The pond lay clear and blue in the morning light, as you have seen it so many times. In the shallows a man's waterlogged shirt undulated gently. A few flies came out to greet me and convoy me to your cove, past the No Bathing signs on which the fellows and the girls had scrawled their names. I felt strangely excited suddenly to be snooping around your premises, tiptoeing along watchfully, as though not to tread by mistake upon the intervening century. Before I got to the cove I heard something which seemed to me quite wonderful: I heard your frog, a full clear *troonk*, guiding me, still hoarse and solemn, bridging the years as the robins had bridged them in the sweetness of the village evening. But he soon quit, and I came on a couple of young boys throwing stones at him.

Your front yard is marked by a bronze tablet set in a stone. Four small granite posts, a few feet away, show where the house was. On top of the tablet was a pair of faded blue bathing trunks with a white stripe. Back of it is a pile of stones, a sort of cairn, left by your visitors as a tribute I suppose. It is a rather ugly little heap of stones, Henry. In fact the hillside itself seems faded, browbeaten; a few tall skinny pines, bare of lower limbs, a smattering of young maples in suitable green, some birches and oaks, and a number of trees felled by the last big wind. It was from the bole of one of these fallen pines, torn up by the roots, that I extracted the stone which I added to the cairn—a sentimental act in which I was interrupted by a small terrier from a nearby picnic group, who confronted me and wanted to know about the stone.

I sat down for a while on one of the posts of your house to listen to the bluebottles and the dragonflies. The invaded glade sprawled shabby and mean at my feet, but the flies were tuned to the old vibration. There were the remains of a fire in your ruins, but I doubt that it was yours; also two beer bottles trodden into the soil and become part of earth. A young oak had taken root in your house, and two or three ferns, unrolling like the ticklers at a banquet. The only other furnishings were a DuBarry pattern sheet, a page torn from a picture magazine, and some crusts in wax paper.

Before I quit I walked clear round the pond and found the place where you used to sit on the northeast side to get the sun in the fall, and the beach where you got sand for scrubbing your floor. On the eastern side of the pond, where the highway borders it, the State has built dressing rooms for swimmers, a float with diving towers, drinking fountains of porcelain, and rowboats for hire. The pond is in fact a State Preserve, and carries a twenty-dollar fine for picking wild flowers, a decree signed in all solemnity by your fellow-citizens Walter C. Wardwell, Erson B. Barlow, and Nathaniel I. Bowditch. There was a smell of creosote where they had been building a wide wooden stairway to the road and the parking area. Swimmers and boaters were arriving; bodies plunged vigorously into the water and emerged wet and beautiful in the bright air. As I left, a boatload of town boys were splashing about in mid-pond, kidding and fooling, the young fellows singing at the tops of their lungs in a wild chorus:

> Amer-ica, Amer-i-ca, God shed his grace on thee,
> And crown thy good with brotherhood
> From sea to shi-ning sea!

I walked back to town along the railroad, following your custom. The rails were expanding noisily in the hot sun, and on the slope of the roadbed the wild grape and the blackberry sent up their creepers to the track.

The expense of my brief sojourn in Concord was:

Canvas shoes	$1.95	
Baseball bat	.25	gifts to take
Left-handed fielder's glove	1.25	back to a boy
Hotel and meals	4.25	
In all	$7.70	

As you see, this amount was almost what you spent for food for eight months. I cannot defend the shoes or the expenditure for shelter and food: they reveal a meanness and grossness in my nature which you would find contemptible. The baseball equipment, however, is the kind of impediment with which you were never on even terms. You must remember that the house where you practiced the sort of economy which I respect was haunted only by mice and squirrels. You never had to cope with a short-stop.

UNDERSTANDING THE TEXT

1. Why do you think White decided to cast this essay in the form of a letter to Thoreau? What effect is created by the use of this form? How does the tone differ from that of other essays you have read?
2. For what reasons does White find Thoreau's ideas relevant to the situation of twentieth-century Americans? To what extent are these reasons directly stated, and to what extent are they implied? When they are implied, what technique does White use to convey them?
3. What impression does White give of present-day mechanized civilization? Does he pass any judgment on this civilization? If so, how?
4. Study closely the descriptive details which White notes in the concluding section dealing with Walden Pond and its surroundings. What principles have guided White in selecting these details? How does the conception they create accord with the general purpose of the essay?
5. The first specific scene which White describes is that of a woman cutting the grass with a power lawn mower. Why does he give this incident such prominence?
6. Why does he describe in great detail the way he locks up the car for the night?
7. In this account of locking up the car, explain the point of the very simple sentence structure: "It is what we all do, Henry. It is called locking the car. It is said to confuse thieves and keep them from making off with the laprobe. Four doors to lock behind one robe."
8. What commentary on Thoreau's experiment is implied in the final sentence, "You never had to cope with a shortstop"?

TOPICS FOR DISCUSSION AND WRITING

9. Write a description of a place which has changed perceptibly since your last visit. See if you can choose details which present the place as it now is and which make it possible for you to bring out economically the significant changes from the way it used to be.
10. Most of us have had the experience of going to a place, perhaps a historic site or a famous city, and finding it somewhat different from what we had learned of it through reading. If you have had such an experience, write an essay describing it.

11. Similarly, when we meet a person about whom we have often heard our friends speak, we are likely to discover that our preconception of his character and personality is not entirely accurate. Write an essay describing a person who, when you became acquainted with him, turned out to be different from what you had anticipated.

12. Students who enter college usually find that, although many things are just as they expected them to be, other aspects of campus life are different from their preconceptions. Set down your impressions of some phase of your college experience, developing the essay in such a way that it shows the extent to which the actuality of college corresponds with your expectations.

Walden—1954

E. B. WHITE

IN HIS journal for July 10–12, 1841, Thoreau wrote: "A slight sound at evening lifts me up by the ears, and makes life seem inexpressibly serene and grand. It may be in Uranus, or it may be in the shutter." The book into which he later managed to pack both Uranus and the shutter was published in 1854, and now, a hundred years having gone by, *Walden*, its serenity and grandeur unimpaired, still lifts us up by the ears, still translates for us that language we are in danger of forgetting, "which all things and events speak without metaphor, which alone is copious and standard."

Walden is an oddity in American letters. It may very well be the oddest of our distinguished oddities. For many it is a great deal too odd, and for many it is a particular bore. I have not found it to be a well-liked book among my acquaintances, although usually spoken of with respect, and one literary critic for whom I have the highest regard can find no reason why anyone gives *Walden* a second thought. To admire the book is, in fact, something of an embarrassment, for the mass of men have an indistinct notion that its author was a sort of Nature Boy.

I think it is of some advantage to encounter the book at a period in one's life when the normal anxieties and enthusiasms and rebellions of youth closely resemble those of Thoreau in that spring of 1845 when he borrowed an axe, went out to the woods, and began to whack down some trees for timber. Received at such a juncture, the book is like an invitation to life's dance, assuring the troubled recipient that no matter what befalls him in the way of success or failure he will always be welcome at the party—that the music is played for him, too, if he will but listen and move his feet. In effect, that is what the book is—an invitation, unengraved; and

Reprinted from *The Yale Review*, Autumn, 1954. Copyright, Yale University Press. Used by permission of the author and the editors.

it stirs one as a young girl is stirred by her first big party bid. Many think it a sermon; many set it down as an attempt to rearrange society; some think it an exercise in nature-loving; some find it a rather irritating collection of inspirational puffballs by an eccentric show-off. I think it none of these. It still seems to me the best youth's companion yet written by an American, for it carries a solemn warning against the loss of one's valuables, it advances a good argument for traveling light and trying new adventures, it rings with the power of positive adoration, it contains religious feeling without religious images, and it steadfastly refuses to record bad news. Even its pantheistic note is so pure as to be noncorrupting— pure as the flute-note blown across the pond on those faraway summer nights. If our colleges and universities were alert, they would present a cheap pocket edition of the book to every senior upon graduating, along with his sheepskin, or instead of it. Even if some senior were to take it literally and start felling trees, there could be worse mishaps: the axe is older than the Dictaphone and it is just as well for a young man to see what kind of chips he leaves before listening to the sound of his own voice. And even if some were to get no farther than the table of contents, they would learn how to name eighteen chapters by the use of only thirty-nine words and would see how sweet are the uses of brevity.

If Thoreau had merely left us an account of a man's life in the woods, or if he had simply retreated to the woods and there recorded his complaints about society, or even if he had contrived to include both records in one essay, *Walden* would probably not have lived a hundred years. As things turned out, Thoreau, very likely without knowing quite what he was up to, took man's relation to nature and man's dilemma in society and man's capacity for elevating his spirit and he beat all these matters together, in a wild free interval of self-justification and delight, and produced an original omelette from which people can draw nourishment in a hungry day. *Walden* is one of the first of the vitamin-enriched American dishes. If it were a little less good than it is, or even a little less queer, it would be an abominable book. Even as it is, it will continue to baffle and annoy the literal mind and all those who are unable to stomach its caprices and imbibe its theme. Certainly the plodding economist will continue to have rough going if he hopes to emerge from the book with a clear system of economic thought. Thoreau's assault on the Concord society of the mid-nineteenth century has the quality of a modern Western: he rides into the subject at top speed, shooting in all directions. Many of his shots ricochet and nick him on the rebound, and throughout the melee there is a horrendous cloud of inconsistencies and contradictions, and when the shooting dies down and the air clears, one is impressed chiefly by the courage of the rider and by how splendid it was that somebody should have ridden in there and raised all that ruckus.

When he went to the pond, Thoreau struck an attitude and did so deliberately, but his posturing was not to draw the attention of others to him but rather to draw his own attention more closely to himself. "I learned this at least by my experiment: that if one advances confidently in the direction of his dreams, and endeavors to live the life which he has imagined, he will meet with a success unexpected in common hours." The sentence has the power to resuscitate the youth drowning in his sea of doubt. I recall my exhilaration upon reading it, many years ago, in a time of hesitation and despair. It restored me to health. And now in 1954 when I salute Henry Thoreau on the hundredth birthday of his book, I am merely paying off an old score—or an installment on it.

In his journal for May 3–4, 1838—Boston to Portland—he wrote: "Midnight—head over the boat's side—between sleeping and waking—with glimpses of one or more lights in the vicinity of Cape Ann. Bright moonlight—the effect heightened by seasickness." The entry illuminates the man, as the moon the sea on that night in May. In Thoreau the natural scene was heightened, not depressed, by a disturbance of the stomach, and nausea met its match at last. There was a steadiness in at least one passenger if there was none in the boat. Such steadiness (which in some would be called intoxication) is at the heart of *Walden*—confidence, faith, the discipline of looking always at what is to be seen, undeviating gratitude for the life-everlasting that he found growing in his front yard. "There is nowhere recorded a simple and irrepressible satisfaction with the gift of life, any memorable praise of God." He worked to correct that deficiency. *Walden* is his acknowledgment of the gift of life. It is the testament of a man in a high state of indignation because (it seemed to him) so few ears heard the uninterrupted poem of creation, the morning wind that forever blows. If the man sometimes wrote as though all his readers were male, unmarried, and well-connected, it is because he gave his testimony during the callow years, and, for that matter, never really grew up. To reject the book because of the immaturity of the author and the bugs in the logic is to throw away a bottle of good wine because it contains bits of the cork.

Thoreau said he required of every writer, first and last, a simple and sincere account of his own life. Having delivered himself of this chesty dictum, he proceeded to ignore it. In his books and even in his enormous journal, he withheld or disguised most of the facts from which an understanding of his life could be drawn. *Walden*, subtitled "Life in the Woods," is not a simple and sincere account of a man's life, either in or out of the woods; it is an account of a man's journey into the mind, a toot on the trumpet to alert the neighbors. Thoreau was well aware that no one can alert his neighbors who is not wide awake himself, and he went to the woods (among other reasons) to make sure that he would stay awake during his broadcast. What actually took place during the years 1845–47 is largely unrecorded, and the reader is excluded from the private life of the author, who supplies almost no gossip about himself, a great deal about his neighbors and about the universe.

As for me, I cannot in this short ramble give a simple and sincere account of my own life, but I think Thoreau might find it instructive to know that this memorial essay is being written in a house that, through no intent on my part, is the same size and shape as his own domicile on the pond—about ten by fifteen, tight, plainly finished, and at a little distance from my Concord. The house in which I sit this morning was built to accommodate a boat, not a man, but by long experience I have learned that in most respects it shelters me better than the larger dwelling where my bed is, and which, by design, is a manhouse not a boathouse. Here in the boathouse I am a wilder and, it would appear, a healthier man, by a safe margin. I have a chair, a bench, a table, and I can walk into the water if I tire of the land. My house fronts a cove. Two fishermen have just arrived to spot fish from the air—an osprey and a man in a small yellow plane who works for the fish company. The man, I have noticed, is less well equipped than the hawk, who can dive directly on his fish and carry it away, without telephoning. A mouse and a squirrel share the house with me. The building is, in fact, a multiple dwelling, a semidetached affair. It is because I am semidetached while here that I find it possible to transact this private business with the fewest obstacles.

There is also a woodchuck here, living forty feet away under the wharf. When the wind is right, he can smell my house; and when the wind is contrary, I can smell his. We both use the wharf for sunning, taking turns, each adjusting his schedule to the other's convenience. Thoreau once ate a woodchuck. I think he felt he owed it to his readers, and that it was little enough, considering the indignities they were suffering at his hands and the dressing-down they were taking. (Parts of *Walden* are pure scold.) Or perhaps he ate the woodchuck because he believed every man should acquire strict business habits, and the woodchuck was destroying his market beans. I do not know. Thoreau had a strong experimental streak in him. It is probably no harder to eat a woodchuck than to construct a sentence that lasts a hundred years. At any rate, Thoreau is the only writer I know who prepared himself for his great ordeal by eating a woodchuck; also the only one who got a hangover from drinking too much water. (He was drunk the whole time, though he seldom touched wine or coffee or tea.)

Here in this compact house where I would spend one day as deliberately as Nature if I were not being pressed by *The Yale Review*, and with a woodchuck (as yet uneaten) for neighbor, I can feel the companionship of the occupant of the pondside cabin in Walden woods, a mile from the village, near the Fitchburg right of way. Even my immediate business is no barrier between us: Thoreau occasionally batted out a magazine piece, but was always suspicious of any sort of purposeful work that cut into his time. A man, he said, should take care not to be thrown off the track by every nutshell and mosquito's wing that falls on the rails.

There has been much guessing as to why he went to the pond. To set it down to escapism is, of course, to misconstrue what happened. Henry went forth to battle when he took to the woods, and *Walden* is the report of a man torn by two powerful and opposing drives—the desire to enjoy the world (and not be derailed by a mosquito wing) and the urge to set the world straight. One cannot join these two successfully, but sometimes, in rare cases, something good or even great results from the attempt of the tormented spirit to reconcile them. Henry went forth to battle, and if he set the stage himself, if he fought on his own terms and with his own weapons, it was because it was his nature to do things differently from most men, and to act in a cocky fashion. If the pond and the woods seemed a more plausible site for a house than an in-town location, it was because a cowbell made for him a sweeter sound than a churchbell. *Walden*, the book, makes the sound of the cowbell, more than a churchbell, and proves the point, although both sounds are in it, and both remarkably clear and sweet. He simply preferred his churchbell at a little distance.

I think one reason he went to the woods was a perfectly simple and commonplace one—and apparently he thought so, too. "At a certain season of our life," he wrote, "we are accustomed to consider every spot as the possible site of a house." There spoke the young man, a few years out of college, who had not yet broken away from home. He hadn't married, and he had found no job that measured up to his rigid standards of employment, and like any young man, or young animal, he felt uneasy and on the defensive until he had fixed himself a den. Most young men, of course, casting about for a site, are content merely to draw apart from their kinfolks. Thoreau, convinced that the greater part of what his neighbors called good was bad, withdrew from a great deal more than family: he pulled out of everything for a while, to serve everybody right for being so stuffy, and to try his own prejudices on the dog.

The house-hunting sentence above, which starts the Chapter called "Where I Lived, and What I Lived For," is followed by another passage that is worth quoting here because it so beautifully illustrates the offbeat prose that Thoreau was master of, a prose at once strictly disciplined and wildly abandoned. "I have surveyed the country on every side within a dozen miles of where I live," continued this delirious young man. "In imagination I have bought all the farms in succession, for all were to be bought, and I knew their price. I walked over each farmer's premises, tasted his wild apples, discoursed on husbandry with him, took his farm at his price, at any price, mortgaging it to him in my mind; even put a higher price on it—took everything but a deed of it—took his word for his deed, for I dearly love to talk—cultivated it, and him too to some extent, I trust, and withdrew when I had enjoyed it long enough, leaving him to carry it on." A copydesk man would get a double hernia trying to clean up that sentence for the management, but the sentence needs no fixing, for it perfectly captures the meaning of the writer and the quality of the ramble.

"Wherever I sat, there I might live, and the landscape radiated from me accordingly." Thoreau, the home-seeker, sitting on his hummock with the entire State of Massachusetts radiating from him, is to me the most humorous of the New England figures, and *Walden* the most humorous of the books, though its humor is almost continuously subsurface and there is nothing funny anywhere, except a few weak jokes and bad puns that rise to the surface like a perch in the pond that rose to the sound of the maestro's flute. Thoreau tended to write in sentences, a feat not every writer is capable of, and *Walden* is, rhetorically speaking, a collection of certified sentences, some of them, it would now appear, as indestructible as they are errant. The book is distilled from the vast journals, and this accounts for its intensity: he picked out bright particles that pleased his eye, whirled them in the kaleidoscope of his content, and produced the pattern that has endured—the color, the form, the light.

On this its hundredth birthday, Thoreau's *Walden* is pertinent and timely. In our uneasy season, when all men unconsciously seek a retreat from a world that has got almost completely out of hand, his house in the Concord woods is a haven. In our culture of gadgetry and the multiplicity of convenience, his cry "Simplicity, simplicity, simplicity!" has the insistence of a fire alarm. In the brooding atmosphere of war and the gathering radioactive storm, the innocence and serenity of his summer afternoons are enough to burst the remembering heart, and one gazes back upon that pleasing interlude—its confidence, its purity, its deliberateness —with awe and wonder, as one would look upon the face of a child asleep.

"This small lake was of most value as a neighbor in the intervals of a gentle rain-storm in August, when, both air and water being perfectly still, but the sky overcast, midafternoon had all the serenity of evening, and the wood-thrush sang around, and was heard from shore to shore." Now, in the perpetual overcast in which our days are spent, we hear with extra perception and deep gratitude that song, tying century to century.

I sometimes amuse myself by bringing Henry Thoreau back to life and showing him the sights. I escort him into a phone booth and let him dial Weather. "This is a delicious evening," the girl's voice says, "when the whole body is one sense, and imbibes delight through every pore." I show him the spot in the Pacific where an island used to be, before some magician made it vanish. "We know not where we are," I murmur. "The light which puts out our eyes is darkness to us. Only that day dawns to which we are awake." I thumb through the latest copy of *Vogue* with him. "Of two patterns which differ only by a few threads more or less of a particular color," I read, "the one will be sold readily, the other lie on the shelf, though it frequently happens that, after the lapse of a season, the latter becomes the most fashionable." Together we go outboarding on the Assabet, looking for what we've lost—a hound, a bay horse, a turtledove. I show him a distracted farmer who is trying to repair a hay baler before the thunder shower breaks. "This farmer," I remark, "is endeavoring to solve the problem of a livelihood by a formula more complicated than the problem itself. To get his shoe strings he speculates in herds of cattle."

I take the celebrated author to Twenty-One for lunch, so the waiters may study his shoes. The proprietor welcomes us. "The gross feeder," remarks the proprietor, sweeping the room with his arm, "is a man in the larva stage." After lunch we visit a classroom in one of those schools conducted by big corporations to teach their superannuated executives how to retire from business without serious injury to their health. (The shock to men's systems these days when relieved of the exacting routine of amassing wealth is very great and must be cushioned.) "It is not necessary," says the teacher to his pupils, "that a man should earn his living by the sweat of his brow, unless he sweats easier than I do. We are determined to be starved before we are hungry."

I turn on the radio and let Thoreau hear Winchell beat the red hand around the clock. "Time is but the steam I go a-fishing in," shouts Mr. Winchell, rattling his telegraph key. "Hardly a man takes a half hour's nap after dinner, but when he wakes he holds up his head and asks, 'What's the news?' If we read of one man robbed, or murdered, or killed by accident, or one house burned, or one vessel wrecked, or one steamboat blown up, or one cow run over on the Western Railroad, or one mad dog killed, or one lot of grasshoppers in the winter—we need never read of another. One is enough."

I doubt that Thoreau would be thrown off balance by the fantastic sights and sounds of the twentieth century. "The Concord nights," he once wrote, "are stranger than the Arabian nights." A four-engined air liner would merely serve to confirm his early views on travel. Everywhere he would observe, in new shapes and sizes, the old predicaments and follies of men—the desperation, the impedimenta, the meanness—along with the visible capacity for elevation of the mind and soul. "This curious world which we inhabit is more wonderful than it is convenient; more beautiful than it is useful; it is more to be admired and enjoyed than used." He would see that today ten thousand engineers are busy making sure that the world shall be convenient if they bust doing it, and others are determined to increase its usefulness even though its beauty is lost somewhere along the way.

At any rate, I'd like to stroll about the countryside in Thoreau's company for a day, observing the modern scene, inspecting today's snowstorm, pointing out the sights, and offering belated apologies for my sins. Thoreau is unique among writers in that those who admire him find him uncomfortable to live with—a regular hairshirt of a man. A little band of dedicated Thoreauvians would be a sorry sight indeed: fellows who hate compromise and have compromised, fellows who love wildness and have lived tamely, and at their side, censuring them and chiding them, the ghostly figure of this upright man, who long ago gave corroboration to impulses they perceived were right and issued warnings against the things they instinctively knew to be their enemies. I should hate to be called a Thoreauvian, yet I wince every time I walk into the barn I'm pushing before me, seventy-five feet by forty, and the author of *Walden* has served as my conscience through the long stretches of my trivial days.

Hairshirt or no, he is a better companion than most, and I would not swap him for a soberer or more reasonable friend even if I could. I can re-read his famous invitation with undiminished excitement. The sad thing is that not more acceptances have been received, that so many decline for one reason or another, pleading some previous engagement or ill health. But the invitation stands. It will beckon as long as this remarkable book stays in print—which will be as long as there are August afternoons in the intervals of a gentle rainstorm, as long as there are ears to catch the faint sounds of the orchestra. I find it agreeable to sit here this morning, in a house of correct proportions, and hear across a century of time his flute, his frogs, and his seductive summons to the wildest revels of them all.

UNDERSTANDING THE TEXT

1. In the fifteen years following the publication of the earlier essay, did White change his opinion of Thoreau's work and its meaning for contemporary Americans? Which of the two essays is more serious in tone? Do White's allusions to the twentieth century world suggest any reasons for this difference in seriousness?

2. Compare the premises used to evaluate Thoreau's significance in this essay with those employed in the 1939 essay.

3. In which of the two essays are White's bases for judgment stated more explicitly?

4. Which sections of the second essay most closely resemble the first in technique of presentation?

5. To what extent is White interested in clearing up misconceptions of the meaning of *Walden?* What kinds of people does he assume will be unable to understand the book?

6. What figure of speech does White use for his first full statement of what *Walden* really is? Does he return to this metaphor anywhere in the essay? How is this metaphor related to the rest of what he has to say about Thoreau?

7. Why does White include a description of the boathouse in which the essay was written?

TOPICS FOR DISCUSSION AND WRITING

8. Lowell and White touch on many of the same points in their interpretations of Thoreau. Both agree, for example, that Thoreau and his book are eccen-

tric. Yet their interpretations differ to a marked degree. Compare and contrast Lowell's and White's views of Thoreau, making clear the way their varying premises—on the relationship of the individual and society, for instance—influence their estimates.

9. Do you agree with White's criticism of the quality of twentieth-century mechanized civilization? Would it be possible to write a description covering some of the same details but interpreting them favorably, or would you need to discover and select additional details?

10. From these two essays on Thoreau, what self-characterization of E. B. White emerges? What kind of person does he seem to be?

11. White suggests that Thoreau is an especially valuable writer for young people. What kind of book do you consider particularly important for young people starting out in life? Write an essay on this topic, indicating clearly the reasons for your choice. You may, if you wish, single out a particular writer, or you may prefer to discuss a kind of writing which seems valuable to you.

12. White speaks of Thoreau as "this delirious young man." What does he mean to suggest by the adjective "delirious"? Would the meaning have been different if Lowell had called Thoreau "delirious"?

13. Comment on what White means when he says, at the beginning of the essay, that Thoreau "managed to pack both Uranus and the shutter" into *Walden*.

The American Loneliness

THORNTON WILDER

~

I

WALKING to the auditorium where I am to lecture on Thoreau I pass Hollis Hall in which he lived as an undergraduate.

I think we can understand why on graduation he changed his name—David Henry became Henry David, peremptorily. Like Emerson before him he was a scholarship student. During his first year he had one coat—his mother and aunt had made it for him out of green homespun. That year the right students were wearing black. All his life he railed with particular passion against any discrimination that is based on dress. A classmate tells us that, as a student, Thoreau in conversation did not raise his eyes from the ground and that his hands were continually moist. That chapter over, he changed his name.

As I pass Hollis I become uncomfortable; I feel those extraordinary blue eyes not on me, but directed over me, in taciturn reproach. He set down a portrait of himself and he took pains with its details. He wished it to be known that he was direct, simple, forthright, candid, and uncomplicated. Many have taken him at his word; but no, his life and personality have more important things to tell us.

How hard it is to discuss Thoreau in the presence of the young. Many aspects of his life and thought lie in that sole territory which is inaccessible to young men and women. I never feel an incomprehension on their part when I treat of death or loss or passion; their imaginations can extend themselves—by that principle which Goethe called "anticipation"—to such matters. What is difficult is to treat of the slow attrition of the soul by the conduct of life, of our revolt against the workaday—the background of such works as Le Misanthrope *and* Don Quixote. *I must tell these young people, who are hurrying by me, that Thoreau met defeat in his impassioned demands upon Love, Friendship, and Nature; and yet I must tell them that at the same time he was an American who fought some of our battles for us, whose experience we are to follow with a sort of anxious suspense. The rewards we obtain from the contemplation of Thoreau, however, begin their consolatory and inspiriting effect upon us as we move through our forties.*

I wish I were somewhere else.

Ladies and gentlemen:—

We were talking last time about how difficult it is to be an American. We spoke of the support which a European receives from all those elements we call environment—place, tradition, customs: "I am I because my neighbors know me." Their environment is so thickly woven, so solid, that the growing boy and girl have something to kick against. The American, on the other hand, is at sea—disconnected from place, distrustful of authority, thrown back upon himself.

Here I am again.

And suddenly, as my eyes rest on the upturned faces before me, I am encouraged. It is in many ways a sad story I have to tell. Whenever I think of Thoreau I feel a weight about my heart, a greater weight than descends in thoughts of Poe or Emily Dickinson. Yet all of us here are Americans. My subject is the loneliness that accompanies independence and the uneasiness that accompanies freedom. These experiences are not foreign to anyone here. So forward.

Perceptive visitors to America from Europe are uniformly struck by what they call an "American loneliness" which they find no less present in that fretful and often hollow gregariousness we talked about last time.

Now there are several forms of this loneliness, and the one that occurs to us first is the sentimental form. In America the very word is sentimental and it makes us uncomfortable even to employ it. Yet we see this kind of loneliness about us everywhere; like the loneliness which springs from pride it is a consequence, a deformation, and a malady of that deeper form which we are about to discuss. Both proceed from the fact that the religious ideas current in America are still inadequate to explain the American to himself. The sentimental loneliness arises from the sense that he is a victim, that he was slighted when fortune distributed her gifts (though it is notably prevalent among those who seem to "have everything"); the proud loneliness arises from the sense of boundlessness which we described as related to the American geography and is found among those who make boundless moral demands on themselves and others.

Thoreau illustrates certain American traits connected with loneliness in an extreme and exaggerated form. He finally lost his battle—the typical American battle of trying to convert a loneliness into an enriched and fruitful solitude—but before he died (at forty-four, murmuring: "It is better some things should end") he furnished us many a bulletin of the struggle, many an insight, and many an aid.

Another of the most famous pages in American literature is that wherein Thoreau gives his reasons for going to live in solitude at Walden Pond.

"I went to the woods because I wished to live deliberately, to front only the essential facts of life, and see if I could not learn what it had to teach, and not, when I came to die, discover that I had not lived. . . . nor did I wish to practise resignation, unless it were quite necessary. . . . if [life] proved to be mean, why then to get the whole and genuine meanness of it, and publish its meanness to the world; or if it were sublime, to know it by experience, and be able to give a true account of it in my next excursion."

Thoreau's books are a sort of cento of transcriptions and amplifications of entries in his Journal. Here is what he wrote on the third day of his residence at the pond (July 6, 1845): "I wish to meet the facts of life— the vital facts, which are the phenomena or actuality which the Gods meant to show us—face to face, and so I came here. Life! who knows what it is, what it does?"

There are several things to notice about these passages: among them, first, that he will put his question as though no one had ever said anything valuable before; and, second, that in order to ask what life is, it is necessary to remove oneself from the human community.

Americans constantly feel that the whole world's thinking has to be done over again. They did not only leave the Old World, they repudiated it. Americans start from scratch. This is revolt indeed. All authority is suspect. And this is boundless presumption. I quoted Whitman's words in our last session ("It almost seems as if a poetry . . . suitable to the human soul were never possible before"). Poe, clutching some mathematics and physics he had acquired during a brief stay at West Point, launched into a description of how the universe came into being, and deduced the nature of

God from his theory of the galaxies. He called his work *Eureka* and did not leave us in doubt that he felt that he had succeeded where the greatest minds had failed. Professional astronomers dismiss it with a smile, but we notice that the great French poet Paul Valéry, who occupied himself with mathematics for thirty years, tells us how great a role his book played in the growth of his thought. ("*L'idée fondamentale de Poe n'en est pas moins une profonde et souveraine idée.*")[1]

Thoreau did some reading at Walden Pond, but it is astonishing how small a part it plays in this central inquiry of his life. He invokes neither the great philosophers nor the founders of religions. Every American is an autodidact; every American feels himself capable of being the founder of his own religion. At the end of the passage I have quoted from the Journal there is an allusion to his reading of the Sanskrit scriptures. It is an ironic jest: "to give a true account of it in my next excursion." He does not believe that our souls return to inhabit other bodies, though billions have reposed in that idea all that they know of hope and courage. He makes a jest of it—fit example, to him, of the uselessness of *other people's* thinking. There is something of this religious and metaphysical pioneer in us all. How often I have heard people say: "No, Mr. Wilder, we don't go to church. My husband and I each have our own religion—here—inside!" What student at the height of a lofty argument has not been heard to cry: "Listen, everybody! My theory is *this* . . ."?

To others this must all seem very deplorable. To Americans it is wearing and costing and often desolating; but such is the situation. The die is cast; and our interest in Thoreau is precisely that we see one of ourselves fighting, struggling, and finally fainting in this inescapable American situation. Thoreau asks, What is life? and he asks it in a world from which any considerable reliance on previous answers is denied him, and through his long inquiry he heard the closing of three doors—doors to great areas of experience on which he counted for aid and illumination, the doors to Love, Friendship, and Nature.

Here are the reverberations of these closing doors:—

LOVE (October 27, 1851, aged 34): "The obstacles which the heart meets with are like granite blocks which one alone cannot remove. She who was the morning light is now neither the morning star nor the evening star. We meet but to find each other further asunder. . . ."

FRIENDSHIP (March 4, 1856, aged 38): "I had two friends. The one offered me friendship on such terms that I could not accept it, without a

---

[1] "Poe's fundamental idea is nonetheless profound and masterly."

sense of degradation. He would not meet me on equal terms, but only to be to some extent my patron. . . . Our relation was one long tragedy. . . ."

NATURE: As early as July 16, 1851, Thoreau was saying, "Methinks my present experience is nothing; my past experience is all in all. I think that no experience which I have today comes up to, or is comparable with, the experiences of my boyhood. . . . Formerly, methought, nature developed as I developed, and grew up with me. My life was ecstasy. . . ."

II

The story of Thoreau's love is only beginning to be pieced together. The obstacles that separated him from this woman were indeed granite blocks. The expressions he gives to his love in his Journal are often strange "whirling words": "My sister, it is glorious to me that you live! . . . It is morning when I meet thee in a still cool dewy white sun light in the hushed dawn—my young mother—I thy eldest son" (lightly crossed through: "thy young father") ". . . whether art thou my mother or my sister—whether am I thy son or thy brother. . . . Others are of my kindred by blood or of my acquaintance but you are part of me. I cannot tell where you leave off and I begin." In another passage, Journal 1850, he says: "I am as much thy sister as thy brother. Thou art as much my brother as my sister."

We have reason to be surprised that the erotic emotion expresses itself in images borrowed from the family relationships. Yet such a coloring is present elsewhere in our writers of this period, in Whitman, in Melville (*Pierre*), and in Poe. In America the family is the nexus of an unusually powerful ambivalence. On the one hand, the child strains to break away and lead his own life. The young seldom settle down near their parents' home; less and less frequently do the parents end their days in the homes of their children; I have remarked that young people are increasingly eager for the moment when they are no longer financially dependent on their parents. On the other hand, the American—as we were saying—is exceptionally aware of the multitude of the human race; his loneliness is enhanced by his consciousness of those numbers. The family is at once an encroachment on his individualism and a seductive invitation to rejoin the human community at a level where he does not feel himself to be strange. Moreover, individualism has its arrogance. It has long been a tag that every American is king. Royalty marries only royalty. Other people aren't good enough. Thoreau elevates the woman he loves to this kinship. Poe's mother died when he was three; he lived the latter part of his life with his aunt and married his cousin. The blocks of granite which separated Thoreau from this "sister" were not all outside of him. The door of love closed and he never returned to it.

It was the friendship with Ralph Waldo Emerson that Thoreau described as "one long tragedy." The second friend who proved unworthy was William Ellery Channing, who seems to have enjoyed shocking Thoreau with an occasional ribaldry. Tragedy we too can call it, for few men could more have needed friendship, and few have been less ready to accommodate themselves to it. He wrote (June 11, 1855): "What if we feel a yearning to which no breast answers? I walk alone, my heart is full. Feelings impede the current of my thoughts. I knock on the earth for my friend. I expect to meet him at every turn; but no friend appears, and perhaps none is dreaming of me." Emerson knew that he was incapable of friendship, and the knowledge caused him some pain—brief pain, for Emerson had a short way with moral discomfiture; he mounted up into pink clouds and began to give voice to abstractions. This woeful triangle skirts the comic. A letter has recently come to light which gives Channing's view of a friendship with Emerson. Channing wrote to Elizabeth Hoar from New Bedford on December 23, 1856: ". . . how strange it seems to hear W. [Waldo] lecturing on friendship. If he knew all the hearts he has frozen, he might better read something on the fall of human hopes. . . . I have never parted from him without the bitterest regret, not for having parted, but for having come. . . ."

Individualism! It is the point of honor of men and nations in this century. Every nation boasts that it is a nation of individualists and implies that the other nations are composed of sheep. ("You Americans—you all eat the same things; you repeat the same slogans; you read the same book of the month; the very streets in which you live have not even names, but merely numbers and letters!") Yet no man (and no nation) is as individualistic as he thinks he is; each is so in one area of his existence, and the extent to which he is—fortunately!—conformist in others is not apparent to him. Friendship is not incompatible with individualism, as the great pages of Montaigne have shown us, but it was incompatible in the lives of our Concord philosophers. Thousands of school children were formerly required to read Emerson's chaotic essay on the subject. For generations Emerson's style had the power to put the judgment to sleep, but one wonders what the teachers made of that farewell address to "our dearest friends": "Who are you? Unhand me: I will be dependent no more."

Thoreau's inability to come to terms with friendship was aggravated by the vastness of his expectations. To this day many an American is breaking his life on an excessive demand for the perfect, the absolute, the boundless in realms where it is accorded to few—in love and friendship, for example. The doctrines of moderation and the golden mean may have flourished in Rome and in China (overcrowded and overgoverned countries), but they do not flourish here, save as counsels of despair. The injunction to be content with your lot and in the situation where God has placed you is not an expression of New World thinking. We do not feel ourselves to be subject to lot and we do not cast God in the role of a civil administrator or of a feudal baron.

III

Thoreau goes to the pond, then, to find an answer to the question, What is life? He will not admit other thinkers to his deliberations, and his answer will not reflect any *close* relation with his fellow men. With what frustrated passion, then, he turned to nature. Nature meant primarily the flora and fauna of the Concord River valley, though he made some trips elsewhere. Now that region has no tigers, avalanches, coral vipers, Black Forests, deserts, or volcanoes. Margaret Fuller warned her Concord friends of the dangers of accustoming themselves to a view of nature which omitted both cruelty and grandeur. On his walks Thoreau came upon some malodorous plants (June 26, 1852): "For what purpose has nature made a flower to fill the lowlands with the odor of carrion?" The question seems, to us, both biologically and philosophically a little *simpliste*.

Enough has already been written about the absence of a sense of evil in the work of the Concord essayists. It is only one of the elements that resulted in the gradually progressive grayness of the last volumes of Thoreau's Journal. Far more important is the fact that Thoreau asked of nature a gift which nature cannot, without coöperation, accord. He asked a continual renewal of moments of youthful ecstasy. Unhappy, indeed, is the boy or girl who has not known those moments of inexplicable rapture in the open air. There is a corresponding experience accorded to those in later years—awe. In ecstasy the *self* is infused with happiness; in awe the self recedes before a realization of the vastness and mystery of the nonself. Many never cross the bridge from one to the other. Thoreau despised and dreaded Science; to inquire too narrowly into the laws of nature seemed to him to threaten those increasingly infrequent visitations of irrational joy. "If you would obtain insight, avoid anatomy," he wrote. With

what a sad smile Goethe would have shaken his head over these words—
for it was precisely from his studies of the skeleton of the vertebrates and
the structure of plants that Goethe's life was flooded, even in the eighties,
with an awe which retained much of the character of a juvenile ecstasy.
Indeed, Goethe at eighty would not have written the words which Thoreau wrote at thirty-three: "In youth, before I lost any of my senses, I
can remember that I was all alive, and inhabited my body with inexpressible satisfaction . . . !" As the years passed, Thoreau increasingly mourned
his lost youth and the intoxication which nature had afforded him then.
For a time the humming of the telegraph wires aroused transports; it was
his "redeemer"; then they too lost their peculiar powers. Finally, in his
last years he turns from the almost passive notation of the phenomena
about him and introduces into his observations an element of progression
and exploration into the unknown. He counts the rings in stumps and
makes notes on the succession of trees. Those who are conversant with
these things tell us that he is discovering the science of ecology. He seems,
however, to be deriving no warming satisfaction from this innovation; his
notes lie buried in his Journal and the work is repeated independently by
others.

I am eager to arrive at all the things that call forth our admiration for
Thoreau, but I must delay a moment to point out that we have brushed
against two traits in him which are not characteristic of the American:
the fixed orientation toward childhood, and the view of nature as engaged
in close personal conversation with man. These are characteristic, however, of the region from which he came.

A portion of Massachusetts and several states of our South are enclaves
of residual areas of European feeling. They were cut off, or resolutely cut
themselves off, from the advancing tide of the country's modes of consciousness. Place, environment, relations, repetitions are the breath of their
being. One evidence of it is a constant preoccupation with how old one is
and a striking obsession with early youth (how many of the brilliant novels
which have lately come to us from the South turn upon childhood). In
New York and Chicago and the West, one's age is of relatively little importance; those who are *active* between twenty-five and sixty are contemporaries. They dine and dance and work and enjoy themselves together.
This is bound up with the American sense of time which I shall develop in
later lectures. Time is something we create, we call into being, not something we submit to—an order outside us.

Similarly, there are aspects of Thoreau's relation to nature that are not those we feel to be prevalent elsewhere among us. The gods of glade and brook and pond are not the gods of plain, seacoast, forest, desert, and mountain. The former are almost in reach; one can imagine oneself in dialogue with them; they can enter into an almost personal relation with those who have turned from the company of men. But the gods of great space are enigmatic; we are never sure that we have read aright the message of their beauty and terror; we do not hastily put words into their mouths. Yet the more we feel an "otherness" in nature, the more we recognize that we ourselves are natural. "It appears to be a law," wrote Thoreau, in April, 1852, "that you cannot have a deep sympathy with both man and nature." "I loved nature because she is not man, but a retreat from him." There is no such law, nor have any other American voices expressed any sentiment like it, unless we take note of the moment in Emily Dickinson's life when she wrote: "I thought that nature was enough/Till human nature came." Nature failed Thoreau, as it will ultimately fail anyone who wishes to divide it up, to pick and choose only limited congenial aspects of it, for ecstasy or for retreat, or who wishes to employ one aspect of it to confound another.

And the question: "Life! who knows what it is, what it does?" It would seem that Thoreau had considerably compromised his inquiry by divesting himself of the testimony and the companionship of others and by repeating his question to a wooded vale.

Yet millions have testified and are testifying to the powerful clarifications that he brought back from Walden Pond. And all his triumphs came from his embattled individualism, from pushing it to the limits that border on absurdity, and from facing—"face to face"—the loneliness consequent upon it. He came back with the answer that life, thought, culture, religion, government—everything—arises from subjectivity, from inwardness. Our sole self is the first and last judge of values, including the values of communal life.

Here I traced briefly the long, gradual millenniary convergence of emphasis on the individual—religion's, government's, art's; and showed how through an historical accident the settling of America, by that "selection of a selection" of European individualists, constituted an acceleration, perhaps a "leap" in the forward movement of this centering of emphasis.

Thoreau does not urge us to live in shacks merely to save money and time; to eschew railroad trains, newspapers, and the postal service; to lay in two sets of washable clothing and a bar of soap; to refuse these jobs which deform our souls between nine and five. These are not ends in themselves. "Simplify, simplify, simplify!" All these are injunctions in order that we may refine our ear to the promptings of our subjective, inward self. The evil of community is that it renders us stupid—and cowardly. *Walden* is a manual of self-reliance so much more profound than Emerson's famous essay that the latter seems to be merely on the level of that advice to melancholics which directs them to take walks and drink a lot of milk.

Thoreau did not merely meditate about the problem of living: he costingly, searchingly exemplified it, and his work rings with the validity of that single-minded commitment. One of the rewards of independence, apparently, is that you are certain that you are the master of your choices, you are not left to doubt whether or not you are free.

Yet there is no air of triumph about the latter end of Thoreau's life. It is difficult to be an American. In some aspects of his life and thought Thoreau is one of our most conspicuous, most outrageous Americans. But the spiritual situation in which these citizens of the New World find themselves is so new, so demanding, and so uncharted, that only by keeping in contact with its total demands can one maintain one's head above the surface. A partial American will drown. Thoreau did not grasp the New World sense of the innumerability of the human race—nor did Emerson, for all his employment of the word "universal." Thoreau had a parochial, a wood-lot view of nature and her mighty laws. Is there a Thoreau who can tell us that once one has grasped and accepted a basic solitude, all the other gifts come pouring back—love, friendship, and nature? One reads the life story of Thoreau with anxious suspense.

And Abraham Lincoln?

And Melville—and Poe?

UNDERSTANDING THE TEXT

1. With which of the other writers on Thoreau—Lowell, Canby, and White —does Wilder have the most in common?

2. What views of American and European character, respectively, provide the framework for Wilder's remarks on Thoreau? What distinction between the two cultures is most important for Wilder?

3. Aside from his quotations from Thoreau, how does Wilder try to bring out the existence and nature of what he calls the "American loneliness"?

4. What purpose is served in the essay by the section in which Wilder relates how Thoreau failed to find satisfaction, successively, in Love, Friendship, and Nature?

5. What premises concerning proper relationships among individuals are implied in Wilder's criticism of Emerson's ideas on friendship? How is his treatment of this topic related to the theme of the whole essay?

6. For what reasons does Wilder think that Thoreau's attitude toward nature was unsatisfactory? What would be the basis of a satisfactory relationship with nature?

7. Wilder reaches the conclusion "It is difficult to be an American." How appropriately does this statement follow from the rest of the essay?

8. What is the purpose of the italicized passages which Wilder has included in his text?

TOPICS FOR DISCUSSION AND WRITING

9. Wilder reports a widespread feeling that "Americans start from scratch." Would Lowell agree that this is necessarily true?

10. Both Lowell and Wilder have serious doubts about the soundness of Thoreau's attitude towards nature. Compare the different grounds on which the two critics base their doubts.

11. In this essay Wilder is writing about a typical American trait. How appropriately can Thoreau be used as an example of "typical" American thought or behavior? Does Wilder show any awareness that the objection suggested in this question might be raised?

12. On the basis of the passage from *Walden* and the writings of the four critics, write an essay summarizing Thoreau's message and its meaning for Americans today. You may base your judgments on grounds suggested by one or more of the critics, or you may, preferably, employ premises of your own which are not identical with those of the critics.

13. Compare and contrast the ideas, expressed or implied, which each of the four critics holds concerning the proper relationship between the individual and society, and indicate how the critics' views on this key point affect their interpretation of Thoreau.

14. Can you think of any general ideas, in addition to those developed by these critics, which might be profitably used as criteria for an evaluation of Thoreau's character and work?

3. Developing the Subject: Some Possible Procedures

Definition

MARSTON BATES, The Biotic Community

R. M. MACIVER, Community, Association, and Institution

LOUIS KRONENBERGER, The Crank, the Eccentric, and the Individualist

Characterization

ANTHONY ASHLEY COOPER, First Lord Shaftesbury, An English Squire of the Seventeenth Century: Mr. Henry Hastings

THOMAS BABINGTON MACAULAY, The English Squire in the Seventeenth Century

MARK TWAIN, The House Beautiful

Classification and Analysis

R. M. MACIVER, Civilization and Culture

WILLIAM JAMES, The Social Value of the College-Bred

GEOFFREY SCOTT, The Criticism of Architecture

LORD MOULTON, Law and Manners

Comparison and Contrast

EDWARD GIBBON, Rome Under the Tyranny

MOSES COIT TYLER, Two Classes of Englishmen in the Seventeenth Century

ANTHONY TROLLOPE, The Englishman and the American

116

Example and Analogy

PHILIP WYLIE, Science Has Spoiled My Supper
ALISTAIR COOKE, No Sympathy for Apathy
SIR JAMES JEANS, Why the Sky Looks Blue

Causes and Effects

JAMES MADISON, *The Federalist*, No. 10
FLETCHER PRATT, The Indecisiveness of Decisions

Indirect Argument

ROBERT M. COATES, The Law
E. M. FORSTER, My Wood
JONATHAN SWIFT, A Modest Proposal

IN THE identification of his subject and the adoption of the point of view
which will give meaning to his theme, the writer may not be consciously
aware of all the decisions he has necessarily been making. If he is a perceptive person, he will be able, just by doing what comes natural to him, to see
significance in the world about him. Even in these stages, however, as we
have suggested, the writer can often deepen and clarify his insights if he
pauses to ask some questions of himself, to inquire why, given his fundamental beliefs, he wished to interpret his subject in a particular way. Self-
interrogation before the act of writing may forestall self-reproach after the
piece is finished.

The conscious realization that he confronts a choice among alternative
procedures is even more insistent when the writer begins to develop his
subject. Now his task is to settle upon a framework, a method of organization, which will guide him as he sets down on paper the observations and
reflections which constitute his conception of the subject. The nature of
language being what it is, he cannot simply thrust the subject before the
reader, gesture eloquently, and say happily, "Look!" He must, instead, hit
upon a way of presenting the details of his conception so that they will
cease to be mere *details* and will become, for the reader, significant parts of
what the writer wishes to convey. Most of us have seen, as we travel along
the highway, the sequential billboards which coax the motorist to buy a
particular brand of shaving cream. By itself, each sign is meaningless;
placed in the proper order, the half-dozen signs form a whimsical sales

message. Similarly, the details with which any writer works begin to make sense only when they are organized, and organized in a way that is appropriate to the writer's purpose.

The essays in the following section provide examples of a number of useful and common ways to develop a subject. We emphasize immediately that these seven methods of organizing material—from definition through indirect argument—do not form an exhaustive list. The subtitle of the section, "Some Possible Procedures," means just what it says. There are millions of things to write about, and millions of ways to write about them. It is true, however, that certain methods of casting material into a systematic and rational order have turned out to be particularly valuable. The thoughts of no two men are identical, but there are likely to be important similarities in the way most men of a particular civilization go about the business of thinking. Down through the time-span covered by the written records of Western civilization men have defined, have classified and analyzed, have drawn comparisons, have traced out causes and effects. These common processes of thought are reflected in the equally common patterns of organization through which men have communicated to each other their observations of the natural or social world, their hopes and fears, and their most far-flung speculations. Some of the most persistent of these patterns we have chosen to illustrate in the selections that follow.

In all our discourse, even the most casual conversation, we make constant use of these and other principles of organization. Suppose we eavesdrop on a student bull session which is considering the case of Coach Harry Huddle, whose football team has lost five games in a row. One participant leads off by suggesting that a good coach should possess patience, prudence, and foresight, and that Coach Huddle has none of these qualities. Whether he knows it or not, the speaker is employing *definition* and *classification;* he has defined what is for him the good coach and has excluded Coach Huddle from this particular category. Another student traces the *causes*—poor conditioning, low spirit, faulty strategy—of the most recent defeat; these causes may be cited, in turn, as *examples* of the coach's inadequacy. Someone else inevitably develops a wistful *comparison* between Huddle and the coach of a neighboring college whose team is headed for the Rose Bowl. And the evening is likely to end when someone produces a full-blown *characterization* of the luckless Huddle.

Thus, whenever we speak or write, if what we say is to have some meaning for our listeners or readers, we must discover or devise some way to present our ideas in a systematic fashion. As you read and study the essays in this section, you will note that, although a particular kind of organization is likely to be dominant in each piece, it will be accompanied and supported by other procedures. For example, in the essay by Fletcher Pratt on the Battle of Gettysburg, the author's principal way of organizing his thoughts is to explore the causes of the Confederate defeat. In setting down these causes, however, the writer employs several other approaches: he compares the opposing forces with respect to the strength of their armies and the quality of their military leadership, and he offers an incisive characterization of General Lee. An even more complex interplay of modes of developing a topic can be studied in the tenth *Federalist* paper. In this argument Madison is especially interested in showing that certain forms of political organization will encourage factional strife, while other forms will discourage internal party warfare. That is, Madison is developing his subject according to a basic cause-effect pattern. But he underpins this central structure by careful definition of such key words as "faction" and "republic," by telling comparisons, and by judiciously chosen examples. These essays, then, as well as others which you will be interested in noting for yourself in the following pages, demonstrate that, just as chemical elements are ordinarily found in compounds, so these schemes for developing a subject are used, not in pure isolation, but in conjunction with each other. Indeed, one sign of the skillful writer is his ability, while maintaining the clarity of his main line of thought, to introduce in an easy and natural way the necessary secondary patterns.

All this suggests that the good writer uses these methods of organization with considerable flexibility, and that the good reader will not rely upon hard-and-fast formulas in appraising the way a writer has handled this part of his work. Both writer and reader need to be sensitive to the fact that there are several different ways of developing each of the procedures illustrated here, and that the writer's choice of a particular method will be determined by his purpose and his conception of the subject. The operation of choice is clearly evident, for instance, if the writer wishes to compare and contrast two things—two persons, or two cultures, or two ideas. The writer may proceed by describing the first thing rather fully before he goes on to an account of the second element in his comparison. This is what Edward Gibbon and Anthony Trollope do in the essays which appear in this section. Or the writer may choose to treat one aspect of the first thing, then take up the corresponding aspect of the second thing, and so on. In still another method, the writer may decide to discuss first the similarities between the two things he is comparing and then the differences between them. In each case, the writer's decision is governed by his conception of the task he has undertaken to accomplish. If he wishes the reader to grasp as wholes the two things he is comparing, he uses the first method. If he wishes to direct particular attention to the significant parts of the things he is comparing, he is likely to use the second method. If he wishes to demonstrate that things which appear similar are really unlike each other, or that things which appear dissimilar are really like each other, he can use the third method. These three general methods of organizing a comparison and contrast can be seen in operation every time there is a hot political campaign, since speakers and writers will often wish to draw distinctions among the various competing parties. A speaker who argues that no specific issues divide the two major parties, but that his own party, because of superior general morale, can be relied upon to govern more efficiently, might profitably employ the first, or whole-by-whole, kind of comparison. On the other hand, a speaker who contends that the two parties are basically at odds on important questions—foreign policy, or agricultural programs, or attitudes toward labor unions—would probably organize his comparison in the second, or part-by-part, manner. Finally, an embattled independent spokesman who wished to show that the two parties, beneath superficial differences, were as much alike as Tweedledum and Tweedledee, might choose the third method, developing first the external points of difference and then bearing down on the basic kinship between the parties.

We have described in some detail several possible approaches to the working out of a comparison and contrast, because this particular mode of organization demonstrates in clear-cut fashion something which is true of other ways of developing a subject. That is, each of these methods of organization should be thought of as an infinitely variable procedure for setting forth one's thoughts and observations; none of them is an intellectual basket into which facts and ideas can be thrown mechanically. The kinds of organization represented in this section, then, are offered as a valuable check-list to assist writer and reader alike in recognizing several important ways a subject may be given the kind of shape, sequence, and form which is indispensable for communication. The questions appended to each of the following essays suggest some of the specific considerations which writers and readers need to keep in mind in dealing with each of these categories. But the paramount consideration for the writer is imaginative adaptability in the use of these procedures, so that, as he develops the subject, his primary intentions are illuminated and the dimensions of his subject are fully revealed.

The Biotic Community

MARSTON BATES

~

THE LOGICAL basis for the examination of relationships among organisms is not individual organisms, or different kinds of organisms, but the biotic community. Here we encounter a problem in definition.

THE DEFINITION OF COMMUNITY

Most ecologists have worked in the temperate zone in pine forests or beech forests, and they have come to think of the biotic community as determined by a particular dominant kind of organism. The dominant is thought of as controlling the whole community either through sheer numbers of individuals, or bulk of protoplasm, or all-pervading biological effect. The whole assemblage of organisms living in a pine or beech forest is obviously dominated by the pines or beeches, so that these form a convenient guide to the limits of that particular community.

In the tropical forest, one looks in vain for any particular kind of organism that dominates in the sense that the pine or beech dominates its forest. My experience in the tropics has thus made me very dubious about the whole ecological idea of dominants. The idea works all right in the pine woods, but even in the temperate zone one must stretch the imagination to apply it in a lake or a stream or on the sea coast.

I think the essential element in the concept of the community is the interdependence of its various members to form a functioning unit. It is the next distinctive general organizational level above that of the individual and the population. Individuals of a given kind are organized, through their genetic relationships, into populations; but the behavior and history of these specific populations can only be understood in relation to the behavior and history of the other populations with which they occur. The community, it seems to me, might be defined as the smallest group of such populations that can be studied and understood as a more or less self-sufficient unit.

We thus arrive at a parallel with Toynbee's definition of an equally difficult concept, that of a "civilization." A biotic community might well be defined as "an intelligible field of study" from the point of view of the relations among different kinds of organisms. It is a unit of ecological study, just as civilization is a unit of historical study.

Toynbee has pointed out that English history is in no sense intelligible if taken as a field in itself. From its first clear chapter, the conversion of its people to Christianity, to its last, the establishment of industrial economy, the course of events in England fails to make sense except through the consideration of events in neighboring national states. But in tracing the genesis of these events, the student finds that it is not necessary to cover the whole world as a field, but that more or less definite limits in time and space are reached, limits which Toynbee in the present instance takes to define the particular field of Western Christian civilization. Within this field, the majority of relationships are directed inward, as they are in his other contemporaneous civilizations, the Orthodox Christian, the Islamic, the Hindu, and the Far-Eastern.

A concept like that of the "intelligible field of study" does not give a sharply defined series of units: but the material to be studied, at this level, is not composed of sharply defined units. Human culture is a continuum, but it is a continuum with pronounced modes both in time and in space, and the problem is to recognize these modes and to trace their development and characteristics. Even such an apparently isolated phenomenon as the Mayan civilization is related to the general nexus of culture. It must have started with people who had brought certain cultural equipment with them when they parted from the Old World along the bridge of the Aleutian Islands or across the Pacific, and this cultural equipment would be the common relationship between the civilizations developed in the Old and New Worlds. Among Old World civilizations, the relationships are, of course, numerous, in part obvious, and of a variety of sorts. The important thing is that these relationships are external, that is, their study is not essential to an understanding of the development of events within the civilization.

It is not particularly strange that civilization and biotic communities should be subject to the same type of definition process, since both are biological phenomena, involving the aggregation of individual organisms.

There would be even less difficulty in making the analogy if Toynbee had been concerned with "cultures" instead of with "civilizations," which are essentially a particular kind of cultural development. Civilizations happen to be the only cultural groupings that have got much involved with the special problem of history. If one were studying human ethnology, rather than history, interest would focus on the development of cultural relationships in general, and civilization would fall into perspective as a particular type of development shown by a few scattered cultures.

THE LIMITS OF THE COMMUNITY

An oak tree may seem a world in itself. It may have hundreds of organisms of dozens of kinds that depend on it for food; it may give support to Spanish moss and other epiphytes; protection to birds that nest in its branches. The leaves that it drops decay, and the characteristics of the litter of oak leaves may determine the kind of soil organisms, and the direction of soil development.

But this complex of organisms does not form a community. It is not an intelligible unit of study. If we start to analyze the relationships of the various organisms associated with the oak tree, we find ourselves constantly led away from that association into some larger grouping. The caterpillars that feed on the oak leaves are developmental stages of a butterfly that gets food from the goldenrod in a clearing. The birds nesting in the oak tree forage through the nearby forest, and their behavior cannot be understood in terms of the tree, but only in terms of the forest. Similarly, we find that the association of organisms in the soil depends not so much on the fact that they are under an oak tree, as on being part of the oak forest.

Our biotic community, then, is the forest, not the association in the tree. The complex of organisms making up the forest does form an intelligible field of study, where the events and relationships can be understood with only casual and occasional reference to external phenomena. The range of the birds nesting in our particular tree depends on the relations with birds in neighboring trees, on the "territory" in the forest that is available for each family. The kind of food that they are able to gather depends on a selection from the kinds available in the forest. The number of caterpillars of a given kind eating the leaves of the oak tree depends on the density of population of that particular species in the forest, which is a matter of balance of parasites, climatic relations, and so forth. The characteristics of the forest as a whole can be related to the regional climate, to the physical and chemical factors of the general environment. The climate within the forest can be understood in relation to the density and size of the trees. The forest constitutes a biotic community.

A pool in our forest may, or may not, be inhabited by a distinct community: the answer would soon become obvious in the course of study of the organisms in the pool. If the pool formed an intelligible unit without special reference to the forest, it would certainly form a separate community. But we might find that the behavior of the inhabitants of the pool was constantly conditioned by the character of the forest. The kind of plants growing in the pool might depend on the shade relations with the oaks growing around the margin. A good proportion of the animals in the pool would probably turn out to be insect larvae, and the kinds of insects in the particular pool might depend on whether the adults were able to fit into the conditions in the surrounding forest. The acidity of the water in the pool might depend on the soil character of the forest and on organic matter washed into it from the forest in rains. If, in studying our pool, we found that we had thus constantly to refer back to the forest, we could hardly consider it as more than a special sort of "niche" in the general forest community.

On the other hand, a small lake would probably turn out to form an intelligible field of study in itself. The naturalist studying the lake could likely get along very well with only occasional and casual reference to the communities inhabiting its shores. To understand the physical environment of the lake, he would have to study its mode of origin, whether from glacial action, from uplift across a stream drainage system, or from some more remote sequence of geological events. He would be concerned with the depth of the lake and with the regional climate and its relation to temperatures at various depths. The kind of fish populations inhabiting the lake and their density would depend on host-prey relations among these populations, on the sort of breeding places available in marginal vegetation, and their extent. Even the larval insects found in the vegetation at the lake margins would probably depend more on the characteristics of the lake community than on the characteristics of the forest community adjoining the lake.

If the lake were big enough, we might find that it was inhabited by a series of communities which formed intelligible fields of study in themselves. The problem of study of great lakes thus approaches in nature the problem of studying life in the sea. The lake takes on the character of a geographical region, inhabited by many kinds of communities, tied together chiefly by factors of the regional climate, and the regional geological history.

A biotic community may form an intelligible field of study, but it is never a completely isolated field of study. The birds that nest in the oak community may spend the winter in South America. Large mammals, especially predators such as the puma and jaguar, range through all kinds of communities, although the activities of a particular individual are usually confined to a rather limited area, perhaps a single community. The fluctuations in density of a particular species of organism in a given community may depend on factors that affect the population in the whole geographical region.

UNDERSTANDING THE TEXT

1. According to Bates, in what way have most ecologists defined the term "biotic community"?
2. Why does he find this definition inadequate?
3. On what basis does Bates create his definition of the term?
4. How does Toynbee's definition of the concept of civilization help Bates clarify his own definition? On what grounds does Bates justify the similarity of definition for "civilization" and "biotic community"?
5. In the last half of this essay, Bates extends, amplifies, and sharpens the meaning of his basic definition. What techniques does he employ in thus developing his definition?
6. In terms of his definition, why does Bates regard the forest, rather than the oak tree, as the biotic community?
7. What is the purpose of the caution mentioned in the final paragraph?

TOPICS FOR DISCUSSION AND WRITING

8. What does Bates's heading, "The Limits of the Community," suggest about the purpose of definition?
9. Judging from Bates's procedure, what considerations affect the kind of definitions one frames and uses? Is the *subject* of one's study the sole source of the definition? Or does the *purpose* of the study also influence the way one defines a thing or an idea?
10. How does the definition elaborated in Bates's essay differ from the sort of definition found in ordinary dictionaries?
11. Write an essay in which you present and explain the meaning one of the following terms has for you: well-adjusted personality, standard of living, separation of governmental powers, spectator sports, school spirit, freedom of the press, conscience, liberal education.
12. What kind of audience and what purpose have you assumed in writing this essay in definition? Indicate how your definition might have been modified if your purpose had been different.

Community, Association, and Institution

R. M. MacIVER

IT IS most desirable that every student of social science should learn to attach a definite and single meaning to the primary terms of his vocabulary. Just as the physicist gives precision to such terms as "atom," "force," "momentum," etc., and the biologist to such terms as "cell," "life," "organism," etc., so must the sociologist to the terms which express social characters and relations. It is even more necessary to insist on such precision in our study, because our terms are not themselves technical. They are terms of everyday speech, and so are often employed loosely and interchangeably. We must begin, therefore, by attaching distinct meanings to our essential terms "society," "community," "association," and "institution."

"Society" we shall use in the very widest sense, to include every kind and degree of relationship entered into by men—and any other social creatures—with one another. All our other terms will then express particular types or varieties of social fact or situation. Society, when used without qualification, means the whole system of social relationships.

"Community" properly signifies any whole area of social life, such as a village, or town, or country. It is any circle in which a common life is lived, within which people more or less freely relate themselves to one another in the various aspects of life, and thus exhibit common social characteristics. It is inevitable that people who over any length of time enter freely into social relationships should develop social likenesses, should have some common social ideas, common customs, common traditions, and the sense of belonging together. A community may be small or great. A great community, such as a nation, will enclose a number of smaller communities, localities, and groups with more intense and more numerous common

Reprinted from *The Elements of Social Science* (1921) by R. M. MacIver. Used by permission of the publishers, Methuen & Company, Ltd.

qualities. Small communities are sometimes semi-isolated in the midst of greater ones, especially in countries to which immigrants flock and where they form, as it were, islands of their own peculiar life. Thus it is seen that community is a matter of degree. What we should particularly bear in mind is that community means *any circle of common life*. Common life is more than organization or relationship. When we use the term "society" we think more particularly of organization, but when we use the term "community" we should think of something greater—the life whence organization springs and of which organization is but the means.

The distinction between "community" and "association" is apparent if we take one or two examples. We should call a city a community, but not, in our sense, a church or a college or trade union or a local or city council. We should call a country a community, but not a national association of traders or manufacturers. The church or the trade union or the manufacturers' association or any corporate body is an organization existing within some community. It is an organization deliberately formed for the collective pursuit of some interest or set of interests which the members of it share. But such interest or set of interests is always narrower than the whole range of a common life. It is partial, however important it may be. Hence it has to be specially organized. It pursues in a definite way definite purposes which are not comprehensive of all the purposes of its members, still less of all the purposes of the whole community to which they belong. A community, on the other hand, is integral, not partial. It does not exist for the pursuit of special interests. It is not deliberately created. It has no beginning, no hour of birth. It is simply the whole circle of common life, more comprehensive, more spontaneous than any association.

One remarkable feature of more recent social development has been the multiplication of associations within the community. In former times a few types of associations seemed to suffice: state and church and guild, for example. To-day there are myriads in every developed community. Every single interest or purpose that men share with any other men now prompts to an association. These are of all kinds and degrees of permanence. Some exist to achieve an immediate purpose, say the passing of some piece of legislation, and if and when that purpose is achieved the association ceases to exist. Others stand for permanent purposes of human life, in which class come the family and the state. We shall have occasion later to classify the various types of association, and shall then see more fully the infinite ramifications of associational activity in the modern community.

We have called the family and the state associations. These offer good criteria of the distinction between association and community. In the primitive social world the family—or more strictly the kin-group—was almost comprehensive with community. To-day the family is very distinctly an association. It is not the whole common life of its members, but a specially organized part of it, deliberately established in the first instance by the marriage contract. All associations, unlike community itself, rest on a specific covenant, whether expressed or implied, of its adult members.

So with the state, the most comprehensive of them all and therefore the most easily confounded with community. It is highly important that we should realize that the state is not a community, not a whole common life, but only a particular association for its furtherance. The identification of community and the state has led, alike in theory and in practice, to disastrous conclusions. This false conception, accepted by a long line of political theorists, has lent support to the principle of the unlimited sovereignty of the individual state, such that it owes no express obligation to others, being by nature a completely independent and morally unlimited power. It has justified the exclusiveness of governments by which, under the stimulation of selfish interests, they have denied the common interest which binds people to people, and striven to isolate, only in fact to frustrate and to destroy, the conditions of the welfare of each. Within the state it has led to tyrannous encroachment over the free life of other associations, to a coercive uniformity in respect of religion, education, language, and opinion, against which the creative spirit in man has had to wage incessant war. The state is an association of fundamental value, because to it belongs the establishment and maintenance of the whole system of enforceable rights and obligations, the basis of order and of liberty. It is an essential association of community, but it is not community. Nor can it fulfil its vast social function aright unless that distinction is realized.

A further distinction may now be made, between "community" and "association" on the one hand and "institution" on the other. To illustrate, we should call monogamy an institution, but the family an association; the party-system an institution, but the state an association; baptism an institution, but the church an association. Institutions are established and recognized forms of relationship between social beings. They may be so established either by particular associations, as in the instances abovementioned, or by the community in general. Established customs or "folkways" belong to the latter class. Not infrequently an association takes over for special protection some institution which originally was a spontaneous creation of community. This is specially the way of the state. It has, for example, taken over the institution of property, originally a communal institution, and made it a legal institution. Social institutions make a great network of organization, which both serves and controls the life of men in society. There is always a danger of institutions becoming stereotyped, of their coming, by age or habituation, to seem to exist in their own right, or of their growing into an engine of power quietly manipulated by a dominant few or many, and thus exercising a social control divorced from the principle of social service. Every progressive community needs therefore continuously to examine its institutions so that they shall the better serve the changing needs of the age.

UNDERSTANDING THE TEXT

1. What is the logical relationship between the terms MacIver is particularly concerned with—"community," "association," "institution"—and the term "society"?

2. What advantages does MacIver secure by defining all three key terms at the same time? What difficulties would he have encountered if he had tried to define the terms separately, with pages of exposition intervening?

3. How important is his use of examples in expanding and clarifying the meaning of the terms? For which of the terms does he find it necessary to supply the greatest number of examples? Why?

4. What role does this set of definitions play in permitting MacIver to present a particular interpretation of government? What attitude toward social change is implied by the way MacIver expands his definition of "institution"?

5. It may be useful, logically, to think of definition as the act first of locating a thing or idea within a broad classification, and then of differentiating it from other members of the same class. Thus, the term "freshman" might be defined simply as "a college student who is in his first year." Here the phrase "a college student" identifies the broad classification which is relevant, and the qualification "who is in his first year" makes the differentiation from other subclasses. To what extent does MacIver's procedure illustrate this method of definition?

TOPICS FOR DISCUSSION AND WRITING

6. Compare MacIver's definition of "community" and Bates's definition of "biotic community." Are the two writers assigning essentially the same meaning to the word "community"?

7. Real-estate men opening up a new area almost always invite the public to

inspect a new "community," rather than a new "town" or "subdivision." Discuss the possible reasons for this choice in diction.

8. Judging from these essays, and from other examples of definition which you recall, is it possible to define a single thing, or does definition necessarily deal with classes of things or ideas?

9. In a paper, discuss the premises concerning government which led MacIver to cite the state as an example of "association." Indicate and explain the premises which might cause another writer to classify the state under "community" or some other heading.

10. Can you suggest other clusters of related concepts which, in a way similar to MacIver's procedure, might best be defined together? For example, three methods of teaching—the lecture, the recitation, the discussion—might appropriately be defined in this way. Write an essay defining clearly, with whatever amplification is needed, such a group of related terms.

The Crank, the Eccentric, and
the Individualist

LOUIS KRONENBERGER

OUR WELL-FOUNDED distaste for cranks has . . . rather blurred our ability to tell a crank from a mere eccentric, or even an eccentric from an individual. On a very rough-and-ready basis we might define an eccentric as a man who is a law unto himself, and a crank as one who, having determined what the law is, insists on laying it down to others. An eccentric[1] puts ice cream on steak simply because he likes it; should a crank do so, he would endow the act with moral grandeur and straightway denounce as sinners (or reactionaries) all who failed to follow suit. The crank, however, seldom deals in anything so agreeable as steak or ice cream; the crank prefers the glories of health bread or the splendors of soybeans. Cranks, at their most familiar, are a sort of peevish prophets, and it's not enough that they should be in the right; others must also be in the wrong. They are by definition obsessed, and, by connotation, obsessed with something odd. They mistake the part for the whole, the props for the play, the inconvenience for the efficacy; they are spoil-sport humanitarians, full of the sour milk of human kindness.[2]

The crank is for several reasons a fairly common figure in American

[1] Many "eccentrics" are, of course, mere poseurs and publicity seekers. But many are real, and I speak here only of such.

[2] They can be useful, at moments even invaluable, goads; but they fail of love no less than of humor, and seem most ready to plow the earth where they can spoil the lawn. John the Baptist *requires* the wilderness, and even a man of the critical excellence of Mr. F. R. Leavis evokes the workhouse. After all the gush of the Janeites, Mr. and Mrs. Leavis are well worth hearing on Jane Austen; but they, in the end, misrepresent her no less. They are the sort of people who, in assessing champagne, would give no consideration to the fizz.

life. To begin with, our reaction against cranks has helped breed more of them. A society that worships good-guyism brands the mere dissenter a misfit, and people who are shunned as square pegs will soon find something deeply immoral about round holes. A society, again, that runs to fads and crazes, that has a natural turn for the ingenious and inventive, will encourage some of its members to be cranks and will doom others. There must be, so to speak, lots of factory-damaged human products that, from being looked upon as rejects, come to crankhood rather than true creativity. Careerwise, there is frequently a missed-the-boat quality in cranks, a psychological origin for their moral obsessiveness; and their "flourishing" off failure is tied up with their having failed at the outset. The crank not only increasingly harangues his audience, but the audience increasingly yawns at, and even walks out on, the crank.[3]

Where a crank is either a moral crusader by nature or a man at war with his surroundings, an eccentric is neither given to crusading nor oppressed by the world. Perhaps a certain amount of enjoyment is essential to the eccentric—his life is satisfactory *because* it is pleasant—as a certain lack of enjoyment is essential to the crank. The great blessing of eccentricity is that, since it is a law unto itself, one isn't constantly torn between what is expedient on the one side and what is personally desirable on the other. Something of an anarchist (as your crank is something of a bigot), the eccentric will often display very unsound, or unsocial, habits and beliefs. But there is nothing self-righteous about his wrongheadedness; he doesn't drag God into keeping a pet leopard in his back yard, or Americanism into going in for rifle practice at 2:00 A.M.

True eccentrics, I would think, are fairly rare, for they must not only differ from other people but be quite indifferent to other people's ways: they must, in other words, be as well adjusted as they are odd. So soon as maladjustment enters in, they cease to be characters and turn into cases. On the other hand, many people who with a little encouragement might emerge as eccentrics are, from childhood on, judged—and hence turned into—misfits. Where their peculiarities are mocked, and certainly where they are penalized, the results can be very unhappy. In America, where even the slightest individualist must resist great pressure, the true eccentric is never free from it. In England there is a proud tradition of eccentricity:

[3] Just as many eccentrics are poseurs, so many cranks are charlatans. The charlatan shrewdly exploits human weakness where the true crank rails against it; the charlatan, preaching some form of nudism or trial marriage, some "holy" brand of licentiousness or God-sent type of laxative, may end up a millionaire. But the true crank has only a chip on his shoulder or bee in his bonnet, not a card up his sleeve.

the English are far more given than we are to keeping strange pets, collecting strange objects, pursuing strange hobbies, adopting strange careers; even where they most conform, as in their club life, they will behave toward one another with what, to other races, seems a wild and splendid strangeness. This is so true that England's—and sometimes New England's—eccentrics have often a great air about them, possess style rather than mere singularity. Consider how Julia Margaret Cameron would walk the two miles from her house to the railway station stirring a cup of tea as she went. In England and New England on the one hand, and in most of America on the other, there may be a quite opposite basis for eccentricity: in the one case, the law unto oneself born of social privilege; in the other, the self-made born of being left out of things. The English eccentric suggests a grande dame, the American a spinster.

The individualist is by no means an eccentric. He is for one thing aware of alternatives; he chooses—for the most part consciously—between the expedient and the self-satisfying; he refuses to play ball rather than doesn't know a game is in progress; and he will seldom seem freakish or even picturesque. Yet, more and more, the individualist is being looked on as an eccentric and perhaps even a crank; though this attitude is scarcely deliberate on the public's part, it yet subconsciously—or by force of repetition —constitutes a gimmick, a pressure to make people conform. The other method of diminishing individualism in America has been to foster and develop "personality." Though the difference between "personality" and individuality is vast, there exists a strong, however thoughtless, tendency to identify the one with the other. So greatly has conformity triumphed that, no matter how orthodox a man's opinions or conventional his behavior, if he happens to express or conduct himself with the slightest vividness or briskness, he is rated and touted a "person"—what might be supposed an individual! Actually, he may not even have an iota of real personality, may just possess a breezy, adaptable, quick-on-the-trigger manner that enables him to be the life of the party or the spark plug of the conference. In the same way, a woman with a gift for dinner-party chatter and a feminine, discreetly flirtatious air will be thought to have enormous personality.

And though such mere types must be written off, there yet *are* a great many Americans with true personality—with an easy charm, a distinctive way of doing and saying things, a regional tang, a surviving girlishness or small-boy quality. They have the appeal, at the very least, of not being like everyone else. But that, in the cliché sense, they are "real persons" is to be doubted. One may go a year without hearing them utter an original, not to say controversial, remark, or seeing them perform a striking, not to say truly unorthodox, act. The centrifugal and extrovert charm of personality is in many ways hostile to individualism, which more naturally manifests itself in withdrawal than in contact, in quiet dissent than in eager acquiescence. Personality and individuality are by no means mutually exclusive, nor is genuine personality necessarily engaging nor genuine individuality necessarily difficult. But the fact remains that we regard personality as a decided blessing, as something a man can't have too much of, and individuality as, oftener than not, a handicap. Individuality is almost by definition antisocial; and the sound "social" maneuver—or it were perhaps better called instinct—is to discredit individuality and eventually outlaw it through enabling people to live *colorfully* alike. As for "personality," it has passed from having great social to acquiring great economic importance: it is the prime mark, and prize asset, of the salesman. And ours is the country where, in order to sell your product, you don't so much point out its merits as you first work like hell to sell yourself.

UNDERSTANDING THE TEXT

1. To what more inclusive group of human beings might these three types— the crank, the eccentric, and the individualist—be regarded as belonging?
2. What primary characteristic does Kronenberger use to define each of the three types?
3. What relationship exists among the three characteristics used as defining criteria?
4. In your judgment, do Kronenberger's definitions serve equally well in contrasting all three classes? That is, are the crank and the eccentric separated from each other with about the same degree of sharpness as the eccentric and the individualist are distinguished?
5. Can you see any reason why the author fails to give the "personality" a separate category and special definition? What is the relationship between the individualist and the personality? Is it the same as the relationship between the eccentric and the poseur, and the crank and the charlatan?
6. What reasons does the author suggest for the large number of cranks in America? Does he use any of these reasons to explain the development of eccentrics or individualists?
7. According to Kronenberger, how do English and American social conditions differ in their effects upon human behavior and attitudes?
8. How do you account for the particular order in which the essayist takes up these three types? How would the effect have been changed if he had begun with the individualist and ended with the crank?

9. Look closely at the material which Kronenberger has placed in the three footnotes. Why do you suppose he decided to exclude these points from the main text?

TOPICS FOR DISCUSSION AND WRITING

10. To what extent can Kronenberger's essay be regarded as an argument? What general ideas about desirable human behavior and satisfactory social conditions are implied in the way he defines the three types?

11. Consult a dictionary and see if you can discover the probable origins of the terms "crank" and "eccentric" as applied to human personality. Are these definitions by origin—sometimes called *etymological* definitions—generally consistent with the way Kronenberger defines the terms?

12. Using your dictionary, check the etymology of each of the following terms: *amateur, connoisseur,* and *dilettante.* Write a brief paper comparing their meanings by etymology with the primary meanings the words currently suggest.

13. Are Kronenberger's definitions applicable to the students on an American campus? What kinds of student behavior would be regarded as crankish? As eccentric? As individualistic?

14. Does Kronenberger's general assessment of American social pressures on the individual hold good for social conditions on the campus?

15. Choose one of the following pairs of terms, and write an essay in which, by definition, you distinguish between the terms: *politics* and *statesmanship, knowledge* and *know-how, the grind* and *the serious student, common sense* and *intelligence, the scientist* and *the engineer.*

16. Compare the purpose of Kronenberger's definitions with the purposes of those presented in the foregoing essays by Bates and MacIver. How is the difference in purpose reflected in the techniques Kronenberger uses to develop his definitions?

17. Do you observe any particularly noticeable quality in Kronenberger's diction, especially in his use of figures of speech? What effect is created by the kinds of metaphor he employs?

An English Squire of the Seventeenth Century:
Mr. Henry Hastings

ANTHONY ASHLEY COOPER,
FIRST LORD SHAFTESBURY

❦

MR. HASTINGS, by his quality, being the son, brother, and uncle to the Earls of Huntingdon, and his way of living, had the first place amongst us. He was peradventure an original in our age, or rather the copy of our nobility in ancient days in hunting and not warlike times; he was low, very strong and very active, of a reddish flaxen hair, his clothes always green cloth, and never all worth when new five pounds. His house was perfectly of the old fashion, in the midst of a large park well stocked with deer, and near the house rabbits to serve his kitchen, many fish-ponds, and great store of wood and timber; a bowling-green in it, long but narrow, full of high ridges, it being never levelled since it was ploughed; they used round sand bowls, and it had a banqueting-house like a stand, a large one built in a tree. He kept all manner of sport-hounds that ran buck, fox, hare, otter, and badger, and hawks long and short winged; he had all sorts of nets for fishing; he had a walk in the New Forest and the manor of Christ Church. This last supplied him with red deer, sea and river fish; and indeed all his neighbors' grounds and royalties were free to him, who bestowed all his time in such sports, but what he borrowed to caress his neighbors' wives and daughters, there being not a woman in all his walks of the degree of a yeoman's wife or under, and under the age of forty, but it was extremely her fault if he were not intimately acquainted with her. This made him

Reprinted from *Fragment of Autobiography, from birth 1621 to 1639*, probably composed late in Shaftesbury's life. Source: W. D. Christie, *A Life of Anthony Ashley Cooper, First Earl of Shaftesbury, 1621–1683* (1871).

very popular, always speaking kindly to the husband, brother, or father, who was to boot very welcome to his house whenever he came. There he found beef pudding and small beer in great plenty, a house not so neatly kept as to shame him or his dirty shoes, the great hall strewed with marrow bones, full of hawks' perches, hounds, spaniels, and terriers, the upper sides of the hall hung with the fox-skins of this and the last year's skinning, here and there a polecat intermixed, guns and keepers' and huntsmen's poles in abundance. The parlor was a large long room, as properly furnished; on a great hearth paved with brick lay some terriers and the choicest hounds and spaniels; seldom but two of the great chairs had litters of young cats in them, which were not to be disturbed, he having always three or four attending him at dinner, and a little white round stick of fourteen inches long lying by his trencher, that he might defend such meat as he had no mind to part with to them. The windows, which were very large, served for places to lay his arrows, crossbows, stonebows, and other such like accoutrements; the corners of the room full of the best chose hunting and hawking poles; an oyster-table at the lower end, which was of constant use twice a day all the year round, for he never failed to eat oysters before dinner and supper through all seasons: the neighboring town of Poole supplied him with them. The upper part of this room had two small tables and a desk, on the one side of which was a church Bible, on the other the Book of Martyrs; on the tables were hawks' hoods, bells, and such like, two or three old green hats with their crowns thrust in so as to hold ten or a dozen eggs, which were of a pheasant kind of poultry he took much care of and fed himself; tables, dice, cards, and boxes were not wanting. In the hole of the desk were store of tobacco-pipes that had been used. On one side of this end of the room was the door of a closet, wherein stood the strong beer and the wine, which never came thence but in single glasses, that being the rule of the house exactly observed, for he never exceeded in drink or permitted it. On the other side was a door into an old chapel not used for devotion; the pulpit, as the safest place, was never wanting of a cold chine of beef, pasty of venison, gammon of bacon, or great apple-pie, with thick crust extremely baked. His table cost him not much, though it was very good to eat at, his sports supplying all but beef and mutton, except Friday, when he had the best sea-fish as well as other fish he could get, and was the day that his neighbors of best quality most visited him. He never wanted a London pudding, and always sung it in with "my part lies therein-a." He drank a glass of wine or two at meals, very often syrup of gilliflower in his sack, and had always a tun glass without feet stood by him holding a pint of small beer, which he often stirred with a great sprig of rosemary. He was well natured, but soon angry, called his servants bastard and cuckoldy knaves, in one of which he often spoke truth to his own knowledge, and sometimes in both, though of the same man. He lived to a hundred, never lost his eyesight, but always writ and read without spectacles, and got to horse without help. Until past fourscore he rode to the death of a stag as well as any.

UNDERSTANDING THE TEXT

1. In two or three sentences, summarize in general terms the central impression of Mr. Henry Hastings' character which this sketch conveys.
2. What kinds of detail does Shaftesbury supply in order to explain the sort of man Hastings was? To what extent does he try to penetrate "inside" Hastings, to interpret his mind and spirit?
3. What type of diction is dominant in the passage?
4. Cite examples of the way the author's diction and choice of details underline the physical profusion and sensuous vitality of Hastings' life.
5. How does Shaftesbury organize the details in the sketch? As he canvasses the details of Hastings' physical surroundings, what plan of progression does he follow?
6. In the first sentence Shaftesbury describes his subject's family and social status in these words: "being the son, brother, and uncle to the Earls of Huntingdon." How are the fact itself and the author's way of putting it characteristic of the piece as a whole?
7. Only one kind of possession seems to be in short supply in the Hastings household. What is it? Is this dearth consistent with the profusion of other things?

TOPICS FOR DISCUSSION AND WRITING

8. Write a description of the home of a person you know. Select details which will give the reader a clear physical impression of the place, and which will also convey some conception of the person who lives in it.
9. As an exercise, see if you can communicate a clear-cut conception of a person's character simply by describing his physical appearance, including his clothing. Try to use only concrete language, and avoid general interpretative statements about his character.
10. Comment on the uses and limitations of the kind of characterization represented by this sketch. If this method were applied to a person somewhat more complex and intellectual than Hastings, what difficulties might the writer encounter?

11. Write a comparison of the description of Hastings' house and Mark Twain's description of "The House Beautiful" (pp. 145–149), giving particular attention to the way each writer manages in his description to suggest the character of the occupant.

The English Squire in the Seventeenth Century

THOMAS BABINGTON MACAULAY

WE SHOULD be much mistaken if we pictured to ourselves the squires of the seventeenth century as men bearing a close resemblance to their descendants, the county members and chairmen of quarter sessions with whom we are familiar. The modern country gentleman generally receives a liberal education, passes from a distinguished school to a distinguished college, and has ample opportunity to become an excellent scholar. He has generally seen something of foreign countries. A considerable part of his life has generally been passed in the capital; and the refinements of the capital follow him into the country. There is perhaps no class of dwellings so pleasing as the rural seats of the English gentry. In the parks and pleasure grounds, nature, dressed yet not disguised by art, wears her most alluring form. In the buildings, good sense and good taste combine to produce a happy union of the comfortable and the graceful. The pictures, the musical instruments, the library, would in any other country be considered as proving the owner to be an eminently polished and accomplished man. A country gentleman who witnessed the Revolution was probably in receipt of about a fourth part of the rent which his acres now yield to his posterity. He was, therefore, as compared with his posterity, a poor man, and was generally under the necessity of residing, with little interruption, on his estate. To travel on the Continent, to maintain an establishment in London, or even to visit London frequently, were pleasures in which only the great proprietors could indulge. It may be confidently affirmed that of the squires whose names were then in the Commissions of Peace and Lieutenancy not one in twenty went to town once in five years, or had ever in his life wandered so far as Paris. Many lords of manors had received an

Reprinted from *The History of England from the Accession of James II*, Chapter 3 (1848).

education differing little from that of their menial servants. The heir of an estate often passed his boyhood and youth at the seat of his family with no better tutors than grooms and gamekeepers, and scarce attained learning enough to sign his name to a Mittimus. If he went to school and to college, he generally returned before he was twenty to the seclusion of the old hall, and there, unless his mind were very happily constituted by nature, soon forgot his academical pursuits in rural business and pleasures. His chief serious employment was the care of his property. He examined samples of grain, handled pigs, and, on market days, made bargains over a tankard with drovers and hop merchants. His chief pleasures were commonly derived from field sports and from an unrefined sensuality. His language and pronunciation were such as we should now expect to hear only from the most ignorant clowns. His oaths, coarse jests, and scurrilous terms of abuse, were uttered with the broadest accent of his province. It was easy to discern, from the first words which he spoke, whether he came from Somersetshire or Yorkshire. He troubled himself little about decorating his abode, and, if he attempted decoration, seldom produced anything but deformity. The litter of a farmyard gathered under the windows of his bedchamber, and the cabbages and gooseberry bushes grew close to his hall door. His table was loaded with coarse plenty; and guests were cordially welcomed to it. But, as the habit of drinking to excess was general in the class to which he belonged, and as his fortune did not enable him to intoxicate large assemblies daily with claret or canary, strong beer was the ordinary beverage. The quantity of beer consumed in those days was indeed enormous. For beer then was to the middle and lower classes, not only all that beer now is, but all that wine, tea, and ardent spirits now are. It was only at great houses, or on great occasions, that foreign drink was placed on the board. The ladies of the house, whose business it had commonly been to cook the repast, retired as soon as the dishes had been devoured, and left the gentlemen to their ale and tobacco. The coarse jollity of the afternoon was often prolonged till the revellers were laid under the table.

It was very seldom that the country gentleman caught glimpses of the great world; and what he saw of it tended rather to confuse than to enlighten his understanding. His opinions respecting religion, government, foreign countries and former times, having been derived, not from study, from observation, or from conversation with enlightened companions, but from such traditions as were current in his own small circle, were the opinions of a child. He adhered to them, however, with the obstinacy which is generally found in ignorant men accustomed to be fed with flattery. His animosities were numerous and bitter. He hated Frenchmen and Italians, Scotchmen and Irishmen, Papists and Presbyterians, Independents and Baptists, Quakers and Jews. Towards London and Londoners he felt an aversion which more than once produced important political effects. His wife and daughter were in tastes and acquirements below a housekeeper or a stillroom maid of the present day. They stitched and spun, brewed gooseberry wine, cured marigolds, and made the crust for the venison pasty.

From this description it might be supposed that the English esquire of the seventeenth century did not materially differ from a rustic miller or alehouse keeper of our time. There are, however, some important parts of his character still to be noted, which will greatly modify this estimate. Unlettered as he was and unpolished, he was still in some most important points a gentleman. He was a member of a proud and powerful aristocracy, and was distinguished by many both of the good and of the bad qualities which belong to aristocrats. His family pride was beyond that of a Talbot or a Howard. He knew the genealogies and coats of arms of all his neighbors, and could tell which of them had assumed supporters without any right, and which of them were so unfortunate as to be great grandsons of aldermen. He was a magistrate, and, as such, administered gratuitously to those who dwelt around him a rude patriarchal justice, which, in spite of innumerable blunders and of occasional acts of tyranny, was yet better than no justice at all. He was an officer of the trainbands; and his military dignity, though it might move the mirth of gallants who had served a campaign in Flanders, raised his character in his own eyes and in the eyes of his neighbors. Nor indeed was his soldiership justly a subject of derision. In every county there were elderly gentlemen who had seen service which was no child's play. One had been knighted by Charles the First, after the battle of Edgehill. Another still wore a patch over the scar which he had received at Naseby. A third had defended his old house till Fairfax had blown in the door with a petard. The presence of these old Cavaliers, with their old swords and holsters, and with their old stories about Goring and Lunsford, gave to the musters of militia an earnest and warlike aspect which would otherwise have been wanting. Even those country gentlemen who were too young to have themselves exchanged blows with the cuirassiers of the Parliament had, from childhood, been surrounded with the traces of recent war, and fed with stories of the martial exploits of their fathers and uncles. Thus the character of the English esquire of the seventeenth century was compounded of two elements which we seldom or never find united. His ignorance and uncouthness, his low tastes and gross phrases, would, in our time, be considered as indicating a nature and a breeding thoroughly plebeian. Yet he was essentially a patrician, and had, in large measure, both the virtues and the vices which flourish among men set from their birth in high place, and used to respect themselves and to be respected by others. It is not easy for a generation accustomed to find chivalrous sentiments only in company with liberal studies and polished manners to image to itself a man with the deportment, the vocabulary, and the accent of a carter, yet punctilious on matters of genealogy and precedence, and ready to risk his life rather than see a stain cast on the honor of his house. It is however only by thus joining together things seldom or never found together in our own experience, that we can form a just idea of that rustic aristocracy which constituted the main strength of the armies of Charles the First, and which long supported, with strange fidelity, the interest of his descendants.

UNDERSTANDING THE TEXT

1. What is the purpose of the sketch of the contemporary (nineteenth-century) English gentleman with which Macaulay begins? How does this purpose guide him in selecting aspects of the country gentleman's life for inclusion in the brief sketch?

2. When he gets to his real subject, the English squire of the seventeenth century, how does Macaulay organize his account of the squire's physical routine and customary activities?

3. What circumstance is brought forward to account for the squire's enforced rural residence, lack of education, and narrowness of experience?

4. To what extent can the remainder of the squire's personal traits and social habits be regarded as corollaries of his narrowly provincial life?

5. To what pattern do the squire's political ideas conform? Are the origins of his politics similar to the origins of his social habits?

6. What specific virtues does Macaulay find in the typical old-time squire? Why does he regard his possession of these virtues as something of a paradox?

7. In view of the final sentence of the passage, for what reason did Macaulay probably reserve his discussion of the squire's virtues until after he had recounted his vices?

TOPICS FOR DISCUSSION AND WRITING

8. How similar is Macaulay's typical seventeenth-century squire to Mr. Henry Hastings of the preceding sketch? List the characteristics which the indi-

vidual and the type have in common. Do any of the specific illustrative details occur in both pieces?

9. Write a comparison of the seventeenth-century squire described by Macaulay and the eighteenth-century country gentleman described by Cecil in "The Whig World" (pp. 424–433).

10. Which of the common procedures for developing a subject, in addition to characterization itself, are used in this passage? The central sketch may be regarded as an analysis of a typical character. On what basis is the analysis carried out?

The House Beautiful

MARK TWAIN

WE TOOK passage in a Cincinnati boat for New Orleans; or on a Cincinnati boat—either is correct; the former is the Eastern form of putting it, the latter the Western.

Mr. Dickens declined to agree that the Mississippi steamboats were "magnificent," or that they were "floating palaces"—terms which had always been applied to them; terms which did not over-express the admiration with which the people viewed them.

Mr. Dickens's position was unassailable, possibly; the people's position was certainly unassailable. If Mr. Dickens was comparing these boats with the crown jewels; or with the Taj, or with the Matterhorn; or with some other priceless or wonderful thing which he had seen, they were not magnificent—he was right. The people compared them with what *they* had seen; and, thus measured, thus judged, the boats were magnificent—the term was the correct one, it was not at all too strong. The people were as right as was Mr. Dickens. The steamboats were finer than anything on shore. Compared with superior dwelling-houses and first-class hotels in the valley, they were indubitably magnificent, they were "palaces." To a few people living in New Orleans and St. Louis they were not magnificent, perhaps; not palaces; but to the great majority of those populations, and to the entire populations spread over both banks between Baton Rouge and St. Louis, they were palaces; they tallied with the citizen's dream of what magnificence was, and satisfied it.

Every town and village along that vast stretch of double river-frontage had a best dwelling, finest dwelling, mansion—the home of its wealthiest and most conspicuous citizen. It is easy to describe it: large grassy yard,

Reprinted from *Life on the Mississippi* by Mark Twain. Used by permission of the publishers, Harper & Brothers.

with paling fence painted white—in fair repair; brick walk from gate to door; big, square, two-story "frame" house, painted white and porticoed like a Grecian temple—with this difference, that the imposing fluted columns and Corinthian capitals were a pathetic sham, being made of white pine, and painted; iron knocker; brass door-knob—discolored, for lack of polishing. Within, an uncarpeted hall, of planed boards; opening out of it, a parlor, fifteen feet by fifteen—in some instances five or ten feet larger; ingrain carpet; mahogany center-table; lamp on it, with green-paper shade—standing on a gridiron, so to speak, made of high-colored yarns, by the young ladies of the house, and called a lamp-mat; several books, piled and disposed, with cast-iron exactness, according to an inherited and unchangeable plan; among them, Tupper, much penciled; also, *Friendship's Offering*, and *Affection's Wreath*, with their sappy inanities illustrated in die-away mezzotints; also, Ossian; *Alonzo and Melissa*, maybe *Ivanhoe;* also "Album," full of original "poetry" of the Thou-hast-wounded-the-spirit-that-loved-thee breed; two or three goody-goody works—*Shepherd of Salisbury Plain*, etc.; current number of the chaste and innocuous *Godey's Lady's Book,* with painted fashion-plate of wax-figure women with mouths all alike—lips and eye-lids the same size—each five-foot woman with a two-inch wedge sticking from under her dress and letting on to be half of her foot. Polished air-tight stove (new and deadly invention), with pipe passing through a board which closes up the discarded good old fireplace. On each end of the wooden mantel, over the fireplace, a large basket of peaches and other fruits, natural size, all done in plaster, rudely, or in wax, and painted to resemble the originals—which they don't. Over middle of mantel, engraving—"Washington Crossing the Delaware"; on the wall by the door, copy of it done in thunder-and-lightning crewels by one of the young ladies—work of art which would have made Washington hesitate about crossing, if he could have foreseen what advantage was going to be taken of it. Piano—kettle in disguise—with music, bound and unbound, piled on it, and on a stand near by: "Battle of Prague"; "Bird Waltz"; "Arkansas Traveler"; "Rosin the Bow"; "Marseillaise Hymn"; "On a Lone Barren Isle" (St. Helena); "The Last Link Is Broken"; "She Wore a Wreath of Roses the Night When Last We Met"; "Go, Forget Me, Why Should Sorrow o'er That Brow a Shadow Fling"; "Hours That Were to Memory Dearer"; "Long, Long Ago"; "Days of Absence"; "A Life on the Ocean Wave, a Home on the Rolling Deep"; "Bird at Sea"; and spread open on the rack where the plaintive singer has left it, "*Ro*-holl on, silver *moo*-hoon, guide the *trav*-el-err on his *way*," etc. Tilted pensively against the piano, a guitar—guitar capable of playing the Spanish fandango by itself, if you give it a start. Frantic work of art on the wall—pious motto, done on the premises, sometimes in colored yarns, sometimes in faded grasses: progenitor of the "God Bless Our Home" of modern commerce. Framed in black moldings on the wall, other works of art, conceived and committed on the premises, by the young ladies; being grim black-and-white crayons; landscapes, mostly: lake, solitary sailboat, petrified clouds, pregeological trees on shore, anthracite precipice; name of criminal conspicuous in the corner. Lithograph, "Napoleon Crossing the Alps." Lithograph, "The Grave at St. Helena." Steel plates, Trumbull's "Battle of Bunker Hill," and the "Sally from Gibraltar." Copper plates, "Moses Smiting the Rock," and "Return of the Prodigal Son." In big gilt frame, slander of the family in oil: papa holding a book ("Constitution of the United States"); guitar leaning against mamma, blue ribbons fluttering from its neck; the young ladies, as children, in slippers and scalloped pantalettes, one embracing toy horse, the other beguiling kitten with ball of yarn, and both simpering up at mamma, who simpers back. These persons all fresh, raw, and red—apparently skinned. Opposite, in gilt frame, grandpa and grandma, at thirty and twenty-two, stiff, old-fashioned, high-collared, puff-sleeved, glaring pallidly out from a background of solid Egyptian night. Under a glass French clock dome, large bouquet of stiff flowers done in corpsy-white wax. Pyramidal what-not in the corner, the shelves occupied chiefly with bric-à-brac of the period, disposed with an eye to best effect: shell, with the Lord's Prayer carved on it; another shell—of the long-oval sort, narrow, straight orifice, three inches long, running from end to end—portrait of Washington carved on it; not well done; the shell had Washington's mouth, originally—artist should have built to that. These two are memorials of the long-ago bridal trip to New Orleans and the French Market. Other bric-à-brac: Californian "Specimens"—quartz, with gold wart adhering; old Guinea-gold locket, with circlet of ancestral hair in it; Indian arrowheads, of flint; pair of bead moccasins, from uncle who crossed the Plains; three "alum" baskets of various colors—being skeleton-frame of wire, clothed on with cubes of crystallized alum in the rock-candy style—works of art which were achieved by the young ladies; their doubles and duplicates to be found upon all what-nots in the land; convention of desiccated bugs and butterflies pinned to a card; painted toy dog, seated upon bellows attachment—drops its under-jaw and squeaks when pressed upon; sugar-candy rabbit—limbs and features merged together, not strongly defined; pewter presidential-campaign medal; miniature cardboard wood-sawyer, to be attached to the stovepipe and operated by the heat; small Napoleon, done in wax; spread-open daguerreotypes of dim children, parents, cousins, aunts, and friends, in all attitudes but customary ones; no templed portico at back, and manufactured landscape stretching away in the distance—that came in later, with the photograph; all these vague figures lavishly chained and ringed—metal indicated and secured from doubt by stripes and splashes of vivid gold bronze; all of them too much combed, too much fixed up; and all of them uncomfortable in inflexible Sunday clothes of a pattern which the spectator cannot realize could ever have been in fashion; husband and wife generally grouped together— husband sitting, wife standing, with hand on his shoulder—and both preserving, all these fading years, some traceable effect of the daguerreotypist's brisk "Now smile, if you please!" Bracketed over what-not—place of special sacredness—an outrage in water-color, done by the young niece that came on a visit long ago, and died. Pity, too; for she might have repented of this in time. Horsehair chairs, horsehair sofa which keeps sliding from under you. Window-shades, of oil stuff, with milkmaids and ruined castles stenciled on them in fierce colors. Lambrequins dependent from gaudy boxings of beaten tin, gilded. Bedrooms with rag carpets; bedsteads of the "corded" sort, with a sag in the middle, the cords needing tightening; snuffy feather-bed—not aired often enough; cane-seat chairs, splint-bottomed rocker; looking-glass on wall, school-slate size, veneered frame; inherited bureau; wash-bowl and pitcher, possibly—but not certainly; brass candlestick, tallow candle, snuffers. Nothing else in the room. Not a bathroom in the house; and no visitor likely to come along who has ever seen one.

That was the residence of the principal citizen, all the way from the suburbs of New Orleans to the edge of St. Louis. When he stepped aboard a big fine steamboat, he entered a new and marvelous world: chimney-tops cut to counterfeit a spraying crown of plumes—and maybe painted red; pilot-house, hurricane-deck, boiler-deck guards, all garnished with white wooden filigree-work of fanciful patterns; gilt acorns topping the derricks; gilt deer-horns over the big bell; gaudy symbolical picture on the paddle-box, possibly; big roomy boiler-deck, painted blue, and furnished with Windsor arm-chairs; inside, a far-receding snow-white "cabin"; porcelain knob and oil-picture on every stateroom door; curving patterns of filigree-work touched up with gilding, stretching overhead all down the converging vista; big chandeliers every little way, each an April shower of glittering glass-drops; lovely rainbow-light falling everywhere from the colored glazing of the skylights; the whole a long-drawn, resplendent tunnel, a be-wildering and soul-satisfying spectacle! in the ladies' cabin a pink and white Wilton carpet, as soft as mush, and glorified with a ravishing pattern of gigantic flowers. Then the Bridal Chamber—the animal that invented that idea was still alive and unhanged, at that day—Bridal Chamber whose pre-tentious flummery was necessarily overawing to the now tottering intellect of that hosannahing citizen. Every stateroom had its couple of cozy clean bunks, and perhaps a looking-glass and a snug closet; and sometimes there was even a wash-bowl and pitcher, and part of a towel which could be told from mosquito-netting by an expert—though generally these things were absent, and the shirt-sleeved passengers cleansed themselves at a long row of stationary bowls in the barber shop, where were also public towels, public combs, and public soap.

Take the steamboat which I have just described, and you have her in her highest and finest, and most pleasing, and comfortable, and satisfactory estate. Now cake her over with a layer of ancient and obdurate dirt, and you have the Cincinnati steamer awhile ago referred to. Not all over—only inside; for she was ably officered in all departments except the steward's.

But wash that boat and repaint her, and she would be about the counter-part of the most complimented boat of the old flush times: for the steam-boat architecture of the West has undergone no change; neither has steam-boat furniture and ornamentation undergone any.

UNDERSTANDING THE TEXT

1. Twain is concerned with the difference between Dickens' judgment of the Western steamboat and the people's judgment. What is the basis, in Twain's opinion, of this difference? What is Twain's description of the House Beau-tiful designed to show about the people's attitude toward the steamboat? What are the dominant impressions Twain seeks to convey in his descrip-tion of the house?

2. Do you see any principle of order in the sequence in which Twain arranges the details of his description of the House Beautiful?

3. To what parts of the house or the house furnishings does Twain give the greatest emphasis? How does he secure this emphasis? Why does he empha-size these aspects? Does he omit altogether anything that a "normal" de-scription of a house would probably include? Why?

4. Twain arranges his composition in such a way that the description of the house is given in a single very long paragraph, much longer than any of the other paragraphs in the essay. What does he accomplish by this method of

arrangement? Would the essay have been more effective if the description of the house had been broken up into several shorter paragraphs, each dealing with one aspect of the appearance of the house?

5. Why is Twain's description of the steamboat so much shorter than his description of the house? So much less detailed? Why does Twain, even in this rather brief description of the steamboat, devote more space to the bathing arrangements than he does in the long description of the house?

6. Define as carefully as you can the peculiarities of Twain's sentence structure in the descriptive passages. How do the sentences here differ from the sentences in the first three paragraphs? What does Twain accomplish by this method of writing his description?

7. What qualities do the works of art in the house have in common? How are these qualities related to Twain's explanation of the attitude of Westerners toward the steamboats?

8. What is Twain's own judgment of the House Beautiful and of the Western steamboat? Make a list of all the kinds of signs from which you infer his judgment. How far is Twain from Dickens in what he thinks about the steamboats?

TOPICS FOR DISCUSSION AND WRITING

9. This is a "composite" description, in which characteristic details are fitted together to form a picture of a typical house of a certain kind. In this respect the method Twain follows is similar to that followed by Macaulay and Trollope in other essays in this section. Read those essays and note the methods of composite description used in them.

10. Suppose that you have read an account of America by a contemporary foreign visitor which contains a severe criticism of some feature of the American landscape—clusters of neon signs in big cities, for example, or highway billboards, or skyscrapers, or superhighways. Using Twain's method, write a paper in which you account for a favorable American judgment by referring it to some other expression of American taste.

11. Write a composite description, aiming at effects similar to those Twain achieves, of a kind of building you are familiar with: movie theater, railroad station, doctor's waiting room, fraternity house, etc.

12. Twain implies in his third paragraph that judgments of beauty are purely relative—that they depend entirely on the standard of comparison the individual judge happens to adopt. Does Twain's essay suggest that he really holds this view? Consider your own opinions on the judgment of beauty or value and see if you can explain and defend your assumptions.

Civilization and Culture

R. M. MacIVER

SOCIETY has an inner environment which it makes, besides the outer which it only moulds. The former consists in the whole apparatus of custom and institution, the complex and multiform mechanism of order, the devices and instruments by which nature is controlled, the modes of expression and communication, the comforts, refinements, and luxuries which determine standards of living, and the economic system through which they are produced and distributed. It includes all that human intelligence and art have wrought to make the world a home for the human spirit. It includes alike the technological and the institutional equipment, parliaments and telephone exchanges, corporation charters and railroads, insurance agencies and automobiles. This whole apparatus of life we shall here call civilization. It is obvious that the political system belongs to this region and constitutes one great division of it.

From civilization we must distinguish culture as its animating and creating spirit. Civilization is the instrument, the body, even the garment of culture. Civilization expresses itself in politics, in economics, in technology, while culture expresses itself in art, in literature, in religion, in morals. Our culture is what we are, our civilization is what we use. There is a technique of culture, but the culture itself is not technique. Culture is the fulfilment of life, revealed in the things we want in themselves, and not in their results. No one wants banking systems and factories and ballot-boxes for any intrinsic significance they possess. If we could attain the products without the process we would gladly dispense with the latter. But the objects of culture have a direct significance. It is the difference between the mode of achieving and the thing achieved, between the way of living and

Reprinted from *The Modern State* (1926) by R. M. MacIver. Used by permission of the publishers, The Clarendon Press, Oxford.

the life led. The interest in technique is derivative, though like any other it may come to engross the mind, but the interest in culture is primary.

There is a great difference between an object of civilization and a work of culture. An institutional or technical achievement raises, so to speak, the level of civilization. It is an improvement on the past. Once the spinning-machine or the railway-locomotive or the typewriter is discovered, men go on developing it. Civilization is cumulative. The new model betters the old, and renders it obsolete. The achievement perpetuates itself and is the basis of further achievement. Civilization is rightly described as a "march," for each step leads to another and is always forward. Great historical catastrophes can interrupt this cumulation, but nothing seems able to break it altogether. It is a poor age indeed that does not add some stones to this rising edifice of civilization. But culture is not cumulative. It has to be won afresh by each new generation. It is not a simple inheritance like civilization. It is true that here too past attainment is the basis of present achievement, but there is no surety that the present will equal, still less that it will improve on, the past. The heights reached by Greek art and Greek drama are not held by succeeding ages. The achievement of Dante or of Shakespeare is not equalled by those who follow them. What Archimedes or Galileo or Newton discovered is the basis of further discovery that exceeds any of theirs, but what Sophocles or Michael Angelo or Milton expressed is not expressed better or more fully by others who have their works before them. We do not deny that there is advance in culture also, but it is no steady advance. It is variable and seems capricious, subject to retreats and setbacks.

The reason thereof suggests another difference between civilization and culture. Culture must always be won afresh, because it is a direct expression of the human spirit. In a very real sense a musician composes only for musicians and an artist paints only for artists. A poet can write only for those who have themselves the poetic quality. Every work of art implies at least two artists, he who creates and he who understands, and so with all the achievements of culture. Cultural expression is communication between likes and is possible only by reason of their likeness. The work of the artist is only for other artists, but the work of the engineer is not for other engineers. The bridge-builder does not construct for other bridge-builders, but for those who themselves may appreciate nothing of his skill. Millions may use a technical invention without the least understanding of it. Devices for use are in fact the more perfect the less understanding they require, and the aim of the inventor is to make his invention, in the American phrase, "fool-proof." We would get an entirely false conception of the intelligence and capacity of our age, and an entirely false standard of comparison between it and other ages, if we judged it by its institutions and its technical equipment. Our estimate would be much more just if we judged it by the books men read and write, by the ideals they cherish, by the pleasures they pursue, by the religions which they practise, by all the things they really care about and think about.

It follows that one people can borrow civilization from another people in a way in which culture cannot be borrowed. Technical devices can be transplanted without change. Institutional devices, being more nearly related to the form of culture which they serve, undergo some change when they are borrowed. The barbarian can learn more easily to use the rifle than the ballot-box. The institutions of Western democracy do not accommodate themselves without strain to the social life of the Orient or even of South America. Nevertheless they are transferable to a degree, and have in fact been adopted in many countries to which they were not native. But a culture cannot be adopted. A culture may be assimilated gradually, by peoples who are ready for it and who are brought into constant contact with it, but even so they inevitably change it in making it their own. When extraneous considerations lead to the nominal acceptance of an alien culture it becomes a travesty or an empty form. The extraordinary transmogrifications of Christianity in the course of two thousand years, involving not merely the restatement but often the rejection of its original principles, offer a splendid illustration of the truth that a culture cannot be "adopted." The culture of a people expresses their character and can express nothing else. Hence civilization is far more pervasive than culture. Japan can speedily adopt the civilization of the West, but it neither can nor cares to adopt its culture. Of course we must not imply that the two factors are entirely separate. Civilization, whether native or adopted, is a kind of social environment, and human beings respond in similar ways to similar conditions. Civilization and culture necessarily react on one another. Nevertheless it seems clear that cultures can remain distinctive within the form of a common civilization. Given the means of communication, it is inevitable that civilization should become, in its larger aspects, one and universal. But under this seeming uniformity of life great cultural differences remain, both within and between the peoples of the earth.

One further distinction can now be made. We have pointed out that civilization, in contrast to culture, is cumulative. This is true in another sense also. Means can be massed into great engines of power. Systems can be extended into vaster systems. But culture resists the mechanics of addition and multiplication. I have elsewhere expressed this truth as follows: "We can add the wealth of a group or a nation and get some kind of a total. We can add its man-power and get a total. But we cannot make a sum of its health or its habits or its culture. A thousand weak purposes cannot be rolled into one strong purpose as a thousand weak units of force are joined into one strong force. We cannot add wisdom as we can add wealth. A thousand mediocrities do not sum up into one genius."

UNDERSTANDING THE TEXT

1. Can you identify the broader conception of which the two ideas discussed here—civilization and culture—are, in a manner of speaking, parts?
2. What criteria does MacIver employ to carry out his analysis—to distinguish, that is, between civilization and culture?
3. Of the several points of contrast between the two ideas developed by the author, which seem to you central to the analysis? Which serve mainly to bring the distinction into sharper focus, once it has been made?
4. In view of the scale of this essay, discuss the way MacIver uses examples to clarify the distinctions he draws between the two ideas.
5. MacIver develops the distinction between the two terms by proceeding through a series of points of contrast. An alternative method would have been to define one term fully, and then proceed to the other. Considering the purpose of the passage, do you believe that the method he employs is superior to this possible alternative?
6. Do you notice anything particularly striking about the kind of sentence structure MacIver usually employs? What effect does it create?
7. Why do you think the author begins by introducing the idea of civilization and then that of culture, instead of handling them in the reverse order?

TOPICS FOR DISCUSSION AND WRITING

8. Write an essay stating and explaining your reaction to the idea expressed by MacIver in the passage beginning, "In a very real sense a musician composes only for musicians and an artist paints only for artists."
9. Do you agree with MacIver that it is misleading to judge an age by its civilization, and that it would be much more just to evaluate it in terms of its cultural achievements? Develop your ideas on this question into an essay.
10. Would the particular distinction MacIver makes between civilization and culture be universally acceptable? How would the premises implied in this passage—concerning human nature, for example—have to be altered if one wished to argue that no such distinction exists, and that all "cultural" manifestations are really a part of what MacIver calls civilization?

The Social Value of the College-Bred[1]

WILLIAM JAMES

OF WHAT use is a college training? We who have had it seldom hear the question raised; we might be a little nonplussed to answer it offhand. A certain amount of meditation has brought me to this as the pithiest reply which I myself can give: The best claim that a college education can possibly make on your respect, the best thing it can aspire to accomplish for you, is this: that it should *help you to know a good man when you see him.* This is as true of women's as of men's colleges; but that it is neither a joke nor a one-sided abstraction I shall now endeavor to show.

What talk do we commonly hear about the contrast between college education and the education which business or technical or professional schools confer? The college education is called higher because it is supposed to be so general and so disinterested. At the "schools" you get a relatively narrow practical skill, you are told, whereas the "colleges" give you the more liberal culture, the broader outlook, the historical perspective, the philosophic atmosphere, or something which phrases of that sort try to express. You are made into an efficient instrument for doing a definite thing, you hear, at the schools; but, apart from that, you may remain a crude and smoky kind of petroleum, incapable of spreading light. The universities and colleges, on the other hand, although they may leave you less efficient for this or that practical task, suffuse your whole mentality with something more important than skill. They redeem you, make you well-bred; they make "good company" of you mentally. If they find you with a naturally boorish or caddish mind, they cannot leave you so, as a technical school may leave you. This, at least, is pretended; this is what we hear among col-

[1] Address delivered at a meeting of the Association of American Alumnae at Radcliffe College, November 7, 1907, and first published in *McClure's Magazine* for February, 1908.

lege-trained people when they compare their education with every other sort. Now, exactly how much does this signify?

It is certain, to begin with, that the narrowest trade or professional training does something more for a man than to make a skilful practical tool of him—it makes him also a judge of other men's skill. Whether his trade be pleading at the bar or surgery or plastering or plumbing, it develops a critical sense in him for that sort of occupation. He understands the difference between second-rate and first-rate work in his whole branch of industry; he gets to know a good job in his own line as soon as he sees it; and getting to know this in his own line, he gets a faint sense of what good work may mean anyhow, that may, if circumstances favor, spread into his judgments elsewhere. Sound work, clean work, finished work: feeble work, slack work, sham work—these words express an identical contrast in many different departments of activity. In so far forth, then, even the humblest manual trade may beget in one a certain small degree of power to judge of good work generally.

Now, what is supposed to be the line of us who have the higher college training? Is there any broader line—since our education claims primarily not to be "narrow"—in which we also are made good judges between what is first-rate and what is second-rate only? What is especially taught in the colleges has long been known by the name of the "humanities," and these are often identified with Greek and Latin. But it is only as literatures, not as languages, that Greek and Latin have any general humanity-value; so that in a broad sense the humanities mean literature primarily, and in a still broader sense the study of masterpieces in almost any field of human endeavor. Literature keeps the primacy; for it not only *consists* of masterpieces, but is largely *about* masterpieces, being little more than an appreciative chronicle of human master-strokes, so far as it takes the form of criticism and history. You can give humanistic value to almost anything by teaching it historically. Geology, economics, mechanics, are humanities when taught with reference to the successive achievements of the geniuses to which these sciences owe their being. Not taught thus literature remains grammar, art a catalogue, history a list of dates, and natural science a sheet of formulas and weights and measures.

The sifting of human creations!—nothing less than this is what we ought to mean by the humanities. Essentially this means biography; what our colleges should teach is, therefore, biographical history, that not of politics merely, but of anything and everything so far as human efforts and conquests are factors that have played their part. Studying in this way, we learn what types of activity have stood the test of time; we acquire standards of the excellent and durable. All our arts and sciences and institutions are but so many quests of perfection on the part of men; and when we see how diverse the types of excellence may be, how various the tests, how flexible the adaptations, we gain a richer sense of what the terms "better" and "worse" may signify in general. Our critical sensibilities grow both more acute and less fanatical. We sympathize with men's mistakes even in the act of penetrating them; we feel the pathos of lost causes and misguided epochs even while we applaud what overcame them.

Such words are vague and such ideas are inadequate, but their meaning is unmistakable. What the colleges—teaching humanities by examples which may be special, but which must be typical and pregnant—should at least try to give us, is a general sense of what, under various disguises, *superiority* has always signified and may still signify. The feeling for a good human job anywhere, the admiration of the really admirable, the disesteem of what is cheap and trashy and impermanent,—this is what we call the critical sense, the sense for ideal values. It is the better part of what men know as wisdom. Some of us are wise in this way naturally and by genius; some of us never become so. But to have spent one's youth at college, in contact with the choice and rare and precious, and yet still to be a blind prig or vulgarian, unable to scent out human excellence or to divine it amid its accidents, to know it only when ticketed and labelled and forced on us by others, this indeed should be accounted the very calamity and shipwreck of a higher education.

The sense for human superiority ought, then, to be considered our line, as boring subways is the engineer's line and the surgeon's is appendicitis. Our colleges ought to have lit up in us a lasting relish for the better kind of man, a loss of appetite for mediocrities, and a disgust for cheapjacks. We ought to smell, as it were, the difference of quality in men and their proposals when we enter the world of affairs about us. Expertness in this might well atone for some of our awkwardness at accounts, for some of our ignorance of dynamos. The best claim we can make for the higher education, the best single phrase in which we can tell what it ought to do for us, is, then, exactly what I said: it should enable us to *know a good man when we see him.*

UNDERSTANDING THE TEXT

1. In what respects, according to James, do college education and vocational training belong to the same class of activity? In what respects do they belong to different classes?

2. In the development of James's argument, which is more important, the similarities or the differences between college education and vocational training?

3. As James analyzes the objectives of college education, several of his key terms are *the humanities, literature, history,* and *criticism.* What relationship does he see among these terms? Are they parallel in importance and status, or are some more inclusive than others?

4. For James what is the most important objective of college education? How does the study of the humanities lead to the fulfillment of this objective?

5. James urges the need for cultivating a sense of superiority, an admiration for the admirable, a feeling for a good job well done. What specific kind of excellence do you think he is talking about? Is it primarily intellectual excellence, or aesthetic excellence, or moral excellence? What evidence in the text supports your opinion on this?

6. In the second paragraph the author develops a common contrast between college education and vocational education. How does his choice of words in this paragraph serve to convey the impression that this contrast is perhaps less sharp and less significant than most people think?

7. Near the end of the essay James refers twice to the "sense of superiority," as well as to "the critical sense" and "the sense for ideal values." In this part of the essay can you discover several choices of diction which are especially consistent with this reiteration of the word "sense"?

TOPICS FOR DISCUSSION AND WRITING

8. Immediately after defining the humanities as "the sifting of human creations," James goes on to say, "Essentially this means biography." Do you agree that what James calls biographical history is essential to the proper study of the humanities? Are there any other ways in which this sifting process could be encouraged?

9. Would any course dealing with humanistic subject matter—that is, with the great works of the human past—meet James's standards for a proper college education? Or, to measure up, would the course need to be taught with a particular set of emphases?

10. Some people argue that, if one wishes to develop a trustworthy understanding of the past, second-rate works are more valuable than masterpieces, because they are more representative and less unusual. What do you think of this argument?

11. Write a paper in which you adopt and support a position on the following statement: "If the purpose of a college education is to cultivate the student's sense of excellence, curricular materials should be primarily contemporary,

since a person can most effectively learn to exercise judgment upon matters which are directly related to his own present-day problems and interests."

12. Which of your courses seem to you most directly concerned with the objectives of college education as defined by James? Write an essay comparing your courses in terms of James's criteria.

13. If you are taking a course with direct vocational objectives, compose an essay describing the extent to which the course, in addition to providing technical training, aids in developing the general sense of excellence advocated by James.

14. "If the purpose of going to college is to know a good man when you see him, the best policy is to major in extracurricular activities." Comment on the validity of this statement.

The Criticism of Architecture

GEOFFREY SCOTT

"WELL-BUILDING hath three conditions: Commodity, Firmness, and Delight." From this phrase of an English humanist[1] a theory of architecture might take its start. Architecture is a focus where three separate purposes have converged. They are blended in a single method; they are fulfilled in a single result; yet in their own nature they are distinguished from each other by a deep and permanent disparity. The criticism of architecture has been confused in its process; it has built up strangely diverse theories of the art, and the verdicts it has pronounced have been contradictory in the extreme. Of the causes which have contributed to its failure, this is the chief: that it has sought to force on architecture an unreal unity of aim. "Commodity, firmness, and delight"; between these three values the criticism of architecture has insecurely wavered, not always distinguishing very clearly between them, seldom attempting any statement of the relation they bear to one another, never pursuing to their conclusion the consequences which they involve. It has leaned now this way and now that, and struck, between these incommensurable virtues, at different points, its arbitrary balance.

Architecture, the most complex of the arts, offers to its critics many paths of approach, and as many opportunities for avoiding their goal. At the outset of a fresh study in this field, it is well, at the risk of pedantry, to define where these paths lead.

[1] Sir Henry Wotton, *Elements of Architecture.* He is adapting Vitruvius, Bk. I, chap. iii.

Reprinted from *The Architecture of Humanism* by Geoffrey Scott with the permission of Charles Scribner's Sons and Constable and Company Ltd.

160

Architecture requires "firmness." By this necessity it stands related to science, and to the standards of science. The mechanical bondage of construction has closely circumscribed its growth. Thrust and balance, pressure and its support, are at the root of the language which architecture employs. The inherent characters of marble, brick, wood and iron have moulded its forms, set limits to its achievement, and governed, in a measure, even its decorative detail. On every hand the study of architecture encounters physics, statics, and dynamics, suggesting, controlling, justifying its design. It is open to us, therefore, to look in buildings for the logical expression of material properties and material laws. Without these, architecture is impossible, its history unintelligible. And if, finding these everywhere paramount, we seek, in terms of material properties and material laws, not merely to account for the history of architecture, but to assess its value, then architecture will be judged by the exactness and sincerity with which it expresses constructive facts, and conforms to constructive laws. That will be the scientific standard for architecture: a logical standard so far as architecture is related to science, and no further.

But architecture requires "commodity." It is not enough that it should possess its own internal coherence, its abstract logic of construction. It has come into existence to satisfy an external need. That, also, is a fact of its history. Architecture is subservient to the general uses of mankind. And, immediately, politics and society, religion and liturgy, the large movements of races and their common occupations, become factors in the study. These determine what shall be built, and, up to a point, in what way. The history of civilisation thus leaves in architecture its truest, because its most unconscious record. If, then, it is legitimate to consider architecture as an expression of mechanical laws, it is legitimate, no less, to see in it an expression of human life. This furnishes a standard of value totally distinct from the scientific. Buildings may be judged by the success with which they supply the practical ends they are designed to meet. Or, by a natural extension, we may judge them by the value of those ends themselves; that is to say, by the external purposes which they reflect. These, indeed, are two very different questions. The last makes a moral reference which the first avoids, but both spring, and spring inevitably, from the link which architecture has with life—from that "condition of well-building" which Wotton calls commodity.

And architecture requires "delight." For this reason, interwoven with practical ends and their mechanical solutions, we may trace in architecture a third and different factor—the disinterested desire for beauty. This desire does not, it is true, culminate here in a purely aesthetic *result*, for it has to deal with a concrete basis which is utilitarian. It is, none the less, a purely aesthetic *impulse*, an impulse distinct from all the others which architecture may simultaneously satisfy, an impulse by virtue of which architecture becomes art. It is a separate instinct. Sometimes it will borrow a suggestion from the laws of firmness or commodity; sometimes it will run counter to them, or be offended by the forms they would dictate. It has its own standard, and claims its own authority. It is possible, therefore, to ask how far, and how successfully, in any architectural style, this aesthetic impulse has been embodied; how far, that is to say, the instincts which, in the other arts, exert an obvious and unhampered activity, have succeeded in realising themselves also through this more complicated and more restricted instrument. And we can ask, still further, whether there may not be aesthetic instincts, for which this instrument, restricted as it is, may furnish the sole and peculiar expression. This is to study architecture, in the strict sense, as an art.

Here, then, are three "conditions of well-building," and corresponding to them three modes of criticism, and three provinces of thought.

Now what, in fact, is the result? The material data of our study we certainly possess in abundance: the statistics of architecture, the history of existing works, their shape and size and authorship, have long been investigated with the highest scholarship. But when we ask to be given not history but criticism, when we seek to know what is the value of these works of art, viewed in themselves or by comparison with one another, and why they are to be considered worthy of this exact attention, and whether one is to be considered more deserving of it than another, and on what grounds, the answers we obtain may be ready and numerous, but they are certainly neither consistent nor clear.

The criticism of architecture has been of two kinds. The first of these remains essentially historical. It is content to describe the conditions under which the styles of the past arose. It accepts the confused and partly fortuitous phenomenon which architecture actually is, and estimates the phenomenon by a method as confused and fortuitous as itself. It passes in and out of the three provinces of thought, and relates its subject now to science, now to art, and now to life. It treats of these upon a single plane, judging one building by standards of constructive skill, another by standards of rhythm and proportion, and a third by standards of practical use or by the moral impulse of its builders. This medley of elements, diverse and uncommensurated as they are, can furnish no general estimate or true comparison of style.

Doubtless, *as a matter of history*, architecture has not come into existence in obedience to any *a priori* aesthetic. It has grown up around the practical needs of the race, and in satisfying these it has been deflected, now by the obstinate claims of mechanical laws, now by a wayward search for beauty. But the problem of the architect and that of the critic are here essentially different. The work of the architect is synthetic. He must take into simultaneous account our three "conditions of well-building," and find some compromise which keeps a decent peace between their claims. The task of the critic, on the contrary, is one of analysis. He has to discover, define, and maintain the ideal standards of value in each province. Thus the three standards of architecture, united in practice, are separable, and must be separated, in thought. Criticism of the historical type fails to apply an ideal and consistent analysis, for the insufficient reason that the *practice* of architecture has, of necessity, been neither consistent nor ideal. Such criticism is not necessarily misleading. Its fault is more often that it leads nowhere. Its judgments may be individually accurate, but it affords us no general view, for it adopts no fixed position. It is neither simple, nor comprehensive, nor consistent. It cannot, therefore, furnish a theory of style.

The second type of criticism is more dangerous. For the sake of simplicity it lays down some "law" of architectural taste. Good design in architecture, it will say, should "express the uses the building is intended to serve"; "it should faithfully state the facts of its construction," or again it should "reflect the life of a noble civilisation." Then, having made these plausible assumptions, it drives its theory to a conclusion, dwells on the examples that support its case, and is willing, for the sake of consistency, to condemn all architecture in which the theory is not confirmed. Such general anathemas are flattering alike to the author and his reader. They greatly simplify the subject. They have a show of logic. But they fail to explain why the styles of architecture which they find it necessary to condemn have in fact been created and admired. Fashion consequently betrays these faultless arguments; for whatever has once genuinely pleased is likely to be again found pleasing; art and the enjoyment of art continue in the condemned paths undismayed; and criticism is left to discover a sanction for them, if it can, in some new theory, as simple, as logical, and as insufficient as the first.

The true task of criticism is to understand such aesthetic pleasures as have in fact been felt, and then to draw whatever laws and conclusions it may from that understanding. But no amount of reasoning will create, or can annul, an aesthetic experience; for the aim of the arts has not been logic, but delight. The theory of architecture, then, requires logic; but it requires, not less, an independent sense of beauty. Nature, unfortunately, would seem to unite these qualities with extreme reluctance.

Obviously, there is room for confusion. The "condition of delight" in architecture—its value as an art—may conceivably be found to *consist in* its firmness, or in its commodity, or in both; or it may consist in something else different from, yet dependent upon these; or it may be independent of them altogether. In any case, these elements are, at first sight, distinct. There is no reason, *prima facie*, to suppose that there exists between them a pre-established harmony, and that in consequence a perfect principle of building can be laid down which should, in full measure, satisfy them all. And, in the absence of such a principle, it is quite arbitrary to pronounce dogmatically on the concessions which art should make to science or utility. Unless it can be proved that these apparently different values are in reality commensurable, there ought to be three separate schemes of criticism: the first based on construction, the second on convenience, the third on aesthetics. Each could be rational, complete, and, within its own province, valid. Thus by degrees might be obtained what at present is certainly lacking—the data for a theory of architecture which should not be contradicted at once by the history of taste.

UNDERSTANDING THE TEXT

1. Although Scott discusses the nature of architecture before he examines the criticism of architecture, he is primarily interested in the criticism of architecture. How does he make this clear in his opening paragraph?
2. What is the chief cause for the contradictory results achieved by the various theories of architecture?
3. Summarize, in a paragraph, the distinctions between "firmness," "commodity," and "delight," and the relations between them.
4. How is Scott's discussion of the criticism of architecture subdivided?
5. What do the two sorts of architectural criticism which Scott examines have in common? How are they different? Why is the second kind more dangerous?
6. Show how the distinctions Scott draws among "firmness," "commodity," and "delight" are used in the discussion of the criticism of architecture in the second half of the essay.

7. Explain the assumption in this sentence: "The history of civilisation thus leaves in architecture its truest, because its most unconscious record."
8. Scott devotes a paragraph (p. 163) to a contrast between the work of the architect and the work of the critic of architecture. Explain the contrast and show how it functions at this point in the essay.
9. Explain the meanings of the following words in their contexts: *disparity, incommensurable, pedantry, fortuitous, anathemas.*

TOPICS FOR DISCUSSION AND WRITING

10. Scott, like Lord Moulton, is trying to persuade his readers that essential distinctions should be preserved in a subject that is often treated as if it were all of a piece. Scott is discussing the way men talk about architecture and Moulton is discussing the way men act, but apart from these differences do you see any similarities in the way the two writers go about their work of distinction and analysis?
11. Find support in the essay for Scott's statement (p. 160) that architecture is the most complex of the arts.
12. Write two paragraphs setting forth in your own words the aims and the methods which good criticism of architecture, according to Scott, should observe.

Law and Manners

LORD MOULTON

IN ORDER to explain this extraordinary title I must ask you to follow me in examining the three great domains of Human Action. First comes the domain of Positive Law, where our actions are prescribed by laws binding upon us which must be obeyed. Next comes the domain of Free Choice, which includes all those actions as to which we claim and enjoy complete freedom. But between these two there is a third large and important domain in which there rules neither Positive Law nor Absolute Freedom. In that domain there is no law which inexorably determines our course of action, and yet we feel that we are not free to choose as we would. The degree of this sense of a lack of complete freedom in this domain varies in every case. It grades from a consciousness of a Duty nearly as strong as Positive Law, to a feeling that the matter is all but a question of personal choice. Some might wish to parcel out this domain into separate countries, calling one, for instance, the domain of Duty, another the domain of Public Spirit, another the domain of Good Form; but I prefer to look at it as all one domain, for it has one and the same characteristic throughout—it is the domain of Obedience to the Unenforceable. The obedience is the obedience of a man to that which he cannot be forced to obey. He is the enforcer of the law upon himself.

One of the reasons why I have chosen this as the subject on which to speak is that I have spent my life as a commissioner for delimiting the frontier line which divides this domain from the realm of Positive Law. I have had to decide so frequently whether Law could say, "You must," or regretfully to say, "I must leave it to you." This is the land in which all those whom the Law cannot reach take refuge. It might be thought from such a description that I wished to annex that country and bring it under

Reprinted from *The Atlantic Monthly*, July, 1924.

the rule of Positive Law. That is not the case. The infinite variety of circumstances surrounding the individual and rightly influencing his action make it impossible to subject him in all things to rules rigidly prescribed and duly enforced. Thus there was wisely left the intermediate domain which, so far as Positive Law is concerned, is a land of freedom of action, but in which the individual should feel that he was not wholly free. This country which lies between Law and Free Choice I always think of as the domain of Manners. To me, Manners in this broad sense signifies the doing that which you should do although you are not obliged to do it. I do not wish to call it Duty, for that is too narrow to describe it, nor would I call it Morals for the same reason. It might include both, but it extends beyond them. It covers all cases of right doing where there is no one to make you do it but yourself.

All these three domains are essential to the properly organized life of the individual, and one must be on one's guard against thinking that any of them can safely be encroached upon. That Law must exist needs no argument. But, on the other hand, the domain of Free Choice should be dear to all. This is where spontaneity, originality, and energy are born. The great movements which make the history of a country start there. It covers a precious land where the actions of men are not only such as they choose, but have a right to claim freedom even from criticism. Men must keep safely guarded this right to follow the bent of their nature in proper cases and act as they would without anyone having the right to utter a word of dictation or command. This country forms the other frontier of the domain of Manners and delimits it on the side farthest away from that of Positive Law.

The dangers that threaten the maintenance of this domain of Manners arise from its situation between the region of Absolute Choice and the region of Positive Law. There are countless supporters of the movements to enlarge the sphere of Positive Law. In many countries—especially in the younger nations—there is a tendency to make laws to regulate everything. On the other hand, there is a growing tendency to treat matters that are not regulated by Positive Law as being matters of Absolute Choice. Both these movements are encroachments on the middle land, and to my mind the real greatness of a nation, its true civilization, is measured by the extent of this land of Obedience to the Unenforceable. It measures the extent to which the nation trusts its citizens, and its existence and area testify to the way they behave in response to that trust. Mere obedience to Law does not measure the greatness of a Nation. It can easily be obtained by a strong executive, and most easily of all from a timorous people. Nor is the licence of behavior which so often accompanies the absence of Law, and which is miscalled Liberty, a proof of greatness. The true test is the extent to which the individuals composing the nation can be trusted to obey self-imposed law.

In the changes that are taking place in the world around us, one of those which is fraught with grave peril is the discredit into which this idea of the middle land is falling. I will give two examples. First, I will take freedom of debate in the houses of legislature such as our own House of Commons. For centuries the members had unrestricted freedom of debate, and no inconvenience was felt. But in recent times some members of this House have said to themselves: "We have unrestricted freedom of debate. We will use it so as to destroy debate. The absence of imposed restriction enables us to do it." This obstruction was developed, and it has destroyed freedom of debate, and, indeed, all useful debate in practically every legislature. The freedom due to absence of positive restriction has been treated by the individual members as leaving their use of debate a matter of Absolute Choice, fettered with no duty that they were bound to regard. They shut their eyes to the fact that the freedom was given to them in trust to help forward debate, and that it was incumbent on them so to use it. Clumsy and even mischievous regulations have necessarily been introduced which fetter debate but prevent its being absolutely stifled. The old freedom cannot now be entrusted to the members, because when they possessed it they did not respond to it by the exercise of that moral sense which would have led them to treat it as a trust, and not as an absolute possession, unburdened by obligations which they should compel themselves to regard.

It is not only the conduct of individual members of the legislature that furnishes an illustration. The conduct of the legislatures themselves furnishes an equally striking one. It is the fundamental principle of democracies to bow to the decision of the majority. But in accepting this we do not surrender ourselves to the rule of the majority in all things, but only in those things which are of a kind fit to be regulated by Government. We do not admit, for instance, the right of the majority to decide whom we should marry or what should be our religion. These are but types of a vast number of matters of great interest in life which we hold to be outside the decision of a majority, and which are for the individual alone to decide. But in form the power of a Government has no restrictions. It has the power to do everything, and too often it forgets that this limitless power does not leave the scope of its legislation a matter of absolute choice on its part, but a choice fettered by a duty to act according to the trust reposed in it, and to abstain from legislating in matters where legislation is not truly within its province. And what is true as to the scope of legislation is also true to a great extent as to the nature of that legislation. But there is a widespread tendency to regard the fact that they can do a thing as meaning that they may do it. There can be no more fatal error than this. Between "can do" and "may do" ought to exist the whole realm which recognizes the sway of duty, fairness, sympathy, taste, and all the other things that make life beautiful and society possible. It is this confusion between "can do" and "may do" which makes me fear at times lest in the future the worst tyranny will be found in democracies. Interests which are not strongly represented in parliament may be treated as though they had no rights by Governments who think that the power and the will to legislate amount to a justification of that legislation. Such a principle would be death to liberty. No part of our life would be secure from interference from without. If I were asked to define tyranny, I would say it was yielding to the lust of governing. It is only when Governments feel it an honorable duty not to step beyond that which was in reality, and not only in form, put into their hands that the world will know what true Freedom is. . . .

Now I can tell you why I chose the title "Law and Manners." It must be evident to you that Manners must include all things which a man should impose upon himself, from duty to good taste. I have borne in mind the great motto of William of Wykeham—*Manners Makyth Man*. It is in this sense—loyalty to the rule of Obedience to the Unenforceable, throughout the whole realm of personal action—that we should use the word "Manners" if we would truly say that "Manners makyth Man."

UNDERSTANDING THE TEXT

1. On what basis does Moulton distinguish among the three great domains of human action?
2. What does the domain of Obedience to the Unenforceable have in common with the domain of Positive Law? What does it have in common with the domain of Free Choice? In what essential respects is the domain of Obedience to the Unenforceable different from each of the other two domains? Show how the term "Obedience to the Unenforceable" combines features of the other two realms. Locate a sentence in which Moulton defines manners.
3. Why is the greatness of a nation—"its true civilization"—measured by the extent of the domain of Manners?
4. How, in Moulton's view, is the domain of Manners threatened?

5. Moulton gives two examples of the way in which the domain of Manners is being discredited. Explain how the examples work. How effective are these two examples in establishing his point?

6. Why does Moulton fear that in the future the worst tyranny will be found in democracies?

7. Give examples of duty, public spirit, and good form to show how, as Moulton says in the opening paragraph, they all involve the individual's enforcement of the law upon himself.

8. Why do you think Moulton called his essay "Law and Manners," giving prominence to two of the three domains, instead of, say, "Law, Manners, and Choice"?

TOPICS FOR DISCUSSION AND WRITING

9. Write a paragraph comparing Moulton's procedure in differentiating manners from law and free choice with MacIver's procedure in differentiating civilization and culture.

10. Write a comparison of Moulton's conception of manners and that in Morton J. Cronin's essay on "The Tyranny of Democratic Manners" (pp. 537–543).

11. In Moulton's terms, what would be the difference between good manners and bad manners?

12. If manners, as Moulton says, is a man's enforcement of the law upon himself, or his obedience to that which he cannot be forced to obey, then there is implied a law or standard which he is to enforce or obey. Where does this law or standard of manners come from? In considering this problem you may get some help from Moulton's discussion of the behavior of legislators (p. 168), especially the sentence "They shut their eyes . . . so to use it."

Rome Under the Tyranny

EDWARD GIBBON

IF A man were called to fix the period in the history of the world, during which the condition of the human race was most happy and prosperous, he would, without hesitation, name that which elapsed from the death of Domitian to the accession of Commodus [96–180 A.D.]. The vast extent of the Roman empire was governed by absolute power, under the guidance of virtue and wisdom. The armies were restrained by the firm but gentle hand of four successive emperors, whose characters and authority commanded involuntary respect. The forms of the civil administration were carefully preserved by Nerva, Trajan, Hadrian, and the Antonines, who delighted in the image of liberty, and were pleased with considering themselves as the accountable ministers of the laws. Such princes deserved the honour of restoring the republic, had the Romans of their days been capable of enjoying a rational freedom.

The labours of these monarchs were overpaid by the immense reward that inseparably waited on their success; by the honest pride of virtue, and by the exquisite delight of beholding the general happiness of which they were the authors. A just, but melancholy reflection embittered, however, the noblest of human enjoyments. They must often have recollected the instability of a happiness which depended on the character of a single man. The fatal moment was perhaps approaching, when some licentious youth, or some jealous tyrant, would abuse, to the destruction, that absolute power, which they had exerted for the benefit of their people. The ideal restraints of the senate and the laws might serve to display the virtues, but could never correct the vices, of the emperor. The military force was a blind and irresistible instrument of oppression; and the corruption of Roman manners would always supply flatterers eager to applaud, and minis-

Reprinted from *The Decline and Fall of the Roman Empire* (1776), Chapter 3.

ters prepared to serve, the fear or the avarice, the lust or the cruelty, of their masters.

These gloomy apprehensions had been already justified by the experience of the Romans. The annals of the emperors exhibit a strong and various picture of human nature, which we should vainly seek among the mixed and doubtful characters of modern history. In the conduct of those monarchs we may trace the utmost lines of vice and virtue; the most exalted perfection, and the meanest degeneracy of our own species. The golden age of Trajan and the Antonines had been preceded by an age of iron. It is almost superfluous to enumerate the unworthy successors of Augustus. Their unparalleled vices, and the splendid theater on which they were acted, have saved them from oblivion. The dark unrelenting Tiberius, the furious Caligula, the feeble Claudius, the profligate and cruel Nero, the beastly Vitellius, and the timid inhuman Domitian, are condemned to everlasting infamy. During fourscore years (excepting only the short and doubtful respite of Vespasian's reign) Rome groaned beneath an unremitting tyranny, which exterminated the ancient families of the republic, and was fatal to almost every virtue and every talent that arose in that unhappy period.

Under the reign of these monsters, the slavery of the Romans was accompanied with two peculiar circumstances, the one occasioned by their former liberty, the other by their extensive conquests, which rendered their condition more completely wretched than that of the victims of tyranny in any other age or country. From these causes were derived, 1. The exquisite sensibility of the sufferers; and, 2. The impossibility of escaping from the hand of the oppressor.

I. When Persia was governed by the descendants of Sefi, a race of princes whose wanton cruelty often stained their divan, their table, and their bed with the blood of their favorites, there is a saying recorded of a young nobleman, That he never departed from the sultan's presence, without satisfying himself whether his head was still on his shoulders. The experience of every day might almost justify the scepticism of Rustan. Yet the fatal sword, suspended above him by a single thread, seems not to have disturbed the slumbers, or interrupted the tranquillity, of the Persian. The monarch's frown, he well knew, could level him with the dust; but the stroke of lightning or apoplexy might be equally fatal; and it was the part of a wise man to forget the inevitable calamities of human life in the enjoyment of the fleeting hour. He was dignified with the appellation of the king's slave; had, perhaps, been purchased from obscure parents, in a country which he had never known; and was trained up from his infancy in the severe discipline of the seraglio. His name, his wealth, his honours, were the gift of a master, who might, without injustice, resume what he had bestowed. Rustan's knowledge, if he possessed any, could only serve to confirm his habits by prejudices. His language afforded not words for any form of government, except absolute monarchy. The history of the East informed him, that such had ever been the condition of mankind. The Koran, and the interpreters of that divine book, inculcated to him, that the sultan was the descendant of the prophet, and the viceregent of heaven; that patience was the first virtue of a Mussulman, and unlimited obedience the great duty of a subject.

The minds of the Romans were very differently prepared for slavery. Oppressed beneath the weight of their own corruption and of military violence, they for a long while preserved the sentiments, or at least the ideas, of their free-born ancestors. The education of Helvidius and Thrasea, of Tacitus and Pliny, was the same as that of Cato and Cicero. From Grecian philosophy, they had imbibed the justest and most liberal notions of the dignity of human nature, and the origin of civil society. The history of their own country had taught them to revere a free, a virtuous, and a victorious commonwealth; to abhor the successful crimes of Caesar and Augustus; and inwardly to despise those tyrants whom they adored with the most abject flattery. As magistrates and senators, they were admitted into the great council, which had once dictated laws to the earth, whose name still gave a sanction to the acts of the monarch, and whose authority was so often prostituted to the vilest purposes of tyranny. Tiberius, and those emperors who adopted his maxims, attempted to disguise their murders by the formalities of justice, and perhaps enjoyed a secret pleasure in rendering the senate their accomplice as well as their victim. By this assembly, the last of the Romans were condemned for imaginary crimes and real virtues. Their infamous accusers assumed the language of independent patriots, who arraigned a dangerous citizen before the tribunal of his country; and the public service was rewarded by riches and honours. The servile judges professed to assert the majesty of the commonwealth, violated in the person of its first magistrate, whose clemency they most applauded when they trembled the most at his inexorable and impending cruelty. The tyrant beheld their baseness with just contempt, and encountered their secret sentiments of detestation with sincere and avowed hatred for the whole body of the senate.

II. The division of Europe into a number of independent states, connected, however, with each other, by the general resemblance of religion, language, and manners, is productive of the most beneficial consequences to the liberty of mankind. A modern tyrant, who should find no resistance either in his own breast, or in his people, would soon experience a gentle restraint from the example of his equals, the dread of present censure, the advice of his allies, and the apprehension of his enemies. The object of his displeasure, escaping from the narrow limits of his dominions, would easily obtain, in a happier climate, a secure refuge, a new fortune adequate to his merit, the freedom of complaint, and perhaps the means of revenge. But the empire of the Romans filled the world, and when that empire fell into the hands of a single person, the world became a safe and dreary prison for his enemies. The slave of Imperial despotism, whether he was condemned to drag his gilded chain in Rome and the senate, or to wear out a life of exile on the barren rock of Seriphus, or the frozen banks of the Danube, expected his fate in silent despair. To resist was fatal, and it was impossible to fly. On every side he was encompassed with a vast extent of sea and land, which he could never hope to traverse without being discovered, seized, and restored to his irritated master. Beyond the frontiers, his anxious view could discover nothing, except the ocean, inhospitable deserts, hostile tribes of barbarians, of fierce manners and unknown language, or dependent kings, who would gladly purchase the emperor's protection by the sacrifice of an obnoxious fugitive. "Wherever you are," said Cicero to the exiled Marcellus, "remember that you are equally within the power of the conqueror."

UNDERSTANDING THE TEXT

1. For what purpose does Gibbon introduce the contrast between the situation and mental state of the typical Persian and the poignant plight of the Romans under the tyranny? What particular circumstance affecting the Romans under oppression is he attempting to explain?

2. What specific aspects of the Persian's life, thought, and history does Gibbon mention? To what extent are the corresponding aspects treated in his sketch of the Romans' situation?

3. Do these specific points of comparison and contrast appear in the same order in the two sketches? If not, how do they differ?

4. In view of the purpose of the contrast, can you suggest a hypothesis to explain why Gibbon treats the Persian as a single person, while in the second sketch he speaks of "the Romans" and uses the plural number throughout?

5. What is the function of the second contrast in the passage—that between the situation of political dissenters in an eighteenth-century Europe composed

of independent states and the fate of men who fell out of favor in the days when the Roman Empire encompassed the civilized world?

6. Gibbon reports that the eighteenth-century exile could easily obtain "a secure refuge, a new fortune adequate to his merit, the freedom of complaint, and perhaps the means of revenge." In the description of the Roman exile's situation, what terms does he use to sum up the refugee's expectations?

TOPICS FOR DISCUSSION AND WRITING

7. The contrast between the Persian and the Romans is organized according to the whole-by-whole method; that is, the Persian's situation is described fully before Gibbon turns to that of the Romans. As an exercise, revise the passage, supplying the necessary transitions, according to the part-by-part method; treat each aspect for both the Persian and the Romans, and then proceed to the next aspect. After you have finished, evaluate the effectiveness of the two procedures.

8. Choose two vocations in which you are interested and concerning which you have some knowledge, and write an essay comparing and contrasting typical representatives of the two vocations. In the contrast, cover the points which would be of interest to students facing a choice between the fields.

9. Suppose that the comparison and contrast assigned in question 8 were part of an article addressed specifically to teachers engaged in training people for the vocation. Of the points of comparison and contrast included in the original essay, which ones might now be made less prominent or perhaps even omitted? Which might be built up? What new elements might be added to the comparison?

Two Classes of Englishmen
in the Seventeenth Century

MOSES COIT TYLER

⌒‿⌒

THE PERSONAL traits of the original New-Englanders were in many ways remarkable. To know these people we need to know the people from whom they came. The English race has been described as one having practical sagacity rather than ideas; as being weighted by grossness of fibre, sluggishness, animal instincts, earthly preferences; as caring more for dull precedents than for brilliant intuitions; as making whatever progress it achieves by feeling its way safely step by step, rather than by projecting its way boldly from the beginning with the easy infallibility of abstract reasoners. There is some truth in this description; but it is far from being the whole truth. Especially far is it from being the whole truth if applied to the English people as they were in the first half of the seventeenth century. At that time, though they were apparently divided into many classes, they were really divided into only two:—first, the disciples of things as they are; second, the disciples of things as they ought to be.[1] Without doubt, in the first of these two classes were included vast numbers of thoughtful and noble natures, who with intelligent deliberation accepted things as established notwithstanding their faults, rather than encounter the frightful risk of having all things unsettled, and of making them worse in the very attempt to make them better; but in this class, likewise, were included the still larger number of those whose natures were neither noble

[1] Of course this distinction is to be seen among any people who have begun to think; but it is particularly to be seen among the English people at the period just mentioned. At that time they were especially given to thinking, and their thinking was turned in an uncommon degree to this particular dispute between what is and what ought to be,—in which dispute, indeed, they were then taking sides openly, with dangerous weapons in their hands.

From *A History of American Literature, 1607–1765* (1878).

nor thoughtful, and whose conservatism was only the expression of their intellectual torpor, their frivolity, their sensualism, their narrowness, or their cowardice. As to the second class, it certainly included many base persons also, many crackbrained and shallow persons, multitudes who shouted and wrangled for change, impelled to it by all sorts of contemptible motives,—aimless discontent, curiosity, lust, lawlessness, folly, cruelty, ambition, hope of pillage amid the wreck of other people's possessions. Nevertheless in this class, if anywhere, were to be found those men, whether many or few, in whom at that time centred for the English-speaking race the possibility of any further progress in human society; the men who not only dared to have ideas, but dared to put them together and to face the logical results of them; who regarded their own souls, and truth, more than they did gold, or respectability, or bodily comfort, or life; who had a high and stout confidence that as God in wisdom had made the world, so man by increasing in wisdom might improve his own condition in the world; and who proposed then and there, if possible, to bring all things in religion and in politics to some genuine test, in which nothing foolish should be retained because it was old, and nothing wise rejected because it was new. At no other time, probably, has there been in England a greater activity of brain directed toward researches into the very roots of things, than there was during that time; and never in England has the class of persons just described been larger in numbers, wider in the range of its individual peculiarities, more heterogeneous, more resolute, or more hopeful.

It was principally out of this second class, this vast, loosely connected, and deeply excited class of Englishmen in the seventeenth century—the Englishmen who were not sluggish, were not living for physical comfort, were not ruled by animal instincts, were not tied to precedents, were not afraid of ideas—that the twenty-one thousand people came who between 1620 and 1640 populated New England. Primarily, then, these first New-Englanders were thinkers in some fashion; they assumed the right to think, the utility of thinking, and the duty of standing by the fair conclusions of their thinking, even at very considerable cost. Of course among them were representatives of all degrees of intellectual radicalism, from the wealthy, reputable, and moderate non-conformists of Massachusetts Bay, down to the lowly and discreet separatists of Plymouth, and still further down to that inspired concourse of crotchety and pure-hearted enthusiasts, the Anabaptists, Antinomians, Quakers, Ranters, and Seekers, who found their first earthly paradise in Rhode Island. But the one grand distinction between the English colonists in New England and nearly all other English colonists in America was this, that while the latter came here chiefly for some material benefit, the former came chiefly for an ideal benefit. In its inception New England was not an agricultural community, nor a manufacturing community, nor a trading community: it was a thinking community; an arena and mart for ideas; its characteristic organ being not the hand, nor the heart, nor the pocket, but the brain.

UNDERSTANDING THE TEXT

1. What central characteristic does Tyler use to distinguish the two classes of Englishmen in the seventeenth century?
2. To each class Tyler attributes a series of traits. What is the relationship, in each case, between these traits and the characteristic which serves to distinguish the classes?
3. Does each class have a separate package of traits, or do the traits in one class stand in a logical relationship with those of the other class?
4. In the third sentence the author summarizes a conventional view of English character. How does this summary, and especially the way Tyler presents it, function in preparing for the more extensive comparison and contrast?
5. How does Tyler attempt to protect himself against the possible charge that his contrast is oversimplified? Do you think the attempt is successful?
6. Which side of Tyler's comparison and contrast receives the more substantial development? How do you account for this?
7. Near the end of the passage Tyler divides the New Englanders into several subclasses: the men of Massachusetts Bay, the men of Plymouth, and the "enthusiasts." What connection do you see between this classification and his treatment, earlier in the passage, of the thinking class in England?
8. At the close of the passage Tyler makes a brief comparison between the New Englanders and the other English settlers in America. How is this concluding comparison connected with the central contrast developed earlier in the piece?

TOPICS FOR DISCUSSION AND WRITING

9. This essay and those by Gibbon and Trollope are concerned with comparing and contrasting large groups of people. How similar in procedures of comparison are the three essays? Can you explain any differences by referring to the authors' varying purposes?
10. Consult a standard reference in American history—a textbook or a more specialized work—and see if modern historians accept, accept with qualifica-

tion, or reject Tyler's explanation of the motives which brought about the settlement of New England.

11. Close reading of the Tyler passage may suggest that he is really describing four groups of Englishmen: good reformers, bad reformers, noble conservatives, and ignoble conservatives. Try rewriting the passage with an organization based on these four categories. What changes does this revision produce in the effect of the passage?

12. Current magazines often publish articles comparing the characteristics of various national or cultural groups—Americans and Russians, Asians and Westerners, etc. Consult the guide to periodical literature in your library, look up several articles whose titles indicate that they engage in this kind of comparison, and prepare a report on the way the comparisons are handled.

13. If a group of persons is to be compared with another group, it must have enough homogeneity to be regarded as a class. What groups of students on your campus seem to you to be homogeneous enough to constitute a class which could be compared profitably with another group?

The Englishman and the American

ANTHONY TROLLOPE

~

THE VISITOR to New York must seek his gratification and obtain his instruction from the habits and manners of men. The American, though he dresses like an Englishman, and eats roast beef with a silver fork—or sometimes with a steel knife—as does an Englishman, is not like an Englishman in his mind, in his aspirations, in his tastes, or in his politics. In his mind he is quicker, more universally intelligent, more ambitious of general knowledge, less indulgent of stupidity and ignorance in others, harder, sharper, brighter with the surface brightness of steel, than is an Englishman; but he is more brittle, less enduring, less malleable, and I think less capable of impressions. The mind of the Englishman has more imagination, but that of the American more incision. The American is a great observer, but he observes things material rather than things social or picturesque. He is a constant and ready speculator; but all speculations, even those which come of philosophy, are with him more or less material. In his aspirations the American is more constant than an Englishman—or I should rather say he is more constant in aspiring. Every citizen of the United States intends to do something. Every one thinks himself capable of some effort. But in his aspirations he is more limited than an Englishman. The ambitious American never soars so high as the ambitious Englishman. He does not even see up to so great a height; and when he has raised himself somewhat above the crowd becomes sooner dizzy with his own altitude. An American of mark, though always anxious to show his mark, is always fearful of a fall. In his tastes the American imitates the Frenchman. Who shall dare to say that he is wrong, seeing that in general matters of design and luxury the French have won for themselves the foremost name? I will

Reprinted from *North America* (1862).

not say that the American is wrong, but I cannot avoid thinking that he is so. I detest what is called French taste; but the world is against me. When I complained to a landlord of an hotel out in the West that his furniture was useless; that I could not write at a marble table whose outside rim was curved into fantastic shapes; that a gold clock in my bedroom which did not go would give me no aid in washing myself; that a heavy, immoveable curtain shut out the light; and that *papier-maché* chairs with small fluffy velvet seats were bad to sit on—he answered me completely by telling me that his house had been furnished not in accordance with the taste of England, but with that of France. I acknowledged the rebuke, gave up my pursuits of literature and cleanliness, and hurried out of the house as quickly as I could. All America is now furnishing itself by the rules which guided that hotel-keeper. I do not merely allude to actual household furniture—to chairs, tables, and detestable gilt clocks. The taste of America is becoming French in its conversation, French in its comforts and French in its discomforts, French in its eating, and French in its dress, French in its manners, and will become French in its art. There are those who will say that English taste is taking the same direction. I do not think so. I strongly hope that it is not so. And therefore I say that an Englishman and an American differ in their tastes.

But of all the differences between an Englishman and an American that in politics is the strongest, and the most essential. I cannot here, in one paragraph, define that difference with sufficient clearness to make my definition satisfactory; but I trust that some idea of that difference may be conveyed by the general tenor of my book. The American and the Englishman are both republicans. The governments of the States and of England are probably the two purest republican governments in the world. I do not, of course, here mean to say that the governments are more pure than others, but that the systems are more absolutely republican. And yet no men can be much further asunder in politics than the Englishman and the American. The American of the present day puts a ballot-box into the hands of every citizen and takes his stand upon that and that only. It is the duty of an American citizen to vote, and when he has voted he need trouble himself no further till the time for voting shall come round again. The candidate for whom he has voted represents his will, if he have voted with the majority, and in that case he has no right to look for further influence. If he have voted with the minority, he has no right to look for any influence at all. In either case he has done his political work, and may go about his business till the next year or the next two or four years shall have come round. The Englishman, on the other hand, will have no ballot-box, and is by no means inclined to depend exclusively upon voters or upon voting. As far as voting can show it, he desires to get the sense of the country; but he does not think that that sense will be shown by universal suffrage. He thinks that property amounting to a thousand pounds will show more of that sense than property amounting to a hundred; but he will not on that account go to work and apportion votes to wealth. He thinks that the educated can show more of that sense than the uneducated; but he does not therefore lay down any rule about reading, writing, and arithmetic, or apportion votes to learning. He prefers that all these opinions of his shall bring themselves out and operate by their own intrinsic weight. Nor does he at all confine himself to voting in his anxiety to get the sense of the country. He takes it in any way that it will show itself, uses it for what it is worth—or perhaps for more than it is worth—and welds it into that gigantic lever by which the political action of the country is moved. Every man in Great Britain, whether he possesses any actual vote or no, can do that which is tantamount to voting every day of his life, by the mere expression of his opinion. Public opinion in America has hitherto been nothing, unless it has managed to express itself by a majority of ballot-boxes. Public opinion in England is everything, let votes go as they may. Let the people want a measure, and there is no doubt of their obtaining it. Only the people must want it—as they did want Catholic emancipation, reform, and corn-law repeal—and as they would want war if it were brought home to them that their country was insulted.

In attempting to describe this difference in the political action of the two countries, I am very far from taking all praise for England or throwing any reproach on the States. The political action of the States is undoubtedly the more logical and the clearer. That indeed of England is so illogical and so little clear that it would be quite impossible for any other nation to assume it, merely by resolving to do so. Whereas the political action of the States might be assumed by any nation tomorrow, and all its strength might be carried across the water in a few written rules as are the prescriptions of a physician or the regulations of an infirmary. With us the thing has grown of habit, has been fostered by tradition, has crept up uncared for and in some parts unnoticed. It can be written in no book, can be described in no words, can be copied by no statesmen, and I almost believe can be understood by no people but that to whose peculiar uses it has been adapted.

UNDERSTANDING THE TEXT

1. How clearly does Trollope indicate the criteria according to which he is comparing the Englishman and the American?
2. Of the four points of comparison he uses, which does he develop most fully?
3. In your judgment, which of the four does Trollope treat most effectively and interestingly? What makes you choose this one?
4. Can you suggest any reason for the order in which he takes up the four elements of the comparison? Which of the four is the most general?
5. In what part of the essay does Trollope express his own opinions and preferences most directly? Does the tone of the essay change at this point?
6. You will note that, in his discussion of taste, Trollope has a good deal to say about American furnishings, but does not develop the contrast by characterizing English taste. How do you account for this omission?
7. Indicate the general ideas which Trollope uses to illuminate the contrast between American and British politics. In his view, what basic political habits account for the political differences he observes?
8. Would American and British politics, as Trollope describes them, be a part of "civilization" or "culture," according to MacIver's definitions of these terms (pp. 151–154)?

TOPICS FOR DISCUSSION AND WRITING

9. Develop in a paragraph the meaning of this statement from Trollope: "The political action of the States is undoubtedly the more logical and the clearer."
10. Do you believe that Trollope's assertion that Americans attach great importance to elections but lose interest in government between elections holds good today? Is public opinion still as passive as he describes it?
11. If you were developing a contrast between the Englishman and the American today, would you find Trollope's four criteria relevant and useful? What additional points of comparison would you be inclined to use?
12. From your experience and observation, do you believe that there are significant differences, at least in a good many cases, between persons who come from a large family and those who come from a small family or are only children? Present your ideas on this question in an essay comparing a "typical" only child with a "typical" person from a large family.
13. Write a brief comparison between the views of Trollope and Wilder on the British and the American character.

Science Has Spoiled My Supper

PHILIP WYLIE

I AM a fan for Science. My education is scientific and I have, in one field, contributed a monograph to a scientific journal. Science, to my mind, is applied honesty, the one reliable means we have to find out truth. That is why, when error is committed in the name of Science, I feel the way a man would if his favorite uncle had taken to drink.

Over the years, I have come to feel that way about what science has done to food. I agree that America can set as good a table as any nation in the world. I agree that our food is nutritious and that the diet of most of us is well-balanced. What America eats is handsomely packaged; it is usually clean and pure; it is excellently preserved. The only trouble with it is this: year by year it grows less good to eat. It appeals increasingly to the eye. But who eats with his eyes? Almost everything used to taste better when I was a kid. For quite a long time I thought that observation was merely another index of advancing age. But some years ago I married a girl whose mother is an expert cook of the kind called "old-fashioned." This gifted woman's daughter (my wife) was taught her mother's venerable skills. The mother lives in the country and still plants an old-fashioned garden. She still buys dairy products from the neighbors and, in so far as possible, she uses the same materials her mother and grandmother did—to prepare meals that are superior. They are just as good, in this Year of Grace, as I recall them from my courtship. After eating for a while at the table of my mother-in-law, it is sad to go back to eating with my friends —even the alleged "good cooks" among them. And it is a gruesome experience to have meals at the best big-city restaurants.

Take cheese, for instance. Here and there, in big cities, small stores and delicatessens specialize in cheese. At such places, one can buy at least some of the first-rate cheeses that we used to eat—such as those we had with pie and in macaroni. The latter were sharp but not too sharp. They were a little crumbly. We called them American cheeses, or even rat cheese; actually they were Cheddars. Long ago, this cheese began to be supplanted by a material called "cheese foods." Some cheese foods and "processed" cheese are fairly edible; but not one comes within miles of the old kinds—for flavor.

A grocer used to be very fussy about his cheese. Cheddar was made and sold by hundreds of little factories. Representatives of the factories had particular customers, and cheese was prepared by hand to suit the grocers, who knew precisely what their patrons wanted in rat cheese, pie cheese, American and other cheeses. Some liked them sharper; some liked them yellower; some liked anise seeds in cheese, or caraway.

What happened? Science—or what is called science—stepped in. The old-fashioned cheeses didn't ship well enough. They crumbled, became moldy, dried out. "Scientific" tests disclosed that a great majority of the people will buy a less-good-tasting cheese if that's all they can get. "Scientific marketing" then took effect. Its motto is "Give the people the least quality they'll stand for." In food, as in many other things, the "scientific marketers" regard quality as secondary so long as they can sell most persons anyhow; what they are after is "durability" or "shippability."

It is not possible to make the very best cheese in vast quantities at a low average cost. "Scientific sampling" got in its statistically nasty work. It was found that the largest number of people will buy something that is bland and rather tasteless. Those who prefer a product of a pronounced and individualistic flavor have a variety of preferences. Nobody is altogether pleased by bland foodstuff, in other words; but nobody is very violently put off. The result is that a "reason" has been found for turning out zillions of packages of something that will "do" for nearly all and isn't even imagined to be superlatively good by a single soul!

Economics entered. It is possible to turn out in quantity a bland, impersonal, practically imperishable substance more or less resembling, say, cheese—at lower cost than cheese. Chain groceries shut out the independent stores and "standardization" became a principal means of cutting costs.

Imitations also came into the cheese business. There are American duplications of most of the celebrated European cheeses, mass-produced and cheaper by far than the imports. They would cause European food-lovers to gag or guffaw—but generally the imitations are all that's available in the supermarkets. People buy them and eat them.

Perhaps you don't like cheese—so the fact that decent cheese is hardly ever served in America any more, or used in cooking, doesn't matter to you. Well, take bread. There has been (and still is) something of a hullabaloo about bread. In fact, in the last few years, a few big bakeries have taken to making a fairly good imitation of real bread. It costs much more than what is nowadays called bread, but it is edible. Most persons, however, now eat as "bread" a substance so full of chemicals and so barren of cereals that it approaches a synthetic.

Most bakers are interested mainly in how a loaf of bread looks. They are concerned with how little stuff they can put in it—to get how much money. They are deeply interested in using chemicals that will keep bread from molding, make it seem "fresh" for the longest possible time, and so render it marketable and shippable. They have been at this monkeyshine for a generation. Today a loaf of "bread" looks deceptively real; but it is made from heaven knows what and it resembles, as food, a solidified bubble bath. Some months ago I bought a loaf of the stuff and, experimentally, began pressing it together, like an accordion. With a little effort, I squeezed the whole loaf to a length of about one inch.

Yesterday, at the home of my mother-in-law, I ate with country-churned butter and home-canned wild strawberry jam several slices of actual bread, the same thing we used to have every day at home. People who have eaten actual bread will know what I mean. They will know that the material commonly called bread is not even related to real bread, except in name.

II

For years, I couldn't figure out what had happened to vegetables. I knew, of course, that most vegetables, to be enjoyed in their full deliciousness, must be picked fresh and cooked at once. I knew that vegetables cannot be overcooked and remain even edible, in the best sense. They cannot stand on the stove. That set of facts makes it impossible, of course, for any American restaurant—or, indeed, any city-dweller separated from supply by more than a few hours—to have decent fresh vegetables. The Parisians manage by getting their vegetables picked at dawn and rushed in farmers' carts to market, where no middleman or marketman delays produce on its way to the pot.

Our vegetables, however, come to us through a long chain of command. There are merchants of several sorts—wholesalers before the retailers, commission men, and so on—with the result that what were once edible products become, in transit, mere wilted leaves and withered tubers.

Homes and restaurants do what they can with this stuff—which my mother-in-law would discard on the spot. I have long thought that the famed blindfold test for cigarettes should be applied to city vegetables. For I am sure that if you puréed them and ate them blindfolded, you couldn't tell the beans from the peas, the turnips from the squash, the Brussels sprouts from the broccoli.

It is only lately that I have found how much science has to do with this reduction of noble victuals to pottage. Here the science of genetics is involved. Agronomists and the like have taken to breeding all sorts of vegetables and fruits—changing their original nature. This sounds wonderful and often is insane. For the scientists have not as a rule taken any interest whatsoever in the taste of the things they've tampered with!

What they've done is to develop "improved" strains of things for every purpose but eating. They work out, say, peas that will ripen all at once. The farmer can then harvest his peas and thresh them and be done with them. It is extremely profitable because it is efficient. What matter if such peas taste like boiled paper wads?

Geneticists have gone crazy over such "opportunities." They've developed string beans that are straight instead of curved, and all one length. This makes them easier to pack in cans, even if, when eating them, you can't tell them from tender string. Ripening time and identity of size and shape are, nowadays, more important in carrots than the fact that they taste like carrots. Personally, I don't care if they hybridize onions till they are as big as your head and come up through the snow; but, in doing so, they are producing onions that only vaguely and feebly remind you of onions. We are getting some varieties, in fact, that have less flavor than the water off last week's leeks. Yet, if people don't eat onions because they taste like onions, what in the name of Luther Burbank do they eat them for?

The women's magazines are about one third dedicated to clothes, one third to mild comment on sex, and the other third to recipes and pictures of handsome salads, desserts, and main courses. "Institutes" exist to experiment and tell housewives how to cook attractive meals and how to turn leftovers into works of art. The food thus pictured looks like famous paintings of still life. The only trouble is it's tasteless. It leaves appetite unquenched and merely serves to stave off famine.

I wonder if this blandness of our diet doesn't explain why so many of us are overweight and even dangerously so. When things had flavor, we knew what we were eating all the while—and it satisfied us. A teaspoonful of my mother-in-law's wild strawberry jam will not just provide a gastronome's ecstasy: it will entirely satisfy your jam desire. But, of the average tinned or glass-packed strawberry jam, you need half a cupful to get the idea of what you're eating. A slice of my mother-in-law's apple pie will satiate you far better than a whole bakery pie.

That thought is worthy of investigation—of genuine scientific investigation. It is merely a hypothesis, so far, and my own. But people—and their ancestors—have been eating according to flavor for upwards of a billion years. The need to satisfy the sense of taste may be innate and important. When food is merely a pretty cascade of viands, with the texture of boiled cardboard and the flavor of library paste, it may be the instinct of *genus homo* to go on eating in the unconscious hope of finally satisfying the ageless craving of the frustrated taste buds. In the days when good-tasting food was the rule in the American home, obesity wasn't such a national curse.

How can you feel you've eaten if you haven't tasted, and fully enjoyed tasting? Why (since science is ever so ready to answer the beck and call of mankind) don't people who want to reduce merely give up eating and get the nourishment they must have in measured doses shot into their arms at hospitals? One ready answer to that question suggests that my theory of overeating is sound: people like to taste! In eating, they try to satisfy that like.

The scientific war against deliciousness has been stepped up enormously in the last decade. Some infernal genius found a way to make biscuit batter keep. Housewives began to buy this premixed stuff. It saved work, of course. But any normally intelligent person can learn, in a short period, how to prepare superb baking powder biscuits. I can make better biscuits, myself, than can be made from patent batters. Yet soon after this fiasco became an American staple, it was discovered that a half-baked substitute for all sorts of breads, pastries, rolls, and the like could be mass-manufactured, frozen—and sold for polishing off in the home oven. None of these two-stage creations is as good as even a fair sample of the thing it imitates. A man of taste, who had eaten one of my wife's cinnamon buns, might use the premixed sort to throw at starlings—but not to eat! Cake mixes, too, come ready-prepared—like cement and not much better-tasting compared with true cake.

It is, however, "deep-freezing" that has really rung down the curtain on

American cookery. Nothing is improved by the process. I have yet to taste a deep-frozen victual that measures up, in flavor, to the fresh, unfrosted original. And most foods, cooked or uncooked, are destroyed in the deep freeze for all people of sense and sensibility. Vegetables with crisp and crackling texture emerge as mush, slippery and stringy as hair nets simmered in Vaseline. The essential oils that make peas peas—and cabbage cabbage—must undergo fission and fusion in freezers. Anyhow, they vanish. Some meats turn to leather. Others to wood pulp. Everything, pretty much, tastes like the mosses of tundra, dug up in midwinter. Even the appearance changes, oftentimes. Handsome comestibles you put down in the summer come out looking very much like the corpses of woolly mammoths recovered from the last Ice Age.

Of course, all this scientific "food handling" tends to save money. It certainly preserves food longer. It reduces work at home. But these facts, and especially the last, imply that the first purpose of living is to avoid work—at home, anyhow.

Without thinking, we are making an important confession about ourselves as a nation. We are abandoning quality—even, to some extent, the quality of people. The "best" is becoming too good for us. We are suckling ourselves on machine-made mediocrity. It is bad for our souls, our minds, and our digestion. It is the way our wiser and calmer forebears fed, not people, but hogs: as much as possible and as fast as possible, with no standard of quality.

The Germans say, "*Mann ist was er isst*—Man is what he eats." If this be true, the people of the U.S.A. are well on their way to becoming a faceless mob of mediocrities, of robots. And if we apply to other attributes the criteria we apply these days to appetite, that is what would happen! We would not want bright children any more; we'd merely want them to look bright—and get through school fast. We wouldn't be interested in beautiful women—just a good paint job. And we'd be opposed to the most precious quality of man: his individuality, his differentness from the mob.

There are some people—sociologists and psychologists among them—who say that is exactly what we Americans are doing, are becoming. Mass man, they say, is on the increase. Conformity, standardization, similarity—all on a cheap and vulgar level—are replacing the great American ideas of colorful liberty and dignified individualism. If this is so, the process may well begin, like most human behavior, in the home—in those homes where a good meal has been replaced by something-to-eat-in-a-hurry. By something not very good to eat, prepared by a mother without very much to do, for a family that doesn't feel it amounts to much anyhow.

I call, here, for rebellion.

UNDERSTANDING THE TEXT

1. According to Wylie, what is wrong with the food Americans eat? What makes it bad? What are the author's standards of comparison?

2. How does Wylie organize his indictment? What specific examples of culinary malpractice does he cite?

3. Why do you suppose he leads off by considering the sad case of cheese? To what extent are the declining quality of cheese, and the causes which produced the decline, typical of Wylie's general findings?

4. In what sense is "science" to blame for the regrettable state of affairs Wylie describes?

5. Is Wylie careful to confine his examples to foods which have been made bad through scientific ministrations, or does he include examples of foods which are just plain bad, either intrinsically or because of inept cooking?

6. Which examples of the "scientific war against deliciousness" does the author reserve for the conclusion of his essay? Why are they presented last?

7. What impression of the author's character and temperament do you gain from the essay? What qualities of style convey this impression?

8. How does Wylie extend and generalize his concern in the closing paragraphs?

TOPICS FOR DISCUSSION AND WRITING

9. If you were to write an essay complaining about the kind of food we eat, what examples other than those adduced by Wylie would you include? Which of his examples do you find most persuasive?

10. Examine a paper you have already written, and see if by the judicious use of example you can make it clearer, more forceful, and more lively.

11. On the basis of this essay and that by Jeans, what is the essential difference between analogy and example?

12. Write a paragraph describing the effect created by Wylie's vehemence and exuberance of statement. Do you think that the kind of style he uses here would be appropriate and effective for all subjects? How does it work out here?

No Sympathy for Apathy

ALISTAIR COOKE

NOT LONG ago the gentle E. M. Forster spoke before the American Academy of Arts and Letters. To an audience of distinguished poets, painters, historians, and novelists he set up an ideal for the conquering American, whose expression is a little bloodshot these days from being told so often he has come to his first high peak of world power. It was this: "Man's best chance for harmony lies in apathy, uninventiveness and inertia. . . . Universal exhaustion would certainly be a new experience. The human race has never undergone it, and it is still too perky to admit that it might result in a sprouting of new growth through decay."

Mr. Forster said this with a weary face and that air of a meditative child whispering in the wilderness which makes him sound sometimes like Gandhi and sometimes like Christopher Robin. Americans may well be depressed by this advice, for they are temperamentally the last people likely to take it. And it was offered to them at a tantalizing time, in the first flush of summer. Only those who have endured a summer on the Atlantic seaboard can know how at that season "Man's best chance for harmony" does seem to lie in getting down enough beer, expiring enough sweat, and keeping at bay, as a distant rustle in the kitchen, the nightly invasions of the cockroach. This coast has theoretically a Northern climate, but New York is at the latitude of Madrid. And the summer comes in with a crash of thunder, and thereafter the heat broods over the city till it has turned it rancid.

The city's deep streets are hot as the funnels of a stove, the bedrooms like bakeries. From cabs parked on street corners the high voices of baseball commentators rattle out from portable radios, and all there is of the

Reprinted from *One Man's America* by Alistair Cooke, by permission of Alfred A. Knopf, Inc. Copyright, 1952, by Alistair Cooke.

driver slumped inside is one fat, shirtless arm over the door. The Elevated bangs past tenements with all their windows open, dank laundry over the ledges, and vast women shuffling around inside carrying frying-pans or little flower-pots. You see old men sitting on the stoops, and babies spilling over the sidewalks, and cars hooting at little boys darting into the roadway waving baseball bats. You get into a bus and somebody goes down hard on your toe—my toe, that is. And I look up and see through a radiating haze a large pink woman shouting, "Will you keep your feet to yourself? Somebody's going to be killed one of these days." And as the bus grinds into gear, and the sudden whiff of carbon monoxide comes up, I hear the voice of a thin man opposite mutter unsmilingly, "It's a cinch it won't be you, lady." For three months we shall pad around through sweating streets and blinding light, over grass burned from yellow to brown, and down into the stew of the subway.

But even when the summer exhausts people, and they fall over, the attitudes of their fatigue are nothing short of violent. I walked through Central Park the other day—not a good day, there was high humidity and the sun burned like a copper vat. Nobody could say that the people in the park I saw were full of perkiness or inventiveness. But even in exhaustion, it is rare to see an American who looks cowed or meek. The immense bulk of cheerful derelicts snoozed under trees. Two sailors were spread-eagled in possession of a whole bench to themselves. And though their brows were glistening with sweat, their eyes roved after the girls as sassily as ever. A Negro, fast asleep, sprawled on and over and under a bench, in a position of helpless independence.

These, after all, were the people with a day off, or bums out of a job, or men just arrived in a new port. Everybody else was at work. And when I went down into the subway, the concentration of human sweat and aliveness was immense. I had been going down, day after day in line of duty, to the hearings of a now celebrated perjury trial, and this entailed taking a subway train six miles from my office.

The train I took was an express and does it in seven dreadful minutes. It starts at Forty-second Street, makes only one intermediate stop at Fourteenth Street, and next comes to rest, panting and dripping oil, under Foley Square, where the law courts are. At Forty-second Street the platform was choked with every sort of American face, and body, and shirt, and human shape, and color of eye and hair, and swarthy males and pretty girls and not so pretty girls, with the trim, bright clothes, the vivid line of scarlet mouth, the flaring nostrils—the animal stare that is the surest sign of the unconscious, uncontemplative American appetite for life, and an acceptance of it no matter how restless, loud, hot, or atomic it may be. The train came shrieking round the curve, stopped with a shudder, and flung its doors open. A writhing mass of humans fell out, and another mass of humans fell in. One puffing fat man, carrying his coat, his shirt transparent as flypaper, fell almost on to a very dark, charming-looking girl in front of me. In a flash, her face went into a spasm of anger. She shot black eyes at the big oaf and said in an intense, contemptuous snarl, "Take it easy! Don't be so—*cute!*" Then we all shoved in, the doors crashed, and her face was calm and charming again as the train swayed and screamed at a perilous pace downtown.

Only an hour later this incident touched off a pathetic irony. In court the defendant's accuser was being questioned about what had been undoubtedly a fairly troubled life. The defense counsel asked him if his brother had committed suicide, at the age of twenty-two. He said yes, he had. The counsel read a sentence from the young man, who had tried to persuade his brother to join him in a suicide pact. The sad young man, who in the end went it alone, had written: "We are gentle people, incapable of coping with the world." I thought of the brunette with the black eyes, who snarled at the clumsy fat man and then composed her face again without shame or afterthought. She, evidently, could cope. And though a snarl is not an expression taught in the nicest girls' schools, it is an instinctive thing, and on her it looked healthy.

Perhaps New York and other American cities are no place for sensitive souls. And certainly to people who come from places where there is a gentler tradition of public manners and behavior, New York is raw and terrifying—but, they also always seem bound to add, intensely alive. The question then comes up—how normal, how healthy, is spontaneous and intense feeling? The Americans prize it, not only in their theater and their literature, but in their young. They would no doubt like their children to be delicate and courteous, but if they have to choose they will take them —with a proud sigh—brassy and wild. Even their psychiatrists imply the better chance for happiness of the "outgoing" child rather than (with an ominous note) the "withdrawn" child. So shyness is not only at a discount. It is one of the warning signs of emotional trouble that the child-doctors and child-clinics drop hints to the parent about.

This, I believe, is one of the great differences between the culture of America and the culture of Europe. In Tennessee Williams's poignant play, *A Streetcar Named Desire*, the only scene is a basement flat in a

poor section of New Orleans in the thunderous midsummer. Four men—
factory workers, ex-G.I.'s, a garage mechanic—are playing poker. The
hero is a Polish-American, thick-spoken, laconic, with a magnificent body.
His wife is a cheerful girl, leaving the poker-players to their game and
gossiping—through one of those bead curtains—with her sister, a gentle,
neurotic, fanciful girl schoolteacher. Suddenly there is a quarrel and the
poker game is up in the air. And so too are the table and the beer bottles. The air is thick with flying wedges of bodies and loud cursing. The
husband throws everybody out. He is drunk, anyway, but he too is sensitive in his lumbering way and he can't stand the giggles of the girls in the
next room. He smashes the radio the gentle girl keeps turning on. It is a
terrible scene. The next morning the place is a shambles. The two sisters
come into the disheveled room. The wife stretches luxuriously, looks at
the wreckage and the splintered bottles, and laughs. The visiting sister is
furious and begs her to leave the husband. She launches into a frantic appeal for what she takes to be the best values of a civilized life between
men and women. The wife listens ruefully. Maybe she's right. Then the
husband ambles in. And the wife takes a flying leap across the stage and
is high in his arms.

This is a universal situation. But in the sounds that the audience make,
the way they take it, the feeling comes across on our side of the footlights
that the sister is in a bad way, that everything that is lusty and normal
is on the wife's side. "That sister," said a man walking out in the inter-
mission, "is crazy as a coot."

In this culture, then, what chance is there for warming to "inertia, apathy, uninventiveness," which have quite seriously been the mainstay of
some Oriental peoples?

I go home and open the paper, and rustle through the ads in a magazine.
A man has invented a gadget which can make a blind man fly a plane
with safety. All the women's ads are for ways and means to be "alluring,
vital, the life of the party." The workmen are already laying steam-pipes
under the motor parkways, so that next winter the snows will melt as they
fall and leave a naked, safe highway in the middle of the blanketed countryside. The campaigns get more active every day in the big cities for sub-
scription funds to keep cancer research going at its current unprecedented
pace. The farmers of Kansas own more private planes than those of any
other state. Bomb or no bomb, Manhattan is loud with the demolition of
whole blocks of little buildings and the drilling of foundations for twenty-
and thirty- and forty-story skyscrapers that are shooting up all over town.

In Albany the state historical museum has given a black eye to despairing educators and anxious parents by putting on an elaborate exhibition: "Two thousand years of the comic strip," from ancient pictographs to the comic supplements of today's newspapers.

And on the political scene, countless men in Washington are angry or panicky enough to start investigations into everything from the care of the atomic bomb to the shortcomings of history teachers in the public schools. What comes out of these investigations is a lot of energy thrown into violent accusation, Congressmen listening and challenging eight hours a day, stenotypists working like wood-ticks, and the restless citizen getting the satisfaction not, perhaps, of the truth, but of knowing that somebody is on his toes and watching out for him.

An American newspaperman just back from Europe told me the other day he'd been struck by the more leisurely and meditative tone of the best European political reporting. "You people," he said, "must be trained in a library. But with us, whether we're writing about an oil deal, or China, or the economic reports of the United Nations, we are always looking for a guy with a gun."

He shook his head. But that was pure politeness. There was an unregenerate gleam in his eye. He went off—to look for the guy with a gun, leaving the solid implication that America may end in spontaneous combustion, but never in "apathy, inertia, uninventiveness."

UNDERSTANDING THE TEXT

1. From what point of view does Cooke develop his generalization about the vigor of Americans? Does he approve or disapprove of this trait? What makes you think so?

2. What is the function of the quotation from E. M. Forster at the beginning of the essay? Study the way the author introduces the quotation. With what words and metaphors does he characterize E. M. Forster? What does the tone of his first reference, in the second sentence, to the "conquering American" suggest about the attitude he will take in the essay which follows?

3. In order to move smoothly into the body of the essay, how does the author use the fact that E. M. Forster made his speech in the summertime?

4. From what areas of American life does Cooke draw examples to prove that Americans are an almost frighteningly energetic people?

5. Of the incidents he cites, which seem to you most valuable in supporting his argument? Why? Are they intrinsically more persuasive, or has their value been enhanced by the way Cooke is able to treat them?

6. What qualities of Cooke's style serve to reinforce the impression of rush and vitality he is trying to convey? In this connection, study and discuss the passage describing a subway ride.
7. To what extent does Cooke state, and to what extent does he imply, a contrast between American energy and the more leisurely tempo of Europe?
8. Does the author express, or imply, any kind of judgment, either favorable or adverse, on the Americans' inability to be apathetic?

TOPICS FOR DISCUSSION AND WRITING

9. Most of Cooke's examples of American drive and bustle are drawn from his experiences in New York City. Do you think his conclusions would have been substantially modified if he had been writing about small-town and rural America?
10. Think for a few minutes about any large group of people that you know something about—Americans, or the people in your part of the country, or the students at your college—and see if you can frame a statement which seems to be true of most of them. From this statement develop an essay in which you support your main point with abundant use of specific observations and incidents.
11. Judging from the text itself, do you think Cooke's essay was written originally for a British or an American audience? Why?
12. Write a stylistic analysis of the following sentence: "Mr. Forster said this with a weary face and that air of a meditative child whispering in the wilderness which makes him sound sometimes like Gandhi and sometimes like Christopher Robin." Comment on such features as the choice of words, the point of the allusions, the sentence structure, and any qualities of sound and rhythm which seem significant to you.
13. What impression of the American character might emerge from a day's drive on a busy express highway? Write an account of such a journey in which you attempt to develop an interpretation of the way the drivers act.
14. Is the American energy described by Cooke identical with the American restlessness noted by Tocqueville?

Why the Sky Looks Blue

SIR JAMES JEANS

‹•›

IMAGINE that we stand on an ordinary seaside pier, and watch the waves rolling in and striking against the iron columns of the pier. Large waves pay very little attention to the columns—they divide right and left and re-unite after passing each column, much as a regiment of soldiers would if a tree stood in their road; it is almost as though the columns had not been there. But the short waves and ripples find the columns of the pier a much more formidable obstacle. When the short waves impinge on the columns, they are reflected back and spread as new ripples in all directions. To use the technical term, they are "scattered." The obstacle provided by the iron columns hardly affects the long waves at all, but scatters the short ripples.

We have been watching a sort of working model of the way in which sunlight struggles through the earth's atmosphere. Between us on earth and outer space the atmosphere interposes innumerable obstacles in the form of molecules of air, tiny droplets of water, and small particles of dust. These are represented by the columns of the pier.

The waves of the sea represent the sunlight. We know that sunlight is a blend of many colors—as we can prove for ourselves by passing it through a prism, or even through a jug of water, or as nature demonstrates to us when she passes it through the raindrops of a summer shower and pro-duces a rainbow. We also know that light consists of waves, and that the different colors of light are produced by waves of different lengths, red light by long waves and blue light by short waves. The mixture of waves which constitutes sunlight has to struggle past the columns of the pier. And these obstacles treat the light waves much as the columns of the pier treat the sea-waves. The long waves which constitute red light are hardly

Reprinted from *The Stars in Their Courses* by Sir James Jeans. Used by permission of the publishers, Cambridge University Press.

affected but the short waves which constitute blue light are scattered in all directions.

Thus the different constituents of sunlight are treated in different ways as they struggle through the earth's atmosphere. A wave of blue light may be scattered by a dust particle, and turned out of its course. After a time a second dust particle again turns it out of its course, and so on, until finally it enters our eyes by a path as zigzag as that of a flash of lightning. Consequently the blue waves of the sunlight enter our eyes from all directions. And that is why the sky looks blue.

UNDERSTANDING THE TEXT

1. In presenting the seaside analogy in the first paragraph, does Jeans introduce any details which are not used in the subsequent explanation of why the sky looks blue?
2. Are there any elements in the explanation which are not prepared for in the analogy?
3. How successfully does Jeans move back and forth between the analogy and the explanation? Point out the specific transitional words and phrases which he employs.
4. Why, in the opening paragraph, does he introduce the technical term "scattered"?
5. Jeans's diction in this piece is marked by a willingness to repeat key words several times in a short passage. Do you consider this repetition a strength or a weakness?

TOPICS FOR DISCUSSION AND WRITING

6. What function does a good analogy serve in writing? Judging from this example, what qualities should it possess? Is the subject of the analogy likely to be more or less concrete than the idea being explained? On analogy see Supplement 1 (p. 626).
7. This is a brief passage, and the analogy is a clear-cut one. Without consulting the text, "rewrite" the essay. Do not attempt to recall Jeans's language, but concentrate on achieving an orderly presentation of the relationship between the analogy and the explanation.
8. It would be possible, of course, for a writer to present his real subject first, and then clarify it with an appropriate analogy. Why do you think Jeans introduced the analogy before proceeding to his actual point?
9. What kinds of subjects do you think would lend themselves particularly well to clarification by analogy?

The Federalist, *No. 10*

JAMES MADISON

TO THE PEOPLE OF THE STATE OF NEW YORK:

Among the numerous advantages promised by a well-constructed Union, none deserves to be more accurately developed than its tendency to break and control the violence of faction. The friend of popular governments never finds himself so much alarmed for their character and fate as when he contemplates their propensity to this dangerous vice. He will not fail, therefore, to set a due value on any plan which, without violating the principles to which he is attached, provides a proper cure for it. The instability, injustice, and confusion introduced into the public councils, have, in truth, been the mortal diseases under which popular governments have everywhere perished; as they continue to be the favorite and fruitful topics from which the adversaries to liberty derive their most specious declamations. The valuable improvements made by the American constitutions on the popular models, both ancient and modern, cannot certainly be too much admired; but it would be an unwarrantable partiality, to contend that they have as effectually obviated the danger on this side, as was wished and expected. Complaints are everywhere heard from our most considerate and virtuous citizens, equally the friends of public and private faith, and of public and personal liberty, that our governments are too unstable, that the public good is disregarded in the conflicts of rival parties, and that measures are too often decided, not according to the rules of justice and the rights of the minor party, but by the superior force of an interested and overbearing majority. However anxiously we may wish that these complaints had no foundation, the evidence of known facts will not permit us to deny that they are in some degree true. It will be found, indeed, on a candid review of our situation, that some of the distresses un-

Originally printed in the *New York Packet*, November 23, 1787.

der which we labor have been erroneously charged on the operation of our governments; but it will be found, at the same time, that other causes will not alone account for many of our heaviest misfortunes; and, particularly, for that prevailing and increasing distrust of public engagements, and alarm for private rights, which are echoed from one end of the continent to the other. These must be chiefly, if not wholly, effects of the unsteadiness and injustice with which a factious spirit has tainted our public administrations.

By a faction, I understand a number of citizens, whether amounting to a majority or minority of the whole, who are united and actuated by some common impulse of passion, or of interest, adverse to the rights of other citizens, or to the permanent and aggregate interests of the community.

There are two methods of curing the mischiefs of faction: the one, by removing its causes; the other, by controlling its effects.

There are again two methods of removing the causes of faction: the one, by destroying the liberty which is essential to its existence; the other, by giving to every citizen the same opinions, the same passions, and the same interests.

It could never be more truly said than of the first remedy, that it was worse than the disease. Liberty is to faction what air is to fire, an aliment without which it instantly expires. But it could not be less folly to abolish liberty, which is essential to political life, because it nourishes faction, than it would be to wish the annihilation of air, which is essential to animal life, because it imparts to fire its destructive agency.

The second expedient is as impracticable as the first would be unwise. As long as the reason of man continues fallible, and he is at liberty to exercise it, different opinions will be formed. As long as the connection subsists between his reason and his self-love, his opinions and his passions will have a reciprocal influence on each other; and the former will be objects to which the latter will attach themselves. The diversity in the faculties of men, from which the rights of property originate, is not less an insuperable obstacle to a uniformity of interests. The protection of these faculties is the first object of government. From the protection of different and unequal faculties of acquiring property, the possession of different degrees and kinds of property immediately results; and from the influence of these on the sentiments and views of the respective proprietors, ensues a division of the society into different interests and parties.

The latent causes of faction are thus sown in the nature of man; and we see them everywhere brought into different degrees of activity, according to the different circumstances of civil society. A zeal for different opinions concerning religion, concerning government, and many other points, as well of speculation as of practice; an attachment to different leaders ambitiously contending for preeminence and power; or to persons of other descriptions whose fortunes have been interesting to the human passions, have, in turn, divided mankind into parties, inflamed them with mutual animosity, and rendered them much more disposed to vex and oppress each other than to co-operate for their common good. So strong is this propensity of mankind to fall into mutual animosities, that where no substantial occasion presents itself, the most frivolous and fanciful distinctions have been sufficient to kindle their unfriendly passions and excite their most violent conflicts. But the most common and durable source of factions has been the various and unequal distribution of property. Those who hold and those who are without property have ever formed distinct interests in society. Those who are creditors, and those who are debtors, fall under a like discrimination. A landed interest, a manufacturing interest, a mercantile interest, a moneyed interest, with many lesser interests, grow up of necessity in civilized nations, and divide them into different classes, actuated by different sentiments and views. The regulation of these various and interfering interests forms the principal task of modern legislation, and involves the spirit of party and faction in the necessary and ordinary operations of the government.

No man is allowed to be a judge in his own cause, because his interest would certainly bias his judgment, and, not improbably, corrupt his integrity. With equal, nay with greater reason, a body of men are unfit to be both judges and parties at the same time; yet what are many of the most important acts of legislation, but so many judicial determinations, not indeed concerning the rights of single persons, but concerning the rights of large bodies of citizens? And what are the different classes of legislators but advocates and parties to the causes which they determine? Is a law proposed concerning private debts? It is a question to which the creditors are parties on one side and the debtors on the other. Justice ought to hold the balance between them. Yet the parties are, and must be, themselves the judges; and the most numerous party, or, in other words, the most powerful faction must be expected to prevail. Shall domestic manufactures be encouraged, and in what degree, by restrictions on foreign manufactures? are questions which would be differently decided by the landed and the manufacturing classes, and probably by neither with a sole regard to justice and the public good. The apportionment of taxes on the various descriptions of property is an act which seems to require the most exact impartiality; yet there is, perhaps, no legislative act in which greater opportunity and temptation are given to a predominant party to trample on the rules of justice. Every shilling with which they overburden the inferior number, is a shilling saved to their own pockets.

It is in vain to say that enlightened statesmen will be able to adjust these clashing interests, and render them all subservient to the public good. Enlightened statesmen will not always be at the helm. Nor, in many cases, can such an adjustment be made at all without taking into view indirect and remote considerations, which will rarely prevail over the immediate interest which one party may find in disregarding the rights of another or the good of the whole.

The inference to which we are brought is that the *causes* of faction cannot be removed, and that relief is only to be sought in the means of controlling its *effects*.

If a faction consists of less than a majority, relief is supplied by the republican principle, which enables the majority to defeat its sinister views by regular vote. It may clog the administration, it may convulse the society; but it will be unable to execute and mask its violence under the forms of the Constitution. When a majority is included in a faction, the form of popular government, on the other hand, enables it to sacrifice to its ruling passion or interest both the public good and the rights of other citizens. To secure the public good and private rights against the danger of such a faction, and at the same time to preserve the spirit and the form of popular government, is then the great object to which our inquiries are directed. Let me add that it is the great desideratum by which this form of government can be rescued from the opprobrium under which it has so long labored, and be recommended to the esteem and adoption of mankind.

By what means is this object attainable? Evidently by one of two only: Either the existence of the same passion or interest in a majority at the same time must be prevented, or the majority, having such coexistent passion or interest, must be rendered, by their number and local situation, unable to concert and carry into effect schemes of oppression. If the impulse and the opportunity be suffered to coincide, we well know that neither moral nor religious motives can be relied on as an adequate control. They are not found to be such on the injustice and violence of individuals, and lose their efficacy in proportion to the number combined together, that is, in proportion as their efficacy becomes needful.

From this view of the subject it may be concluded that a pure democracy, by which I mean a society consisting of a small number of citizens, who assemble and administer the government in person, can admit of no cure for the mischiefs of faction. A common passion or interest will, in almost every case, be felt by a majority of the whole; a communication and concert result from the form of government itself; and there is nothing to check the inducements to sacrifice the weaker party or an obnoxious individual. Hence it is that such democracies have ever been spectacles of turbulence and contention; have ever been found incompatible with personal security or the rights of property; and have in general been as short in their lives as they have been violent in their deaths. Theoretic politicians, who have patronized this species of government, have erroneously supposed that by reducing mankind to a perfect equality in their political rights, they would at the same time, be perfectly equalized and assimilated in their possessions, their opinions, and their passions.

A republic, by which I mean a government in which the scheme of representation takes place, opens a different prospect, and promises the cure for which we are seeking. Let us examine the points in which it varies from pure democracy, and we shall comprehend both the nature of the cure and the efficacy which it must derive from the union.

The two great points of difference between a democracy and a republic are: first, the delegation of the government, in the latter, to a small number of citizens elected by the rest; secondly, the greater number of citizens, and greater sphere of country, over which the latter may be extended.

The effect of the first difference is, on the one hand, to refine and enlarge the public views, by passing them through the medium of a chosen body of citizens, whose wisdom may best discern the true interest of their country, and whose patriotism and love of justice will be least likely to sacrifice it to temporary or partial considerations. Under such a regulation, it may well happen that the public voice, pronounced by the representatives of the people, will be more consonant to the public good than if pronounced by the people themselves, convened for the purpose. On the other hand, the effect may be inverted. Men of factious tempers, of local prejudices, or of sinister designs, may, by intrigue, by corruption, or by other means, first obtain the suffrages, and then betray the interests, of the people. The question resulting is, whether small or extensive republics are more favorable to the election of proper guardians of the public weal; and it is clearly decided in favor of the latter by two obvious considerations:

In the first place, it is to be remarked that, however small the republic may be, the representatives must be raised to a certain number, in order to guard against the cabals of a few; and that, however large it may be, they must be limited to a certain number, in order to guard against the confusion of a multitude. Hence, the number of representatives in the two cases not being in proportion to that of the two constituents, and being proportionally greater in the small republic, it follows that, if the proportion of fit characters be not less in the large than in the small republic, the former will present a greater option, and consequently a greater probability of a fit choice.

In the next place, as each representative will be chosen by a greater number of citizens in the large than in the small republic, it will be more difficult for unworthy candidates to practice with success the vicious arts by which elections are too often carried; and the suffrages of the people, being more free, will be more likely to center in men who possess the most attractive merit and the most diffusive and established characters.

It must be confessed that in this, as in most other cases, there is a mean, on both sides of which inconveniences will be found to lie. By enlarging too much the number of electors, you render the representative too little acquainted with all their local circumstances and lesser interests; as by reducing it too much, you render him unduly attached to these, and too little fit to comprehend and pursue great and national objects. The federal Constitution forms a happy combination in this respect; the great and aggregate interests being referred to the national, the local and particular to the State legislatures.

The other point of difference is, the greater number of citizens and extent of territory which may be brought within the compass of republican than of democratic government; and it is this circumstance principally which renders factious combinations less to be dreaded in the former than in the latter. The smaller the society, the fewer probably will be the distinct parties and interests composing it; the fewer the distinct parties and interests, the more frequently will a majority be found of the same party; and the smaller the number of individuals composing a majority, and the smaller the compass within which they are placed, the more easily will they concert and execute their plans of oppression. Extend the sphere, and you take in a greater variety of parties and interests; you make it less probable that a majority of the whole will have a common motive to invade the rights of other citizens; or if such a common motive exists, it will be more difficult for all who feel it to discover their own strength, and to act in unison with each other. Besides other impediments, it may be remarked that, where there is a consciousness of unjust or dishonorable purposes, communication is always checked by distrust in proportion to the number whose concurrence is necessary.

Hence, it clearly appears, that the same advantage which a republic has over a democracy, in controlling the effects of faction, is enjoyed by a large over a small republic,—is enjoyed by the Union over the States composing it. Does the advantage consist in the substitution of representatives whose enlightened views and virtuous sentiments render them superior to local prejudices and to schemes of injustice? It will not be denied that the representation of the Union will be most likely to possess these requisite endowments. Does it consist in the greater security afforded by a greater variety of parties against the event of any one party being able to outnumber and oppress the rest? In an equal degree does the increased variety of parties comprised within the Union increase this security. Does it, in fine, consist in the greater obstacles opposed to the concert and accomplishment of the secret wishes of an unjust and interested majority? Here, again, the extent of the Union gives it the most palpable advantage.

The influence of factious leaders may kindle a flame within their particular States, but will be unable to spread a general conflagration through the other States. A religious sect may degenerate into a political faction in a part of the Confederacy; but the variety of sects dispersed over the entire face of it must secure the national councils against any danger from that source. A rage for paper money, for an abolition of debts, for an equal division of property, or for any other improper or wicked project, will be less apt to pervade the whole body of the Union than a particular member of it; in the same proportion as such a malady is more likely to taint a particular county or district than an entire State.

In the extent and proper structure of the Union, therefore, we behold a republican remedy for the diseases most incident to republican government. And according to the degree of pleasure and pride we feel in being republicans, ought to be our zeal in cherishing the spirit and supporting the character of Federalists.

PUBLIUS

UNDERSTANDING THE TEXT

1. What specific objection to popular government is Madison answering in this paper?
2. Madison states that there are two methods of removing the causes of faction. The first method would be to destroy the liberty which breeds faction. What kind of argument does he use to show that this method is unwise?

3. How does he demonstrate that the second method of removing the causes of faction—i.e., giving all men the same opinions and interests—is impracticable? In this part of the argument, what relationship does he assume to exist among opinions, passions, and economic interests?

4. If the causes of faction cannot be removed, how can the effects of a majority faction be controlled?

5. According to Madison, why is a pure democracy unable to prevent a majority faction from acting in concert against the public interest?

6. For what reasons is a republic likely to be more successful than a democracy in controlling the effects of faction?

7. Why, finally, is a large republic, like the United States, best fitted of all to prevent a majority faction from dominating the government?

TOPICS FOR DISCUSSION AND WRITING

8. Aside from the primary emphasis on the causes and effects of faction, how many different methods of organization are used in this argument? Check the list of procedures illustrated in this section of the book, and see which ones are represented in this essay.

9. In the eighteenth century the emerging political parties were often described as factions. How accurately could Madison's definition of faction be applied to present-day American political parties? To what extent does each of the two major parties unite citizens who are "actuated by some common impulse of passion, or of interest"?

10. If, as Madison argues, the views and interests of the majority are not to be the determining factors in government, what should be the source of political action? What do you think Madison means by the "public interest"? How would this differ from the interest of the dominant majority faction?

11. Compare the assumptions on human nature and political conduct which underlie *Federalist* No. 10 with the assumptions concerning the same matters in Franklin's speech opposing the payment of government salaries (pp. 48–51).

12. Do you believe that political parties organized on the basis of clear principle, rather than on a come-one-come-all appeal, would make for more effective and juster government? In an essay state and argue your views on this question.

13. Write a paragraph presenting your reaction to the following statement: "In a democracy the decision of the majority is the measure of sound policy and true justice."

The Indecisiveness of Decisions

FLETCHER PRATT

SIR EDWARD CREASY considered Gettysburg one of the fifteen decisive battles of the world, and with Gettysburg, Stephen V. Benét sweeps the pieces from the board, holding the result no longer in doubt; the mate will follow in a given number of moves. It is probable that a Jung word-association test on most people, with "Civil War" as the impulse-phrase, would produce either "Gettysburg" or "Gettysburg Address" as a response.

This is reasonable with regard to the address, which contains all of American aspiration and consecration, of reverence for the past and hope for the future, from the Declaration of Independence to the release of the slaves. But it is profoundly untrue with regard to the battle, which decided nothing except that the South could not conquer the North. The South had never supposed that it could; more, it had never wanted to. The whole Southern scheme of life was based on the idea that only beings on a lower plane of existence should be conquered, and the Yankee, though an inferior and rather obnoxious organism, was tacitly accorded the status of a reasonable being.

The invasion of the Southern states by the armies of the Union was immediately political in its object—to secure possession of the fountainheads of authority and return those states to their allegiance, a kind of exalted police duty. When Grant took Vicksburg a large part of his army ceased field operations to enter directly upon such political duties. The National army in Missouri did hardly anything else. Lee's invasion of Pennsylvania, on the other hand, was political only at the second remove; it did not aim at destroying the established governments in the Northern states, but only at subjecting them to a certain amount of pressure. It was undertaken for purely military reasons, and although most of the failures of the Confederacy were political (failure to win the border states, to persuade England to intervene) the Gettysburg offensive failed on military and not on political grounds.

In view of the fact that the event of the battle was so shocking to contemporaries who had come to regard the words "Lee" and "victory" as synonymous, it is worth while discovering what those grounds were. Pickett's magnificent charge has an inevitable attraction for the eye; one tends to be satisfied with the explanation that it was made and repulsed and that Lee admitted it was an error of judgment to order it. But this does not carry us far in the direction of discovering why the error in judgment occurred or why the charge was repulsed. It was not merely that the movement was too bold, or wrong in a technical, chess-game sense; the maneuver round Pope's flank at Second Manassas was just as bold, the encircling columns at Savage Station were just as bad tactically, Jackson's sweep at Chancellorsville was positively foolhardy—but all of them succeeded brilliantly.

Lee himself thought the explanation was the lack of Jackson; he was mistaken. The Army of Northern Virginia was all it had ever been in personnel and leadership, and Lee's own judgment was less bad than he and some of the recent critics who claim he underestimated Meade would like to have us think. He read Meade's mind as closely as he had Pope's or Hooker's—an unenterprising man with considerable ability at handling defensive positions. It was not Meade he underestimated but the Army of the Potomac, the Northern people, the thing he had failed to comprehend from the first. For if any one fact emerges from the tangled account of Gettysburg it is this—that the Union victory was achieved by no one man, but by the cooperation of a large number of men, each appearing, as though by a miracle, in exactly the right place.

When the II Corps is caught isolated on the first day, it is Reynolds, the most complete soldier in the army, who sees the importance of Gettysburg and places the corps in position to hold it; when he falls, it is Doubleday, a fourth-rate tactician simply too unskillful to retreat, who keeps the corps there; of all possible officers, it has to be Howard, burning to erase the stigma of Chancellorsville, who next comes on the field; and as the rebels are making their sunset attack, who should turn up but reckless Judson Kilpatrick to overawe them with an insane cavalry movement. It is the same on the second day; Warren, the engineer, appears at Little Round Top at the crucial moment; the perfectly drilled V Corps arrives to stop

Hood. The stars in their courses fought against the Confederacy, right on through Pickett's charge that would have gone through any line not held by Hancock. Such a chapter of coincidence is impossible; when accident is repeated a dozen times the accidental explanation will no longer serve and we must look further.

The accidental explanation will not serve. Gettysburg is simply one step farther along the line than Chancellorsville. If Antietam should have been a portent to Lee, Chancellorsville should have sent cold shivers up his spine. He won a great victory there, but it was a strategic victory only, a triumph over the mind of Joseph Hooker, not over the Union army. In all the previous battles minor Union commanders had failed or regiments had broken. At Chancellorsville their conduct was as flawless as that of the Confederates, only the general did not know how to use his machine. "Be sure to put in *all* your men" was Lincoln's parting caution to Hooker before the battle, but the combination had been too big for him to grasp, and two of his corps only got in to cover the retreat.

Hooker had been trying to manage the complicated attacking maneuver; Meade was not only a better soldier, he also had a simpler problem; he simply could not help putting in all his men. Lee attacked him at every point in succession; all he had to do was keep a clear head and stand his ground. He had seen enough of war by this time—any of the Union generals had seen enough of war by this time—to do that; the rest followed as logically as conclusion succeeds premise. The appearances of Reynolds, Doubleday, Kilpatrick and the others at the right moments were not accidents but incidents; the Union infantry was full of generals who knew how to take advantage of the ground, the cavalry was loaded with valiant youths. What Lee attacked at Glendale was an armed mob; what he attacked at Second Bull Run was a group of quarrelsome old men; at Chancellorsville, he attacked a man; but at Gettysburg he came into collision with a system. The Army of the Potomac had developed to such an extent it no longer needed brains; it needed only someone to see that it did not fall over its own feet, which Meade was quite capable of doing.

He had not Lee's intellect, but he had an instrument infinitely more powerful than Lee's, and in the succeeding Mine Run campaign the combination worked out to a state of perfect equilibrium, which may be expressed mathematically:

Army of Northern Virginia	+	Lee	=	Army of the Potomac	+	Meade
2	+	4	=	4	+	2

The danger for the Confederacy obviously lay in the fact that its figures were constant; it could hardly improve upon the tactical genius of Lee, which was a maximum, nor could it increase the numbers of its soldiers, whereas the Army of the Potomac was guaranteed an unlimited supply of recruits and might some day produce a general who was a 3 or even a 4.

In other words, in the political factor, the thing that made the Army of the Potomac a 4 with an inexhaustible reservoir of other 4s behind it was the real danger; the spirit of voluntary combination. The South, a democracy of the classical type, believed combination on such a scale, such regulation, impossible without the sacrifice of individuality; they conceived of the Republic as the narrowly knitted federal league prescribed by the letter of the Constitution. They looked upon it much as Chios or Mitylene on the Athenian League of Pericles.

They did not realize that the North had developed a much stronger and more imperial structure, a type of polity new in the world. Combination is not new in the world; the Romans were a people of combination; the Germans are, so are the Japanese. But all the classical combinations had obtained their strength by making the individual one grain of sugar in the sack, with no thought or will or direction save those furnished by the mass. They ruthlessly harried the oddity, even the oddity of genius, such as Scipio or Schubert. The Northern type of combination—which became the American type, since it triumphed—was something much more complex and valuable, and constitutes this nation's one outstanding contribution to the science of human relations, a contribution not even yet thoroughly understood.

It lies not in that spirit of voluntary combination alone, but in the ability to form combinations for certain objectives, maintaining perfect freedom of action in all other respects; to divide the mind into water-tight compartments, as it were, to give complete obedience in one direction while maintaining complete independence in others. The ideal has not always been attained, it is true; it tends to shade into the more restrictive type of combination, as in the case of prohibition; but it has remained the ideal, and the ideal has been held in an amazing number of cases.

Americans are a race of "joiners"; they should exult over the fact, it is their greatest title to fame. It enables them to form an association for the improvement of musical taste without inquiring into the social status of the members, and one for sending a rocket to the moon without examining their private morals. In Europe such bodies would be impossible unless the members were *gemütlich, sympathique,* all around the compass; every association is necessarily a general association, throwing the members together at all points.

Americans are a race of joiners; it has enabled them to form those strange caravans that subdued a continent, and those research bodies which are the glory of science. The husking-bee, the house-building-bee, are the characteristic American institutions. Once their purpose is accomplished, they disband and no more is heard of them.

This implies an extraordinary flexibility of mind and a high degree of tolerance. The fault, the fatal fault of the Confederacy was that its system possessed neither. Tolerance was reserved for the small circle of the elect. It was intolerant of any but received opinion; it was inflexible, Chinese, dead, static. It was not without splendid virtues; ability (when found in the right places) made its way more swiftly to the top through the loose Southern organization than through the tighter organization of Northern society. But such ability, unless it were genius itself, arrived at the top not quite capable of performing its tasks. The Northern system furnished talent with such an elaborate apparatus of training and support that it became the equal of genius. It is not without significance that the Southern commanders at the beginning of the war—Lee, Longstreet, Johnston, Bragg, Forrest—were still the Southern commanders at the end of the war, mostly older men, while the Union, with an air of prestidigitation, was producing such young tigers as Sheridan, Custer, Wilson, Upton and Kilpatrick. The South, like most aristocracies, was deficient in education, both of the corporate body and of the individual member.

It also had the other common aristocratic defect, interior disunity. Your people of combination finds its problems simplified; it can continue to serve an idea, the purpose of the group, although the personal representative of that idea may be somewhat unlovely. Individualism can offer only personality as a focus for devotion, and the South was, unfortunately, not rich in attractive personalities. Jefferson Davis was a brilliant intellectual but the last man in the world to excite sentimental enthusiasms, as cold as an iceberg; and his most prominent and capable assistant, Judah P. Benjamin, was draped in the strangeness of the alien. The successive commanders in the West (after the fall of Albert Sidney Johnston)—Joe Johnston, Pemberton, Bragg—were all of the Davis type, forceful, intellectual, precise and chilling. Their very existence generated quarrel and complaint.

All the more, then, does the personality of Robert E. Lee stand out against this background. He had that rarest of qualities, character, the unmistakable willingness to follow his view of the right, be the consequences what they would; the unselfed ability to subordinate his own feelings to the general good. He had a strong sense of justice overlaid with so deep a sympathy for human shortcomings that he was never unable to forgive the wrong and parole the prisoner. And, as it happened, he was the intellectual as well as the moral superior of the other Confederate leaders. It was no wonder that he acquired a personal following not surpassed by that of Washington, perhaps not equaled by that of Washington. "Country be damned!" exclaimed Henry Wise in the hour when everything was crumbling, at Appomattox. "There is no country. There has been no country, general, for a year or more. You are the country for these men. They have fought for you. If you demand the sacrifice there are still thousands of us who will die for you."

As time went on, as defeat sharpened the tempers and dulled the minds of the other rebel leaders, Lee became the only cohesive force within the Confederacy; in the last days the government practically abdicated in favor of a kind of Lee dictatorship, which might have saved the day if it had come sooner. For it is the virtue of the aristocratic democracy that it can produce such characters, that it can find men to entrust with its liberties during an emergency when monarchy alone, the single control, will give it the strength to beat off the attacks to which it is subjected.

Lee's one defect as a leader was that he really was the kind of plaster saint Lincoln is in danger of being made by admiring schoolboys. There was something unearthly about the man's best moments. He was foreordained to failure by a devotion to duty so inhuman that it would not let him step a hair's breadth beyond the legal bounds of his office, even to save the Confederacy. He had no humor and none of that talent for intrigue without which real statesmanship is unattainable.

Lincoln, on the other hand, would have delighted Machiavelli. One can picture the astute Florentine in ecstasies over the maneuver for eliminating Hooker and the Chase-led "Radicals"—"A masterpiece of duplicity!" Yet Lincoln bore as good a moral character as Lee; better, for he took his morals into the tumults of the market-place while the Southerner was hiding his precious integrity behind the monastery wall of Duty. There is not a single step in the Hooker business where Lincoln can be shown to have acted with anything but the utmost sincerity and frankness; that is what makes it so interesting—it is intrigue on a new basis, strictly moral. Look at the record—Lincoln objected to retaining Hooker on grounds of his inefficiency; he was overruled by the pro-Hooker faction. He denied the general the reinforcements he had asked because Hooker had already shown himself incapable of bringing what troops he had into action and because he already had more troops than Lee; when the general protested by resigning he accepted the resignation.

The only point at which a weakness can be suspected is in permitting the radicals to foist Hooker upon him, and even here Lincoln was obedient to the spirit of the state over which he presided; a spirit of control by the general intelligence instead of individual intelligence.

The North obtained its monarchial singleness of control by combination; the South essayed to obtain it through personality, but it moved too slowly. By his personal prestige, Lee might cover the effects of the terrible defeat of Gettysburg, and he did so. Nobody in the South felt that Gettysburg was anything but a repairable error of judgment, like McClellan's during the Seven Days. But Lee commanded only the Army of Northern Virginia; his authority could do nothing to gloss over the fatal blows the Confederacy received in the West. In the last analysis, the rock on which the new republic split was the Rock of Chickamauga. Technically, the battle was a victory; actually it was a defeat, the most crushing, the most decisive any Southern army suffered.

UNDERSTANDING THE TEXT

1. What general procedure does Pratt follow in seeking a cause for the Southern setback at Gettysburg? What broad, all-embracing explanation of the outcome of the battle proves satisfactory to him? How does he arrive at this explanation?

2. On what grounds does Pratt brush aside, first, such commonly cited causes as the failure of Pickett's charge, the absence of Jackson, and bad judgment on Lee's part?

3. How does Pratt support his first tentative general statement of causation, ". . . the Union victory was achieved by no one man, but by the cooperation of a large number of men, each appearing, as though by a miracle, in exactly the right place"?

4. In closing the final link in his causal chain, how successfully does Pratt tie the growing strength of the Army of the Potomac to what he calls "the spirit of voluntary combination"?

5. What mental and social characteristics does Pratt associate with "the Northern type of combination"? What contrasting characteristics does he discern in Southern society?

6. What connection is there between the way he contrasts the characters of Lee and Lincoln and the way he distinguishes between Southern and North-

ern society? To what extent does he interpret each leader as representing the strengths and weaknesses of a particular social system?

TOPICS FOR DISCUSSION AND WRITING

7. Is Pratt's theory concerning voluntary combination in the North contradicted by the fact that the Army of the Potomac included many thousands of conscript soldiers?

8. Could Pratt's interpretation of Northern versus Southern society be used to explain, not only the eventual Northern triumph, but also the Southern successes at the outset of the war?

9. From your observation of American life, how pervasive and influential do you find the spirit of voluntary combination in the twentieth century? What similarities do you note between this concept and what MacIver describes as "association" (pp. 126–129)? Does the broadening scope of governmental activity threaten the role of voluntary combinations? In an essay describe as precisely as you can the function of voluntary combination in America today.

10. Select a decisive event in recent history, or in your personal experience, and write an essay setting forth what seem to you its most important causes.

The Law

ROBERT M. COATES

THE FIRST intimation that things were getting out of hand came one early-fall evening in the late nineteen-forties. What happened, simply, was that between seven and nine o'clock on that evening the Triborough Bridge had the heaviest concentration of outbound traffic in its entire history.

This was odd, for it was a weekday evening (to be precise, a Wednesday), and though the weather was agreeably mild and clear, with a moon that was close enough to being full to lure a certain number of motorists out of the city, these facts alone were not enough to explain the phenomenon. No other bridge or main highway was affected, and though the two preceding nights had been equally balmy and moonlit, on both of these the bridge traffic had run close to normal.

The bridge personnel, at any rate, was caught entirely unprepared. A main artery of traffic, like the Triborough, operates under fairly predictable conditions. Motor travel, like most other large-scale human activities, obeys the Law of Averages—that great, ancient rule that states that the actions of people in the mass will always follow consistent patterns—and on the basis of past experience it had always been possible to foretell, almost to the last digit, the number of cars that would cross the bridge at any given hour of the day or night. In this case, though, all rules were broken.

The hours from seven till nearly midnight are normally quiet ones on the bridge. But on that night it was as if all the motorists in the city, or at any rate a staggering proportion of them, had conspired together to upset tradition. Beginning almost exactly at seven o'clock cars poured onto the bridge in such numbers and with such rapidity that the staff at the toll booths was overwhelmed almost from the start. It was soon apparent that

Reprinted from *The New Yorker*, November 29, 1947. Permission the author. Copr., 1947, The New Yorker Magazine, Inc.

this was no momentary congestion, and as it became more and more obvious that the traffic jam promised to be one of truly monumental proportions, added details of police were rushed to the scene to help handle it.

Cars streamed in from all directions—from the Bronx approach and the Manhattan one, from 125th Street and the East River Drive. (At the peak of the crush, about eight-fifteen, observers on the bridge reported that the drive was a solid line of car headlights as far south as the bend at Eighty-ninth Street, while the congestion crosstown in Manhattan disrupted traffic as far west as Amsterdam Avenue.) And perhaps the most confusing thing about the whole manifestation was that there seemed to be no reason for it.

Now and then, as the harried toll-booth attendants made change for the seemingly endless stream of cars, they would question the occupants, and it soon became clear that the very participants in the monstrous tieup were as ignorant of its cause as anyone else was. A report made by Sergeant Alfonse O'Toole, who commanded the detail in charge of the Bronx approach, is typical. "I kept askin' them," he said, " 'Is there night football somewhere that we don't know about? Is it the races you're goin' to?' But the funny thing was half the time they'd be askin' *me*. 'What's the crowd for, Mac?' they would say. And I'd just look at them. There was one guy I mind, in a Ford convertible with a girl in the seat beside him, and when he asked me, I said to him, 'Hell, you're *in* the crowd, ain't you?' I said. 'What brings *you* here?' And the dummy just looked at me. 'Me?' he says. 'I just come out for a drive in the moonlight. But if I'd known there'd be a crowd like this . . .' he says. And then he asks me, 'Is there any place I can turn around and get out of this?' " As the *Herald Tribune* summed things up in its story next morning, it "just looked as if everybody in Manhattan who owned a motorcar had decided to drive out on Long Island that evening."

The incident was unusual enough to make all the front pages next morning, and because of this, many similar events, which might otherwise have gone unnoticed, received attention. The proprietor of the Aramis Theatre, on Eighth Avenue, reported that on several nights in the recent past his auditorium had been practically empty, while on others it had been jammed to suffocation. Lunchroom owners noted that increasingly their patrons were developing a habit of making runs on specific items; one day it would be the roast shoulder of veal with pan gravy that was ordered almost exclusively, while the next everyone would be taking the Vienna loaf, and the roast veal went begging. A man who ran a small notions store in Bayside revealed that over a period of four days two hundred and seventy-four successive customers had entered his shop and asked for a spool of pink thread.

These were news items that would ordinarily have gone into the papers as fillers or in the sections reserved for oddities. Now, however, they seemed to have a more serious significance. It was apparent at last that something decidedly strange was happening to people's habits, and it was as unsettling as those occasional moments on excursion boats when the passengers are moved, all at once, to rush to one side or the other of the vessel. It was not till one day in December when, almost incredibly, the Twentieth Century Limited left New York for Chicago with just three passengers aboard that business leaders discovered how disastrous the new trend could be, too.

Until then, the New York Central, for instance, could operate confidently on the assumption that although there might be several thousand men in New York who had business relations in Chicago, on any single day no more—and no less—than some hundreds of them would have occasion to go there. The play producer could be sure that his patronage would sort itself out and that roughly as many persons would want to see the performance on Thursday as there had been on Tuesday or Wednesday. Now they couldn't be sure of anything. The Law of Averages had gone by the board, and if the effect on business promised to be catastrophic, it was also singularly unnerving for the general customer.

The lady starting downtown for a day of shopping, for example, could never be sure whether she would find Macy's department store a seething mob of other shoppers or a wilderness of empty, echoing aisles and unoccupied salesgirls. And the uncertainty produced a strange sort of jitteriness in the individual when faced with any impulse to action. "Shall we do it or shan't we?" people kept asking themselves, knowing that if they did do it, it might turn out that thousands of other individuals had decided similarly; knowing, too, that if they *didn't*, they might miss the one glorious chance of all chances to have Jones Beach, say, practically to themselves. Business languished, and a sort of desperate uncertainty rode everyone.

At this juncture, it was inevitable that Congress should be called on for action. In fact, Congress called on itself, and it must be said that it rose nobly to the occasion. A committee was appointed, drawn from both Houses and headed by Senator J. Wing Slooper (R.), of Indiana, and though after considerable investigation the committee was forced reluctantly to conclude that there was no evidence of Communist instigation, the unconscious subversiveness of the people's present conduct was obvious at a glance. The problem was what to do about it. You can't indict a whole nation, particularly on such vague grounds as these were. But, as Senator Slooper boldly pointed out, "You can control it," and in the end a system of re-education and reform was decided upon, designed to lead people back to—again we quote Senator Slooper—"the basic regularities, the homely averageness of the American way of life."

In the course of the committee's investigations, it had been discovered, to everyone's dismay, that the Law of Averages had never been incorporated into the body of federal jurisprudence, and though the upholders of States' Rights rebelled violently, the oversight was at once corrected, both by Constitutional amendment and by a law—the Hills-Slooper Act —implementing it. According to the Act, people were *required* to be average, and, as the simplest way of assuring it, they were divided alphabetically and their permissible activities catalogued accordingly. Thus, by the plan, a person whose name began with "G," "N," or "U," for example, could attend the theatre only on Tuesdays, and he could go to baseball games only on Thursdays, whereas his visits to a haberdashery were confined to the hours between ten o'clock and noon on Mondays.

The law, of course, had its disadvantages. It had a crippling effect on theatre parties, among other social functions, and the cost of enforcing it was unbelievably heavy. In the end, too, so many amendments had to be added to it—such as the one permitting gentlemen to take their fiancées (if accredited) along with them to various events and functions no matter what letter the said fiancées' names began with—that the courts were frequently at a loss to interpret it when confronted with violations.

In its way, though, the law did serve its purpose, for it did induce—rather mechanically, it is true, but still adequately—a return to that average existence that Senator Slooper desired. All, indeed, would have been well if a year or so later disquieting reports had not begun to seep in from the backwoods. It seemed that there, in what had hitherto been considered to be marginal areas, a strange wave of prosperity was making itself felt. Tennessee mountaineers were buying Packard convertibles, and Sears, Roebuck reported that in the Ozarks their sales of luxury items had gone up nine hundred per cent. In the scrub sections of Vermont, men who formerly had barely been able to scratch a living from their rock-strewn acres were now sending their daughters to Europe and ordering expensive cigars from New York. It appeared that the Law of Diminishing Returns was going haywire, too.

UNDERSTANDING THE TEXT

1. Does Coates convey any serious reflection through this indirect means? If so, what is it?

2. Discuss the way in which, after the first sentence hints that something unusual is going to be recounted, the author builds up suspense concerning the exact nature of his surprise. At what point in the essay does it become clear that the disappearance of the Law of Averages is the subject to be developed?

3. What tone has Coates adopted for telling this whimsical fable? Identify the characteristics of the style which help to establish this particular tone, and point to any particularly good examples of the dominant stylistic effect.

4. How effectively does Coates dramatize the aimlessness of the people who thronged across the Triborough Bridge the night the phenomenon was first noted?

5. Comment on the appropriateness of the specific incidents Coates mentions to bring out the continuing course of the mysterious change in people's habits. Which examples seem to you most effective? What is the final stage of the civic disintegration caused by the inability of people to act according to average expectations?

6. Study the manner in which Coates treats the Congressional action to enforce averageness on the population. What contribution does this section make to the total effect of the essay?

7. What is the purpose of the unexpected twist at the end of the fable?

TOPICS FOR DISCUSSION AND WRITING

8. Write a paragraph in which you attempt to set down straightforwardly the points you believe Coates is making by implication in this essay.

9. On the basis of the three illustrative essays presented here, write a definition of the term "indirect argument." How would you differentiate the form from other kinds of writing? What special qualities do successful examples of the type appear to possess? Mention any other indirect arguments with which you are familiar. Consider Barzun's "Myths for Materialists" (pp. 487–495) as another "indirect" argument.

10. Obviously, in writing this kind of essay, it is necessary for the author to develop his ruse with enough subtlety so that the reader's interest in the unfolding of the meaning is aroused and maintained. At one extreme, then, the writer's error would be to tip his hand so completely that the reader feels no sense of discovery. What would be the nature of the writer's error at the other extreme?

My Wood

E. M. FORSTER

A FEW years ago I wrote a book which dealt in part with the difficulties of
the English in India. Feeling that they would have had no difficulties in
India themselves, the Americans read the book freely. The more they read
it the better it made them feel, and a cheque to the author was the result.
I bought a wood with the cheque. It is not a large wood—it contains
scarcely any trees, and it is intersected, blast it, by a public footpath. Still,
it is the first property that I have owned, so it is right that other people
should participate in my shame, and should ask themselves, in accents that
will vary in horror, this very important question: What is the effect of
property upon the character? Don't let's touch economics; the effect of
private ownership upon the community as a whole is another question—a
more important question, perhaps, but another one. Let's keep to psychology. If you own things, what's their effect on you? What's the effect
on me of my wood?

In the first place, it makes me feel heavy. Property does have this effect.
Property produces men of weight, and it was a man of weight who failed to
get into the Kingdom of Heaven. He was not wicked, that unfortunate
millionaire in the parable, he was only stout; he stuck out in front, not to
mention behind, and as he wedged himself this way and that in the crys-
talline entrance and bruised his well-fed flanks, he saw beneath him a
comparatively slim camel passing through the eye of a needle and being
woven into the robe of God. The Gospels all through couple stoutness
and slowness. They point out what is perfectly obvious, yet seldom
realized: that if you have a lot of things you cannot move about a lot, that

furniture requires dusting, dusters require servants, servants require insurance stamps, and the whole tangle of them makes you think twice before you accept an invitation to dinner or go for a bathe in the Jordan. Sometimes the Gospels proceed further and say with Tolstoy that property is sinful; they approach the difficult ground of asceticism here, where I cannot follow them. But as to the immediate effects of property on people, they just show straightforward logic. It produces men of weight. Men of weight cannot, by definition, move like the lightning from the East unto the West, and the ascent of a fourteen-stone bishop into a pulpit is thus the exact antithesis of the coming of the Son of Man. My wood makes me feel heavy.

In the second place, it makes me feel it ought to be larger.

The other day I heard a twig snap in it. I was annoyed at first, for I thought that someone was blackberrying, and depreciating the value of the undergrowth. On coming nearer, I saw it was not a man who had trodden on the twig and snapped it, but a bird, and I felt pleased. My bird. The bird was not equally pleased. Ignoring the relation between us, it took fright as soon as it saw the shape of my face, and flew straight over the boundary hedge into a field, the property of Mrs. Henessy, where it sat down with a loud squawk. It had become Mrs. Henessy's bird. Something seemed grossly amiss here, something that would not have occurred had the wood been larger. I could not afford to buy Mrs. Henessy out, I dared not murder her, and limitations of this sort beset me on every side. Ahab did not want that vineyard—he only needed it to round off his property, preparatory to plotting a new curve—and all the land around my wood has become necessary to me in order to round off the wood. A boundary protects. But—poor little thing—the boundary ought in its turn to be protected. Noises on the edge of it. Children throw stones. A little more, and then a little more, until we reach the sea. Happy Canute! Happier Alexander! And after all, why should even the world be the limit of possession? A rocket containing a Union Jack, will, it is hoped, be shortly fired at the moon. Mars. Sirius. Beyond which . . . But these immensities ended by saddening me. I could not suppose that my wood was the destined nucleus of universal dominion—it is so very small and contains no mineral wealth beyond the blackberries. Nor was I comforted when Mrs. Henessy's bird took alarm for the second time and flew clean away from us all, under the belief that it belonged to itself.

In the third place, property makes its owner feel that he ought to do something to it. Yet he isn't sure what. A restlessness comes over him, a vague sense that he has a personality to express—the same sense which, without any vagueness, leads the artist to an act of creation. Sometimes I think I will cut down such trees as remain in the wood, at other times I want to fill up the gaps between them with new trees. Both impulses are pretentious and empty. They are not honest movements towards money-making or beauty. They spring from a foolish desire to express myself and from an inability to enjoy what I have got. Creation, property, enjoyment form a sinister trinity in the human mind. Creation and enjoyment are both very, very good, yet they are often unattainable without a material basis, and at such moments property pushes itself in as a substitute, saying, "Accept me instead—I'm good enough for all three." It is not enough. It is, as Shakespeare said of lust, "The expense of spirit in a waste of shame": it is "Before, a joy proposed; behind, a dream." Yet we don't know how to shun it. It is forced on us by our economic system as the alternative to starvation. It is also forced on us by an internal defect in the soul, by the feeling that in property may lie the germs of self-development and of exquisite or heroic deeds. Our life on earth is, and ought to be, material and carnal. But we have not yet learned to manage our materialism and carnality properly; they are still entangled with the desire for ownership, where (in the words of Dante) "Possession is one with loss."

And this brings us to our fourth and final point: the blackberries.

Blackberries are not plentiful in this meagre grove, but they are easily seen from the public footpath which traverses it, and all too easily gathered. Foxgloves, too—people will pull up the foxgloves, and ladies of an educational tendency even grub for toadstools to show them on the Monday in class. Other ladies, less educated, roll down the bracken in the arms of their gentlemen friends. There is paper, there are tins. Pray, does my wood belong to me or doesn't it? And, if it does, should I not own it best by allowing no one else to walk there? There is a wood near Lyme Regis, also cursed by a public footpath, where the owner has not hesitated on this point. He has built high stone walls each side of the path, and has spanned it by bridges, so that the public circulate like termites while he gorges on the blackberries unseen. He really does own his wood, this able chap. Dives in Hell did pretty well, but the gulf dividing him from Lazarus could be traversed by vision, and nothing traverses it here. And perhaps I shall come to this in time. I shall wall in and fence out until I really taste the sweets of property. Enormously stout, endlessly avaricious, pseudo-creative, intensely selfish, I shall weave upon my forehead the quadruple crown of possession until those nasty Bolshies come and take it off again and thrust me aside into the outer darkness.

UNDERSTANDING THE TEXT

1. Although Forster writes mainly about his own experience, about the effect of the wood on him, it seems clear that he wants us to see the larger implications of his experience. Show how he brings about this indirect result.

2. Restate in general terms the four effects that Forster's wood had on him. Begin your statement "Property has four main effects upon the character of the owner. . . ."

3. Do Forster's opening sentences—that he bought his wood with the proceeds from American sales of his book on the difficulties of the English in India—have any relevance to the discussion, apart from providing a sort of narrative introduction?

4. Why is it "right" (paragraph 1) that other people should participate in Forster's shame? What is his shame?

5. What effect does Forster create by joining in one sentence (in paragraph 2) accepting an invitation to dinner and going for a bathe in the Jordan? Locate other examples of similar couplings of apparently incongruous elements. Define their contribution to the tone of the essay.

6. Explain the references to Canute and Alexander in paragraph 4.

7. What is Forster implying when he says that the bird "flew clean away from us all, under the belief that it belonged to itself"? Point to earlier references to the bird that prepare for this sentence.

8. Forster says that the passage from Dante, "Possession is one with loss," brings us to his fourth point, about the blackberries. Explain the reasoning by which it brings us to this point.

9. Show how the words "enormously stout, endlessly avaricious, pseudo-creative, intensely selfish" summarize Forster's experience.

TOPICS FOR DISCUSSION AND WRITING

10. Write a paragraph defining the basic attitude toward property that underlies Forster's essay. Do not overlook the sentence "Our life on earth is, and ought to be, material and carnal."

11. When Forster talks in paragraph 2 about how the wood makes him feel heavy, how property produces "men of weight," he can scarcely expect us to believe that owning a wood is likely to make a man fat. And in any case he has told us that he is going to describe the effects of ownership on character, not on body size. What condition of character is Forster pointing to when he talks about heaviness and weight?

12. Using the implications of the essay, write a paragraph characterizing the person who might ask Forster's question (paragraph 1) in an accent entirely lacking in horror.

13. Write a comparison between Forster and Coates, or Forster and Swift, with respect to their management of indirect argument.

A Modest Proposal

for Preventing the Children of Ireland from Being a Burden to Their Parents or Country

JONATHAN SWIFT

IT IS a melancholy object to those who walk through this great town or travel in the country, when they see the streets, the roads, and cabin-doors crowded with beggars of the female sex, followed by three, four, or six children, all in rags, and importuning every passenger for an alms. These mothers instead of being able to work for their honest livelihood, are forced to employ all their time in strolling to beg sustenance for their helpless infants, who, as they grow up, either turn thieves for want of work, or leave their dear native country, to fight for the Pretender in Spain, or sell themselves to the Barbadoes.

I think it is agreed by all parties, that this prodigious number of children in the arms, or on the backs, or at the heels of their mothers, and frequently of their fathers, is in the present deplorable state of the kingdom a very great additional grievance; and therefore whoever could find out a fair, cheap, and easy method of making these children sound and useful members of the common-wealth, would deserve so well of the public as to have his statue set up for a preserver of the nation.

But my intention is very far from being confined to provide only for the children of professed beggars; it is of a much greater extent, and shall take in the whole number of infants at a certain age, who are born of parents in effect as little able to support them, as those who demand our charity in the streets.

As to my own part, having turned my thoughts, for many years, upon this important subject, and maturely weighed the several schemes of other projectors, I have always found them grossly mistaken in their computation. It is true, a child just dropt from its dam, may be supported by her milk for a solar year with little other nourishment, at most not above the value of two shillings, which the mother may certainly get, or the value in scraps, by her lawful occupation of begging; and it is exactly at one year old that I propose to provide for them in such a manner, as, instead of being a charge upon their parents, or the parish, or wanting food and raiment for the rest of their lives, they shall, on the contrary, contribute to the feeding and partly to the clothing of many thousands.

There is likewise another great advantage in my scheme, that it will prevent those voluntary abortions, and that horrid practice of women murdering their bastard children, alas! too frequent among us—sacrificing the poor innocent babes, I doubt, more to avoid the expense than the shame —which would move tears and pity in the most savage and inhuman breast.

The number of souls in this kingdom being usually reckoned one million and a half, of these I calculate there may be about two hundred thousand couples whose wives are breeders; from which number I subtract thirty thousand couples, who are able to maintain their own children, although I apprehend there cannot be so many, under the present distresses of the kingdom; but this being granted, there will remain an hundred and seventy thousand breeders. I again subtract fifty thousand, for those women who miscarry, or whose children die by accident or disease within the year. There only remain an hundred and twenty thousand children of poor parents annually born: The question therefore is, How this number shall be reared, and provided for? which, as I have already said, under the present situation of affairs, is utterly impossible by all the methods hitherto proposed; for we can neither employ them in handicraft or agriculture; we neither build houses, (I mean in the country) nor cultivate land: They can very seldom pick up a livelihood by stealing till they arrive at six years old, except where they are of towardly parts, although, I confess, they learn the rudiments much earlier; during which time they can however be properly looked upon only as probationers; as I have been informed by a principal gentleman in the county of Cavan, who protested to me, that he never knew above one or two instances under the age of six, even in a part of the kingdom so renowned for the quickest proficiency in that art.

I am assured by our merchants, that a boy or a girl before twelve years old, is no saleable commodity, and even when they come to this age, they will not yield above three pounds, or three pounds and half a crown at most, on the exchange; which cannot turn to account either to the parents or kingdom, the charge of nutriment and rags having been at least four times that value.

I shall now therefore humbly propose my own thoughts, which I hope will not be liable to the least objection.

I have been assured by a very knowing American of my acquaintance in London, that a young healthy child well nursed is at a year old a most delicious nourishing and wholesome food, whether stewed, roasted, baked, or boiled; and I make no doubt that it will equally serve in a fricassee, or a ragout.

I do therefore humbly offer it to publick consideration, that of the hundred and twenty thousand children, already computed, twenty thousand may be reserved for breed, whereof only one fourth part to be males; which is more than we allow to sheep, black cattle, or swine; and my reason is that these children are seldom the fruits of marriage, a circumstance not much regarded by our savages; therefore one male will be sufficient to serve four females. That the remaining hundred thousand may, at a year old, be offered in the sale to the persons of quality and fortune through the kingdom; always advising the mother to let them suck plentifully in the last month, so as to render them plump and fat for a good table. A child will make two dishes at an entertainment for friends; and when the family dines alone, the fore or hind quarter will make a reasonable dish, and seasoned with a little pepper or salt will be very good boiled on the fourth day, especially in winter.

I have reckoned upon a medium that a child just born will weigh 12 pounds, and in a solar year, if tolerably nursed, increaseth to 28 pounds.

I grant this food will be somewhat dear, and therefore very proper for landlords, who, as they have already devoured most of the parents, seem to have the best title to the children.

Infants' flesh will be in season throughout the year, but more plentiful in March, and a little before and after; for we are told by a grave author, an eminent French physician, that fish being a prolific diet, there are more children born in Roman Catholic countries about nine months after Lent than at any other season; therefore, reckoning a year after Lent, the markets will be more glutted than usual, because the number of popish infants is at least three to one in this kingdom: and therefore it will have one other collateral advantage, by lessening the number of papists among us.

I have already computed the charge of nursing a beggar's child (in which list I reckon all cottagers, laborers, and four-fifths of the farmers) to be about two shillings per annum, rags included; and I believe no gentleman would repine to give ten shillings for the carcass of a good fat child, which, as I have said, will make four dishes of excellent nutritive meat, when he hath only some particular friend or his own family to dine with him. Thus the squire will learn to be a good landlord, and grow popular among his tenants; the mother will have eight shillings net profit, and be fit for work till she produces another child.

Those who are more thrifty (as I must confess the times require) may flay the carcass, the skin of which artificially dressed will make admirable gloves for ladies, and summer boots for fine gentlemen.

As to our city of Dublin, shambles may be appointed for this purpose in the most convenient parts of it, and butchers we may be assured will not be wanting; although I rather recommend buying the children alive and dressing them hot from the knife, as we do roasting pigs.

A very worthy person, a true lover of his country, and whose virtues I highly esteem, was lately pleased in discoursing on this matter to offer a refinement upon my scheme. He said that many gentlemen of this kingdom, having of late destroyed their deer, he conceived that the want of venison might be well supplied by the bodies of young lads and maidens, not exceeding fourteen years of age nor under twelve; so great a number of both sexes in every country being now ready to starve for want of work and service; and these to be disposed of by their parents if alive, or otherwise by their nearest relations. But with due deference to so excellent a friend, and so deserving a patriot, I cannot be altogether in his sentiments; for as to the males, my American acquaintance assured me from frequent experience, that their flesh was generally tough and lean, like that of our schoolboys, by continual exercise, and their taste disagreeable, and to fatten them would not answer the charge. Then as to the females, it would, I think with humble submission, be a loss to the publick, because they soon would become breeders themselves: And besides it is not improbable that some scrupulous people might be apt to censure such a practice (although indeed very unjustly) as a little bordering upon cruelty, which, I confess, hath always been with me the strongest objection against any project, how well soever intended.

But in order to justify my friend, he confessed, that this expedient was put into his head by the famous Psalmanazar, a native of the island Formosa, who came from thence to London, above twenty years ago, and in conversation told my friend, that in his country when any young person happened to be put to death, the executioner sold the carcass to persons of quality, as a prime dainty, and that, in his time, the body of a plump girl of fifteen, who was crucified for an attempt to poison the Emperor, was sold to his Imperial Majesty's prime minister of state, and other great mandarins of the court, in joints from the gibbet, at four hundred crowns. Neither indeed can I deny, that if the same use were made of several plump young girls in this town, who, without one single groat to their fortunes, cannot stir abroad without a chair, and appear at a play-house and assemblies in foreign fineries which they never will pay for, the kingdom would not be the worse.

Some persons of a desponding spirit are in great concern about that vast number of poor people, who are aged, diseased, or maimed, and I have been desired to employ my thoughts what course may be taken, to ease the nation of so grievous an encumbrance. But I am not in the least pain upon that matter, because it is very well known, that they are every day dying, and rotting, by cold, and famine, and filth, and vermin, as fast as can be reasonably expected. And as to the younger laborers, they are now in almost as hopeful a condition. They cannot get work, and consequently pine away for want of nourishment, to a degree, that if at any time they are accidentally hired to common labour, they have not strength to perform it, and thus the country and themselves are happily delivered from the evils to come.

I have too long digressed, and therefore shall return to my subject. I think the advantages by the proposal which I have made are obvious and many, as well as of the highest importance.

For *first*, as I have already observed, it would greatly lessen the number of papists, with whom we are yearly over-run, being the principal breeders of the nation, as well as our most dangerous enemies, and who stay at home on purpose with a design to deliver the kingdom to the Pretender, hoping to take their advantage by the absence of so many good Protestants, who have chosen rather to leave their country, than stay at home, and pay tithes against their conscience to an Episcopal curate.

Secondly, the poorer tenants will have something valuable of their own, which by law may be made liable to distress and help to pay their landlord's rent, their corn and cattle being already seized, and money a thing unknown.

Thirdly, whereas the maintenance of an hundred thousand children, from two years old and upward, cannot be computed at less than ten shillings apiece per annum, the nation's stock will be thereby increased fifty thousand pounds per annum, besides the profit of a new dish introduced to the tables of all gentlemen of fortune in the kingdom who have any refinement in taste. And the money will circulate among ourselves, the goods being entirely of our own growth and manufacture.

Fourthly, the constant breeders, beside the gain of eight shillings sterling per annum by the sale of their children, will be rid of the charge of maintaining them after the first year.

Fifthly, this food would likewise bring great custom to taverns, where the vintners will certainly be so prudent as to procure the best receipts for dressing it to perfection, and consequently have their houses frequented by all the fine gentlemen who justly value themselves upon their knowledge in good eating; and a skillful cook, who understands how to oblige his guests, will contrive to make it as expensive as they please.

Sixthly, this would be a great inducement to marriage, which all wise nations have either encouraged by rewards or enforced by laws and penalties. It would increase the care and the tenderness of mothers toward their children, when they were sure of a settlement for life to the poor babes, provided in some sort by the public, to their annual profit instead of expense. We should soon see an honest emulation among the married women, which of them could bring the fattest child to the market. Men would become as fond of their wives during the time of their pregnancy as they are now of their mares in foal, their cows in calf, their sows when they are ready to farrow; nor offer to beat or kick them (as is too frequent a practice) for fear of a miscarriage.

Many other advantages might be enumerated. For instance, the addition of some thousand carcasses in our exportation of barreled beef, the propagation of swine's flesh, and improvement in the art of making good bacon, so much wanted among us by the great destruction of pigs, too frequent at our tables; which are no way comparable in taste or magnificence to a well-grown, fat, yearling child, which roasted whole will make a considerable figure at a lord mayor's feast or any other public entertainment. But this and many others I omit, being studious of brevity.

Supposing that one thousand families in this city would be constant customers for infants' flesh, besides others who might have it at merry meetings, particularly at weddings and christenings, I compute that Dublin would take off annually about twenty thousand carcasses; and the rest of the kingdom (where probably they will be sold somewhat cheaper) the remaining eighty thousand.

I can think of no one objection that will possibly be raised against this proposal, unless it should be urged that the number of people will be thereby much lessened in the kingdom. This I freely own, and 'twas indeed one principal design in offering it to the world. I desire the reader will observe that I calculate my remedy for this one individual kingdom of Ireland, and for no other that ever was, is, or, I think, ever can be upon earth. Therefore let no man talk to me of other expedients: of taxing our absentees at five shillings a pound: of using neither clothes, nor household furniture, except what is of our own growth and manufacture: of utterly rejecting the materials and instruments that promote foreign luxury: of curing the expensiveness of pride, vanity, idleness, and gaming in our women: of introducing a vein of parsimony, prudence and temperance: of learning to love our country, wherein we differ even from Laplanders, and the inhabitants of Topinamboo: of quitting our animosities, and factions, nor act any longer like the Jews, who were murdering one another at the very moment their city was taken: of being a little cautious not to sell our country and consciences for nothing: of teaching landlords to have at least one degree of mercy towards their tenants. Lastly, of putting a spirit of honesty, industry, and skill into our shop-keepers, who, if a resolution could now be taken to buy only our native goods, would immediately unite to cheat and exact upon us in the price, the measure, and the goodness, nor could ever yet be brought to make one fair proposal of just dealing, though often and earnestly invited to it.

Therefore I repeat, let no man talk to me of these and the like expedients, till he hath at least some glimpse of hope, that there will ever be some hearty and sincere attempt to put them in practice.

But as to my self, having been wearied out for many years with offering vain, idle, visionary thoughts, and at length utterly despairing of success, I fortunately fell upon this proposal, which as it is wholly new, so it hath something solid and real, of no expense and little trouble, full in our own power, and whereby we can incur no danger in disobliging England. For this kind of commodity will not bear exportation, the flesh being of too tender a consistence, to admit a long continuance in salt, although perhaps I could name a country, which would be glad to eat up our whole nation without it.

After all, I am not so violently bent upon my own opinion, as to reject any offer, proposed by wise men, which shall be found equally innocent, cheap, easy, and effectual. But before something of that kind shall be advanced in contradiction to my scheme, and offering a better, I desire the author or authors, will be pleased maturely to consider two points. *First*, as things now stand, how they will be able to find food and raiment for a hundred thousand useless mouths and backs. And *Secondly*, there being a round million of creatures in human figure throughout this kingdom, whose whole subsistence put into a common stock would leave them in debt two millions of pounds sterling, adding those who are beggars by profession, to the bulk of farmers, cottagers and labourers, with their wives and children, who are beggars in effect; I desire those politicians, who dislike my overture, and may perhaps be so bold to attempt an answer, that they will first ask the parents of these mortals, whether they would not at this day think it a great happiness to have been sold for food at a year old, in the manner I prescribe, and thereby have avoided such a perpetual scene of misfortunes as they have since gone through, by the oppression of land-lords, the impossibility of paying rent without money or trade, the want of common sustenance, with neither house nor clothes to cover them from the inclemencies of the weather, and the most inevitable prospect of en-tailing the like or greater miseries upon their breed for ever.

I profess, in the sincerity of my heart, that I have not the least personal interest in endeavoring to promote this necessary work, having no other motive than the public good of my country, by advancing our trade, pro-viding for infants, relieving the poor, and giving some pleasure to the rich. I have no children by which I can propose to get a single penny; the youngest being nine years old, and my wife past child-bearing.

UNDERSTANDING THE TEXT

1. In what character does the speaker present himself? Make clear in detail how Swift's handling of his material permits the speaker's character to emerge. What is the speaker's nationality?

2. To what audience does the speaker seem to be addressing his proposal? To what audience do you think Swift's real argument is addressed?

3. Why does the speaker enlarge on the advantages of his scheme before he explains what his scheme is? Here, as in almost every other question about the content and method of this essay, you will probably find it necessary to give two different answers, one from the point of view of the strategy of the speaker and one from the point of view of Swift's actual aims.

4. What previous proposals for dealing with the children of the poor does the speaker refer to? Do you suppose these were actually proposed? If not, to what aspects of the actual Irish situation do you think they correspond?

5. Make a list of the distinct methods Swift uses to increase the monstrousness of his modest proposal.

6. What is the value of such expressions as "a child just dropt from its dam," "breeders," "creatures in human figure"? Can you find other examples of this sort of linguistic tactic?

7. Discuss the value of the complete title in relation to Swift's purpose.

8. What methods of dealing with Irish poverty does Swift really favor? How are these made clear? How are they protected from the general irony of the essay?

9. Is there any way of determining where Swift puts the blame for conditions in Ireland? Is anything besides the attitude and actions of the English responsible for these conditions? What is the evidence for your answer?

10. The speaker makes a good deal of the "logic" of his proposal. Clearly, in a grim way, Swift thinks there is logic in it too. The speaker's proposal is logical if we grant a fundamental premise about the treatment of the Irish. What is that premise?

11. Swift of course counts on the fact that his audience will recoil in horror from the speaker's proposal, and that they will reject the fundamental premise on which the proposal rests. Obviously, if he could not count on this—if the English were really willing to accept the implied premise—Swift's irony would be pointless. What underlying trait of the English character does Swift take for granted when he counts on their rejection of the speaker's basic premise?

TOPICS FOR DISCUSSION AND WRITING

12. Discuss the paragraph beginning "I can think of no one objection . . ." (p. 229), and the paragraph following. What purpose do these paragraphs serve? Are they "in character"? Do they fully preserve the ironic tone?

13. This essay is usually regarded as one of the great masterpieces of irony in English. How does irony differ from sarcasm? One of the essential properties of irony is usually said to be a perceptible difference between the surface meaning of a statement and what is really intended. What problems does this essential condition create for the ironist? Under what circumstances do you think irony would have its greatest force? What conditions might make it fail altogether?

14. It is clearly essential to the success of Swift's essay that the speaker's "proposal" should seem monstrous and inhuman; Swift is careful to underline its monstrousness. Would it have been possible for him to have gone too far in this direction? Try to think of some of the ways in which he might have carried this line of development too far, as a means of defining the tact with which Swift has done his work.

15. Try a "modest proposal" of your own on some subject with which you are familiar. Be careful to adopt the right character for your purpose and to keep your irony consistent.

16. What does Swift's method in "A Modest Proposal" have in common with Coates's "The Law" and Barzun's "Myths for Materialists"?

4. Language: The Writer's Resources and Responsibilities

GEORGE ORWELL, Politics and the English Language
JAMES THURBER, The Psychosemanticist Will See You Now,
    Mr. Thurber
DWIGHT MACDONALD, The Bible in Modern Undress
THEODORE BAIRD, Darwin and the Tangled Bank

THE ASPECTS of writing discussed and illustrated in the preceding sections raise questions which the writer handles mainly in terms of ideas, observations, schemes of organization. They are aspects of writing that lie largely in the domain of *thought*. This is not to say that they do not involve words: a great share of our thinking, perhaps all of our thinking, about subjects, approaches, and procedures is done in words. But language is not the first object of our attention when we deal with these problems. Now, however, we turn to the problem of *language* itself, to the writer's big question, "How shall I put it?"

This is a good place to pause and note once more what was said earlier about the relations between the different parts of the writing process. They have been separated here for emphasis and illustration. But they are not really separate. They are mutually interacting parts of a complex whole. Nevertheless, all the other parts of the writing process are in a sense subordinate to the use of language. The meaning a writer wants to communicate cannot exist apart from the verbal expression he gives it. The writer's meaning *is* his language, and his language *is* his meaning. A piece of writing succeeds when the expression sets up in the reader precisely that sequence of feelings, ideas, and impressions which the writer intends to convey. The writing, therefore, is the pay-off.

From what has just been said it follows that there is always, at least hypothetically, a best form of words for what the writer is trying to say: a mode of statement that uniquely fits his meaning. Few of us regularly achieve this ideal in our own writing. But we meet it often enough to give it substance. We know it in the work of the greatest writers—in Shakespeare, for example:

> Tomorrow and tomorrow and tomorrow
> Creeps in this petty pace from day to day,
> To the last syllable of recorded time;
> And all our yesterdays have lighted fools
> The way to dusty death.

This, we feel, is not merely the best way to say what Macbeth is saying. It is the only way to say it. So intimate is the congruence of language and meaning here that some nuance of meaning would be destroyed or altered with any change, however slight, in the language.

This is the ideal. Most of us, most of the time, will inevitably fall below it, forced to content ourselves with an approximation to that absolute coincidence of form and meaning. The wider the gap between our thought and our expression, the further we and our readers will be from knowing precisely what we intend to say, and the more frequently we and our readers will be trapped by vague, weak, or ill-sorted language into supposing we mean something that we don't intend at all. So we will follow the lead of all good writers and *revise* what we have written. We will ask, "Does this really say what I want to say?" "Can I get it clearer?" "Will the reader, with nothing but these words to guide him, surely see what I want him to see?" As a Supplement to this book, we have included a section on revision, where you can see several writers in the act of asking just such questions about their work, trying to get the closest possible fit between their meaning and their expression.

Whatever his subject, the writer needs two sorts of equipment in order to answer the question "How shall I put it?" He has to have an adequate command of the resources of language, and he has to have a sense of his responsibilities in using these resources.

Viewing the problem in purely operational terms, language is to the writer what tools are to the cabinetmaker. Depending on how many he has, how many different purposes they are adapted to, and how skillfully he can handle them, his range will be broad or narrow, his work well suited or ill suited to its intended use, and his products sturdy or shaky. The act of writing is the act of putting down words in a certain order. If we put *these* words down in *this* order we reject, whether consciously or not, *those other* words and *those other* orders. A sentence is a commitment. And the question is, what have I committed myself to? In order to examine his commitment and, if it fails to meet his view of the matter, to alter it before it is too late, the writer must have alternative ways of stating his meaning. He may feel vaguely discontented with the way he has said something, but he can't really do anything about it unless he has a set of substitute forms of expression which he can try until he finds just the right ones. He has to know what *those other* words and *those other* orders are, because they may be just the ones he finally wants. He has to have, in short, an adequate command of the resources of language. The primary resources with which most of us are likely to be concerned are *diction, figurative expression*, and the *structure and rhythm of sentences*. Or, to put the matter another way, we have to make decisions about the *meanings* of our words, about the *application of meanings*, literal and direct or figurative and transferred, and about the *disposition* or *arrangement* of words into larger units of meaning—phrases, clauses, sentences.

The question of *diction* is essentially the question of the right choice of words. The writer's vocabulary must be large enough to afford him a range of choices. For this reason, the questions in this book frequently ask you to use the dictionary on words that may be unfamiliar to you. The writer must not only *know* a tolerably large number of words, he must know them *accurately*, in their various shades of meaning, in their connotations as well as their denotations, for words are seldom fully synonymous, and choice must be guided by the cluster of associated meanings that the history of almost every word has given it. The writer's choice from the stock in his word-hoard will be controlled by two other criteria —*language level* and *consistency of diction*. He has to be aware of the differences between the general vocabulary and the restricted vocabularies of trades, professions, sections, and other restricted groups. He must be sensitive to the associations which much of our language has with the conditions of its use—the level of slang or vulgar speech, the level of informal or conversational speech and writing, and the level of more formal and deliberate utterance. He will select his language so as to fit its conventional status to the use he has in mind, avoiding the treatment of trivial topics in grave language or weighty subjects in slang. And the writer will be careful, in view of the influence which these conventional associations have on the way we respond to words, to keep his language pitched at a consistent level—consistent with itself, with the role he has adopted, and with the occasion on which he is writing, avoiding shifts from one level to another, unless he mixes levels for humorous or satiric effect.

Figurative expression is the application of words to ideas or things outside the normal range of their meanings. When Thurber says that the psychosemanticist will treat "the havoc wrought by verbal artillery upon the fortress of reason," when Orwell talks about stereotyped phrases "tacked together like the sections of a prefabricated hen-house," they are using figures of speech which bring the meanings and associations of one set of terms to bear on subjects to which they are not usually applied. They are extending the meanings of the words they use figuratively, pulling them out of restricted contexts and stretching them around new objects. More important, they are creating *new* meanings and revealing aspects of their subjects that we would be unaware of, or less vividly aware of, if they had stuck to literal statements. The invention of apt figures of speech requires a certain quality of mind that not everyone possesses—not even all good prose writers. It is probably better to stick to plain statement than to risk spoiling our prose with poor figures. But figurative language offers rich possibilities. It can illustrate and vivify; it can help make unfamiliar subjects intelligible; it can express meanings for which there are no alternative literal formulations. Figurative language can contribute to writing of all sorts, technical as well as familiar, as Theodore Baird makes clear in his discussion of the metaphors at the heart of Darwin's *Origin of Species*. Wherever it is used, figurative language—whether it be a single word or a continuous metaphor or simile working through several sentences or even a whole composition—ought to meet certain standards. It ought to be *fresh*: a cliché, a standard metaphor—one of the sections of Orwell's prefabricated henhouse—battered from repeated use, will not serve to build a new meaning. It ought to be *appropriate*, which is another way of saying that it ought to fit not only the subject but the occasion, the attitude we intend to convey, and the readers we envisage. And it ought to be *consistent*: metaphors ought not to be mixed, and a figure of speech, if it is extended, ought to be developed in the terms originally established.

Choice of effective diction and skillful use of figurative language are two ingredients of good writing. A third is *structure and rhythm*, the arrangement or combination of words into larger units of meaning. It was said of the American philosopher William James that he wrote philosophy like a novelist, and of his brother, the novelist Henry James, that he wrote novels like a philosopher. The one wrote in predominantly short, direct, relatively simple sentences, using plain diction; the other's sentences were long, complicated, full of qualifying elements and suspended constructions, using a much more elaborate vocabulary. As this judgment implies, we regularly associate certain sorts of sentences and certain sorts of rhythms with certain sorts of speakers, subjects, and occasions. When we read Wylie's "Science Has Spoiled My Supper," for example, we hear in his colloquial phraseology, his abrupt transitions, his short, simple sentences, his rhetorical questions, and his pell-mell forward rush the individualized speaking voice of a man getting something off his chest. When we read the full, complex sentences of Gibbon or Macaulay, with their elaborate systems of dependent constructions, their stately rhythms, and their formal diction, we have a sense not only of the utmost deliberation on subjects of great import but of voices impersonal and calm, rendering measured judgment from positions of authority. The writer has his choice of a rich variety of sentence patterns and rhythmic sequences, offering endless gradations in stress, subordination, and coherence, and adaptable to many different subjects, moods, tones, and characters. The essays in this section and in the remainder of the book should help you familiarize yourself with some of these; the questions, by asking you to consider the contribution which the writer's habits of sentence arrangement make to his meaning, should help you to develop good habits of your own.

Effective use of language depends, then, on a command of the resources of statement adequate to the range of choices the writer needs to make. But the writer also needs equipment of a different sort if he is to use language well. Writing, as E. B. White says, is an "act of faith, not a trick of grammar." Technique and verbal resources are indispensable, but writing cannot be mechanized. It is a mode of action, and as with all action, its quality is ultimately determined by the attitude from which it springs. Quite simply, the writer must feel his responsibilities: responsibility to his reader, to protect the trust on which all communication depends; responsibility to himself, to make what he says declare his mind; responsibility to his subject, to deliver it whole and unmarred; responsibility to the language, to keep our most precious cultural possession clean and ready for use. Several of the essayists in this section are concerned about the relation between writing and the character of the writer, between language habits and habits of thought. In their different ways, they make it clear that insensitivity to language is a sign of more radical insensitivity, and that the degradation of words accompanies and may even cause degradation of thought and feeling. A sentence, as we said earlier, is a commitment. It is an act of choice. It reveals, for good or ill, and for all to see, a mind in operation. The writer's use of language will finally depend on the depth of his commitment and his awareness of responsibility. Style, as the philosopher Whitehead says, is "the ultimate morality of mind."

Politics and the English Language

GEORGE ORWELL

MOST people who bother with the matter at all would admit that the English language is in a bad way, but it is generally assumed that we cannot by conscious action do anything about it. Our civilization is decadent, and our language—so the argument runs—must inevitably share in the general collapse. It follows that any struggle against the abuse of language is a sentimental archaism, like preferring candles to electric light or hansom cabs to aeroplanes. Underneath this lies the half-conscious belief that language is a natural growth and not an instrument which we shape for our own purposes.

Now, it is clear that the decline of a language must ultimately have political and economic causes: it is not due simply to the bad influence of this or that individual writer. But an effect can become a cause, reinforcing the original cause and producing the same effect in an intensified form, and so on indefinitely. A man may take to drink because he feels himself to be a failure, and then fail all the more completely because he drinks. It is rather the same thing that is happening to the English language. It becomes ugly and inaccurate because our thoughts are foolish, but the slovenliness of our language makes it easier for us to have foolish thoughts. The point is that the process is reversible. Modern English, especially written English, is full of bad habits which spread by imitation and which can be avoided if one is willing to take the necessary trouble. If one gets rid of these habits one can think more clearly, and to think clearly is a necessary first step towards political regeneration: so that the fight against bad English is not frivolous and is not the exclusive concern of professional writers. I will come back to this presently, and I hope that by that time the meaning of what I have said here will have become clearer. Meanwhile, here are five specimens of the English language as it is now habitually written.

These five passages have not been picked out because they are especially bad—I could have quoted far worse if I had chosen—but because they illustrate various of the mental vices from which we now suffer. They are a little below the average, but are fairly representative samples. I number them so that I can refer back to them when necessary:

(1) I am not, indeed, sure whether it is not true to say that the Milton who once seemed not unlike a seventeenth-century Shelley had not become, out of an experience ever more bitter in each year, more alien [*sic*] to the founder of that Jesuit sect which nothing could induce him to tolerate.

Professor Harold Laski (Essay in *Freedom of Expression*).

(2) Above all, we cannot play ducks and drakes with a native battery of idioms which prescribes such egregious collocations of vocables as the Basic *put up with* for *tolerate* or *put at a loss* for *bewilder*.

Professor Lancelot Hogben (*Interglossa*).

(3) On the one side we have the free personality: by definition it is not neurotic, for it has neither conflict nor dream. Its desires, such as they are, are transparent, for they are just what institutional approval keeps in the forefront of consciousness; another institutional pattern would alter their number and intensity; there is little in them that is natural, irreducible, or culturally dangerous. But *on the other side,* the social bond itself is nothing but the mutual reflection of these self-secure integrities. Recall the definition of love. Is not this the very picture of a small academic? Where is there a place in this hall of mirrors for either personality or fraternity?

Essay on psychology in *Politics* (New York).

(4) All the "best people" from the gentlemen's clubs, and all the frantic fascist captains, united in common hatred of Socialism and bestial horror of the rising tide of the mass revolutionary movement, have turned to acts of provocation, to foul incendiarism, to medieval legends of poisoned wells, to legalize their own destruction of proletarian organizations, and rouse the agitated petty-bourgeoisie to chauvinistic fervour on behalf of the fight against the revolutionary way out of the crisis.

Communist pamphlet.

(5) If a new spirit *is* to be infused into this old country, there is one thorny and contentious reform which must be tackled, and that is the humanization and galvanization of the B.B.C. Timidity here will bespeak canker and atrophy of the soul. The heart of Britain may be sound and of strong beat, for instance, but the British lion's roar at present is like that of Bottom in Shakespeare's *Mid-*

summer Night's Dream—as gentle as any sucking dove. A virile new Britain cannot continue indefinitely to be traduced in the eyes, or rather ears, of the world by the effete languors of Langham Place, brazenly masquerading as "standard English." When the Voice of Britain is heard at nine o'clock, better far and infinitely less ludicrous to hear aitches honestly dropped than the present priggish, inflated, inhibited, school-ma'amish arch braying of blameless bashful mewing maidens!

Letter in Tribune.

Each of these passages has faults of its own, but, quite apart from avoidable ugliness, two qualities are common to all of them. The first is staleness of imagery: the other is lack of precision. The writer either has a meaning and cannot express it, or he inadvertently says something else, or he is almost indifferent as to whether his words mean anything or not. This mixture of vagueness and sheer incompetence is the most marked characteristic of modern English prose, and especially of any kind of political writing. As soon as certain topics are raised, the concrete melts into the abstract and no one seems able to think of turns of speech that are not hackneyed: prose consists less and less of *words* chosen for the sake of their meaning, and more and more of *phrases* tacked together like the sections of a prefabricated hen-house. I list below, with notes and examples, various of the tricks by means of which the work of prose-construction is habitually dodged:

Dying metaphors. A newly-invented metaphor assists thought by evoking a visual image, while on the other hand a metaphor which is technically "dead" (e.g., *iron resolution*) has in effect reverted to being an ordinary word and can generally be used without loss of vividness. But in between these two classes there is a huge dump of worn-out metaphors which have lost all evocative power and are merely used because they save people the trouble of inventing phrases for themselves. Examples are: *Ring the changes on, take up the cudgels for, toe the line, ride roughshod over, stand shoulder to shoulder with, play into the hands of, no axe to grind, grist to the mill, fishing in troubled waters, on the order of the day, Achilles' heel, swan song, hotbed*. Many of these are used without knowledge of their meaning (what is a "rift," for instance?), and incompatible metaphors are frequently mixed, a sure sign that the writer is not interested in what he is saying. Some metaphors now current have been twisted out of their original meaning without those who use them even being aware of the fact. For example, *toe the line* is sometimes written *tow the line*. Another example is *the hammer and the anvil*, now always used with the implication that the anvil gets the worst of it. In real life it is always the anvil that breaks the hammer, never the other way about: a writer who stopped to think what he was saying would be aware of this, and would avoid perverting the original phrase.

Operators, or *verbal false limbs.* These save the trouble of picking out appropriate verbs and nouns, and at the same time pad each sentence with extra syllables which give it an appearance of symmetry. Characteristic phrases are: *render inoperative, militate against, make contact with, be subjected to, give rise to, give grounds for, have the effect of, play a leading part (role) in, make itself felt, take effect, exhibit a tendency to, serve the purpose of, etc., etc.* The keynote is the elimination of simple verbs. Instead of being a single word, such as *break, stop, spoil, mend, kill,* a verb becomes a *phrase,* made up of a noun or adjective tacked on to some general-purposes verb such as *prove, serve, form, play, render.* In addition, the passive voice is wherever possible used in preference to the active, and noun constructions are used instead of gerunds (*by examination of* instead of *by examining*). The range of verbs is further cut down by means of the *-ize* and *de-* formations, and banal statements are given an appearance of profundity by means of the *not un-* formation. Simple conjunctions and prepositions are replaced by such phrases as *with respect to, having regard to, the fact that, by dint of, in view of, in the interests of, on the hypothesis that;* and the ends of sentences are saved from anticlimax by such resounding commonplaces as *greatly to be desired, cannot be left out of account, a development to be expected in the near future, deserving of serious consideration, brought to a satisfactory conclusion,* and so on and so forth.

Pretentious diction. Words like *phenomenon, element, individual* (as noun), *objective, categorical, effective, virtual, basic, primary, promote, constitute, exhibit, exploit, utilize, eliminate, liquidate,* are used to dress up simple statements and give an air of scientific impartiality to biased judgments. Adjectives like *epoch-making, epic, historic, unforgettable, triumphant, age-old, inevitable, inexorable, veritable,* are used to dignify the sordid processes of international politics, while writing that aims at glorifying war usually takes on an archaic colour, its characteristic words being: *realm, throne, chariot, mailed fist, trident, sword, shield, buckler, banner, jackboot, clarion.* Foreign words and expressions such as *cul de sac, ancien régime, deus ex machina, mutatis mutandis, status quo, gleichschaltung, weltanschauung,* are used to give an air of culture and elegance. Except for the useful abbreviations *i.e., e.g.,* and *etc.,* there is no real need for any of the hundreds of foreign phrases now current in English. Bad writers, and especially scientific, political and sociological writers, are nearly always haunted by the notion that Latin or Greek words are grander than Saxon ones, and unnecessary words like *expedite, ameliorate, predict, extraneous, deracinated, clandestine, subaqueous* and hundreds of others constantly gain ground from their Anglo-Saxon opposite numbers.[1] The jargon peculiar to Marxist writing (*hyena, hangman, cannibal, petty bourgeois, these gentry, lacquey, flunkey, mad dog, White Guard,* etc.) consists largely of words and phrases translated from Russian, German or French; but the normal way of coining a new word is to use a Latin or Greek root with the appropriate affix and, when necessary, the -ize formation. It is often easier to make up words of this kind (*deregionalize, impermissible, extramarital, non-fragmentatory* and so forth) than to think up the English words that will cover one's meaning. The result, in general, is an increase in slovenliness and vagueness.

Meaningless words. In certain kinds of writing, particularly in art criticism and literary criticism, it is normal to come across long passages which are almost completely lacking in meaning.[2] Words like *romantic, plastic, values, human, dead, sentimental, natural, vitality,* as used in art criticism, are strictly meaningless, in the sense that they not only do not point to any discoverable object, but are hardly even expected to do so by the reader. When one critic writes, "The outstanding feature of Mr. X's work is its living quality," while another writes, "The immediately striking thing about Mr. X's work is its peculiar deadness," the reader accepts this as a simple difference of opinion. If words like *black* and *white* were involved, instead of the jargon words *dead* and *living,* he would see at once that language was being used in an improper way. Many political words are similarly abused. The word *Fascism* has now no meaning except in so far as it signifies "something not desirable." The words *democracy, socialism, freedom, patriotic, realistic, justice,* have each of them several different meanings which cannot be reconciled with one another. In the case of a word

[1] An interesting illustration of this is the way in which the English flower names which were in use till very recently are being ousted by Greek ones, *snapdragon* becoming *antirrhinum, forget-me-not* becoming *myosotis,* etc. It is hard to see any practical reason for this change of fashion: it is probably due to an instinctive turning-away from the more homely word and a vague feeling that the Greek word is scientific.

[2] Example: "Comfort's catholicity of perception and image, strangely Whitmanesque in range, almost the exact opposite in aesthetic compulsion, continues to evoke that trembling atmospheric accumulative hinting at a cruel, an inexorably serene timelessness . . . Wrey Gardiner scores by aiming at simple bull's-eyes with precision. Only they are not so simple, and through this contented sadness runs more than the surface bitter-sweet of resignation." (*Poetry Quarterly.*)

like *democracy*, not only is there no agreed definition, but the attempt to make one is resisted from all sides. It is almost universally felt that when we call a country democratic we are praising it: consequently the defenders of every kind of régime claim that it is a democracy, and fear that they might have to stop using the word if it were tied down to any one meaning. Words of this kind are often used in a consciously dishonest way. That is, the person who uses them has his own private definition, but allows his hearer to think he means something quite different. Statements like *Marshal Pétain was a true patriot*, *The Soviet Press is the freest in the world*, *The Catholic Church is opposed to persecution*, are almost always made with intent to deceive. Other words used in variable meanings, in most cases more or less dishonestly, are: *class, totalitarian, science, progressive, reactionary, bourgeois, equality*.

Now that I have made this catalogue of swindles and perversions, let me give another example of the kind of writing that they lead to. This time it must of its nature be an imaginary one. I am going to translate a passage of good English into modern English of the worst sort. Here is a well-known verse from *Ecclesiastes:*

I returned and saw under the sun, that the race is not to the swift, nor the battle to the strong, neither yet bread to the wise, nor yet riches to men of understanding, nor yet favour to men of skill; but time and chance happeneth to them all.

Here it is in modern English:

Objective consideration of contemporary phenomena compels the conclusion that success or failure in competitive activities exhibits no tendency to be commensurate with innate capacity, but that a considerable element of the unpredictable must invariably be taken into account.

This is a parody, but not a very gross one. Exhibit (3), above, for instance, contains several patches of the same kind of English. It will be seen that I have not made a full translation. The beginning and ending of the sentence follow the original meaning fairly closely, but in the middle the concrete illustrations—race, battle, bread—dissolve into the vague phrase "success or failure in competitive activities." This had to be so, because no modern writer of the kind I am discussing—no one capable of using phrases like "objective consideration of contemporary phenomena"— would ever tabulate his thoughts in that precise and detailed way. The whole tendency of modern prose is away from concreteness. Now analyze these two sentences a little more closely. The first contains 49 words but only 60 syllables, and all its words are those of everyday life. The second contains 38 words of 90 syllables: 18 of its words are from Latin roots, and one from Greek. The first sentence contains six vivid images, and only one phrase ("time and chance") that could be called vague. The second contains not a single fresh, arresting phrase, and in spite of its 90 syllables it gives only a shortened version of the meaning contained in the first. Yet without a doubt it is the second kind of sentence that is gaining ground in modern English. I do not want to exaggerate. This kind of writing is not yet universal, and outcrops of simplicity will occur here and there in the worst-written page. Still, if you or I were told to write a few lines on the uncertainty of human fortunes, we should probably come much nearer to my imaginary sentence than to the one from *Ecclesiastes*.

As I have tried to show, modern writing at its worst does not consist in picking out words for the sake of their meaning and inventing images in order to make the meaning clearer. It consists in gumming together long strips of words which have already been set in order by someone else, and making the results presentable by sheer humbug. The attraction of this way of writing is that it is easy. It is easier—even quicker, once you have the habit—to say *In my opinion it is a not unjustifiable assumption that* than to say *I think*. If you use ready-made phrases, you not only don't have to hunt about for words; you also don't have to bother with the rhythms of your sentences, since these phrases are generally so arranged as to be more or less euphonious. When you are composing in a hurry—when you are dictating to a stenographer, for instance, or making a public speech—it is natural to fall into a pretentious, Latinized style. Tags like *a consideration which we should do well to bear in mind* or *a conclusion to which all of us would readily assent* will save many a sentence from coming down with a bump. By using stale metaphors, similes and idioms, you save much mental effort, at the cost of leaving your meaning vague, not only for your reader but for yourself. This is the significance of mixed metaphors. The sole aim of a metaphor is to call up a visual image. When these images clash—as in *The Fascist octopus has sung its swan song, the jackboot is thrown into the melting pot*—it can be taken as certain that the writer is not seeing a mental image of the objects he is naming; in other words he is not really thinking. Look again at the examples I gave at the beginning of this essay. Professor Laski (1) uses five negatives in 53 words. One of these is superfluous, making nonsense of the whole passage, and in addition there is the slip *alien* for *akin*, making further nonsense, and several avoidable pieces of clumsiness which increase the general vagueness. Professor Hogben (2) plays ducks and drakes with a battery which is able to write prescriptions, and, while disapproving of the everyday phrase *put up with*, is unwilling to look *egregious* up in the dictionary and see what it means. (3), if one takes an uncharitable attitude towards it, is simply meaningless: probably one could work out its intended meaning by reading the whole of the article in which it occurs. In (4), the writer knows more or less what he wants to say, but an accumulation of stale phrases chokes him like tea leaves blocking a sink. In (5), words and meaning have almost parted company. People who write in this manner usually have a general emotional meaning—they dislike one thing and want to express solidarity with another—but they are not interested in the detail of what they are saying. A scrupulous writer, in every sentence that he writes, will ask himself at least four questions, thus: What am I trying to say? What words will express it? What image or idiom will make it clearer? Is this image fresh enough to have an effect? And he will probably ask himself two more: Could I put it more shortly? Have I said anything that is avoidably ugly? But you are not obliged to go to all this trouble. You can shirk it by simply throwing your mind open and letting the ready-made phrases come crowding in. They will construct your sentences for you—even think your thoughts for you, to a certain extent—and at need they will perform the important service of partially concealing your meaning even from yourself. It is at this point that the special connection between politics and the debasement of language becomes clear.

In our time it is broadly true that political writing is bad writing. Where it is not true, it will generally be found that the writer is some kind of rebel, expressing his private opinions and not a "party line." Orthodoxy, of whatever color, seems to demand a lifeless, imitative style. The political dialects to be found in pamphlets, leading articles, manifestoes, White Papers and the speeches of under-secretaries do, of course, vary from party to party, but they are all alike in that one almost never finds in them a fresh, vivid, home-made turn of speech. When one watches some tired hack on the platform mechanically repeating the familiar phrases—*bestial atrocities, iron heel, bloodstained tyranny, free peoples of the world, stand shoulder to shoulder*—one often has a curious feeling that one is not watching a live human being but some kind of dummy: a feeling which suddenly becomes stronger at moments when the light catches the speaker's spectacles and turns them into blank discs which seem to have no eyes behind them. And this is not altogether fanciful. A speaker who uses that kind of phraseology has gone some distance towards turning himself into a machine. The appropriate noises are coming out of his larynx, but his brain is not involved as it would be if he were choosing his words for himself. If the speech he is making is one that he is accustomed to make over and over again, he may be almost unconscious of what he is saying, as one is when one utters the responses in church. And this reduced state of consciousness, if not indispensable, is at any rate favorable to political conformity.

In our time, political speech and writing are largely the defense of the indefensible. Things like the continuance of British rule in India, the Russian purges and deportations, the dropping of the atom bombs on Japan, can indeed be defended, but only by arguments which are too brutal for most people to face; and which do not square with the professed aims of political parties. Thus political language has to consist largely of euphemism, question-begging and sheer cloudy vagueness. Defenseless villages are bombarded from the air, the inhabitants driven out into the countryside, the cattle machine-gunned, the huts set on fire with incendiary bullets: this is called *pacification*. Millions of peasants are robbed of their farms and sent trudging along the roads with no more than they can carry: this is called *transfer of population* or *rectification of frontiers*. People are imprisoned for years without trial, or shot in the back of the neck or sent to die of scurvy in Arctic lumber camps: this is called *elimination of unreliable elements*. Such phraseology is needed if one wants to name things without calling up mental pictures of them. Consider for instance some comfortable English professor defending Russian totalitarianism. He cannot say outright, "I believe in killing off your opponents when you can get good results by doing so." Probably, therefore, he will say something like this:

While freely conceding that the Soviet régime exhibits certain features which the humanitarian may be inclined to deplore, we must, I think, agree that a certain curtailment of the right to political opposition is an unavoidable concomitant of transitional periods, and that the rigours which the Russian people have been called upon to undergo have been amply justified in the sphere of concrete achievement.

The inflated style is itself a kind of euphemism. A mass of Latin words falls upon the facts like soft snow, blurring the outlines and covering up all the details. The great enemy of clear language is insincerity. When there is a gap between one's real and one's declared aims, one turns as it were instinctively to long words and exhausted idioms, like a cuttlefish squirting out ink. In our age there is no such thing as "keeping out of politics." All issues are political issues, and politics itself is a mass of lies, evasions, folly, hatred and schizophrenia. When the general atmosphere is bad, language must suffer. I should expect to find—this is a guess which I have not sufficient knowledge to verify—that the German, Russian and Italian languages have all deteriorated in the last ten or fifteen years, as a result of dictatorship.

But if thought corrupts language, language can also corrupt thought. A bad usage can spread by tradition and imitation, even among people who should and do know better. The debased language that I have been discussing is in some ways very convenient. Phrases like *a not unjustifiable assumption, leaves much to be desired, would serve no good purpose, a consideration which we should do well to bear in mind*, are a continuous temptation, a packet of aspirins always at one's elbow. Look back through this essay, and for certain you will find that I have again and again committed the very faults I am protesting against. By this morning's post I have received a pamphlet dealing with conditions in Germany. The author tells me that he "felt impelled" to write it. I open it at random, and here is almost the first sentence that I see: "(The Allies) have an opportunity not only of achieving a radical transformation of Germany's social and political structure in such a way as to avoid a nationalistic reaction in Germany itself, but at the same time of laying the foundations of a co-operative and unified Europe." You see, he "feels impelled" to write—feels, presumably, that he has something new to say—and yet his words, like cavalry horses answering the bugle, group themselves automatically into the familiar dreary pattern. This invasion of one's mind by ready-made phrases (*lay the foundations, achieve a radical transformation*) can only be prevented if one is constantly on guard against them, and every such phrase anaesthetizes a portion of one's brain.

I said earlier that the decadence of our language is probably curable. Those who deny this would argue, if they produced an argument at all, that language merely reflects existing social conditions, and that we cannot influence its development by any direct tinkering with words and constructions. So far as the general tone or spirit of a language goes, this may be true, but it is not true in detail. Silly words and expressions have often disappeared, not through any evolutionary process but owing to the conscious action of a minority. Two recent examples were *explore every avenue* and *leave no stone unturned*, which were killed by the jeers of a few journalists. There is a long list of flyblown metaphors which could similarly be got rid of if enough people would interest themselves in the job;

and it should also be possible to laugh the *not un-* formation out of existence,[3] to reduce the amount of Latin and Greek in the average sentence, to
drive out foreign phrases and strayed scientific words, and, in general, to
make pretentiousness unfashionable. But all these are minor points. The
defense of the English language implies more than this, and perhaps it is
best to start by saying what it does *not* imply.

To begin with, it has nothing to do with archaism, with the salvaging of
obsolete words and turns of speech, or with the setting-up of a "standard
English" which must never be departed from. On the contrary, it is especially concerned with the scrapping of every word or idiom which has out-
worn its usefulness. It has nothing to do with correct grammar and syntax,
which are of no importance so long as one makes one's meaning clear, or
with the avoidance of Americanisms, or with having what is called a "good
prose style." On the other hand it is not concerned with fake simplicity and
the attempt to make written English colloquial. Nor does it even imply in
every case preferring the Saxon word to the Latin one, though it does imply using the fewest and shortest words that will cover one's meaning.
What is above all needed is to let the meaning choose the word, and not the
other way about. In prose, the worst thing one can do with words is to
surrender to them. When you think of a concrete object, you think word-
lessly, and then, if you want to describe the thing you have been visualiz-
ing, you probably hunt about till you find the exact words that seem to fit
it. When you think of something abstract you are more inclined to use
words from the start, and unless you make a conscious effort to prevent it,
the existing dialect will come rushing in and do the job for you, at the expense of blurring or even changing your meaning. Probably it is better to
put off using words as long as possible and get one's meaning as clear as one
can through pictures or sensations. Afterwards one can choose—not simply
accept—the phrases that will best cover the meaning, and then switch
round and decide what impressions one's words are likely to make on another person. This last effort of the mind cuts out all stale or mixed images,
all prefabricated phrases, needless repetitions, and humbug and vagueness
generally. But one can often be in doubt about the effect of a word or a
phrase, and one needs rules that one can rely on when instinct fails. I think
the following rules will cover most cases:

(i) Never use a metaphor, simile or other figure of speech which you are
used to seeing in print.

---

[3] One can cure oneself of the *not un-* formation by memorizing this sentence: *A
not unblack dog was chasing a not unsmall rabbit across a not ungreen field.*

(ii) Never use a long word where a short one will do.

(iii) If it is possible to cut a word out, always cut it out.

(iv) Never use the passive where you can use the active.

(v) Never use a foreign phrase, a scientific word or a jargon word if you can think of an everyday English equivalent.

(vi) Break any of these rules sooner than say anything outright barbarous.

These rules sound elementary, and so they are, but they demand a deep change of attitude in anyone who has grown used to writing in the style now fashionable. One could keep all of them and still write bad English, but one could not write the kind of stuff that I quoted in those five specimens at the beginning of this article.

I have not here been considering the literary use of language, but merely language as an instrument for expressing and not for concealing or preventing thought. Stuart Chase and others have come near to claiming that all abstract words are meaningless, and have used this as a pretext for advocating a kind of political quietism. Since you don't know what Fascism is, how can you struggle against Fascism? One need not swallow such absurdities as this, but one ought to recognize that the present political chaos is connected with the decay of language, and that one can probably bring about some improvement by starting at the verbal end. If you simplify your English, you are freed from the worst follies of orthodoxy. You cannot speak any of the necessary dialects, and when you make a stupid remark its stupidity will be obvious, even to yourself. Political language—and with variations this is true of all political parties, from Conservatives to Anarchists— is designed to make lies sound truthful and murder respectable, and to give an appearance of solidity to pure wind. One cannot change this all in a moment, but one can at least change one's own habits, and from time to time one can even, if one jeers loudly enough, send some worn-out and useless phrase—some *jackboot, Achilles' heel, hotbed, melting pot, acid test, veritable inferno* or other lump of verbal refuse—into the dustbin where it belongs.

UNDERSTANDING THE TEXT

1. In relation to what broader conditions or causes does Orwell consider the state of the English language? What specific methods does he use to establish connections between language and this broader context?

2. What two qualities does Orwell find in the sample passages with which he begins his essay? How general does he believe these qualities to be in modern writing? How do the four "tricks by means of which the work of prose-

construction is habitually dodged" contribute to these qualities in modern style?

3. What view of language, writing, and human nature underlies Orwell's conviction that "the decadence of our language is probably curable"? What specific remedies does he propose to cure it?

4. Which of Professor Laski's five negatives is "superfluous, making nonsense of the sentence"? Rewrite the Laski sentence.

5. What does *egregious* mean? What word should Professor Hogben have used?

6. What are the "six vivid images" in the sentence Orwell quotes from *Ecclesiastes?*

7. Orwell says that in his translation of the passage from *Ecclesiastes* eighteen of the words have Latin roots and one has a Greek root. Can you identify them?

8. Rewrite the sentence Orwell quotes from the pamphlet on conditions in Germany (p. 248), removing the causes of Orwell's objections.

9. Orwell has a good deal to say about figures of speech, and he uses a good many in his own writing. List and classify the figures of speech he uses, and test them against the criteria he lays down for the use of figurative language.

10. What do the following words mean in their contexts: *decadent, archaism, inadvertently, hackneyed, evocative, banal, euphemism?*

TOPICS FOR DISCUSSION AND WRITING

11. "The sole aim of a metaphor is to call up a visual image." Discuss this dictum. Is it true of Orwell's metaphors?

12. Orwell invites us to "Look back through this essay, and for certain you will find that I have again and again committed the very faults I am protesting against." Can you find any places where Orwell has?

13. Could it be argued that Orwell is attempting to locate too narrow a cause for the pervasive effect he deals with? Can you think of other important causes of the defects in language and style that he describes?

14. What assumption does Orwell make in order to argue that one can bring about some political improvement by starting at the verbal end? Does Thurber make this assumption in the essay following?

15. What is Orwell's view of politics? Could you hold a different view of politics and yet share Orwell's views about language?

16. Apply Orwell's six rules to your next paper.

17. Read Orwell's essay "Shooting an Elephant" (pp. 436–442) and see if you can find any consistency in the political attitudes expressed in the two essays.

18. Which of the various methods of procedure in writing illustrated in Section 3 does Orwell use in this essay? Does one of them predominate?

The Psychosemanticist Will See You Now,
Mr. Thurber

JAMES THURBER

I BELIEVE there are no scientific investigators that actually call themselves psychosemanticists, but it is surely time for these highly specialized therapeuticians to set up offices. They must not be carelessly confused with psychosomaticists, who study the effects of mental weather upon the ramparts of the body. The psychosemanticists will specialize in the havoc wrought by verbal artillery upon the fortress of reason. Their job will be to cope with the psychic trauma caused by linguistic meaninglessness, to prevent the language from degenerating into gibberish, and to save the sanity of persons threatened by the onset of polysyllabic monstrosititis.

We have always been a nation of categorizationists, but what was once merely a national characteristic is showing signs of malignancy. I shall not attempt to discover the incipient primary lesion, for I am not a qualified research scholar in this field. Indeed, for having had the impudence to trespass thus far I shall no doubt be denounced by the classificationists as a fractional impactionist (one who hits subjects a glancing blow), an unauthorized incursionist, a unilateral conclusionist, and a presumptuous deductionist. Our national predilection for ponderous phraseology has been traced by one authority as far back as the awkward expression "taxation without representation" (unjust impost). It is interesting to note that the irate American colonists of that period in our history would be categorized today as "anti-taxation-without-representationists."

Not long ago, for the most recent instance in my collection, Senator Lyndon Johnson was described by a Washington newspaperman as a prag-

Reprinted from *The New Yorker*, May 28, 1955. Permission the author. Copr., 1955, The New Yorker Magazine, Inc.

matic functionalist, a term that was used in a laudatory sense. It isn't always easy nowadays to tell the laudatory from the derogatory at first glance, but we should be glad that this Democratic leader is not a dogmatic divisionary or an occlusive impedimentarian. The most alarming incidence of verbal premalignancy occurs, of course, in this very area of politics, but let us skip over such worn and familiar double-jointedisms as creeping Socialists, disgruntled ex-employees, ritualistic liberals, massive retaliationists, agonized reappraisalists, unorthodox thinkers, unwitting handmaidens (male), to name only a few out of hundreds, and take a look at excessive prewar anti-Fascism, a colossal (I use the adjective as a noun, in the manner of television's "spectacular") that was disgorged a few years ago. Here the classificatory degradationists brought a time element into what might be called the post-evaluation of political morality. The operation of this kind of judgment during and after the Civil War would have thrown indelible suspicion upon all the Northern patriots, including Abraham Lincoln, who wanted Robert E. Lee to take command of the Federal Armies in the field. They would be known today as "overenthusiastic pre-Manassas pro-Leeists."

The carcinomenclature of our time is, to be sure, an agglomerative phenomenon of accumulated concretions, to which a dozen different types of elaborative descriptivists have contributed—eminently the old Communist intellectuals, with their "dialectical materialists," "factional deviationists," "unimplemented obscurantists," and so on, and so on. Once the political terminologists of all parties began to cross-infect our moribund vocabulary, the rate of degeneration became appalling. Elephantiasis of cliché set in, synonym atrophied, the pulse of inventiveness slowed alarmingly, and paraphrase died of impaction. Multiple sclerosis was apparent in the dragging rhythms of speech, and the complexion of writing and of conversation began to take on the tight, dry parchment look of death. We have become satisfied with gangrenous repetitions of threadbarisms, like an old man cackling in a chimney corner, and the onset of utter meaninglessness is imminent.

The symptoms of this ominous condition show up most clearly in the tertiary stage of "controversial figure." The most complicated specimen of this type of modern American is the man of unquestionable loyalty, distinguished public service, and outstanding ability and experience who has nonetheless "lost his usefulness." Actually, this victim of verbositosis has not lost his usefulness, his nation has lost it. It doesn't do the national psyche any good to realize that a man may be cut off in the full flower of his usefulness, on the ground that that is not what it is. I trust I have made the urgent need for psychosemanticists apparent, even though I have admittedly become contaminated in the process, and I doubt whether my own psychosemanticist, after treating me, will ever be able to turn to my wife and say cheerfully, "Madam, your husband will write clearly again."

Before visiting my hypothetical psychosemanticist for a brief imaginary interview, I feel that I should get something reassuring into this survey of depressing ailments of the tongue. We have, then, cured, or at least survived, various incipient mouth maladies in the past. There was a moment when "globaloneyism," growing out of the Timethod of wordoggle, seemed likely to become epidemic, but it fortunately turned out to be no worse than a touch of pig Latin or a slight case of Knock, Knock, Who's There? Congress was not prepared to adopt the telescoping of words, which takes both time and ingenuity, and unless an expression becomes absorbed by Congressionalese, it has little chance of general survival. This brings me to what may easily be the direct cause of my being bundled off to the psychosemanticist's before long: the beating the word "security" is taking in this great, scared land of ours. It is becoming paralyzed. This is bound to occur to any forceful word when it loses its quality of affirmation and is employed exclusively in a connotation of fear, uncertainty, and suspicion. The most frequent use of "security" (I hate to add to its shakiness with quotation marks, which have taken on a tone of mockery in our day) is in "security risk," "weakest link in our chain of security," and "lulled into a false sense of security." Precision of speech and meaning takes a small tossing around in the last of those three phrases. "Lulled" is actually what happens to a nation after it has been argued, tricked, maneuvered, reasoned, coaxed, cajoled, or jockeyed into a false sense of security, but the inflexibility that has descended upon us has ruled out the once noble search for the perfect word and the exact expression. What Eric Partridge calls "a poverty of linguistic resource" is exemplified by the practically exclusive use of two verbs in any public-forum discussion of national security. It is threatened or it is bolstered; I never heard of its being supported, reinforced, fortified, buttressed, or shored up, and only very rarely is it menaced, endangered, or in jeopardy.

The word "insecurity," by the way, seems to have been taken over by the psychiatrists as their personal property. In politics, as in penology, "security" itself has come to mean "insecurity." Take, for example, this sentence: "He was considered a 'maximum security' prisoner because of his police record and was never allowed out of his cell block." Similarly,

"security data" means data of the kind calculated to scare the living daylights out of you, if not, indeed, your pants off. I could prove that
"maximum," in the case of the prisoner mentioned above, really means
"minimum," but I don't want to get us in so deep that we can't get out.
The present confused usage of "security" may have originated with the
ancient Romans. Anyway, here is what Cassell's Latin Dictionary has to
say about *securitas:* "I. *freedom from care.* A. In a good sense, *peace of
mind, quiet,* Cic. B. In a bad sense, *carelessness, indifference,* Tac. II.
Transf., *freedom from danger, security,* Tac."

A vital and restless breed of men, given to tapping our toes and drum-
ming with our fingers, infatuated with every new crazy rhythm that rears
its ugly beat, we have never truly loved harmony, the graceful structure of
shapes and tones, and for this blindness and deafness we pay the awful
price of continuous cacophony. It gets into language as well as music; we
mug melody for the sake of sound effects, and the louder and more disso-
nant they are, the better we seem to like them. Our national veins have
taken in the singing blood of Italy, Wales, Ireland, and Germany, but the
transfusion has had no beneficial effect. Great big blocky words and phrases
bumble off our tongues and presses every day. In four weeks of purposeful
listening to the radio and reading the newspapers I have come up with a
staggering list, full of sound and fury, dignifying nothing: "automation,"
"roadability," "humature," "motivational cognition" (this baby turned up
in a series of travel lectures and was never defined), "fractionalization,"
"varietism," "redesegregation," "additive," "concertization" (this means
giving a concert in a hall, and is not to be confused with cinematization or
televisionization). The colloquial deformity "knowledgeable," which
should have been clubbed to death years ago, when it first began crawling
about like the late Lon Chaney, has gained new life in recent months. It is
a dented derby of a word, often found in the scrawny company of such
battered straw hats as "do-gooder," "know-how," "update," "uptake" (I
recently uptook the iodine uptake test for thyroidism), and others so ugly
and strange I can't decipher them in my notes. One of them looks like "de-
egghead," which would mean to disintellectualize or mentally emasculate
—a crippling operation approved of by an alarming number of squash-
heads, in Washington and elsewhere.

During my month of vigil and research, I heard an able physiologist who
has a radio program say, quite simply, "We do not use up all the food we
take in." He wasn't allowed to get away with that piece of clarity, however. "Ah," cut in his announcer, for the benefit of those no longer able to

understand simplicity, "the utilization factor!" I turned from this station to a droning psychologist, just in time to hear him say, "The female is sometimes the sexual aggressor." Here a familiar noun of mental illness and military invasion was clumsily at work beating in the skull of love with a verbal bung-starter. The sweetheart now often wears the fustian of the sick man and the Caesar. In the evening, I tuned in on one of the space-patrol programs that gleefully exude the great big blockyisms. "Your astrogation bank will tell you!" cried the captain of a space ship to another interplanetary pilot, meaning his navigational instruments. In a fairy tale, an astrogation bank would be a "star panel," but the quality of fairy tale is nowhere to be found in these dime novels of the constellations.

One Sunday morning, my head aching with "kiss-close" and "swivel-chair-it," meaning, I guess, "at kissing distance" and "maul it over in your executive brain," respectively, I stumbled upon a small radio station that had been captured by a man of God, ominous and squealful, who was begging his listeners to live on their knees, not as slaves but as supplicants. This particular fundamentalist, or maybe it is fundamentalitarian, had probably never heard of the great protest "I would rather die on my feet than live on my knees." But these yammering eschatologists, and many of their followers, have even less respect for the glory and grace of English than the unsaved politicians. "Let us cease to sugar-coat, let us cease to whitewash, let us cease to bargain-counter the Bible!" the speaker implored us. He finished second in vulgarity, I regret to say, to a reverend I had heard earlier in the year, who shouted, "I didn't cook up this dish, God cooked it up. I'm just dishing it out to ye!" The line between holiness and blasphemy becomes even thinner when some of the lay testimonialists begin ranting. "I own a shoe store in New Jersey," one of them confessed, "but Jesus Christ is my senior partner."

A recent investigation of the worries and concerns of five thousand selected Americans revealed that we are preoccupied almost wholly with the personal and private, and are troubled only mildly by political anxieties, including the danger of war, the state of civil liberties, and the internal Communist threat. This does not come as a surprise to me, since the nature of our national concern about Communism is proved to be personal by such expressions as "anti-anti-Communists" and "anti-anti-anti-Communists." The first actually means men who are against men who are against Communists, and the second, when you unravel it, means men who are against men who are against men who are against Communists. In these wonderful examples of our love of formidable elaborationisms, concept and doctrine are put aside, and personalities take their place. What we have left is pure personalism—a specific reactionary who is against a specific liberal who is against Senator McCarthy, let us say. The multiplicity of prefixes, another sign of linguistic poverty, was touched with a fine and healthful irony in Quincy Howe's invention of the phrase "ex-ex-Communist." (Many will claim that for their own, but Mr. Howe got to it first.) One would think that Americans would be worried, or at least concerned, by a man who may have ceased to be a man who may have ceased to be a Communist, but the Worry Research I have mentioned showed that this isn't so. We are worried about health, family matters, and money, and we have no time for a man who may be lying about lying. Incidentally, a fairly new advertising slogan, "The portable portable," fits neatly into modern jargon: the type-writer that you can carry that you can carry.

While I was exploring the decline of expression in America, I spent a week in a hospital. Medical science has done much for humanity, but not in the area of verbal communication. It should undergo a prefectomy, and have some of its prefixes taken out. I should like to see the "semi" re-moved from "semi-private," a dispiriting word that originated in hospitals; there must be a less depressing way of describing a room with two or more beds. I am also for taking the "sub" out of "sub-clinical," and starting all over again with the idea in mind of making the word mean something. In-cidentally, I discovered at the hospital the difference between "to be hos-pitalized" and "to become hospitalized." The first means to be placed in a hospital, and the second has two meanings: to get so that you can't stand it in the hospital any longer, and to like it so much there that you don't want to leave.

Lying in bed brooding over these matters, I turned on the radio and heard an American describe another American as "an old-time A.D.A. type of anti-Jeffersonian radical"—a beautiful specimen of bumblery. Sir Win-ston Churchill, in the exhilarating years of his public life, turned out many phrases as sharp as stilettos—for one example, "squalid gamin." But you can count on your fingers the Americans, since the Thomas Paine of "the summer soldier and the sunshine patriot," who have added bright, clear phrases to our language. If you can bumble an opponent to death why stab him seems to be the general feeling among our politicians, some of whom have got through the ten years since the war ended with only five adjec-tives of derogation: naïve, hostile, unrealistic, complacent, and irresponsi-ble. All these slither easily, if boggily, into bumblery, and the bumbler is spared the tedious exercising of his mental faculties.

The day I got dressed and was about to leave the hospital, I heard a nurse and an interne discussing a patient who had got something in his eye. "It's a bad city to get something in your eye in," the nurse said. "Yes," the interne agreed, "but there isn't a better place to get something in your eye out in." I rushed past them with my hair in my wild eyes, and left the hospital. It was high time, too.

When and if I find a reputable psychosemanticist, I want to take up with him something that happened to me one night more than two years ago. It may be the basis of my etymological or philological problems, if that's what they are—words, especially big ones, are beginning to lose their meaning for me. Anyway, I woke up one summer night, from a deep dream of peacelessness, only to realize that I had been startled by nothing whatever into a false sense of insecurity. I had a desperate feeling that I was being closed in on, that there was a menace in the woods behind my house or on the road in front of it, watchful, waiting, biding its time. A few weeks later I bought a .38-calibre Smith & Wesson police revolver, which startled my wife into a genuine sense of insecurity. She hid the gun somewhere, and the cartridges somewhere else, and I still don't know where they are. I have often thought of telling my psychosemanticist about it, and I sometimes have the feeling that I did call on him and that the interview went like this:

"Doesn't your wife's hiding the gun worry you?" he asked.

"No," I said.

"It would me," he confessed.

"It would *what* you?" I demanded.

It seemed to disturb him. "*What* would what me?" he asked cautiously.

I suddenly couldn't think of a thing. I didn't even know what what was, but I had to say something, so I said something: "Ill fares the land, to galloping fears a prey, where gobbledygook accumulates, and words decay."

I had just reached that Goldsmith paraphrase when a sub-researcher brought me the news from Washington that a movement is afoot in the nation's capital to cut down on bumblery, clarify officialese, and discourage certain platitudes (but not enough), in the wistful hope of bringing grace and meaning to the writing of English by government employees. I was glad to discover "finalize" among the banned gargoyles, but I don't see how the lawyers in Washington are going to get along without "predecease." The reformers, by the way, don't seem to know that this monster spawned an equally clumsy offspring, "survivorship." The main reason for this reform is to save filing space and money, but the economic aspect of the project does not depress me too much. It is a hopeful step in the direction of sense and sanity.

Come on, let's go out and get a breath of fresh air.

UNDERSTANDING THE TEXT

1. Thurber uses a medical-psychological metaphor as the frame for his argument. Trace the specific details that keep the medical-psychological theme before the reader through the essay. What is the special appropriateness of this metaphor? Does it allow Thurber to make any points that would be difficult to make otherwise? Does the extended metaphor have a cumulative effect as the essay proceeds? Does it suggest any relevant meanings beyond those Thurber explicitly mentions?

2. What specific categories of writing and speaking does Thurber examine? Does he take them up in any significant order?

3. Thurber makes use of certain general premises in his discussion. An example is the sentence which begins the paragraph on p. 255: A "vital and restless breed of men . . . cacophony." What use does he make of this general statement about Americans? Can you find other explicit statements of Thurber's general views? How does he introduce them and how does he relate them to his theme?

4. More often, Thurber's assumptions are implicit in the judgments he makes, in his observations, and in his style. Consider such a sentence as "Here a familiar noun of mental illness and military invasion was clumsily at work beating in the skull of love with a verbal bung-starter" (p. 256). What assumptions and values underlie this statement? Find other examples of implicit assumptions, and show how they help organize Thurber's approach to his subject.

5. The last item in Thurber's list of exhibits before he relates his dream and visits the psychosemanticist is the episode of the nurse and the interne (p. 258). Does this seem to you a climactic episode? In what ways does it serve to sum up what has gone before? Does it seem to you significant that both the nurse and the interne use very simple language, with none of the "big blocky" words Thurber has described earlier?

6. What is the function, in Thurber's total plan, of the paragraph beginning "One Sunday morning . . ." (p. 256)?

7. What does Thurber mean by "what might be called the post-evaluation of political morality" (p. 253)? Why does he use language of this sort? How do expressions of this kind fit in with the "psychosemantic" theme of the essay?

8. Suppose that instead of saying "Similarly, 'security data' means data of the kind calculated to scare the living daylights out of you, if not, indeed, your

pants off" Thurber had said "data of the kind which reveals a determination to overthrow the government or betray national secrets to a foreign power"? What attitude is implied by each of these statements? How is the attitude implied by Thurber's words consistent with his general theme?

9. Thurber gives "unjust impost" as a substitute for the ponderous phraseology of "taxation without representation." Give similar substitutes, if you can, for "unauthorized incursionist," "unilateral conclusionist," and "presumptuous deductionist."

10. The following are based on famous lines in English literature:
   a. "Full of sound and fury, dignifying nothing."
   b. "Woke up from a deep dream of peacelessness."
   c. "Ill fares the land, to galloping fears a prey, where gobbledygook accumulates, and words decay."
   Consult a dictionary of quotations, if you don't recognize these offhand, and try to make clear what Thurber's parodies contribute.

11. What is "the Timethod of wordoggle"? Does Thurber himself use this method anywhere in the essay?

12. Can you say why *knowledgeable* is a "dented derby of a word," and why *know-how* is a "battered straw hat"?

TOPICS FOR DISCUSSION AND WRITING

13. From your reading, add to Thurber's list of "big blocky words and phrases," and try to find some other adjectives used as nouns, like *colossal* and *spectacular*.

14. Rewrite the following sentence in literal terms: "Elephantiasis of cliché set in, synonym atrophied, the pulse of inventiveness slowed alarmingly, and paraphrase died of impaction."

15. What is Thurber's political attitude? Write a paragraph in which you analyze his views on security.

16. Like Orwell, Thurber gives special attention to the relation between politics and language. Write a paper comparing the views of the two writers on this topic.

17. Keeping in mind the stylistic criteria used by Orwell and Thurber, write an essay analyzing and evaluating a contemporary piece of political writing —a newspaper editorial, magazine article, pamphlet, or the like.

The Bible in Modern Undress

DWIGHT MACDONALD

ON SEPTEMBER 30th of last year, two million people in over three thousand communities in the United States and Canada attended meetings celebrating the appearance of the Revised Standard Version of the Bible. Within eight weeks, over sixteen hundred thousand copies were sold; the total to date is two million three hundred thousand, and it is still on the best-seller lists. The publishers, Thomas Nelson & Sons, have spent a million dollars on a promotional campaign. The Revised Standard Version is "authorized"; that is, the National Council of the Churches of Christ, which includes all the major Protestant denominations, was in charge of the committee of Biblical scholars that prepared it, and most of the denominations have authorized its use in their churches. The committee, headed by Dean Luther A. Weigle of the Yale Divinity School, spent fifteen years on the task. They encountered many and great problems of scholarship, of interpretation, of archeology, theology, philology, and English usage, but the greatest problem was a competitor that has been in the field for over three centuries and has been fatal to the ambitions of all contenders up to now. This was, of course, the King James Version. Although Dean Weigle's committee was instructed to revise not the King James but a revision of it made in 1901, the American Standard Version, they well understood which was the champion they had to beat. For the King James Version has long occupied a unique place in both the culture and the religion of English-speaking peoples.

In January, 1604, King James I summoned the leading divines of the Church of England to a conference at Hampton Court Palace to settle matters in dispute between the High Church and the Puritan factions. The dis-

The New Yorker, November 14, 1953. Reprinted by permission; © 1953 The New Yorker Magazine, Inc.

pute was not resolved, and James's successor was to lose his head in consequence, but the conference bore rich and unexpected fruit. One of the Puritans' grievances was that the authorized English Bible was not true to the original; Dr. John Reynolds, a leading Puritan and the president of Corpus Christi College, proposed a new translation. An ardent scholar and theologian, James accepted the proposal with enthusiasm and appointed fifty-four scholars, from Oxford, Cambridge, and Westminster. The work was begun in 1607 and completed in the incredibly short space of four years. In 1611, the result, "The Holy Bible, Conteyning the Old Testament and the New: Newly translated out of the Originall tongues & with the former translations diligently compared and reuised by his Maiesties speciall Commandement. Appointed to be read in Churches," came off the press. The King James Version is probably the greatest translation ever made. It is certainly "The Noblest Monument of English Prose," as the late John Livingston Lowes called his essay on the subject. "Its phraseology," he wrote, "has become part and parcel of our common tongue. . . . Its rhythms and cadences, its turns of speech, its familiar imagery, its very words are woven into the texture of our literature. . . . The English of the Bible . . . is characterized not merely by a homely vigor and pithiness of phrase but also a singular nobility of diction and by a rhythmic quality which is, I think, unrivalled in its beauty."

The King James Bible came at the end of the Elizabethan age, between Shakespeare and Milton, when Englishmen were using words more passionately, richly, vigorously, wittily, and sublimely than ever before or since. Although none of the divines and scholars who made it were literary men, their language was touched with genius—the genius of a period when style was the common property of educated men rather than an individual achievement. It also came at a time when Englishmen were intensely concerned with religion. "Theology rules there," Grotius wrote of England in 1613. In the King James Bible, the artistic flowering of the Renaissance and the religious fervor of the Reformation united to produce a masterpiece. Like the Gothic cathedrals, it was a collective expression of a culture and, like them, it was not built all at once but grew slowly over a considerable period of time. The speed with which it was accomplished was possible only because it was not so much a new translation as a synthesis of earlier efforts, the final form given to a continuous process of creation, the climax to the great century of English Bible translation. "Truly, good Christian reader," wrote Dr. Miles Smith in the preface, "we never thought from the beginning that we should neede to make a new Translation nor yet to make of a bad one a good one . . . but to make a good one better, or out of many good ones one principall good one. That hath bene our indeavour, that our marke. . . . So if we, building upon their foundation that went before us, and being holpen by their labours, doe endeavour to make that better which they left so good, no man, we are sure, hath cause to mislike us, and, they, we perswade our selves, if they were alive, would thanke us." No man, surely, has cause to mislike the King James translators, and many men have cause to thank them.

The Englishing of the Bible—except for some earlier fragments—probably began with the Venerable Bede, who is thought to have completed a translation of the four Gospels just before he died, in 735. The first translation of the whole Bible into English was done under the supervision of John Wycliffe, "the morning star of the Reformation," and appeared in 1382. The Lollards, or poor preachers, who walked through England teaching his doctrines, used his Bible, in which, for the first time, the common people could hear the complete word of God in their own language. Bede and Wycliffe translated not from the original Greek and Hebrew but from the Latin Vulgate. The first translation from an original tongue was William Tyndale's New Testament, put out in 1525. The fall of Constantinople to the Turks in 1453 and the expulsion of the Jews from Spain and Portugal toward the end of that century sent many Greek and Hebrew scholars into exile all over Europe, thus giving a tremendous impetus to the study of their languages. This providentially coincided with the beginning of the Reformation—providentially because translating the Bible into living languages was one of the reformers' chief ways of bringing the word of God directly to the people. Luther, whose German translation of the Bible has a quality and importance comparable to the King James Version, befriended Tyndale, whose New Testament was printed in the Lutheran stronghold of Worms. "If God spare my lyfe," Tyndale defiantly wrote to a Catholic cleric, "ere many yeares I wyl cause a boye that dryveth the plough shall know more of the scripture than thou doest." His life was spared just long enough; in 1536 he was burned at the stake in Belgium for heresy, but while he was in prison, in the last year of his life, he continued to work on his translation of the Old Testament, and managed to complete the bulk of it. Tyndale's Bible was the first and by all odds the greatest of a spate of translations that poured forth during the century, and it was drawn on far more heavily by the King James translators than any other version. The other important translations were Miles Coverdale's (1535); the Matthews Bible (1537), a combination of Coverdale and Tyndale done by a disciple of Tyndale, John Rogers, who was later martyred under Bloody Mary; the Great Bible (1539), the first Authorized Version, prepared by Coverdale at the request of Henry VIII; the Genevan Bible, also known as the Breeches Bible because Adam's fig leaf was rendered "breeches," which was issued in 1560 in Calvinist Geneva by a group of English Protestant refugees from Bloody Mary's persecution, went through a hundred and forty editions (being popular partly because of its literary quality and partly because of its legible Roman type and its handy quarto size, as against the cumbersome black-letter folios of previous Bibles), and was the Bible of the Pilgrims and of Cromwell's Ironsides; and the Bishops' Bible (1568), an authorized revision of the Great Bible that was to the High Church party what the Genevan Bible was to the Puritans. The King James Version was officially a revision of the Bishops' Bible, but those who made the revision paid very little attention to it, relying mostly on Tyndale, Coverdale, and the Genevan Bible, in that order. Thus the Puritans, though they got no satisfaction out of the Hampton Court conference, had their way with the new Bible.

For the next two and a half centuries, the King James Version (K.J.V. for short) was *the* Bible to English-speaking people. Close to a hundred complete or partial translations were made during this time, but none was either authorized or widely used. Toward the end of the nineteenth century, however, archeology and Biblical scholarship had made such progress that the Church of England appointed an interdenominational committee of scholars to revise K.J.V. The heaviest changes were made in the New Testament, for the K.J.V. translators had used a Greek text established by Beza, Stephanus, and Erasmus and based on late and inaccurate medieval manuscripts; much older manuscripts, some going back to the third century, were now available, and the Victorian scholars Hort and Westcott had established from them a text that differed in 5,788 instances from the Beza-Stephanus-Erasmus text. The Hebrew text of the Old Testament was essentially the tenth-century "Masoretic" text used by the K.J.V. translators, but since 1611 a number of important Greek versions, some from the fourth century, had come to light.

Thus when the nineteenth-century revisionists began their fifteen-year task, in 1870, they had an enormous advantage in scholarly knowledge over their speedier predecessors. This, it turned out, was not enough. When they brought out their New Testament, it was the publishing sensation of the century; despite an advance sale of a million, long lines formed in front of English bookstores on the day of publication; two Chicago newspapers got the full text by cable and ran it as a serial; three million copies were sold the first year. K.J.V. had won acceptance slowly, but the 1885 revision went up like a rocket—and came down like one. The men who made K.J.V. were both scholars and stylists; their Victorian successors, living in a more specialized age, were only scholars. Literal accuracy, rather than beauty or even sense, was their aim, to achieve which they adopted such absurd translating rules as always using the same English word for a given Greek or Hebrew word regardless of context, and sticking to the word order of the original. The result often read like an interlinear "trot." After the excitement had died down, the public returned to K.J.V. In 1901, the American Standard Version, an authorized adaptation of the 1885 English version, appeared. Although more successful, this also failed to replace K.J.V. The work under consideration here, the Revised Standard Version (R.S.V.), issued with such fanfare last fall, is the latest great effort to supersede K.J.V.

R.S.V. was undertaken partly because Biblical scholarship has made enormous progress since 1900. Since then, a vast number of Greek papyri have been unearthed in Egypt. Some, among them the Chester Beatty papyri, are fragments of very early Biblical manuscripts. Most of them are business documents, private letters, wills, and other records of everyday life that, according to the R.S.V. scholars, "prove that 'Biblical Greek' was really the spoken vernacular of the first century A.D.—not the classical Greek which the King James translators assumed it to be." Even more important was the discovery of some Old Testament Hebrew and Aramaic manuscripts believed to date back to the time of Christ, or a full thousand years before the earliest hitherto known examples. A Bedouin shepherd looking for a lost goat in a cave on the shores of the Dead Sea came on some parchment scrolls that turned out to contain the complete text of Isaiah and a commentary on Habakkuk. Hundreds of other fragments of ancient scrolls were later found in the same cave. (On April 1st of this year, G. Lankester Harding, Director of Antiquities for the government of Jordan, announced that Arab shepherds had made an even richer find among the caves of the Dead Sea,—seventy Hebrew, Aramaic, and Greek scrolls of around the time of Christ, which contain no less than nineteen books of the Old Testament, including Genesis, Exodus, Psalms, Ecclesiastes, and Daniel. Terming this "perhaps the most sensational archaeological event of our time," Mr. Harding predicted it would keep Biblical scholars busy "for the next generation at least." It is unfortunate that Mr. Harding chose April Fool's Day to make his announcement, but, assuming he is not the most ambitious hoaxer in history, his evaluation of the new find seems moderate enough.)

The chief motive behind R.S.V., however, was stylistic rather than scholarly. The Revisers felt, correctly, that the 1885 English revision and the 1901 American version were "literal, word-for-word translations" that "sacrificed much of the beauty and power of the earlier version." They therefore set out to produce a version that would, on the one hand, "combine accuracy with the simplicity, directness, and spiritual power of K.J.V." and, on the other, be more readable for the American public of today. In pursuing this aim, they have made numerous departures from K.J.V. in ways that seem to me legitimate, and many, many more in ways that do not. Let us begin with the former.

There are, first, the changes in translation. Being no specialist on the subject, I can only assume that where R.S.V. differs in meaning from K.J.V., the translation has been improved. (Considering the immense advances in archeology, philology, and other sciences since 1611, this is a reasonable assumption.) I am also willing to accept the Revisers' assurance that no changes have been made for doctrinal reasons. Two changes are of special importance. The Roman Catholic Church has long used John 10:16, as rendered in K.J.V., to support its claim to being the only true church: "Other sheep I have, which are not of this fold . . . and there shall be one fold, and one shepherd." R.S.V. alters this to "And I have other sheep, that are not of this fold. . . . So there shall be one flock, one shepherd." The K.J.V. version was influenced by the Catholic Vulgate, which translates two different Greek words as "fold." According to the R.S.V. translators, however, the true meaning is that, while there is more than one fold (or church), there is only one flock (the Christians in general). The revision that has raised the greatest doctrinal ruckus is the change in Isaiah 7:14 from "Behold, a virgin shall conceive" to "Behold, a young woman shall conceive." The verse is important as a prophecy of Christ's birth. One hard-shell Southern Baptist minister burned the page on the lawn of his church. Some fundamentalists have raised the Communist issue, notably the Reverend Carl McIntire, of Collingswood, New Jersey, who charges that some of the translators are "Leftists" and denounces R.S.V. as impious tampering with God's word. McIntire is a defrocked Presbyterian who has set up a minuscule but peppery International Council of Christian Churches to combat the National Council of the Churches, R.S.V.'s sponsor, which he believes to be tainted with "Leftism." He is currently wrangling with the State Department, which refuses to let him use West Germany as a base from which to launch balloons to bear small Bibles (K.J.V.) behind the Iron Curtain. To offset fundamentalist attacks, the publishers of R.S.V. have circulated a rebuttal pointing out, among other things, that scholars now agree that the Hebrew word *almah* means simply "young woman," while the Greek word *parthenos*, used in the New Testament account of Christ's birth, means "virgin" and is so translated, and that R.S.V. has been endorsed by the Southern Baptist Seminary and by the revivalist Billy Graham.

The great majority of the translating changes, while often important, are of little or no doctrinal significance. When K.J.V. has Pilate say of Jesus, "Nothing worthy of death is done unto Him," the sense clearly demands R.S.V.'s "has been done *by* Him." The "unto" may well have been a misprint, just as the "at" in K.J.V.'s "strain at a gnat" is undoubtedly a misprint for "out." (The early editions of K.J.V. were full of printer's errors. One was known as "the Wicked Bible" because the printer dropped the "not" out of the Seventh Commandment, producing "Thou shalt commit adultery." In another, the 119th Psalm's "Princes have persecuted me without a cause" became, appositely, "Printers have, etc.") Another famous K.J.V. phrase, "Thou madst him [man] a little lower than the angels" (Hebrews 2:7), is now revised to "Thou didst make him for a little while lower than the angels." In I John 4:19, K.J.V. has "We love Him [God] because he first loved us," but the Revisers, finding no "Him" in the Greek, render it "We love, because He first loved us." "Abstain from all appearance of evil" (I Thessalonians 5:22) now reads "Abstain from every form of evil." "Supposing that gain is godliness" (I Timothy 6:5) now reads "Imagining that godliness is a means of gain," and Paul's "For I know nothing by myself" is now "I am not aware of anything against myself." Often the old meanings are painful to give up, but accuracy, of course, must come first. In "For what shall it profit a man if he shall gain the whole world and lose his own soul," the last word is now rendered as "life," while the Kingdom of God is no longer "within you" but "in the midst of you," a comedown from the mystical to the sociological. Some important words were mistranslated in K.J.V. Thus the Greek *doulos* is always given as "servant," though it actually means "slave," an error that gave the false impression that Jesus and Paul were not concerned with the greatest social evil of their day. The Hebrew *Sheol* often appears in K.J.V. as "hell," though it is really a general term for the afterlife, like Hades, and not a place of punishment. Tyndale correctly translated the Greek *agape* as "love," but K.J.V., influenced by the Vulgate, in which the word is translated by the Latin *caritas*, changed it to "charity." R.S.V. returns to Tyndale's rendering, which gives more sense to such phrases as "faith, hope, and love." It also uses "steadfast love" as an attribute of God in place of K.J.V.'s "mercy," another example of a gain in accuracy producing a literary loss, as happens in "His steadfast love endures forever." Very occasionally, when the Revisers feel that an inaccurate phrase is too hallowed to monkey with, they allow it to stand, as when they leave "the valley of the shadow of death" in the Twenty-third Psalm, though everywhere else they change "shadow of death" to the more literal "deep darkness" or "gloom."

The other kind of legitimate change in R.S.V. is made to clear up obscurities. The Revisers state that K.J.V. contains over three hundred words whose meanings have changed so much that they are now misleading. In the K.J.V., "suffer" is used for "let," "let" for "prevent," and "prevent" for "precede" ("I prevented the dawning of the morning" in the 119th Psalm means merely "I rose before dawn"). Other examples are "careless" for "in security," "cleanness of teeth" for "famine," "communicate" for "share," "leasing" for "lies," "feebleminded" for "fainthearted," "reins" for "kidneys," and "virtue" for "power." Some words have become obsolete, among them "days-man" (umpire), "chapmen" (traders), "publicans" (tax collectors), "ouches" (jewel settings), and "neesings" (sneezings). Certain stylistic improvements, too, lead toward clarity. The startling advice, in I Corinthians 10:24, to "Let no man seek his own, but every man another's wealth" turns out to mean "Let no man seek his own good, but the good of his neighbor." In Job 40:8, R.S.V.'s "Will you even put me in the wrong?" is clearer than K.J.V.'s "Wilt thou also disannul my judgment?" And in Proverbs 28:21, R.S.V. is clearer with "To show partiality is not good" than K.J.V. with "To have respect of persons is not good." One is baffled by K.J.V.'s rendering of Genesis 29:17—"Leah was tender-eyed, but Rachel was beautiful"—but not by R.S.V.'s "Leah's eyes were weak." I had always thought Paul's "It is better to marry than burn" meant "burn in hellfire," but R.S.V. makes it "aflame with passion," which is unambiguous if banal. Job 13:12 is obscure in K.J.V. ("Your remembrances are like unto ashes, your bodies to bodies of clay") but not in R.S.V. ("Your maxims are proverbs of ashes, your defenses are defenses of clay"). The word "thank" always bothered me in Jesus's "For if ye love them which love you, what thank have ye? For sinners also love those that love them." R.S.V. clears it up with "What credit is that to you?" In addition to such improvements in detail here and there, some parts of the New Testament are better rendered in R.S.V. than in K.J.V., notably the Acts of the Apostles and much of the Pauline epistles. This is because the Acts and the Epistles are largely narrative or argumentative prose, written in a rather flat, workmanlike Greek, and clearness is what is needed and what R.S.V. can supply.

Had the Revisers limited themselves to these changes, surely no man would have cause to mislike them. But they have gone beyond legitimate and useful revision to produce a work whose literary texture is quite different from K.J.V., and they have mutilated or completely destroyed many of the phrases made precious by centuries of religious feeling and cultural tradition. Their intention was to revise the 1901 American Standard Version "in the direction of the . . . classic English style of the King James Version," but though they apparently think they have done so, they have actually shown little respect for K.J.V. For they also had a more important aim: to produce a Bible "written in language direct and clear and meaningful to people today," a Bible as close as possible to "the life and language of the common man in our day." In this they have succeeded all too well, but they don't seem to realize that this success conflicts with the first aim. The closer the Bible is brought to the "direct and clear and meaningful" sort of journalistic writing the American masses are now accustomed to, the farther it must depart from the language of Shakespeare and Milton. This is an age of prose, not of poetry, and R.S.V. is a prose Bible, while K.J.V. is a poetic one.

True, the morning stars still sing together, man is still born unto trouble as the sparks fly upward, the lilies of the field still eclipse Solomon in all his glory, Ecclesiastes still preaches "vanity of vanities," and David still laments over Saul and Jonathan, "How are the mighty fallen! Tell it not in Gath, publish it not in the streets of Ashkelon." So, too, our bombers tried to spare the more celebrated monuments of Europe, though "military necessity" often compelled their destruction. The Revisers' military necessity is the language of the Common Man. Reading their work is like walking through an old city that has just been given, if not a saturation bombing, a thorough going-over. One looks about anxiously. Is this gone? Does that still survive? Surely they might have spared *that!* And even though many of the big landmarks are left—their fabric weakened by the Revisers' policy of modernizing the grammatical usage—so many of the lesser structures have been razed that the whole feel of the place is different. In Cologne, the cathedral still stands, alone and strange, in the midst of miles of rubble.

If the Revisers had changed K.J.V. only where modern scholarship found its translation defective, one would hardly notice the alterations. But what they are really translating is not the original Greek and Hebrew but the English of the King James Version, and the language they have put it into is modern expository prose, direct and clear, and also flat, insipid, and mediocre. To accomplish this alchemy in reverse, they have had to do a number of things. They have, first of all, modernized the usage. "Thou," "ye," "thy," and "thine" are replaced by "you" and "your"; the obsolete verb endings "-est" and "-eth" are dropped; inverted word order is generally avoided; "unto" becomes "to," "whither" "where," "whatsoever" "whatever," and so on. This was done not for comprehensibility, since any literate person knows what the old forms mean, but as part of the policy of making the Bible more "accessible" to the modern reader or listener. And, indeed, R.S.V. does slip more smoothly into the modern ear, but it also slides out more easily; the very strangeness and antique ceremony of the old forms made them linger in the mind. The 1901 American Standard Version kept the old usage, and I think rightly. For there are other considerations, too. One is the loss of familiarity. It is extraordinary what a difference modernization makes; even passages otherwise undisturbed have a blurred, slightly off-register effect. The Hebrew Old Testament is an archaic document, far more primitive even than Homer, and the old usage seems more appropriate. "Thus saith the Lord" is more Lordly than "Thus says the Lord," "Praise ye the Lord!" is more exalted than "Praise the Lord!" The Ten Commandments lose when the awesome "Thou shalt not" is stepped down to the querulous "You shall not"; the prophet Nathan's terrible denunciation to King David, "Thou art the man!," collapses in the police-report "You are the man!," and God's solemn words to Adam, "Dust thou art, and unto dust shalt thou return," are flattened in the conversational "You are dust, and to dust you shall return." A better case can be made for modernizing the New Testament's usage, since it was written in the everyday Greek of the common people. But the Common Man of the first century A.D. was a considerably more poetic and (if he was a Christian) devout creature than his similar of the twentieth century, and the religious passion of Jesus and Paul, transcending modern experience, needs an exalted idiom to be adequately conveyed. "Verily, verily I say unto you" gets it better than "Truly, truly I say to you"; Jesus's "Suffer the little children to come unto me" (Mark 10:14) is more moving than R.S.V.'s "Let the children come to me," which sounds like a mother at a picnic.

The Revisers state that the old usage has been preserved in "language addressed to God or in exalted poetic apostrophe." The first exemption has been respected—why God's own language should not also be permitted some antique elevation I cannot see—but the second often has not. Surely the Psalms are "exalted poetic apostrophe," yet in the Nineteenth Psalm, "Day unto day uttereth speech, and night unto night showeth knowledge" is diminished to "Day to day pours forth speech, and night to night declares knowledge." Even the sacred (one would think) Twenty-third Psalm comes out a bit fuzzy: "He makes me lie down" for the rhythmic "He maketh me to lie down," and instead of the triumphant "Yea, though I walk through the valley of the shadow of death" the tamer "Even though I walk." The most damaging effect of modernizing the usage is the alteration of rhythm, which is all-important in a book so often read aloud; quite aside from literary grace, the ceremonial effect of the Bible is enhanced by the interesting, varied, and suitable rhythms of K.J.V. But to (partially) avoid inversion, the Revisers render "Male and female created He them" (Genesis 1:27) "Male and female He created them," breaking the rhythm's back simply by changing the position of two words. In K.J.V., Ecclesiastes moves to a slow, mourning music:

What profit hath a man of all his labor which he taketh under the sun? One generation passeth and another generation cometh, but the earth abideth forever. . . . For there is no remembrance of the wise more than of the fool for ever, seeing that which now is in the days to come shall all be forgotten. And how dieth the wise man? As the fool.

This now steps along to a brisker, less complex, and also less authoritative measure:

What does a man gain by all the toil at which he toils under the sun? A generation goes and a generation comes, but the earth remains forever. . . . For of the wise man as of the fool there is no enduring remembrance, seeing that in the days to come all will have been long forgotten. How the wise man dies just like the fool!

Ruth's familiar and moving "Whither thou goest, I will go" loses its cadenced charm when it is transmuted into "Where you go, I will go." So, too, Philippians 4:8 ("Finally, brethren, whatsoever things are true, whatsoever things are honest, whatsoever things are just") is robbed of its earnest gravity when it is speeded up by replacing "whatsoever" with "whatever," just as Matthew 11:28 ("Come unto me, all ye that labor and are heavy laden") becomes inappropriately brisk when it is modernized to "Come to me, all who labor." I won't comment on changing Luke 16:3

from "I cannot dig; to beg I am ashamed" to "I am not strong enough to dig, and I am ashamed to beg."

In this modernization there is an understandable, if misguided, principle at work. But many changes seem to derive not from principle but merely from officiousness, from the restlessness that causes people to pluck imaginary or microscopic bits of fluff off coat lapels. Too frequently some great and familiar phrase is marred or obliterated for the sake of a trivial change in the sense, or none at all. "Den of thieves" is now "den of robbers," "Let the dead bury their dead" is now "Leave the dead to bury their own dead," "maid" becomes "maiden" in "the way of a man with a maid," hypocrites are "whitewashed tombs" instead of the familiar "whited sepulchres," "O death where is thy sting, O grave where is thy victory?" yields to the just-out-of-focus "O death where is thy victory, O death where is thy sting?," and Jesus's "Can the blind lead the blind? Shall they not both fall into the ditch?" is capriciously rephrased into "Can a blind man lead a blind man? Will they not both fall into a pit?"

More numerous are the changes that involve a slight change in sense. But granting that Joseph really wore not "a coat of many colors" but "a long robe with sleeves," that the Gadarene swine were really the Gerasene swine and Calvary was more properly called The Skull, that "the children of Israel" is less accurate than "the people of Israel" and that these children, or people, refrained from putting their new wine into old wineskins and not old bottles, that the Old Testament desert actually blossomed not like a rose but like a crocus, that Job really put the price of wisdom above pearls and not above rubies, that the silver cord was "snapped" rather than "loosed," that the widow gave not her "mites" but "two copper coins," that the writing on Belshazzar's wall was not "Mene mene tekel upharsin" but "Mene mene tekel and parsin," that the Psalmist saw the wicked man "towering like a cedar" instead of "spreading himself like a green bay tree," that Adam was not "of the earth, earthy" but "from the earth, a man of dust," and that "my cup overflows" and "by the mouth of babes and infants" are more up-to-date locutions than "my cup runneth over" and "out of the mouth of babes and sucklings"—granting all this, it is still doubtful that such trivial gains in accuracy are not outweighed by the loss of such long-cherished beauty of phrasing. Might not the Revisers have let well enough, and indeed a good deal better than well enough, alone?

Other doubts swarm. I can't understand why "The spirit of God moved upon the face of the waters" had to be changed to "was moving over the face of the waters" or why the Nineteenth Psalm had to be altered from

"The heavens declare the glory of God" to "The heavens are telling the glory of God." I don't know why "there shall be weeping and gnashing of teeth" (Matthew 22:13) had to become "there men will weep and gnash their teeth" or why Paul's magnificent eloquence (in K.J.V., at least) has to be hamstrung by pettifogging and needless alterations. For example, in I Corinthians 13:1, "Though I speak with the tongues of men and of angels, and have not charity, I am become as sounding brass or a tinkling cymbal" is mutilated to "a noisy gong or a clanging cymbal," and in Ephesians 6:12, the familiar grandeur of "For we wrestle not against flesh and blood but against principalities, against powers, against the rulers of the darkness of this world, against spiritual wickedness in high places" is revised to "For we are not contending against flesh and blood but against the principalities, against the powers, against the world rulers of this present darkness, against the spiritual hosts of wickedness in the heavenly places." Substituting "noisy gong" for "sounding brass" and the weak, abstract "contending" for the vivid "wrestle" seems to me malicious mischief, if not assault and battery.

They have even rewritten the Lord's Prayer. "As we forgive our debtors" is changed to "as we also have forgiven our debtors," a bit of lint-picking that might have been forgone in the interest of tradition—and euphony. "For Thine is the kingdom, and the power, and the glory, for-ever. Amen" is omitted (though given in a footnote) because they believe it a corruption of the original text. But, after all, the fact that Bernini's colonnades were not part of the original plan of St. Peter's is hardly a rea-son for doing away with them. Some of the manuscripts discovered last spring in that Dead Sea cave may turn out to be more ancient and uncor-rupted than anything discovered up to now. They may also turn out to differ importantly from what has been known for the last thousand years as "The Bible." Maybe the Ten Commandments are a late interpolation. But if they are, I should think that even the Revisers would hesitate to give the public this Bible, pure and uncorrupted though it be, in place of the familiar text.

The *raison d'être* of R.S.V., however, is not scholarly but stylistic; to produce a more "readable" Bible. This being an age much more matter-of-fact than the seventeenth century—or the first century, for that matter—an age more used to skimming rapidly over a large quantity of journalistic prose than to dwelling intensively on a few poetic works, to make the Bi-ble "readable" means to have it "make sense" to a reader who wants to know simply What's It All About. Poetic intensity or prophetic exaltation interferes with this easy, rapid assimilation partly because such language is idiosyncratic and partly because it strikes down to depths of response which it takes time and effort for the reader to reach. Literature, and especially religious literature, is not primarily concerned with being clear and reasonable; it is connotative rather than direct, suggestive rather than explicit, decorative and incantatory rather than functional. To make the Bible readable in the modern sense means to flatten out, tone down, and convert into tepid expository prose what in K.J.V. is wild, full of awe, poetic, and passionate. It means stepping down the voltage of K.J.V. so it won't blow any fuses. The Revisers have admirably and horribly succeeded; babes and sucklings (or infants) can play with R.S.V. without the slightest danger of electrocution.

In K.J.V., God describes the battle horse to Job: "Hast thou given the horse strength? Hast thou clothed his neck with thunder? . . . The glory of his nostrils is terrible. . . . He saith among the trumpets, Ha, Ha." R.S.V. steps it down to "Do you give the horse his might? Do you clothe his neck with strength? . . . His majestic snorting is terrible. . . . When the trumpet sounds, he says, 'Aha!' " The trick is turned by replacing the metaphorical "thunder" with the literal "strength," by converting the thrilling "glory of his nostrils" into the prosaic "majestic snorting" (a snort can be many things, but never majestic), and toning down the wild "Ha, Ha" into the conversational "Aha!" A like fate has overtaken the Sermon on the Mount. Comparing this as rendered in K.J.V. and in R.S.V. is like hearing a poet read his verses while someone stands by and paraphrases. The exalted has become flat, the pungent bland, the rhythm crippled, phrases dear for centuries to English-speaking people have disappeared or are maimed. For example:

But let your communication be "Yea, Yea," "Nay, Nay."
Let what you say be simply, "Yes" or "No."

Behold the fowls of the air.
Look at the birds of the air.

And why take ye thought for raiment? Consider the lilies of the field, how they grow; they toil not, neither do they spin; and yet I say unto you that even Solomon in all his glory was not arrayed like one of these.

And why are you anxious about clothing? Consider the lilies of the field, how they grow; they neither toil nor spin; yet I tell you, even Solomon, etc. . . .

Enter ye in at the strait gate: for wide is the gate and broad is the way that leadeth to destruction, and many there be which go in thereat; because strait is the gate and narrow is the way which leadeth unto life, and few there be that find it.

Enter by the narrow gate: for the gate is wide and the way is easy that leads to destruction, and those who enter by it are many. For the gate is narrow and the way is hard that leads to life, and those who find it are few.

Wherefore by their fruits ye shall know them.
Thus you will know them by their fruits.

The Song of Solomon is now slightly off key. "Our vines have tender grapes" has become "Our vineyards are in blossom"—the Revisers have a weakness for Spelling It Out. Instead of "Thy navel is like a round goblet, which wanteth not liquor" we get "Your navel is a rounded bowl that never lacks mixed wine," which disturbingly suggests a cocktail party; the lyrical "How fair and how pleasant art thou, O love, for delights!" is changed into the mawkish and stumbling "How fair and pleasant you are, O loved one, delectable maiden!" Repetition, another poetic (and hieratic) device, is generally avoided, perhaps because it is felt to be of no expository value. The K.J.V. Lord cries out, "I have seen, I have seen the affliction of my people" (Acts 7:34), but the R.S.V. Lord merely states, "I have surely seen the ill-treatment of my people." The ominous and brooding effect, in the description of hell in Mark 9, of repeating in verses 44, 46, and 48, the great line "Where their worm dieth not and the fire is not quenched" is escaped by omitting verses 44 and 46.

There *is* an attempt at poetry; a fancy "literary" word is often used in place of a homely one. Now, as Wordsworth observed, a simple word is always more poetic than a "poetic" one. A stylistic virtue of K.J.V. is the tact with which it uses stately, sonorous Latin-root abstract words *and* humble, concrete Anglo-Saxon words, each in its appropriate place. If the Revisers pull to earth K.J.V.'s swelling Latin passages, they also give a bogus elevation, a false refinement to its direct, homely passages; if they tone down some strings, they tone up others, adjusting them all to produce a dead monotone. Thus "dirt" becomes "mire" (Psalms 18:42), "clothes" "mantle" (Matthew 24:18), "I brake the jaws of the wicked" "I broke the fangs of the unrighteous" (Job 29:17), in each case a more archaic word being put in place of a modern (but homely) one. In K.J.V. sin "lieth" at the door, but it is "couching" in R.S.V.; the blind "see" and the hungry "are filled" in K.J.V., but in R.S.V. they "receive their sight" and "are satisfied"; K.J.V. renders I Samuel 4:22: "The glory is departed from Israel, for the ark of God is taken," but this is too stark for R.S.V., which changes it to "the ark of God has been captured." Often the Revisers inflate the simplicity and understatement of K.J.V. into prose resembling cotton candy. The lovely phrase in Ecclesiastes 12:5, "Man goeth to his long home," with its sombre, long-drawn-out "o"s and its austere melancholy, is Spelled Out into "Man goes to his eternal home," which sounds like a mortician's ad. K.J.V. often uses concrete action words to metaphorically suggest an abstract meaning, but R.S.V. prefers less vivid abstractions. In her perceptive article in the *Ladies' Home Journal* on the two versions, Dorothy Thompson gave a perfect example of this. Psalms 42:1 reads, in K.J.V., "As the hart panteth after the water brooks, so panteth my soul after Thee, O God." R.S.V. makes it "As a hart longs for flowing streams, so longs my soul for Thee, O God!" As Miss Thompson remarked, a hart pants but does not long, or if he does, he can, being inarticulate, express his emotions only in some action like panting. The passionate vigor of K.J.V. depends on the hart's being an animal, not a sentimental human being in a deerskin. If, however, there is a chance for a good, safe cliché—another method of making the Bible more "readable" —R.S.V. reverses this process; "When he thought thereon, he wept" becomes "He broke down and wept," "All things have I seen in the days of my vanity" becomes "In my vain life I have seen everything," and "They were pricked in their heart" becomes "They were cut to the heart."

R.S.V. has also departed from simplicity in certain matters of "taste," mostly involving sex. If only to avoid adolescent giggles in church, some Elizabethan terms must be avoided in this degenerate and refined age—as in I Samuel 25:22, in which the expression "any that pisseth against the wall" is discreetly omitted—but Nice Nellie is altogether too prominent. Thus "whore" is rendered "harlot," although the former term is still current while the latter is archaic (but, for that very reason, Nicer). Thus the wise and the foolish virgins have become "maidens," as well as more archaic and less sexy, costing us, incidentally, still another familiar expression. "My bowels boiled" is now "My heart is in turmoil," "sore boils" are "loathsome sores," "dung hill" is "ash heap." The Revisers even fear "belly." "Fill his belly with the east wind" becomes "fill himself" and Psalms 22:10 is changed from "I was cast upon Thee from the womb; Thou art my God from my mother's belly" to "upon Thee was I cast from my birth, and since my mother bore me Thou hast been my God," which is also a good example of Spelling It Out. " 'Belly,' " says H. W. Fowler in *Modern English Usage*, "is a good word now almost done to death by genteelism."

"The King James Bible," write the Revisers, apropos the failure of the

1885 and the 1901 revisions to replace it, "has still continued to hold its place upon the lecterns of the majority of churches. . . . Congregations have gone on loving it best because it seemed to them incomparably beautiful." One wonders how they could think their version preserves this beauty. K.J.V.'s "dignity and profundity," they go on, "are the result of the utmost clarity, directness, and simplicity. These qualities have been earnestly sought in R.S.V." But K.J.V. also has very different qualities—strange, wild, romantic, complex turns of style, since Elizabethan English was as much in the rococo as in the classic mode. This is especially true of the Old Testament. Clarity, directness, and simplicity are hardly an adequate definition of the qualities of poetry. Milton's "simple, sensuous, and passionate" is more adequate; R.S.V. usually achieves the first, rarely the second (rhythm being the chief sensuous element in poetry), and almost never the third. "Poetry differs from prose in the concrete colors of its diction. It is not enough for it to furnish a meaning to philosophers. It must also appeal to emotions with the charm of direct impression, flashing through regions where the intellect can only grope. Poetry must render what is said, not what is merely meant." So writes the prince of modern translators, Ezra Pound, who might have made a much better job of the new Bible than the Dean of the Yale Divinity School and his learned but unliterate colleagues.

"Our conversation [compared to that of the Elizabethans] is direct and tense; our narrative . . . swift and unadorned," the Revisers state. "Our words are likely to be shorter and our sentences, too. . . . Therefore in this translation, it has been a constant purpose to make every word and sentence clear, to avoid involved constructions, and to make the current of the central thought flow in such a straight sure channel that the minds of the listeners will be carried forward unmistakably and not dropped into verbal whirlpools by the way. . . . The style is, as nearly as possible, such as the rank and file of Bible readers today will understand with as little difficulty as possible . . . so as to permit the attention of the hearer or reader to center on the message and not be diverted by the language." But style is not mere decoration, and it is precisely the function of language to "divert" the reader; form, in a work of art like K.J.V., cannot be separated from content, nor can the central current be separated from "verbal whirlpools." It is true that today K.J.V. is harder to read than R.S.V. This difficulty, though, is not a defect but the inevitable accompaniment of virtues that R.S.V. has had to remove in order to remove the difficulty. The difficulty in reading K.J.V. is simply that it is high art, which will always demand more from the reader, for it makes its appeal on so many planes. *Ulysses* and *The Waste Land*, while modern works, are more difficult in this sense than an eighteenth-century newspaper. It is the price of artistic quality, and the Revisers are unwilling to pay it. Probably the main obstacle in K.J.V. today is its archaic style—the obsolete grammatical usage, the inversions, and all the other devices of Elizabethan English. But our culture is lucky—or was until R.S.V. came along—in having in K.J.V. a great literary monument to which, because it also happens to have a religious function, practically everybody, no matter how unliterary or meagrely educated, was at some time exposed, in church or Sunday school or at home.

And why this itch for modernizing anyway? Why is it not a good thing to have variety in our language, to have a work whose old-fashioned phrases exist in the living language, to preserve in one area of modern life the old forms of speech, so much more imaginative and moving than our own nervous, pragmatic style? As it enriches us to leave beautiful old buildings standing when they are no longer functional or to perform Shakespeare without watering his poetry down into prose, so with the Bible. The noblest ancient fane must be trussed and propped and renovated now and then, but why do it in the slashing style of the notorious Gothic "restorations" of Viollet-le-Duc? In any event, I think the Revisers exaggerate the difficulty of K.J.V. Almost all of it is perfectly understandable to anyone who will give a little thought and effort to it, plus some of that over-valued modern commodity, time. Those who won't can hardly claim a serious interest in the Bible as either literature or religion.

Writing of the 1885 revised version, Allen Wikgren observes, in *The Interpreter's Bible*, "Purchasers found themselves in possession of a text in which the number of changes far exceed all previous estimates. Of some 180,000 words in the New Testament, alterations amounted to an estimated 30,000, or an average of 4½ per verse. . . . It was not long, however, before the number and character of the changes provoked a strong reaction. . . . Charges of unnecessary departure from the familiar phraseology, undue literalism, elaborate overcorrection, destruction of beauty and rhythm, impoverishment of the English language and the like flew thick and fast." All but the second of these charges can be sustained against R.S.V., even though it has not gone so far as such other modern versions as those of Moffatt, Rieu, and Smith-Goodspeed. Whether it will be any more successful in replacing K.J.V. than the 1885 version was remains to be seen. If it is, what is now simply a blunder—a clerical error, so to speak—will become a catastrophe. Bland, flavorless mediocrity will have replaced the pungency of genius. And if the salt have lost his savor, wherewith shall it be salted? That is to say (R.S.V.): if salt has lost its taste, how shall its saltness be restored?

UNDERSTANDING THE TEXT

1. Why, after his opening paragraph, does Macdonald devote two long paragraphs to a brief history and characterization of the King James Version of the Bible?

2. What is the function in Macdonald's essay of the history of Biblical translation given next (pp. 263–265)?

3. In a paragraph summarize the similarities and differences between the 1885 Standard Version, described on pp. 264–265, and the King James Version.

4. Why was the Revised Standard Version undertaken? How did the translators of the R.S.V. view their task in relation to the Standard Version and to the King James Version?

5. List what Macdonald regards as the different kinds of legitimate departures of the R.S.V. from the K.J.V.

6. Explain Macdonald's metaphor of the "alchemy in reverse" which the R.S.V. translators have brought about.

7. What are the main kinds of departures of the R.S.V. from the King James text that Macdonald condemns?

8. Explain the grounds of his objection in each case.

9. In the modernizations which Macdonald illustrates on pp. 269–272, there is, he says, "an understandable, if misguided, principle at work." What is the principle, how is it understandable, and why does Macdonald think it is misguided?

10. Euphony is harmonious or pleasing sound. Explain why Macdonald says that the change from "As we forgive our debtors" to "As we also have forgiven our debtors" might have been forgone in the interest of euphony.

11. What effort did the R.S.V. translators make to achieve literary or poetic effects? Explain why Macdonald regards this effort as a mistake.

TOPICS FOR DISCUSSION AND WRITING

12. One of Macdonald's major contentions is that the R.S.V. is a "prose" Bible, while the K.J.V. is a "poetic" one. Collect from the essay material for two paragraphs defining Macdonald's conception of a poetic and of a prose style.

13. The translators of the R.S.V. attempted to adapt their style to the understanding of the modern reader; the value they chiefly sought was ease of

communication. Macdonald's objections to the R.S.V. translation arise in large measure from his concern for other values which are lost in the translation. Write a paragraph defining the values which Macdonald wishes to preserve.

14. Macdonald's diction is frequently racy and informal—e.g., "went up like a rocket," "doctrinal ruckus," "monkey with," "stepped-down," "thorough going-over," "itch for modernizing," etc. Collect other examples of this sort of diction from the essay. Write a paragraph on the appropriateness of diction of this kind to Macdonald's criticism of the R.S.V. translators.

Darwin and the Tangled Bank

THEODORE BAIRD

DETAILS of the scene can be filled in. They were both very great men. Carlyle was eighty. On his latest birthday he had been much honored. From Prussia came a decoration—"The Star . . . is really very pretty . . . hung with a black ribbon, with silver edges. . . . Had they sent me a ¼ lb. of good Tobacco the addition to my happiness had probably been . . . greater!" From America and Harvard came an honorary LL.D., and Disraeli, beginning his letter, "A Government should recognize intellect," offered him the Grand Cross of the Bath.

Darwin was sixty-six, and *The Origin* had been published for sixteen years. At home and abroad learned societies had delighted in recognizing him, and he too was entitled to wear the star with the black silver-edged ribbon, the Prussian *Pour le Mérite*. In the public mind he played a unique part, for his name had been appropriated to stand for what vast numbers of people professed to be against, Darwinism. He had been abused, denounced and reviled. Carlyle, in ordinary conversation, but not to the man's face, had had his say often enough: our descent from the apes is a humiliating discovery, which scientists had much better have kept to themselves, and, in short, he would like to lay his stick over Darwin's back. "I find no one," he told Allingham, "who has the deep abhorrence of [Darwinism] . . . that I have in my heart of hearts!" Here then was a combination of persons more crucial than in the famous meeting of the libertine Wilkes and the moralist Johnson; here was personified the clash between science and literature, empiricism and intuition.

We owe our knowledge of what they talked about to Carlyle's brief report. "I asked him," he said, "if he thought there was a possibility of men

Reprinted from *The American Scholar*, Autumn, 1946. Copyright, 1946, by the United Chapters of Phi Beta Kappa. Used by permission of the author and the editor.

turning into apes again. . . . [Darwin] laughed much at this, and came back to it over and over again." Completely won over by Darwin personally, Carlyle was pleased with the meeting, and he told Allingham, who thought the phrase curious, that Darwin was a "pleasant, *jolly*-minded man." What Darwin thought of this exchange may well be contained in the sentence where he says of Carlyle, "As far as I could judge, I never met a man with a mind so ill adapted for scientific research."

Plainly Carlyle belongs to literature. Darwin's position is obscure. A popular textbook places him at the opposite pole, remarking that his work "cannot be said to belong to literature, if in the definition of literary work is presupposed an effort towards artistic expression." Yet Darwin, who certainly never thought of himself as a writer like Carlyle, was deeply concerned with literary composition, as the extensive remarks to Bates of the *Amazon* reveal. There were people who were born writers, he admitted, but he found the work hard. He had found it a good plan whenever he was in difficulties to fancy that some one had entered the room and asked him what he is doing; then he would try to explain "what it is all about." He added, "I think too much pains cannot be taken in making the style transparently clear and throwing eloquence to the dogs." The effort toward expression was there, and it would be a harsh critic who did not find artistic the result in the *Voyage of the Beagle*.

Darwin's subject—the face of the earth, the processes of nature—had long been within the scope of literature, and in his attitude there was nothing consciously novel. In the presence of the mystery or the beauty or the violence of nature, with the accompanying possible responses of worship or pleasure or shock, a writer could say, "Here it is, look at it," while simultaneously he communicated to the reader the effect, "How divine"; "How lovely"; or "How horrible." This, indeed, is the literary experience—seeing the object, feeling an emotion. And it is this which Darwin communicates on page after page of the *Journal and Remarks* made on the voyage around the world of H.M.S. Beagle. His emotions he records in the plain and modest language of the eighteenth century. They are none the less strong.

Naturally many were pleasurable. In reflecting on the five years' experience, he says he enjoyed himself deeply. His biggest word, *sublime*, he applies to large effects, like the forests of Brazil, "where the powers of life are predominant," or to Tierra del Fuego, "where Death and Decay prevail." Milder adjectives are *glorious, beautiful, delicious, striking, pretty*, and he is moved to speak of the "inexpressible charm" of life in the open air: the deathlike stillness of the plains, the Gauchos making their beds round the fire, the dogs keeping watch. More than once he deliberately took thought how to convey to the reader the pleasure he felt: "I wish to find language to express my ideas. Epithet after epithet was found too weak to convey to those who have not visited the intertropical regions the sensations of delight which the mind experiences."

Yet violence, destruction and death were everywhere part of the charming landscape, like the slowly wheeling condor in the sky. The observer's experience is complicated, and the emotions mixed. In the foreground there is ever present the human being—the Fuegian savage, described in pages comparable to Swift on the Yahoo, slavery in Brazil, the conflict of races in New Zealand. "Wherever the European has trod, death seems to pursue the aboriginal." The same kind of fact met him everywhere. There was the cormorant playing with the fish it caught: "Eight times successively the bird let its prey go, then dived after it." There were the seals lying in astonishing numbers on the rocks, watched in the sky all the while "by the patient but inauspicious eyes of the turkey-buzzard. This disgusting bird. . . ."

Inanimate nature provoked even more violent response. The concepts of time and space, which might be enlarged by the attentive perusal of the paragraphs in Lyell's *Principles of Geology* on prepossessions in regard to the duration of past time, were shattered by the presence before his eyes of bones and shells and mountain ranges and in his ears the sound of running water. By immediate observation Darwin was forced to review his prepossessions, to consider how time in sufficient quantities could be conceived of; and the language he uses indicates how great was his perplexity. "It is impossible to reflect on the changed state of the American continent," he says, "without the deepest astonishment. . . . Certainly, no fact in the long history of the world is so startling as the wide and repeated exterminations of its inhabitants."

He returns to this problem, and once with especial solemnity. Climbing a pass in the Andes he saw and heard the muddy, steeply inclined mountain streams, whose roar was like that of the sea. "Amidst the din of rushing waters, the noise of the stones, as they rattled one over another, was most distinctly audible even from a distance. . . . The sound spoke eloquently to the geologist, the thousands and thousands of stones, which, striking against each other, made the one dull uniform sound, were all hurrying in one direction. It was like thinking on time, where the minute that now glides past is irrecoverable. So it was with these stones; the ocean is their eternity, and each note of that wild music told of one more step toward their destiny."

Often he had seen beds of mud and sand and shingle thousands of feet thick, and he had been inclined to exclaim that such enormous masses could never have been formed by natural causes, grain on grain. "But . . . when listening to the rattling noise of these torrents, and calling to mind that whole races of animals have passed away from the face of the earth, and that during this whole period, night and day, these stones have gone rattling onwards in their course, I have thought to myself, can any mountains, any continent, withstand such waste?" Any continent—as if nothing could be more stable. Yet even this prepossession was destroyed by the "perfect horror" of the earthquake at Valdivia. "I falter where I firmly trod," says Tennyson, and every reader knows his words are metaphorical, alluding to instabilities of faith, but for Darwin the quaking of the earth was a literal experience with consequences on his systematic thinking. "The earth, the very emblem of solidity, has moved beneath our feet," he says, "like a thin crust over a fluid."

In this mixed response to nature—so beautiful, so horrible—Darwin was, of course, like many another man. Among his contemporaries the serious writers were making it their business to convey this very tension, to frame statements about it, even to resolve it, and in so doing they used traditional forms of speech, metaphors. They spoke as if an analogy between their manner of speaking and the universe really existed; and their readers, making the proper allowances, knew what they meant. It is unlikely that anyone ever asked Tennyson whether "God's finger touch'd him, and he slept," is an accurate verbal equivalent for the bursting of a blood vessel, nor was Carlyle besought to define in operational language his splendid, ringing phrases. Communication between author and reader was sustained by words which always meant more than their literal paraphrase, and the meaning was an insight, an intuition.

When in the *Origin* Darwin came to express how Nature as a whole seemed to him, he, too, used a metaphor. Nature, he said, is like something else, a struggle for existence, in which the fittest survive. The public instantly knew what he meant, recognizing the similarity as true (the Social Darwinians) or as false (the anti-Darwinians). And as a metaphor it must stand for some general experience, some common feeling about life, like that contained in the comparison with a flame ("Out, out, brief candle") or with a growing thing ("All flesh is as grass"). It implies what was by the middle of the nineteenth century a familiar literary attitude, the act of witnessing and feeling about, as at a play. It involves recognition of hero and villain, conflict, victory and defeat, and the conversion of painful emotions into pleasure. The dramatist asserts that everything turns out right, and the audience is satisfied, the tension relaxed. "Now cracks a noble heart. Good night, sweet prince, and flights of angels sing thee to thy rest!"

Educated readers were accustomed to the most exquisite verbal consolations about the death of Hamlet or the fall of man or the decline of the Roman Empire, and the ultimate, the inexpressible meanings resided in metaphor, as in the similarity of "good night," "rest," and "death." The transfer of this trained literary attitude to nature and its processes was apparently not difficult. A handful of seeds thrown on the ground becomes a drama. No matter how painful some moments, the spectator is finally satisfied. True, a number of seeds did not germinate, others were starved out, parasites and disease were shockingly destructive, but the play has a good ending—the survivors are the better plants. The complicated literary expression known as tragedy had recognized a paradox, that death is sometimes better than life, so that we applaud defeat. The metaphor of struggle for existence revises this proposition to read, life *is* better than death, the living *are* better than the dead. If nature is horrible, it is finally beautiful.

This kind of interpretation was to be expected from readers brought up on the prophetic writing of the nineteenth century. Carlyle could proclaim that the Universe is made by Law, that the great Soul of the World is just. "Look thou, if thou have eyes or soul left, into this great shoreless Incomprehensible: in the heart of its tumultuous Appearances, Embroilments, and mad Time-vortexes, is there not, silent, eternal, an All-just, an All-Beautiful . . ." and so on, ending, "This is not a figure of speech; this is a fact."

But Darwin was using language in quite another manner. He took pains to say that the struggle for existence is not a fact but only a figure of speech. He stops dead in his tracks, when first using the term, to explain, "I use this term in a large and metaphorical sense," and he defines exactly what in nature he is pointing at. Two dogs in a time of dearth may be truly said to struggle for life as they fight for a bone. Second, the phrase is extended to include the relation of dependence: a plant on the edge of a desert is dependent on sufficient moisture, a mistletoe is dependent on the apple tree. Third, the phrase includes success in leaving progeny. These three different kinds of behavior are represented by the shorthand notation, struggle for existence. And in detail Darwin was careful not to confuse his manner of speaking with the thing spoken of. Thus he writes, every single organic being *"may be said* to be striving. . . ."

Some readers knew well enough what Darwin was talking about. Asa

Gray straightened out a correspondent who could not see how plants "struggled" since they had neither consciousness nor will, by replying that something really did happen in nature, "call the action what you please— competition (that is open to the same objection), collision, or what not— it is just what I should think Darwin was driving at," and he refers him to the relevant passages of definition in *The Origin*. Here is a language difficulty. What phrase can stand for "the action" of nature, since it contains in it so many separate items, capable of expression in so many possible relationships? Any one metaphor—struggle, competition, collision—is little better than another, since none can express nature in its entirety. To understand the meaning of the phrase the reader must comprehend the grandly complex context, established by the author, in which nature appears as a multiplicity, so varied in its movements, that only the most wide-ranging mind can take it in.

Yet the parallel phrase, survival of the fittest, seems to imply that nature turns out right and that the best man wins. Each creature tends to become more and more improved, and this improvement leads to gradual advance in organization. This, says Darwin, is an intricate subject. Only a careless reader could suppose that Darwin saw clear direction in any given moment or event, that he was ever in a position to applaud the hero or hiss the villain, like the spectator in the theater—for at great length he expresses objections and qualifications to his own theory. A sequence of events can be labeled "improvement," but this word is not a fact, it is only a figure of speech. What exactly does it refer to in nature? Naturalists are not agreed among themselves, as they shift their points of view and adopt different scales of measurement. It can be defined—in words—as high differentiation and specialization of the several organs, but how do they apply to a particular organism, how as a means of comparison of two organisms? What, for example, is to be said of the many low forms which have not advanced since the dawn of life, where no sequence of improvement is perceptible, which, nevertheless, when dissected, reveal to the naturalist "their really wondrous and beautiful organization"? Then there are cases of "what we must call retrogression of organization," and how does that fit into movement going in one direction? As for the comparison of different types, to make an ascending scale seems hopeless, for "who will decide whether a cuttlefish be higher than a bee?"

The objection that a theory which must be so qualified is of little use is obviously wrong. Asa Gray and other readers knew what Darwin was talking about. Darwin's position as a writer was identical with that of the historian. Gibbon had been able to speak of events as true—in a certain way. He defined his scale, civilization under the Antonines, and, at the other extreme, the illiterate barbarian, so that the basic metaphor of decline and fall refers to something more expressed than the reader's personal scale of civilization. In detail, of course, he could not be sure of very much. The precise behavior of a particular Scythian during every moment of his life was unknown to him or to any man, but the general westward movement, in "waves," of the pastoral tribes of Asia, is an historical fact.

The figure of speech, then, points to a complicated event. A blow by blow account, with victory and defeat determined by the universal umpire, the score carefully kept, is impossible in the struggle of any organism's existence. How little he knew in detail Darwin is constantly reminding the reader: "We know hardly anything about. . . . If we make due allowance for our profound ignorance. . . . This ought to convince us of our ignorance. . . ." Granting, however, the enormous limitations of knowledge under which the historian and the scientist labor, we do know what they are driving at: that life has flourished in many forms, that whole races have disappeared, yet the historical record can be made out by the trained observer, and this record can be expressed in a large, metaphorical sense.

The basic figure for this process is the tree of life—the trunk, the branches and twigs, some living, some dead, all representing complex relationships. "I believe," said Darwin, "this simile largely speaks the truth," and for a page and item by item he works out the similitude of that great tree "which fills with its dead and broken branches the crust of the earth, and covers the surface with its ever-branching and beautiful ramifications." The related movement which takes place while the tree grows, one part living, another part dying, one part branching out and continuing the succession—this is the struggle for existence. The way in which this movement takes place is natural selection. And as for the survival of the fittest, "The inhabitants of the world at successive periods in its history have beaten their predecessors in the race for life, and are, in so far *higher* in the scale." This is, indeed, largely the truth. On the diagram known as a family tree the living are higher on the scale than the dead. A temporal relation is represented spatially.

Darwin's use of language is consistent. If in addition to the analysis of metaphor a glossary is compiled of key words, such as *law, facts, nature, species, variety, variation,* and if the crucial word in each definition is followed up, it will appear that Darwin's verbal universe is expressed and his language system complete. From the pages of *The Origin* can be constructed a recognizable, going world. It would contain an enormous number of separate things, accurately observed: animals and insects and plants, continents and oceans. Life and death take place, the surface of the earth moves like a thin crust over a fluid, and whole races pass away. The causes are all natural. There would also be a consciously placed, self-disciplined observer, a man aware of his own ignorance. For him exists a language problem, to use words not as revelations of his own inner self but as pointers to actions outside the observer, and he solves it by limiting exactly the degree of similitude implied by his metaphor.

This observer is also much moved by what he sees. Privately, we know, Darwin took intense delight in the act of observing. His son writes: "I used to like to hear him admire the beauty of a flower; it was a kind of gratitude to the flower itself. . . ." The emotions expressed so modestly in *The Voyage of the Beagle* recur in more generalized form in *The Origin*. Wonder and amazement predominate. "No one," he says, "can have marveled more than I have done at the extinction of species." In the last stately pages of *The Origin* he, too, resolves the tension of nature, so horrible, so beautiful. "When I view all beings . . ." he says, "as the lineal descendants of some few beings which lived long before the first bed of the Cambrian system was deposited, they seem to me to become ennobled." And as he contemplated the tangled bank, clothed with plants, the birds singing, insects flitting about, and in the damp earth the worms crawling—the struggle for existence going on before his eyes while he paused in his morning stroll on the Sand Walk; as he reflected that these elaborate forms have all been produced by laws acting around us, and that from the war of nature, from famine and death, has come the production of the higher animals—then he says, "There is grandeur in this view of life. . . ."

Galton's praise of Darwin, that he had "studied veracity as the highest of arts," belongs to him both as an observer and as a writer. Actually it is hard to see how these two processes can be separated and distinguished. It is easier to conclude that in 1859, at one of the great moments in modern thought, literature and science were united.

UNDERSTANDING THE TEXT

1. What purpose does the meeting between Darwin and Carlyle serve in Baird's essay? Is it essential to his argument, or is it merely a useful way of introducing a point which might have been made in other ways? Does it

have any special values as a method of *beginning* the essay? Is Carlyle referred to after the opening paragraphs?

2. In his discussion of the way Darwin revealed the emotional effects of his experiences on the voyage of the *Beagle*, Baird gives special attention to Darwin's responses to violence, destruction, and death in the animate and inanimate worlds. Apart from the value of the passages which he quotes in showing that Darwin was sensitive to the emotional quality of his surroundings, is there any special reason, in relation to the main argument of the essay, why Baird should stress Darwin's response to the violence of nature?

3. "Struggle for existence" is one of three famous Darwinian phrases which Baird mentions. What are the others? Are they also metaphors?

4. According to Baird, Darwin includes three kinds of behavior in the term "struggle for existence." What are they?

5. Why, according to Baird, was Darwin so careful to make it clear that "the struggle for existence is not a fact but only a figure of speech"?

6. In what important ways did Darwin's use of the metaphor of struggle, life, and death differ from the traditional literary use of the metaphor?

7. From what literary work is Baird quoting at the end of the paragraph at the top of p. 285?

TOPICS FOR DISCUSSION AND WRITING

8. State in a paragraph what Darwin's problem of expression was, as Baird sees it.

9. Read the essay by Henry Myers on "Literature, Science, and Democracy" (pp. 578–588). Like Baird, Myers is concerned with the relations between literature and science. Write a critical comparison between the ways these two writers conceive of the problem of literature and science and the ways in which they deal with it. Would Myers be likely to agree that in Darwin's work "literature and science were united"?

10. Read Loren Eiseley's "The Fire Apes" (pp. 561–575). Write an essay in which you apply to it the sort of analysis of metaphor in scientific writing which Baird applies to Darwin. Does Eiseley make significant or merely illustrative use of metaphor? What are his dominant metaphorical terms? What role do they play in his treatment of his subject? Does he seem to be aware, as Darwin was, of the limitations of metaphor in scientific writing?

11. Does the use of figures of speech for the larger conceptions of science seem to you inescapable, as it seemed to Darwin? Examine from this point of view some of the central terms of a science you are studying. Such terms as "light waves," "current," "magnetic field," "attraction," "repulsion," and "cosmic ray" are examples you might consider.

PART TWO

Writers at Large

5. Biography: The Personal Record

Wilmarth S. Lewis, The Difficult Art of Biography
Alfred Kazin, Summer: The Way to Highland Park
Graham Greene, The Revolver in the Corner Cupboard
James Boswell, Dr. Johnson Dines with Jack Wilkes
Lytton Strachey, The Sad Story of Dr. Colbatch
Otis Ferguson, Young Man with a Horn Again

The Difficult Art of Biography

WILMARTH S. LEWIS

JUST about everyone likes biography. The reason for this is not hard to find. It is the pleasure we get in identifying ourselves with real people who have attained eminence of some sort. By the magic of biography we are transported out of ourselves into kings and queens, generals, poets, lovers, and bankers; we become Eleanor of Aquitaine or George Washington or Babe Ruth. Such being the power of biography, it is remarkable that of all the forms of the literary art it has had the fewest successes:

From *The Yale Review*, Autumn, 1954; copyright Yale University Press. Reprinted by permission of the author and publisher.

there has been composed in our language only one life that everybody agrees is a masterpiece.

Writing on biography recently Sir Harold Nicolson gave the "Oxford English Dictionary's" definition of it: "the history of the lives of individual men, as a branch of literature." "This excellent definition," he goes on, "contains within itself three principles that any serious biographer should observe. A biography must be 'history,' in the sense that it must be accurate and depict a person in relation to his times. It must describe an 'individual,' with all the gradations of human character, and not merely present a type of virtue or of vice. And it must be composed as 'a branch of literature,' in that it must be written in grammatical English and with an adequate feeling for style."

In a full-dress biography the history begins before the birth of the principal figure; it reaches back into his family, to father, mother, and grandparents, and picks out in the further past any ancestors who have escaped oblivion. The hero then appears, and the story of his life is unfolded to the best of the biographer's abilities as a scholar, as a person, and as a writer.

In collecting his materials the author who is writing the life of a contemporary has certain obvious advantages: he can interview his man and his family, friends, and enemies. He can get answers that a biographer writing in the future will perhaps have to search many books to find, and which he may not find in the end. The contemporary has the additional advantage of knowing how his subject dressed and walked and ate; above all, how he spoke. "In the intervals of articulating," Boswell tells us, Johnson "made various sounds with his mouth, sometimes as if ruminating, or what is called chewing the cud, sometimes giving a half whistle, sometimes making his tongue play backwards from the roof of his mouth, as if clucking like a hen, and sometimes protruding it against his upper gums in front, as if pronouncing quickly under his breath, *too, too, too;* all this accompanied sometimes with a thoughtful look, but more frequently with a smile." These "minute singularities" noted by an eyewitness who was also a genius make the great man live. The notes of some such eyewitness of the first emperors supplied Suetonius a century after their deaths with his most telling touches: Caesar on a litter carried home from the Capitol "with one arm hanging down"; Augustus "wrapped in four tunics and a heavy toga, besides an undershirt, a woolen chest-protector and wraps for his thighs and shins," rolling dice with little boys. The contemporary biographer will perhaps have the gift the blind have, the ability to sense the state of his man's mind and spirit and to know when he is troubled or serene. If the biographer has this insight it will be his supreme advantage; if he lacks it his work will not reach the first rank.

The contemporary biographer has a still further advantage which is so obvious that it might be overlooked: the advantage of living in the same time as his subject. Were Mr. Aneurin Bevan to write the life of Sir Winston Churchill he would come to his task with grave handicaps, but he would have one advantage that Sir Winston's biographers in future centuries will lack. This is that both were born in a horse-drawn age. Mr. Bevan would have a further advantage in writing his biography, that of being a generation younger than his subject, the same advantage that Boswell and Lockhart had. This advantage is illustrated by the stereoscope, whose slightly divergent photographs give a third dimension to the Taj Mahal or Niagara Falls. You might almost be there, you feel, as you place the frame upon your nose with a gasp of delight. The slightly different point of view of a younger contemporary gives to the subject he is examining the same sense of a third dimension.

It may take much study and thought to discover the details of the setting in which the subject of the biography moved. Mr. Bevan in his life of Churchill will not think of England as it is today when he writes of Sir Winston's part in the Boer War, nor will he present Sir Winston in the First World War in the uniform of the Boer War. In the dozen years that intervened between those wars England and the world had changed. The automobile had appeared, for one thing; suffragettes for another; Blériot had flown the Channel; strange and alarming things had happened in the arts: just as the man in the street was getting used to Monet and Whistler he was called upon to admire the "Nude Descending the Staircase" and ladies with both eyes on the same side of their noses—or did *they* come later? Mr. Bevan will perhaps have to look that point up. Although he will be writing inside the time and so will be more likely to avoid anachronisms than would a later biographer, he, too, must verify his references and allusions. Since Mr. Bevan will have to do so, think what Churchill's biographers of the 24th century will have to do! They will acquire the reputation of being learned men when they discover that television was invented after the bicycle and that ladies began smoking cigarettes at about the same time that they gave up wearing black stockings into the sea. Even well-educated men and women in the year 2300 will not have realized that ladies did wear black stockings into the sea—to say nothing of corsets, and what, by the way, *were* corsets? The historians of the 24th century will have to discriminate, one by one, the differences in thought, speech, customs, and manners that evolved during Churchill's lifetime. Many of these changes will leap to the eye; many, the tacit assumptions of our day, will have to be recovered when the age is, so to say, off its guard.

Such a moment came when Horace Walpole went to hear the Cock Lane Ghost. "We set out from the Opera," Walpole wrote, "changed our clothes at Northumberland House, the Duke of York, Lady Northumberland, Lady Mary Coke, Lord Hertford, and I, all in one hackney coach, and drove to the spot; it rained torrents; yet the lane was full of mob, and the house so full we could not get in—at last they discovered it was the Duke of York, and the company squeezed themselves into one another's pockets to make room for us." There are three tacit assumptions in this passage: that this richly dressed group changed into their ordinary day dress before going into the slums, that they gave up their carriages for the 18th-century equivalent of a taxi, and that "the mob" respected the Duke of York, the King's uncle, enough to make way for him and his party. These three facts were taken for granted by Walpole and his correspondent. He did not write, "You know that if we had gone to Cock Lane in our fine clothes and carriages we might have been pelted with filth and abuse." This glimpse of unmusical people escaping from the opera to go to a more amusing show makes us feel close to 1762. We share their curiosity about the ghost, we understand why they changed their clothes, and why "the mob" was polite to them and not hostile. In these recognitions we find the familiar amid the strange. Were we to return to London in 1762 the strange amid the familiar would shock, sicken, and edify us. The waning survivals of still earlier centuries would confront us on every hand, survivals of ancient manners, customs, and attitudes of mind, such things as visiting madhouses to laugh at the inmates or seeing two women, stripped to the waist, fighting each other with broken bottles, or a party of pleasure on the Thames singing, as they rowed along, to the accompaniment of oboes, bassoons, and violins.

Being in tune with a remote period is like listening to a radio station while motoring. As you approach the limit of its range the program begins to fade. You turn up the volume higher and higher, and when you can turn it no higher you strain to hear. At last you go around a bend in the road or down a long hill and there is silence. So it is as we travel away from our own time into the past. We who were born in the last century can tune in on the 18th century (we, too, were born in a horse-drawn age), but it will be very hard for those born after 1930 to do so: too much has happened in the past fifty years.

The best biographers burst through the time barrier. In spite of all the handicaps of differing speech and customs, they are able to convey to us the essence of the people that they are writing about. They do this by reporting incidents and occasions, many of which appear to be trivial, but which reveal character. Such revelations occur on almost every page of Boswell, as you will find if you will open his book at random. Take that evening when Johnson dined at General Paoli's and had a tiff with Sir Joshua Reynolds on the subject of drinking wine. Boswell tells us about it in dialogue: "JOHNSON (who from drinking only water, supposed everybody who drank wine to be elevated), 'I won't argue any more with you, Sir. You are too far gone.' SIR JOSHUA, 'I should have thought so indeed, Sir, had I made such a speech as you have now done.' JOHNSON (drawing himself in, and, I really thought blushing) 'Nay, don't be angry. I did not mean to offend you.'"

Or, to go back many centuries, take that moment at the well outside the city of Nahor when Abraham's servant had offered Isaac in marriage to Rebekah and had given her a golden earring and two bracelets of ten shekels weight of gold. Rebekah put them on and ran to show them off to her brother Laban. Or, that other time when "the mother of Sisera looked out at a window, and cried through the lattice, 'Why is his chariot so long in coming? Why tarry the wheels of his chariot?'" not knowing what we know, that the stars in their courses have fought against Sisera. The recorders of these moments have reached across the centuries to speak to you and to me and to the men and women of this planet as long as it lasts.

And what advantage has the noncontemporary biographer? The first, I think, is perspective. The hero's career has been studied, his work has been appraised, a sounder judgment of his significance has been reached. The dust storm of opinion and emotion that swirled about him and made dispassionate contemporary appraisal impossible has blown away. "New" material has come to light that has brought him and his age into focus: private letters and diaries and memoirs in which facts and opinions and interviews have been revealed that the subject may have known nothing about, or have forgotten if he ever did know them.

A second advantage that the later biographer has is that he is free to say what he likes without regard to the feelings of living persons or their immediate families, an easiness that increases with the years. The man who writes about Caligula is not constrained by the thought of Caligula's family, but the biographer of a great poet who died only fifty years ago must bear in mind not only what is in good taste, but what is legally perilous in the event that the great poet has a grandson in the hardware business in Weehawken who may consult his lawyer if the biographer reveals that the ethereal Helen of his grandfather's sonnets was something more substantial than a disembodied spirit.

All biographers, those writing of contemporaries and those writing of figures of the past, share certain dangers and disadvantages. The chief danger, I think, is that the biographer will identify himself with his subject. This danger is present whether the central figure is a good man or a bad man, alive or dead, but it is a danger that is particularly strong when the subject is dead. When the subject is alive the author may meet him and see and feel his weaknesses. When the subject is dead the author does not have this salutary corrective. As his study deepens he discovers engaging qualities in the great man that he had not realized were there, hints and signs of humanity and humility that had gone unnoticed by earlier biographers, amiable qualities that place the subject in a new light and show him innocent of many—of most, of all—the charges brought against him. At this point the hero has become a pattern for schoolboys and the biographer a crusader determined to right the injustice done him. To do this the base and ignorant persons who have traduced the hero must be dragged forward to receive their due from an awakened and angry public. In carrying out this agreeable duty the biographer becomes one with his subject: the great man's loves and hates are his loves and hates; criticism of the great man is criticism of the biographer, whose book has now ceased to be the life that the subject lived and has turned into a polemical apology for the author himself.

The chief disadvantage that all biographers share, I think, is ignorance, ignorance of what actually took place in the hero's life. We read of his modest and afflicted beginning; everything seems to be against him, and then—presto! he has arrived. It is never quite clear how; the trick remains a mystery. To be sure, there was that man who gave him a dollar, or published his first verses, or told him to go west, but there must have been much more to it than that. Some of the jars and accidents of the hero's daily life we may know, but what about the inspirations and sudden insights that enabled him to rise above them? The subject himself can seldom recall the answers to these questions in later life because time blots out and twists recollections of what actually took place.

Furthermore, the course of our lives is continually being determined by matters of which we have no knowledge whatever. A man may be chosen—or turned down—for a job that means success or failure in the world's eyes and never learn why he was chosen or rejected. Such decisions are often made as a result of small incidents; the deciding vote may be cast by a man who thinks of the candidate at one observed moment when he appeared admirable—or foolish: a chance remark, a gesture, a smile at the right or wrong time, may change the course of a man's life. How much do we know—does the subject himself ever know—of these critical moments? And of the strength of a man's good and evil components, the struggle in him of ambition and selflessness, or retaliation and charity, the spiritual causes of his illnesses and recoveries—all biographers, no matter how skilful in research they may be, are ultimately left to grope in that region of their subject's souls that Plutarch likens to the unknown portions on old maps where "all beyond is nothing but monsters and tragic fictions." Boswell had the advantage of holding countless conversations with Johnson, of reading his prayers and meditations, and of recovering hundreds of his private letters; yet even Boswell does not tell us why Johnson had to touch lampposts and count his steps. We can guess, but we cannot know.

The first two principles of biography, you recall, are the accurate history of the individual related to his time and the gradations of his character. We now come to the third principle, the principle that biography is "a branch of literature." Few today have the leisure or the will to pursue the art of writing as that art used to be practiced, and few know the works that have formed the best literary styles in English. Lack of familiarity with the Greek and Latin classics and the Authorized Version of the English Bible is not made up for by weaker substitutes, especially when they are presented in the new dialect evolved by the academic profession. Fortunately, in every respectable school and college and university there are diehards who refuse to speak and write this patois. These resolute conservatives are keeping the English language alive in our country, and they are not doing it in secret: this resistance movement does not hide in cellars. Its members are audible, and if only the biographers of the future will listen to them they may yet produce lives that will belong to "a branch of literature."

All biographers hope that they will turn out to be Pygmalions, and that the figure upon which they have spent so much time and affection will come to life. If this miracle is to take place, Pygmalion must do more than execute his work with the utmost skill. He must give his figure those other touches that belong to it and to none other, but he must do still more than that; he must quicken it with those touches that the reader will find in himself, revelations of duplicity inspired by the deepest instincts as well as nobility brought out by suffering: Rebekah showing Jacob how to trick Isaac into getting his father's blessing in Esau's stead, and David crying "Absalom, my son! my son!" In such passages the miracle does occur.

Biography demands much of its practitioners: study, accuracy, insight, and artistry. Its power and responsibility are immense. The subject's life, his many thousand hours, may be set aside by posterity if his biographer is careless or frivolous, idolatrous, or unjust. Immortality on earth is the gift the biographer has to confer. If in the verdict of the best judges in his own and succeeding ages he has made the gift, he will have won, as his reward, immortality for himself.

UNDERSTANDING THE TEXT

1. Lewis derives from Sir Harold Nicolson three principles which he uses to organize his analysis of biography. What are these principles? Mark off the paragraphs in Lewis' discussion which fall under each principle.

2. In addition to using Nicolson's three principles as a way of organizing his analysis, Lewis also uses two other sets of terms—the relative advantages of the contemporary and the non-contemporary biographer, and the opportunities vs. the dangers which beset all biographers. Mark off in the text the places where these two sets of terms come into play. How are these two distinctions related to the three principles of biography which Lewis derives from Nicolson?

3. Why, in listing the advantages of the contemporary biographer, does Lewis say that it is "above all" an advantage to know how his subject spoke?

4. Why does Lewis, speaking of the chronology of modern painting, ask, of the ladies with both eyes on the same side of their noses, "or did *they* come later?" Is his point here the same as the point he makes by asking, later in the same paragraph, "and what, by the way, *were* corsets?"

5. Why does Lewis say that a visit to the London of 1762, in addition to shocking and sickening, would also "edify" us?

6. In his next to last paragraph, Lewis says that if his figure is to come to life, the biographer must "quicken it with those touches that the reader will find in himself." Why does he select these particular touches to illustrate the point? What do they have in common? What view of human nature do they

imply? Compare the point Lewis is making here with the point he makes in his opening paragraph about the pleasure of biography.

TOPICS FOR DISCUSSION AND WRITING

7. Using the method Lewis employs in uncovering the tacit assumptions in Walpole's account of his visit to Cock Lane, write a paragraph uncovering the tacit assumptions in a section of Boswell's account of Johnson and Wilkes.

8. Lewis gives several examples (p. 294) of the biographer's use of apparently trivial details to reveal character. Write a paragraph, based on one of the biographical essays in this section, showing how such revelatory information is used.

9. When Lewis, at the end of his first paragraph, speaks of the one biography in English that everybody agrees is a masterpiece, he is referring to Boswell's *Life of Johnson*. Taking the selection on pp. 310–318 as a sample, write three paragraphs in which you consider how well Boswell fulfills the criteria of biographical writing set forth in Lewis' essay.

10. Look up the Cock Lane Ghost and write a paragraph showing why it interested a party of eighteenth-century sightseers.

Summer: The Way to Highland Park

ALFRED KAZIN

THAT summer I had my first regular job. Carrying a blue canvas bag in which I kept a book for private reading, I went about the streets of middle Brooklyn all through the long blazing afternoons picking up specimens from drugstores to be delivered to a urinalysis lab on Nostrand Avenue. Between drugstores on my route I often stopped to read in various small parks along the way. I remember how that faint distant odor curiously reminiscent of stale ground-up peanuts clung to the blue surface of the *David Copperfield* I was always reading on the job, and that whenever I got lost in reading and rode far past my destination, usually found that I had used up the carfare the boss had given me and that I would have to walk it the rest of the way. But then, in the brilliant heat, the jars and flasks wrapped in brown paper bags tinkling against each other as I walked, that faint odor of stale ground-up peanuts lingering along the cracks in the pavement, I gave myself to those streets I was lost in as if I were swimming in the weather.

It was the intense silence and heat of those summer streets that delivered me to all my joy. Whenever I guiltily thrust *David Copperfield* back into my canvas bag and started out fresh from some strange streetcar crossing, I would rush off in a panic, thinking only of the time I had lost and what the boss would say. Then the silence of summer would fall on the top of my head, cleaving me through and through, as if the front of my face alone were rushing ahead to the next drugstore on my list, while my spine dawdled in amazement. There was suddenly anywhere to go now; I had the whole long afternoon to walk around in. My summer's time had come; my own time had come at last. There was a deep aromatic coolness behind the awning of each new drugstore that was made up of cleanness and camphor and the toilet water seeping out of the vials on the counter, of the thick black type and the priestly face on Father John's Cough Medicine, of the clink of an empty spoon against the smooth top of the soda fountain counter, of the dry fizz of soda water backing out of the taps, of the stiff "American" dignity and starched linen jackets on all those strange new Gentile druggists. The insides of all drugstores summer afternoons were hermetically deep. When I walked into one under the awning, out of the glare, it was like floating down to the bottom of a lake with my eyes wide open among the rushes.

That particular great day in the heat, the unending heat, I was walking somewhere off Gates Avenue, and saw that they had unfurled awnings even over the El stations. I could hear the plash of a fountain in a school courtyard across the street; one whole side of that block was lined with trees. How hot it was that afternoon. The dust never stirred on the leaves of the nearest trees; the pavements were so fierce that I kept walking under the awnings of chain groceries to cool my breath and to sniff at the fresh watered celery stalks on the open stands and the clean, shaded interiors that smelled of coffee beans and of biscuits. When I walked back into the sun, every mica dot glittered in the pavement. From time to time, the hot streets were racked by some dry, distant thunder from the El. How hot it was that afternoon, how silent and hot. As I started down that lonely stretch of sidewalk somewhere off Gates Avenue, everything moved so slowly that I could almost count the drops of sweat bubbling on a girl's upper lip, the sounds of my heart dreamily pounding into my ears from the end of a long corridor as she passed me, breasts rustling in her blouse, her blouse gleaming in the sun like a second sheath of skin. All around me the city seemed entirely at rest. There were so few passers-by that I could feel the awnings over the shops pulling away from me in amazement and scorn, was queerer and more alone to myself than ever as I passed up that street with a trickle from some loosened jar seeping out of my bag.

And then it came. All the way down that street, there seemed to be nothing but myself with a bag, the blazingly hot and empty afternoon, and silence through which I pressed my way. But the large shadow on the pavement was me, the music in my head was me, the indescribable joy I felt was me. I was so happy, I could not tell what I felt apart from the evenness of the heat in which I walked. The sweat poured out of my body in relief. I was me, me, me, and it was summer.

UNDERSTANDING THE TEXT

1. Kazin first gives a generalized account of his experiences, forming a picture of a composite or typical day, and then he passes to "that particular great day in the heat." Is there any difference in the amount or kind of detail he presents in the two parts of his narrative?

2. What was the meaning for Kazin of "that particular day"? How did it differ from other days? What sort of discovery did he make on that day?

3. What is the significance of the silence and the heat in the experience Kazin describes?

4. What particular sounds does Kazin record? Which of the senses are particularly appealed to in his descriptions?

5. Explain the meaning of each of the following:
   a. "Then the silence . . . dawdled in amazement."
   b. "The insides of all drugstores summer afternoons were hermetically deep."
   c. "And then it came."
   d. "I was me, me, me, and it was summer."

6. The phrase "as if I were swimming in the weather" (p. 302) involves a certain intermingling of elements—air being treated as water, walking being treated as swimming. Does Kazin elsewhere in the essay mingle the powers of the senses or attribute to certain objects qualities proper to other objects? What is the point of this in the process of discovery he is relating?

TOPICS FOR DISCUSSION AND WRITING

7. Write an essay in which you try to recapture the feelings and sensations of a day in your life memorable not for any great happening but for some discovery you made about yourself.

8. Write an essay telling about your experience in your first job.

The Revolver in the Corner Cupboard

GRAHAM GREENE

—————

I CAN remember very clearly the afternoon I found the revolver in the brown deal corner cupboard in the bedroom which I shared with my elder brother. It was the early autumn of 1922. I was seventeen and terribly bored and in love with my sister's governess—one of those miserable, hopeless, romantic loves of adolescence that set in many minds the idea that love and despair are inextricable and that successful love hardly deserves the name. At that age one may fall irrevocably in love with failure, and success of any kind loses half its savour before it is experienced. Such a love is surrendered once and for all to the singer at the pavement's edge, the bankrupt, the old school friend who wants to touch you for a dollar. Perhaps in many so conditioned it is the love for God that mainly survives, because in his eyes they can imagine themselves remaining always drab, seedy, unsuccessful, and therefore worthy of notice.

The revolver was a small genteel object with six chambers like a tiny egg stand, and there was a cardboard box of bullets. It has only recently occurred to me that they may have been blanks; I always assumed them to be live ammunition, and I never mentioned the discovery to my brother because I had realized the moment I saw the revolver the use I intended to make of it. (I don't to this day know why he possessed it; certainly he had no license, and he was only three years older than myself. A large family is as departmental as a Ministry.)

My brother was away—probably climbing in the Lake District—and until he returned the revolver was to all intents mine. I knew what to do with it because I had been reading a book (the name Ossendowski comes to mind as the possible author) describing how the White Russian officers, condemned to inaction in South Russia at the tail-end of the counter-revolutionary war, used to invent hazards with which to escape boredom. One man would slip a charge into a revolver and turn the chambers at random, and his companion would put the revolver to his head and pull the trigger. The chance, of course, was six to one in favour of life.

How easily one forgets emotions. If I were dealing now with an imaginary character, I would feel it necessary for verisimilitude to make him hesitate, put the revolver back into the cupboard, return to it again after an interval, reluctantly and fearfully, when the burden of boredom became too great. But in fact I think there was no hesitation at all, for the next I can remember is crossing Berkhamsted Common, gashed here and there between the gorse bushes with the stray trenches of the first Great War, towards the Ashridge beeches. Perhaps before I had made the discovery, boredom had already reached an intolerable depth.

I think the boredom was far deeper than the love. It had always been a feature of childhood: it would set in on the second day of the school holidays. The first day was all happiness, and, after the horrible confinement and publicity of school, seemed to consist of light, space and silence. But a prison conditions its inhabitants. I never wanted to return to it (and finally expressed my rebellion by the simple act of running away), but yet I was so conditioned that freedom bored me unutterably.

The psycho-analysis that followed my act of rebellion had fixed the boredom as hypo fixes the image on the negative. I emerged from those delightful months in London spent at my analyst's house—perhaps the happiest months of my life—correctly orientated, able to take a proper extrovert interest in my fellows (the jargon rises to the lips), but wrung dry. For years, it seems to me, I could take no aesthetic interest in any visual thing at all: staring at a sight that others assured me was beautiful, I would feel nothing. I was fixed in my boredom. (Writing this I come on a remark of Rilke: "Psycho-analysis is too fundamental a help for me, it helps you once and for all, it clears you up, and to find myself finally cleared up one day might be even more helpless than this chaos.")

Now with the revolver in my pocket I was beginning to emerge. I had stumbled on the perfect cure. I was going to escape in one way or another, and because escape was inseparably connected with the Common in my mind, it was there that I went.

The wilderness of gorse, old trenches, abandoned butts was the unchanging backcloth of most of the adventures of childhood. It was to the

Common I had decamped for my act of rebellion some years before, with the intention, expressed in a letter left after breakfast on the heavy black sideboard, that there I would stay, day and night, until either I had starved or my parents had given in; when I pictured war it was always in terms of this Common, and myself leading a guerilla campaign in the ragged waste, for no one, I was persuaded, knew its paths so intimately (how humiliating that in my own domestic campaign I was ambushed by my elder sister after a few hours).

Beyond the Common lay a wide grass ridge known for some reason as Cold Harbour to which I would occasionally with some fear take a horse, and beyond this again stretched Ashridge Park, the smooth olive skin of beech trees and the thick last year's quagmire of leaves, dark like old pennies. Deliberately I chose my ground, I believe without any real fear —perhaps because I was uncertain myself whether I was play-acting; perhaps because so many acts which my elders would have regarded as neurotic, but which I still consider to have been under the circumstances highly reasonable, lay in the background of this more dangerous venture.

There had been, for example, perhaps five or six years before, the disappointing morning in the dark room by the linen cupboard on the eve of term when I had patiently drunk a quantity of hypo under the impression that it was poisonous: on another occasion the blue glass bottle of hay fever lotion which as it contained a small quantity of cocaine had probably been good for my mood: the bunch of deadly nightshade that I had eaten with only a slight narcotic effect: the twenty aspirins I had taken before swimming in the empty out-of-term school baths (I can still remember the curious sensation of swimming through wool): these acts may have removed all sense of strangeness as I slipped a bullet into a chamber and, holding the revolver behind my back, spun the chambers round.

Had I romantic thoughts about the governess? Undoubtedly I must have had, but I think that at the most they simply eased the medicine down. Boredom, aridity, those were the main emotions. Unhappy love has, I suppose, sometimes driven boys to suicide, but this was not suicide, whatever a coroner's jury might have said of it: it was a gamble with six chances to one against an inquest. The romantic flavour—the autumn scene, the small heavy compact shape lying in the fingers—that perhaps was a tribute to adolescent love, but the discovery that it was possible to enjoy again the visible world by risking its total loss was one I was bound to make sooner or later.

I put the muzzle of the revolver in my right ear and pulled the trigger.

There was a minute click, and looking down at the chamber I could see that the charge had moved into place. I was out by one. I remember an extraordinary sense of jubilation. It was as if a light had been turned on. My heart was knocking in its cage, and I felt that life contained an infinite number of possibilities. It was like a young man's first successful experience of sex—as if in that Ashridge glade one had passed a test of manhood. I went home and put the revolver back in the corner cupboard.

The odd thing about this experience was that it was repeated several times. At fairly long intervals I found myself craving for the drug. I took the revolver with me when I went up to Oxford and I would walk out from Headington towards Elsfield down what is now a wide arterial road, smooth and shiny like the walls of a public lavatory. Then it was a sodden unfrequented country lane. The revolver would be whipped behind my back, the chambers twisted, the muzzle quickly and surreptitiously inserted beneath the black and ugly winter tree, the trigger pulled.

Slowly the effect of the drug wore off—I lost the sense of jubilation, I began to gain from the experience only the crude kick of excitement. It was like the difference between love and lust. And as the quality of the experience deteriorated so my sense of responsibility grew and worried me. I wrote a very bad piece of free verse (free because it was easier in that way to express my meaning without literary equivocation) describing how, in order to give a fictitious sense of danger, I would "press the trigger of a revolver I already know to be empty." This piece of verse I would leave permanently on my desk, so that if I lost my gamble, there would be incontrovertible evidence of an accident, and my parents, I thought, would be less troubled than by an apparent suicide—or than by the rather bizarre truth.

But it was back at Berkhamsted that I paid a permanent farewell to the drug. As I took my fifth dose it occurred to me that I wasn't even excited: I was beginning to pull the trigger about as casually as I might take an aspirin tablet. I decided to give the revolver—which was six-chambered—a sixth and last chance. Twirling the chambers round, I put the muzzle to my ear for the last time and heard the familiar empty click as the chambers revolved. I was through with the drug, and walking back over the Common, down the new road by the ruined castle, past the private entrance to the gritty old railway station—reserved for the use of Lord Brownlow—my mind was already busy on other plans. One campaign was over, but the war against boredom had got to go on.

I put the revolver back in the corner cupboard, and going downstairs

I lied gently to my parents that a friend had invited me to join him in Paris.

UNDERSTANDING THE TEXT

1. What meaning do you attach to "the discovery that it was possible to enjoy again the visible world by risking its total loss"? How important is this insight in the organization of Greene's narrative?

2. Greene develops his narrative generally in straight chronological sequence, but there are several inset recapitulations of earlier events in his life. Where do these occur? Why are they introduced in this way instead of being incorporated into the narrative in their proper chronological positions? To have followed the latter method, Greene would have had to extend considerably the time span of his narrative. What would have been lost by this?

3. Consider the following sentences:

"But in fact I think there was no hesitation at all."

"The revolver would be whipped behind my back."

"The odd thing about this experience was that it was repeated several times."

Can you find other examples of sentences in which Greene avoids the active voice and the first personal pronoun? What would be the effect of saying, e.g., "But in fact I think I did not hesitate at all"? How do you interpret this feature of Greene's style in relation to his purpose?

4. What is Greene's *present* attitude toward the events of his youth that he narrates here? How is that attitude revealed?

5. What sorts of details of the physical setting of the action does Greene give? On what principle does he seem to have chosen them?

6. Greene uses a rather large number of parentheses. Can you classify the sorts of things he says parenthetically? Is there any special justification for using so many of them? Compare Greene's use of parentheses with E. B. White's in "The Door."

TOPICS FOR DISCUSSION AND WRITING

7. Why does Greene refer to the revolver as a drug?

8. From the scattered references he gives in the essay—with what supplementary help you need from your own imagination—write a narrative of the act of rebellion that had occurred before the events described here.

9. Take either of the following as the text for a paragraph:

"A large family is as departmental as a Ministry."

"One campaign was over, but the war against boredom had got to go on."

10. Describe a particular place that has a special significance for you, as the Berkhamsted Common had for Greene.

Dr. Johnson Dines with Jack Wilkes

JAMES BOSWELL

MAY 1776:

I am now to record a very curious incident in Dr. Johnson's Life, which fell under my own observation; of which *pars magna fui*, and which I am persuaded will, with the liberal-minded, be much to his credit.

My desire of being acquainted with celebrated men of every description, had made me, much about the same time, obtain an introduction to Dr. Samuel Johnson and to John Wilkes, Esq. Two men more different could perhaps not be selected out of all mankind. They had even attacked one another with some asperity in their writings; yet I lived in habits of friendship with both. I could fully relish the excellence of each; for I have ever delighted in that intellectual chemistry, which can separate good qualities from evil in the same person.

Sir John Pringle, "mine own friend and my Father's friend," between whom and Dr. Johnson I in vain wished to establish an acquaintance, as I respected and lived in intimacy with both of them, observed to me once, very ingeniously, "It is not in friendship as in mathematics, where two things, each equal to a third, are equal between themselves. You agree with Johnson as a middle quality, and you agree with me as a middle quality; but Johnson and I should not agree." Sir John was not sufficiently flexible; so I desisted; knowing, indeed, that the repulsion was equally strong on the part of Johnson; who, I know not from what cause, unless his being a Scotchman, had formed a very erroneous opinion of Sir John. But I conceived an irresistible wish, if possible, to bring Dr. Johnson and Mr. Wilkes together. How to manage it, was a nice and difficult matter.

My worthy booksellers and friends, Messieurs Dilly in the Poultry, at whose hospitable and well-covered table I have seen a greater number of

Reprinted from *The Life of Samuel Johnson, LL.D.* (1791).

literary men, than at any other, except that of Sir Joshua Reynolds, had invited me to meet Mr. Wilkes and some more gentlemen on Wednesday, May 15. "Pray," said I, "let us have Dr. Johnson."—"What, with Mr. Wilkes? not for the world," said Mr. Edward Dilly. "Dr. Johnson would never forgive me." "Come," said I, "if you'll let me negotiate for you, I will be answerable that all shall go well." DILLY: "Nay, if you will take it upon you, I am sure I shall be very happy to see them both here."

Notwithstanding the high veneration which I entertained for Dr. Johnson, I was sensible that he was sometimes a little actuated by the spirit of contradiction, and by means of that I hoped I should gain my point. I was persuaded that if I had come upon him with a direct proposal, "Sir, will you dine in company with Jack Wilkes?" he would have flown into a passion, and would probably have answered, "Dine with Jack Wilkes, Sir! I'd as soon dine with Jack Ketch."[1] I therefore, while we were sitting quietly by ourselves at his house in an evening, took occasion to open my plan thus: "Mr. Dilly, Sir, sends his respectful compliments to you, and would be happy if you would do him the honour to dine with him on Wednesday next along with me, as I must soon go to Scotland." JOHNSON: "Sir, I am obliged to Mr. Dilly. I will wait upon him—" BOSWELL: "Provided, Sir, I suppose, that the company which he is to have, is agreeable to you." JOHNSON: "What do you mean, Sir? What do you take me for? Do you think I am so ignorant of the world, as to imagine that I am to prescribe to a gentleman what company he is to have at his table?" BOSWELL: "I beg your pardon, Sir, for wishing to prevent you from meeting people whom you might not like. Perhaps he may have some of what he calls his patriotic friends with him." JOHNSON: "Well, Sir, and what then? What care *I* for his *patriotic friends*? Poh!" BOSWELL: "I should not be surprised to find Jack Wilkes there." JOHNSON: "And if Jack Wilkes *should* be there, what is that to *me*, Sir? My dear friend, let us have no more of this. I am sorry to be angry with you; but really it is treating me strangely to talk to me as if I could not meet any company whatever, occasionally." BOSWELL: "Pray forgive me, Sir; I meant well. But you shall meet whoever comes, for me." Thus I secured him, and told Dilly that he would find him very well pleased to be one of his guests on the day appointed.

Upon the much-expected Wednesday, I called on him about half an hour before dinner, as I often did when we were to dine out together, to see that he was really in time, and to accompany him. I found him

[1] Jack Ketch: the common name for the public executioner.

buffeting his books, as upon a former occasion, covered with dust, and making no preparation for going abroad. "How is this, Sir?" said I. "Don't you recollect that you are to dine at Mr. Dilly's?" JOHNSON: "Sir, I did not think of going to Dilly's; it went out of my head. I have ordered dinner at home with Mrs. Williams." BOSWELL: "But, my dear Sir, you know you were engaged to Mr. Dilly, and I told him so. He will expect you, and will be much disappointed if you don't come." JOHNSON: "You must talk to Mrs. Williams about this."

Here was a sad dilemma. I feared that what I was so confident I had secured would yet be frustrated. He had accustomed himself to show Mrs. Williams such a degree of humane attention, as frequently imposed some restraint upon him; and I knew that if she should be obstinate, he would not stir. I hastened downstairs to the blind lady's room, and told her I was in great uneasiness, for Dr. Johnson had engaged to me to dine this day at Mr. Dilly's, but that he had told me he had forgotten his engagement and had ordered dinner at home. "Yes, sir," said she, pretty peevishly, "Dr. Johnson is to dine at home." "Madam," said I, "his respect for you is such, that I know he will not leave you, unless you absolutely desire it. But as you have so much of his company, I hope you will be good enough to forgo it for a day, as Mr. Dilly is a very worthy man, has frequently had agreeable parties at his house for Dr. Johnson, and will be vexed if the Doctor neglects him today. And then, Madam, be pleased to consider my situation: I carried the message, and I assured Mr. Dilly that Dr. Johnson was to come, and no doubt he has made a dinner, and invited a company, and boasted of the honour he expected to have. I shall be quite disgraced if the Doctor is not there." She gradually softened to my solicitations, which were certainly as earnest as most entreaties to ladies upon any occasion, and was graciously pleased to empower me to tell Dr. Johnson, "That all things considered, she thought he should certainly go." I flew back to him, still in dust, and careless of what should be the event, "indifferent in his choice to go or stay," but as soon as I had announced to him Mrs. Williams' consent, he roared, "Frank, a clean shirt," and was very soon dressed. When I had him fairly seated in a hackney coach with me, I exulted as much as a fortune hunter who has got an heiress into a post chaise with him to set out for Gretna Green.

When we entered Mr. Dilly's drawing room, he found himself in the midst of a company he did not know. I kept myself snug and silent, watching how he would conduct himself. I observed him whispering to Mr. Dilly, "Who is that gentleman, Sir?" "Mr. Arthur Lee." JOHNSON:

"Too, too, too" (under his breath), which was one of his habitual mutterings. Mr. Arthur Lee could not but be very obnoxious to Johnson, for he was not only a *patriot*, but an *American*. He was afterwards minister from the United States at the court of Madrid. "And who is the gentleman in lace?" "Mr. Wilkes, Sir." This information confounded him still more; he had some difficulty to restrain himself and, taking up a book, sat down upon a window seat and read, or at least kept his eye upon it intently for some time, till he composed himself. His feelings, I dare say, were awkward enough. But he no doubt recollected his having rated me for supposing that he could be at all disconcerted by any company, and he, therefore, resolutely set himself to behave quite as an easy man of the world, who could adapt himself at once to the disposition and manners of those whom he might chance to meet.

The cheering sound of "Dinner is upon the table" dissolved his reverie, and we *all* sat down without any symptom of ill humour. There were present, beside Mr. Wilkes, and Mr. Arthur Lee, who was an old companion of mine when he studied physic at Edinburgh, Mr. (now Sir John) Miller, Dr. Lettsom, and Mr. Slater, the druggist. Mr. Wilkes placed himself next to Dr. Johnson, and behaved to him with so much attention and politeness that he gained upon him insensibly. No man ate more heartily than Johnson, or loved better what was nice and delicate. Mr. Wilkes was very assiduous in helping him to some fine veal. "Pray give me leave, Sir—It is better here—A little of the brown—Some fat, Sir—A little of the stuffing—Some gravy—Let me have the pleasure of giving you some butter—Allow me to recommend a squeeze of this orange—or the lemon, perhaps, may have more zest." "Sir, Sir, I am obliged to you, Sir," cried Johnson, bowing and turning his head to him with a look for some time of "surly virtue," but, in a short while, of complacency.

Foote being mentioned, Johnson said, "He is not a good mimic." One of the company added, "A merry Andrew, a buffoon." JOHNSON: "But he has wit, too, and is not deficient in ideas, or in fertility and variety of imagery, and not empty of reading; he has knowledge enough to fill up his part. One species of wit he has in an eminent degree, that of escape. You drive him into a corner with both hands, but he's gone, Sir, when you think you have got him—like an animal that jumps over your head. Then he has a great range for his wit; he never lets truth stand between him and a jest, and he is sometimes mighty coarse. Garrick is under many restraints from which Foote is free." WILKES: "Garrick's wit is more like Lord Chesterfield's." JOHNSON: "The first time I was in company with

Foote was at Fitzherbert's. Having no good opinion of the fellow, I was resolved not to be pleased; and it is very difficult to please a man against his will. I went on eating my dinner pretty sullenly, affecting not to mind him. But the dog was so very comical, that I was obliged to lay down my knife and fork, throw myself back upon my chair, and fairly laugh it out. No, Sir, he was irresistible. He upon one occasion experienced, in an extraordinary degree, the efficacy of his powers of entertaining. Amongst the many and various modes which he tried of getting money, he became a partner with a small-beer brewer, and he was to have a share of the profits for procuring customers amongst his numerous acquaintance. Fitzherbert was one who took his small beer; but it was so bad that the servants resolved not to drink it. They were at some loss how to notify their resolution, being afraid of offending their master, who they knew liked Foote much as a companion. At last they fixed upon a little black boy, who was rather a favourite, to be their deputy, and deliver their remonstrance; and having invested him with the whole authority of the kitchen, he was to inform Mr. Fitzherbert, in all their names, upon a certain day, that they would drink Foote's small beer no longer. On that day Foote happened to dine at Fitzherbert's, and this boy served at table; he was so delighted with Foote's stories and merriment and grimace that, when he went downstairs, he told them, 'This is the finest man I have ever seen. I will not deliver your message. I will drink his small beer.'"

Somebody observed that Garrick could not have done this. WILKES: "Garrick would have made the small beer still smaller. He is now leaving the stage; but he will play Scrub[2] all his life." I knew that Johnson would let nobody attack Garrick but himself, as Garrick once said to me, and I had heard him praise his liberality; so to bring out his commendation of his celebrated pupil, I said, loudly, "I have heard Garrick is liberal." JOHNSON: "Yes, Sir, I know that Garrick has given away more money than any man in England that I am acquainted with, and that not from ostentatious views. Garrick was very poor when he began life; so when he came to have money, he probably was very unskilful in giving away, and saved when he should not. But Garrick began to be liberal as soon as he could; and I am of opinion, the reputation of avarice which he has had, has been very lucky for him, and prevented his having many enemies. You despise a man for avarice, but do not hate him. Garrick might have been much better attacked for living with more splendour than is suitable to a player: if they had had the wit to have assaulted him in that quarter, they might

[2] *Scrub:* a servant in Farquhar's *The Beaux' Stratagem.*

have galled him more. But they have kept clamouring about his avarice, which has rescued him from much obloquy and envy."

Talking of the great difficulty of obtaining authentic information for biography, Johnson told us, "When I was a young fellow I wanted to write the 'Life of Dryden,' and in order to get materials, I applied to the only two persons then alive who had seen him; these were old Swinney, and old Cibber. Swinney's information was no more than this, 'That at Will's coffee-house Dryden had a particular chair for himself, which was set by the fire in winter, and was then called his winter-chair; and that it was carried out for him to the balcony in summer, and was then called his summer-chair.' Cibber could tell no more but 'That he remembered him a decent old man, arbiter of critical disputes at Will's.' You are to consider that Cibber was then at a great distance from Dryden, had perhaps one leg only in the room, and durst not draw in the other." Boswell: "Yet Cibber was a man of observation?" Johnson: "I think not." Boswell: "You will allow his *Apology* to be well done." Johnson: "Very well done, to be sure, Sir. That book is a striking proof of the justice of Pope's remark:

> Each might his several province well command,
> Would all but stoop to what they understand."

Boswell: "And his plays are good." Johnson: "Yes; but that was his trade; *l'esprit du corps;* he had been all his life among players and play-writers. I wondered that he had so little to say in conversation, for he had kept the best company, and learned all that can be got by the ear. He abused Pindar to me, and then showed me an Ode of his own, with an absurd couplet, making a linnet soar on an eagle's wing. I told him that when the ancients made a simile, they always made it like something real."

Mr. Wilkes remarked, that "among all the bold flights of Shakespeare's imagination, the boldest was making Birnam-wood march to Dunsinane; creating a wood where there never was a shrub; a wood in Scotland! ha! ha! ha!" And he also observed, that "the clannish slavery of the Highlands of Scotland was the single exception to Milton's remark of 'The Mountain Nymph, sweet Liberty,' being worshipped in all hilly countries."— "When I was at Inverary (said he,) on a visit to my old friend, Archibald, Duke of Argyle, his dependents congratulated me on being such a favourite of his Grace. I said, 'It is then, gentlemen, truly lucky for me; for if I had displeased the Duke, and he had wished it, there is not a Campbell among you but would have been ready to bring John Wilkes's head to him in a charger. It would have been only

'Off with his head! So much for Aylesbury.'

I was then member for Aylesbury."

Dr. Johnson and Mr. Wilkes talked of the contested passage in Horace's *Art of Poetry*, "*Difficile est propriè communia dicere.*" Mr. Wilkes, according to my note, gave the interpretation thus: "It is difficult to speak with propriety of common things; as, if a poet had to speak of Queen Caroline drinking tea, he must endeavour to avoid the vulgarity of cups and saucers." But upon reading my note, he tells me that he meant to say, that "the word *communia*, being a Roman law term, signifies here things *communis juris*, that is to say, what have never yet been treated by any body; and this appears clearly from what followed,

'——*Tuque*
Rectiùs Iliacum carmen deducis in actus,
Quàm si proferres ignota indictaque primus.'

You will easier make a tragedy out of the *Iliad* than on any subject not handled before." JOHNSON: "He means that it is difficult to appropriate to particular persons qualities which are common to all mankind, as Homer has done."

WILKES: "We have no City Poet now; that is an office which has gone into disuse. The last was Elkanah Settle. There is something in *names* which one cannot help feeling. Now *Elkanah Settle* sounds so *queer*, who can expect much from that name? We should have no hesitation to give it for John Dryden, in preference to Elkanah Settle, from the names only, without knowing their different merits." JOHNSON: "I suppose, Sir, Settle did as well for aldermen in his time as John Home could do now. Where did Beckford and Trecothick learn English?"

Mr. Arthur Lee mentioned some Scotch who had taken possession of a barren part of America, and wondered why they should choose it. JOHNSON: "Why, sir, all barrenness is comparative. The *Scotch* would not know it to be barren." BOSWELL: "Come, come, he is flattering the English. You have now been in Scotland, Sir, and say if you did not see meat and drink enough there." JOHNSON: "Why, yes, Sir, meat and drink enough to give the inhabitants sufficient strength to run away from home." All these quick and lively sallies were said sportively, quite in jest, and with a smile, which showed that he meant only wit. Upon this topic he and Mr. Wilkes could perfectly assimilate; here was a bond of union between them, and I was conscious that, as both of them had visited Caledonia, both were fully satisfied of the strange narrow ignorance of those who imagine that it is a land of famine. But they amused themselves with persevering in the old jokes. When I claimed a superiority for Scotland over England in one respect, that no man can be arrested there for a debt merely because another swears it against him, but there must first be the judgment of a court of law ascertaining its justice; and that a seizure of the person, before judgment is obtained, can take place only if his creditor should swear that he is about to fly from the country or, as it is technically expressed, is *in meditatione fugae*. WILKES: "That, I should think, may be safely sworn of all the Scotch nation." JOHNSON (to Mr. Wilkes): "You must know, Sir, I lately took my friend Boswell, and showed him genuine civilized life in an English provincial town. I turned him loose at Lichfield, my native city, that he might see for once real civility, for you know he lives among savages in Scotland, and among rakes in London." WILKES: "Except when he is with grave, sober, decent people, like you and me." JOHNSON (smiling): "And we ashamed of him."

They were quite frank and easy. Johnson told the story of his asking Mrs. Macaulay to allow her footman to sit down with them, to prove the ridiculousness of the arguments for the equality of mankind; and he said to me afterwards, with a nod of satisfaction, "You saw Mr. Wilkes acquiesced." Wilkes talked with all imaginable freedom of the ludicrous title given to the Attorney General, *Diabolus Regis*, adding, "I have reason to know something about that officer, for I was prosecuted for a libel." Johnson, who many people would have supposed must have been furiously angry at hearing this talked of so lightly, said not a word. He was now, *indeed*, "a good-humored fellow."

After dinner we had an accession of Mrs. Knowles, the Quaker lady, well known for her various talents, and of Mr. Alderman Lee. Amidst some patriotic groans, somebody (I think the alderman) said, "Poor old England is lost." JOHNSON: "Sir, it is not so much to be lamented that old England is lost, as that the Scotch have found it." WILKES: "Had Lord Bute governed Scotland only, I should not have taken the trouble to write his eulogy, and dedicate *Mortimer* to him."

Mr. Wilkes held a candle to show a fine print of a beautiful female figure which hung in the room, and pointed out the elegant contour of the bosom with the finger of an arch connoisseur. He afterwards in a conversation with me waggishly insisted that all the time Johnson showed visible signs of a fervent admiration of the corresponding charms of the fair Quaker.

This record, though by no means so perfect as I could wish, will serve to give a notion of a very curious interview, which was not only pleasing at the time, but had the agreeable and benignant effect of reconciling any animosity, and sweetening any acidity, which, in the various bustle of political contest, had been produced in the minds of two men, who, though widely different, had so many things in common—classical learning, modern literature, wit, and humour, and ready repartee—that it would have been much to be regretted if they had been for ever at a distance from each other.

Mr. Burke gave me much credit for this successful *negotiation;* and pleasantly said that "there was nothing to equal it in the whole history of the *Corps Diplomatique.*"

I attended Dr. Johnson home, and had the satisfaction to hear him tell Mrs. Williams how much he had been pleased with Mr. Wilkes's company, and what an agreeable day he had passed.

UNDERSTANDING THE TEXT

1. To what trait of Johnson's character does Boswell appeal in proposing the dinner at Dilly's?
2. Is there any suspense in Boswell's narrative? From what circumstances does it arise? Does Boswell treat these circumstances so as to get the most suspense out of them?
3. What is the point of Boswell's remarks about Sir John Pringle in paragraph 2? Would anything be lost if this paragraph were omitted?
4. Does Johnson reveal anything about himself in his story about Foote that is relevant to his own conduct with Wilkes?
5. We must assume that Boswell records only a portion of what was said at the dinner. What principles does he seem to have used in making his selection?
6. One of Boswell's greatest talents as a biographer was his ability to steer the conversation so that Johnson and others would be kept supplied with interesting and provocative topics on which to discourse. Is there any evidence in this narrative of Boswell at work in this way?
7. Make clear the meanings of each of the following words in its context: *repulsion, snug, assiduous, avarice, obloquy, ostentatious, connoisseur, waggishly, assimilate, benignant, repartee.*

TOPICS FOR DISCUSSION AND WRITING

8. Consult an encyclopedia or a biographical dictionary for the political careers and views of Wilkes and Johnson.

9. Are there any signs that Boswell attempted to insure the accuracy of his record by checking his notes with the participants afterwards?

10. Johnson says that "You despise a man for avarice, but do not hate him." Write a paragraph commenting on this precept.

11. Boswell gives relatively little evaluation and interpretation, allowing the speeches to stand pretty much by themselves. Write a brief evaluative comparison of Johnson and Wilkes on the basis of the information which Boswell's narrative provides.

12. Describe an experience in which you arranged a social occasion involving persons who you knew disliked each other, or one in which you had suddenly to cope with conflicting personalities, or one in which you *were* one of the conflicting personalities.

13. Samuel Johnson remarked that "They only who live with a man can write his life with any genuine exactness and discrimination; and few people who have lived with a man know what to remark about him." Using Boswell, Strachey, and Ferguson as sources of examples, write an appraisal of biographical method on the basis of this precept. Consider especially the kinds of observations the contemporary biographer and the later biographer are in favorable positions to make, and the special limitations under which each works.

The Sad Story of Dr. Colbatch

LYTTON STRACHEY

THE REV. DR. COLBATCH could not put up with it any more. Animated by the highest motives, he felt that he must intervene. The task was arduous, odious, dangerous; his antagonist most redoubtable; but Dr. Colbatch was a Doctor of Divinity, Professor of Casuistry in the University of Cambridge, a Senior Fellow of Trinity College, and his duty was plain; the conduct of the Master could be tolerated no longer; Dr. Bentley must go.

In the early years of the eighteenth century the life of learning was agitated, violent, and full of extremes. Everything about it was on the grand scale. Erudition was gigantic, controversies were frenzied, careers were punctuated by brutal triumphs, wild temerities, and dreadful mortifications. One sat, bent nearly double, surrounded by four circles of folios, living to edit Hesychius and confound Dr. Hody, and dying at last with a stomach half-full of sand. The very names of the scholars of those days had something about them at once terrifying and preposterous: there was Graevius, there was Wolfius, there was Cruquius; there were Torrentius and Rutgersius; there was the gloomy Baron de Stosch, and there was the deplorable De Pauw. But Richard Bentley was greater than all these. Combining extraordinary knowledge and almost infinite memory with an acumen hardly to be distinguished from inspiration, and a command of logical precision which might have been envied by mathematicians or generals in the field, he revivified with his daemonic energy the whole domain of classifical scholarship. The peer of the mightiest of his predecessors—of Scaliger, of Casaubon—turning, in skillful strength, the magic glass of science, he brought into focus the world's comprehension of ancient literature with a luminous exactitude of which they had never dreamed. His prowess had first declared itself in his *Dissertation upon the Epistles of Phalaris,* in which he had obliterated under cartloads of erudition and ridicule the miserable Mr. Boyle. He had been rewarded, in the year 1700, when he was not yet forty, with the Mastership of Trinity; and then another side of his genius had appeared. It became evident that he was not merely a scholar, that he was a man of action and affairs, and that he intended to dominate over the magnificent foundation of Trinity with a command as absolute as that which he exercised over questions in Greek grammar. He had immediately gathered into his own hands the entire control of the College; he had manipulated the statutes, rearranged the finances, packed the Council; he had compelled the Society to rebuild and redecorate, at great expense, his own Lodge; he had brought every kind of appointment—scholarships, fellowships, livings—to depend simply upon his will. The Fellows murmured and protested in vain; their terrible tyrant treated them with scant ceremony. "You will die in your shoes!" he had shouted at one tottering Senior who had ventured to oppose him; and another fat and angry old gentleman he had named "The College Dog." In fact, he treated his opponents as if they had been corrupt readings in an old manuscript. At last there was open war. The leading Fellows had appealed to the Visitor of the College, the Bishop of Ely, to remove the Master; and the Master had replied by denying the Bishop's competence and declaring that the visitatorial power lay with the Crown. His subtle mind had detected an ambiguity in the Charter; the legal position was, indeed, highly dubious; and for five years, amid indescribable animosities, he was able to hold his enemies at bay. In the meantime, he had not been idle in other directions; he had annihilated Le Clerc, who, ignorant of Greek, was rash enough to publish a Menander; he had produced a monumental edition of Horace; and he had pulverized Freethinking in the person of Anthony Collins. But his foes had pressed upon him; and eventually it had seemed that his hour was come. In 1714 he had been forced to appear before the Bishop's court; his defense had been weak; the Bishop had drawn up a judgment of deprivation. Then there had been a *coup de théâtre.* The Bishop had suddenly died before delivering judgment. All the previous proceedings lapsed, and Bentley ruled once more supreme in Trinity.

It was at this point that the Rev. Dr. Colbatch, animated by the highest motives, felt that he must intervene. Hitherto he had filled the *rôle* of a peacemaker; but now the outrageous proceedings of the triumphant

Master—who, in the flush of victory, was beginning to expel hostile Fellows by force from the College, and had even refused to appoint Dr. Colbatch himself to the Vice-Mastership—called aloud for the resistance of every right-thinking man. And Dr. Colbatch flattered himself that he could resist to some purpose. He had devoted his life to the study of the law; he was a man of the world; he was acquainted with Lord Carteret; and he had written a book on Portugal. Accordingly, he hurried to London and interviewed great personages, who were all of them extremely sympathetic and polite; then he returned to Trinity, and, after delivering a fulminating sermon in the chapel, he bearded the Master at a College meeting, and actually had the nerve to answer him back. Just then, moreover, the tide seemed to be turning against the tyrant. Bentley, not content with the battle in his own College, had begun a campaign against the University. There was a hectic struggle, and then the Vice-Chancellor, by an unparalleled exercise of power, deprived Bentley of his degrees: the Master of Trinity College and the Regius Professor of Divinity was reduced to the status of an undergraduate. This delighted the heart of Dr. Colbatch. He flew to London, where Lord Carteret, as usual, was all smiles and agreement. When, a little later, the College living of Orewell fell vacant, Dr. Colbatch gave a signal proof of his power; for Bentley, after refusing to appoint him to the living, at last found himself obliged to give way. Dr. Colbatch entered the rectory in triumph; was it not clear that that villain at the Lodge was a sinking man? But, whether sinking or no, the villain could still use a pen to some purpose. In a pamphlet on a proposed edition of the New Testament, Bentley took occasion to fall upon Dr. Colbatch tooth and nail. The rector of Orewell was "a casuistic drudge," a "plodding pupil of Escobar," an insect, a snarling dog, a gnawing rat, a maggot, and a cabbage-head. His intellect was as dark as his countenance; his "eyes, muscles, and shoulders were wrought up into the most solemn posture of gravity"; he grinned horribly; he was probably mad; and his brother's beard was ludicrously long.

On this Dr. Colbatch, chattering with rage, brought an action against the Master for libel in the Court of the Vice-Chancellor. By a cunning legal device Bentley arranged that the action should be stopped by the Court of King's Bench. Was it possible that Dr. Colbatch's knowledge of the law was not impeccable? He could not believe it, and forthwith composed a pamphlet entitled *Jus Academicum*, in which the whole case, in all its bearings, was laid before the public. The language of the pamphlet was temperate, the references to Bentley were not indecently severe; but, unfortunately, in one or two passages some expressions seemed to reflect upon the competence of the Court of the King's Bench. The terrible Master saw his opportunity. He moved the Court of the King's Bench to take cognizance of the *Jus Academicum* as a contempt of their jurisdiction. A cold shiver ran down Dr. Colbatch's spine. Was it conceivable? . . . But no! He had friends in London, powerful friends, who would never desert him. He rushed to Downing Street; Lord Townshend was reassuring; so was the Lord Chief Justice; and so was the Lord Chancellor. "Here," said Lord Carteret, waving a pen, "is the magician's wand that will always come to the rescue of Dr. Colbatch." Surely all was well. Nevertheless, he was summoned to appear before the Court of King's Bench in order to explain his pamphlet. The judge was old and testy; he misquoted Horace—"Jura negat sibi nata, nihil non abrogat"[1]; "*Arrogat,* my lord!" said Dr. Colbatch. A little later the judge once more returned to the quotation, making the same error. "*Arrogat,* my lord!" cried Dr. Colbatch for the second time. Yet once again, in the course of his summing-up, the judge pronounced the word "abrogat"; "*Arrogat,* my lord!" screamed, for the third time, Dr. Colbatch. The interruption was fatal. The unhappy man was fined £50 and imprisoned for a week.

A less pertinacious spirit would have collapsed under such a dire misadventure; but Dr. Colbatch fought on. For ten years more, still animated by the highest motives, he struggled to dispossess the Master. Something was gained when yet another Bishop was appointed to the See of Ely—a Bishop who disapproved of Bentley's proceedings. With indefatigable zeal Dr. Colbatch laid the case before the Bishop of London, implored the Dean and Chapter of Westminster to interfere, and petitioned the Privy Council. In 1729 the Bishop of Ely summoned Bentley to appear before him; whereupon Bentley appealed to the Crown to decide who was the Visitor of Trinity College. For a moment Dr. Colbatch dreamed of obtaining a special Act of Parliament to deal with his enemy; but even he shrank from such a desperate expedient; and at length, in 1732, the whole case came up for decision before the House of Lords. At that very moment Bentley published his edition of *Paradise Lost,* in which all the best passages were emended and rewritten—a book remarkable as a wild aberra-

---

[1] The line, with Dr. Colbatch's correction, means "He denies that laws were framed against him; he arrogates everything to himself"; the full text in Horace adds *armis,* "by force of arms"; this is given as the definition of a tyrant.

tion of genius, and no less remarkable as containing, for the first time in
print, "tow'ring o'er the alphabet like Saul," the great Digamma. If
Bentley's object had been to impress his judges in his favour, he failed; for
the House of Lords decided that the Bishop of Ely was the Visitor. Once
more Bentley was summoned to Ely House. Dr. Colbatch was on tenter-
hooks; the blow was about to fall; nothing could avert it now, unless—he
trembled—if the Bishop were to die again? But the Bishop did not die; in
1734 he pronounced judgment; he deposed Bentley.

So, after thirty years, a righteous doom had fallen upon that proud and
wicked man. Dr. Colbatch's exultation was inordinate: it was only equalled,
in fact, by his subsequent horror, indignation, and fury. For Bentley had
discovered in the Statutes of the College a clause which laid it down that,
when the Master was to be removed, the necessary steps were to be taken
by the Vice-Master. Now the Vice-Master was Bentley's creature; he
never took the necessary steps; and Bentley never ceased, so long as he
lived, to be Master of Trinity. Dr. Colbatch petitioned the House of Lords,
he applied to the Court of King's Bench, he beseeched Lord Carteret—all
in vain. His head turned; he was old, haggard, dying. Tossing on his bed at
Orewell, he fell into a delirium; at first his mutterings were inarticulate;
but suddenly, starting up, a glare in his eye, he exclaimed, with a strange
emphasis, to the utter bewilderment of the bystanders, "*Arrogat*, my lord!"
and immediately expired.

UNDERSTANDING THE TEXT

1. Analyze the ironic elements in Strachey's presentation of Colbatch's career.
2. Describe the point of view which Strachey uses in the essay. Through whose
   eyes or in terms of whose attitudes are the events narrated? Does Strachey
   maintain a single point of view throughout the essay, or does he shift from
   one to another? If you find he does the latter, when does the point of view
   shift, and for what reasons?
3. What seems to be Strachey's attitude toward Colbatch? Toward Bentley?
   Toward eighteen-century scholarship? Is it possible to make out the more
   general conceptions and values in terms of which Strachey views the persons
   and events he describes?
4. Was Dr. Colbatch really "animated by the highest motives" in intervening?
   What characteristics of Strachey's writing help you to answer this question?
   Why does Strachey repeat this phrase on pp. 321 and 323?
5. Consider the following alternative sequence of items in the fourth sentence
   of the paragraph beginning "It was at this point . . ." (p. 321):
   "He had written a book on Portugal; he was a friend of Lord Carteret; he

had devoted his life to the study of the law; and he was a man of the world."
What is the value of Strachey's order for his purpose?

6. Consider the effects of the following substitutions: *a mountain of erudition* for *cartloads of erudition* (p. 321); *seething with rage* for *chattering with rage* (p. 322); *such a blow to his hopes* for *such a dire misadventure* (p. 323); *but he shrank* for *but even he shrank* (p. 323).

7. Explain the meanings of the following words in their contexts: *temerities, acumen, daemonic, genius, livings, coup de théâtre, aberration.*

TOPICS FOR DISCUSSION AND WRITING

8. In your own words, write a sketch of Dr. Colbatch's character as Strachey would have us believe it was.

9. Using the facts that Strachey gives, construct an account of Colbatch's feud with Bentley in which Colbatch will appear in a favorable light.

10. Write a paragraph explaining the point Strachey is making in his description of Dr. Colbatch's death.

11. We can assume that Strachey had available when he wrote a good many facts about Colbatch's career that he decided not to include. Here are some facts that he omitted and that it is safe to say he knew:

   a. Through the good offices of Bentley, Colbatch was selected, in 1701, to be tutor to the Earl of Hertford, eldest son of the Duke of Somerset, Chancellor of Cambridge University.

   b. Through Bentley's patronage, Colbatch held an appointment in Salisbury Cathedral from 1702 to 1720, worth £20 a year.

   c. Colbatch achieved a considerable reputation for his lectures on moral philosophy at Cambridge.

   d. Colbatch published a pamphlet defending Bentley's view that holders of divinity degrees should have priority over holders of M.A. degrees in the assignment of college rooms or college livings.

   e. In 1714, Colbatch refused Bentley's offer of the vice-mastership of Trinity College.

   f. In 1727 Bentley presented Colbatch with the old Trinity College clock for Colbatch's church at Orewell.

   g. Colbatch in his will left an income of £30 a year to a charity school at Orewell.

Consider these facts and see if you can determine why Strachey may have decided to leave them out of his essay. What different kinds of reasons for omission do you find? Select two or three of these facts and decide where you would insert them in Strachey's essay, if they were to be included, and consider how you would express each fact in order to preserve the total effect that Strachey is aiming at.

12. Read the life of Colbatch in the *Dictionary of National Biography* and write a critical comparison of its interpretation of Colbatch's career and Strachey's.

13. Do you think there is any justification for the sort of treatment to which Strachey subjects Colbatch? Colbatch was not, after all, a very important person. Why does Strachey go to so much trouble to have fun with him?

Young Man with a Horn Again

OTIS FERGUSON

IT IS almost ten years since Bix Beiderbecke died, shortly after his twenty-eighth birthday; it is at least twelve years since he played the bulk of his music. But he is as new and wonderful now as he was in those fast days on the big time, the highest expression of jazz when jazz was still young, the golden boy with the cornet he would sometimes carry around under his arm in a paper bag. Columbia has just reissued some of the famous recordings (Album C-29; 8 ten-inch sides, $2.50). They aren't the half of it, not the tenth of what was recorded, of course; and most of them aren't even among the best. But Columbia has acquired some of the masters of the old Okeh company, and now resurrects "Royal Garden Blues," "Goose Pimples," "Thou Swell," etc., for those with ears.

I suppose the kids growing up in the belief that Glenn Miller is what it really takes to blow the roof off would wonder, in the midst of this rather dated small-band clamor, what they were listening to and why. Well, it's just jazz, kids, and as far as groups in general go, not the best of its period. But Bix, the fellow riding above and ahead and all around with that clear-bell horn, Bix had swing before the phonies knew the word. He had it at its best and purest, for he had not only the compelling life of syncopation, the ease within an intense and relentless rhythm; he had music in a way of invention that is only found when you find a good song, inevitable, sweet and perfect. He could take off out of any chord sequence, any good or silly tune, and wheel and lift with his gay new melodic figures as free of strain in the air as pigeons. He had a sense of harmonic structure that none can learn and few are born with; he had absolute pitch and absolute control of his instrument—in fact, no trumpet player I've ever heard

Reprinted from *The New Republic*, November 18, 1940. Used by permission of *The New Republic*.

could be so reckless and yet so right, so assured in all the range from tender
to brash, from sorrow to a shout; his tone was as perfect without artifice as
water in the brooks, and his lip and tongue and valve-work so exact in all
registers that he could jump into a line of notes and make it sound like
he'd slapped every one of them square in the face. With this technical assurance, he never had to cramp and plan and fuss himself: he could start at
any point, and land on a dime.

This makes it sound too tossed off. He worked on his music, and worried always. Any jealous little stinkfinger (and there were plenty around to
envy and fear his talent) could always bring him down by low-rating the
thing he'd just played; any musician who had something was the object of
his admiration. He never got over feeling uneasy about his lack of facility
in sight reading—but it was too natural and easy to play it by ear. He had
a memory in music like nobody's business, and could and at certain hilarious times did imitate a corny solo just preceding his, so closely note for
note that the only one who wasn't holding his sides was the soloist himself,
who figgered that young feller was rarin' to go.

I don't know anybody who did more in the way of opening up the set
rhythm of jazz. Everything is written in four-four time, and the pace can
be said to vary through twelve or fifteen standard tempos, from slow-drag
to fast-jump. But Bix as he went along actually wrote his own time signature over the implied beat for dancing, by subtleties of phrasing, by delayed attack or a quick rush on ahead, and by the varying duration of a
note.

It was no mere gut-bucket, emotion without control, virtuosity without
pattern, louder and faster and higher. He sweat, and for all the ease of his
solo in flight, the men around him could see the lines tighten in his face
every time he stood up. One of the easy remarks in jazz is: He played it
fifteen times, every one different. Bix played it different, all right. But
when he got just the note of the chord, just the intervals, just the main
line the way he wanted—that was his structure and there couldn't be a
better, so why go off into new scales and razz-mah-tazz? At times—and
you can hear it proved on half a dozen records—he would get a way of
playing for the brass section and have the arranger leave that chorus blank;
then he would get the boys together outside and play a phrase and then
another, and then go back and play it in chords, patiently, carefully, just
as he used to do with the glee club back in grade school in Davenport,
note for note and chord for chord, until that part of the arrangement was a

section in solo, established in the book and no need for writing. It couldn't be written anyway.

And all of this makes him sound too perfect, as well, like a church-going cousin always being thrown up in your face. He was perfect only in music, and in the simple goodness and loyalty that was always there under the rusty tux with the soup stains, the underwear and sox you never could get off him for sending to the laundry until they fell off, and he'd borrowed them from you in the first place, like as not. As a kid he had wanted to be Douglas Fairbanks; he kept himself in trim and was great at skating, swimming, jumping over walls and the like, an all-around first in his neighborhood, and so generally hardy that an old sweater was all he found necessary for an Iowa winter. But music as it became a profession and almost a religion shut out his concern for just about everything else. Things were always happening to him, partly because he couldn't spare the time to study about them—missing the train, losing his tie, falling off the stand in a whirlwind of music racks, getting thrown out of the hotel.

Of his considerable achievements as a rumpot, people still speak with wonder and endlessly, and there were indeed some funny times, before the dark days. But one of his troubles was a capacity rare in brass men: he could tie quite a handsome one on without going technically fuzzy and lip-numb, so that he could stand up and get off those clear round notes as innocent as pie, and then solemnly take his seat in the middle of the whole boilerworks of a drummer's outfit. He lacked a natural brake in that; and his constitution was so good to start with that he wasn't retarded physically until he'd blown the fuse on the whole works. Also, he could make as big money as you want without having a dime, a very rough man on a dollar bill. Also, while no one ever suffered musical fools more gladly, stood by for and worked over them, he had no use for any stuffed shirt in music or anything else, except as a target for a slingshot. He'd run into any such rich spreading trees as quick and head-on as the horse in the fable: he wasn't blind, he just didn't give a damn.

The story of his musical career is outlined in the book "Jazz Men" about as well as it can be. The dates, the cities, the things done, the people met are established enough by now for a pattern, if only in fragments. But he had started in music early, and there is not so much known about that. His family was well off; his father was a good solid lumber merchant; his mother an amateur musician. There was always a piano in the house and there was a phonograph when few people had them. Bix (his real name was

Leon Bismarck, for it was a family of German-American extraction) was a perfectly normal boy, except that he was always fussing around with music. He had a sister and an older brother, who was enough a hero to him so that he swiped the nickname Bix from him, and would not part with it. He lived in a big house across a sloping playground from the school, and the school was more a center of life than schools usually get to be.

There was the playground, the sliding and skating and wrassling, but there was also a lot of singing: the kind of spontaneous thing where a whole grade of kids will enjoy their cantatas and what-not so much that they not only start a ball rolling through the classes in general but work at it and get pretty good. They used to have the run of the school at night for rehearsal; they used to have a barber-shop quartet out on the fire-escape. In one grade they wanted a piano for their own room, so they arranged a local concert, which was so successful they gave another, and before the year was out they had the piano, bought and paid for. One of those happy things that cannot be incubated, taught or fostered.

Anyhow, Bix went through all the grades without being kept back, and in this social-musical atmosphere he was the number-one boy. Anything he heard he could play on the piano; anything he could play he could figure out the parts for, and teach the others to sing in chords. He liked music and music liked him and gave him a place, and the world was very young. Then on top of that, first off the crank-winding phonograph and later up the river from New Orleans in boats, came jazz, with horns. He got a cornet and taught himself to play it, for that was the kind of instrument it took to blast out this new thing in music. He got quite a little drunk on the excitement of it and did not want to be Douglas Fairbanks any more. His family began to worry about him, for it was one of those happy families that enjoy their group with pride and a fierce concern that it shall have the best. They sent Bix from high school to Lake Forest Military Academy, thinking to get him away from the bad balance of nothing but music. But Lake Forest was near Chicago, and Chicago was jazz then. It was as though jazz were a house that had been built just for him. And he moved in.

I was no intimate, but I think I could say in general why he blew up. It was partly the pace, of course, and taking it too fast. He began to see the little fellows with green beards walking up and down on his chest, and Whiteman sent him back to Davenport, to get squared up. He was too far gone for any working band at that time, which was 1928. At home, he came out of it. He was shaky but still good, and he jobbed around with his old friend from grade-school, Larry Andrews, and watched his hand when he held it out every morning to see if it still looked as though he were waving at somebody. He had been at the top but somewhere along the line, some time or other, he'd taken a fall. And he wasn't sure in his own heart he would fit back there again, even if he stayed off brass rails. He was honestly anxious. Was it just liquor that had pulled the knife on him? Maybe it was something else too?

It was, all right. He lifted his horn over the sixty-odd dancers or the beer tables of this cover-your-expenses circuit, and the other musicians (if no one else) would shake their heads and marvel; and it was the same as in the first days when he showed up in an Indiana town where the boys had thought they were really going, and played a few sets, and as one of them reports today, a day in which he is pretty famous, "I tell you the tears stood in my eyes, I couldn't get out the next number in the book."

He stayed on the wagon and the music was as good as ever—which he proved later on the last recording date he had before he died, with Hoagy Carmichael's pick-up band. But what he couldn't see, the nameless thing that was his trouble, had got him down. First he'd wanted to be "as good" as the men out front whose music had excited him. Then he wanted to stay good, and be if possible better. This was a preoccupation to bridge the years from the rusty clangor of the Wolverines to the bright lights of the Goldkette and Whiteman shows; this and the handy gin pitcher kept him assuming that if he felt low and the road ahead was flat and lonesome, it was just a hangover, just feeling low, let's sick a hare on the hound that bit me. Actually something else had been creeping up, something he never saw clearly. He had come to the top like a cork, and he had no more place to go.

And still he had to be going, he had to travel, so completely a musician that music was his ticket and there was no other line. He didn't go much for women. He was loyal, true and happy in his friendships with men, even self-effacing, but his friends were, after all, musicians. It had to be music for him, and as far as he could see when he could see, he wanted neither the money, nor the place, nor the show. But what else? He dreamed of being a composer. He had written some piano pieces and he wanted to do something even more ambitious. But what? He had no equipment, not the kind of equipment that a so-called legitimate musician acquires from study of the great body of Western music, which has had its best time in other times and is now gone fairly sterile. He didn't know what to do, and listened with awe to Debussy records (Debussy is for some strange reason a great favorite of good jazz men), and would sequester himself and sit morosely at the piano, fingering the chords of a new music without being able to reconcile the old, which he didn't comprehend, with the new, which was in him as natural as a voice in your throat and which he had spent his brief lifetime tuning for song.

From the top of folk music as folk music, there is no place to go, actually. Jazz is a folk music, but Bix had never taken time to think of things like that: jazz was the country where he grew up, the fine high thing, the sun coming up to fill the world through the morning.

He never heard about what was troubling him and only knew it was trouble. He came back to the big time eventually, but he could no longer stay on it, he played here and there, hole and corner, but he was too unreliable now for the standard type of show—and the big time was letting jazz go underground quietly by these days, for whatever life there had been in bands like Pollack, Goldkette, Whiteman in 1927–28 was no longer in demand by 1930, and even the great jumping Negro outfits were either breaking up or hightailing off to Europe. Bix played for dances and recordings, and went back to the bottle and was not seen in the better places; and even moped around fearing he had lost his sense of perfect pitch; but when he lifted that stumpy dented cornet at the fraction of a second after the release, for dancing or just for the record in a dead studio, it came tumbling and leaping out as complete and lovely as ever. What he could always do he could still do, from the jazz-band tone to the sadness. But what he had was more than enough, and he didn't know where to put it.

Perhaps you will have to hear him a lot; perhaps you won't have any ear for the jazz music that grew up around you and in your time, and so will never hear the voice, almost as if speaking; but there is something in these records that goes beyond a mere instrument or the improviser on it, some unconquerable bright spirit that leaves no slops even in confusion and defeat and darkness gathering; some gallant human thing which is as near to us as it is completely marvelous, and which makes only just and apposite that end of a career so next to the heart of all who would like this country to be a country of happy people, singing. In the summer of 1931 Bix Beiderbecke got out of a sick bed, and against the best advice, to ride a rickety bus to a place some fellows were playing a dance. He had promised the fellows he would go for the date, which would fall through if there were not some stubby cornet lifting over the boys and girls on the floor, and through the close air to the roof, some special glad thing to dance by. So he went, walking up to the bus and from the bus to the band room with that peculiar purposeful air of walking a straight line to some immediate destination, eyes going neither left nor right. He had promised to play; he played, and music was around him like rain falling once more. That was all.

He got pneumonia out of it, of course, and died of that a few days later. That is, they buried the body. For those who had been around and those to come after there was something, grown in this country out of the Iowa dirt, that didn't die and could not be buried so long as there should be a record left in the world, and a turntable to spin it on.

UNDERSTANDING THE TEXT

1. This essay was written on the occasion of the issue of an album of Beiderbecke records in 1940. Can you detect any evidences of its date?

2. What is Ferguson's explanation of Beiderbecke's crackup? How much weight does he give to the fact that Beiderbecke drank a great deal? Does he imply that Beiderbecke might have made a comeback had it not been for his last illness? How early in the essay does Ferguson refer to the trait of character to which he attributes Beiderbecke's failure?

3. How much of the essay can you account for by using this description as a theme statement: "the golden boy with the trumpet he would sometimes carry around under his arm in a paper bag"?

4. Consider the following sentence: "He liked music and music liked him and gave him a place, and the world was very young." Both in structure and tone, how characteristic of Ferguson's writing is this sentence? Is it appropriate to Ferguson's purpose in this essay?

5. Toward the end of the essay Ferguson describes Beiderbecke's last performance: "music was around him like rain falling once more." What is the appropriateness, in Ferguson's analysis of Bix's character and playing, of this comparison? Does he use similar figures of speech elsewhere in the essay?

6. What trait of character which Ferguson has mentioned earlier in the essay is suggested in Beiderbecke's "walking up to the bus and from the bus to the band room with that peculiar purposeful air of walking a straight line to some immediate destination, eyes going neither left nor right" (pp. 332–333)? Why is it introduced at this point in the narrative?

7. Paragraph 6 of the essay is related to paragraph 5 in a way that parallels the relation between paragraph 3 and paragraph 2. What is the similarity between the two pairs of paragraphs? What progression is there between the two groups? What is the function of paragraph 4?

TOPICS FOR DISCUSSION AND WRITING

8. Why does Ferguson say that the end of Beiderbecke's career was "only just and apposite"? Do you agree? Set forth the reasons for your agreement or disagreement in one paragraph.

9. Using the materials Ferguson provides, write a 1000-word account of Beiderbecke's career in your own words.

10. Write a critical analysis of Ferguson's style, identifying its outstanding features and appraising its effectiveness.

11. Why do you think Ferguson omits an account of Beiderbecke's career between his discovery of jazz and his first crackup?

12. Write on the following sentence: "From the top of folk music as folk music, there is no place to go, actually."

13. Do you agree that jazz is folk music?

6. History: The Record of Society

Getting at the Truth

MARCHETTE CHUTE

THIS is a rather presumptuous title for a biographer to use, since truth is a very large word. In the sense that it means the reality about a human being it is probably impossible for a biographer to achieve. In the sense that it means a reasonable presentation of all the available facts it is more nearly

Reprinted from *The Saturday Review*, September 19, 1953, by permission of the author and *The Saturday Review*.

possible, but even this limited goal is harder to reach than it appears to be. A biographer needs to be both humble and cautious when he remembers the nature of the material he is working with, for a historical fact is rather like the flamingo that Alice in Wonderland tried to use as a croquet mallet. As soon as she got its neck nicely straightened out and was ready to hit the ball, it would turn and look at her with a puzzled expression, and any biographer knows that what is called a "fact" has a way of doing the same.

Here is a small example. When I was writing my forthcoming biography, "Ben Jonson of Westminster," I wanted to give a paragraph or two to Sir Philip Sidney, who had a great influence on Jonson. No one thinks of Sidney without thinking of chivalry, and to underline the point I intended to use a story that Sir Fulke Greville told of him. Sidney died of gangrene, from a musket shot that shattered his thigh, and Greville says that Sidney failed to put on his leg armor while preparing for battle because the marshal of the camp was not wearing leg armor and Sidney was unwilling to do anything that would give him a special advantage.

The story is so characteristic both of Sidney himself and of the misplaced high-mindedness of late Renaissance chivalry that I wanted to use it, and since Sir Fulke Greville was one of Sidney's closest friends the information seemed to be reliable enough. But it is always well to check each piece of information as thoroughly as possible and so I consulted another account of Sidney written by a contemporary, this time a doctor who knew the family fairly well. The doctor, Thomas Moffet, mentioned the episode but he said that Sidney left off his leg armor because he was in a hurry.

The information was beginning to twist in my hand and could no longer be trusted. So I consulted still another contemporary who had mentioned the episode, to see which of the two he agreed with. This was Sir John Smythe, a military expert who brought out his book a few years after Sidney's death. Sir John was an old-fashioned conservative who advocated the use of heavy armor even on horseback, and he deplored the current craze for leaving off leg protection, "the imitating of which . . . cost that noble and worthy gentleman Sir Philip Sidney his life."

So here I was with three entirely different reasons why Sidney left off his leg armor, all advanced by careful writers who were contemporaries of his. The flamingo had a legitimate reason for looking around with a puzzled expression.

The only thing to do in a case like this is to examine the point of view of the three men who are supplying the conflicting evidence. Sir Fulke

Greville was trying to prove a thesis: that his beloved friend had an extremely chivalric nature. Sir John Smythe also was trying to prove a thesis: that the advocates of light arming followed a theory that could lead to disaster. Only the doctor, Thomas Moffet, was not trying to prove a thesis. He was not using his own explanation to reinforce some point he wanted to make. He did not want anything except to set down on paper what he believed to be the facts; and since we do not have Sidney's own explanation of why he did not put on leg armor, the chances are that Dr. Moffet is the safest man to trust.

For Moffet was without desire. Nothing can so quickly blur and distort the facts as desire—the wish to use the facts for some purpose of your own—and nothing can so surely destroy the truth. As soon as the witness wants to prove something he is no longer impartial and his evidence is no longer to be trusted.

The only safe way to study contemporary testimony is to bear constantly in mind this possibility of prejudice and to put almost as much attention on the writer himself as on what he has written. For instance, Sir Anthony Weldon's description of the Court of King James is lively enough and often used as source material; but a note from the publisher admits that the pamphlet was issued as a warning to anyone who wished to "side with this bloody house" of Stuart. The publisher, at any rate, did not consider Weldon an impartial witness. At about the same time Arthur Wilson published his history of Great Britain, which contained an irresistibly vivid account of the agonized death of the Countess of Somerset. Wilson sounds reasonably impartial; but his patron was the Earl of Essex, who had good reason to hate that particular countess, and there is evidence that he invented the whole scene to gratify his patron.

Sometimes a writer will contradict what he has already written, and in that case the only thing to do is to investigate what changed his point of view. For instance, in 1608 Captain John Smith issued a description of his capture by Powhatan, and he made it clear that the Indian chief had treated him with unwavering courtesy and hospitality. In 1624 the story was repeated in Smith's "General History of Virginia," but the writer's circumstances had changed. Smith needed money, "having a prince's mind imprisoned in a poor man's purse," and he wanted the book to be profitable. Powhatan's daughter, the princess Pocahontas, had recently been in the news, for her visit to England had aroused a great deal of interest among the sort of people that Smith hoped would buy his book. So Smith supplied a new version of the story, in which the once-hospitable Powhatan would have permitted the hero's brains to be dashed out if Pocahontas had not saved his life. It was the second story that achieved fame, and of course it may have been true. But it is impossible to trust it because the desire of the writer is so obviously involved; as Smith said in his prospectus, he needed money and hoped that the book would give "satisfaction."

It might seem that there was an easy way for a biographer to avoid the use of this kind of prejudiced testimony. All he has to do is to construct his biography from evidence that cannot be tampered with—from parish records, legal documents, bills, accounts, court records, and so on. Out of these solid gray blocks of impersonal evidence it should surely be possible to construct a road that will lead straight to the truth and that will never bend itself to the misleading curve of personal desire.

This might be so if the only problem involved were the reliability of the material. But there is another kind of desire that is much more subtle, much more pervasive, and much more dangerous than the occasional distortions of fact that contemporary writers may have permitted themselves to make; and this kind of desire can destroy the truth of a biography even if every individual fact in it is as solid and as uncompromising as rock. Even if the road is built of the best and most reliable materials it can still curve away from the truth because of this other desire that threatens it: the desire of the biographer himself.

A biographer is not a court record or a legal document. He is a human being, writing about another human being, and his own temperament, his own point of view, and his own frame of reference are unconsciously imposed upon the man he is writing about. Even if the biographer is free from Captain Smith's temptation—the need for making money—and wants to write nothing but the literal truth, he is still handicapped by the fact that there is no such thing as a completely objective human being.

An illustration of what can happen if the point of view is sufficiently strong is the curious conclusion that the nineteenth-century biographers reached about William Shakespeare. Shakespeare joined a company of London actors in 1594, was listed as an actor in 1598 and 1603, and was still listed as one of the "men actors" in the company in 1609. Shortly before he joined this company Shakespeare dedicated two narrative poems to the Earl of Southampton, and several years after Shakespeare died his collected plays were dedicated to the Earl of Pembroke. This was his only relationship with either of the two noblemen, and there is nothing to connect him with them during the fifteen years in which he belonged to the same acting company and during which he wrote nearly all his plays.

But here the desire of the biographers entered in. They had been reared in the strict code of nineteenth-century gentility and they accepted two ideas without question. One was that there are few things more important than an English lord; the other was that there are few things less important than a mere actor. They already knew the undeniable fact that Shakespeare was one of the greatest men who ever lived; and while they could not go quite so far as to claim him as an actual member of the nobility, it was clear to them that he must have been the treasured friend of both the Earl of Southampton and the Earl of Pembroke and that he must have written his plays either while basking in their exalted company or while he was roaming the green countryside by the waters of the river Avon. (It is another basic conviction of the English gentleman that there is nothing so inspiring as nature.) The notion that Shakespeare had spent all these years as the working member of a company of London actors was so abhorrent that it was never seriously considered. It could not be so; therefore it was not.

These biographers did their work well. When New South Wales built its beautiful memorial library to Shakespeare, it was the coat of arms of the Earl of Southampton that alternated with that of royalty in dignified splendor over the bookshelves. Shakespeare had been recreated in the image of desire, and desire will always ignore whatever is not relevant to its purpose. Because the English gentlemen did not like Shakespeare's background it was explained away as though it had never existed, and Shakespeare ceased to be an actor because so lowly a trade was not suited to so great a man.

All this is not to say that a biography should be lacking in a point of view. If it does not have a point of view it will be nothing more than a kind of expanded article for an encyclopedia—a string of facts arranged in chronological order with no claim to being a real biography at all. A biography must have a point of view and it must have a frame of reference. But it should be a point of view and a frame of reference implicit in the material itself and not imposed upon it.

It might seem that the ideal biographical system, if it could be achieved, would be to go through the years of research without feeling any kind of emotion. The biographer would be a kind of fact-finding machine and then suddenly, after his years of research, a kind of total vision would fall upon him and he would transcribe it in his best and most persuasive English for a waiting public. But research is fortunately not done by machinery, nor are visions likely to descend in that helpful manner. They are the product not only of many facts but also of much thinking, and it is only when the biographer begins to get emotional in his thinking that he ought to beware.

It is easy enough to make good resolutions in advance, but a biographer cannot altogether control his sense of excitement when the climax of his years of research draws near and he begins to see the pieces fall into place. Almost without his volition, A, B, and D fit together and start to form a pattern, and it is almost impossible for the biographer not to start searching for C. Something turns up that looks remarkably like C, and with a little trimming of the edges and the ignoring of one very slight discrepancy it will fill the place allotted for C magnificently.

It is at this point that the biographer ought to take a deep breath and sit on his hands until he has had time to calm down. He has no real, fundamental reason to believe that his discovery is C, except for the fact that he wants it to be. He is like a man looking for a missing piece in a difficult jigsaw puzzle, who has found one so nearly the right shape that he cannot resist the desire to jam it into place.

If the biographer had refused to be tempted by his supposed discovery of C and had gone on with his research, he might have found not only the connecting, illuminating fact he needed but much more besides. He is not going to look for it now. Desire has blocked the way. And by so much his biography will fall short of what might have been the truth.

It would not be accurate to say that a biographer should be wholly lacking in desire. Curiosity is a form of desire. So is the final wish to get the material down on paper in a form that will be fair to the reader's interest and worthy of the subject. But a subconscious desire to push the facts around is one of the most dangerous things a biographer can encounter, and all the more dangerous because it is so difficult to know when he is encountering it.

The reason Alice had so much trouble with her flamingo is that the average flamingo does not wish to be used as croquet mallet. It has other purposes in view. The same thing is true of a fact, which can be just as self-willed as a flamingo and has its own kind of stubborn integrity. To try to force a series of facts into a previously desired arrangement is a form of misuse to which no self-respecting fact will willingly submit itself. The best and only way to treat it is to leave it alone and be willing to follow where it leads, rather than to press your own wishes upon it.

To put the whole thing into a single sentence: you will never succeed in getting at the truth if you think you know, ahead of time, what the truth ought to be.

UNDERSTANDING THE TEXT

1. Judging from the examples given by the author, what are the most important general reasons for unreliability in contemporary accounts of historical events?

2. Can you think of causes, other than those cited by Miss Chute, which might damage the accuracy of a historical record? Why do you think she has concentrated on one particular source of error?

3. How is the author's treatment of her second main topic, the possible distortion introduced by the present-day biographer, related to her discussion of the first topic, the uncertainty of the sources? What do the present-day biographer and the writer of the original record have in common?

4. In the structure of this essay what is the function of the comment on nineteenth-century biographers of Shakespeare?

5. From Miss Chute's account of the way a biographer proceeds, what human traits account for the temptation "to push the facts around"? Is the temptation, as she describes it, peculiar to writers of biography and history, or does it operate in other phases of life?

6. Can you detect any general ideas concerning the purpose of biography which influence the exposition in this essay? Should biography celebrate the great men of the past? Should it strive to point out moral examples? Should it attempt, through inference, a full re-creation of the man's life?

7. Define as precisely as you can the views which the author sets forth concerning the relationship between individual facts and a general line of interpretation in historical writing.

TOPICS FOR DISCUSSION AND WRITING

8. In a brief paper indicate and describe the standards which you would use to judge the credibility of a person who gave you an oral report of a meeting you did not attend, or an accident you did not see. If the report were given to you in writing, are there additional criteria you might wish to consider?

9. Marchette Chute says at one point that the biographer's point of view and frame of reference should be "implicit in the material itself and not imposed upon it." Do you agree with this statement, in this form, or should it be qualified by some consideration of the purpose of the work? In thinking about this question, you will find it helpful to review the introduction to Section 2 of this book.

10. "Every age writes its own history." Write an essay commenting upon the foregoing statement in the light of Miss Chute's cautions about the danger of distorting historical fact.

11. Go to a standard encyclopedia and read the biographical entry for a well-known historical figure. Pick out a single clear-cut statement of fact concerning the person. Then consult other and more detailed biographical or historical sources in your library, and see if you can discover and evaluate the authority on which the statement of fact rests.

12. Consult the guide to periodical literature in your library, and locate at least two articles dealing with a contemporary figure or event. Read the articles and develop an essay comparing their treatments of the subject. Make clear whether the differences you discern are primarily in general interpretation, in specific interpretation of a series of facts, or in the facts themselves.

13. Join at least two of your classmates in agreeing to write a narrative account of an event which all three of you have observed. Then compare the three accounts and compose an appendix in which you point out differences in factual substance and in interpretation.

14. Make a list of the attributes which you believe the ideal historian or biographer should possess, and then use this as the basis of a paragraph.

15. Similarly, draw up a list of the matters which should be kept in mind by the thoughtful reader of history or biography, and incorporate these into a paper on the way a reader should approach works of this kind.

The Private History of a Campaign That Failed

MARK TWAIN

—————◦—————

YOU HAVE heard from a great many people who did something in the war; is it not fair and right that you listen a little moment to one who started out to do something in it, but didn't? Thousands entered the war, got just a taste of it, and then stepped out again permanently. These, by their very numbers, are respectable, and therefore entitled to a sort of voice—not a loud one, but a modest one; not a boastful one, but an apologetic one. They ought not to be allowed much space among better people —people who did something. I grant that; but they ought at least to be allowed to state why they didn't do anything, and also to explain the process by which they didn't do anything. Surely this kind of light must have a sort of value.

Out West there was a good deal of confusion in men's minds during the first months of the great trouble—a good deal of unsettledness, of leaning first this way, then that, then the other way. It was hard for us to get our bearings. I call to mind an instance of this. I was piloting on the Mississippi when the news came that South Carolina had gone out of the Union on the 20th of December, 1860. My pilot mate was a New Yorker. He was strong for the Union; so was I. But he would not listen to me with any patience; my loyalty was smirched, to his eye, because my father had owned slaves. I said, in palliation of this dark fact, that I had heard my father say, some years before he died, that slavery was a great wrong and that he would free the solitary Negro he then owned if he could think it right to give away the property of the family when he was so straitened in means. My mate retorted that a mere impulse was nothing—anybody could pretend to a good

Reprinted from *The American Claimant* by Mark Twain. Used by permission of the publishers, Harper & Brothers. Originally published in *Century Magazine*, December, 1885.

impulse, and went on decrying my Unionism and libeling my ancestry. A month later the secession atmosphere had considerably thickened on the Lower Mississippi, and I became a rebel; so did he. We were together in New Orleans the 26th of January, when Louisiana went out of the Union. He did his full share of the rebel shouting but was bitterly opposed to letting me do mine. He said that I came of bad stock—of a father who had been willing to set slaves free. In the following summer he was piloting a Federal gunboat and shouting for the Union again, and I was in the Confederate army. I held his note for some borrowed money. He was one of the most upright men I ever knew but he repudiated that note without hesitation because I was a rebel and the son of a man who owned slaves.

In that summer—of 1861—the first wash of the wave of war broke upon the shores of Missouri. Our state was invaded by the Union forces. They took possession of St. Louis, Jefferson Barracks, and some other points. The Governor, Claib Jackson, issued his proclamation calling out fifty thousand militia to repel the invader.

I was visiting in the small town where my boyhood had been spent, Hannibal, Marion County. Several of us got together in a secret place by night and formed ourselves into a military company. One Tom Lyman, a young fellow of a good deal of spirit but of no military experience, was made captain; I was made second lieutenant. We had no first lieutenant; I do not know why; it was long ago. There were fifteen of us. By the advice of an innocent connected with the organization we called ourselves the Marion Rangers. I do not remember that any one found fault with the name. I did not; I thought it sounded quite well. The young fellow who proposed this title was perhaps a fair sample of the kind of stuff we were made of. He was young, ignorant, good-natured, well-meaning, trivial, full of romance, and given to reading chivalric novels and singing forlorn love-ditties. He had some pathetic little nickel-plated aristocratic instincts and detested his name, which was Dunlap; detested it partly because it was nearly as common in that region as Smith, but mainly because it had a plebeian sound to his ear. So he tried to ennoble it by writing it in this way: *d'Unlap*. That contented his eye but left his ear unsatisfied, for people gave the new name the same old pronunciation—emphasis on the front end of it. He then did the bravest thing that can be imagined, a thing to make one shiver when one remembers how the world is given to resenting shams and affectations; he began to write his name so: *d'Un Lap*. And he waited patiently through the long storm of mud that was flung at this work of art and he had his reward at last, for he lived to see that name accepted and the emphasis put where he wanted it by people who had known him all his life, and to whom the tribe of Dunlaps had been as familiar as the rain and the sunshine for forty years. So sure of victory at last is the courage that can wait. He said he had found by consulting some ancient French chronicles that the name was rightly and originally written d'Un Lap, and said that if it were translated into English it would mean Peterson: *Lap*, Latin or Greek, he said, for stone or rock, same as the French *pierre*, that is to say, Peter: *d'*, of or from: *un*, a or one; hence, d'Un Lap, of or from a stone or a Peter; that is to say, one who is the son of a stone, the son of a Peter—Peterson. Our militia company were not learned and the explanation confused them; so they called him Peterson Dunlap. He proved useful to us in his way; he named our camps for us and he generally struck a name that was "no slouch," as the boys said.

That is one sample of us. Another was Ed Stevens, son of the town jeweler—trim-built, handsome, graceful, neat as a cat; bright, educated, but given over entirely to fun. There was nothing serious in life to him. As far as he was concerned, this military expedition of ours was simply a holiday. I should say that about half of us looked upon it in the same way; not consciously, perhaps, but unconsciously. We did not think; we were not capable of it. As for myself, I was full of unreasoning joy to be done with turning out of bed at midnight and four in the morning for a while, grateful to have a change, new scenes, new occupations, a new interest. In my thoughts that was as far as I went; I did not go into the details; as a rule one doesn't at twenty-four.

Another sample was Smith, the blacksmith's apprentice. This vast donkey had some pluck, of a slow and sluggish nature, but a soft heart; at one time he would knock a horse down for some impropriety and at another he would get homesick and cry. However, he had one ultimate credit to his account which some of us hadn't; he stuck to the war and was killed in battle at last.

Jo Bowers, another sample, was a huge, good-natured, flax-headed lubber; lazy, sentimental, full of harmless brag, a grumbler by nature; an experienced, industrious, ambitious, and often quite picturesque liar, and yet not a successful one, for he had had no intelligent training but was allowed to come up just any way. This life was serious enough to him, and seldom satisfactory. But he was a good fellow, anyway, and the boys all liked him. He was made orderly sergeant; Stevens was made corporal.

These samples will answer—and they are quite fair ones. Well, this herd of cattle started for the war. What could you expect of them? They did as well as they knew how but, really, what was justly to be expected of them? Nothing, I should say. That is what they did.

We waited for a dark night, for caution and secrecy were necessary; then toward midnight we stole in couples and from various directions to the Griffith place, beyond the town; from that point we set out together on foot. Hannibal lies at the extreme southeastern corner of Marion County, on the Mississippi River; our objective point was the hamlet of New London, ten miles away, in Ralls County.

The first hour was all fun, all idle nonsense and laughter. But that could not be kept up. The steady trudging came to be like work; the play had somehow oozed out of it; the stillness of the woods and the somberness of the night began to throw a depressing influence over the spirits of the boys, and presently the talking died out and each person shut himself up in his own thoughts. During the last half of the second hour nobody said a word.

Now we approached a log farm-house where, according to report, there was a guard of five Union soldiers. Lyman called a halt; and there, in the deep gloom of the overhanging branches, he began to whisper a plan of assault upon that house, which made the gloom more depressing than it was before. It was a crucial moment; we realized with a cold suddenness that here was no jest—we were standing face to face with actual war. We were equal to the occasion. In our response there was no hesitation, no indecision: we said that if Lyman wanted to meddle with those soldiers, he could go ahead and do it, but if he waited for us to follow him, he would wait a long time.

Lyman urged, pleaded, tried to shame us, but it had no effect. Our course was plain, our minds were made up: we would flank the farm-house —go out around. And that was what we did.

We struck into the woods and entered upon a rough time, stumbling over roots, getting tangled in vines and torn by briers. At last we reached an open place in a safe region and sat down, blown and hot, to cool off and nurse our scratches and bruises. Lyman was annoyed but the rest of us were cheerful; we had flanked the farm-house, we had made our first military movement and it was a success; we had nothing to fret about, we were feeling just the other way. Horse-play and laughing began again; the expedition was become a holiday frolic once more.

Then we had two more hours of dull trudging and ultimate silence and depression; then about dawn we straggled into New London, soiled, heel-blistered, fagged with our little march, and all of us except Stevens in a

sour and raspy humor and privately down on the war. We stacked our
shabby old shotguns in Colonel Ralls's barn and then went in a body and
breakfasted with that veteran of the Mexican War. Afterward he took us to
a distant meadow, and there in the shade of a tree we listened to an old-
fashioned speech from him, full of gunpowder and glory, full of that ad-
jective-piling, mixed metaphor and windy declamation which were regarded as eloquence in that ancient time and that remote region; and then
he swore us on the Bible to be faithful to the State of Missouri and drive all
invaders from her soil, no matter whence they might come or under what
flag they might march. This mixed us considerably, and we could not
make out just what service we were embarked in, but Colonel Ralls, the
practised politician and phrase-juggler, was not similarly in doubt; he knew
quite clearly that he had invested us in the cause of the Southern Confederacy. He closed the solemnities by belting around me the sword which his
neighbor, Colonel Brown, had worn at Buena Vista and Molino del Rey;
and he accompanied this act with another impressive blast.

Then we formed in line of battle and marched four miles to a shady and
pleasant piece of woods on the border of the far-reaching expanses of a
flowery prairie. It was an enchanting region for war—our kind of war.

We pierced the forest about half a mile and took up a strong position,
with some low, rocky, and wooded hills behind us and a purling, limpid
creek in front. Straightway half the command were in swimming and the
other half fishing. The ass with the French name gave this position a romantic title, but it was too long, so the boys shortened and simplified it to
Camp Ralls.

We occupied an old maple-sugar camp, whose half-rotted troughs were
still propped against the trees. A long corn-crib served for sleeping-quar-
ters for the battalion. On our left, half a mile away, were Mason's farm
and house, and he was a friend to the cause. Shortly after noon the farmers
began to arrive from several directions with mules and horses for our use,
and these they lent us for as long as the war might last, which they judged
would be about three months. The animals were of all sizes, all colors, and
all breeds. They were mainly young and frisky, and nobody in the command could stay on them long at a time, for we were town boys and ignorant of horsemanship. The creature that fell to my share was a very small
mule, and yet so quick and active that it could throw me without difficulty,
and it did this whenever I got on it. Then it would bray—stretching its
neck out, laying its ears back, and spreading its jaws till you could see
down to its works. It was a disagreeable animal in every way. If I took it

by the bridle and tried to lead it off the grounds, it would sit down and brace back and no one could budge it. However, I was not entirely destitute of military resources and I did presently manage to spoil this game, for I had seen many a steamboat aground in my time and knew a trick or two which even a grounded mule would be obliged to respect. There was a well by the corn-crib; so I substituted thirty fathom of rope for the bridle, and fetched him home with the windlass.

I will anticipate here sufficiently to say that we did learn to ride after some days' practice, but never well. We could not learn to like our animals; they were not choice ones and most of them had annoying peculiarities of one kind or another. Stevens's horse would carry him, when he was not noticing, under the huge excrescences which form on the trunks of oak-trees, and wipe him out of the saddle; in this way Stevens got several bad hurts. Sergeant Bowers's horse was very large and tall, with slim, long legs, and looked like a railroad bridge. His size enabled him to reach all about, and as far as he wanted to, with his head; so he was always biting Bowers's legs. On the march, in the sun, Bowers slept a good deal, and as soon as the horse recognized that he was asleep he would reach around and bite him on the leg. His legs were black and blue with bites. This was the only thing that could ever make him swear, but this always did; whenever his horse bit him he always swore, and of course Stevens, who laughed at everything, laughed at this and would even get into such convulsions over it as to lose his balance and fall off his horse; and then Bowers, already irritated by the pain of the horse-bite, would resent the laughter with hard language, and there would be a quarrel; so that horse made no end of trouble and bad blood in the command.

However, I will get back to where I was—our first afternoon in the sugar-camp. The sugar-troughs came very handy as horse-troughs and we had plenty of corn to fill them with. I ordered Sergeant Bowers to feed my mule, but he said that if I reckoned he went to war to be a dry-nurse to a mule it wouldn't take me very long to find out my mistake. I believed that this was insubordination, but I was full of uncertainties about everything military, and so I let the thing pass and went and ordered Smith, the blacksmith's apprentice, to feed the mule; but he merely gave me a large, cold, sarcastic grin, such as an ostensibly seven-year-old horse gives you when you lift his lip and find he is fourteen, and turned his back on me. I then went to the captain and asked if it were not right and proper and military for me to have an orderly. He said it was but as there was only one orderly in the corps, it was but right that he himself should have Bowers

on his staff. Bowers said he wouldn't serve on anybody's staff, and if anybody thought he could make him, let him try it. So, of course, the thing
had to be dropped; there was no other way.

Next, nobody would cook; it was considered a degradation; so we had
no dinner. We lazied the rest of the pleasant afternoon away, some dozing
under the trees, some smoking cob-pipes and talking sweethearts and war,
some playing games. By late supper-time all hands were famished and to
meet the difficulty all hands turned to on an equal footing, and gathered
wood, built fires, and cooked the meal. Afterward everything was smooth
for a while; then trouble broke out between the corporal and the sergeant,
each claiming to rank the other. Nobody knew which was the higher office; so Lyman had to settle the matter by making the rank of both officers
equal. The commander of an ignorant crew like that has many troubles
and vexations which probably do not occur in the regular army at all.
However, with the song-singing and yarn-spinning around the camp-fire,
everything presently became serene again, and by and by we raked the
corn down level in one end of the crib and all went to bed on it, tying a
horse to the door, so that he would neigh if any one tried to get in.[1]

We had some horsemanship drill every forenoon; then, afternoons, we
rode off here and there in squads a few miles and visited the farmers' girls,
and had a youthful good time and got an honest good dinner or supper,
and then home again to camp, happy and content.

For a time life was idly delicious, it was perfect; there was nothing to
mar it. Then came some farmers with an alarm one day. They said it was
rumored that the enemy were advancing in our direction from over Hyde's
prairie. The result was a sharp stir among us, and general consternation. It
was a rude awakening from our pleasant trance. The rumor was but a rumor—nothing definite about it; so in the confusion we did not know which
way to retreat. Lyman was for not retreating at all in these uncertain circumstances, but he found that if he tried to maintain that attitude he would
fare badly, for the command were in no humor to put up with insubordination. So he yielded the point and called a council of war, to consist of

---

[1] It was always my impression that that was what the horse was there for, and I
know that it was also the impression of at least one other of the command, for we
talked about it at the time and admired the military ingenuity of the device; but
when I was out West three years ago, I was told by Mr. A. G. Fuqua, a member of
our company, that the horse was his, that the leaving him tied at the door was a
matter of mere forgetfulness, and that to attribute it to intelligent invention was to
give him quite too much credit. In support of his position he called my attention to
the suggestive fact that the artifice was not employed again. I had not thought of that
before.

himself and the three other officers; but the privates made such a fuss about
being left out that we had to allow them to remain, for they were already
present and doing the most of the talking too. The question was, which
way to retreat; but all were so flurried that nobody seemed to have even a
guess to offer. Except Lyman. He explained in a few calm words that, inas-
much as the enemy were approaching from over Hyde's prairie, our course
was simple: all we had to do was not to retreat *toward* him; any other direction would answer our needs perfectly. Everybody saw in a moment
how true this was, and how wise, so Lyman got a great many compliments.
It was now decided that we should fall back on Mason's farm.

It was after dark by this time and as we could not know how soon the
enemy might arrive, it did not seem best to try to take the horses and
things with us; so we only took the guns and ammunition, and started at
once. The route was very rough and hilly and rocky, and presently the
night grew very black and rain began to fall; so we had a troublesome time
of it, struggling and stumbling along in the dark, and soon some person
slipped and fell, and then the next person behind stumbled over him and
fell, and so did the rest, one after the other; and then Bowers came, with
the keg of powder in his arms, while the command were all mixed together, arms and legs, on the muddy slope; and so he fell, of course, with
the keg, and this started the whole detachment down the hill in a body,
and they landed in the brook at the bottom in a pile, and each that was
undermost pulling the hair and scratching and biting those that were on
top of him, and those that were being scratched and bitten scratching and
biting the rest in their turn, and all saying they would die before they
would ever go to war again if they ever got out of this brook this time,
and the invader might rot for all they cared, and the country along with
him—and all such talk as that, which was dismal to hear and take part in, in
such smothered, low voices, and such a grisly dark place and so wet, and
the enemy, maybe, coming any moment.

The keg of powder was lost, and the guns too; so the growling and complaining continued straight along while the brigade pawed around the pasty
hillside and slopped around in the brook hunting for these things; consequently we lost considerable time at this; and then we heard a sound and
held our breath and listened, and it seemed to be the enemy coming,
though it could have been a cow, for it had a cough like a cow; but we
did not wait but left a couple of guns behind and struck out for Mason's
again as briskly as we could scramble along in the dark. But we got lost
presently among the rugged little ravines and wasted a deal of time finding

the way again, so it was after nine when we reached Mason's stile at last; and then before we could open our mouths to give the countersign several dogs came bounding over the fence with great riot and noise, and each of them took a soldier by the slack of his trousers and began to back away with him. We could not shoot the dogs without endangering the persons they were attached to; so we had to look on helpless at what was perhaps the most mortifying spectacle of the Civil War. There was light enough and to spare, for the Masons had now run out on the porch with candles in their hands. The old man and his son came and undid the dogs without difficulty, all but Bowers's; but they couldn't undo his dog, they didn't know his combination; he was of the bull kind and seemed to be set with a Yale time-lock; but they got him loose at last with some scalding water, of which Bowers got his share and returned thanks. Peterson Dunlap afterward made up a fine name for this engagement, and also for the night march which preceded it, but both have long ago faded out of my memory.

We now went into the house and they began to ask us a world of questions, whereby it presently came out that we did not know anything concerning who or what we were running from; so the old gentleman made himself very frank and said we were a curious breed of soldiers and guessed we could be depended on to end up the war in time, because no government could stand the expense of the shoe-leather we should cost it trying to follow us around. "Marion *Rangers!* good name, b'gosh!" said he. And wanted to know why we hadn't had a picket-guard at the place where the road entered the prairie, and why we hadn't sent out a scouting party to spy out the enemy and bring us an account of his strength, and so on, before jumping up and stampeding out of a strong position upon a mere vague rumor—and so on, and so forth, till he made us all feel shabbier than the dogs had done, not half so enthusiastically welcome. So we went to bed shamed and low-spirited, except Stevens. Soon Stevens began to devise a garment for Bowers which could be made to automatically display his battle-scars to the grateful or conceal them from the envious, according to his occasions; but Bowers was in no humor for this, so there was a fight, and when it was over Stevens had some battle-scars of his own to think about.

Then we got a little sleep. But after all we had gone through, our activities were not over for the night, for about two o'clock in the morning we heard a shout of warning from down the lane, accompanied by a chorus from all the dogs, and in a moment everybody was up and flying around to find out what the alarm was about. The alarmist was a horseman who gave notice that a detachment of Union soldiers was on its way from Hannibal with orders to capture and hang any bands like ours which it could find, and said we had no time to lose. Farmer Mason was in a flurry this time himself. He hurried us out of the house with all haste, and sent one of his negroes with us to show us where to hide ourselves and our telltale guns among the ravines half a mile away. It was raining heavily.

We struck down the lane, then across some rocky pasture-land which offered good advantages for stumbling; consequently we were down in the mud most of the time, and every time a man went down he blackguarded the war and the people that started it and everybody connected with it, and gave himself the master dose of all for being so foolish as to go into it. At last we reached the wooded mouth of a ravine, and there we huddled ourselves under the streaming trees and sent the negro back home. It was a dismal and heart-breaking time. We were like to be drowned with the rain, deafened with the howling wind and the booming thunder, and blinded by the lightning. It was indeed a wild night. The drenching we were getting was misery enough, but a deeper misery still was the reflection that the halter might end us before we were a day older. A death of this shameful sort had not occurred to us as being among the possibilities of war. It took the romance all out of the campaign and turned our dreams of glory into a repulsive nightmare. As for doubting that so barbarous an order had been given, not one of us did that.

The long night wore itself out at last, and then the negro came to us with the news that the alarm had manifestly been a false one and that breakfast would soon be ready. Straightway we were light-hearted again, and the world was bright and life as full of hope and promise as ever—for we were young then. How long ago that was! Twenty-four years.

The mongrel child of philology named the night's refuge Camp Devastation and no soul objected. The Masons gave us a Missouri country breakfast in Missourian abundance, and we needed it: hot biscuits, hot "wheat bread," prettily criss-crossed in a lattice pattern on top, hot cornpone, fried chicken, bacon, coffee, eggs, milk, buttermilk, etc., and the world may be confidently challenged to furnish the equal of such a breakfast, as it is cooked in the South.

We stayed several days at Mason's, and after all these years the memory of the dullness and stillness and lifelessness of that slumberous farm-house still oppresses my spirit as with a sense of the presence of death and mourning. There was nothing to do, nothing to think about; there was no interest in life. The male part of the household were away in the fields all day, the women were busy and out of our sight; there was no sound but the plaintive wailing of a spinning-wheel, forever moaning out from some distant room, the most lonesome sound in nature, a sound steeped and sodden with homesickness and the emptiness of life. The family went to bed about dark every night, and as we were not invited to intrude any new customs we naturally followed theirs. Those nights were a hundred years long to youths accustomed to being up till twelve. We lay awake and miserable till that hour every time, and grew old and decrepit waiting through the still eternities for the clock-strikes. This was no place for town boys. So at last it was with something very like joy that we received news that the enemy were on our track again. With a new birth of the old warrior spirit we sprang to our places in line of battle and fell back on Camp Ralls.

Captain Lyman had taken a hint from Mason's talk, and he now gave orders that our camp should be guarded against surprise by the posting of pickets. I was ordered to place a picket at the forks of the road in Hyde's prairie. Night shut down black and threatening. I told Sergeant Bowers to go out to that place and stay till midnight; and, just as I was expecting, he said he wouldn't do it. I tried to get others to go but all refused. Some excused themselves on account of the weather, but the rest were frank enough to say they wouldn't go in any kind of weather. This kind of thing sounds odd now, and impossible, but there was no surprise in it at the time. On the contrary, it seemed a perfectly natural thing to do. There were scores of little camps scattered over Missouri where the same thing was happening. These camps were composed of young men who had been born and reared to a sturdy independence, and who did not know what it meant to be ordered around by Tom, Dick, and Harry, whom they had known familiarly all their lives in the village or on the farm. It is quite within the probabilities that this same thing was happening all over the South. James Redpath recognized the justice of this assumption and furnished the following instance in support of it. During a short stay in East Tennessee he was in a citizen colonel's tent one day talking, when a big private appeared at the door and, without salute or other circumlocution, said to the colonel:

"Say, Jim, I'm a-goin' home for a few days."

"What for?"

"Well, I hain't b'en there for a right smart while, and I'd like to see how things is comin' on."

"How long are you going to be gone?"

" 'Bout two weeks."

"Well, don't be gone longer than that, and get back sooner if you can."

That was all, and the citizen officer resumed his conversation where the private had broken it off. This was in the first months of the war, of course. The camps in our part of Missouri were under Brigadier-General Thomas H. Harris. He was a townsman of ours, a first-rate fellow and well liked, but we had all familiarly known him as the sole and modest-salaried operator in our telegraph-office, where he had to send about one despatch a week in ordinary times and two when there was a rush of business; consequently, when he appeared in our midst one day on the wing, and delivered a military command of some sort in a large military fashion, nobody was surprised at the response which he got from the assembled soldiery.

"Oh, now, what'll you take to *don't,* Tom Harris?"

It was quite the natural thing. One might justly imagine that we were hopeless material for war. And so we seemed, in our ignorant state; but there were those among us who afterward learned the grim trade; learned to obey like machines; became valuable soldiers; fought all through the war, and came out at the end with excellent records. One of the very boys who refused to go out on picket duty that night and called me an ass for thinking he would expose himself to danger in such a foolhardy way, had become distinguished for intrepidity before he was a year older.

I did secure my picket that night—not by authority but by diplomacy. I got Bowers to go by agreeing to exchange ranks with him for the time being, and go along and stand the watch with him as his subordinate. We stayed out there a couple of dreary hours in the pitchy darkness and the rain, with nothing to modify the dreariness but Bowers's monotonous growlings at the war and the weather; then we began to nod and presently found it next to impossible to stay in the saddle; so we gave up the tedious job and went back to the camp without waiting for the relief guard. We rode into camp without interruption or objection from anybody and the enemy could have done the same, for there were no sentries. Everybody was asleep; at midnight there was nobody to send out another picket, so none was sent. We never tried to establish a watch at night again, as far as I remember, but we generally kept a picket out in the daytime.

In that camp the whole command slept on the corn in the big corn-crib; and there was usually a general row before morning, for the place was full of rats and they would scramble over the boys' bodies and faces, annoying and irritating everybody, and now and then they would bite some one's toe, and the person who owned the toe would start up and magnify his English and begin to throw corn in the dark. The ears were half as heavy as bricks and when they struck they hurt. The persons struck would respond and inside of five minutes every man would be locked in a deathgrip with his neighbor. There was a grievous deal of blood shed in the corn-crib, but this was all that was spilt while I was in the war. No, that is not quite true. But for one circumstance it would have been all. I will come to that now.

Our scares were frequent. Every few days rumors would come that the enemy were approaching. In these cases we always fell back on some other camp of ours; we never stayed where we were. But the rumors always turned out to be false, so at last even we began to grow indifferent to them. One night a negro was sent to our corn-crib with the same old warning: the enemy was hovering in our neighborhood. We all said let him hover. We resolved to stay still and be comfortable. It was a fine warlike resolution, and no doubt we all felt the stir of it in our veins—for a moment. We had been having a very jolly time, that was full of horse-play and school-boy hilarity, but that cooled down now and presently the fast-waning fire of forced jokes and forced laughs died out altogether and the company became silent. Silent and nervous. And soon uneasy—worried—apprehensive. We had said we would stay and we were committed. We could have been persuaded to go, but there was nobody brave enough to suggest it. An almost noiseless movement presently began in the dark by a general but unvoiced impulse. When the movement was completed each man knew that he was not the only person who had crept to the front wall and had his eye at a crack between the logs. No, we were all there; all there with our hearts in our throats and staring out toward the sugar-troughs where the forest footpath came through. It was late and there was a deep woodsy stillness everywhere. There was a veiled moonlight, which was only just strong enough to enable us to mark the general shape of objects. Presently a muffled sound caught our ears and we recognized it as the hoof-beats of a horse or horses. And right away a figure appeared in the forest path; it could have been made of smoke, its mass had so little sharpness of outline. It was a man on horseback and it seemed to me that there were others behind him. I got hold of a gun in the dark, and pushed it through a crack between the logs, hardly knowing what I was doing, I was so dazed with fright. Somebody said "Fire!" I pulled the trigger. I seemed to see a hundred flashes and hear a hundred reports; then I saw the man fall down out of the saddle. My first feeling was of surprised gratification; my first impulse was an apprentice-sportsman's impulse to run and pick up his game. Somebody said, hardly audibly, "Good—we've got him!—wait for the rest." But the rest did not come. We waited—listened —still no more came. There was not a sound, not the whisper of a leaf; just perfect stillness, an uncanny kind of stillness which was all the more uncanny on account of the damp, earthy, late-night smells now rising and pervading it. Then, wondering, we crept stealthily out and approached the man. When we got to him the moon revealed him distinctly. He was lying on his back with his arms abroad, his mouth was open and his chest heaving with long gasps, and his white shirt-front was all splashed with blood. The thought shot through me that I was a murderer, that I had killed a man, a man who had never done me any harm. That was the coldest sensation that ever went through my marrow. I was down by him in a moment, helplessly stroking his forehead, and I would have given anything then— my own life freely—to make him again what he had been five minutes before. And all the boys seemed to be feeling in the same way; they hung over him, full of pitying interest, and tried all they could to help him and said all sorts of regretful things. They had forgotten all about the enemy; they thought only of this one forlorn unit of the foe. Once my imagination persuaded me that the dying man gave me a reproachful look out of his shadowy eyes, and it seemed to me that I could rather he had stabbed me than done that. He muttered and mumbled like a dreamer in his sleep about his wife and his child; and I thought with a new despair, "This thing that I have done does not end with him; it falls upon *them* too, and they never did me any harm, any more than he."

In a little while the man was dead. He was killed in war, killed in fair and legitimate war, killed in battle, as you may say, and yet he was as sincerely mourned by the opposing force as if he had been their brother. The boys stood there a half-hour sorrowing over him and recalling the details of the tragedy, and wondering who he might be and if he were a spy, and saying that if it were to do over again they would not hurt him unless he attacked them first. It soon came out that mine was not the only shot fired; there were five others—a division of the guilt which was a great relief to me since it in some degree lightened and diminished the burden I was carrying. There were six shots fired at once; but I was not in my right mind at the time, and my heated imagination had magnified my own shot into a volley.

The man was not in uniform and was not armed. He was a stranger in the country, that was all we ever found out about him. The thought of him got to preying upon me every night; I could not get rid of it. I could not drive it away, the taking of that unoffending life seemed such a wanton thing. And it seemed an epitome of war, that all war must be just that—the killing of strangers against whom you feel no personal animosity, strangers whom in other circumstances you would help if you found them in trouble, and who would help you if you needed it. My campaign was spoiled. It seemed to me that I was not rightly equipped for this awful business; that war was intended for men, and I for a child's nurse. I resolved to retire from this avocation of sham soldiership while I could save some remnant of my self-respect. These morbid thoughts clung to me against reason, for at bottom I did not believe I had touched that man. The law of probabilities decreed me guiltless of his blood, for in all my small experience with guns I had never hit anything I had tried to hit and I knew I had done my best to hit him. Yet there was no solace in the thought. Against a diseased imagination demonstration goes for nothing.

The rest of my war experience was of a piece with what I have already told of it. We kept monotonously falling back upon one camp or another and eating up the country. I marvel now at the patience of the farmers and their families. They ought to have shot us; on the contrary, they were as hospitably kind and courteous to us as if we had deserved it. In one of these camps we found Ab Grimes, an Upper Mississippi pilot who afterward became famous as a dare-devil rebel spy, whose career bristled with desperate adventures. The look and style of his comrades suggested that they had not come into the war to play and their deeds made good the conjecture later. They were fine horsemen and good revolver shots, but their favorite arm was the lasso. Each had one at his pommel and could snatch a man out of the saddle with it every time, on a full gallop, at any reasonable distance.

In another camp the chief was a fierce and profane old blacksmith of sixty, and he had furnished his twenty recruits with gigantic home-made bowie-knives, to be swung with two hands like the *machetes* of the Isthmus. It was a grisly spectacle to see that earnest band practising their murderous cuts and slashes under the eye of that remorseless old fanatic.

The last camp which we fell back upon was in a hollow near the village of Florida, where I was born, in Monroe County. Here we were warned one day that a Union colonel was sweeping down on us with a whole regiment at his heel. This looked decidedly serious. Our boys went apart and consulted; then we went back and told the other companies present that the war was a disappointment to us and we were going to disband. They were getting ready themselves to fall back on some place or other, and we were only waiting for General Tom Harris, who was expected to arrive at any moment; so they tried to persuade us to wait a little while, but the majority of us said no, we were accustomed to falling back and didn't need any of Tom Harris's help, we could get along perfectly well without him—and save time, too. So about half of our fifteen, including myself, mounted and left on the instant; the others yielded to persuasion and stayed—stayed through the war.

An hour later we met General Harris on the road, with two or three people in his company, his staff probably, but we could not tell; none of them were in uniform; uniforms had not come into vogue among us yet. Harris ordered us back; but we told him there was a Union colonel coming with a whole regiment in his wake and it looked as if there was going to be a disturbance, so we had concluded to go home. He raged a little but it was of no use; our minds were made up. We had done our share, had killed one man, exterminated one army, such as it was; let him go and kill the rest and that would end the war. I did not see that brisk young general again until last year; then he was wearing white hair and whiskers.

In time I came to know that Union colonel whose coming frightened me out of the war and crippled the Southern cause to that extent—General Grant. I came within a few hours of seeing him when he was as unknown as I was myself; at a time when anybody could have said, "Grant? —Ulysses S. Grant? I do not remember hearing the name before." It seems difficult to realize that there was once a time when such a remark could be rationally made; but there *was*, and I was within a few miles of the place and the occasion, too, though proceeding in the other direction.

The thoughtful will not throw this war paper of mine lightly aside as being valueless. It has this value: it is a not unfair picture of what went on in many and many a militia camp in the first months of the rebellion, when the green recruits were without discipline, without the steadying and heartening influence of trained leaders; when all their circumstances were new and strange and charged with exaggerated terrors, and before the invaluable experience of actual collision in the field had turned them from rabbits into soldiers. If this side of the picture of that early day has not before been put into history, then history has been to that degree incomplete, for it had and has its rightful place there. There was more Bull Run material scattered through the early camps of this country than exhibited itself at Bull Run. And yet it learned its trade presently and helped to fight the great battles later. I could have become a soldier myself if I had waited. I had got part of it learned; I knew more about retreating than the man that invented retreating.

UNDERSTANDING THE TEXT

1. What point of view does Mark Twain adopt toward the events he is narrating? How does the opening paragraph help to establish this point of view?

2. What principles direct Mark Twain in his choice of the incidents he describes? In other words, what characteristics of the Marion Rangers do these incidents bring out?

3. The author describes four "samples" of the men who made up the company of Rangers. Why do you suppose he chose to write about these particular four men? Which of the four does he characterize most fully? Why?

4. In what way does Twain make clear the indecision which prevailed, at the beginning of the war, over which side to support?

5. Does Mark Twain suggest any attitudes toward social relationships which may account, in part, for the lack of discipline among the Rangers? Why, for example, are the men unimpressed by orders from Brigadier-General Harris?

6. What is the purpose of the footnote dealing with the reason the horse was tied to the corn-crib door?

7. Can you detect any change in tone, in point of view toward the subject, as Mark Twain narrates the events leading up to the shooting of the solitary horseman?

8. Comment on the fact that the Rangers are able to learn nothing about the man they killed. How is this fact related to Mark Twain's view of the significance of the "campaign"?

9. Discuss the kind and the purpose of the style Mark Twain employs in the following passages: (1) "It was a crucial moment; we realized with a cold suddenness that here was no jest—we were standing face to face with actual war. We were equal to the occasion. In our response there was no hesitation, no indecision: we said that if Lyman wanted to meddle with those soldiers, he could go ahead and do it, but if he waited for us to follow him, he would wait a long time." (2) "Lyman was for not retreating at all in these uncertain circumstances, but he found that if he tried to maintain that attitude he would fare badly, for the command were in no humor to put up with insubordination."

TOPICS FOR DISCUSSION AND WRITING

10. Does Mark Twain believe that this "private history" has any importance for an understanding of the beginnings of the Civil War? Write a paragraph developing the meaning of this sentence: "There was more Bull Run material scattered through the early camps of this country than exhibited itself at Bull Run."

11. What traits common in American civilian life might work against the creation of military discipline? What traits might aid in the establishment of discipline? Do you think the situation has changed much since the period Mark Twain describes? Write an essay embodying, developing, and organizing your answers to these questions.

12. How might the events of this campaign have been narrated by each of the following: a Union officer trying to clean up partisan resistance in Missouri; a Confederate officer trying to strengthen and organize such resistance; Peterson d'Un Lap?

13. At some time or other, most of us have engaged in an activity which was part of a larger whole of which we knew little or nothing. We may, for instance, have served on committees to raise money for purposes which were quite vague to us. If you have had such an experience, write a narrative concerning it, choosing details which, in addition to making clear what went on in your own small circle, underline your lack of knowledge as to how this activity fitted into the larger scheme.

14. Write an essay characterizing three or four persons who, in your opinion, are fair "samples" of the students in a particular campus club or activity.

15. Write an interpretation of this campaign in terms of the generalization about Northern and Southern society that Pratt develops in his analysis of the Battle of Gettysburg (pp. 207–213).

Progress

CARL BECKER

———— ⌢⌣ ————

"THOUGHT," says Pascal, "makes the greatness of man." The universe
can destroy an individual by a mere breath; but even if the entire force of
the universe were employed to destroy a single man, the man "would still
be more noble than that which destroys him, since he is aware of his own
death and of the advantage which the universe has over him: of all this the
universe knows nothing." This awareness of himself and of the universe is
no doubt what chiefly distinguishes man from all other forms of life. Man
alone is conscious in the sense that he alone can stand outside of himself,
as it were, and watch himself functioning for a brief span in the universe
of which he is part. Man alone can coördinate memory of things past, perception of things present, anticipation of things to come, sufficiently so at
least to know that he, like generations before him and after him, will live
his brief span and will die. It is in virtue of this awareness, and somewhat
in proportion to its intensity, that man alone asks the fundamental questions. Why and for what purpose this brief and precarious existence in a
universe that endures? What is man's relation to the universe that is sometimes friendly, sometimes hostile, but in the end always fatal to him? How
may he elude its hostility, win its favor, find compensations for the intolerable certainty of the death which it will inflict upon him? The answers which men have given to these questions are to be found in the
various myths, religious doctrines, philosophical and ethical interpretations which they have accepted, and in those unconsciously held preconceptions which in every age so largely shape their thought and conduct.
The modern idea of progress belongs in this category of answers to necessary but insoluble questions. Like the myths of primitive peoples and the

Reprinted from *The Encyclopedia of the Social Sciences*, Volume XII. Copyright,
1934, by The Macmillan Company. Used by permission of the publishers.

religious and philosophical beliefs of more advanced societies, it springs from the nature of man as a conscious creature, who finds existence intolerable unless he can enlarge and enrich his otherwise futile activities by relating them to something more enduring and significant than himself.

Although grounded in the nature of man as a conscious creature, the idea of progress belongs historically to the European tradition, and its origin may be derived from two sources. One of these is the classical conception of history as an endless series of cycles; the other is the Hebraic-Christian doctrine of messianic intervention and salvation.

In Greek mythology the reign of Cronus was regarded as a golden age when men lived like gods free from toil and grief. The present appeared to be a period of degeneration, and improvement or progress could be conceived only in terms of regeneration—a return to the lost golden age. After the myth ceased to be believed, the Greeks continued to look back to the time of great lawgivers, such as Lycurgus and Solon, whose work they idealized, and forward to the time when other great lawgivers would appear and give them better laws again. "Until philosophers become kings . . . ," said Plato, "cities will not cease from ill." Yet however often restoration was accomplished by inspired lawgivers or philosopher-kings, fate and human frailty would again bring degeneration; so that, since "time is the enemy of man," most classical writers regarded human history as an endless series of cycles, a continual repetition of the familiar phenomena of recovery and degeneration. The rational mind, according to Marcus Aurelius, "stretches forth into the infinitude of Time, and comprehends the cyclical Regeneration of all things, and . . . discerns that our children will see nothing fresh, just as our fathers too never saw anything more than we" (*The Communings with Himself of Marcus Aurelius Antoninus,* tr. by C. R. Haines, Loeb Classical Library, London 1916, bk. XI, sect. I). To regenerate the Roman Empire was obviously less easy than to construct a constitution for a small city-state; and Marcus Aurelius, philosopher-king though he was, instead of giving new laws to society recommended that the individual cultivate resignation. The later centuries of the Roman Empire, when resignation became at once more necessary and more difficult, were therefore a suitable time for the hopeless classical doctrine of endless cycles to be replaced by the Hebraic-Christian doctrine of messianic intervention and salvation.

The Jews like the Greeks looked back to a golden age, but it was identified with the creation of the world and with the Garden of Eden, in which the first men lived in innocence. Like the Greeks the Jews regarded the present as a period of degeneration, but they attributed the "fall" to Adam's disobedience to God's commands. God was at once the omniscient creator of the world and the supreme lawgiver, so that regeneration was identified with the coming of a God-inspired king of the house of David. Multiplied reverses and the destruction of the Hebraic state gave to this doctrine a less political, a more mystical and transcendent character. The once actual but now vanished kingdom was replaced by an ideal Israel, symbolized as the "son of man"; and the idea of a God-inspired king was replaced by the idea of a messiah who would effect a catastrophic intervention in the affairs of men and pronounce a doomlike judgment on the world. The Christian myth was but an elaboration of these ideas. Jesus, son of man, son of God, was the Messiah. But the end was not yet. The death of Jesus was expiation for the sins of men, faith in Him the means of salvation. Jesus the man was dead, but Christ the Lord still lived and would come again; then the earthly city would be destroyed and all the faithful be gathered with God in the heavenly city, there to dwell in perfection forever.

The weakness of the classical version of degeneration and recovery was that it offered no ultimate hope; of the Jewish, that its promise was for the chosen people only. The strength of the Christian version was that, conceiving human history as a cosmic drama in which all men played their predestined part, it offered to all the hope of eternal life as a compensation for the frustrations of temporal existence: by transferring the golden age from the past to the future it substituted an optimistic for a disillusioned view of human destiny. It is easily to be understood that such a view won wide assent in the Roman Empire during the centuries (300–500) of declining prosperity and increasing oppression or that it served so well to make existence tolerable in the relatively anarchic, isolated and static society of western Europe from the dissolution of the Roman Empire to the Renaissance of classical learning. But it lost its hold on the imaginations of men as a result of profound changes in the outward conditions of life which occurred in western Europe from the fourteenth to the nineteenth century. Among these changes were the rise of ordered secular governments, the growth of towns and industry, the geographical discoveries and the extension of commerce which brought western Europe into direct contact with alien customs and ideas, and above all the rise of an educated middle class whose interests were hampered by a form of society in which both the power and the doctrines of the Christian church supported the autocracy of kings and the privileges of a landed aristocracy. It was in this time of revolt against ecclesiastical and secular authority that the Christian doctrine of salvation was gradually transformed into the modern idea of progress.

So long as Christian philosophy was little questioned, men could afford to ignore the factual experience of mankind since they were so well assured of its ultimate significance. But the declining influence of the church was accompanied by an increasing interest in the worldly activities of men in the past. Italian humanists turned to the study of classical writers; Protestant reformers appealed from current theologians to the beliefs and practises of the primitive church. Thus was born the modern historical approach to problems, and human life came increasingly to be regarded rather as a historical process than as a finished drama to be played out according to a divine plan. Seen in historical perspective, classical civilization emerged for the humanists as a resplendent epoch from which the middle period of ecclesiastical ascendancy was manifestly a degeneration. Until the seventeenth century secular thought and learning turned for inspiration to the past—to the golden ages of Pericles and Augustus; and classical writers were idealized as models to be imitated, to be equaled if possible but hardly to be surpassed. In all this there was nothing that could not be found in the Greek notion of history with its cycles of recovery and degeneration, and but for two general influences modern thought might have been no more than a return to the classical view of human destiny.

One of these influences was Christian philosophy itself. Although it was gradually discredited as an account of events historically verifiable, Christian philosophy had so thoroughly habituated men to the thought of an ultimate happy destiny that they could never be content with a pale imitation of Greek pessimism. The other influence was experimental science which, in proportion as it displaced the Christian notion of a utopian existence after death to be brought about by the miraculous intervention of God, opened up the engaging prospect of indefinite improvement in this life to be effected by the application of human reason to the mastery of the physical and social environment which determines men's lives for good or ill.

In the seventeenth century Galileo and Newton made possible a new attitude toward nature. Nature was now seen to be friendly to man since the universe behaved in a uniform way according to universal natural laws—a behavior capable of being observed and measured and subjected to the uses of men. God was still the supreme lawgiver, the author of the universe; but His will was revealed in the great book of nature which men were to study in order to interpret, and to interpret in order that their ideas and customs might attain an increasing perfection by being brought into greater harmony with the laws of nature and of nature's God. God's revelation to men was thus made not through an inspired book or a divinely established church but through His works, and man had been endowed with reason precisely that he might learn through the course of the centuries what that revelation was. It was therefore no longer so necessary to think of the golden age of Greece and Rome as unsurpassable. "Those whom we call the ancients were really those who lived in the youth of the world," said Pascal, and "as we have added the experience of the ages between us and them to what they knew, it is in ourselves that is to be found that antiquity which we venerate in others." In the ascription of antiquity to the race there is still the implication of degeneration; but if a continuously richer experience made the moderns wiser than the ancients, it was not difficult to hit upon the idea that future generations would, in virtue of the same advantages, surpass the moderns. "We have admired our ancestors less," said Chastellux, "but we have loved our contemporaries better, and have expected more of our descendants (*"De la félicité publique*, 2 vols., new ed. Paris 1822, vol. ii, p. 71). Thus in the eighteenth century the modern idea of progress was born. Under the pressure of social discontents the dream of perfection, that necessary compensation for the limitations of the present state, having long been identified with the golden age or the Garden of Eden or life eternal in the heavenly city of God, was at last projected into the temporal life of man on earth and identified with the desired and hoped for regeneration of society.

As formulated by the *philosophes* the doctrine of progress was but a modification, however important, of the Christian doctrine of redemption; what was new in it was faith in the goodness of man and the efficacy of conscious reason to create an earthly utopia. The French Revolution was the outward expression of this faith. In the nineteenth century the doctrine of progress still reigned and won even a wider popular support, but it was somewhat differently conceived. After the disillusionment occasioned by the revolution and the Napoleonic conquests the prevailing desire was for social stability and national independence. The rationalization of this desire was provided by the historians and jurists who formulated the notion of historical continuity and deprecated the attempt to transform institutions according to a rational plan. Change was considered necessary but was thought to be beneficial only when it issued spontane-

ously from national tradition; the concept of natural law was not abandoned, but it was regarded as implicit in historical evolution rather than
as a conclusion from abstract reason. Law is not made by the legislator,
said Savigny, any more than language is made by the grammarian. Ranke,
who influenced three generations of historians, viewed progress as something to be discovered by tracing the history of each nation just as it had
occurred and by noting the peculiar contribution which each nation at the
appropriate moment had made to European civilization. Hegel formulated the point of view of early nineteenth century jurists and historians in
his *Philosophie der Geschichte*. A reason of nature working over the heads
of men, a transcendent *Vernunft* reconciling within its cloudy recesses innumerable and conflicting *Verstände*, progressively realized itself in the
actual events of history.

After the middle of the century natural science invested the doctrine of
progress with a more materialistic implication. Progress was still regarded
as the result of a force external to man; but the force was to be found not
above but inherent in the phenomenal world. This view found support
in the Darwinian theory of struggle for existence and survival of the fittest
and in Schopenhauer's doctrine of the will as an aspect of a universal blind
force. Guided by these preconceptions thinkers abandoned the effort to
hasten progress by describing utopias and turned to the search for the inevitable law by which progress had been and would be achieved. Of the
many efforts of this sort the most important were those of Auguste Comte
and Karl Marx. Comte looked upon history as the result of the instinctive
effort of men to ameliorate their condition—an effort which could be observed to fall into three stages of culture, the theological, the metaphysical
and the positive, or scientific. Marx, interpreting the historic process in
terms of Hegel's famous dialectic, found the determining force in the economic class conflict which, having substituted the nineteenth century
capitalist competitive society for the aristocratic landed society of the
Middle Ages and early modern times, would in turn replace the capitalist
competitive society of the nineteenth century by the proletarian communist society of the future.

Of the many theories of progress formulated in the nineteenth century
the only one that had much influence on the thought of common men was
that of Marx. Yet the idea of progress, vaguely conceived as a rapid improvement in general prosperity and happiness, became a living force. The
chief reason for this was no doubt the rapid changes in the outward conditions of life consequent upon the technological revolution. The common

man, before whose eyes the marvels of science and invention were constantly displayed, noted the unprecedented increase in wealth, the growth of cities, the new and improved methods of transportation and communication, the greater security from disease and death and all the conveniences of domestic life unknown to previous generations, and accepted the doctrine of progress without question: the world was obviously better than it had been, obviously would be better than it was. The precise objective toward which the world was progressing remained, however, for the common man and for the intellectual, somewhat vague.

Thus the nineteenth century doctrine of progress differed somewhat from that of the eighteenth. The difference may be expressed, with some exaggeration in the contrast, by saying that whereas the eighteenth century held that man can by taking thought add a cubit to his stature, the nineteenth century held that a cubit would be added to his stature whether he took thought or not. This latter faith that the stars were carrying men on to better things received a rude shock during the World War and subsequently; and there may be noted two significant changes in the present attitude toward the doctrine of progress. Certain thinkers, notably Spengler, are returning to the Greek notion of cycles, now formulated in terms of the rise, flourishing and decline of "cultures." Others are reverting to the eighteenth century idea that by deliberate purpose and the rational use of knowledge man can reconstruct society according to a more just and intelligible design. To this class belong those who have faith in communism, fascism and the planned capitalist society.

The doctrine of progress is peculiarly suited to western society in modern times; that is, a highly dynamic society capable of seeing its achievements against a long historical background. From the practical and from the rational point of view there is no reason to suppose that it will have a more enduring virtue than other doctrines which it has supplanted. If, as may well happen, the possibilities of scientific discovery and of technological invention should sometime be exhausted, the outward conditions of life might become sufficiently stabilized so that the idea of progress would cease to be relevant. Rationally considered, the idea of progress is always at war with its premises. It rests upon the notion of a universe in perpetual flux; yet the idea of progress has always carried the implication of finality, for it seems to be meaningless unless there is movement toward some ultimate objective. The formal theories of progress are all vitiated by this radical inconsistency. In Hegel's scheme the objective was freedom, already realized in the Prussian state. In Comte's theory the objective was the final positive stage into which Europe had already entered. Marx criticized Hegel for explaining history by a process which would not explain the future, but he is himself open to the criticism of having explained history in terms of a class conflict which would end with the establishment of a classless society. It is easy to picture history as a process working toward an ultimate good if the world is to come to an end when that good is attained; but if the universe as presented by modern science is to be accepted—a universe in perpetual flux—then a law of history which at some determinate time ceases to apply leaves much to be desired.

Thus the final good, absolute standards of value, are sought in vain; there is merely a universe in which the ideas of things as well as the things themselves arise out of temporary conditions and are transformed with the modification of the conditions out of which they arose. On this assumption we must dispense with the notion of finality, must suppose that the idea of progress and all of its special formulations are but temporary insights useful for the brief moment in which they flourish. "In escaping from the illusion of finality, is it legitimate to exempt that dogma itself? Must not it, too, submit to its own negation of finality? Will not that process of change, for which Progress is the optimistic name, compel 'Progress' too to fall from the commanding position in which it is now, with apparent security, enthroned?" (Bury, J. B., *The Idea of Progress*, p. 352). The price we pay for escaping from the illusion of finality is the recognition that nothing, not even the belief that we have escaped that illusion, is likely to endure. All philosophies based upon the absolute and the unconditioned have their defects; but all philosophies based upon the universal relativity of things have their defects also, a minor one being that they must be prepared, at the appropriate moment, to commit hara-kiri in deference to the ceaseless change which they postulate.

Belief in progress as a fact depends upon the standard of value chosen for measuring it and upon the time perspective in which it is measured. If we look back a hundred years, it is obvious that there has been progress in the mastery of physical forces. If we look back two thousand years, it is uncertain whether there has been much if any progress in intelligence and the art of living. If we look back two hundred and fifty thousand years, it is apparent that there has been progress in all those aspects of life which civilized men regard as valuable. All these judgments are based on standards of value appreciable by the mind of civilized man. But if we take a still longer perspective and estimate the universe as a whole, as an omniscient intelligence indifferent to human values might estimate it, in terms of cosmic energy, then progress and the very existence of man himself become negligible and meaningless. In such a perspective we should see the whole life of man on the earth as a mere momentary ripple on the surface of one of the minor planets in one of the minor stellar systems.

UNDERSTANDING THE TEXT

1. According to Becker, what purpose do general interpretations of history, such as the idea of progress, serve for the people who hold them?
2. Becker says that "the doctrine of progress is peculiarly suited to western society in modern times." For what reason does he lead up to his discussion of the idea in contemporary times with such a long historical account?
3. Indicate the various stages which Becker points out in the historical evolution of the idea of progress. How does he account for the modifications in the idea, the changes from one period to the next?
4. What kinds of evidence does he bring forward to demonstrate the special form the idea possessed in a particular historical period?
5. Does Becker himself seem to be making any assumptions about the uniformity of the ideas held by people who lived in the same historical epoch?
6. Becker writes, "Rationally considered, the idea of progress is always at war with its premises." What does this statement mean? Do you see any connection between this criticism and the fact that Becker begins his account of the idea by mentioning two sources: the classical conception of history as a series of cycles and the Hebraic-Christian doctrine of messianic intervention?
7. Judging from the essay, do you think that Becker himself is guided by any assumptions concerning man's place in the universe? If so, how do these assumptions affect the way he treats the idea of progress?
8. What do you think was Becker's chief purpose in writing this essay? Was he interested primarily in tracing the history of the idea of progress, in analyzing it philosophically, or in showing how general ideas are modified by historical circumstances?

TOPICS FOR DISCUSSION AND WRITING

9. Becker concludes his historical sketch of the idea of progress by referring to the First World War and its aftermath. If the account had been carried through World War II and the years immediately following it, what changes in interpretation, if any, would have been required?
10. Do you believe that the life of mankind generally is improving or degenerating? Support your opinion in an essay which makes clear the criteria on which you base your judgment.

11. Select a special area of human life—religion, or family relationships, or recreational opportunity, for example—and write a paper showing whether, as you see it, there has been progress or decline in this area during recent years.

12. Pick a particular technological advance—the advent of television, the development of superhighways, the use of automatic processes in factories and offices—and write an essay describing the social gains and losses which have accompanied its development.

13. Developing broad interpretations of history is only one way in which men have found meaning in their existence on earth. What are some other ways?

14. Can you identify any general ideas which most of the people you know take for granted, feel no need of questioning or proving, and use as the bases for their thinking and acting?

Point of View in History:
The Defeat of Braddock

NO TWO accounts of the same event by different writers are likely to be quite the same, even when they are based on the same facts. We have all noticed, in reading reports of an incident in two newspapers, or in listening to friends recount the same happening, how different the alternative versions can be. We can identify common notes, but the tunes are not the same. Sometimes we can locate the causes of the differences without much trouble: the writers may be more or less truthful; they may have had different opportunities to observe what happened or to gather evidence about it; they may be more or less qualified as witnesses or reporters; they may have special biases or prejudices that lead them to omit or to slant the evidence. Disagreements between accounts of the same event are often so striking and their causes frequently so obvious and discreditable that we are sometimes inclined to dismiss one or another of them as false, and to suppose that there is one true and adequate version of an event, to which all versions should aspire. For very simple happenings this is perhaps a realizable aim. But as soon as we consider complex events, and especially those whose treatment requires interpretation and judgment, we see that it is a theoretical possibility at best. Differences between accounts of the same happening are by no means confined to partisans, and they cannot always be resolved by appealing to bias or any other simple cause.

Trained historians, who we may suppose, in the absence of contrary evidence, are doing their best to give true and intelligible accounts of the past, frequently differ in their versions of the same happening. Sometimes, of course, these differences are traceable to differences in the accuracy or fullness of the data on which their narratives are based. Historical research is constantly turning up new evidence that enables later historians to improve, sometimes in minor and sometimes in important ways, on the work of their predecessors. But apart from this cause of variation, there are others less obvious but no less powerful: differences in the scope and detail of the history, in the assumptions the historians use to assess evidence, in the standards of value by which they judge character and action, in the larger framework of events in relation to

371

which they treat a particular episode. These and other variables enter into every historical narrative, affecting the scale, the order, and the interpretation of the facts. Taken together, these conditioning influences determine the "point of view" in history. The various elements that make up the historian's point of view may be more or less justified or adequate or illuminating, but in some form or other they are inescapable if the historian is to control and interpret his material. Intelligent reading and appraisal of historical writing requires a sensitivity to the various influences that give each history its particular shape and meaning.

To provide materials for a study of these influences and of the ways in which they affect different accounts of the same event (different uses of the same "facts") we have chosen four treatments of one of the best-known episodes of American pre-Revolutionary history—the defeat of General Edward Braddock and his British and Colonial troops at the hands of the French and Indian defenders of Fort Duquesne on 9 July 1755.

Francis Parkman's account of Braddock's defeat is included in his *Conspiracy of Pontiac* (1851), a volume which was a forerunner to Parkman's monumental history of the conflict between France and England for mastery of the New World. A few years after Parkman's book appeared, Washington Irving, then the dean of American writers, published (1855–1859) the five volumes of his *Life of George Washington*. It was Irving's last work (he died shortly after the fifth volume was published), written in the decline of his powers; but it was a remarkable achievement of American biography, and the first scholarly life of Washington. Irving devotes a chapter to Braddock's defeat because Washington, as Braddock's American aide, was prominent on the field that day.

Our last two historians are also contemporaries, and again one deals with the battle as an episode in the Anglo-French colonial rivalry and one with the battle as an incident in the life of George Washington. L. H. Gipson's six-volume history of "The British Empire before the American Revolution" devotes several volumes to the struggles between the British and the French. The defeat of Braddock figures prominently in *The Great War for Empire: The Years of Defeat, 1754–1757*. Douglas Southall Freeman, like Irving, is the biographer of Washington. He is also one of America's most distinguished military historians: his *R. E. Lee* and *Lee's Lieutenants* are classic works. Freeman's five-volume *George Washington* is the most detailed and scholarly biography of Washington so far published. His account of the battle occurs in the second volume, *The Young Washington*.

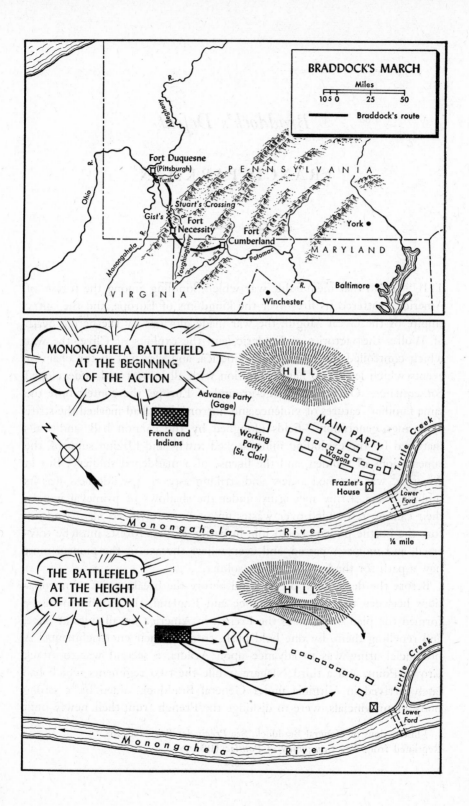

BRADDOCK'S MARCH

Miles
105 0   25   50

Braddock's route

Allegheny R.

Ohio R.

Monongahela R.

Fort Duquesne
(Pittsburgh)

Turtle Cr.

Stuart's Crossing

Gist's

Fort
Necessity

Youghiogheny R.

Fort
Cumberland

Potomac

P E N N S Y L V A N I A

York

M A R Y L A N D

Baltimore

R.

Winchester

V I R G I N I A

MONONGAHELA BATTLEFIELD
AT THE BEGINNING
OF THE ACTION

HILL

Advance Party
(Gage)

French and
Indians

N

Working
Party
(St. Clair)

MAIN PARTY

Wagons

Turtle Creek

Frazier's
House

Lower
Ford

M o n o n g a h e l a   R i v e r

⅛ mile

THE BATTLEFIELD
AT THE HEIGHT
OF THE ACTION

HILL

Turtle Creek

Lower
Ford

M o n o n g a h e l a   R i v e r

Braddock's Defeat

FRANCIS PARKMAN

THUS began that memorable war which, kindling among the forests of America, scattered its fires over the kingdoms of Europe, and the sultry empire of the Great Mogul; the war made glorious by the heroic death of Wolfe, the victories of Frederic, and the exploits of Clive; the war which controlled the destinies of America, and was first in the chain of events which led on to her Revolution with all its vast and undeveloped consequences. On the old battle-ground of Europe, the contest bore the same familiar features of violence and horror which had marked the strife of former generations—fields ploughed by the cannon ball, and walls shattered by the exploding mine, sacked towns and blazing suburbs, the lamentations of women, and the license of a maddened soldiery. But in America, war assumed a new and striking aspect. A wilderness was its sublime arena. Army met army under the shadows of primeval woods; their cannon resounded over wastes unknown to civilized man. And before the hostile powers could join in battle, endless forests must be traversed, and morasses passed, and everywhere the axe of the pioneer must hew a path for the bayonet of the soldier.

Before the declaration of war, and before the breaking off of negotiations between the courts of France and England, the English ministry formed the plan of assailing the French in America on all sides at once, and repelling them, by one bold push, from all their encroachments.[1] A provincial army was to advance upon Acadia, a second was to attack Crown Point, and a third Niagara; while the two regiments which had lately arrived in Virginia under General Braddock, aided by a strong body of provincials, were to dislodge the French from their newly-built

---

[1] Instructions of General Braddock. See *Précis des Faits*, 160, 168.
Reprinted from *The Conspiracy of Pontiac* (1851).

fort of Du Quesne. To Braddock was assigned the chief command of all the British forces in America; and a person worse fitted for the office could scarcely have been found. His experience had been ample, and none could doubt his courage; but he was profligate, arrogant, perverse, and a bigot to military rules.[2] On his first arrival in Virginia, he called together the governors of the several provinces, in order to explain his instructions and adjust the details of the projected operations. These arrangements complete, Braddock advanced to the borders of Virginia, and formed his camp at Fort Cumberland, where he spent several weeks in training the raw backwoodsmen, who joined him, into such discipline as they seemed capable of; in collecting horses and wagons, which could only be had with the utmost difficulty; in railing at the contractors, who scandalously cheated him; and in venting his spleen by copious abuse of the country and the people. All at length was ready, and early in June, 1755, the army left civilization behind, and struck into the broad wilderness as a squadron puts out to sea.

It was no easy task to force their way over that rugged ground, covered with an unbroken growth of forest; and the difficulty was increased by the needless load of baggage which encumbered their march. The crash of falling trees resounded in the front, where a hundred axemen labored with ceaseless toil to hew a passage for the army.[3] The horses strained their utmost strength to drag the ponderous wagons over roots and stumps, through gullies and quagmires; and the regular troops were daunted by the depth and gloom of the forest which hedged them in on either hand, and closed its leafy arches above their heads. So tedious was

[2] The following is Horace Walpole's testimony, and writers of better authority have expressed themselves, with less liveliness and piquancy, to the same effect:—

"Braddock is a very Iroquois in disposition. He had a sister, who, having gamed away all her little fortune at Bath, hanged herself with a truly English deliberation, leaving only a note upon the table with those lines, 'To die is landing on some silent shore,' &c. When Braddock was told of it, he only said, 'Poor Fanny! I always thought she would play till she would be forced to *tuck herself up.*'"

Here follows a curious anecdote of Braddock's meanness and profligacy, which I omit. The next is more to his credit. "He once had a duel with Colonel Gumley, Lady Bath's brother, who had been his great friend. As they were going to engage, Gumley, who had good humor and wit (Braddock had the latter), said, 'Braddock, you are a poor dog! Here, take my purse. If you kill me, you will be forced to run away, and then you will not have a shilling to support you.' Braddock refused the purse, insisted on the duel, was disarmed, and would not even ask his life. However, with all his brutality, he has lately been governor of Gibraltar, where he made himself adored, and where scarce any governor was endured before."—*Letters to Sir H. Mann*, CCLXV. CCLXVI.

Washington's opinion of Braddock may be gathered from his Writings, II. 77.

[3] MS. *Diary of the Expedition*, in the British Museum.

their progress, that, by the advice of Washington, twelve hundred chosen men moved on in advance with the lighter baggage and artillery, leaving the rest of the army to follow, by slower stages, with the heavy wagons. On the eighth of July, the advanced body reached the Monongahela, at a point not far distant from Fort du Quesne. The rocky and impracticable ground on the eastern side debarred their passage, and the general resolved to cross the river in search of a smoother path, and recross it a few miles lower down, in order to gain the fort. The first passage was easily made, and the troops moved, in glittering array, down the western margin of the water, rejoicing that their goal was well nigh reached, and the hour of their expected triumph close at hand.

Scouts and Indian runners had brought the tidings of Braddock's approach to the French at Fort du Quesne. Their dismay was great, and Contrecœur, the commander, thought only of retreat; when Beaujeu, a captain in the garrison, made the bold proposal of leading out a party of French and Indians to waylay the English in the woods, and harass or interrupt their march. The offer was accepted, and Beaujeu hastened to the Indian camps.

Around the fort and beneath the adjacent forest were the bark lodges of savage hordes, whom the French had mustered from far and near; Ojibwas and Ottawas, Hurons and Caughnawagas, Abenakis and Delawares. Beaujeu called the warriors together, flung a hatchet on the ground before them, and invited them to follow him out to battle; but the boldest stood aghast at the peril, and none would accept the challenge. A second interview took place with no better success; but the Frenchman was resolved to carry his point. "I am determined to go," he exclaimed. "What, will you suffer your father to go alone?"[4] His daring proved contagious. The warriors hesitated no longer; and when, on the morning of the ninth of July, a scout ran in with the news that the English army was but a few miles distant, the Indian camps were at once astir with the turmoil of preparation. Chiefs harangued their yelling followers, braves bedaubed themselves with war-paint, smeared themselves with grease, hung feathers in their scalp-locks, and whooped and stamped till they had wrought themselves into a delirium of valor.

[4] Sparks's *Life and Writings of Washington*, II. 473. I am indebted to the kindness of President Sparks for copies of several French manuscripts, which throw much light on the incidents of the battle. These manuscripts are alluded to in the Life and Writings of Washington.

That morning, James Smith, an English prisoner recently captured on the frontier of Pennsylvania, stood on the rampart, and saw the half-frenzied multitude thronging about the gateway, where kegs of bullets and gunpowder were broken open, that each might help himself at will.[5] Then band after band hastened away towards the forest, followed and supported by nearly two hundred and fifty French and Canadians, commanded by Beaujeu. There were the Ottawas, led on, it is said, by the remarkable man [Pontiac] whose name stands on the title-page of this history; there were the Hurons of Lorette under their chief, whom the French called Athanase,[6] and many more, all keen as hounds on the scent of blood. At about nine miles from the fort, they reached a spot where the narrow road descended to the river through deep and gloomy woods, and where two ravines, concealed by trees and bushes, seemed formed by nature for an ambuscade. Beaujeu well knew the ground; and it was here that he had resolved to fight; but he and his followers were well nigh too late; for as they neared the ravines, the woods were resounding with the roll of the British drums.

It was past noon of a day brightened with the clear sunlight of an American midsummer, when the forces of Braddock began, for a second time, to cross the Monongahela, at the fording-place, which to this day bears the name of their ill-fated leader. The scarlet columns of the British regulars, complete in martial appointment, the rude backwoodsmen with shouldered rifles, the trains of artillery and the white-topped wagons, moved on in long procession through the shallow current, and slowly mounted the opposing bank.[7] Men were there whose names have become historic: Gage, who, twenty years later, saw his routed battalions recoil in disorder from before the breastwork on Bunker Hill; Gates, the future

---

[5] *Smith's Narrative.* This interesting account has been several times published. It may be found in Drake's *Tragedies of the Wilderness.*

[6] "Went to Lorette, an Indian village about eight miles from Quebec. Saw the Indians at mass, and heard them sing psalms tolerably well—a dance. Got well acquainted with Athanase, who was commander of the Indians who defeated General Braddock, in 1755—a very sensible fellow."—*MS. Journal of an English Gentleman on a Tour through Canada, in 1765.*

[7] "My feelings were heightened by the warm and glowing narration of that day's events, by Dr. Walker, who was an eye-witness. He pointed out the ford where the army crossed the Monongahela (below Turtle Creek, 800 yards). A finer sight could not have been beheld,—the shining barrels of the muskets, the excellent order of the men, the cleanliness of their appearance, the joy depicted on every face at being so near Fort du Quesne—the highest object of their wishes. The music re-echoed through the hills. How brilliant the morning—how melancholy the evening!"—*Letter of Judge Yeates, dated August, 1776.* See Haz. Pa. Reg., VI. 104.

conqueror of Burgoyne; and one destined to a higher fame,—George Washington, a boy in years, a man in calm thought and self-ruling wisdom.

With steady and well ordered march, the troops advanced into the great labyrinth of woods which shadowed the eastern borders of the river. Rank after rank vanished from sight. The forest swallowed them up, and the silence of the wilderness sank down once more on the shores and waters of the Monongahela.

Several engineers and guides and six light horsemen led the way; a body of grenadiers under Gage was close behind, and the army followed in such order as the rough ground would permit, along a narrow road, twelve feet wide, tunnelled through the dense and matted foliage. There were flanking parties on either side, but no scouts to scour the woods in front, and with an insane confidence Braddock pressed on to meet his fate. The van had passed the low grounds that bordered the river, and were now ascending a gently rising ground, where, on either hand, hidden by thick trees, by tangled undergrowth and rank grasses, lay the two fatal ravines. Suddenly, Gordon, an engineer in advance, saw the French and Indians bounding forward through the forest and along the narrow track, Beaujeu leading them on, dressed in a fringed hunting-shirt, and wearing a silver gorget on his breast. He stopped, turned, and waved his hat, and his French followers, crowding across the road, opened a murderous fire upon the head of the British column, while, screeching their war-cries, the Indians thronged into the ravines, or crouched behind rocks and trees on both flanks of the advancing troops. The astonished grenadiers returned the fire, and returned it with good effect; for a random shot struck down the brave Beaujeu, and the courage of the assailants was staggered by his fall. Dumas, second in command, rallied them to the attack; and while he, with the French and Canadians, made good the pass in front, the Indians from their lurking places opened a deadly fire on the right and left. In a few moments, all was confusion. The advance guard fell back on the main body, and every trace of subordination vanished. The fire soon extended along the whole length of the army, from front to rear. Scarce an enemy could be seen, though the forest resounded with their yells; though every bush and tree was alive with incessant flashes; though the lead flew like a hailstorm, and the men went down by scores. The regular troops seemed bereft of their senses. They huddled together in the road like flocks of sheep; and happy did he think himself who could wedge his way into the midst of the crowd, and place a barrier of human flesh between his life and the shot of the ambushed marksmen. Many were seen eagerly loading their muskets, and then firing them into the air, or shooting their own comrades in the insanity of their terror. The officers, for the most part, displayed a conspicuous gallantry; but threats and commands were wasted alike on the panic-stricken multitude. It is said that at the outset Braddock showed signs of fear; but he soon recovered his wonted intrepidity. Five horses were shot under him, and five times he mounted afresh.[8] He stormed and shouted, and, while the Virginians were fighting to good purpose, each man behind a tree, like the Indians themselves, he ordered them with furious menace to form in platoons, where the fire of the enemy mowed them down like grass. At length, a mortal shot silenced him, and two provincials bore him off the field. Washington rode through the tumult calm and undaunted. Two horses were killed under him, and four bullets pierced his clothes;[9] but his hour was not come, and he escaped without a wound. Gates was shot through the body, and Gage also was severely wounded. Of eighty-six officers, only twenty-three remained unhurt; and of twelve hundred soldiers who crossed the Monongahela, more than seven hundred were killed and wounded. None suffered more severely than the Virginians, who had displayed throughout a degree of courage and steadiness which put the cowardice of the regulars to shame. The havoc among them was terrible, for of their whole number scarcely one-fifth left the field alive.[10]

The slaughter lasted three hours; when, at length, the survivors, as if impelled by a general impulse, rushed tumultuously from the place of carnage, and with dastardly precipitation fled across the Monongahela. The enemy did not pursue beyond the river, flocking back to the field to collect the plunder, and gather a rich harvest of scalps. The routed troops pursued their flight until they met the rear division of the army, under Colonel Dunbar; and even then their senseless terrors did not abate. Dunbar's soldiers caught the infection. Cannon, baggage, provisions and wag-

---

[8] Letter—*Captain Orme, his aide-de-camp, to* ——, July 18.

[9] Sparks, I. 67.

[10] "The Virginia troops showed a good deal of bravery, and were nearly all killed; for I believe, out of three companies that were there, scarcely thirty men are left alive. Captain Peyrouny, and all his officers, down to a corporal, were killed. Captain Polson had nearly as hard a fate, for only one of his was left. In short, the dastardly behavior of those they call regulars exposed all others, that were inclined to do their duty, to almost certain death; and at last, in despite of all the efforts of the officers to the contrary, they ran, as sheep pursued by dogs, and it was impossible to rally them."—*Writings of Washington*, II. 87.

The English themselves bore reluctant testimony to the good conduct of the Virginians.—See Entick, *Hist. Late War*, 147.

ons were destroyed, and all fled together, eager to escape from the shadows of those awful woods, whose horrors haunted their imagination. They passed the defenceless settlements of the border, and hurried on to Philadelphia, leaving the unhappy people to defend themselves as they might against the tomahawk and scalping-knife.

The calamities of this disgraceful rout did not cease with the loss of a few hundred soldiers on the field of battle; for it brought upon the provinces all the miseries of an Indian war. Those among the tribes who had thus far stood neutral, wavering between the French and English, now hesitated no longer. Many of them had been disgusted by the contemptuous behavior of Braddock. All had learned to despise the courage of the English, and to regard their own prowess with unbounded complacency. It is not in Indian nature to stand quiet in the midst of war; and the defeat of Braddock was a signal for the western savages to snatch their tomahawks and assail the English settlements with one accord, murdering and pillaging with ruthless fury, and turning the frontier of Pennsylvania and Virginia into one wide scene of havoc and desolation.

From The Life of George Washington

WASHINGTON IRVING

IN CONSEQUENCE of adhering to technical rules and military forms, General Braddock had consumed a month in marching little more than a hundred miles. The tardiness of his progress was regarded with surprise and impatience even in Europe, where his patron, the Duke of Brunswick, was watching the events of the campaign he had planned. "The Duke," writes Horace Walpole, "is much dissatisfied at the slowness of General Braddock, *who does not march as if he was at all impatient to be scalped.*" The insinuation of the satirical wit was unmerited. Braddock was a stranger to fear; but in his movements he was fettered by system.

Washington was warmly received on his arrival, especially by his fellow aides-de-camp, Morris and Orme. He was just in time, for the attack upon Fort Duquesne was to be made on the following day. The neighboring country had been reconnoitered to determine upon a plan of attack. The fort stood on the same side of the Monongahela with the camp; but there was a narrow pass between them of about two miles, with the river on the left and a very high mountain on the right, and in its present state quite impassable for carriages. The route determined on was to cross the Monongahela by a ford immediately opposite to the camp; proceed along the west bank of the river, for about five miles, then recross by another ford to the eastern side, and push on to the fort. The river at these fords was shallow, and the banks were not steep.

According to the plan of arrangement, Lieutenant-Colonel Gage, with the advance, was to cross the river before daybreak, march to the second ford, and recrossing there, take post to secure the passage of the main force. The advance was to be composed of two companies of grenadiers,

From Volume I (1855).

one hundred and sixty infantry, the independent company of Captain Horatio Gates, and two six-pounders.

Washington, who had already seen enough of regular troops to doubt their infallibility in wild bush-fighting, and who knew the dangerous nature of the ground they were to traverse, ventured to suggest, that on the following day the Virginia rangers, being accustomed to the country and to Indian warfare, might be thrown in the advance. The proposition drew an angry reply from the general, indignant very probably, that a young provincial officer should presume to school a veteran like himself.

Early next morning (July 9th), before daylight, Colonel Gage crossed with the advance. He was followed, at some distance, by Sir John St. Clair, quartermaster-general, with a working party of two hundred and fifty men, to make roads for the artillery and baggage. They had with them their wagons of tools, and two six-pounders. A party of about thirty savages rushed out of the woods as Colonel Gage advanced, but were put to flight before they had done any harm.

By sunrise the main body turned out in full uniform. At the beating of "the general," their arms, which had been cleansed the night before, were charged with fresh cartridges. The officers were perfectly equipped. All looked as if arrayed for a *fête*, rather than a battle. Washington, who was still weak and unwell, mounted his horse, and joined the staff of the general, who was scrutinizing everything with the eye of a martinet. As it was supposed the enemy would be on the watch for the crossing of the troops, it had been agreed that they should do it in the greatest order, with bayonets fixed, colors flying, and drums and fifes beating and playing.[1] They accordingly made a gallant appearance as they forded the Monongahela, and wound along its banks, and through the open forests, gleaming and glittering in the morning sunshine, and stepping buoyantly to the "Grenadiers' March."

Washington, with his keen and youthful relish for military affairs, was delighted with their perfect order and equipment, so different from the rough bush-fighters, to which he had been accustomed. Roused to new life, he forgot his recent ailments, and broke forth in expressions of enjoyment and admiration, as he rode in company with his fellow aides-de-camp, Orme and Morris. Often, in after life, he used to speak of the effect upon him of the first sight of a well-disciplined European army, marching in high confidence and bright array, on the eve of a battle.

About noon they reached the second ford. Gage, with the advance,

[1] Orme's *Journal.*

was on the opposite side of the Monongahela, posted according to orders; but the river bank had not been sufficiently sloped. The artillery and baggage drew up along the beach and halted until one, when the second crossing took place, drums beating, fifes playing, and colors flying as before. When all had passed, there was again a halt close by a small stream called Frazier's Run, until the general arranged the order of march.

First went the advance, under Gage, preceded by the engineers and guides, and six light horsemen.

Then, Sir John St. Clair and the working party, with their wagons and the two six-pounders. On each side were thrown out four flanking parties.

Then, at some distance, the general was to follow with the main body, the artillery and baggage were preceded and flanked by light horse and squads of infantry; while the Virginian and other provincial troops, were to form the rear-guard.

The ground before them was level until about half a mile from the river, where a rising ground, covered with long grass, low bushes, and scattered trees sloped gently up to a range of hills. The whole country, generally speaking, was a forest with no clear opening but the road, which was about twelve feet wide, and flanked by two ravines, concealed by trees and thickets.

Had Braddock been schooled in the warfare of the woods, or had he adopted the suggestions of Washington, which he rejected so impatiently, he would have thrown out Indian scouts or Virginian rangers in the advance, and on the flanks, to beat up the woods and ravines; but, as has been sarcastically observed, he suffered his troops to march forward through the centre of the plain, with merely their usual guides and flanking parties, "as if in a review in St. James's Park."

It was now near two o'clock. The advanced party and the working party had crossed the plain and were ascending the rising ground. Braddock was about to follow with the main body, and had given the word to march, when he heard an excessively quick and heavy firing in front. Washington, who was with the general, surmised that the evil he had apprehended had come to pass. For want of scouting parties ahead, the advance parties were suddenly and warmly attacked. Braddock ordered Lieutenant-Colonel Burton to hasten to their assistance with the vanguard of the main body, eight hundred strong. The residue, four hundred, were halted, and posted to protect the artillery and baggage.

The firing continued with fearful yelling. There was a terrible uproar. By the general's orders an aide-de-camp spurred forward to bring him an account of the nature of the attack. Without waiting for his return the general himself, finding the turmoil increase, moved forward, leaving Sir Peter Halkett with the command of the baggage.[2]

The van of the advance had indeed been taken by surprise. It was composed of two companies of pioneers to cut the road, and two flank companies of grenadiers to protect them. Suddenly the engineer who preceded them to mark out the road gave the alarm, "French and Indians!" A body of them was approaching rapidly, cheered on by a Frenchman in gayly fringed hunting-shirt, whose gorget showed him to be an officer. There was sharp firing on both sides at first. Several of the enemy fell; among them their leader; but a murderous fire broke out from among trees and a ravine on the right, and the woods resounded with unearthly whoops and yellings. The Indian rifle was at work, levelled by unseen hands. Most of the grenadiers and many of the pioneers were shot down. The survivors were driven in on the advance.

Gage ordered his men to fix bayonets and form in order of battle. They did so in hurry and trepidation. He would have scaled a hill on the right whence there was the severest firing. Not a platoon would quit the line of march. They were more dismayed by the yells than by the rifles of the unseen savages. The latter extended themselves along the hill and in the ravines; but their whereabouts was only known by their demoniac cries and the puffs of smoke from their rifles. The soldiers fired wherever they saw the smoke. Their officers tried in vain to restrain them until they should see their foe. All orders were unheeded; in their fright they shot at random, killing some of their own flanking parties, and of the vanguard, as they came running in. The covert fire grew more intense. In a short time most of the officers and many of the men of the advance were killed or wounded. Colonel Gage himself received a wound. The advance fell back in dismay upon Sir John St. Clair's corps, which was equally dismayed. The cannon belonging to it were deserted.

Colonel Burton had come up with the reinforcement, and was forming his men to face the rising ground on the right, when both of the advanced detachments fell back upon him, and all now was confusion.

By this time the general was upon the ground. He tried to rally the men. "They would fight," they said, "if they could see their enemy; but

[2] Orme's *Journal*.

it was useless to fire at trees and bushes, and they could not stand to be shot down by an invisible foe."

The colors were advanced in different places to separate the men of the two regiments. The general ordered the officers to form the men, tell them off into small divisions, and advance with them; but the soldiers could not be prevailed upon either by threats or entreaties. The Virginia troops, accustomed to the Indian mode of fighting, scattered themselves, and took post behind trees, whence they could pick off the lurking foe. In this way they, in some degree, protected the regulars. Washington advised General Braddock to adopt the same plan with the regulars; but he persisted in forming them into platoons; consequently they were cut down from behind logs and trees as fast as they could advance. Several attempted to take to the trees, without orders, but the general stormed at them, called them cowards, and even struck them with the flat of his sword. Several of the Virginians, who had taken post and were doing good service in this manner, were slain by the fire of the regulars, directed wherever a smoke appeared among the trees.

The officers behaved with consummate bravery; and Washington beheld with admiration those who, in camp or on the march, had appeared to him to have an almost effeminate regard for personal ease and convenience, now exposing themselves to imminent death, with a courage that kindled with the thickening horrors. In the vain hope of inspiriting the men to drive off the enemy from the flanks and regain the cannon, they would dash forward singly or in groups. They were invariably shot down; for the Indians aimed from their coverts at every one on horseback, or who appeared to have command.

Some were killed by random shot of their own men, who, crowded in masses, fired with affrighted rapidity, but without aim. Soldiers in the front ranks were killed by those in the rear. Between friend and foe, the slaughter of the officers was terrible. All this while the woods resounded with the unearthly yellings of the savages, and now and then one of them, hideously painted, and ruffling with feathered crest, would rush forth to scalp an officer who had fallen, or seize a horse galloping wildly without a rider.

Throughout this disastrous day, Washington distinguished himself by his courage and presence of mind. His brother aides, Orme and Morris, were wounded and disabled early in the action, and the whole duty of carrying the orders of the general devolved on him. His danger was imminent and incessant. He was in every part of the field, a conspicuous mark for the murderous rifle. Two horses were shot under him. Four bullets passed through his coat. His escape without a wound was almost miraculous. Dr. Craik, who was on the field attending to the wounded, watched him with anxiety as he rode about in the most exposed manner, and used to say that he expected every moment to see him fall. At one time he was sent to the main body to bring the artillery into action. All there was likewise in confusion; for the Indians had extended themselves along the ravine so as to flank the reserve and carry slaughter into the ranks. Sir Peter Halkett had been shot down at the head of his regiment. The men who should have served the guns were paralyzed. Had they raked the ravines with grape-shot the day might have been saved. In his ardor Washington sprang from his horse, wheeled and pointed a brass field-piece with his own hand, and directed an effective discharge into the woods; but neither his efforts nor example were of avail. The men could not be kept to the guns.

Braddock still remained in the centre of the field, in the desperate hope of retrieving the fortunes of the day. The Virginia rangers, who had been most efficient in covering his position, were nearly all killed or wounded. His secretary, Shirley, had fallen by his side. Many of his officers had been slain within his sight, and many of his guard of Virginia light horse. Five horses had been killed under him; still he kept his ground, vainly endeavoring to check the flight of his men, or at least to effect their retreat in good order. At length a bullet passed through his right arm, and lodged itself in his lungs. He fell from his horse, but was caught by Captain Stewart of the Virginia guards, who, with the assistance of another American, and a servant, placed him in a tumbril. It was with much difficulty they got him out of the field—in his despair he desired to be left there.[3]

The rout now became complete. Baggage, stores, artillery, everything was abandoned. The wagoners took each a horse out of his team, and fled. The officers were swept off with the men in this headlong flight. It was rendered more precipitate by the shouts and yells of the savages, numbers of whom rushed forth from their coverts, and pursued the fugitives to the river side, killing several as they dashed across in tumultuous confusion. Fortunately for the latter, the victors gave up the pursuit in their eagerness to collect the spoil.

The shattered army continued its flight after it had crossed the Monon-

[3] *Journal of the Seamen's Detachment.*

gahela, a wretched wreck of the brilliant little force that had recently gleamed along its banks, confident of victory. Out of eighty-six officers, twenty-six had been killed, and thirty-six wounded. The number of rank and file killed and wounded was upwards of seven hundred. The Virginia corps had suffered the most; one company had been almost annihilated, another, beside those killed and wounded in the ranks, had lost all its officers, even to the corporal.

About a hundred men were brought to a halt about a quarter of a mile from the ford of the river. Here was Braddock, with his wounded aides-de-camp and some of his officers, Dr. Craik dressing his wounds, and Washington attending him with faithful assiduity. Braddock was still able to give orders, and had a faint hope of being able to keep possession of the ground until reinforced. Most of the men were stationed in a very advantageous spot about two hundred yards from the road; and Lieutenant-Colonel Burton posted out small parties and sentinels. Before an hour had elapsed most of the men had stolen off. Being thus deserted, Braddock and his officers continued their retreat; he would have mounted his horse, but was unable, and had to be carried by soldiers. Orme and Morris were placed on litters borne by horses. They were subsequently joined by Colonel Gage with eighty men whom he had rallied.

Washington, in the meantime, notwithstanding his weak state, being found most efficient in frontier service, was sent to Colonel Dunbar's camp, forty miles distant, with orders for him to hurry forward provisions, hospital stores, and wagons for the wounded, under the escort of two grenadier companies. It was a hard and a melancholy ride throughout the night and the following day. The tidings of the defeat preceded him, borne by the wagoners, who had mounted their horses, on Braddock's fall, and fled from the field of battle. They had arrived, haggard, at Dunbar's camp at midday; the Indian yells still ringing in their ears. "All was lost!" they cried. "Braddock was killed! They had seen wounded officers borne off from the field in bloody sheets! The troops were all cut to pieces!" A panic fell upon the camp. The drums beat to arms. Many of the soldiers, wagoners, and attendants, took to flight; but most of them were forced back by the sentinels.

Washington arrived at the camp in the evening, and found the agitation still prevailing. The orders which he brought were executed during the night, and he was in the saddle early in the morning accompanying the convoy of supplies. At Gist's plantation, about thirteen miles off, he met Gage and his scanty force escorting Braddock and his wounded officers. Captain Stewart and a sad remnant of the Virginia light horse still accompanied the general as his guard. The captain had been unremitting in his attentions to him during the retreat. There was a halt of one day at Dunbar's camp for the repose and relief of the wounded. On the 13th they resumed their melancholy march, and that night reached the Great Meadows.

The proud spirit of Braddock was broken by his defeat. He remained silent the first evening after the battle, only ejaculating at night: "Who would have thought it!" He was equally silent the following day; yet hope still seemed to linger in his breast, from another ejaculation: "We shall better know how to deal with them another time!"[4]

He was grateful for the attentions paid to him by Captain Stewart and Washington, and more than once, it is said, expressed his admiration of the gallantry displayed by the Virginians in the action. It is said, moreover, that in his last moments, he apologized to Washington for the petulance with which he had rejected his advice, and bequeathed to him his favorite charger, and his faithful servant, Bishop, who had helped to convey him from the field.

Some of these facts, it is true, rest on tradition, yet we are willing to believe them, as they impart a gleam of just and generous feeling to his closing scene. He died on the night of the 13th, at the Great Meadows, the place of Washington's discomfiture in the previous year. His obsequies were performed before break of day. The chaplain having been wounded, Washington read the funeral service. All was done in sadness, and without parade, so as not to attract the attention of lurking savages, who might discover and outrage his grave. It is doubtful even whether a volley was fired over it, that last military honor which he had recently paid to the remains of an Indian warrior. The place of his sepulture, however, is still known, and pointed out.

Reproach spared him not, even when in his grave. The failure of the expedition was attributed, both in England and America, to his obstinacy, his technical pedantry, and his military conceit. He had been continually warned to be on his guard against ambush and surprise, but without avail. Had he taken the advice urged on him by Washington and others, to employ scouting parties of Indians and rangers, he would never have been so signally surprised and defeated.

---

[4] Captain Orme, who gave these particulars to Dr. Franklin, says that Braddock "died a few minutes after." This, according to his account, was on the second day; whereas the general survived upwards of four days. Orme, being conveyed on a litter at some distance from the general, could only speak of his moods from hearsay.

Still his dauntless conduct on the field of battle shows him to have been a man of fearless spirit; and he was universally allowed to be an accomplished disciplinarian. His melancholy end, too, disarms censure of its asperity. Whatever may have been his faults and errors, he in a manner expiated them by the hardest lot that can befall a brave soldier, ambitious of renown—an unhonored grave in a strange land; a memory clouded by misfortune and a name forever coupled with defeat.

The Disaster at the Monongahela

L. H. GIPSON

WHEN General Braddock finally moved his army with its siege artillery through the Appalachian barrier over indescribable mountain roads, he performed what one writer has described as the "eighth wonder of the world."[1] I know of no other feat in the annals of the military history of North America that can be compared with it—certainly not Burgoyne's campaign or even Arnold's intrepid and painful expedition up the Kennebec and down the Chaudière in 1775, which may be more nearly likened in difficulty to Washington's movement from Great Meadows to Mount Braddock and then back again in 1754. It will be noted that when the Ordnance Board sent to Virginia in 1753 a number of four-pounder cannon in place of the small three-pounders requested, the Virginians were dismayed at the possibility of ever getting them over the mountains and finally, after repeated efforts, gave it up as futile. But Braddock brought with him real siege guns in the form of great eight-inch howitzers, large twelve-pounders, as well as six-pounders, and the smaller cohorn mortars. Some of the twelve-pounders, in fact, came from the upper-tier battery of the H.M.S. *Norwich*, in need of new masts and tied up at Alexandria, and were so huge that that old sea-dog Admiral Keppel, who furnished them to Braddock on request, declared in writing to the Admiralty:

I have very strong doubts that these additional Guns to the Train will prove so heavy that they [the army] will meet with great, and perhaps, insurmountable difficulties in getting them over the Mountains.[2]

[1] A. B. Hulbert, *Braddock's Road*, p. 116.
[2] Letter of March 14, 1755, P.R.O., Admiralty, In-Letters, 1746–63, 480:1060. On March 18 Keppel wrote: ". . . I own I have my Fears that the heavy Guns must be left off this Side the Hill [Allegheny Mountains]" (*ibid.*, 480:1085).

But Braddock was determined that what appeared to be an impossibility should be achieved. He would take this heavy artillery over every obstacle to have it available for pulverizing the French fort. Anticipating the difficulties that would be encountered, he also received from Keppel thirty sailors who could help the army over rivers in floats and boats and who also could make "leeff tackles,"[3] by means of which the howitzers and the great guns could be lifted over barriers too precipitous for horses to pull them.[4] These monsters finally appeared, as by a miracle, in the neighbourhood of Fort Duquesne, and, with the smaller cannon, were left behind by the British in the panic that followed the defeat. The French, however, apparently appalled at the time by the problem of transporting them even eight miles over fairly smooth terrain, spiked and dismantled them and then proceeded to take the six-pounders to the fort to strengthen their defences.[5]

Even after Braddock had stripped his army of all nonessentials, it was stretched out for three or four miles. Now moving along the single road blasted from the mountain sides or blazed through virgin forests of immense white pines and northern cypress and equally immense hardwoods with interlocking branches so dense that, in the words of Sir John St. Clair, a man might go "Twenty Miles without seeing before him ten yards";[6] then wading through swampy lands filled with venomous snakes that struck and killed or through underbrush alive with wood-ticks that stung like scorpions; again, balancing itself on rocky ledges or worming its way among boulders and the stumps of trees, on and on it moved, ever inching its way with deadly persistence toward its goal. Over Great Savage Mountain it passed; then crept through the Little Shades of Death; traversed Tumblestones and on through the Shades of Death; then it moved over the Great Crossings of the Youghiogheny, on to Great Meadows and the ruins of Fort Necessity, up over a spur of the rocky Laurel Range and down the valley to Stewarts Crossing; then, leaving Chestnut Range on the right, it proceeded on to Mount Pleasant. Horses fell dead in their traces, wagons were racked to pieces, the men became sickly on a diet of salt meat; even Washington, with his iron constitution,

---

[3] A leeff tackle was used to control the weather leech or forward leech of a fore-and-aft sail. It consisted of a double and a single pulley with ropes and hooks so arranged that in lifting a weight, power is multiplied three or four times.

[4] P.R.O., Admiralty, In-Letters, 480:1061.

[5] Later the big guns were, it is true, taken to Niagara and to Frontenac and some were used against Fort Oswego (Sargent, *op. cit.*, p. 257).

[6] Pargellis, *op. cit.*, p. 94.

was taken down with the bloody flux before he reached the Great Crossings of the Youghiogheny on June 28.[7] While the army, after it left Great Meadows, had some stragglers picked off by the lurking enemy Indians, the latter, under French leaders, at first shrewdly directed their chief attacks against the frontier settlements or isolated families of Maryland and Virginia. This had the effect of placing the people living in this region "in such Frights and Apprehensions" that they fled for security to certain advantageous points. But Braddock was not to be diverted by these acts and marched ahead, very properly leaving to the colonial militia of the two provinces the responsibility of providing protection to their own inhabitants.[8]

In the course of this historic march many adjustments were made. On June 11 at a council of war—after Lieutenant Colonel Burton, who was with the advanced party, had reported that he was able to make but five miles in two days "on a better road than we were to expect afterwards, occasioned by the extreme faintness and deficiency of the horses"[9]—it was agreed to send back to Fort Cumberland two of the six-pounders and four cohorns and some of the ammunition, as well as all the King's wagons that Braddock had brought with him, since these were found to be too heavy for the task. The lighter country wagons were now substituted for these and the load was limited to fourteen hundred pounds—far short of a ton's weight. To draw each light wagon, four hourses were provided; to pull each of the great howitzers, seven of the strongest horses were selected, and five of the strongest for each of the twelve-pounders. Each bat horse was limited to two hundred pounds, a very reasonable pack; but the horses furnished on contract by the Virginians were so defective —"the offcasts of Indian Traders"—that they could hardly carry a hundredweight. Representing to his officers the great need for horses and how important it was therefore to eliminate all but the most essential baggage and to send this back to Fort Cumberland, the general made an appeal to them to surrender their extra mounts. Washington led the way in giving up his best horse; his example was generally followed, with the result that "near a hundred able horses were given to the public serv-

---

[7] *Writings of Washington* (ed. Fitzpatrick), I, 139.

[8] "I don't think the General has sent . . . any parties whatsoever, after those troublesome Indians," wrote Admiral Keppel on July 6 from Hampton Roads; "his not doing it will in all Probability be a disappointment to the French . . . for I cannot help thinking but they have sent the Indians so near, in order to tempt him to weaken his Army, by sending detachments after them" (P.R.O., Admiralty, In-Letters, 480:1188).

[9] Orme's "Journal," Sargent, *op. cit.*, p. 331.

ice."[10] After two days spent in adjusting loads the army again moved forward over the "excessively mountainous and rocky" road. On the 15th, in passing the summit of Savage Mountain, involving a continuous rocky ascent of almost two miles and in many places extremely steep, one half of the soldiers were detailed to help push the wagons and gun carriages up the grade when the horses became faint and many died; then came the dangerous descent from the summit, described as "very rugged and almost perpendicular," where some of the wagons were dashed to pieces and others shattered. Many horses that survived the ordeal were now mere wrecks. Even before this passage Washington had expressed the fear that unless some of the wagons were eliminated and pack-horses substituted for carrying the stores and provisions, the difficulties of continuing the march might prove insurmountable.[11] Yet he did not despair. Writing to his brother Samuel on the same day—that is, the 14th—he declared that

. . . we have gone thus far, and shall continue on to Fort Duquisne; where, I hope the dispute will soon be decided. . . .[12]

From the summit of Savage Mountain other ranges of the Appalachian chain towered to the west before the eyes of the determined leaders. Could the army continue onward? Others than Washington had now come to the conviction that it would be "impossible to proceed with such a number of carriages."[13] At Little Meadows Braddock therefore summoned his second council of war since leaving Fort Cumberland. His high regard for Washington led him to get his private opinion of the expedition before the council was held. Speaking of this informal conference, Washington declared:

I urg'd it in the warmest terms I was Master of to push on; if we even did it with a chos'n Detacht. for that purpose, with the Artillery and such other things as were absolutely necessary; leav'g the baggage and other Convoys with the Remainder of the Army, to follow by slow and regular Marches, which they might do safely, while we were advanced in Front.[14]

The advice of Washington was sound and the council of war, acting upon it, determined that a flying column supported by artillery should

[10] *Ibid.*, pp. 331–2.
[11] *Writings* (ed. Fitzpatrick), I, 140.
[12] *Ibid.*, I, 141.
[13] Orme's "Journal," Sargent, *op. cit.*, p. 335.
[14] *Writings*, I, 143.

move ahead at the greatest speed possible in order to arrive at Fort Duquesne before the expected French reinforcements. Twelve hundred
troops in all—composed of some of the best of the grenadiers and of the
rank and file, with pioneers, artillerymen, the party of seamen, and the
light horse—were detailed as a special task force. Each soldier was supplied with a hundred rounds of ammunition. Four of the great howitzers,
each with fifty rounds, four of the twelve-pounders, each with eighty
rounds, together with some of the six-pounders were also included. On the
18th of June four hundred men supported by six-pounders, under command of Colonel Gage, later of Revolutionary War fame, moved forward
with their axes to blaze the way; the following day Halkett's regiment and
then the remainder of the selected force plunged into the forest gloom.
It seemed that much greater speed could now be attained: the howitzers
and their caissons were pulled by nine of the strongest horses instead of
seven, the twelve-pounders by seven, and the wagons containing the ammunition and other matériel by six; while great strings of bat horses carried a month's provisions for the entire force.[15] But still there were delays
as the army was obliged to wait for the pioneers to prepare the way for
the passage of the artillery train and the ammunition wagons—now
through swamps and springs, now over mountains, and most of the time
through dense forest. To Washington, who had fallen ill and was impatient for action, it was intolerable

. . . that instead of pushing on with vigour, without regarding a little rough
Road, they were halting to level every Mold [sic] Hill, and to erect Bridges
over every Brook; by which means we were 4 Days gett'g 12 Miles. . . .[16]

But one must feel that the youthful aide-de-camp was wrong. Many,
many weary miles lay ahead for man and beast. Far beyond over rough
mountainous country was still the great Laurel Range, which the preceding year had taken such a frightful toll of both horses and wagons that
when Washington himself had had to retreat from Gist's Plantation, his
men were obliged to pull the swivels and carry the supplies on their backs.
But now the horses were pulling howitzers and twelve-pounders and other
large cannon with the caissons, and wagons loaded with ammunition and
other matériel. This demanded the utmost care because of the great dead
weight, lest at best the horses should have their shoulders irreparably
galled and consequently become useless and at worst should fall dead of

[15] Orme's "Journal," Sargent, *op. cit.*, p. 336.
[16] *Writings* (ed. Fitzpatrick), I, 144.

overexertion. In explaining the slowness of his progress St. Clair, in charge of the pioneers, records in his Journal:

The Roads are either Rocky or full of Boggs, we are obliged to blow the Rocks and lay Bridges every Day.[17]

All this took time, but time well spent.[18] Moreover, the general, to save his precious horses, provided that at very precipitous places the guns and wagons should be handled by his soldiers using the tackle blocks and assisted by the sailors. Again this took time.

In fact, General Braddock, in spite of undeniable faults of character and unmeasured censure later heaped upon him, was not an unworthy leader of so desperate an adventure. Although a man of years, he pursued his objectives "with a great deal of vigour and Vivacity," according to Sir John St. Clair;[19] there was an absence of that brutality which some writers have assumed he possessed; he had even words of praise for his two Irish regiments, who, he reported,

. . . behave well and shew great Spirit and Zeal for the Service, which will be a good Example to the rest.[20]

His humaneness is also indicated by the records of the courts-martial, which he repeatedly overruled by mitigating the severe punishment decreed against his soldiers.[21] He knew the limits of exertion of those who marched with packs and of horses dragging loads, and thoughtfully ordered frequent and proper rests. If, on the one hand, he lashed out against those in America who would not honour their contracts and acted fraudulently in their transactions with the army, he may be pardoned since he had a keen sense of the great responsibilities he had assumed in undertaking so difficult a campaign. On the other hand, those who had proved to be worthy of his trust and friendship were treated most courteously and generously; some received almost fatherly consideration. For example,

[17] Pargellis, *op. cit.*, p. 95.

[18] I may perhaps be permitted to state that during the years that I lived in the Far West, where I was reared, I came to have personal knowledge of the serious problems involved in carrying freight over mountain roads by the use of horses and wagons—especially over newly opened roads filled with what one might regard superficially as minor obstructions. A horse is a highly expendable asset.

[19] Pargellis, *op. cit.*, p. 94.

[20] *Ibid.*, p. 83.

[21] His "Orderly Books" are in the Congressional Library. Among the Ayer Collection in the Newberry Library is the transcription of a copy of these made by George Washington. These books throw much light upon Braddock's military arrangements. Orme's "Journal" also repeats many of the orders.

when Washington became violently ill, the general ordered his own physician to attend him and detailed a body of soldiers to stand guard over him when his army moved forward. He also promised not to attack the French before his young aide-de-camp could join the advanced detachment, and he kept his word; then when the battle was joined, he refused to permit the young man, still weak and suffering from his ailment, to expose himself unnecessarily to the enemy's fire. Further, as a good soldier he sought advice and, when it seemed sound, acted upon it.[22] Personally without fear, he helped to instil confidence in others, especially the soldiers of his Irish regiments, who at first were deeply apprehensive of the great forest that had swallowed them up. His military conceptions and his tactical arrangements were sound and most errors of judgment in connection with the campaign were committed by others, his military superiors or inferiors; yet his correspondence is remarkably free from any censure of his fellow officers. Finally, an examination of his orders shows that he felt under necessity to take the utmost precautions against surprise attacks, whether on the march or in camp. To illustrate: While in the vicinity of the first branch of the Youghiogheny, as his army was skirting "an immense mountain," reports came of the presence of the enemy; thereupon he ordered a detachment of a hundred men to occupy the eminence until his artillery and baggage train should pass by this dangerous point. Scouting parties, pickets, and sentries he constantly employed; moreover, strong detachments preceded and followed and, when possible, flanked the army as an additional precaution against surprise, especially when rivers had to be crossed.

On June 30 the army passed over the Youghiogheny at Stewarts Crossing and then proceeded on to Salt Lick Creek, now called Jacob's Creek, where Braddock called his third council of war to consider Sir John St. Clair's recommendations that the force should halt there and send back all the horses to bring up the rest of the forces commanded by Colonel Dunbar, who was struggling along with a great wagon train and an utterly inadequate number of horses. After full consideration it was decided that this would involve great delays: it had taken the lighter detachment

[22] For example, before leaving Wills Creek, Braddock called a council of war of his leading officers and informed them that "he had formed a plan of march and encampment . . . that he offered it to them for their opinions, in which he desired they would be very explicit, and make such objections, and offer such amendments, as they should judge proper, by which some general plan might be formed which would effectually answer the end proposed, of marching and encamping with greater security" (Orme's "Journal," Sargent, *op. cit.*, p. 317).

eleven days to come from the position that Dunbar had attained at Squaw's Creek and his force was much more encumbered with baggage. Washington's advice—given at Little Meadows—in favour of "pushing on" was still favoured by Braddock, and the council agreed to it unanimously.[23] Thereupon the army proceeded, with great precautions observed, in the direction of the Monongahela. On July 7 an attempt was made to pass Turtle Creek some miles before its junction with the Monongahela, but was wisely given up in the face of dangers involved in the precipice that bordered it; instead it was decided to move to the left toward the main stream. In approaching it through the valley of Long Run on the 8th, great care was taken by means of powerful detachments to secure control of eminences that dominated both the right and the left flanks of the army. Up to the very day of the great disaster so extraordinary had been all the proper precautions, so efficient the means of overcoming the tremendous problem of transport, so confident the once dispirited and even mutinous soldiers through the example set by the general, that no one doubted or had good reason to doubt the happy outcome of this epic campaign in the wilderness. . . .

According to the French accounts, from the early part of June one expedition after another was sent out from Fort Duquesne for the purpose of turning Braddock aside. On the 6th M. de Normanville led a party of French and Indians that penetrated the wilderness to the site of Fort Necessity; on the 18th M. de Neverville left with one hundred and thirty Indians and a small body of French to harass the enemy; on the 26th nineteen Indians left and returned with a scalp; on the 28th it was a party of one hundred and twenty Indians—Hurons and others—with ten Frenchmen under the command of M. Rigoville; M. Roctoyade also was sent out at that time with another mixed party with the same design. Although these detachments succeeded in firing upon the soldiers and killing some of them, the Indians were disappointed and not a little discouraged since they were unable to secure scalps because of the alertness and good order of the British, who proceeded without interruption in their methodical march. Nevertheless, the last-named two parties and others that

---

[23] Washington did not join Braddock until the 8th of July, when he arrived with the supply wagons coming from Dunbar's contingent with additional food supplies, including livestock. Dunbar had remained at Little Meadows until June 2 and then moved forward slowly. He could not transport all his supplies with the available horses without sending them back with their drivers under military escort to the preceding halting-place—a situation that made rapid movement impossible.

left on the 30th and on July 5 hung upon the flanks of the advancing army until it was within eight leagues of the forks of the Ohio and then most of them returned on July 7 to report their failure to check its progress.[24] In commenting upon this failure Contrecœur declared that

. . . these troops remain so constantly on guard, always marching in battle formation, that all the efforts that our detachments put forth against them are useless.[25]

The conduct of the defenders of Fort Duquesne was at this critical juncture marked by great indecision. For example, on the 6th of July a party of Hurons appeared at the forks with the news that the British were marching forward briskly with their artillery. To secure more accurate information the Chevalier de la Peyrade was sent the same day with a small party; but after going some three or four leagues, his guide, an Iroquois living at the forks, refused to proceed farther. The Ottawa and the Michilimakinac, who were to have gone out on the 6th to strike the British, were detained by the other Indians for a conference with Contrecœur, at which it was at length decided that all the Indians at the forks would proceed together the following day. But on the 7th nothing happened except that two new parties went out by different routes to observe the British; these on their return amply confirmed the accuracy of the earlier information of their near approach. Again the plan to strike the enemy was postponed to the 8th, and it was agreed that every Frenchman and Indian that could be spared from the fort would then march out. But on the 8th, in spite of the fact that Captain de Beaujeu, a man of energy and determination who had led the reinforcements to the forks in the spring, who possessed great influence with the Indians, and who had been appointed to lead the expedition, sang the war-song, the Indians still held back.[26] Now it was the Potawatomi who remained silent on their mats.[27] On the other hand, the Shawnee and the Mingo, living in the region of the forks—the very Indians whom Dinwiddie had sought to pro-

[24] See the Frenchman Godefroy's "Relation" in *Relations diverses sur la bataille du Malangueulé, gagné le 9 Juillet, 1755* (ed. J. M. Shea), pp. 9–10; also among the Chatham Manuscripts (Volume XCVIII, folios 12–19) is to be found a most detailed account, translated into English, of activities at Fort Duquesne between the 6th and 12th of July. A transcript of this is in the Canadian Archives.

[25] Pargellis, *op. cit.*, p. 129.

[26] *Relations diverses sur la bataille du Malangueulé*, p. xi. Beaujeu had commanded both at Detroit and at Niagara.

[27] On July 5 a party of Potawatomi and Missisauga had gone out to strike the British, but they returned without accomplishing anything and apparently deeply impressed with the formidable nature of the invading forces (*ibid.*, p. 10).

tect from the French in sending Washington on his adventure the preceding year and who had for years been showered with presents by
Virginia and Pennsylvania—appeared before Contrecœur and offered to
assist him in opposing the British. He entertained them in a proper manner at the commandery in order to win over the other natives and
complacently granted all their demands. Armed and equipped, they declared themselves ready to set forth immediately with the French. But
Beaujeu proposed that the expedition be once more postponed, now to
the 9th, when he was determined to set forth at daybreak, hoping that all
the Indians would then join him. The French, most of them "in Indian
dress" on that fatal day, to set an example marched two musket-shots
from the fort and then halted, for the Indians had not joined them. There
were one hundred and eight regulars—including Captains Beaujeu, Dumas, and Deligney, four lieutenants, six ensigns, and twenty-three cadets
—and one hundred and forty-six Canadian militia. Beaujeu thereupon, it
is said, dramatically appealed to the Indians, announcing that if need be
he would meet the English alone:

I am determined to go against the enemy! What! Will you allow your father
to go alone?[28]

Even the Potawatomi took fire at this display of courage. Loading themselves with the ammunition from the barrels that had been placed before
the gate of the fort, they now, to the number of over six hundred, raced
forward to join the waiting French troops.

The defenders of Fort Duquesne apparently had hoped—when tidings
were received that Braddock had avoided what might well have been a
trap presented by the more direct approach along the well-established
trail that crossed Turtle Creek—to be able to ambuscade the British as
they crossed or recrossed the Monongahela. But the General, encamped
on the evening of the 8th only two miles from the river, took the precaution to order Lieutenant Colonel Gage, with three hundred and sixty
regulars, supported by Captain Gates's New York Independent Company
and two six-pounders, to march well before daylight in order to protect
the rest of the army as it passed over to the left bank and then back to the
right bank below the mouth of Turtle Creek to regain the well-worn trail
leading to the forks of the Ohio and Fort Duquesne. Gage, moving about
two o'clock in the morning, secured these vital crossings without oppo-

---

[28] "*Relation depuis le départ des Trouppes de Quebec, jusqu'au 30 du mois de
Septembre, 1755,*" Sargent, *op. cit.*, Appendix, p. 411.

sition and for reasons that have been made clear. To the men who made the crossings that morning it must have seemed providential that the enemy had not taken advantage of banks—rising twelve feet perpendicular from the shores—to pour a devastating fire upon those attempting to ford the stream, some three hundred yards in breadth at the points selected. At four o'clock St. Clair's pioneers marched, followed by the rest of the army, which was delayed in getting the heavy artillery across the river and back again. But by early afternoon the whole army was safely back on the right bank and the soldiers, in the words of one of them,

. . . hugg's themselves with joy at our Good Luck in having surmounted our greatest Difficultys. . . .[29]

The taking of Fort Duquesne now seemed assured.

Gage was once again ordered to advance along the trail until three o'clock, when in the more open country to the north—perhaps in one of the areas the French had cleared for field crops—camp would be struck for the day. The trail wound past Frazier's trading house, through a fairly dense growth of trees up along a ridge only some twenty rods in width, into a region which was more open and yet which was flanked on either side by ravines with a dense undergrowth and dominated by a hill likewise covered with underbrush rising from the ravine on the right.[30] Most of the usual precautions were observed. Scouts moved ahead, followed after an interval of some two hundred yards by the vanguard and then the main body of Gage's command protected by flank guards. After these came the pioneers clearing the way for the artillery carriages and the wagons, followed by the gunners with two six-pounders and the ammunition and tool wagons, likewise protected by rear as well as flank guards. After another interval of a quarter of a mile came the main body of troops, including the general's guard, the heavy artillery, the remainder of the wagons, and a herd of cattle. Here at last but three leagues from Fort Duquesne was the place where the enemy would give battle and here the British need of adequate Indian support became painfully apparent.[31]

[29] Royal Engineer Harry Gordon, "Journal of Proceedings from Willes's Creek to the Monongahela," Pargellis, *op. cit.*, pp. 105–6.

[30] One of the most careful studies of the terrain of the battlefield was made by J. K. Lacock in his article, "Braddock's Road" (*Pa. Mag. of Hist. and Biog.*, XXXVIII, 1–38). After the most painstaking examination, he wrote that "the contour of the road over which the line of march extended on the day of the battle was found to be so much altered that even the slightest traces of its course were not perceptible." We are therefore obliged to rely upon contemporary accounts.

[31] The court of inquiry that reported upon the disaster gives as one of the three causes: "The Want of Indians or other irregulars to give timely Notice of the Enemy's

Where were the Catawba, so held in dread by the very Indians living about the forks who had gone to Contrecœur only the day before to express their willingness to help the French destroy the approaching army?[32] Where were the Cherokee, who, together with the Catawba, had stealthily passed and repassed this very spot endless times bent on their deadly missions against the Northern Indians—over the trail that, significantly, was called the Catawba-Cherokee Path? One may affirm with confidence that had Dinwiddie been able to provide only half the number of these Southern Indians that he had promised and that were available, the history of this fatal July 9 would have been very different. For they could have been in possession of the very ravines and the commanding eminence from out of the mystery of which death spoke alike to British grenadier and Virginia rifleman. Lacking this support, there remained as a protection the maintenance of all those safeguards that had preserved the army thus far from surprise and serious attack on its difficult and dangerous march.

It will be noted that when the army on June 19 passed over the Little Crossings on the upper waters of Castleman's River and was obliged to skirt a high mountain, Colonel Gage, leading the vanguard, on his own responsibility very properly ordered a detachment to occupy it; when Braddock moved up with the main force, he in turn, as has been mentioned already, posted a hundred soldiers on it, who remained there until his artillery train and wagons had safely passed by. On the 8th of July similar precautions were observed, as has been emphasized, when the army moved toward the Monongahela down Long Run. But Gage, after his successful crossing and recrossing of that river, was apparently lulled into a false sense of security. Before the attack took place he passed by a dominating hill without bothering to secure it with his vanguard, as did the pioneers under Sir John St. Clair who followed him. Once the opportunity was missed thus to secure the army, it never returned.

When Beaujeu with his French and Indians moving rapidly along the trail came into view, the advanced British scouts fell back upon the van-

---

Approach . . ." (*Corresp. of William Shirley*, II, 313). George Croghan, the famous Pennsylvania Indian trader, declared after the defeat that he was "yet of opinion that had we had fifty Indians instead of eight, that we might in a great measure have prevented the surprise, that day of our unhappy defeat" ("Journal to the Ohio," Du Simitiere Mss., Library Company of Philadelphia).

[32] In a letter dated July 29, 1754, Captain Stobo, one of the two hostages that Washington had given to the French at Fort Necessity, wrote from Fort Duquesne to Governor James Hamilton: "I wish a Peace may be made up between the Catawbas and the nations here; they [the Ohio Indians] are much afraid of them [the Catawba]" (*Pa. Col. Rec.*, VI, 141-2).

guard of grenadiers. The latter formed a skirmish-line and proceeded to open fire. They were soon joined by the gunners with their six-pounders. Beaujeu fell mortally wounded and many of the Canadian militia fled. But Captain Dumas now took over command. In an instant his regular troops and the Indians divided, some racing through the trees to the right and others to the left of the British vanguard. Faced now by a cross-fire delivered under cover of the trees, Gage could have pushed forward and thereby gained the still more open ground and in turn placed the enemy at a serious disadvantage, not only by finding itself ultimately enveloped in the cross-fire of the vanguard and the main body of the British army but by having a force between it and Fort Duquesne. Instead he decided to retreat—his second major error. For in falling back he came within the range of fire of the Indians and French who had poured into the ravines that he had already passed and who also concentrated in force upon the hill that he had also passed without seizing and from which they now "did the greatest Execution on the King's Troops."

But this was not the only serious consequence of Gage's retrograde movement; for he helped mightily to throw into confusion the large detachment immediately sent forward by Braddock to support him. According to Orme, when the firing was heard, the general,

> . . . imagining the advanced parties were very warmly attacked, and being willing to free himself from the incumbrance of the baggage, ordered Lieutenant Colonel Burton to re-enforce them with the vanguard [that is, the vanguard of the main body], and the line to halt. According to this disposition, eight hundred men were detached from the line, free from all embarrassments, and four hundred were left for the defence of the Artillery and baggage, posted in such a manner as to secure them from any attack or insults.[33]

Burton, as he moved forward, sensed the necessity of securing immediate possession of the hill on the right of the road and was making preparations to carry it by assault when the retreating troops of the advance helped to plunge his own command into confusion.[34] This confusion seems to have

---

[33] Orme's "Journal," Sargent, *op. cit.*, p. 354.

[34] This was denied in an "Advertisement" printed in the *Pennsylvania Gazette* of September 4, 1755. Dr. Stanley M. Pargellis in his important article "Braddock's Defeat" (*American Historical Review*, XLI, 251-9) develops and supports the thesis that the battle was lost not because the soldiers did not fight in frontier fashion, not that they displayed cowardice, but on account of the failure of the officers to measure up to their responsibilities and to apply sound tactical principles already laid down in Bland's *Treatise of Military Discipline*. His blame is particularly directed against Braddock rather than against Gage. However, on March 27 Braddock issued permanent orders for the conduct of "firings" and platoons in connection with the cam-

become hopeless when, in addition to the appearance of the retreating troops, which made proper manœuvring of his own force impossible upon a narrow twelve-foot road already swarming with soldiers, the French and Indians now brought his command also under a galling cross-fire, which was the more deadly in its demoralizing effects in that the enemy was hidden, while his troops were in an exposed position in the roadway running along the ridge. What also added immeasurably to the confusion was the forward movement of the baggage train. This, when a quarter of a mile from the scene of action, was ordered to halt by Braddock.

As the firing continued, Braddock rode forward, leaving Sir Peter Halkett in charge of the convoy. Why Sir Peter permitted the convoy to continue along the road in face of a positive command to halt cannot be understood. But when it was brought to a stop, it was planted squarely against Burton's soldiers, who had of course left it in order to be free to manœuvre. Under these trying conditions—with the shrieking of six hundred Indians, the staccato of musketry, the roar of cannon, and the cries of the wounded and dying soldiers all creating a terrifying symphony of death—the only possibility of snatching success from the prospect of total defeat lay in stoically accepting the necessary losses and pushing forward resolutely until the more open country that lay ahead had been reached.[35] This Braddock apparently sought to do, but in vain. For he found himself now in possession of a milling mass of disorganized soldiers firing aimlessly without seeing an enemy. Desperately he tried to drive them back into proper formation with the flat of his sword; desperately he sought to urge them forward. Standards were raised to rally the soldiers; officers responded only to be stricken down as they came out into the open on the flanks. Five horses were shot out from under the general as he recklessly exposed himself before he received his fatal wound and before the battle was lost and the once proud little army with banners flying had become mere hunted fugitives, with most of its officers either dead or wounded.

---

paign (*Major-General Edward Braddock's Orderly Books from February 26 to June 17, 1755* [Cumberland, Md., 1878], pp. v–vi) that were manifestly based upon Bland's *Treatise*. Burton, it appears, attempted to carry out these orders in moving forward from the baggage train, but could not execute the required formation on account of the retrograde movement of Gage's troops and those of St. Clair.

[35] When Lieutenant Colonel Smith was caught by the Minute Men's cross-fire in his retreat from Concord in 1775, in pushing ahead he did the only thing that was practicable under the circumstances. Had he attempted to halt and fight as the colonials were fighting, it is more than likely that his detachment would have been completely decimated.

As to the easy assumption made by many writers in that day and subsequently that the field could have been won had the Virginia and other troops been encouraged to post themselves behind trees and fire at will, this will not bear the test of critical analysis. It would seem that many, if not most, of those who were killed or wounded were shot, not by the enemy that they faced, but by the enemy behind them, who, by their murderous cross-fire, had every advantage in the engagement, which lasted between two and three hours before the British forces fled in wild panic—an engagement that exacted, incidentally, a particularly heavy toll of those who, leaving the ranks, sought under the given conditions to fight in typical backwoodsman style. Of 1,373 non-commissioned officers and privates but 459 were neither killed nor wounded; of 86 officers, but 23.[36] The Virginians, placed as flank guards, were sadly decimated, not only by the fire of the enemy but also, it would appear, by that of the British regulars, blinded by fear and also by the smoke of battle. In the words of Washington:

Our poor Virginians behaved like men, and died like soldiers; for I believe that out of three companies that were there that day, scarce thirty were left alive.

He thereupon asserted:

In short the dastardly behavior of the English soldiers exposed all those who were inclined to do their duty to almost certain death. It is imagined (I believe with great justice, too) that two-thirds of both killed and wounded received their shots from our own cowardly dogs of soldiers, who gathered themselves in a body, contrary to orders, ten and twelve deep, would then level, fire, and shoot down the men before them.[37]

Although the movements of the army after the disaster at the Monongahela will be considered in a subsequent chapter, it may here be said that out of the defeat developed many bitter controversies. Such men as Sir John St. Clair and Colonel Dunbar and their supporters cast the chief

[36] "A list . . . of those killed and wounded, in the Action on the Banks of the Monongahela, 9 July, 1755," C.O. 5:46.

[37] C.O. 5:46. The *Public Advertiser* (London) of August 27, 1755 in its account of the battle quotes the following from a letter from Wills Creek on July 10: "It is rumoured that most of the Officers were killed by the European Troops firing upon them when they endeavoured to rally them; and that very few of our Men were killed by the Enemy; in short that a *full* Account of this Action would disclose such a Scene as was never seen before in our nor perhaps in any other Army." Statements of this type must be placed in the same category as those of such men as Fossit and Allison about the shooting of Braddock.

blame for it upon the general.[38] Their charges involved his decision—
taken after securing Washington's advice, which he acted upon—to separate his army and push forward at maximum speed with a picked detachment. Dunbar, left behind with most of the convoy, bitterly resented
being placed in this position. He and St. Clair favoured the movement of
the whole army in one body; the latter also strongly favoured taking time
to build blockhouses and other defences at strategic points, which would
have delayed the advance upon Fort Duquesne doubtless until the fall.[39]
The strategic move strongly recommended by Washington may have
been unsound, but many strong arguments can be advanced in support of
it. He himself, after due reflection upon the disaster, arrived at conclusions that the historian would do well to ponder. Writing from Mount
Vernon on August 14, 1755, soon after his return from the scene of the
battle, in referring to the difficult position of any commanding officer,
but obviously with Braddock in mind, he notes:

> . . . how little credit is given to a Commander, who perhaps after a defeat, in
> relating the cause justly lays the blame on some individual whose cowardly
> behav'r betray'd the whole to ruin; how little does the World consider the
> Circumstances, and how apt are Mankind to level their vindictive Censures
> against the unfortunate Chief, who perhaps merited least of the blame.[40]

---

[38] For letters written by St. Clair, Dunbar, and others, including Captain Orme,
see Pargellis, *Military Affairs in North America, 1748–1765*, pp. 98–124.

[39] The Forbes expedition did not arrive at the fort until the latter part of November.

[40] *Writings of Washington* (ed. Fitzpatrick), I, 161.

Monongahela
(July 9–31, 1755)

DOUGLAS SOUTHALL FREEMAN

IT IS not in the heart of man, aroused from deep sleep at 2 o'clock in the morning, to have cheer or conscious, pulsing courage; but when the British camp began to stir at that hour on the 9th of July, 1755, there was confidence as well as expectancy in the minds of those who knew the plan for crossing the Monongahela and marching on Fort Duquesne. "The British gentlemen," one provincial officer wrote afterward, "were confident they would never be attacked and would have laid any odds that they never should [be] until they came before the fort—yea some went further and were of the opinion that we should hear the explosion of the French fort blown up and destroyed before we approached it."[1] Careful officers realized, of course, that the advance of the column might be disputed at one ford or the other. Even soldiers of cautious mind felt that if the troops, the artillery and the wagons could get across the Monongahela unresisted, the remainder of the campaign would be easy.

George's responsibility was neither for strategy nor for tactics but for being mounted and afield on the day of all days in his life of twenty-three years. His fever and his pain were gone; but they had left him with his muscles so weakened that he did not know whether he could endure the jolt of a fast-moving horse. He determined to try it, and, to lessen his ordeal, he procured cushions and tied them into his saddle. While George was making his arrangements,[2] Lieutenant Colonel Gage started with

[1] *Stephen-Hardwicke*, loc. cit.
[2] Cf. 29 *G.W.*, 42.

about 350 men[3] and two six-pounder cannon to cross the fords and then to take position beyond the second of them in order to cover the advance of the army.[4] At 4 o'clock, Sir John St. Clair followed the same route with 250 carpenters and pioneers and their wagons.[5] An hour later Braddock's main force took the road. Directly under his charge were the remaining troops, about 750 all told,[6] most of the vehicles, the pack animals, the cattle to be slaughtered for food, and the greater part of the artillery —four twelve-pounders on traveling carriages with limbers, four eight-inch howitzers similarly equipped, and three cohorn mortars.[7]

Starting this mixed column was such slow work that watches pointed to 8 o'clock when Braddock reached the first crossing. As George splashed through the upper ford on his horse, he noticed how low the water was because of the drought that had parched Pennsylvania, Maryland and Virginia.[8] At the level then prevailing, passage of the river was easy. When it had been completed, Braddock formed his line of march and set off, in the footprints of Gage's and St. Clair's men, down a road that had been cut roughly parallel to the stream.[9] The General, George and the others had proceeded a mile only when a messenger brought fine news: Colonel Gage presented his compliments to His Excellency and begged to report that he had completed the second crossing without encountering opposition, and had taken position as ordered, on the right bank where his guns commanded the lower ford.[10] En route to the first shallow, Gage had flushed thirty Indians, who had made off.[11] At the second crossing the men of the advance guard had noticed that the water

[3] The exact strength of this advanced party is variously given. Orme, *op. cit.*, 352–53, stated that it was to consist of two Companies of grenadiers, plus 160 troops of the line, Gates's New York Company (100 enlisted men), and the men in charge of the six-pounders—a total of 460, less the day's absentees. A figure of 300 was given by the engineer, Harry Gordon, in a letter of July 23, 1755, to an unnamed correspondent. This document, containing perhaps the clearest account of the day's events, is printed in *Pargellis*, 104–09.

[4] Orme to Sharpe, July 18, 1755; 1 *Sharpe*, 253. Substantially the same letter was addressed by Orme to several colonial officials. See Pargellis, "Braddock's Defeat," 41 *A.H.R.*, 255, n. 4. These letters and Orme's journal are among the basic sources on the campaign; but, to repeat, Orme was not accurate concerning dates, numbers and hours.

[5] 1 *Sharpe*, 253; *Orme*, 353.

[6] Based on the assumption that the entire force was 1459.

[7] *Pargellis*, 97; unknown French writer in 20 *Penn. Mag.*, 409–11; 3 *Col. MMS rel. à la Nouvelle-France*, 544.

[8] 29 *G.W.*, 42.

[9] *Orme*, 353.

[10] *Orme*, 354.

[11] *Seaman*, Sargent, 384.

still was muddy, as if there had been recent passing, and they had seen many footprints on the river bank.[12] If these particulars were reported to Braddock, no importance was attached to them.

The march along the left bank continued without incident until, at length, the head of the column halted at a point slightly downstream from the mouth of Turtle Creek, which flowed into the Monongahela from the opposite side. As George and his companions looked, they saw on the other bank a sandy[13] bluff about twelve feet high through which St. Clair's men busily were cutting an incline at the point chosen for the passage of the troops.[14] The situation was precisely as the messenger had reported: both the advanced parties were safely across the river at the place where a vigilant and courageous enemy might have repelled them. "Men hugged themselves with joy," one observer wrote, "at our good luck in having surmounted our greatest difficulties."[15] Braddock proceeded, in spite of this clear advantage, to do what his English and German seniors had said an officer should do in a like situation: he ordered all the vehicles drawn up properly on the bank and he posted pickets on the higher ground behind him.[16] Then he, his staff and his line officers had opportunity of examining the country ahead of them as far as it was visible from their position. George had never been on the left bank of the Monongahela, but he had some exciting memories of the side to which he was looking. Almost directly across the river from him was Frazier's trading post and gun shop to which he had come with Christopher Gist and their small party, on the 22nd of November, 1753, while he was carrying the message of Dinwiddie to Fort Le Boeuf.[17] It had been to Frazier's, too, that he and Gist had returned at the end of December, that same year, after their desperate struggle with the ice of the Allegheny.[18] Only nineteen months previously that had been . . . and now the wintry landscape had all turned to verdure . . . and the river bank was crowded with the coats and the cannon of the King.

Downstream from Frazier's, behind the low bluff, the advance of the army was to be through rising ground for a mile or more. Near the river was a fringe of heavy underbrush that extended northward for about 400

[12] Dulany's News Letter, 3 *Penn. Mag.*, 17.
[13] *Pargellis*, 108.
[14] *Orme*, 354.
[15] Gordon in *Pargellis*, 106.
[16] *Orme*, 354.
[17] See *supra*, Vol. I, p. 286.
[18] *Ibid.*

yards.[19] Beyond that elevation could be seen both northward and to the West. There, too, was a forest of large trees less densely set than in many parts of the country through which the expedition had passed.[20] If the landscape was cut by any deep ravines or watercourses, these were not visible.

Inspection was as deliberate as the prospect was beautiful. Completion of the passageway through the bluff occupied St. Clair's men until almost 2 P.M. When the incline at last was ready, Braddock sent Captain Morris[21] to order Gage and St. Clair to start down the ridge with their detachments and to open a road as they advanced. They were instructed to march until 3 o'clock, with the inference that the entire column would then be across the river and would be ready to bivouac for the final advance the next day on Fort Duquesne. The distance from the proposed halting place to the junction of the rivers would not be more than seven miles, no farther than the troops easily could move between suns in a country that presented no great natural obstacle.[22]

Officers on the left bank soon could see Gage's and St. Clair's men leave their posts and disappear. After the last of the advanced parties had cleared the other side of the ford, Braddock gave the word for his column to cross. It was easily and flawlessly done—in George's eyes the most thrilling sight of his entire life.[23] As the men came up the incline from the river, they took their place in the line of march, which now was complete. In front, mounting the ridge, were the guides and a few of Stewart's Company of Virginia light horse. Behind them was the engineer who was marking the route and blazing the trees that had to be felled to provide a roadway. His task was not difficult. The woods were so open that a vehicle could be driven almost anywhere among the trees. Besides, orders were to prepare a twelve-foot road—no wider. All that was needed now, in the judgment of the responsible officers, was room enough for the guns and the wagons. The men could look after themselves.[24]

As the engineer stopped at intervals and hacked the bark, Gage's cov-

[19] On this, the language of Sinclair (*Pargellis*, 103) and of Orme (*op. cit.*, 355) is not altogether clear. The underbrush, which both of them styled "underwood," might have extended downstream, instead of back from the stream, for a quarter of a mile, but the interpretation given in the text seems more probable.
[20] *Orme*, 355; *Pargellis*, 103, 117. The elevation at the highest point of this ground is about 340 feet above that of the opposite bank.
[21] *Pargellis*, 103.
[22] *Orme*, 385.
[23] 2 *Sparks*, 469.
[24] *Pargellis*, 103, 117.

ering party followed in files four deep. On the flanks were the grenadier Companies, spread in parties of twenty men, each under a Sergeant. Next were the carpenters and pioneers, and then the two six-pounders with the ammunition wagon and a guard. Together, these men were the advanced force. Closing on them now was Lieutenant Colonel Burton with the vanguard, most of the wagons and part of the guns. The rearguard, with the remainder of the cannon, was under Col. Sir Peter Halkett.[25] If the proper intervals were being observed, everything was in the best style of the regular establishment. Braddock would not have been ashamed to have organized such a march in Flanders or to have had it made while even His Royal Highness, the Duke of Cumberland, was observing it.

As the rear of the column cleared the curve in the road near Frazier's trading post and started northwestward, George rode forward with the General and the staff. All were in high spirits. Gage was then about three-quarters of a mile beyond the ford;[26] from his front to the last man of the rearguard, the distance was about 1900 yards. Whether this was too great a length of column for advance in the enemy's country or too compact a column for maneuver in the event of attack, no officer troubled himself to consider. It scarcely mattered. If the French had intended to resist the British, they would have done so in the early morning, and at the fords, not beyond on the direct way to the fort.

Half-past two o'clock and close to 1500 men confidently in motion; then, suddenly, the sound of firing from the front, the roll of a volley, more of scattered, heavy fire, another volley! George was stiff in the saddle at the first crash. So was every officer. The troops tightened their grip on their muskets and looked toward their Captains. Braddock listened intently: the fire, he thought, was that of hostile parties heavily engaged. Halt the column; let one of the young aides go forward and find out what was happening.[27]

Harry Gordon, the engineer, had ridden ahead of the advanced guard to find the guides, and he had been looking for them when they had hurried back and had reported the enemy close at hand. As the engineer peered through the open forest ahead of him, he had seen about 300 men, French and Indians, approaching on the run. Most of them were stripped; all were ready for action. At their head was an officer who wore a piece

---

[25] *Pargellis*, 106; *Orme*, 355; *Seaman*, Sargent, 385. Full details of the line of march, not required for the present narrative, will be found in the familiar sketches by Patrick Mackellar. . . .

[26] 1 *Sharpe*, 268.

[27] The aide sent to the front probably was Shirley.

of decorative armor at his neck.[28] He, too, was looking vigilantly ahead, but he had not yet discovered the British.[29] A little later, when the French commander had caught a glimpse of the grenadiers, he had motioned with his arms to right and to left. His men then had divided and had begun to encircle the head and the flanks of the British column.[30]

The hideous Indian warwhoop swelled through the woods and froze the blood of the soldiers who never before had heard that sound. Farther from the front but within earshot, the yell of an invisible enemy was enough to make ignorant men think they had marched into a den of demons.[31] After their first instant of startled fright, the grenadiers delivered a volley and then loaded and fired again. Some of their bullets brought down the conspicuous French officers and a number of Indians.[32] The reply of the attacking force was strong enough to swell the volume of fire the column heard,[33] but the redmen and their white comrades did not intend to form line of battle and exchange volleys with the British in the woods. Before most of the English soldiers saw a single rifleman, the French and Indians disappeared, quickly and mysteriously. The hair-raising whoops continued. Down both flanks the fire spread. Soon it began to strike the British from the high ground on the right of the halted column.[34] All except one of the English flanking parties ran in;[35] one Com-

---

[28] A gorget.

[29] Gordon, Washington and others insisted that the attacking force did not exceed 300 men (cf. *Pargellis*, 106; 1 *G.W.*, 147, 151), but this figure was too low. Included in the column of attack were seventy-two French, 146 Canadians and 637 Indians, a total of 855, according to the Relation depuis le Départ des Trouppes de Québec; Arch de Guerre, photostat, Canadian Arch., Ottawa. Cf. Sargent, *op. cit.*, 223, with notice of other estimates. The Relation du Combat, *loc. cit.*, gives the number as 133 French, 100 Canadians and 600 savages, total 833. Relation de la Bataille du Fort duQuesne, Paris, Aff. Etra. Mém. et Docts., France, 535, p. 110, spoke of "200 youths of great zeal, and at most 600 savages . . ." Gipson, *op. cit.*, 91, counted 108 regulars, including officers, and 146 Canadian militia. For another early French estimate of 250 Canadians and 650 Indians, see Relation de l'action . . . de 9e Juillet . . . *Cumberland Papers*, Box 46–28; Windsor Castle. Cf., also, *Penn. Gazette*, Jan. 8, 1756. The *Gentleman's Mag.*, August, 1755, p. 378, asserted that the French employed 1500 regulars, 600 irregulars and a "considerable number of Indians," but in its September issue, p. 426, the publication stated, on the mistaken assurance of private letters, that "no French troops were present."

[30] *Pargellis*, 106; *Seaman*, Sargent, 387.

[31] 29 *G.W.*, 42. Cf. Relation du Combat, *loc. cit.*: "les cris des Sauvages, dont les bois retentissoient, porterent l'épouvante dans les coeurs des ennemis."

[32] According to a French report in *Penn. Gazette*, Jan. 8, 1756, the number was fifteen Indians and four Canadians, as well as the commander of the force, Daniel Liénard Beaujeu, and two junior officers.

[33] For the heaviness of the fire see the contemporary account in 11 *Penn. Mag.*, 94.

[34] *Pargellis*, 116. Contemporary British and colonial writers did not always convey the same meaning when they spoke of "right" and "left" in the battle of the Monongahela. Officers near the front often used the terms with reference to the head of the

pany of grenadiers and one of carpenters were in danger of being cut off.[36] Almost before the officers could shout their commands, the whole of the advanced force fell back fifty or sixty yards.

There by pleas and threats and by riding among the bewildered troops, the Captains and Lieutenants were able to restore a confused line,[37] but it was for a few minutes only. Bulking above the heads of the crouching troops, the mounted leaders were ideal targets for the invisible marksmen. Down the officers tumbled from their steeds, dead or wounded. Most of those who escaped with their lives lost their horses.[38] Colonel Gage kept his saddle, but he found few subordinates to help him rally men who had no idea how to fight an enemy they could not see. Occasionally, through the thickening smoke, a soldier might get a momentary glimpse of a red face that appeared from behind a large tree. Sometimes, too, if a Briton happened to look in the proper direction at the right moment, he observed a smoke-puff from the ground where an Indian lay hidden in the grass.[39] That was all, except for the rattle of muskets, the whoop, and the thud of the body of man after man.

Now Sir John St. Clair rode up to ascertain what was happening—and got the information in the form of a bullet through his body. He managed to save himself from falling and, though losing blood fast, he returned to his own command and called on Polson's carpenters and on Peyroney's rangers—both of them Virginia commands—to cover the two six-pounders[40] which, with their teams and ammunition-wagon, were between St. Clair's men and his wagons.[41]

In rear of what had been the right flank of the marching column the fire was heavier every minute. Surviving officers who could see anything beyond the smoke-cloud realized soon that the Indians and the Canadians were firing from the hillside to the North of the road that had been cut

column as it was at the moment of attack. Right to them was the northern flank of a front that was facing roughly westward. Later in the action, when the entire column was halted, some of the participants thought of the front as extending from West to East with the front to the North. So considered, the advanced guard was the left-flank element and the rearguard the right. In the present narrative, "the right" and "the left" are employed as those flanks were until the battle front shifted. Notice then is given that "right" spreads East and "left" is toward the West.

[35] *Orme*, 355.
[36] *Seaman*, Sargent, 385.
[37] *Pargellis*, 106.
[38] Franklin, *Autobiography* (Bigelow ed.), 272.
[39] 29 *G.W.*, 42; *Stephen-Hardwicke*.
[40] *Pargellis*, 103. This is St. Clair's own account. As printed, Peyroney's name is Periwee, but there can be no doubt of the identification.
[41] See "F" in Mackellar's first sketch following p. 81.

through the forest.[42] Riflemen concealed there could cross fire with that of savages who had slipped down Gage's left, between the road and the river.[43] With front and both flanks thus enveloped, the British now were within a half-moon[44] of yelling adversaries. The accurate fire of the enemy already was sweeping the whole of the ground occupied by Gage and more and more, every minute, of that held by St. Clair.

Suddenly the rumor spread that the French and Indians were attacking the baggage train.[45] Stunned men under triple fire from an unseen foe did not stop to ask whether the rumor had probability. They concluded instantly that if the enemy was closing on their rear, they soon would be surrounded, scalped, massacred. With one impulse, Gage's men ran eastward, carried St. Clair's workers along, abandoned the two six-pounders —and at a distance of 300 yards stumbled into the uncertain files of Burton's vanguard which, by Braddock's order, had been advancing to their support up the twelve-foot road.[46]

Burton and his officers had halted their men because of the fire from the side of the hill to the North. Already these troops of the van were disturbed and confused, as Gage's and St. Clair's soldiers had been, by the viciousness of fire from invisible, whooping Indians; but the commanders had succeeded partially in getting some of them to form a line, facing North, for an assault on the hill. At the time, the three twelve-pounders with Burton's command were being placed South of the road to deal with the enemy on the side nearer the Monongahela.[47] Burton, in a word, was drawing a confused line along the road, from West to East. With his front to the North, his rear would be exposed to attack from the South if the cannon there could not be used to drive off the enemy. Gage and St. Clair had been perpendicular to the road, with the front to the West. When, therefore, the men of their advanced parties ran back eastward through the woods and reached the vanguard, the new left flank of Burton was rolled up. The line, if it could be so styled, was temporarily a capital T laid on its side, with the top to the West. Then, in their dismay, the remnant of Gage's and of St. Clair's troops began quickly to pull in, so to say, the two sides of the top of the bar until, in a matter of minutes,

[42] The crest of this hill has now (1948) an elevation of 1240 feet.
[43] *Pargellis*, 106.
[44] *Ibid.*, 116.
[45] *Pargellis*, 106.
[46] *Pargellis*, 107; 1 *Sharpe*, 253. Gage or one of his friends anonymously insisted that Burton's men already were "in confusion." See *Penn. Gazette*, Sept. 4, 1755.
[47] *Orme*, 355; Mackellar's sketch No. 2, *loc. cit.*

the front was like a half-opened umbrella lying in the road with the tip pointing toward Fort Duquesne.

Tactically, this opening second phase of the battle would have been a difficult one to correct had like confusion of ranks and direction occurred on a drillfield through the blunder of an incompetent Colonel. As it was, under that persistent fire—from the North, from the West and from the South—the situation was completely beyond the control of the few officers who remained on horseback.[48]

Now Braddock rode up, attended by George.[49] The General had waited only a few minutes at the point where he had heard the first fire and had halted the column. Then, as the continued rattle of muskets had convinced him the action was serious, he had started for the front. At first he was half paralyzed by the indescribable confusion and the unfamiliar ground. Instead of a line, he found a mass of men, ten or twelve deep, who were firing at random, and were shooting many of their comrades in the back.[50] "They kept," said Adam Stephen afterward, "in a mere huddle . . ."[51] Braddock could not decide, on the instant, what to do or how to do it. While he hesitated, St. Clair made his way through the mad, milling press of men and called to the General for God's sake to take the northern hill in order to keep the army from being surrounded. Before the Quartermaster could say more to explain the situation, he lost consciousness because of his wound.[52]

Capt. Thomas Waggener, a veteran of Fort Necessity, had kept his men together and now he undertook to lead them up the hill to the trunk of a great fallen tree that he thought he could use as a parapet. He succeeded in getting there with the loss of three men only, but to his amazement he found himself subjected to the fire of British who mistook his Company for French. Some of the regular officers, seeing his movement, concluded that he and his soldiers were attempting to run away, and they discouraged those who were willing to reenforce him. In getting back under fire,

[48] *Orme*, 355; 1 *Sharpe*, 253.
[49] Shirley probably had been killed before this time by a bullet through his head (1 *Sharpe* 253; *Orme*, P.R.O., C.O. 5:46, p. 68–73), and Morris and Orme in all likelihood had received their disabling wounds, but all that is known of the time of these casualties is that they occurred "early in the engagement" (Washington to his mother [July 18, 1755], 1 *G.W.*, 151). Robert Dobson, senior Captain of the 48th, and a favorite of Braddock's, was assigned as temporary aide after Orme was wounded (*Pargellis*, 119; Sargent, *op. cit.*, 211; 2 *Shirley*, 321).
[50] Washington thought this responsible for two-thirds of the casualties (1 *G.W.*, 150).
[51] *Stephen-Hardwicke*.
[52] *Pargellis*, 103.

the Captain lost all except thirty of his men.[53] George, like Waggener, felt that the high ground could be taken and the enemy driven off, and he appealed to the General to permit him to collect the provincial troops and to send them against the hill in the Indian manner. Braddock merely shook his bewildered head.[54]

The British of the advanced force and of the van crowded more and more closely together by this time, and they fired, for the most part, in aimless confusion. Here and there, a courageous officer was able to keep a grip on a few score men and to give direction to their fire. Presently, too, some of Halkett's troops pushed up the road, but in a few minutes these reenforcements lost heart and added new disorder on the right.[55] Sir Peter Halkett himself was killed early;[56] his junior officers and his soldiers, like those already engaged, could do nothing but load and fire, load and fire. The maddening thing about it was that while man after man dropped with a groan or a dying gasp, most of the troops still could not tell where their enemies were. To this moment of the fight, some British soldiers had not seen a single Frenchman or Indian. If a redman showed himself at all, he might dash out, scalp some dead or wounded soldier, and leap back behind a tree or drop into the concealing grass.[57] This hideous sight and the baffling, futile character of the battle were beginning to demoralize the British. Some, but by no means all, the provincials tried to fight the Indians in their own way.[58]

Braddock at last realized that the hill must be wrested from the savages and that the two six-pounders must be recaptured before they were turned against the bleeding British crowded in the road. He sent George off to find officers and to tell them to organize one party of 150 to charge up the hill and another party of like size to recover the cannon. In de-

---

[53] This is one of the few incidents of the battle concerning which some reservation has to be made. Waggener is identified as commander by Thomas Burd in a letter of July 25, 1755, printed in Watson's *Annals of Philadelphia and Penn. in the Olden Time*, v. 2, p. 139, but the letter echoes much rumor along with some fact. Burd's statement manifestly is incorrect in crediting Waggener with eighty men. None of the Virginia Companies had an enlisted strength above fifty. Cf. *Orme*, 327–29. Washington, writing in 1786, mentioned an advance of "some of the irregulars (as they were called) without direction . . ." (29 *G.W.*, 43). While it is altogether probable that this was Waggener's effort, there is the possibility of error in the confusion of this and some unrecorded attempt to storm the hill.

[54] Washington's restrained later language (1786) was "the propriety of it was not seen until it was too late for execution" (29 *G.W.*, 43).

[55] 29 *G.W.*, 43.

[56] 1 *Sharpe*, 253.

[57] 1 *Sharpe*, 263, 268; *Pargellis*, 111, 117; *Seaman*, Sargent, 386.

[58] 1 *G.W.*, 151; 1 *Entick*, 147; *Stephen-Hardwicke*.

livering these orders, George managed to stay in his saddle despite his weakness. During the action, he had two horses shot under him, but he found another and skillfully made his way through the woods. His tall figure was a mark for hidden riflemen. One of them sent a bullet through his hat; another, a third, and still another slit his uniform with hot lead.[59] He was conspicuous, in the generous words of the wounded Orme, for "the greatest courage and resolution"[60] and, happily, thus far was unscathed.

While George was trying to find Company officers and to get them to attack the hill and recover the guns, Braddock was doing the same thing. Again and again he undertook to rally the men, to form a line and to lead them against the hidden enemy and the high ground North of the road. Nothing could be done. The survivors would not budge from the huddle.[61] At last, in desperation, Braddock decided to withdraw to the right and East in order to cover his wagons and to take from them provisions for use in event he had to leave the field altogether.[62] The General did not proceed far with this shift. Already five bullets had struck one or another of the horses he had ridden; now it was his turn. A missile crashed through his right arm and penetrated his lungs.[63] After he was placed on the ground by the men near him, he remained conscious, but, of course, could not attempt to direct the withdrawal to the wagons which were strung out along the road.

Few of the officers received the order to cover the vehicles, and consequently they continued to exhort the men to attack from the ground where they were crowded together. Lieutenant Colonel Burton, with much spirit, succeeded in getting about 100 soldiers of the 48th Regiment

[59] 1 *G.W.*, 151; 29 *G.W.*, 43.

[60] Cf. 1 *Sharpe*, 253.

[61] Cf. 1 *Sharpe*, 253.

[62] *Orme*, 356; Report of Dunbar and Gage on the Court of Inquiry, 2 *Shirley*, 312. This incident of the battle cannot be timed precisely. Orme placed it before the events presently to be described in the text. Dunbar and Gage did not relate it to any occurrence prior to the climax of the battle. Almost certainly the order was given by Braddock himself and was not distributed generally, but a caveat is necessary.

[63] 1 *Sharpe*, 253. The absurd, familiar story has often been printed that he was shot deliberately by an American, who was infuriated when Braddock killed the man's brother with a sword stroke for alleged skulking. Lowdermilk (*op. cit.*, 177–78) was inclined uncritically to accept this yarn, though Sargent (*op. cit.*, 245 ff) wholly discredited it. Another tradition of the wounding of Braddock (cited in *Lowdermilk*, 162) was that Orme vainly offered sixty guineas to anyone who would carry Braddock from the field. Captain Robert Stewart of the Virginia Troop of light horse, with another officer and Braddock's servant, are said to have taken him off in his own sash, which they unwrapped from around his waist.

to form in line, and then he gave command for a charge up the hill. He led it gallantly, his men followed courageously part of the way to the crest—and then drifted to the right and fell back to the road. The reason was that Burton had received a wound. Without him, the men would not advance.[64] Other officers undertook to do what Burton, for all his effort, had been unable to accomplish. Sometimes in small groups, they started up the grade in the hope their men would attend, but they could not induce the dazed infantry to venture from the road.[65] Other leaders individually stepped out and appealed to their soldiers—all to no purpose. Officers, said Orme, were "absolutely sacrificed."[66]

The situation now was desperate but not altogether hopeless. Two hundred men were held together by uninjured commanders and by officers returning from the surgeons with bandaged wounds. These troops, keeping their heads, still were able to hold the enemy at a distance, though they were deaf to every order to mount the eminence or to rush out and put the six-pounders into action.[67] On the extreme right, also, there was organized resistance without any attempt at a counter-stroke. The Captain on this flank, which had been the rearguard, had time to dispose his men carefully before the redmen appeared. By posting the troops behind trees, he beat off the scattered savages with some loss. No large number of Indians penetrated that far eastward.[68]

While these centres of resistance remained, those officers who had received the order to withdraw to the wagons undertook to do so and to carry their commands with them. They were powerless. The men in the road stayed where they were and continued their blind fire. Orders no longer meant anything. Bewildered though they were and close to exhaustion, the troops seemed to realize, as Adam Stephen put it, that "you might as well send a cow in pursuit of a hare as an English soldier loaded in their way . . . after Canadians in their shirts . . . or naked Indians accustomed to the woods."[69] Nor had these English soldiers in the wilderness failed to notice that when any of their comrades made an attempt to assail the high ground, the fire of the enemy became more rapid.[70] Counter-action was suicide. Hopelessly the men continued to ram home their

---

[64] *Orme*, 356. Burton was listed in Sargent, *op. cit.*, 362, as slightly wounded.
[65] 1 *Sharpe*, 253.
[66] *Ibid*.
[67] *Pargellis*, 107.
[68] *Orme*, 355; *Pargellis*, 117. This rear Company almost certainly was provincial but has not been identified satisfactorily.
[69] *Stephen-Hardwicke*.
[70] *Pargellis*, 107.

charges and to level their pieces aimlessly. Ammunition was almost exhausted;[71] few officers remained on their feet; most of the Lieutenants and Ensigns who kept with the confused mass in the road did not know to whom to look for orders.[72] The cannon were deserted;[73] the rain of bullets from hidden marksmen did not cease or even diminish. That same paralyzing, fiendish whoop of the savages rang through woods carpeted with dead and dying men. Now, as the sun was descending, more and more of the soldiers began to collect around the wagons. "They stood about . . . for some little time without any fire," their senior officers later reported,[74] and then, from their front and rear,[75] they heard a heavier fire. This was more than could be endured by wagoners who had held their teams for hours. Most of the men in charge of the vehicles cut loose the horses, mounted and made off as fast as they could for the ford.[76] Frightened soldiers plunged past comrades of stouter heart and gave themselves to mad panic. "They behaved," said George indignantly, "with more cowardice than it is possible to conceive; . . . they broke and ran as sheep pursued by dogs."[77] Many of the troops threw away arms, even parts of their clothing to speed their flight down to the river[78] through a shallow ravine. Efforts to halt them met—again the words are George's— "with as much success as if we had attempted to have stopped the wild boars of the mountains."[79] Soon the struggling men were crowding and choking the passageway that led down to the crossing.[80]

When all hope of rallying the soldiers on the right bank was gone, George's first duty was to get safely across the river the wounded General whom Robert Stewart had brought from the front. By good fortune, Washington found a little cart that had not lost its team, and into this he and Stewart put Braddock, who still was master of himself. Carefully, too,

[71] *Orme*, 356; 1 *Sharpe*, 253. Gage's men had gone into action with twenty-five rounds (*Halkett's Orderly Book*, July 8, 1755); the amount of ammunition carried by the other troops is not established, but probably was the same (*ibid.*, May 27, 1755).

[72] 29 *G.W.*, 43.

[73] *Pargellis*, 107.

[74] Dunbar and Gage in 2 *Shirley*, 312–13.

[75] Dunbar and Gage (*loc. cit.*) said "front and left flank" and Gordon (*Pargellis*, 107) said "left." They used these terms as they applied at the opening of the action. "Left" now had become more than ever the "rear" of troops who faced North.

[76] Franklin, *Autobiography* (Bigelow ed.), 191.

[77] 1 *G.W.*, 151.

[78] *Orme*, 356.

[79] 1 *G.W.*, 149.

[80] *Pargellis*, 108.

George loaded on the vehicle some of the General's equipage. In the company of the best of the troops,[81] Washington then descended to the bank and, under fire, conveyed the hard-breathing commander over the ford.[82] Had George looked back while he was crossing, he would have seen some battle-maddened Indians plunge into the water and kill exhausted fugitives there. Otherwise, there was no immediate pursuit. Most of the savages remained on the battlefield to plunder the wagons, to rob the dead and, above all, to scalp the wounded and the slain.[83] Among these victims were eight women.[84] George shuddered to think that this massacre might include all the wounded among the 300 persons or more, dead included, he subsequently estimated the army had left behind on the field of slaughter.[85] Had all the wounded been brought off, George could have reconciled himself to the looting of the wagons and even to the scalping of the slain. He told himself then and many times afterward that if the savages had not stopped to pillage, they might have pressed through the Narrows and might have confronted the survivors from the right bank at the upper ford. Had the French and their savage allies done that, then all the British who had escaped from the battleground might have been starved or slaughtered.[86]

With Burton and Orme, who kept afield in spite of their wounds, George now shared the task of trying to restore order among the survivors who were panting on the left bank or were wandering around in a daze. High ground was chosen, about a quarter of a mile from the river and some 200 yards from the road—a position strong enough to be held indefinitely by courageous troops. George and the others reasoned that if the men could be induced to occupy this eminence, they could beat off all attacks till Colonel Dunbar came up.[87] Burton made an appeal to the soldiers and prevailed upon the least shaken of them to serve as outposts.[88] Braddock observed this, approved it, and directed George to ride farther

[81] They probably were the 200 who had kept together.
[82] 29 *G.W.*, 43.
[83] *Orme*, 356; 1 *Sharpe*, 269.
[84] They had remained with the advanced detachment, for one reason or another, after the other women, twenty-four in number, had been sent to Eastern Pennsylvania (*Pargellis*, 108; P.R.O., 98 Chatham Papers, 12 ff). For the order that the soldiers' wives leave the army, June 9, 1755, see *Lowdermilk*, 135–36.
[85] 1 *G.W.*, 149–50. For the difference between Washington's estimate (July 18, 1755) and the actual loss, see *infra*, p. 86.
[86] 29 *G.W.*, 45.
[87] *Orme*, 356.
[88] *Pargellis*, 107; *Orme*, 356–57.

back along the line of the morning advance and to rally the men who had fled in that direction.

Obediently, George turned his horse's head. Beyond the upper ford,[89] he found Lieutenant Colonel Gage. How the commander of the advance party got that far to the rear, George did not ascertain, or if he learned, he did not record.[90] Gage had with him eighty men, whom he apparently had rallied and now had under some discipline.[91] George felt that the officer was doing all that the situation required; so, about sundown, he recrossed the upper ford to return to Braddock. On the way back to the hill the officers had agreed to make their stronghold, George met a grim cavalcade—Braddock and such of the troops as had held to their duty after the first panic was overcome.[92] The other soldiers had slipped away from the eminence and singly or in small groups were trying to put more distance between them and the enemy.[93]

Manifestly it was futile to talk after that of standing fast, of rallying, of getting the men into the ranks, and of recovering the wagons. Nothing remained to do except to organize a retreat and to execute it as quickly as possible without further loss.[94] Colonel Dunbar with the remainder of the second Brigade was supposed to be advancing and at no great distance; he could cover the retreat and could forward provisions and liquor to the hungry and exhausted men.[95]

For sending orders to Dunbar, a mission of darkness and distance, the wounded Braddock looked again to young Washington: there was no one else who both knew the country and could speak in the General's name.[96] Forty-eight hours previously, George had bumped over that road, a weak convalescent in a wagon. Now, having been on horseback for more than twelve mad hours of incredible strain, he had to set out again. He did, though he had to muster all his moral courage to undertake it. With two guides he crossed the upper ford for the fourth time that day and passed the first fugitives.

[89] Most of the participants referred to this as the first ford in writing of the advance and, in describing the retreat, they termed it the second. This may confuse a reader.

[90] Gage subsequently was accused of cowardice in quitting the field. See William Findlay in 14 *Niles Register*, 179.

[91] *Orme*, 357.

[92] 29 *G.W.*, 44; *Orme*, 356.

[93] *Pargellis*, 107; *Orme*, 356-57.

[94] 29 *G.W.*, 44.

[95] 29 *G.W.*, 44; *Orme*, 356-57.

[96] Robert Dobson, temporary aide (see *supra*, n. 49) knew nothing of the country, except for what he had observed during the march to the Monongahela.

UNDERSTANDING THE TEXT

1. Sum up, in two or three sentences, the varying points of view from which each of these writers narrates the defeat of Braddock. Which of the historians emphasizes most forcefully the drama of the conflict? Which ones seem most concerned with establishing a scholarly, objective narrative of the event?

2. Two of the writers—Irving and Freeman—tell the story of Braddock's disaster as part of biographies of George Washington. What effect does this have on their narratives of the battle? Do Irving and Freeman confine themselves to incidents in which Washington participated or which he presumably observed?

3. How do the four writers differ in their estimates of the character and conduct of General Braddock?

4. What kinds of detail does each historian bring forth to support his interpretation of Braddock's performance?

5. Do you detect any differences in the way each of these writers treats the relationship between Braddock and Washington?

6. Some of these historians and other critics damn Braddock as a "textbook general." Show how Gipson attempts to weaken the force of this criticism. In this connection, what is the point of Gipson's long footnote (No. 34) on accepted military tactics?

7. There is some disagreement among the historians as to the value of the tactics which the Virginia riflemen employed. Indicate the nature of this disagreement and the grounds on which the difference of opinion rests. What fact does Gipson cite to throw doubt on the soundness of the Virginians' tactics?

8. How much agreement is there among the four historians on such important factual details as the number of men engaged on both sides, the time of day at which the action started, the duration of the battle, the number of casualties?

9. How successful is each of these narrators in giving the reader a clear understanding of the geography of the battle and the movement of the troops? Compare their accounts on such points as these: (a) the reason for the two crossings of the Monongahela, (b) the physical features of the actual battle-ground, (c) the movements of both sides after the initial encounter.

10. Study closely Freeman's exposition of the way Braddock's troops shifted their positions, and comment on the usefulness of the analogies he employs to clarify these changes.

11. Which historian develops most fully, considering the scale of his narrative, the preparations of the French and Indians at Fort Duquesne? What influence does this fullness have on the effect of his narrative?

12. In explaining the causes of Braddock's defeat, do the historians differ in the amount of emphasis they give to the unorthodox and terrifying quality of Indian warfare? How do you account for any differences in emphasis which you discern?

13. Gipson's history offers an unusually detailed narrative of Braddock's slow progress westward across the mountains. What relationship do you see between Gipson's general conception of the campaign and his decision to describe the journey fully? What impression of Braddock's generalship does the reader receive from the account of the army's westward march?

14. From what kinds of sources have these historians gathered their material? Which sources appear to be the most basic and trustworthy for this particular campaign? To what extent do the writers comment on the usefulness and reliability of the source materials available to them?

15. These historical narratives make considerable use of footnotes for purposes other than documentation of sources. On what principles do the writers appear to have decided that certain kinds of information and comment belong in footnotes rather than in the text itself?

TOPICS FOR DISCUSSION AND WRITING

16. Solely on the basis of the material in these four accounts, write a character sketch of General Braddock. Then go to the library, consult any other sources you can find on Braddock, and revise your paper in the light of the additional information.

17. Again, on the basis of the information presented in these narratives, write a straightforward 1000-word essay into which you attempt to compress the salient features of the action. In developing the details which you decide to include, be sure to maintain a scale consistent with the scope of your narrative.

18. In the library, consult works which provide fuller information than is supplied by these narratives concerning the background of the Braddock campaign. Why was the campaign undertaken? How did it fit into the larger pattern of military operations in North America? What was the general political situation between Great Britain and France? Then write an expository essay explaining why the British decided to send Braddock against Fort Duquesne in 1755.

19. How might a present-day newspaper correspondent describe the battle of the Monongahela? How might his arrangement of the facts differ from that used by the historians? Compose the opening four or five paragraphs of such a newspaper account.

20. Consult an encyclopedia or standard military reference work, and examine its account of the Braddock defeat. Compare this account with the fuller

narratives presented in this section, noting any important differences in facts and interpretations.

21. Would you expect the events of the American Revolution, occurring two decades after Braddock's catastrophe, to have any effect on the way American writers treat the battle of the Monongahela? Can you detect examples of this tendency in any of the four pieces under study?

22. Toward the end of his *Autobiography*, Benjamin Franklin gives an account of his dealings with Braddock and a brief interpretation of the Monongahela campaign. Look this up, study it, and write a paper indicating which of these four historians Franklin agrees with most closely.

23. How do you suppose a French historian would treat this particular battle? At what point would he be likely to begin his narrative? What changes would he wish to make in the scale and proportions of these Braddock-centered narratives? That is, which sections of these narratives would a French writer probably decide to expand, and which would he condense? What additional information, not included in these accounts, might he supply?

24. From these narratives, particularly those of Irving and Freeman, how clearly are you able to trace Washington's actions during the day of the battle? Write a paper in which you attempt to follow Washington through the events of July 9, 1755.

7. Man in a Diversity of Cultures

DAVID CECIL, The Whig World
GEORGE ORWELL, Shooting an Elephant
FRANK GIBNEY, Five Gentlemen of Japan
E. B. WHITE, The Door

The Whig World

DAVID CECIL

THE GREAT Whig country houses of the eighteenth and early nineteenth centuries are among the most conspicuous monuments of English
history. Ornate and massive, with their pedimented porticoes, their spreading balustraded wings, they dominate the landscape round them with a
magnificent self-assurance. Nor are their interiors less imposing. Their
colonnaded entrance halls, whence the Adam staircase sweeps up beneath
a fluted dome; their cream and gilt libraries piled with sumptuous editions
of the classics; their orangeries peopled with casts from the antique; their

saloons hung with yellow silk, and with ceiling and doorways painted in delicate arabesque by Angelica Kauffmann, all combine to produce an extraordinary impression of culture and elegance and established power.

Yet, they are not palaces. There is something easy-going and unofficial about them. Between library and saloon one comes on little rooms, full of sporting prints and comfortable untidiness; the bedrooms upstairs are friendly with chintz and flowered wallpaper. Even the great rooms themselves, with their roomy writing tables, their armchairs, their tables piled with albums and commonplace books, seem designed less for state occasions than for private life: for leisure and lounging, for intimate talk, and desultory reading. And the portraits that glow down from the walls exhibit a similar character. The gentlemen lean back in their hunting coats, the ladies stroll in their parks with spaniels snapping at the ribbons that dangle from the garden hats, slung on their arms. In big and in detail these houses convey an effect of splendid naturalness. In this they are typical of the society which was their creator.

The Whig aristocracy was a unique product of English civilization. It was before all things a governing class. At a time when economic power was concentrated in the landed interest, the Whigs were among the biggest landowners: their party was in office for the greater part of the eighteenth century; during this period they possessed a large proportion of the seats in the House of Commons; they produced more ambassadors and officers of state than the rest of England put together. And they lived on a scale appropriate to their power. "A man," said one of their latest representatives, "can jog along on £40,000 a year." And jog very well they did. They possessed, most of them, a mansion in London and two or three in the country; they moved through the world attended by a vast retinue of servants, of secretaries and chaplains, of companions, librarians and general hangers-on; they never travelled but in their own carriages; they kept open house to a continuous stream of guests, whom they entertained in the baroque and lavish style approved by their contemporaries.

For the elaboration of their life was increased by the period they lived in. The eighteenth century, that accomplished age, did not believe in the artless and the austere. In its view the good man or, as they would have phrased it, "the man of sense and taste," was he whose every activity was regulated in the light of a trained judgment and the experience of the wise in his own and former ages. From his earliest years the Whig nobleman was subjected to a careful education. He was grounded in the classics first by a tutor, then at Eton, then at the University. After this he went abroad for two years' grand tour to learn French and good manners in the best society of the continent. His sisters learnt French and manners equally thoroughly at home; and their demeanour was further improved by a course of deportment. The Whigs' taste was in harmony with the ideal that guided their education. They learnt to admire the grand style in painting, the "correct" in letters, the Latin tradition in oratory. And in everything they paid strict attention to form. Since life to them was so secure and so pleasant, the Whig aristocrats tended to take its fundamental values very much for granted; they concentrated rather on how to live. And here again, their ideal was not an artless one. Their customs, their mode of speech, their taste in decoration, their stylish stiff clothes, are alike marked by a character at once polished and precise, disciplined and florid. If one of them writes a note it is rounded with a graceful phrase, their most extempore speeches are turned with a flourish of rotund rhetoric.

Yet—and here it is that it differs from those of similar societies on the continent—theirs was not an unreal life; no Watteau-like paradise of exquisite trifling and fastidious idleness. For one thing it had its roots in the earth. Founded as their position was on landed property, the Whig aristocracy was never urban. They passed at least half the year in their country seats; and there they occupied themselves in the ordinary avocations of country life. The ladies interested themselves in their children, and visited the poor; the gentlemen looked after their estates, rode to hounds, and administered from the local bench justice to poachers and pilferers. Their days went by, active out-of-door, unceremonious; they wore riding-boots as often as silk stockings. Moreover, they were always in touch with the central and serious current of contemporary life. The fact that they were a governing class meant that they had to govern. The Whig lord was as often as not a minister, his eldest son an M.P., his second attached to a foreign embassy. So that their houses were alive with the effort and hurry of politics. Red Foreign Office boxes strewed the library tables; at any time of day or night a courier might come galloping up with critical news, and the minister must post off to London to attend a Cabinet meeting. He had his work in the country too. He was a landlord and magistrate, often a lord lieutenant. While every few years would come a general election when his sons, if not himself, might have to sally forth to stand on the hustings and be pelted with eggs and dead cats by the free and independent electors of the neighbouring borough. Indeed his was not a protected existence. The eighteenth century was the age of clubs; and Whig society itself was a sort of club, exclusive, but in which those who managed to achieve membership lived on equal terms; a rowdy, rough-and-tumble club, full of conflict and plain speaking, where people were expected to stand up for themselves and take and give hard knocks. At Eton the little dukes and earls cuffed and bullied each other like street urchins. As mature persons in their country homes, or in the pillared rooms of Brooks's Club, their intercourse continued more politely, yet with equal familiarity. While their House of Commons life passed in a robust atmosphere of combat and crisis and defeat. The Whigs despised the royal family; and there was certainly none of the hush and punctilio of court existence about them. Within the narrow limits of their world they were equalitarians.

Their life, in fact, was essentially a normal life, compounded of the same elements as those of general humanity, astir with the same clamour and clash and aspiration and competition as filled the streets round their august dwellings. Only, it was normal life played out on a colossal stage and with magnificent scenery and costumes. Their houses were homes, but homes with sixty bedrooms, set in grounds five miles round; they fought to keep their jobs, but the jobs were embassies and prime ministerships; their sons went to the same universities as humbler students, but were distinguished from them there by a nobleman's gold-tasselled mortarboard. When the Duke of Devonshire took up botany, he sent out a special expedition to the East Indies to search for rare plants; Lord Egremont liked pictures, so he filled a gallery with Claudes and Correggios; young Lord Palmerston was offered the Chancellorship of the Exchequer a year or two after entering Parliament.

This curiously blended life produced a curiously blended type of character. With so many opportunities for action, its interests were predominantly active. Most of the men were engaged in politics. And the women—for they lived to please the men—were political too. They listened, they sympathized, they advised; through them two statesmen might make overtures to each other, or effect a reconciliation. But politics then were not the life sentence to hard labour that in our iron age they have become. Parliament only sat for a few months in the year; and even during the session, debates did not start till the late afternoon. The Whigs had the rest of their time to devote to other things. If they were sporting they raced and hunted; if interested in agriculture they farmed on an ambitious scale; if artistic they collected marbles and medals; if intellectual they read history and philosophy; if literary they composed compliments in verse and sonorous, platitudinous orations. But the chief of their spare time was given up to social life. They gave balls, they founded clubs, they played cards, they got up private theatricals: they cultivated friendship, and every variety, platonic and less platonic, of the art of love. Their ideal was the Renaissance ideal of the whole man, whose aspiration it is to make the most of every advantage, intellectual and sensual, that life has to offer.

In practice, of course, this ideal was not so broad as it sounds. The Whigs could not escape the limitations imposed by the splendour of their circumstances. Like all aristocrats they tended to be amateurs. When life is so free and so pleasant, a man is not likely to endure the drudgery necessary to make himself really expert in any one thing. Even in those affairs of state which took up most of the Whigs' time, they troubled little with the dry details of economic theory or administrative practice. Politics to them meant first of all personalities, and secondly general principles. And general principles to them were an occasion for expression rather than thought. They did not dream of questioning the fundamental canons of Whig orthodoxy. All believed in ordered liberty, low taxation and the enclosure of land; all disbelieved in despotism and democracy. Their only concern was to restate these indisputable truths in a fresh and effective fashion.

Again, their taste was a little philistine. Aristocratic taste nearly always is. Those whose ordinary course of life is splendid and satisfying, find it hard to recognize the deeper value of the exercises of the solitary imagination; art to them is not the fulfilment of the soul, but an ornamental appendage to existence. Moreover, the English nobility were too much occupied with practical affairs to achieve the fullest intellectual life. They admired what was elegant, sumptuous and easy to understand; portraits that were good likenesses and pleasing decorations; architecture which appropriately housed a stately life. In books, they appreciated acute, wittily phrased observation of human nature, or noble sentiments expressed in flowing periods; Cicero, Pope, Horace, Burke. The strange and the harsh they dismissed immediately. Among contemporary authors they appreciated Jane Austen, condemned Crabbe, for the most part, as sordid and low; and neglected Blake almost entirely. If they had read him, they would not have liked him. For—it is another of their limitations—they were not spiritual. Their education did not encourage them to be; and, anyway, they found this world too absorbing to concern themselves much with the next. The bolder spirits among them were atheists. The average person accepted Christianity, but in a straightforward spirit, innocent alike of mysticism and theological exactitude.

Further, their circumstances did not encourage the virtues of self-control. Good living gave them zest; wealth gave them opportunity; and they threw themselves into their pleasures with an animal recklessness at once terrifying and exhilarating to a modern reader. The most respectable people often drank themselves under the table without shocking anyone. "Colonel Napier came in to-night as drunk as an owl," remarks Lady Sarah Napier, of the staid middle-aged gentleman who was her husband. And their drinking was nothing to their gambling. Night after night they played loo and faro from early evening till the candles guttered pale in the light of the risen sun. Lord Stavordale lamented he had not been playing higher, on a night when he won £11,000 in a single hand at hazard. Georgiana, Duchess of Devonshire, cost her husband nearly £1,000,000 in card debts. Rich as they were, they often ruined themselves. The letters of the time are loud with lamentations about the duns coming in and the furniture going out. Nor was their sexual life of a kind to commend them to an austere morality. "I was afraid I was going to have the gout the other day," writes Lord Carlisle to a friend, "I believe I live too chaste: it is not a common fault with me." It was not a common fault with any of them. In fact an unmarried man was thought unpleasantly queer, if he did not keep under his protection some sprightly full-bosomed Kitty Clive or Mrs. Bellamy, whose embraces he repaid with a house in Montpelier Square, a box at the opera, and a smart cabriolet in which to drive her down to Brighthelmstone for a week's amorous relaxation. Nor did he confine himself to professional ladies of pleasure. Even unmarried girls like Lady Hester Stanhope were suspected of having lovers; among married women the practice was too common to stir comment. The historian grows quite giddy as he tries to disentangle the complications of heredity consequent on the free and easy habits of the English aristocracy. The Harley family, children of the Countess of Oxford, were known as the Harleian Miscellany on account of the variety of fathers alleged to be responsible for their existence. The Duke of Devonshire had three children by the Duchess and two by Lady Elizabeth Foster, the Duchess one by Lord Grey; and most of them were brought up together in Devonshire House, each set of children with a surname of its own. "Emily, does it never strike you," writes Miss Pamela Fitzgerald in 1816, "the vices are wonderfully prolific among Whigs? There are such countless illegitimates, such a tribe of children of the mist." It is noteworthy that the author of this lively comment was a carefully brought up young lady of the highest breeding. The free habits of these days encouraged free speech. "Comfortable girls," remarks a middle-aged lady of her growing nieces, "who like a dirty joke." And the men, as can be imagined, were a great deal freer than the women. For all their polish the Whigs were not refined people in the Victorian sense of the word.

It appears in other aspects of their lives. They could be extremely arrogant; treating their inferiors with a patrician insolence which seems to us the reverse of good breeding. Lady Catherine de Bourgh was not the caricature that an ignorant person might suppose. Fashionable young men of refined upbringing amused themselves by watching fights where the Game Chicken battered the Tutbury Pet into unconsciousness with bare and blood-stained fists. And the pamphlets, the squibs, the appalling political cartoons that lay open in the most elegant drawingrooms show that the ladies of the day were not squeamish either.

Still, unseemly as some of its manifestations were, one must admit that there is something extremely attractive in this earthy exuberance. And, as a matter of fact, it was the inevitable corollary of their virtues. English society had the merits of its defects. Its wide scope, its strong root in the earth, gave it an astounding, an irresistible vitality. For all their dissipation there was nothing decadent about these eighteenth century aristocrats. Their excesses came from too much life, not too little. And it was the same vitality that gave them their predominance in public life. They took on the task of directing England's destinies with the same self-confident vigour, that they drank and diced. It was this vigour that made Pitt Prime Minister at twenty-four years old,[1] that enabled the Foxites to keep the flag of liberty flying against the united public opinion of a panic-stricken nation. Nor did they let their pleasures interfere with these more serious activities. After eighteen hours of uninterrupted gambling, Charles Fox would arrive at the House of Commons to electrify his fellow members by a brilliant discourse on American taxation. Rakes and ladies of fashion intersperse their narratives of intrigue with discussions on politics, on literature, even on morals. For they were not unmoral. Their lapses came from passion not from principle; and they are liable at any time to break out in contrite acknowledgments of guilt, and artless resolutions for future improvement. Indeed it was one of the paradoxes

[1] Pitt diverged from the Whigs in later life: but he was brought up among them; and is, so far, representative of the Whig tradition.

created by their mixed composition that, though they were worldly, they were not sophisticated. Their elaborate manners masked simple reactions. Like their mode of life their characters were essentially natural; spontaneous, unintrospective, brimming over with normal feelings, love of home and family, loyalty, conviviality, desire for fame, hero-worship, patriotism. And they showed their feelings too. Happy creatures! They lived before the days of the stiff upper lip and the inhibited public school Englishman. A manly tear stood in their eye at the story of a heroic deed: they declared their loves in a strain of flowery hyperbole. They were the more expressive from their very unselfconsciousness. It never struck them that they needed to be inarticulate to appear sincere. They were equally frank about their less elevated sentiments. Eighteenth century rationalism combined with rural common sense to make them robustly ready to face unedifying facts. And they declared their impressions with a brusque honesty, outstandingly characteristic of them. From Sir Robert Walpole who encouraged coarse conversation on the ground that it was the only form of talk which everyone enjoyed, down to the Duke of Wellington who described the army of his triumphs as composed of "the scum of the earth, enlisted for drink," the Augustan aristocracy, Whig and Tory alike, said what they thought with a superb disregard for public opinion. For if they were not original they were independent-minded. The conventions which bounded their lives were conventions of form only. Since they had been kings of their world from birth they were free from the tiresome inhibitions that are induced by a sense of inferiority. Within the locked garden of their society, individuality flowered riotous and rampant. Their typical figures show up beside the muted introverts of to-day as clear-cut and idiosyncratic as characters in Dickens. They took for granted that you spoke your mind and followed your impulses. If these were odd they were amused but not disapproving. They enjoyed eccentrics; George Selwyn who never missed an execution, Beau Brummel who took three hours to tie his cravat. The firm English soil in which they were rooted, the spacious freedom afforded by their place in the world, allowed personality to flourish in as many bold and fantastic shapes as it pleased.

But it was always a garden plant, a civilized growth. Whatever their eccentricities, the Whig nobles were never provincial and never uncouth. They had that effortless knowledge of the world that comes only to those, who from childhood have been accustomed to move in a complex society; that delightful unassertive confidence possible only to people who have never had cause to doubt their social position. And they carried to the finest degree of cultivation those social arts which engaged so much of their time. Here we come to their outstanding distinction. They were the most agreeable society England has ever known. The character of their agreeability was of a piece with the rest of them; mundane, straightforward, a trifle philistine, largely concerned with gossip, not given to subtle analyses or flights of fancy. But it had all their vitality and all their sense of style. It was incomparably racy and spontaneous and accomplished; based solidly on a wide culture and experience, yet free to express itself in bursts of high spirits, in impulses of appreciation, in delicate movements of sentiment, in graceful compliments. For it had its grace; a virile classical grace like that of the Chippendale furniture which adorned its rooms, lending a glittering finish to its shrewd humour, its sharp-eyed observation, its vigorous disquisitions on men and things. Educated without pedantry, informal but not slipshod, polished but not precious, brilliant without fatigue, it combined in an easy perfection the charms of civilization and nature. Indeed the whole social life of the period shines down the perspective of history like some masterpiece of natural art; a prize bloom, nurtured in shelter and sunshine and the richest soil, the result of generations of breeding and blending, that spreads itself to the open sky in strength and beauty.

It was at its most characteristic in the middle of the century, it was at its most dazzling towards its close. By 1780 a new spirit was rising in the world. Ossian had taught people to admire ruins and ravines, Rousseau to examine the processes of the heart; with unpowdered heads and the ladies in simple muslin dresses, they paced the woods meditating, in Cowperlike mood, on the tender influences of nature. Though they kept the style and good sense of their fathers, their sympathies were wider. At the same time their feelings grew more refined. The hardness, which had marred the previous age, dwindled. Gainsborough, not Hogarth, mirrored the taste of the time; sensibility became a fashionable word. For a fleeting moment Whig society had a foot in two worlds and made the best of both of them. The lucid outline of eighteenth-century civilization was softened by the glow of the romantic dawn.

Dawn—but for them it was sunset. The same spirit that tinged them with their culminating glory was also an omen of their dissolution. For the days of aristocratic supremacy were numbered. By the iron laws which condition the social structure of man's existence, it could only last as long as it maintained an economic predominance. With the coming of the Industrial Revolution this predominance began to pass from the land-lords to other ranks of the community. Already by the close of the century, go-ahead manufacturers in the north were talking of Parliamentary reform; already, in the upper rooms of obscure London alleys, working men met together to clamour for liberty, equality, and fraternity. Within forty years of its zenith, the Whig world was completely swept away. Only a few survivors lingered on to illustrate to an uncomprehending generation the charm of the past. Of these the most distinguished was William Lamb, second Viscount Melbourne.[2]

UNDERSTANDING THE TEXT

1. In his first two paragraphs Cecil develops a contrast between two aspects of the Whig country house. What are they? This contrast, expressed in various terms, runs through the essay as a whole. Identify the different forms in which this basic contrast appears. Show how it is involved in what Cecil describes (p. 427) as the "curiously blended life" of the Whigs and the "curiously blended type of character" produced by that life. How far do you find that this contrast serves to organize Cecil's interpretation of the Whig world?

2. What were the major deficiencies of the Whig world? What were its principal strengths? What does Cecil point to as the outstanding *distinction* of Whig society? In what sense does their outstanding distinction sum up the other qualities, good and bad, that Cecil has analyzed?

3. Although Cecil does not develop his analysis of the Whig world through a systematic comparison with any other society, he frequently makes comparative statements. Make a list of the societies or periods in history to which he compares the Whigs. Does any one predominate?

4. What reasons does Cecil advance to explain the naturalness and "reality" of Whig society? How are these causes related to the general conditions that permitted the Whigs to dominate English society?

5. Notice the procedure Cecil follows in opening his essay: he begins with the exterior of the Whig houses, then moves to the interiors, then to one of the interior furnishings, the portraits of Whig ladies and gentlemen, and finally to the Whigs themselves. Do you see any special advantage in this procedure?

6. Cecil refers to Whig society as a "locked garden" (p. 431). What does this metaphor mean? Is it appropriate to the general lines of Cecil's interpreta-

---

[2] "The Whig World" is the first chapter of Cecil's biography of Lord Melbourne. This final sentence merely introduces the real subject of the book.

tion? Consider its usefulness by tracing the extension of the metaphor of the garden through the remainder of the essay.

7. Occasionally Cecil's tone is ironic, as when he refers to the canons of Whig orthodox opinion as "these indisputable truths." Can you find other examples of ironic statement in the essay? What do they contribute?

8. Consider the exclamatory sentence on p. 431: "Happy creatures!" Does it seem to you to involve a shift in the basic tone that Cecil adopts in the essay?

9. Explain the following allusions: Adam staircase, Angelica Kauffmann, Watteau, Brooks's Club, Harleian Miscellany, Lady Catherine de Bourgh, the Foxites, Ossian, Rousseau.

TOPICS FOR DISCUSSION AND WRITING

10. The Whig world, as Cecil describes it, is a society within a society, a special world within the larger world of England as a whole. What other groups in English society does Cecil mention? How many of the qualities that Cecil finds characteristic of the Whig world are characteristic of eighteenth-century England as a whole and how many are peculiar to the Whigs? Does Cecil show any awareness of this question of common vs. special qualities?

11. Write a paper analyzing the grounds on which Cecil describes and judges the Whigs. You might begin by making as full a list as you can of the assumptions he makes about aristocracy, taste, morality, and other general topics. Sometimes these are stated fully, as in "Like all aristocrats they tended to be amateurs." Sometimes his assumptions are introduced more indirectly, as in the judgment that "they were not unmoral. Their lapses came from passion not from principle." And sometimes you will have to dig well below the surface to locate Cecil's standards of judgment. In your paper try to determine whether there is any center or consistency in Cecil's fundamental views, and make clear your own judgment of them.

12. Cecil is himself an aristocrat, a member of one of England's oldest and most distinguished families. Do you find any reflections of this fact in his essay?

13. Consider this statement: "It never struck them that they needed to be inarticulate to be sincere." Whose view is it that one needs to be inarticulate to be sincere? What is Cecil's attitude toward this view? How far does it seem to you a principle of modern conduct? Write a paragraph discussing a modern hero—in movies, television, the novel, or in real life—from this point of view.

14. What does Cecil mean when he says that the Whig "earthy exuberance" was "the inevitable corollary of their virtues"? Do you agree with this line of reasoning?

15. Comment on Cecil's statement that the Whigs, "though they were worldly, . . . were not sophisticated."

16. Write a comparison between Whig society of the eighteenth century as Cecil describes it and the country squirearchy of the seventeenth century as Macaulay describes it, trying to bring out the traits that seem to have persisted between the two periods and the traits that seem to have changed most considerably.

Shooting an Elephant

GEORGE ORWELL

IN MOULMEIN, in Lower Burma, I was hated by large numbers of people—the only time in my life that I have been important enough for this to happen to me. I was sub-divisional police officer of the town, and in an aimless, petty kind of way anti-European feeling was very bitter. No one had the guts to raise a riot, but if a European woman went through the bazaars alone somebody would probably spit betel juice over her dress. As a police officer I was an obvious target and was baited whenever it seemed safe to do so. When a nimble Burman tripped me up on the football field and the referee (another Burman) looked the other way, the crowd yelled with hideous laughter. This happened more than once. In the end the sneering yellow faces of young men that met me everywhere, the insults hooted after me when I was at a safe distance, got badly on my nerves. The young Buddhist priests were the worst of all. There were several thousands of them in the town and none of them seemed to have anything to do except stand on street corners and jeer at Europeans.

All this was perplexing and upsetting. For at that time I had already made up my mind that imperialism was an evil thing and the sooner I chucked up my job and got out of it the better. Theoretically—and secretly, of course—I was all for the Burmese and all against their oppressors, the British. As for the job I was doing, I hated it more bitterly than I can perhaps make clear. In a job like that you see the dirty work of Empire at close quarters. The wretched prisoners huddling in the stinking cages of the lock-ups, the grey, cowed faces of the long-term convicts, the scarred buttocks of the men who had been flogged with bamboos—all these oppressed me with an intolerable sense of guilt. But I could get nothing into perspective. I was young and ill-educated and I had had to think out my problems in the utter silence that is imposed on every Englishman in the East. I did not even know that the British Empire is dying, still less did I know that it is a great deal better than the younger empires that are going to supplant it. All I knew was that I was stuck between my hatred of the empire I served and my rage against the evil-spirited little beasts who tried to make my job impossible. With one part of my mind I thought of the British Raj as an unbreakable tyranny, as something clamped down, in *saecula saeculorum,* upon the will of prostrate peoples; with another part I thought that the greatest joy in the world would be to drive a bayonet into a Buddhist priest's guts. Feelings like these are the normal by-products of imperialism; ask any Anglo-Indian official, if you can catch him off duty.

One day something happened which in a roundabout way was enlightening. It was a tiny incident in itself, but it gave me a better glimpse than I had had before of the real nature of imperialism—the real motives for which despotic governments act. Early one morning the sub-inspector at a police station the other end of the town rang me up on the 'phone and said that an elephant was ravaging the bazaar. Would I please come and do something about it? I did not know what I could do, but I wanted to see what was happening and I got on to a pony and started out. I took my rifle, an old .44 Winchester and much too small to kill an elephant, but I thought the noise might be useful *in terrorem.* Various Burmans stopped me on the way and told me about the elephant's doings. It was not, of course, a wild elephant, but a tame one which had gone "must." It had been chained up, as tame elephants always are when their attack of "must" is due, but on the previous night it had broken its chain and escaped. Its mahout, the only person who could manage it when it was in that state, had set out in pursuit, but had taken the wrong direction and was now twelve hours' journey away, and in the morning the elephant had suddenly reappeared in the town. The Burmese population had no weapons and were quite helpless against it. It had already destroyed somebody's bamboo hut, killed a cow and raided some fruit-stalls and devoured the stock; also it had met the municipal rubbish van and, when the driver jumped out and took to his heels, had turned the van over and inflicted violences upon it.

The Burmese sub-inspector and some Indian constables were waiting for me in the quarter where the elephant had been seen. It was a very poor quarter, a labyrinth of squalid bamboo huts, thatched with palm-leaf, winding all over a steep hillside. I remember that it was a cloudy, stuffy morning at the beginning of the rains. We began questioning the people as to where the elephant had gone and, as usual, failed to get any definite information. That is invariably the case in the East; a story always sounds clear enough at a distance, but the nearer you get to the scene of events the vaguer it becomes. Some of the people said that the elephant had gone in one direction, some said that he had gone in another, some professed not even to have heard of any elephant. I had almost made up my mind that the whole story was a pack of lies, when we heard yells a little distance away. There was a loud, scandalized cry of "Go away, child! Go away this instant!" and an old woman with a switch in her hand came round the corner of a hut, violently shooing away a crowd of naked children. Some more women followed, clicking their tongues and exclaiming; evidently there was something that the children ought not to have seen. I rounded the hut and saw a man's dead body sprawling in the mud. He was an Indian, a black Dravidian coolie, almost naked, and he could not have been dead many minutes. The people said that the elephant had come suddenly upon him round the corner of the hut, caught him with its trunk, put its foot on his back and ground him into the earth. This was the rainy season and the ground was soft, and his face had scored a trench a foot deep and a couple of yards long. He was lying on his belly with arms crucified and head sharply twisted to one side. His face was coated with mud, the eyes wide open, the teeth bared and grinning with an expression of unendurable agony. (Never tell me, by the way, that the dead look peaceful. Most of the corpses I have seen looked devilish.) The friction of the great beast's foot had stripped the skin from his back as neatly as one skins a rabbit. As soon as I saw the dead man I sent an orderly to a friend's house nearby to borrow an elephant rifle. I had already sent back the pony, not wanting it to go mad with fright and throw me if it smelt the elephant.

The orderly came back in a few minutes with a rifle and five cartridges, and meanwhile some Burmans had arrived and told us that the elephant was in the paddy fields below, only a few hundred yards away. As I started forward practically the whole population of the quarter flocked out of the houses and followed me. They had seen the rifle and were all shouting excitedly that I was going to shoot the elephant. They had not shown much interest in the elephant when he was merely ravaging their homes, but it was different now that he was going to be shot. It was a bit of fun to them, as it would be to an English crowd; besides they wanted the meat. It made me vaguely uneasy. I had no intention of shooting the elephant—I had merely sent for the rifle to defend myself if necessary—and it is always unnerving to have a crowd following you. I marched down the hill, looking and feeling a fool, with the rifle over my shoulder and an ever-growing army of people jostling at my heels. At the bottom, when you got away from the huts, there was a metalled road and beyond that a miry waste of paddy fields a thousand yards across, not yet ploughed but soggy from the first rains and dotted with coarse grass. The elephant was standing eight yards from the road, his left side towards us. He took not the slightest notice of the crowd's approach. He was tearing up bunches of grass, beating them against his knees to clean them and stuffing them into his mouth.

I had halted on the road. As soon as I saw the elephant I knew with perfect certainty that I ought not to shoot him. It is a serious matter to shoot a working elephant—it is comparable to destroying a huge and costly piece of machinery—and obviously one ought not to do it if it can possibly be avoided. And at that distance, peacefully eating, the elephant looked no more dangerous than a cow. I thought then and I think now that his attack of "must" was already passing off; in which case he would merely wander harmlessly about until the mahout came back and caught him. Moreover, I did not in the least want to shoot him. I decided that I would watch him for a little while to make sure that he did not turn savage again, and then go home.

But at that moment I glanced round at the crowd that had followed me. It was an immense crowd, two thousand at the least and growing every minute. It blocked the road for a long distance on either side. I looked at the sea of yellow faces above the garish clothes—faces all happy and excited over this bit of fun, all certain that the elephant was going to be shot. They were watching me as they would watch a conjurer about to perform a trick. They did not like me, but with the magical rifle in my hands I was momentarily worth watching. And suddenly I realized that I should have to shoot the elephant after all. The people expected it of me and I had got to do it; I could feel their two thousand wills pressing me forward, irresistibly. And it was at this moment, as I stood there with the rifle in my hands, that I first grasped the hollowness, the futility of the white man's dominion in the East. Here was I, the white man with his gun, standing in front of the unarmed native crowd—seemingly the leading actor of the piece; but in reality I was only an absurd puppet pushed to and fro by the will of those yellow faces behind. I perceived in this moment that when the white man turns tyrant it is his own freedom that he destroys. He becomes a sort of hollow, posing dummy, the conventionalized figure of a sahib. For it is the condition of his rule that he shall spend his life in trying to impress the "natives," and so in every crisis he has got to do what the "natives" expect of him. He wears a mask, and his face grows to fit it. I had got to shoot the elephant. I had committed myself to doing it when I sent for the rifle. A sahib has got to act like a sahib; he has got to appear resolute, to know his own mind and do definite things. To come all that way, rifle in hand, with two thousand people marching at my heels, and then to trail feebly away, having done nothing—no, that was impossible. The crowd would laugh at me. And my whole life, every white man's life in the East, was one long struggle not to be laughed at.

But I did not want to shoot the elephant. I watched him beating his bunch of grass against his knees, with that preoccupied grandmotherly air that elephants have. It seemed to me that it would be murder to shoot him. At that age I was not squeamish about killing animals, but I had never shot an elephant and never wanted to. (Somehow it always seems worse to kill a *large* animal.) Besides, there was the beast's owner to be considered. Alive, the elephant was worth at least a hundred pounds; dead, he would only be worth the value of his tusks, five pounds, possibly. But I had got to act quickly. I turned to some experienced-looking Burmans who had been there when we arrived, and asked them how the elephant had been behaving. They all said the same thing: he took no notice of you if you left him alone, but he might charge if you went too close to him.

It was perfectly clear to me what I ought to do. I ought to walk up to within, say, twenty-five yards of the elephant and test his behavior. If he charged, I could shoot; if he took no notice of me, it would be safe to leave him until the mahout came back. But also I knew that I was going to do no such thing. I was a poor shot with a rifle and the ground was soft mud into which one would sink at every step. If the elephant charged and I missed him, I should have about as much chance as a toad under a steam roller. But even then I was not thinking particularly of my own skin, only of the watchful yellow faces behind. For at that moment, with the crowd watching me, I was not afraid in the ordinary sense, as I would have been if I had been alone. A white man mustn't be frightened in front of "natives"; and so, in general, he isn't frightened. The sole thought in my mind was that if anything went wrong those two thousand Burmans would see me pursued, caught, trampled on and reduced to a grinning corpse like that Indian up the hill. And if that happened it was quite probable that some of them would laugh. That would never do. There was only one alternative. I shoved the cartridges into the magazine and lay down on the road to get a better aim.

The crowd grew very still, and a deep, low, happy sigh, as of people who see the theatre curtain go up at last, breathed from innumerable throats. They were going to have their bit of fun after all. The rifle was a beautiful German thing with cross-hair sights. I did not then know that in shooting an elephant one would shoot to cut an imaginary bar running from ear-hole to ear-hole. I ought therefore, as the elephant was sideways on, to have aimed straight at his ear-hole; actually I aimed several inches in front of this, thinking the brain would be further forward.

When I pulled the trigger I did not hear the bang or feel the kick—one never does when a shot goes home—but I heard the devilish roar of glee that went up from the crowd. In that instant, in too short a time, one would have thought, even for the bullet to get there, a mysterious, terrible change had come over the elephant. He neither stirred nor fell, but every line of his body had altered. He looked suddenly stricken, shrunken, immensely old, as though the frightful impact of the bullet had paralysed him without knocking him down. At last, after what seemed a long time—it might have been five seconds, I dare say—he sagged flabbily to his knees. His mouth slobbered. An enormous senility seemed to have settled upon him. One could have imagined him thousands of years old. I fired again into the same spot. At the second shot he did not collapse but climbed with desperate slowness to his feet and stood weakly upright, with legs sagging and head drooping. I fired a third time. That was the shot that did for him. You could see the agony of it jolt his whole body and knock the last remnant of strength from his legs. But in falling he seemed for a moment to rise, for as his hind legs collapsed beneath him he seemed to tower upwards like a huge rock toppling, his trunk reaching skywards like a tree. He trumpeted, for the first and only time. And then down he came, his belly towards me, with a crash that seemed to shake the ground even where I lay.

I got up. The Burmans were already racing past me across the mud. It was obvious that the elephant would never rise again, but he was not dead. He was breathing very rhythmically with long rattling gasps, his great mound of a side painfully rising and falling. His mouth was wide open—I could see far down into caverns of pale pink throat. I waited a long time for him to die, but his breathing did not weaken. Finally I fired my two remaining shots into the spot where I thought his heart must be. The thick blood welled out of him like red velvet, but still he did not die. His body did not even jerk when the shots hit him, the tortured breathing continued without a pause. He was dying, very slowly and in great agony, but in some world remote from me where not even a bullet could damage him further. I felt that I had got to put an end to that dreadful noise. It seemed dreadful to see the great beast lying there, powerless to move and yet powerless to die, and not even to be able to finish him. I sent back for my small rifle and poured shot after shot into his heart and down his throat. They seemed to make no impression. The tortured gasps continued as steadily as the ticking of a clock.

In the end I could not stand it any longer and went away. I heard later that it took him half an hour to die. Burmans were bringing dahs and baskets even before I left, and I was told they had stripped his body almost to the bones by the afternoon.

Afterwards, of course, there were endless discussions about the shooting of the elephant. The owner was furious, but he was only an Indian and could do nothing. Besides, legally I had done the right thing, for a mad elephant has to be killed, like a mad dog, if its owner fails to control it. Among the Europeans opinion was divided. The older men said I was right, the younger men said it was a damn shame to shoot an elephant for killing a coolie, because an elephant was worth more than any damn Coringhee coolie. And afterwards I was very glad that the coolie had been killed; it put me legally in the right and it gave me a sufficient pretext for shooting the elephant. I often wondered whether any of the others grasped that I had done it solely to avoid looking a fool.

UNDERSTANDING THE TEXT

1. Orwell tells us that even before the episode of the elephant he had come to the conclusion that imperialism was an evil thing. What sorts of evidence had led him to this conclusion?
2. If Orwell had already made up his mind about the evil of imperialism, what new discovery did he make in the episode with the elephant? Identify the paragraph in which Orwell states what his discovery was.
3. What reasons does Orwell give for his feeling that he ought not to shoot the

elephant? Which reason do you take to have been the most important for Orwell? Why?

4. Notice the vividness with which Orwell describes the dead body of the coolie and the dying elephant, and the relative lack of detail in his description of the Burmans. How do you account for these differences in detail and scale?

5. What is the effect of these sentences about the elephant: "But in falling he seemed for a moment to rise, for as his hind legs collapsed beneath him he seemed to tower upwards like a huge rock toppling, his trunk reaching skywards like a tree."

6. Why do you think Orwell included the final sentence in the next-to-last paragraph?

7. "They had not shown much interest when the elephant was merely ravaging their homes, but it was different now that he was going to be shot." What does this sentence say about the Burmans?

TOPICS FOR DISCUSSION AND WRITING

8. Why is it important to Orwell's point that he should have been the only European present when this episode occurred?

9. Comment on Orwell's observation that "it always seems worse to kill a *large* animal." Why do you think he believes this? Do you agree?

10. This "tiny incident," Orwell says, gave him a glimpse of "the real nature of imperialism—the real motives for which despotic governments act." Write an analysis of the real motives for which despotic governments act, as the essay makes them out, and as they seem to you.

11. In the light of what Orwell says about figures of speech in "Politics and the English Language" (pp. 239–250), write a paragraph evaluating his figures of speech in this essay.

12. Comment on the differences between Orwell's attitude, during this episode, toward the Burmans and toward the elephant. With which does he feel more closely identified? Why?

13. What conventional attitude does Orwell call attention to by putting "natives" in quotation marks (p. 440)? What does this device indicate about Orwell's attitude toward the cultures of the East?

14. Every white man's life in the East, Orwell says, was "one long struggle not to be laughed at." What makes laughter the appropriate defense of subject peoples?

Five Gentlemen of Japan

FRANK GIBNEY

〜

HIROHITO, Yamazaki, Kisei, Shimizu and Sanada—these are five gentlemen of the new Japan. In one sense they have very little in common. Each has his peculiar tastes and talents. Sanada the farmer likes to gather with his neighbors at local shrine festivals or, more regularly, enjoys listening at his radio to the reedy singing of *Naniwabushi*—the old folk songs that do the work of soap operas for the Japanese radio audience. The journalist, Yamazaki, is a subtle and appreciative observer of French films. Louis Jouvet is his favorite actor—a far cry, he feels, from the brassy, shallow types of Hollywood players.

When Hideya Kisei can get away from his duties at home and in the steel mill, he likes to go off by himself on short fishing trips. Admiral Shimizu, who was once quite a tennis player, now prefers golf. He is a long-time member of the Sagami Country Club, which is now improving its 18-hole course some 30 miles south of Tokyo. The Emperor is an adept swimmer. Legend insists that he can hold an umbrella with his toes, while doing a brisk back-stroke. In more serious moments he likes to wade for hours in the rock-girt backwaters near his summer palace on Sagami Bay, gathering new specimens for his marine biology collection.

Knowing these men, one has difficulty fitting them into the usual visual images of the Japanese, put together by foreigners. Only Hirohito is "myopic" and uses glasses constantly; the others have excellent eyesight. Only Sanada and Kisei are short of stature; Shimizu is a six-footer, Yamazaki almost as tall, the Emperor of medium height. None of them has "buck teeth." None of them is continually "grinning," although they have a marked tendency to laugh when they are worried or embarrassed.

It is hard to pour them into the rigid casts of "Japanese character" which foreigners at different times have constructed. It is almost impossible to imagine them as part of a "maddened horde of banzaiing fanatics" charging up a hill in Burma, or bayoneting women and children in the streets of Nanking or Manila. If they are "shifty, treacherous and deceitful, just waiting for their chance to knife you in the back," as some modern American folklore suggests, the deception, which they and 85 million other ostensibly peace-loving Japanese must practice 24 hours every day, is nothing short of supernatural.

It is also hard to fit them into the land of Madame Butterfly and never-ending cherry-blossom festivals, faithfully and gullibly described by generations of Western tourists. Even Henry Adams, normally a perceptive spectator of foreign custom, could spend four months traveling in Japan —at a critical period of Japanese history—and then write to his friends in the United States: "This is a child's country. Men, women and children are taken out of the fairy books. The whole show is out of the nursery. Nothing is serious. All of it toy. . . ."

In its impartial way, history has often supported both these caricatures. On the record, the Japanese have established themselves as a struggling, living conflict of extremes. Their history seems to have more jarring blacks and whites and less comfortable shadings than that of any great nation. Judged from the outside, Japan has acted almost like a puzzling case in a mental hospital, alternating periods of long and moody solitude with violent, destructive energy. The Japanese guide in Kyoto who distributed polite tourist folders to visiting Americans in the thirties was quite possibly the same man who helped burn down Chinese villages during his compulsory military service just a year before. In 1941, Shimizu, Sanada, Kisei, Yamazaki and the Emperor, in varying ways, were all part of a savage total war effort, scarred with its own atrocities. In 1945, in the space of a few hours, the fury seemed to vanish with the defeat. The Japanese opened their souvenir shops again and stood docilely by to await the pleasure of their conquerors, at the start of the least resisted military occupation in history.

*　　*　　*

It it unfair to write of these Japanese in terms of caricature. It is, however, superficial to think of them hopefully as the Westerners of Asia, separated from contemporary Americans, Englishmen or Frenchmen—

and the traditions they hold in common—only by the accidents of geography and a particularly difficult language barrier. For all their disarming individuality, each of the five gentlemen of Japan has had a share in his country's odd behavior. He is also a product of it. For all their familiarity with golf, radios and French film stars, the five are active representatives of the most unified, the most stubborn, the most eccentric national culture of the twentieth century.

There are certain obvious national characteristics which all of them possess. In the normal sense of the term, all of them are hard workers, earnest in their approach to a problem, not too eager to seize new responsibilities, but almost incredibly faithful to those they have. They have a strong feeling for discipline, and a deep sense of family and community loyalty. They are not overly religious, but they pay their debts. They have a good sense of humor, more broad than subtle.

A translation of the Japanese character into English-language virtues and failings is no more productive of a real understanding of the Japanese than the system of Latin parsing is capable of making order out of their primitive, but supple language. The Japanese can be called cruel, they can be called brave, or industrious, or practical-minded, but no amount of categorizing can well describe them, if we do not first examine the premises of their society—the ethos that makes it different from all others.

To get at the basis of Japanese society, one might, like Christian philosophers seeking to describe God, first posit what it is not. The foreigner must imagine a system where the traditional absolute values of Western civilization—the inheritance of Platonism and Christianity—are absent. However calmly Americans and Europeans rationalize their old religious philosophy, it remains true that their cultural heritage, their political and social institutions have been shaped by a belief in absolute values. This the Japanese conspicuously have never had. There are no root words for "good" and "evil" in their language. Well-educated Japanese like Shimizu or Yamazaki have learned in school and at the university that systems of absolute values exist. They are quite conversant with them. But the influence of those systems has played little part in forming their tradition.

When Sakaji Sanada was raising his son Mitsu, talking to him as he led his horse and wagon down the frozen ruts between his house and his farm, he carefully outlined a moral code for his guidance. The basis of this code was not godliness, or abstract honesty, or abstract purity, but something which Sanada and his fellow Japanese call "*shinyo*." *Shinyo* means trust, confidence, reliability. It is the goal of a social morality. To have *shinyo* is to be a man of honor, who fulfills commitments at whatever cost and whose trust in his neighbors is reciprocated by their confidence in him.

The idea of *shinyo* has been important in a society where virtue is more of a horizontal quality than a vertical one. In Japanese society—a strong clan system reinforced by Confucianism and the national religion of Shinto—the goodness of an act depends on the relationship of the doer and the recipient. It is purely circumstantial. Japanese ethics are founded on the social contract, not the abstract value. The highest virtue is loyalty to one's commitments—the hallmark of someone who has *shinyo*. The basest evil is to fail in it.

This system of contracts and commitments threads its way like a giant steel web through every segment of Japanese society. The web binds the individual in all directions—upwards to parents, ancestors, superior officers, downwards to children, employees and servants. Classically, it has only been by achieving equilibrium inside this web that the Japanese finds peace. Like the sinner in the old Buddhist fable, he reaches out from the depths to clutch the fine, but binding strands of the web of Heaven. Holding on to them, he is safe. Once he slips from the web, or loses his place in it, he falls back, doomed, into the void of *Jigoku*, the Buddhist hell. There is no more chance for redemption.

Historically, in the web society of Japan, the individual has had no real existence outside of his group. He has not, like men born in the Christian West, been a soul in his own right, with at least a tradition of God-given natural rights and duties, accountable only to just authority. He has lived only as a member of his family, his community, his nation. Even the gods of his national religion are family spirits, not necessarily good or bad in themselves, but honored because they represent a deep sense of community. Few Japanese have ever escaped the group demands made upon them. If a favor was given to an individual, it was automatically done to his group. One man's misstep, conversely, has generally brought a Confucian shame to fifty or a hundred others.

Fifty years ago Lafcadio Hearn described the stresses of this society: "Today . . . legally, a man can go where he pleases. But as a matter of fact, he can nowhere do as he pleases; for individual liberty is still largely restricted by the survival of community sentiment and old-fashioned custom. In any country community it would be unwise to proclaim such a doctrine as that a man has the right to employ his leisure and his means as he may think proper. No man's time or money or effort can be considered exclusively his own—nor even the body that his ghost inhabits. His right to live in the community rests solely on his willingness to serve the community; and whoever may need his help or sympathy has the privilege of demanding it. That a man's house is his castle cannot be asserted in Japan—except in the case of some high potentate. No ordinary person can shut his door to lock out the rest of the world. Everybody's house must be open to visitors: to close its gates by day would be regarded as an insult to the community—sickness affording no excuse. . . . And to displease the community in which one lives—especially if the community be a rural one—is a serious matter. When a community is displeased it acts as an individual. It may consist of five hundred, a thousand, or several thousand persons; but the thinking of all is the thinking of one."

How obsolete is Hearn's judgment? On the surface the five gentlemen of Japan do not themselves seem to be throttled by this rigid society of their ancestors. Their world is in fact far looser in its demands upon them than it once was. Industrialization and the influence of the West have progressively softened the texture of the web. Defeat in war badly strained it. A military occupation, committed to producing a democratic Japan, pulled and tore at it. But it has not disappeared. It is still the invisible adhesive that seals the nationhood of the Japanese. Shimizu, Sanada, Yamazaki, Kisei and Hirohito were all born within its bonds. Despite their individual work, surroundings and opinions, they have lived most of their lives as cogs geared into a group society. Literally as well as figuratively speaking, none of them has a lock on his house door. In 1948, long after Hearn had gone to his grave, a Japanese sociologist, Takegi Kawashima, could write with much justice about the behavior of his contemporaries:

"The family system is not a moral quality of fidelity at all. It is merely a one-sided duty of a superior to an inferior, or vice-versa. . . . In a social relationship like this the outstanding point of human relationship and the point of greatest importance to us at present is the impossibility for individual responsibility to exist, for within a system like this the follower cannot be aware of himself as having any individual worth. His actions will always be determined by another. Therefore there would never be any occasion for him to judge for himself or act by himself; nor would he have the ability to do so. He will ever be the child of a family, who is not yet an individual, and who will always need protection by the paternal feeling of one with power."

These are hard words. The system they described has been weakened to the breaking point. Perhaps it will not endure much longer. But Dr. Kawashima is a good sociologist, who has backed up his statements with long, detailed observations. If his conclusions are wrong, they are wrong only in degree. The web society may be doomed. But it still presses most Japanese in its bonds. None in Japan is totally free from it. In the story of its hold on the Japanese, and the efforts which they and others have made to modify or break it, lies the crisis and the fascination of modern Japan.

* * *

Of the five Japanese in this story, Sanada, the farmer, is most securely caught by the web—and most comfortable in its bondage. The town he lives in, Shimoyoshida, is a place of 15,000 population, the market center of a poor but sizeable farming community and the trading center of a fairly prosperous silk textile business. It has a hospital and three banks, a modern fire department, advertising offices of five Tokyo newspapers, thirty-odd *pachinko*, or pinball parlors, representing a new Americanized diversion, 2,993 radios, and a large floating population of sight-seeing American G.I.s. But the indigenous life of Shimoyoshida has not changed radically through the centuries. Neighbors cooperate. Marriages are arranged. Impoliteness is a taboo and to neglect repaying a favor, sinful.

Sanada lives in a district, called a *buraku*, named Shinya. There are about 100 households in the *buraku*, with a total of 500 people. There is a good deal of civic loyalty in Shimoyoshida, which finds its most obvious outlet in the annual Shinto festivals, like the display held each September to honor *Ko-no-Hana-Saku-ga Hime*—Princess-who-makes-the-flowers-of-the-trees-to-bloom—the goddess of Mt. Fuji. But Sanada's primary loyalty is to the *buraku*. He and his fellow-farmers help each other each June with the rice planting—and go out into each others' fields—men, women and children—when October comes, to harvest the crop. When a bridge is damaged, Sanada and his neighbors go out to repair it. If a neighbor's house is blown down, Sanada has a rigid obligation to help set it up again.

The measure of this community cooperation is the measure of a man's standing in the village—and his morality. A Shimoyoshida neighbor would not call Sanada an "upright man" in an intransitive sense. He would say that he is upright in discharging this or that obligation, that he is upright because he helps his neighbors and performs his duties to the community. There is no possibility of being considered "good" outside the community framework. Sanada's own hopes and aspirations betray this. His ideal is not an abstract "peace and prosperity." It is *"kyoson kyoei*—work together and prosper together."

Hideya Kisei, the steel worker, lives in an industrial society. The sooty air of Yahata is a world away from the clear country breezes that sweep down past Mt. Fuji. The stale smell of cinders and furnace smoke hangs over the city, not, as in Shimoyoshida, the faint odor of burning charcoal cleaned by the mountain air. But Kisei and his wife, Kiyoko, are as deep in the web as Sanada is. Their sense of responsibility is as great. So are the demands made upon it.

The Kisei family lives in a company house, fifteen minutes by streetcar from the mill. There are several hundred other houses like it in their district, all of them the residences of Yahata steel workers like Kisei. But living in the heart of an industrial society has not prevented the householders from strait-jacketing their lives with the rigid sense of community they learned in their home villages. Kisei and his entire family belong to the *tonarigumi*—the neighborhood association of his area. They have fixed duties to be done for the association—improving the streets, organizing festivals, somewhat the same sort of thing that Sanada does for his *buraku*.

The power of the *tonarigumi*, in fact, was responsible for Kisei's marriage. When the shifts at the mill speeded up near the beginning of World War II, Hideya found that he was unable to keep up with his neighborhood obligations. He was home for barely eight hours each day—and then only to fall into a drugged sleep. The neighbors kindly but firmly suggested that he get married. He would then have a wife to hold up his household's end of its community responsibility.

Kisei agreed. The neighbors scouted around for a suitable bride. When they found one, acting as go-betweens they introduced Kisei to his present wife, Kiyoko, the daughter of another steel worker. In April, 1941, after a traditional Japanese introduction and courtship, they were married. They have lived happily.

The pattern of the Japanese web society that guides *tonarigumi* and *buraku* has also stamped itself on the life of Kisei's mill. He is a *gocho*, or foreman—the lowest supervisory rank at Yahata (and the same word, in-

cidentally, as "corporal" in the Army). Kisei, like all Japanese, takes his
rank and responsibilities seriously. They do not stop outside the plant. As
a *gocho* he has a strong feeling of responsibility not only for helping the
ten men in his crew with their work problems, but with any crises in
their domestic lives. Regularly, twice a month, he takes them out on a
drinking party. He feels that this is a good way of airing any problems
they may have, with a minimum of tension. He accepts the strain on his
budget for the beer and *sake* involved, as one of the corollaries of his job.

In the same way, Kisei is taken out by the two officials above him in
the chain of command at Yahata. In keeping with their higher station, the
kumicho (supervisor) and the *kakaricho* (section chief) throw in a dinner invitation, when they ask Kisei and the other foremen out for drinks.

A degree of social-business relationships exists in every country. On its
face, Kisei's relations with his men might have been drawn out of the un-
written rules for employee relations in some New York corporations.
But nowhere are these relationships so binding, so relentless, so much an
inbred part of the business world, as in the web society of Japan.

Shimizu and Yamazaki, living in the more sophisticated milieux of
Tokyo, are less visibly affected by the demands of the web than the residents of Shimoyoshida *buraku* or the *tonarigumi* in Yahata. But they
have not escaped. Shimizu, as a career naval officer, lived most of his life
in a military society where the rules of loyalty and *shinyo* that pervade
civilian life were cruelly codified. As a technician, who seldom had direct
duties of command, he was not the complete captive of the code, as
others were. He observed whatever obligations he had to, however, and
lived with his society as he found it. He is no social reformer.

Like Kisei, Sanada and Hirohito, his marriage was arranged for him.[1]
His father-in-law, a wealthy farmer in Tochigi Prefecture, was a good
friend of his father's. His wife has been a good and faithful companion.
Like the wives of the others, she stays in the background, exerting her
influence by indirection, dedicating her life to her husband and her children.

The bonds of the web only once made Shimizu wince with pain. When
his arsenal at Toyokawa was bombed, he was shocked by the loss of life
among the 60,000 civilian workers and their families, all living within a
narrow perimeter of wood and paper houses near the factory buildings.

---

[1] This is not altogether just to Hirohito. Although the area of his choices was rigidly limited, he did insist on marrying a princess of the southern Satsuma clan, against
the wishes of his most powerful advisor, Prince Yamagata.

His reaction was as painful and as personal as Hideya Kisei's feelings might have been, if one member of his ten-man crew were scalded at the furnace. There was no reason for him to feel blameful. Toyokawa had been defended as well as the desperate condition of the Japanese forces in 1945 permitted. The bombing was an enemy act, in which he had no conceivable part. But this in no way helped to cast off the responsibility.

The families of the workers, for their part, were bitter and disillusioned. They attacked Shimizu for his "negligence" after the raid, largely because he, as a high-ranking military man, was a handy scapegoat for their defeat and despair. He did not protest the injustice of their accusations. In his neat, five-room house in the Kakinokizaka district of Tokyo, a quiet residential area favored by bankers and comfortably fixed executives, he keeps a list of the dead and the injured. Every morning he prays for them. His conscience hurts him deeply, because he has not enough money to look after their families. In a sense, by the Japanese canons of morality, he has failed in a duty.

Tadao Yamazaki, the newspaper man, is the nearest approach in the web-society to a home-grown iconoclast. His father, a high-school teacher, himself broke away from the traditional Japanese values as he saw them. There were never any Shinto ancestor tablets in the Yamazaki household and his father today does not expect his son to support him in his old age. Yamazaki met his wife Matsui, a college graduate like himself, when he was covering a story for *Asahi*. She was a reporter for *Josei Shimbun*, a women's paper published by the Tokyo YWCA. They fell in love and married, in the Western tradition. There were no go-betweens, nothing was arranged. "Our marriage was from a small romance," Yamazaki describes it.

His views and outlook are more understandable to an American than are those of any of the others. It would hardly be inaccurate to call him a "liberal" in the older American sense, as it was used before many alleged "liberals" became more totalitarian than the totalitarians they attacked. He is open-minded, curious to learn and conscious always that Japan is in a time of dangerous but exciting ferment.

He would not affirm that the web society exists around him. But its evidences are possibly too subtly wound into his life to be noticed. He unconsciously tries to harmonize his traditions with his critical outlook. "As a citizen of Japan I want to abide by the rules that stand," he has said, "simultaneously I want to see our politics from a rational, critical point of view."

Every morning, in the elevator of the *Asahi* building, Yamazaki cannot escape an obligatory round of hieratic bows and salutations as he recognizes his bosses or fellow-employees. In his relations on the newspaper, and with business acquaintances, he exercises a circumspection and a consciousness of rank and position that no American or European of his views and status would think of. He would like Japan to have a real system of social equality, without these shadings of position that dominate every Japanese social circle. But he has an insular resistance to sudden, violent change. The web hangs loosely around him, giving him, with the grace of elbow room, a special kind of perspective. He has the soul of a social reformer. But the presence of the web has kept him from becoming a revolutionary.

At the center of the web society stands the Emperor. He is no casual figurehead, installed to add a symbol value to a system that might work perfectly well without him. His presence and what it stands for make the great difference between the Japanese web system and the "family system" regularized by Confucius in China and found, with local variations, almost everywhere in East Asia. The Chinese family system is an institution. The Japanese family system is both an institution and an instrument. The Chinese family system is a social structure that may be exploited for political purposes, but need not be. The Japanese family system is curiously and confusingly bound up with the Japanese state. Throughout history, the two have challenged separation.

Presiding in a cutaway at the Convocation of the Diet, Hirohito is the national constitutional monarch. Bowing to his ancestors at the Ise Shrine, in the severe black and white of Shinto vestments, he is the national pontiff. Deeper in the hearts of most Japanese, he is the symbol and the purpose of their nationhood, in whom all web commitments begin and end.

No civilized, intelligent society can base its rules of conduct wholly on a system of horizontal contracts. The Japanese is no exception. The Emperor is the institution which gives a moral sanction to the contracts and stamps the web society with a seal of permanence. Japanese have never believed that he was a "God" in the Western sense. What they did believe before 1945—and what quite a few still believe—is that he is a god without a capital "G."

This does not imply obvious superhuman powers. It bases itself on a faith that the Emperor, descending in an unbroken line from the founders of Japan, who were gods, expresses the principle that Japan is a divinely inspired nation with a divine mission. It insists that the Emperor, as a result, can do no wrong. It is only his advisors who must take responsibility to the nation for their blunders. The Emperor is the one living man in the web who has no necessary obligations to his people. He does have an obligation to his divine ancestors, whom he still invokes regularly at the Grand Shrine of Ise, telling them of new developments in the nation and asking their guidance. It is an odd position for a marine biologist to find himself in.

Hirohito himself would like to be a normal constitutional monarch, as would increasingly large numbers of his subjects. But he can only become so if the web society is destroyed. It is dependent on him for its life and perpetuation. His position was bluntly set forth in *Kokutai no Hongi—The Basis of the National Polity*—a book published by the Ministry of Education in 1937 for the edification of teachers and other public officials: "The Emperor is not merely a so-called sovereign, monarch, ruler or administrator, such as is seen among foreign nations, but reigns over this country as a deity incarnate in keeping with the great principle that has come down to us since the founding of the Empire." If Yamazaki is the nearest thing the web society has to an iconoclast, Hirohito is the nearest it comes to having an absolute value.

*   *   *

The existence of this imperially centered web is the central fact of modern Japanese history. It has enabled the Japanese to move as one in the greatest national transformation of modern times; it has also betrayed them into the hands of leaders who were clever enough to find the levers which controlled the dynamics of this national society and use them for their own ends. The repressed individualism of men like Yamazaki and Kisei cries out against it; Shimizu coolly dissects it; Sanada occasionally puzzles over it, without realizing what his worry is about. But, in one way or another, the web still surrounds them, and distinguishes them as a people.

UNDERSTANDING THE TEXT

1. What common Western notions about Japan does Gibney try to dispel in paragraphs 3, 4, and 5? How are these paragraphs unified? What determines the order among them?
2. The Japanese, Gibney says, "have established themselves as a struggling,

living conflict of extremes" (p. 445). What is the importance of this conception of Japanese society in Gibney's analysis as a whole?

3. After setting forth his general conception of Japanese society, Gibney discusses each of his five gentlemen in turn. What determines the order in which he takes them up?

4. What does Gibney mean by the terms "horizontal" and "vertical" in reference to social organization?

5. Make a critical examination of Gibney's metaphor of the web.

6. Which of the five gentlemen is most completely governed by the pattern of Japanese society? In what specific ways does the dominance of the social pattern exhibit itself?

7. Which of the five gentlemen is most free of the restrictions imposed by the pattern of society? What conditions seem to contribute to his relative detachment? In what ways does he accommodate himself to the prevailing pattern of society?

TOPICS FOR DISCUSSION AND WRITING

8. What are the advantages and disadvantages of organizing an analysis of a society in terms of a group of representative individuals? How far, judging by this portion of his book, has Gibney avoided the disadvantages?

9. Suppose you were faced with an assignment like Gibney's. What alternative methods of organizing a treatment of the subject can you think of? What would be their relative advantages and disadvantages with respect to (a) research, (b) organization and expression, (c) reliability of results, (d) general interest?

10. To what extent is American society bound together by "horizontal" ties of group loyalty and responsibility?

11. Gibney says that the Japanese social structure, unlike that of Western countries, does not rest on absolute values. Discuss *shinyo* as a possible absolute value. Give some examples of the absolute values that underlie our society.

12. If you were going to do a study of American society using the procedure Gibney followed, what kinds of Americans would you choose as your subjects? Give reasons for your choices. Would you include any women? Does Gibney's analysis seem to you defective in omitting extended reference to the role of women?

13. Select three or four members of a social group to which you belong or to which you have belonged and characterize each of them in such a way as to show the unifying elements in the social group.

The Door

E. B. WHITE

EVERYTHING (he kept saying) is something it isn't. And everybody is
always somewhere else. Maybe it was the city, being in the city, that made
him feel how queer everything was and that it was something else. Maybe
(he kept thinking) it was the names of the things. The names were tex and
frequently koid. Or they were flex and oid or they were duroid (sani) or
flexsan (duro), but everything was glass (but not quite glass) and the
thing that you touched (the surface, washable, crease-resistant) was rubber, only it wasn't quite rubber and you didn't quite touch it but almost.
The wall, which was glass but thrutex, turned out on being approached
not to be a wall, it was something else, it was an opening or doorway—
and the doorway (through which he saw himself approaching) turned
out to be something else, it was a wall. And what he had eaten not having
agreed with him.

He was in a washable house, but he wasn't sure. Now about those rats,
he kept saying to himself. He meant the rats that the Professor had driven
crazy by forcing them to deal with problems which were beyond the
scope of rats, the insoluble problems. He meant the rats that had been
trained to jump at the square card with the circle in the middle, and the
card (because it was something it wasn't) would give way and let the rat
into a place where the food was, but then one day it would be a trick
played on the rat, and the card would be changed, and the rat would jump
but the card wouldn't give way, and it was an impossible situation (for a
rat) and the rat would go insane and into its eyes would come the un-
speakably bright imploring look of the frustrated, and after the convulsions were over and the frantic racing around, then the passive stage

would set in and the willingness to let anything be done to it, even if it was something else.

He didn't know which door (or wall) or opening in the house to jump at, to get through, because one was an opening that wasn't a door (it was a void, or koid) and the other was a wall that wasn't an opening, it was a sanitary cupboard of the same color. He caught a glimpse of his eyes staring into his eyes, in the thrutex, and in them was the expression he had seen in the picture of the rats—weary after convulsions and the frantic racing around, when they were willing and did not mind having anything done to them. More and more (he kept saying) I am confronted by a problem which is incapable of solution (for this time even if he chose the right door, there would be no food behind it) and that is what madness is, and things seeming different from what they are. He heard, in the house where he was, in the city to which he had gone (as toward a door which might, or might not, give way), a noise—not a loud noise but more of a low prefabricated humming. It came from a place in the base of the wall (or stat) where the flue carrying the filterable air was, and not far from the Minipiano, which was made of the same material nailbrushes are made of, and which was under the stairs. "This, too, has been tested," she said, pointing, but not at it, "and found viable." It wasn't a loud noise, he kept thinking, sorry that he had seen his eyes, even though it was through his own eyes that he had seen them.

First will come the convulsions (he said), then the exhaustion, then the willingness to let anything be done. "And you better believe it *will* be."

All his life he had been confronted by situations which were incapable of being solved, and there was a deliberateness behind all this, behind this changing of the card (or door), because they would always wait till you had learned to jump at the certain card (or door)—the one with the circle —and then they would change it on you. There have been so many doors changed on me, he said, in the last twenty years, but it is now becoming clear that it is an impossible situation, and the question is whether to jump again, even though they ruffle you in the rump with a blast of air— to make you jump. He wished he wasn't standing by the Minipiano. First they would teach you the prayers and the Psalms, and that would be the right door (the one with the circle) and the long sweet words with the holy sound, and that would be the one to jump at to get where the food was. Then one day you jumped and it didn't give way, so that all you got was the bump on the nose, and the first bewilderment, the first young be-wilderment.

I don't know whether to tell her about the door they substituted or not, he said, the one with the equation on it and the picture of the amoeba reproducing itself by division. Or the one with the photostatic copy of the check for thirty-two dollars and fifty cents. But the jumping was so long ago, although the bump is . . . how those old wounds hurt! Being crazy this way wouldn't be so bad if only, if only. If only when you put your foot forward to take a step, the ground wouldn't come up to meet your foot the way it does. And the same way in the street (only I may never get back to the street unless I jump at the right door), the curb coming up to meet your foot, anticipating ever so delicately the weight of the body, which is somewhere else. "We could take your name," she said, "and send it to you." And it wouldn't be so bad if only you could read a sentence all the way through without jumping (your eye) to something else on the same page; and then (he kept thinking) there was that man out in Jersey, the one who started to chop his trees down, one by one, the man who began talking about how he would take his house to pieces, brick by brick, because he faced a problem incapable of solution, probably, so he began to hack at the trees in the yard, began to pluck with trembling fingers at the bricks in the house. Even if a house is not washable, it is worth taking down. It is not till later that the exhaustion sets in.

But it is inevitable that they will keep changing the doors on you, he said, because that is what they are for; and the thing is to get used to it and not let it unsettle the mind. But that would mean not jumping, and you can't. Nobody can not jump. There will be no not-jumping. Among rats, perhaps, but among people never. Everybody has to keep jumping at a door (the one with the circle on it) because that is the way everybody is, specially some people. You wouldn't want me, standing here, to tell you, would you, about my friend the poet (deceased) who said, "My heart has followed all my days something I cannot name"? (It had the circle on it.) And like many poets, although few so beloved, he is gone. It killed him, the jumping. First, of course, there were the preliminary bouts, the convulsions, and the calm and the willingness.

I remember the door with the picture of the girl on it (only it was spring), her arms outstretched in loveliness, her dress (it was the one with the circle on it) uncaught, beginning the slow, clear, blinding cascade— and I guess we would all like to try that door again, for it seemed like the way and for a while it was the way, the door would open and you would go through winged and exalted (like any rat) and the food would be there, the way the Professor had it arranged, everything O.K., and you had chosen the right door for the world was young. The time they changed that door on me, my nose bled for a hundred hours—how do you like that, Madam? Or would you prefer to show me further through this so strange house, or you could take my name and send it to me, for although my heart has followed all my days something I cannot name, I am tired of the jumping and I do not know which way to go, Madam, and I am not even sure that I am not tired beyond the endurance of man (rat, if you will) and have taken leave of sanity. What are you following these days, old friend, after your recovery from the last bump? What is the name, or is it something you cannot name? The rats have a name for it by this time, perhaps, but I don't know what they call it. I call it plexikoid and it comes in sheets, something like insulating board, unattainable and ugli-proof.

And there was the man out in Jersey, because I keep thinking about his terrible necessity and the passion and trouble he had gone to all those years in the indescribable abundance of a householder's detail, building the estate and the planting of the trees and in spring the lawn-dressing and in fall the bulbs for the spring burgeoning, and the watering of the grass on the long light evenings in summer and the gravel for the driveway (all had to be thought out, planned) and the decorative borders, probably, the perennials and the bug spray, and the building of the house from plans of the architect, first the sills, then the studs, then the full corn in the ear, the floors laid on the floor timbers, smoothed, and then the carpets upon the smooth floors and the curtains and the rods therefor. And then, almost without warning, he would be jumping at the same old door and it wouldn't give: they had changed it on him, making life no longer supportable under the elms in the elm shade, under the maples in the maple shade.

"Here you have the maximum of openness in a small room."

It was impossible to say (maybe it was the city) what made him feel the way he did, and I am not the only one either, he kept thinking—ask any doctor if I am. The doctors, they know how many there are, they even know where the trouble is only they don't like to tell you about the prefrontal lobe because that means making a hole in your skull and removing the work of centuries. It took so long coming, this lobe, so many, many years. (Is it something you read in the paper, perhaps?) And now, the strain being so great, the door having been changed by the Professor once too often . . . but it only means a whiff of ether, a few deft strokes, and the higher animal becomes a little easier in his mind and more like the lower one. From now on, you see, that's the way it will be, the ones with the small prefrontal lobes will win because the other ones are hurt too much by this incessant bumping. They can stand just so much, eh, Doctor? (And what is that, pray, that you have in your hand?) Still, you never can tell, eh, Madam?

He crossed (carefully) the room, the thick carpet under him softly, and went toward the door carefully, which was glass and he could see himself in it, and which, at his approach, opened to allow him to pass through; and beyond he half expected to find one of the old doors that he had known, perhaps the one with the circle, the one with the girl her arms outstretched in loveliness and beauty before him. But he saw instead a moving stairway, and descended in light (he kept thinking) to the street below and to the other people. As he stepped off, the ground came up slightly, to meet his foot.

UNDERSTANDING THE TEXT

1. This essay was evoked by the publication of an account of some psychological researches on animals. Hungry rats were presented with colored panels or doors, some of which were fixed and some of which would swing open to reveal food. In time the rats learned which doors to jump at to obtain food and which to avoid. Then the colors were changed, the doors that had opened gave the jumping rats a bump on the nose, and the doors that had been fixed swung open unexpectedly. These changes reduced the rats to neurotic states in which they finally would not jump at all, no matter how hungry they got. What references to these experiments are made in White's essay? To what extent does the essay derive its basic terms and situations from these experiments? What basic analogy does White see between the situation of the experimental animals and the situation of modern man?

2. Where is the speaker? What does he seem to be doing? Can you tell anything about his age, his background, his occupation, his interests?

3. Why do you think White cast the essay into the third person instead of representing the thoughts of the speaker directly, in the first person?

4. Identify the various doors which the speaker has found have been changed on him (the prayers and the Psalms, the one with the equation on it, etc.). What does each door symbolize? What, precisely, does it mean that each of these doors was changed on the speaker?

5. How far can the opening sentence—"Everything (he kept saying) is something it isn't"—be regarded as a topic sentence for the whole piece?

6. What does the speaker mean by saying he is in a "washable house"? Why isn't he sure? Is there any connection between his being in a washable house and the "she" who says "This too has been tested and found viable"? Are there any later references, direct or indirect, to the washable house?

7. "She" first appears in paragraph 3, saying "This too has been tested and found viable." Who is "she"? Where else in the essay does she appear?

8. Suppose the sentences (p. 458), "Nobody can not jump. There will be no not-jumping," had read instead, "Everybody has to jump. There will be no hanging back." What would have been lost?

9. One of the special characteristics of the style of this essay is a kind of syntactical derangement in which sentence elements that would normally be expressed in parallel constructions are expressed instead in non-parallel structures. Consider, for example, the paragraph about the man out in Jersey on p. 459. The words "indescribable abundance of a householder's detail" introduce a long series. The series begins with a participial phrase (*building*), but then shifts from participle to gerund (which looks like a participle but isn't)—"the *planting*," "*the lawn-dressing*"; then to a noun phrase—"the *bulbs*"; back to a gerund—"the *watering*"; and so on. Complete the list for the rest of the paragraph. Rewrite this sentence, observing strict parallelism of construction in the series and making only such changes as parallelism requires. What is the difference in effect between your new version and the original? What do you think is the significance, in the light of White's purpose in the essay, of this stylistic feature? Can you find other examples of this technique? Can you find any related stylistic devices?

10. The essay makes considerable use of repeated words and phrases (e.g., "it was something else," "thrutex"). Find as many of these as you can, trace their occurrences through the essay, and try to make clear their function and value.

TOPICS FOR DISCUSSION AND WRITING

11. What is the "man out in Jersey" doing here?

12. What is your opinion of the last sentence of the opening paragraph?

13. Make a list of departures from normal syntax or "handbook" usage in "The Door" and discuss the reasons for them.

14. Comment on each of the following:
    "Even if a house is not washable, it is worth taking down."
    "(And what is that, pray, that you have in your hand?)"
    "(it was a void, or koid)"
    "He wished he wasn't standing by the Minipiano."
    "As he stepped off, the ground came up slightly, to meet his foot."

15. Write a brief essay in which you attempt to present the problem White is

concerned with here, setting out your views in a literal rather than a symbolic manner.

16. What are the principal features of modern society that this essay takes into account in presenting the plight of the individual in the modern world?

17. Compare the judgments of modern society implied here with those stated or suggested in White's essays on Thoreau (pp. 87–93, 95–103).

8. The American Experience

The Restless Spirit of the Americans in the Midst of Prosperity

ALEXIS DE TOCQUEVILLE

IN CERTAIN remote corners of the Old World you may still sometimes stumble upon a small district which seems to have been forgotten amid the general tumult, and to have remained stationary while everything around it was in motion. The inhabitants are for the most part extremely

Reprinted from *Democracy in America*, Part II, translated by Henry Reeve (1840).

ignorant and poor; they take no part in the business of the country, and they are frequently oppressed by the government; yet their countenances are generally placid, and their spirits light. In America I saw the freest and most enlightened men placed in the happiest circumstances that the world affords: it seemed to me as if a cloud habitually hung upon their brow, and I thought them serious and almost sad even in their pleasures. The chief reason of this contrast is that the former do not think of the ills they endure—the latter are forever brooding over advantages they do not possess. It is strange to see with what feverish ardour the Americans pursue their own welfare; and to watch the vague dread that constantly torments them lest they should not have chosen the shortest path which may lead to it. A native of the United States clings to this world's goods as if he were certain never to die; and he is so hasty in grasping at all within his reach that one would suppose he was constantly afraid of not living long enough to enjoy them. He clutches everything, he holds nothing fast, but soon loosens his grasp to pursue fresh gratifications.

In the United States a man builds a house to spend his latter years in it, and he sells it before the roof is on: he plants a garden, and lets it just as the trees are coming into bearing: he brings a field into tillage, and leaves other men to gather the crops: he embraces a profession, and gives it up: he settles in a place, which he soon afterward leaves, to carry his changeable longings elsewhere. If his private affairs leave him any leisure, he instantly plunges into the vortex of politics; and if at the end of a year of unremitting labour he finds he has a few days' vacation, his eager curiosity whirls him over the vast extent of the United States, and he will travel fifteen hundred miles in a few days to shake off his happiness. Death at length overtakes him, but it is before he is weary of his bootless chase of that complete felicity which is forever on the wing.

At first sight there is something surprising in this strange unrest of so many happy men, restless in the midst of abundance. The spectacle itself is, however, as old as the world; the novelty is to see a whole people furnish an exemplification of it. Their taste for physical gratifications must be regarded as the original source of that secret inquietude that the actions of the Americans betray, and of that inconstancy of which they afford fresh examples every day. He who has set his heart exclusively upon the pursuit of worldly welfare is always in a hurry, for he has but a limited time at his disposal to reach it, to grasp it, and to enjoy it. The recollection of the brevity of life is a constant spur to him. Besides the good things which he possesses, he every instant fancies a thousand others which death will prevent him from trying if he does not try them soon.

This thought fills him with anxiety, fear, and regret, and keeps his mind in ceaseless trepidation, which leads him perpetually to change his plans and his abode. If in addition to the taste for physical well-being a social condition be superadded, in which the laws and customs make no condition permanent, here is a great additional stimulant to this restlessness of temper. Men will then be seen continually to change their track, for fear of missing the shortest cut to happiness. It may readily be conceived that if men, passionately bent upon physical gratifications, desire eagerly, they are also easily discouraged: as their ultimate object is to enjoy, the means to reach that object must be prompt and easy, or the trouble of acquiring the gratification would be greater than the gratification itself. Their prevailing frame of mind, then, is at once ardent and relaxed, violent and enervated. Death is often less dreaded than perseverance in continuous efforts to one end.

The equality of conditions leads by a still straighter road to several of the effects which I have here described. When all the privileges of birth and fortune are abolished, when all professions are accessible to all, and a man's own energies may place him at the top of any one of them, an easy and unbounded career seems open to his ambition, and he will readily persuade himself that he is born to no vulgar destinies. But this is an erroneous notion, which is corrected by daily experience. The same equality which allows every citizen to conceive these lofty hopes renders all the citizens less able to realize them: it circumscribes their powers on every side, while it gives freer scope to their desires. Not only are they themselves powerless, but they are met at every step by immense obstacles, which they did not at first perceive. They have swept away the privileges of some of their fellow-creatures which stood in their way, but they have opened the door to universal competition: the barrier has changed its shape rather than its position. When men are nearly alike, and all follow the same track, it is very difficult for any one individual to walk quick and cleave a way through the dense throng which surrounds and presses him. This constant strife between the propensities springing from the equality of conditions and the means it supplies to satisfy them harasses and wearies the mind.

It is possible to conceive men arrived at a degree of freedom which should completely content them; they would then enjoy their independence without anxiety and without impatience. But men will never establish any equality with which they can be contented. Whatever efforts a people may make, they will never succeed in reducing all the conditions of society to a perfect level; and even if they unhappily attained that ab-

solute and complete depression, the inequality of minds would still remain, which, coming directly from the hand of God, will forever escape
the laws of man. However democratic, then, the social state and the political constitution of a people may be, it is certain that every member of
the community will always find out several points about him that command his own position; and we may foresee that his looks will be dog-
gedly fixed in that direction. When inequality of conditions is the common law of society, the most marked inequalities do not strike the
eye: when everything is nearly on the same level, the slightest are marked
enough to hurt it. Hence the desire of equality always becomes more insatiable in proportion as equality is more complete.

Among democratic nations men easily attain a certain equality of conditions: they can never attain the equality they desire. It perpetually re-
tires from before them, yet without hiding itself from their sight, and in
retiring draws them on. At every moment they think they are about to
grasp it; it escapes at every moment from their hold. They are near
enough to see its charms, but too far off to enjoy them; and before they
have fully tasted its delights they die. To these causes must be attributed
that strange melancholy that oftentimes will haunt the inhabitants of democratic countries in the midst of their abundance, and that disgust at life
that sometimes seizes upon them in the midst of calm and easy circumstances. Complaints are made in France that the number of suicides increases; in America suicide is rare, but insanity is said to be more common
than anywhere else. These are all different symptoms of the same disease.
The Americans do not put an end to their lives, however disquieted they
may be, because their religion forbids it; and among them materialism
may be said hardly to exist, notwithstanding the general passion for physical gratification. The will resists—reason frequently gives way.

In democratic ages enjoyments are more intense than in the ages of
aristocracy, and especially the number of those who partake in them is
larger: but, on the other hand, it must be admitted that man's hopes and
his desires are often blasted, the soul is more stricken and perturbed, and
care itself more keen.

UNDERSTANDING THE TEXT

1. On what scale or level of generality does Tocqueville discuss the "restless
   spirit" of Americans? How much use does he make of specific details and
   examples?
2. What effect is created by the scale Tocqueville employs?

3. Of the different methods of organization illustrated in Part One, Section 3, of this book, which does Tocqueville primarily follow in this essay? Are any other methods used in subordinate ways?

4. In attempting to explain the Americans' restlessness, Tocqueville sets forth two other generalizations about the American character. What are they?

5. In what way does Tocqueville try to show a relationship between each of these subordinate generalizations and the observation that Americans are not a contented people?

6. See if you can trace in detail the logical steps which carry Tocqueville from the second of his explanatory generalizations about Americans to the fact that Americans are unusually restless.

7. What distinction does Tocqueville draw between the effects of freedom and equality, respectively, as social goals?

8. In what sense are suicide in France and insanity in America "different symptoms of the same disease"?

9. What is the purpose of the brief description of European provincial life at the outset of the essay?

10. Analyze the second paragraph, in which Tocqueville illustrates what he means by American restlessness. How satisfactorily and economically do the details included in this sketch convey the general idea the author has in mind?

TOPICS FOR DISCUSSION AND WRITING

11. This essay affords an excellent study in logical implication—that is, in showing how two or more general ideas can be brought into meaningful relationship with each other. As an exercise, see if you can develop a logical connection between these two general statements: (a) Young people think that life is endless, and (b) Young people show little discrimination in choosing the books they read or the movies they see.

12. Write an essay which develops in contemporary terms the ideas expressed in the Tocqueville discussion and which makes considerable use of illustrative incidents and specific details.

13. If you wished to refute the interpretation of the American character offered by Tocqueville, how would you go about it? Could you question the truth of the general statements which are central to the argument? Could you detect flaws in the way Tocqueville establishes connections between the general statements? Write such a refutation.

14. Write a paragraph supporting or contradicting the following statement: "The desire of equality always becomes more insatiable in proportion as equality is more complete."

15. Most observers agree that since World War II Americans have become more

mobile than at any previous time in the twentieth century. Studies show that in many parts of the country an unusually large number of the inhabitants have moved in from other sections. Write a paper setting forth what seem to you the probable causes of this most recent spurt in American "restlessness."

Industrialism and American Ideals

HENRY BAMFORD PARKES

AS INDUSTRIALISM expanded, there was a growing discrepancy between the habits and beliefs of the American people and the realities of their social environment. The character of a people always changes more slowly than their institutions, and the Americans carried over into the more static and regimented society of the big corporations the attitudes they had acquired while they were still pioneers with all the vast resources of an empty wilderness to conquer and exploit. They continued to insist that freedom and equality were actually realized in their society, and to think and act on this assumption in the conduct of their daily lives. This cultural lag produced a schism between idea and reality that may be described as a national neurosis. To use such a word in this context is by no means merely metaphorical. The neurotic individual is the individual who has failed to adjust himself to realities; and when a whole culture exhibits such a failure of adjustment, the result is a growth of neurotic tendencies among the men and women who have been conditioned by it.

The Americans believed that they were a free people. But the wage earner was no longer his own master during the most important part of his daily life—his working hours; he was free only insofar as he could do and say what he liked during his leisure time, and (with considerable limitations) could choose his own form of employment. Unable to participate in making the decisions upon which his livelihood depended, he had become the victim of forces over which he had no control. The Americans believed in equality of opportunity. But the system of property and inheritance laws was creating class divisions as acute as those existing in the Europe from which they had come. Above all, the Americans believed that the individual should struggle to improve his condition and conquer his environment, that if he had energy, courage, and initiative he would surely succeed, and that if he failed it was because of some deficiency within himself. Yet in the new industrial system it was wholly impossible for more than a small minority of the total population to achieve what society regarded as success. The average wage earner must be "fixed to that condition for life." Even among the highly paid and responsible business men and salaried executives only a small fraction were actually able to reach the top. Thus insofar as the American people were committed to the American ideology of personal success, they were attempting to accomplish something that for most of them was impossible. Judged by the prevalent standards of American society, most Americans were compelled to regard themselves as having failed and to attribute their failure to some shortcoming within themselves. This attitude persisted even during periods of economic depression, when millions of men, through no fault of their own, found themselves unemployed. Instead of rebelling against a system that had denied them opportunity, most of the unemployed accepted their fate with a masochistic submissiveness.

Since the big corporations never achieved a total domination over the American economy, this disharmony between idea and reality was by no means universal. Rural and small-town America retained much of the leisureliness and neighborliness of the agrarian past. There was still room for the exercise of initiative, and the Americans continued to be capable of an inventiveness and an adventurousness beyond any other nation. But in the big cities life became competitive, fast-moving, febrile, and neurotic; and to an increasing extent the cities tended to dictate fashions and beliefs and to determine the cultural tone for the rest of the country.

With the transformation of the pioneer into the businessman, money became the principal symbol of success and the main object of ambition. In the strict sense of the word, the Americans were not a materialistic people. They were less concerned with the mere accumulation of material possessions and less careful in their use than were most Europeans. They continued to be the most generous people in the world, and to be extravagantly lavish and wasteful in the spending of their resources. But the business classes sought to prove their strength by the conquest of money, as their ancestors had done by the conquest of the wilderness; and they judged each other in monetary terms. To believe that there might be forms of personal achievement not susceptible to pecuniary measurement was to be slightly eccentric. In the twentieth century, with the growth of the durable consumption-goods industries and the colossal expansion of advertising, the belief that all success was monetary was emphasized and played upon by almost every newspaper, magazine, motion picture, and radio program. The man who could not afford to buy a new car, a new refrigerator, and the most up-to-date plumbing was lacking in virility and had not done his duty by his wife and children.

Such an attitude was incompatible with strict standards of personal and political honesty. In the pursuit of money it was a mistake to be too scrupulous; and laws could usually be circumvented. The Americans had never been a law-abiding people. On the frontier individuals had always defended themselves without relying on any organized enforcement of justice. Outlaws, desperadoes, claim jumpers, cattle rustlers, and other "bad men" had played prominent roles in the legend of the early West. With so individualistic and exuberant a past, it was not to be expected that the Americans would suddenly change their habits when their society became more settled, although the social effects of lawlessness and chicanery were now much more deleterious. Most people kept their financial activities within the letter of the law, but they felt no compunction about twisting its spirit to suit their own convenience. Speculation in stocks and real estate in order to get something for nothing was a national pastime, and was not regarded as in any way reprehensible, in spite of its demonstrably harmful effects upon the economic system. And while a large proportion of the business class hoped to make fortunes by methods that might be unethical but were not illegal, an appreciable element among the poorer classes pursued the same goal by a more direct route. The "bad men" of the frontier and the early West were succeeded, in industrial America, by the big-city gangsters. Skillful criminals sometimes made fortunes, and the disapproval of their more cautious fellow citizens was not always unmixed with envy.

For the aggressive and ambitious individual who felt confident of his power to compete, the life of the big cities had an extraordinary glamor and intoxication. But the plain citizen, insofar as he accepted the standards of his society and regarded monetary success as the main gauge of individual merit, inevitably suffered from a sense of defeat. In this competitive world he could have little feeling of belonging to any social order that was more significant and more enduring than its individual members, and that gave meaning to their lives; such a conception had always been lacking among the Americans. And since he could not conquer his environment, he had to regard himself as its victim, as a man to whom things happened. Whereas the frontier had created culture heroes like Daniel Boone and Mike Fink who stood for physical prowess and mastery, industrial America developed a humor of a new kind, the humor of the little man who always expects defeat—an attitude most perfectly embodied in Charlie Chaplin.[1] Such conditions inevitably undermined self-esteem, dignity, and masculinity, and stimulated neuroticism. What proportion of urban Americans actually suffered from emotional disorders, nervous breakdowns, or outright insanity, it is impossible to say; but any investigation of the subject, such as that undertaken in the case of men of military age during the Second World War, produced startling results.[2] Even before industrialism had conquered the nation De Tocqueville had commented on the high proportion of nervous disorders among the Americans, and had attributed it to the competitiveness of American life.[3]

Growth into psychological maturity requires a healthy self-assurance and self-esteem; and when self-esteem depends upon a competitive success difficult to achieve and always uncertain, then it becomes more difficult for individuals to assume the full emotional responsibilities of adulthood. They may prefer to remain permanently on an adolescent level. Such a prolongation of adolescence became a frequent characteristic of twentieth-century urban Americans, particularly among those business and professional classes who were most involved in the competitive struggle. Their perpetual boyishness was sometimes attributed to the fact that America was a young country in which an adolescent exuberance was somehow appropriate, yet it had by no means been characteristic of the men of the eighteenth century, who had lived at a time when America was even younger; it was a twentieth-century phenomenon. And the emotional immaturity of so many American men led to a further increase in the relative influence of American women. The frontier had already made women more powerful in America than in Europe; and industrial society intensified this tendency. European observers sometimes declared that American society was essentially matriarchal and that women

---

[1] According to James West, Americans living in an old-fashioned agrarian community do not find Charlie Chaplin funny. Dr. Kardiner comments: "Most Plainvillers apparently consider Chaplin just silly. This observation is of considerable importance. It means that the unconscious appeal of Chaplin's bum is less powerful to Plainvillers than to city folks, and that the tensions which this strange vagabond purports to ease are less intense with Plainvillers. This would mean that the Plainviller is more secure and less troubled by the pursuit of goals approved in urban centers." Abram Kardiner, *The Psychological Frontiers of Society*, p. 369.

[2] During the Second World War psychoneurotic disorders were responsible for 1,825,000 draft rejections and for 600,000 discharges.

[3] *Democracy in America*, Vol. II, Second Book, Chap. XIII.

had become the superior class. This development was hastened by the increase in the amount of property held by women and by the gradual abolition during the twentieth century of legal, political, and economic inequalities between the sexes; but its more fundamental causes were emotional. The man of the industrial age was apt to have a neurotic dependence, first upon his mother and afterwards upon his wife, owing to his own insecurity and lack of masculine self-assurance.

On the surface it seemed that this change in the relationship between the sexes could be described eulogistically in terms of feminine emancipation; women, it was often declared, were being liberated from their age-long subordination and were acquiring their own rights to life, liberty, and the pursuit of happiness. There were plenty of indications, however, that neither the American man nor the American woman was deriving full emotional satisfaction from the new order. For the first time in history, sex began to be regarded as a problem, not only in its social and theological implications, but also biologically; there was a rapid increase in the number of divorces; and there was an equally rapid decrease, at least in the cities, in the birth rate. Rural America continued to produce a surplus of children; among the farm population (according to the census of 1930) every ten adults had an average of fourteen children. But in cities with more than one hundred thousand inhabitants every ten adults had an average of only seven children, and among the professional classes, who presumably included the most gifted members of society, the deficit of children amounted to no less than forty per cent. This situation was due to various economic and social as well as emotional factors; but whatever its causes might be, it was an indication of serious maladjustments. A society that was failing to reproduce itself and in which the most talented stocks were steadily becoming extinct, could not be regarded as healthy.

And when sensitive Americans of the twentieth century contrasted their society with that of Europe, they could no longer feel assured that it represented any new and higher principles of social organization. The confidence in America which had been so characteristic of the great men of the eighteenth century had become less plausible. Jefferson's prediction that "when we get piled upon one another as in Europe, we shall become corrupt as in Europe, and go to eating one another as they do there" appeared to have been fulfilled, and with much greater rapidity than Jefferson had expected. This loss of faith in America was by no means characteristic of the nation as a whole. The average twentieth-century citizen continued to believe that men in America were more free and more nearly equal than in Europe, and to take pride in the material achievements of his civilization; and the average citizen did, in fact, continue to have wider opportunities and a higher standard of living in America than anywhere else in the world. But it was no longer possible to define with any clarity what American civilization stood for; liberal idealists in other countries were now inclined to see America, no longer as an inspiring example of freedom and equality, but as a horrifying specimen of capitalist domination. And among the Americans themselves the intellectual classes were increasingly inclined to feel that the hopes of the eighteenth century had somehow been frustrated, that the wealth and power of the industrial age had been purchased at too high a price, and that possibly American civilization from the beginning had been marred by some fatal flaw that would make it permanently inferior to the civilization of Europe.

In the eighteenth century the most gifted and widely cultured of the Americans had been the most convinced of the superiority of American society; but their twentieth-century successors felt no such certainty. The optimism of a Franklin and a Jefferson might be contrasted with the disillusionment of a Henry Adams, who was inclined to regard all Western history since the Middle Ages as a process of steady degeneration, with the tendency of so many American intellectuals to become expatriates, and with the sense of loneliness, of cynicism, and of defeat that pervaded so much of the American literature of the twentieth century.

UNDERSTANDING THE TEXT

1. How does Parkes define the term "neurosis"? How does he use this definition in presenting his views on the way industrialism affected American life?

2. In supporting the statement that American society suffered from a "national neurosis," what examples of disharmony between accepted ideas and social reality does Parkes cite?

3. Once the author has finished describing in general terms the gap he discerns between social ideals and the actual situation, what specific effects does he see flowing from this disharmony?

4. In what order does Parkes present these effects? Can you offer an explanation for the order? Why, for instance, does he discuss the growing importance of money as a symbol of success before he treats the psychological changes in individuals?

5. What use does the author make of the contrast between urban civilization and small-town or rural life?

6. Although Parkes concentrates on showing how industrialism affected American life in the late nineteenth and twentieth centuries, does he relate any of his ideas to the earlier frontier and agrarian America? What characteristics of frontier America does he find carrying over into the new era? What characteristics of the older society are abandoned?

7. How similar are the explanations which Tocqueville and Parkes give for the relatively high rate of insanity among Americans?

8. Can you discern, as a foundation for this essay, any premises concerning the nature of psychological maturity and health?

9. Explain the meaning of the following terms in their contexts: *masochistic, durable consumption-goods, virility, scrupulous, circumvented, chicanery, deleterious, matriarchal, eulogistically, expatriates.*

TOPICS FOR DISCUSSION AND WRITING

10. Parkes assumes that unfortunate consequences are produced when social ideals and social realities are strikingly divergent. What do you think would be the consequences of the opposite extreme—that is, of a society in which ideals and actuality are identical? What kind of society might this be? Develop your reflections on this point into an essay.

11. Can you suggest present-day examples, other than those offered by Parkes, of discrepancy between social ideals and actual conditions? In these cases, does the disharmony create any serious consequences?

12. Choose one of Parkes's central generalizations—concerning the role of women, for example, or the big city, or the significance of money—and in a paper defend or question the author's interpretation of this aspect of American life.

13. Essentially, Parkes's analysis is based on the history of the United States from the emergence of industrialism to World War II. Is the analysis valid today? Are there any points which might be modified if one took into account the history of the postwar years?

14. Comment on the practice of applying to a group or to a nation terms, such as "neurosis," which are ordinarily used in connection with individuals. Can you suggest other words which are sometimes employed in this way? Are there any dangers in this practice?

15. Do you agree with Parkes that the attitude which regards the acquisition of money as the primary form of achievement is "incompatible with strict standards of personal and political honesty"?

The Role of the Undesirables

ERIC HOFFER

IN THE winter of 1934, I spent several weeks in a federal transient camp in California. These camps were originally established by Governor Rolph in the early days of the Depression to care for the single homeless unemployed of the state. In 1934 the federal government took charge of the camps for a time, and it was then that I first heard of them.

How I happened to get into one of the camps is soon told. Like thousands of migrant agricultural workers in California I then followed the crops from one part of the state to the other. Early in 1934 I arrived in the town of El Centro, in the Imperial Valley. I had been given a free ride on a truck from San Diego, and it was midnight when the truck driver dropped me on the outskirts of El Centro. I spread my bedroll by the side of the road and went to sleep. I had hardly dozed off when the rattle of a motorcycle drilled itself into my head and a policeman was bending over me saying, "Roll up, Mister." It looked as though I was in for something; it happened now and then that the police got overzealous and rounded up the freight trains. But this time the cop had no such thought. He said, "Better go over to the federal shelter and get yourself a bed and maybe some breakfast." He directed me to the place.

I found a large hall, obviously a former garage, dimly lit, and packed with cots. A concert of heavy breathing shook the thick air. In a small office near the door, I was registered by a middle-aged clerk. He informed me that this was the "receiving shelter" where I would get one night's lodging and breakfast. The meal was served in the camp nearby. Those who wished to stay on, he said, had to enroll in the camp. He then gave

Reprinted from *Harper's Magazine*, December, 1952. Used by permission of the author.

me three blankets and excused himself for not having a vacant cot. I spread the blankets on the cement floor and went to sleep.

I awoke with dawn amid a chorus of coughing, throat-clearing, the sound of running water, and the intermittent flushing of toilets in the back of the hall. There were about fifty of us, of all colors and ages, all of us more or less ragged and soiled. The clerk handed out tickets for breakfast, and we filed out to the camp located several blocks away, near the railroad tracks.

From the outside the camp looked like a cross between a factory and a prison. A high fence of wire enclosed it, and inside were three large sheds and a huge boiler topped by a pillar of black smoke. Men in blue shirts and dungarees were strolling across the sandy yard. A ship's bell in front of one of the buildings announced breakfast. The regular camp members—there was a long line of them—ate first. Then we filed in through the gate, handing our tickets to the guard.

It was a good, plentiful meal. After breakfast our crowd dispersed. I heard some say that the camps in the northern part of the state were better, that they were going to catch a northbound freight. I decided to try this camp in El Centro.

My motives in enrolling were not crystal clear. I wanted to clean up. There were shower baths in the camp and wash tubs and plenty of soap. Of course I could have bathed and washed my clothes in one of the irrigation ditches, but here in the camp I had a chance to rest, get the wrinkles out of my belly, and clean up at leisure. In short, it was the easiest way out.

A brief interview at the camp office and a physical examination were all the formalities for enrollment.

There were some two hundred men in the camp. They were the kind I had worked and traveled with for years. I even saw familiar faces—men I had worked with in orchards and fields. Yet my predominant feeling was one of strangeness. It was my first experience of life in intimate contact with a crowd. For it is one thing to work and travel with a gang, and quite another thing to eat, sleep, and spend the greater part of the day cheek by jowl with two hundred men.

I found myself speculating on a variety of subjects: the reasons for their chronic bellyaching and beefing—it was more a ritual than the expression of a grievance; the amazing orderliness of the men; the comic seriousness with which they took their games of cards, checkers, and dominoes; the weird manner of reasoning one overheard now and then.

Why, I kept wondering, were these men within the enclosure of a federal transient camp? Were they people temporarily hard up? Would jobs solve all their difficulties? Were we indeed like the people outside?

Up to then I was not aware of being one of a specific species of humanity. I had considered myself simply a human being—not particularly good or bad, and on the whole harmless. The people I worked and traveled with I knew as Americans and Mexicans, whites and Negroes, Northerners and Southerners, etc. It did not occur to me that we were a group possessed of peculiar traits, and that there was something—innate or acquired—in our make-up which made us adopt a particular mode of existence.

It was a slight thing that started me on a new track.

I got to talking to a mild-looking, elderly fellow. I liked his soft speech and pleasant manner. We swapped trivial experiences. Then he suggested a game of checkers. As we started to arrange the pieces on the board, I was startled by the sight of his crippled right hand. I had not noticed it before. Half of it was chopped off lengthwise, so that the horny stump with its three fingers looked like a hen's leg. I was mortified that I had not noticed the hand until he dangled it, so to speak, before my eyes. It was, perhaps, to bolster my shaken confidence in my powers of observation that I now began paying close attention to the hands of the people around me. The result was astounding. It seemed that every other man had had his hand mangled. There was a man with one arm. Some men limped. One young, good-looking fellow had a wooden leg. It was as though the majority of the men had escaped the snapping teeth of a machine and left part of themselves behind.

It was, I knew, an exaggerated impression. But I began counting the cripples as the men lined up in the yard at mealtime. I found thirty (out of two hundred) crippled either in arms or legs. I immediately sensed where the counting would land me. The simile preceded the statistical deduction: we in the camp were a human junk pile.

I began evaluating my fellow tramps as human material, and for the first time in my life I became face-conscious. There were some good faces, particularly among the young. Several of the middle-aged and the old looked healthy and well preserved. But the damaged and decayed faces were in the majority. I saw faces that were wrinkled, or bloated, or raw as the surface of a peeled plum. Some of the noses were purple and swollen, some broken, some pitted with enlarged pores. There were many toothless mouths (I counted seventy-eight). I noticed eyes that were blurred, faded, opaque, or bloodshot. I was struck by the fact that the old men, even the very old, showed their age mainly in the face. Their bodies were still slender and erect. One little man over sixty years of age looked a mere boy when seen from behind. The shriveled face joined to a boyish body made a startling sight.

My diffidence had now vanished. I was getting to know everybody in the camp. They were a friendly and talkative lot. Before many weeks I knew some essential fact about practically everyone.

And I was continually counting. Of the two hundred men in the camp there were approximately as follows:

```
Cripples ............................................ 30
Confirmed drunkards ................................ 60
Old men (55 and over) ............................. 50
Youths under twenty ................................ 10
Men with chronic diseases, heart, asthma, TB .......... 12
Mildly insane ....................................... 4
Constitutionally lazy ................................ 6
Fugitives from justice .............................. 4
Apparently normal ................................. 70
```

(The numbers do not tally up to two hundred since some of the men were counted twice or even thrice—as cripples and old, or as old and confirmed drunks, etc.)

In other words: less than half the camp inmates (seventy normal, plus ten youths) were unemployed workers whose difficulties would be at an end once jobs were available. The rest (60 per cent) had handicaps in addition to unemployment.

I also counted fifty war veterans, and eighty skilled workers representing sixteen trades. All the men (including those with chronic diseases) were able to work. The one-armed man was a wizard with the shovel.

I did not attempt any definite measurement of character and intelligence. But it seemed to me that the intelligence of the men in the camp was certainly not below the average. And as to character, I found much forbearance and genuine good humor. I never came across one instance of real viciousness. Yet, on the whole, one would hardly say that these men were possessed of strong characters. Resistance, whether to one's appetites or to the ways of the world, is a chief factor in the shaping of character; and the average tramp is, more or less, a slave of his few appetites. He generally takes the easiest way out.

The connection between our make-up and our mode of existence as migrant workers presented itself now with some clarity.

The majority of us were incapable of holding onto a steady job. We lacked self-discipline and the ability to endure monotonous, leaden hours. We were probably misfits from the very beginning. Our contact with a steady job was not unlike a collision. Some of us were maimed, some got frightened and ran away, and some took to drink. We inevitably drifted in the direction of least resistance—the open road. The life of a migrant worker is varied and demands only a minimum of self-discipline. We were now in one of the drainage ditches of ordered society. We could not keep a footing in the ranks of respectability and were washed into the slough of our present existence.

Yet, I mused, there must be in this world a task with an appeal so strong that were we to have a taste of it we would hold on and be rid for good of our restlessness.

My stay in the camp lasted about four weeks. Then I found a haying job not far from town, and finally, in April, when the hot winds began blowing, I shouldered my bedroll and took the highway to San Bernardino.

It was the next morning, after I had got a lift to Indio by truck, that a new idea began to take hold of me. The highway out of Indio leads through waving date groves, fragrant grapefruit orchards, and lush alfalfa fields; then, abruptly, passes into a desert of white sand. The sharp line between garden and desert is very striking. The turning of white sand into garden seemed to me an act of magic. This, I thought, was a job one would jump at—even the men in the transient camps. They had the skill and ability of the average American. But their energies, I felt, could be quickened only by a task that was spectacular, that had in it something of the miraculous. The pioneer task of making the desert flower would certainly fill the bill.

Tramps as pioneers? It seemed absurd. Every man and child in California knows that the pioneers had been giants, men of boundless courage and indomitable spirit. However, as I strode on across the white sand, I kept mulling the idea over.

Who were the pioneers? Who were the men who left their homes and went into the wilderness? A man rarely leaves a soft spot and goes deliberately in search of hardship and privation. People become attached to the places they live in; they drive roots. A change of habitat is a painful act of uprooting. A man who has made good and has a standing in his community stays put. The successful business men, farmers, and workers usually stayed where they were. Who then left for the wilderness and the unknown? Obviously those who had not made good: men who went broke or never amounted to much; men who though possessed of abilities were too impulsive to stand the daily grind; men who were slaves of their appetites—drunkards, gamblers, and woman-chasers; outcasts—fugitives from justice and ex-jailbirds. There were no doubt some who went in search of health—men suffering with TB, asthma, heart trouble. Finally there was a sprinkling of young and middle-aged in search of adventure.

All these people craved change, some probably actuated by the naïve belief that a change in place brings with it a change in luck. Many wanted to go to a place where they were not known and there make a new beginning. Certainly they did not go out deliberately in search of hard work and suffering. If in the end they shouldered enormous tasks, endured unspeakable hardships, and accomplished the impossible, it was because they had to. They became men of action on the run. They acquired strength and skill in the inescapable struggle for existence. It was a question of do or die. And once they tasted the joy of achievement, they craved for more.

Clearly the same types of people which now swelled the ranks of migratory workers and tramps had probably in former times made up the bulk of the pioneers. As a group the pioneers were probably as unlike the present-day "native sons"—their descendants—as one could well imagine. Indeed, were there to be today a new influx of typical pioneers, twin brothers of the forty-niners only in a modern garb, the citizens of California would consider it a menace to health, wealth, and morals.

With few exceptions, this seems to be the case in the settlement of all new countries. Ex-convicts were the vanguard in the settling of Australia. Exiles and convicts settled Siberia. In this country, a large portion of our earlier and later settlers were failures, fugitives, and felons. The exceptions seemed to be those who were motivated by religious fervor, such as the Pilgrim Fathers and the Mormons.

Although quite logical, this train of thought seemed to me then a wonderful joke. In my exhilaration I was eating up the road in long strides, and I reached the oasis of Elim in what seemed almost no time. A passing empty truck picked me up just then and we thundered through Banning and Beaumont, all the way to Riverside. From there I walked the seven miles to San Bernardino.

Somehow, this discovery of a family likeness between tramps and pioneers took a firm hold on my mind. For years afterward it kept inter-twining itself with a mass of observations which on the face of them had no relation to either tramps or pioneers. And it moved me to speculate on subjects in which, up to then, I had no real interest, and of which I knew very little.

I talked with several old-timers—one of them over eighty and a native son—in Sacramento, Placerville, Auburn, and Fresno. It was not easy, at first, to obtain the information I was after. I could not make my questions specific enough. "What kind of people were the early settlers and miners?" I asked. They were a hard-working, tough lot, I was told. They drank, fought, gambled, and wenched. They were big-hearted, grasping, pro-fane, and God-fearing. They wallowed in luxury, or lived on next to nothing with equal ease. They were the salt of the earth.

Still it was not clear what manner of people they were.

If I asked what they looked like, I was told of whiskers, broad-brimmed hats, high boots, shirts of many colors, sun-tanned faces, horny hands. Finally I asked: "What group of people in present-day California most closely resemble the pioneers?" The answer, usually after some hesitation, was invariably the same: "The Okies and the fruit tramps."

I tried also to evaluate the tramps as potential pioneers by watching them in action. I saw them fell timber, clear firebreaks, build rock walls, put up barracks, build dams and roads, handle steam shovels, bulldozers, tractors, and concrete mixers. I saw them put in a hard day's work after a night of steady drinking. They sweated and growled, but they did the work. I saw tramps elevated to positions of authority as foremen and superintendents. Then I could notice a remarkable physical transformation: a seamed face gradually smoothed out and the skin showed a healthy hue; an indifferent mouth became firm and expressive; dull eyes cleared and brightened; voices actually changed; there was even an apparent increase in stature. In almost no time these promoted tramps looked as if they had been on top all their lives. Yet sooner or later I would meet up with them again in a railroad yard, on some skid row, or in the fields—tramps again. It was usually the same story: they got drunk or lost their temper and were fired, or they got fed up with the steady job and quit. Usually, when a tramp becomes a foreman, he is careful in his treatment of the tramps under him; he knows the day of reckoning is never far off.

In short, it was not difficult to visualize the tramps as pioneers. I re-flected that if they were to find themselves in a singlehanded life-and-death struggle with nature, they would undoubtedly display persistence. For the pressure of responsibility and the heat of battle steel a character.

The inadaptable would perish, and those who survived would be the equal of the successful pioneers.

I also considered the few instances of pioneering engineered from above —that is to say, by settlers possessed of lavish means, who were classed with the best where they came from. In these instances, it seemed to me, the resulting social structure was inevitably precarious. For pioneering deluxe usually results in a plantation society, made up of large landowners and peon labor, either native or imported. Very often there is a racial cleavage between the two. The colonizing activities of the Teutonic barons in the Baltic, the Hungarian nobles in Transylvania, the English in Ireland, the planters in our South, and the present-day plantation societies in Kenya and other British and Dutch colonies are cases in point. Whatever their merits, they are characterized by poor adaptability. They are likely eventually to be broken up either by a peon revolution or by an influx of typical pioneers—who are usually of the same race or nation as the landowners. The adjustment is not necessarily implemented by war. Even our old South, had it not been for the complication of secession, might eventually have attained stability without war: namely, by the activity of its own poor whites or by an influx of the indigent from other states.

There is in us a tendency to judge a race, a nation, or an organization by its least worthy members. The tendency is manifestly perverse and unfair; yet it has some justification. For the quality and destiny of a nation is determined to a considerable extent by the nature and potentialities of its inferior elements. The inert mass of a nation is in its middle section. The industrious, decent, well-to-do, and satisfied middle classes—whether in cities or on the land—are worked upon and shaped by minorities at both extremes: the best and the worst.

The superior individual, whether in politics, business, industry, science, literature, or religion, undoubtedly plays a major role in the shaping of a nation. But so do the individuals at the other extreme: the poor, the outcasts, the misfits, and those who are in the grip of some overpowering passion. The importance of these inferior elements as formative factors lies in the readiness with which they are swayed in any direction. This peculiarity is due to their inclination to take risks ("not giving a damn") and their propensity for united action. They crave to merge their drab, wasted lives into something grand and complete. Thus they are the first and most fervent adherents of new religions, political upheavals, patriotic hysteria, gangs, and mass rushes to new lands.

And the quality of a nation—its innermost worth—is made manifest by its dregs as they rise to the top: by how brave they are, how humane, how orderly, how skilled, how generous, how independent or servile; by the bounds they will not transgress in their dealings with man's soul, with truth, and with honor.

The average American of today bristles with indignation when he is told that this country was built, largely, by hordes of undesirables from Europe. Yet, far from being derogatory, this statement, if true, should be a cause for rejoicing, should fortify our pride in the stock from which we have sprung.

This vast continent with its towns, farms, factories, dams, aqueducts, docks, railroads, highways, powerhouses, schools, and parks is the handiwork of common folk from the Old World, where for centuries men of their kind had been as beasts of burden, the property of their masters—kings, nobles, and priests—and with no will and no aspirations of their own. When on rare occasions one of the lowly had reached the top in Europe he had kept the pattern intact and, if anything, tightened the screws. The stuffy little corporal from Corsica harnessed the lusty forces released by the French Revolution to a gilded state coach, and could think of nothing grander than mixing his blood with that of the Hapsburg masters and establishing a new dynasty. In our day a bricklayer in Italy, a house painter in Germany, and a shoemaker's son in Russia have made themselves masters of their nations; and what they did was to re-establish and reinforce the old pattern.

Only here, in America, were the common folk of the Old World given a chance to show what they could do on their own, without a master to push and order them about. History contrived an earth-shaking joke when it lifted by the nape of the neck lowly peasants, shopkeepers, laborers, paupers, jailbirds, and drunks from the midst of Europe, dumped them on a vast, virgin continent and said: "Go to it; it is yours!"

And the lowly were not awed by the magnitude of the task. A hunger for action, pent up for centuries, found an outlet. They went to it with ax, pick, shovel, plow, and rifle; on foot, on horse, in wagons, and on flatboats. They went to it praying, howling, singing, brawling, drinking, and fighting. Make way for the people! This is how I read the statement that this country was built by hordes of undesirables from the Old World.

Small wonder that we in this country have a deeply ingrained faith in human regeneration. We believe that, given a chance, even the degraded and the apparently worthless are capable of constructive work and great deeds. It is a faith founded on experience, not on some idealistic theory.

And no matter what some anthropologists, sociologists, and geneticists may tell us, we shall go on believing that man, unlike other forms of life, is not a captive of his past—of his heredity and habits—but is possessed of infinite plasticity, and his potentialities for good and for evil are never wholly exhausted.

UNDERSTANDING THE TEXT

1. In the title and the essay, what meaning does Hoffer give the word "undesirables"? What makes a person an "undesirable"?

2. In a paragraph, summarize what the author conceives the role of the undesirables to be.

3. What is the function of the narrative at the beginning of the essay? What does it tell the reader about the author's right to be heard on this subject? What clues does it provide to the author's character and point of view?

4. How does Hoffer go about studying his fellow residents of the transient camp? What characteristics do the men have in common?

5. How does Hoffer account for the failure of the migrant workers to hold their own in organized society? What premise does he advance about the relationship between character and the ability to work steadily?

6. What similarities does the essayist detect between the transient workers and the pioneers?

7. What evidence does he bring forth to bolster his hunch that the migrant laborers and the pioneers were much like each other? Can you suggest any basic difference between the two which he ignores?

8. According to Hoffer, what kind of work is best suited to the talents and inclinations of the "undesirables"? How does this fact reinforce his central theme?

9. In what way is Hoffer's discussion of "pioneering engineered from above" related to his fundamental point that the itinerant worker and the pioneer are basically similar?

10. Do you discern in the essay any tendency to sentimentalize the subject—to suggest, for example, that being a social derelict is in itself desirable, or pleasant, or charming?

11. What premises about human nature and the possibility of changing it are stated or implied in the essay?

TOPICS FOR DISCUSSION AND WRITING

12. In this essay the author narrates the process of observation and reflection which led him to reach certain conclusions about the "undesirables." He could, of course, have stated his conclusions much more directly, and sup-

pressed or deëmphasized the account of how he developed the ideas. Compare the value of this alternative method with that of the method actually employed by Hoffer.

13. Write an essay in which you describe, as clearly and specifically as you can, how you came to acquire a particular belief or opinion. This might be a belief bearing on morality, human relationships, politics, religion, or any other area of general concern. Your paper should make clear the nature of your ideas on the subject, and should show the stages by which you developed these ideas.

14. The people Hoffer writes about are certainly "restless." Does the author's explanation of their restlessness have any similarities with Tocqueville's interpretation of the instability and mobility of nineteenth-century Americans?

15. Judging from Hoffer's essay, what attitude should society take toward the "undesirables"? Should some kind of program be devised to give them an opportunity to make the best use of their energies? Present your ideas on this question in an essay.

16. Review the interpretation of recent American history given by Parkes in "Industrialism and American Ideals." How would the situation described by Parkes affect the kind of people Hoffer is discussing?

17. In Section 3 of Part One of this book, one of the procedures illustrated is called classification. Would it be possible to explain the structure of Hoffer's essay as a kind of classification?

Myths for Materialists

JACQUES BARZUN

———— ⌣ ————

THE ANGLO-AMERICANS of the twentieth century complained that they had no myths. Their poets, critics and scholars kept bewailing this supposed lack and some even tried to supply it by artificial drafts upon the Irish, Greek or Oriental mythologies. Modern investigation, however, points to the familiar truth that the men of that restless culture were calling for something they already had. Myth, in fact, so pervaded their lives that they could not see it for what it was.

The proof of this statement rests chiefly on the finds recently made in a great hollow formed below the Manhattan schist, probably during the Big (or subatomic) Depression of 1999. Under the usual pile of rubbish in this vast and naturally airtight enclosure, excavation has revealed a group of small buildings, with some adjoining structures shortly to be described; and within the best preserved of these buildings, a large room virtually undamaged. This room may have been the library of a club, or alternatively—for the indications are ambiguous—a dentist's waiting room. In either event, the discovery remains the most significant since that of the lost continent itself. For although the books add little or nothing to our knowledge, the large mass of magazines dating from the middle years of the century constitutes a unique, illuminating, and priceless collection.

I hasten to add that in putting this high value upon it, I have in mind not the reading matter which presumably satisfied the contemporary readers, but the much greater bulk of pictorial representations, often accompanied by text, which resemble earlier fragments identified by the symbol ADVT. Scholars have disputed at length over the exact meaning

Reprinted from *Chimera*, 1946. Used by permission of the author.

of this device. I can now, I believe, settle the principal doubts and establish—or at least confidently advance—a fairly complete theory of the subject. Those pictures, that text, enshrine the mythology of the twentieth century. After examining and comparing some seven thousand pieces, I am in a position to sketch in broad strokes the religious thoughts and the moral feelings evoked by that body of myths.[1]

I may at once explain that I draw my assurance from the curious structures which I referred to as adjoining the buildings recently found. Collapsed through these structures now are, it is clear that they were once meant to stand upright as panels of great size, occupying open spaces set apart to afford the widest visibility. All this suggests a religious consecration of both the site and the structure. On the face of these panels (often marked Outdoor Advt) were the same colored images as in the periodicals, but of heroic proportions and usually accompanied by some pithy aphorism. The number of such dedicated placards in a relatively small area like the one examined justifies my belief that we have in these words and pictures literally the revealed religion of the twentieth century.

It is normal in any culture for the commonest beliefs to be tacit and for the meaning of symbols to be so obvious as never to give rise to any glossary. From the outset, then, we face the double enigma of those four letters ADVT. What was their ordinary meaning and what their ultimate significance? The three main hypotheses regarding the first question are that the mark stands for (1) Advertising, (2) Advantage, and (3) Adventitious. Not the least startling conclusion I have come to is that the symbol denotes all three ideas. There is no discrepancy among them, even though historically the first meaning was the most usual. In twentieth century usage, "advertise" was a verb derived from the character of the Bitch-Goddess of Appearance, whose sacred name is now lost. The four letters stood for something like "Behold Me"—whence the plausible but false etymology of "advert eyes."

Without at first suspecting it, we touch here the central dogma in the Anglo-Americans' religious system. What they called their "modern" civilization was built on the preponderance of one physical sense over all the others, the sense of sight. Their science was not, as with us, the whole of knowledge, but only such knowledge as could be brought within range of the eye, directly or through instruments. They believed only in what they could measure, that is, what they could lay along a ruler, or between two hairlines, or could otherwise visually place. No competent student of their

[1] More exactly, that *mytho-pinaco-prosopopoeia*.

age can deny that they displayed extraordinary ingenuity in achieving this universal reduction of Being to the grasp of a single faculty.

But this monomania entailed an ascetic drying up of the inner life in every member of the culture. It was a prodigal expense of spirit for which ordinary life had to supply emotional compensation. Hence the need for, and the slow creation of, the vast mythology known as Advertising. An "ad"—as it came to be called in demotic speech—was simply the power of things made into pictures. Through the eye was given what actual life denied—beauty, strength, leisure, love, and personal distinction.

"Objects," as one contemporary philosopher confessed, "change their usual faces with the myth maker's emotions."[2] How much did he know of the origin and results of this transformation in the familiar things about him? We cannot tell, but in his day mind control through icons was well-nigh omnipotent. For example, by collating scattered references in the ancient literature with the newly found "ads," it is clear that just at the moment when the myth makers began to invoke the supernatural power of citrus to sustain and embellish existence, technological improvements were depriving the fruit of its natural color, taste and chance of ripening. At the very time when the sense of life as a whole was being atomized into a series of "processes," the mythology was verbally making up for the deficiency by a poetical iteration having Life as its theme. "Vital" became a magic word, as for example in an ad referring to the various kinds of popcorn eaten at breakfast: "Be sure you get the *vital* outer covering of wheat."

About the same period also, the mysterious substances called Vitamins— precious if measured by cost and complex if judged by their name—became the object of an official cult created jointly by mythologers and medicine men. To carry out the myth, Vitamins were chosen by symbolic letters and were weighed in thousands of "life-giving units." A last example will show how unremitting was this grasping after a runaway sense of well-being. Ten, twenty, thirty times a day, the Anglo-Americans were reminded of their need for vigor, for youth, for a "lift" by drug or weed— the worship of Pep. Initiated by one of the national heroes, Ponce de Leon, this quest was originally for a fountain in the south (*soda-fountain*). Many claimed to have found it and "advertised" to that effect; bottled drinks and packaged foods bore the magic syllable. "To be full of Pep" was equivalent to our "enthusiastic" or possessed by the god—the rare state then known in full as *pepsicola*.

We must now turn from the concept to the embodiment, the pictures.

[2] Cassirer.

What strikes the unprejudiced observer at once is the overwhelming emphasis on womanhood—presumably as the inexhaustible fount of human life—and on the situation of sexual approach as the characteristic moment in that life. If one did not know the ways of myth makers, their habit of juxtaposing incompatibles for the sake of a higher truth, one would suppose that the Anglo-Americans were unable to do anything without a member of the opposite sex in a state of provocative or compliant amorousness. In their iconography, seductiveness and sheeps' eyes invariably accompany eating, working, and riding, securing food, clothing, and shelter, listening to music or averting constipation.

An important corollary was that suggestive effects of nudity and drapery were limited, perhaps by law, to the portrayal of women. In all the seven thousand documents examined there occurs not a single instance of Father Paul's Pills showing him in tights, nor of the Chesterfield girl wearing a cassock. Despite this rigid esthetic, based on the complementary traits of the sexes as regards display, all objects whatever acquired an erotic component. The motive is clear enough: the artificial search for life through objects can only be kept at high pitch by associating the objects themselves with the strongest of desires. Advertising maxims were explicit enough: "Look sweeter in a sweater," "Use the soap with sex appeal," etc.

This mythopoeic principle did not, however, rely solely on the mating instinct. It employed two others, closely related—vanity and devotion to the Mother. This last, which goes back very far in the western tradition, was in its latest form singularly debased. Though I am certain that the best literary and pictorial talent of America went into this highly revered and highly paid art of mythography, all the efforts of these creative artists did not succeed in making The Mothers interesting. The type remained domestic and sentimental. One has only to think of the earlier school of Madonna makers, or of the medieval poet von Goethe-Faust, to see the difference.

The decline may well have been due to some obscure physical cause: the American myth-mother is always depicted as frail, grey-haired, with glasses and a senile rictus. Yet by a strange contradiction, the American maiden or young matron is almost always represented as nature makes her during the months of lactation. This is an improbability—or a religious mystery—which I do not pretend to have fathomed.

Contrary to the feeling of all mankind about ancestors, the second appeal, directed at personal vanity, occupies a much larger place than mother worship. Yet the anomaly disappears when we understand the democratic paradox of competition within equality: everyone has a mother; not every-one has a Packard.[3] Moreover, mass production tended to make any class of objects (as of men) virtually identical; some kind of mythical individuality had to be imparted to them in hopes of its transfer to the mass man. More and more, the social self came to depend on the constant tonic of acquiring these specially wrapped goods, these "superheterogene" articles.

I cannot agree with a famous critic of that epoch, Veblen, who spoke of "conspicuous consumption" and attendant waste as the mainspring of "modern" behavior. He described, it seems to me, an earlier age, that of kings and nobles, who translated power into munificence. The common man, on the contrary, receives direct satisfaction from objects, and for the reason I gave earlier: that the goddess ADVT consecrates matter by guaranteeing (1) secret worth and (2) miraculous origin. This is in keep-ing with all we know about myth. The medicine man infuses the magic into the familiar thing; whence the American advertising formulas, "A Wonderful Buy" and "It's Different," i.e., supernatural. A fuller text of the best periods informs us, over a beguiling triptych, "Not just a fur coat, but an important aid to gracious living. It will give your morale a lift, *as well as impress your friends.*" (Italics mine.) No distinction between direct and indirect help to self-esteem could be clearer, and as it happens, the dis-tinction was noted even at the time by the author of the satiric poem, "Civilizoo." As he tersely put it: "Women think fur beauty,/Scholars, books knowledge." Here was no showing off, but simple faith in the fetish.

It would be tedious to enumerate the myriad forms of the faith: they equal the number of consumable articles. Some, however, lent themselves to the arousing of fear preparatory to flattery. To be soothed by posses-sion of the fetish, the citizen must be first alarmed by a dramatization of evil—halitosis, falling hair, teeth, garters, B. O. (undecipherable), as well as by the ever-present threat of Wrong Choice.

In this connection I may instance the farthest reach of magic power found in our documents. As with us, the Anglo-American word for "spir-its" has a double meaning, for alcohol makes man cheerful and enterprising. But the ancients' impressionable souls seem to have drawn virtue not alone from the contents of the bottle; they were affected by the label upon it, which conferred tone or talents on the buyer. Thus a celebrated whisky was normally advertised as being "For Men of Decision." One would have thought that the thing needed was a whisky for men of *In*decision,

---

[3] Highly upholstered locomotive.

but doubtless the poet was using the rhetorical figure known as hypallage—taking the result for the action. In a like manner, medicines, food and personal attire were, whenever possible, held up as proved fetishes.

In discussing any mythology, however "vital," one must consider the treatment accorded to the subject of death. At first, I believed that the ancients ignored it. I knew, to be sure, of a few covert eulogies of funeral parlors, but it was evident that the aim here was still to make the living comfortable. Then it occurred to me that the previously noted tendency to portray happy results without regard to probability might hold a clue to my problem. And it happened that I had on my hands a series of absolutely inexplicable ads. Putting two and two together gave me what I was looking for.

My unexplained series consisted of simple but beautiful compositions depicting entire families sitting about the fire in smooth white uniforms, deceptively like our own suits of underwear. The faces, suggesting the school of Puvis de Chavannes, are full of benignity and repose. The atmosphere, too, is unusual—hardly any luxuries, no hint of the muscular strain, due to toothache or dandruff, financial or scientific anxiety, which meets us elsewhere. More significant still, all marks of sex have disappeared. Young and old seem beyond self-consciousness, or indeed consciousness of any kind. I conclude that we are logically and mythologically bound to accept these beatific groups as showing us the way the ancients represented death.[4] I have in fact found one marked "After the Last Supper," but the words are pencilled in and may lack authority.

If we did not know how uncommon was the belief in an after-life during the twentieth and twenty-first centuries, one could entertain the alternative that these classical figures were meant for angels. But mature reflection rules out this hypothesis; I will at most concede that they may have been Supermen, in the very special condition of immobility. Since all other icons show action, or at least animation, I find it far easier to believe that this sober grouping, these firm outlines, are the work of the religious artist contemplating death. Under conditions then prevailing, it happened more and more frequently that whole families died simultaneously. Their friends coming to pay their last visit, without any hope of reunion hereafter, would find them posed by the undertaker's art in familiar attitudes, clad in ritual white—in fact in that one-piece knitted suit as advertised (with or without buttons) which would match the wreath of lilies and the

---

[4] We find the same serenity in the users of certain soap flakes. This coincidence suggests that the flakes procured euthanasia. One brand was significantly called Lux.

silk-lined coffin. Over the abyss of centuries, one feels a catch in the throat at the thought of these once-living men, in whose desperate symbolism the white of snow, fitting like a new skin, meant death and peace.

Yet despite this symbol of hope, each year in midwinter—on December 25 to be exact—there occurred a nation-wide panic about the renewal of life. It may have come down from the old fear that the earth would not bear in spring. If so, with urbanization and technological farming the fear shifted from the earth to the self. Wearied by a routine divorced from nature, the citizen began to question his own survival. "Who and what am I, why so pale and listless?" Early November saw him sitting before a sunlamp to cure the paleness; the end of the month would see him, and particularly his wife, storming the shops.

It was a saturnalia of devotion to the goddess ADVT. The vernacular name Splurge indeed suggests a baptismal rite—to immerse oneself and wallow in things and be made new by contact. Life was goods after all. By an historical irony, the Anglo-Americans associated this feast with the short-lived founder of Christianity, who always showed the greatest alacrity in leaving his coat in another's hands, and who died possessed of one garment and three nails. His worshippers nonetheless celebrated his birth in a smothering of cloaks, scarfs, ties, silks, baubles and furs. This fact proves again that myth and religion are uncertain allies, but it also enables us to feel the pathos of that puzzling lyric in the American Anthology:

> The first thing to turn green in Spring
> Is the Christmas jewelry.

That "shopping" on these regular occasions was an essential part of mental health is naturally assumed by the advertisers. But the practical proof of the assumption was never more striking than in the serious incidents of the so-called Reconversion Period of the mid-forties. Drained of goods by war, the people nearly perished. They starved, not in their bodies but in their imaginations: six years virtually without the consolation of ads were to them as the suspension of the sacraments would be to us. The shops, though bare, were haunted by women as by insects seeking their prey, while the entire population grew irritable, distempered, antisocial. Women fought over pylon hose (i.e., leg coverings) and men committed suicide for lack of telegrams. Diaries tell us that those who by luck secured even a single object—an icebox or a full-tailed shirt—showed the restorative effect immediately. It was at the worst of these bad times that a laconic sage summed up the mood in the famous phrase, "Money no Object."

Such is, in rough outline, the mythology of the Anglo-Americans as far as archeological research can reconstruct it. I reserve the right to give a fuller account at some later time and to make it more vivid, though I trust not more persuasive, by the addition of plates in color. Meanwhile it may help to settle any lingering doubts if I conclude with a few words on the historical link between the faith in ADVT, on the one hand, and the powerful class of medicine men, on the other.

What distinguishes ADVT from all other great creeds is that its beginnings were perfectly natural and its final form completely miraculous. But at all times it was entangled with established religions. We know that the Greeks, almost as soon as they learned to write, began to inscribe curses on sheets of lead, which were then placed in their temples to call down the vengeance of the god on the person so advertised.

In the early Middle Ages, the public crier could be hired for any sort of advertising and it is on record that new religious dogmas were sometimes entrusted to his powers of publicity. Throughout every period, the marriage market made use of kindred devices and called on the gods to further and sanctify the deed. With the advent of the daily printed sheet, about the middle of the eighteenth century, the real cult of ADVT begins. Dr. Samuel Johnson, an early anthropologist, complains in 1759 of abuses then coming into practice: "It is become necessary to gain attention by magnificence of promises and by eloquence sometimes sublime, sometimes pathetic . . ." and it is "a moral question" whether advertisers do not "play too wantonly with our passions."[5]

But the junction of all the elements into what I ventured to call a *mytho-pinaco-prosopopoeia* (fable in pictures personifying things) came at the end of Dr. Johnson's century, when a medicine man of Bristol, Dr. Joseph Fry, had the revelation that his Maker had chosen him to extend the business of importing cocoa, and had ordained the means. He carried out this injunction in a small way at first, then on a national scale; himself boasting that he was the first man, not indeed to import cocoa; but to import the idea of a *signed guarantee on each and every package* into the distribution of goods. From him were descended the brothers Smith, Lydia Pinkham, and other eponymous figures worthy to rank with Beowulf.

In time, the signed guarantee became superfluous. A strong assertion in print, with an illustration lending color to it, sufficed to make converts. The suffering martyrs to a cough became willing martyrs to *Rem*, the well-named. But an overextension of this true church nearly caused its undoing:

[5] *The Idler*, No. 40.

too many rival assertions neutralized one another. New guarantees were needed, fuller of Authority than manufacturers could command. They appealed, and not in vain, to a new class of medicine men, the laboratory testers.[6] Their success was shown by the fact that in a short time all advertising emanated from a few Oratories and Laboratories, keeping up, for appearance's sake, a pretended competition among products.

In the final phase, the tester was simply symbolized by a white coat, a piece of apparatus, and the look of a seer. Behind him, invisible but using him and his device, was the newest type of Thaumaturgist, to whom no miracles were impossible. I refer to the Expert in Public Relations. He was believed capable of making fraud innocuous, starvation pleasant, and wars remote. It was rumored that such a man had once succeeded in making the public take an interest in the curriculum of a university. But this exaggeration can be dismissed.

Heretics could now and then be found who tried to undermine the common faith. But their small numbers can be inferred from the fact that they were never molested. They might deride mythadology, calling its effect "the massage of the mass age," the larger body of believers could ignore them and sincerely continue their search for myth. Perhaps this was as it should be, for myth will move mankind most when they do not call it so, and what men find indispensable, they preserve. The conveniences of life, as their name implies, are matters of convention; so Chesterfield must forever repeat "They Satisfy," though things in themselves do not. But things enhanced by art and color, sex and slogans, did give the illusions of a lotus-eating life to the men of the strange civilization I have described. The role of ADVT was to suffuse visible matter with invisible virtues, adding to bread the nutrition it had lost and to stone or steel the warmth it had never had.

UNDERSTANDING THE TEXT

1. In what role is the author of this essay pretending to write? How, in the early paragraphs, does he tip off the reader to the fact that this will be something other than straightforward exposition?
2. Identify the targets of Barzun's satire. Do you interpret the essay as primarily (a) a subtle but savage indictment of American materialism, or (b) an ingenious spoof directed against overblown advertising, or (c) a

[6] "A medicine man sits on a deerskin when he makes medicine. He puts herbs in a can, adds water and blows bubbles through a straw to purify it."—From a contemporary account.

parody on the methods of archeological and historical research, or (d) a lively criticism of the tendency to find myths in everything? Which of these descriptions seems to you most accurate?

3. How does the writer attempt to demonstrate that words and pictures in advertisements were "literally the revealed religion of the twentieth century"? What similarities are developed between advertisers and myth-making medicine men?

4. What is the point of the observation that no discrepancy exists among the ideas denoted by the words Advertising, Advantage, and Adventitious?

5. According to Barzun's hypothetical scholar of the future, what fundamental concept underlies the religious cult of the Anglo-Americans of the twentieth century? What is the function of advertising in this cult?

6. When the writer turns to analyzing the advertisements themselves, what basic appeals does he find represented in them? How does he relate this analysis of the advertisements to his central theme concerning the identity of mythology and advertising?

7. Comment on the style in which the essay is written. How appropriate is Barzun's choice of words to the intention of the piece and the author's assumed character? Indicate specific examples of words which are especially apt for maintaining the fiction of mythological research.

8. Point to instances of factual error or misconception (such as the footnote explaining the meaning of "Packard"). Why does Barzun introduce these?

9. Can you suggest any reasons why the author, after concluding the sketch of the Anglo-American "mythology," finishes the essay with a brief history of advertising?

10. What ethical and religious values does Barzun attribute to the society of which his hypothetical scholar is a member? How do these values differ from those of the people he is studying?

TOPICS FOR DISCUSSION AND WRITING

11. Write a 250-word paraphrase setting forth directly the points you believe Barzun is making in this essay.

12. What are the advantages and the limitations of the method Barzun has chosen to present his views? How does the effect of this piece differ from that of an essay beginning conventionally, "Advertising may be regarded as a kind of modern mythology"?

13. In general technique, what other essays in this book does this one resemble? Judging from these examples, what kinds of subjects seem best suited to the indirect approach?

14. Of the essays in this book which are relatively straightforward in technique, do any deal with subjects which might have been treated more indirectly

and imaginatively? Sketch the alternative approach which might have been used.

15. After studying the advertising pages of several current magazines, write an essay in which you attempt to classify the dominant appeals represented in the advertisements. The classification might be made according to any one of a variety of principles—the particular emotions invoked, perhaps, or the basic human situations depicted—but be sure to keep the classification consistent throughout the essay.

16. On the basis of your study of current advertisements, characterize the typical twentieth-century American as he and his life are projected in the advertisements.

17. Can you suggest any other contemporary objects or records that an ingenious archeologist of the remote future might use to reconstruct our present-day "mythology"? If you can, write an essay—straightforward, if you prefer, or ironic in Barzun's manner—based on these materials.

Quincy (1838–1848)

HENRY ADAMS

UNDER the shadow of Boston State House, turning its back on the house of John Hancock, the little passage called Hancock Avenue runs, or ran, from Beacon Street, skirting the State House grounds, to Mount Vernon Street, on the summit of Beacon Hill; and there, in the third house below Mount Vernon Place, February 16, 1838, a child was born, and christened later by his uncle, the minister of the First Church after the tenets of Boston Unitarianism, as Henry Brooks Adams.

Had he been born in Jerusalem under the shadow of the Temple and circumcised in the Synagogue by his uncle the high priest, under the name of Israel Cohen, he would scarcely have been more distinctly branded, and not much more heavily handicapped in the races of the coming century, in running for such stakes as the century was to offer; but, on the other hand, the ordinary traveller, who does not enter the field of racing, finds advantage in being, so to speak, ticketed through life, with the safeguards of an old, established traffic. Safeguards are often irksome, but sometimes convenient, and if one needs them at all, one is apt to need them badly. A hundred years earlier, such safeguards as his would have secured any young man's success; and although in 1838 their value was not very great compared with what they would have had in 1738, yet the mere accident of starting a twentieth-century career from a nest of associations so colonial —so troglodytic—as the First Church, the Boston State House, Beacon Hill, John Hancock and John Adams, Mount Vernon Street and Quincy, all crowding on ten pounds of unconscious babyhood, was so queer as to offer a subject of curious speculation to the baby long after he had witnessed the solution. What could become of such a child of the seventeenth

Reprinted from *The Education of Henry Adams* by Henry Adams. Used by permission of the publishers, Houghton Mifflin Company.

and eighteenth centuries, when he should wake up to find himself required to play the game of the twentieth? Had he been consulted, would he have cared to play the game at all, holding such cards as he held, and suspecting that the game was to be one of which neither he nor any one else back to the beginning of time knew the rules or the risks or the stakes? He was not consulted and was not responsible, but had he been taken into the confidence of his parents, he would certainly have told them to change nothing as far as concerned him. He would have been astounded by his own luck. Probably no child, born in the year, held better cards than he. Whether life was an honest game of chance, or whether the cards were marked and forced, he could not refuse to play his excellent hand. He could never make the usual plea of irresponsibility. He accepted the situation as though he had been a party to it, and under the same circumstances would do it again, the more readily for knowing the exact values. To his life as a whole he was a consenting, contracting party and partner from the moment he was born to the moment he died. Only with that understanding—as a consciously assenting member in full partnership with the society of his age—had his education an interest to himself or to others.

As it happened, he never got to the point of playing the game at all; he lost himself in the study of it, watching the errors of the players; but this is the only interest in the story, which otherwise has no moral and little incident. A story of education—seventy years of it—the practical value remains to the end in doubt, like other values about which men have disputed since the birth of Cain and Abel; but the practical value of the universe has never been stated in dollars. Although every one cannot be a Gargantua-Napoleon-Bismarck and walk off with the great bells of Notre Dame, every one must bear his own universe, and most persons are moderately interested in learning how their neighbors have managed to carry theirs.

This problem of education, started in 1838, went on for three years, while the baby grew, like other babies, unconsciously, as a vegetable, the outside world working as it never had worked before, to get his new universe ready for him. Often in old age he puzzled over the question whether, on the doctrine of chances, he was at liberty to accept himself or his world as an accident. No such accident had ever happened before in human experience. For him, alone, the old universe was thrown into the ash-heap and a new one created. He and his eighteenth-century, troglodytic Boston were suddenly cut apart—separated forever—in act if not in sentiment, by the opening of the Boston and Albany Railroad; the appearance of the first Cunard steamers in the bay; and the telegraphic messages which carried from Baltimore to Washington the news that Henry Clay and James K. Polk were nominated for the Presidency. This was in May, 1844; he was six years old; his new world was ready for use, and only fragments of the old met his eyes.

Of all this that was being done to complicate his education, he knew only the color of yellow. He first found himself sitting on a yellow kitchen floor in strong sunlight. He was three years old when he took this earliest step in education; a lesson of color. The second followed soon; a lesson of taste. On December 3, 1841, he developed scarlet fever. For several days he was as good as dead, reviving only under the careful nursing of his family. When he began to recover strength, about January 1, 1842, his hunger must have been stronger than any other pleasure or pain, for while in after life he retained not the faintest recollection of his illness, he remembered quite clearly his aunt entering the sick-room bearing in her hand a saucer with a baked apple.

The order of impressions retained by memory might naturally be that of color and taste, although one would rather suppose that the sense of pain would be first to educate. In fact, the third recollection of the child was that of discomfort. The moment he could be removed, he was bundled up in blankets and carried from the little house in Hancock Avenue to a larger one which his parents were to occupy for the rest of their lives in the neighboring Mount Vernon Street. The season was midwinter, January 10, 1842, and he never forgot his acute distress for want of air under his blankets, or the noises of moving furniture.

As a means of variation from a normal type, sickness in childhood ought to have a certain value not to be classed under any fitness or unfitness of natural selection; and especially scarlet fever affected boys seriously, both physically and in character, though they might through life puzzle themselves to decide whether it had fitted or unfitted them for success; but this fever of Henry Adams took greater and greater importance in his eyes, from the point of view of education, the longer he lived. At first, the effect was physical. He fell behind his brothers two or three inches in height, and proportionally in bone and weight. His character and processes of mind seemed to share in this fining-down process of scale. He was not good in a fight, and his nerves were more delicate than boys' nerves ought to be. He exaggerated these weaknesses as he grew older. The habit of doubt; of distrusting his own judgment and of totally rejecting the judgment of the world; the tendency to regard every question as open; the hesitation to act except as a choice of evils; the shirking of responsibility; the love of line, form, quality; the horror of ennui; the passion for companionship and the antipathy to society—all these are well-known qualities of New England character in no way peculiar to individuals but in this instance they seemed to be stimulated by the fever, and Henry Adams could never make up his mind whether, on the whole, the change of character was morbid or healthy, good or bad for his purpose. His brothers were the type; he was the variation.

As far as the boy knew, the sickness did not affect him at all, and he grew up in excellent health, bodily and mental, taking life as it was given; accepting its local standards without a difficulty, and enjoying much of it as keenly as any other boy of his age. He seemed to himself quite normal, and his companions seemed always to think him so. Whatever was peculiar about him was education, not character, and came to him, directly and indirectly, as the result of that eighteenth-century inheritance which he took with his name.

The atmosphere of education in which he lived was colonial, revolutionary, almost Cromwellian, as though he were steeped, from his greatest grandmother's birth, in the odor of political crime. Resistance to something was the law of New England nature; the boy looked out on the world with the instinct of resistance; for numberless generations his predecessors had viewed the world chiefly as a thing to be reformed, filled with evil forces to be abolished, and they saw no reason to suppose that they had wholly succeeded in the abolition; the duty was unchanged. That duty implied not only resistance to evil, but hatred of it. Boys naturally look on all force as an enemy, and generally find it so, but the New Englander, whether boy or man, in his long struggle with a stingy or hostile universe, had learned also to love the pleasure of hating; his joys were few.

Politics, as a practice, whatever its professions, had always been the systematic organization of hatreds, and Massachusetts politics had been as harsh as the climate. The chief charm of New England was harshness of contrasts and extremes of sensibility—a cold that froze the blood, and a heat that boiled it—so that the pleasure of hating—one's self if no better victim offered—was not its rarest amusement; but the charm was a true and natural child of the soil, not a cultivated weed of the ancients. The violence of the contrast was real and made the strongest motive of education. The double exterior nature gave life its relative values. Winter and summer, cold and heat, town and country, force and freedom, marked two modes of life and thought, balanced like lobes of the brain. Town was winter confinement, school, rule, discipline; straight, gloomy streets, piled with six feet of snow in the middle; frosts that made the snow sing under wheels or runners; thaws when the streets became dangerous to cross; society of uncles, aunts, and cousins who expected children to behave themselves, and who were not always gratified; above all else, winter represented the desire to escape and go free. Town was restraint, law, unity. Country, only seven miles away, was liberty, diversity, outlawry, the endless delight of mere sense impressions given by nature for nothing, and breathed by boys without knowing it.

Boys are wild animals, rich in the treasures of sense, but the New England boy had a wider range of emotions than boys of more equable climates. He felt his nature crudely, as it was meant. To the boy Henry Adams, summer was drunken. Among senses, smell was the strongest—smell of hot pine-woods and sweet-fern in the scorching summer noon; of new-mown hay; of ploughed earth; of box hedges; of peaches, lilacs, syringas; of stables, barns, cowyards; of salt water and low tide on the marshes; nothing came amiss. Next to smell came taste, and the children knew the taste of everything they saw or touched; from pennyroyal and flagroot to the shell of a pignut and the letters of a spelling-book—the taste of A-B, AB, suddenly revived on the boy's tongue sixty years afterwards. Light, line, and color as sensual pleasures, came later and were as crude as the rest. The New England light is glare, and the atmosphere harshens color. The boy was a full man before he ever knew what was meant by atmosphere; his idea of pleasure in light was the blaze of a New England sun. His idea of color was a peony, with the dew of early morning on its petals. The intense blue of the sea, as he saw it a mile or two away, from the Quincy hills; the cumuli in a June afternoon sky; the strong reds and greens and purples of colored prints and children's picture-books, as the American colors then ran; these were ideals. The opposites or antipathies, were the cold grays of November evenings, and the thick, muddy thaws of Boston winter. With such standards, the Bostonian could not but develop a double nature. Life was a double thing. After a January blizzard, the boy who could look with pleasure into the violent snow-glare of the cold white sunshine, with its intense light and shade, scarcely knew what was meant by tone. He could reach it only by education.

Winter and summer, then, were two hostile lives, and bred two separate

natures. Winter was always the effort to live; summer was tropical license.
Whether the children rolled in the grass, or waded in the brook, or swam
in the salt ocean, or sailed in the bay, or fished for smelts in the creeks, or
netted minnows in the salt-marshes, or took to the pine-woods and the
granite quarries, or chased muskrats and hunted snapping-turtles in the
swamps, or mushrooms or nuts on the autumn hills, summer and country
were always sensual living, while winter was always compulsory learning.
Summer was the multiplicity of nature; winter was school.

The bearing of the two seasons on the education of Henry Adams was
no fancy; it was the most decisive force he ever knew; it ran through life,
and made the division between its perplexing, warring, irreconcilable problems, irreducible opposites, with growing emphasis to the last year of
study. From earliest childhood the boy was accustomed to feel that, for
him, life was double. Winter and summer, town and country, law and
liberty, were hostile, and the man who pretended they were not, was in his
eyes a schoolmaster—that is, a man employed to tell lies to little boys.
Though Quincy was but two hours' walk from Beacon Hill, it belonged in
a different world. For two hundred years, every Adams, from father to
son, had lived within sight of State Street, and sometimes had lived in it,
yet none had ever taken kindly to the town, or been taken kindly by it.
The boy inherited his double nature. He knew as yet nothing about his
great-grandfather, who had died a dozen years before his own birth: he
took for granted that any great-grandfather of his must have always been
good, and his enemies wicked; but he divined his great-grandfather's character from his own. Never for a moment did he connect the two ideas of
Boston and John Adams; they were separate and antagonistic; the idea of
John Adams went with Quincy. He knew his grandfather John Quincy
Adams only as an old man of seventy-five or eighty who was friendly and
gentle with him, but except that he heard his grandfather always called
"the President," and his grandmother "the Madam," he had no reason to
suppose that his Adams grandfather differed in character from his Brooks
grandfather who was equally kind and benevolent. He liked the Adams
side best, but for no other reason than that it reminded him of the country, the summer, and the absence of restraint. Yet he felt also that Quincy
was in a way inferior to Boston, and that socially Boston looked down on
Quincy. The reason was clear enough even to a five-year old child.
Quincy had no Boston style. Little enough style had either; a simpler
manner of life and thought could hardly exist, short of cave-dwelling. The
flint-and-steel with which his grandfather Adams used to light his own

fires in the early morning was still on the mantelpiece of his study. The idea of a livery or even a dress for servants, or of an evening toilette, was next to blasphemy. Bathrooms, water-supplies, lighting, heating, and the whole array of domestic comforts, were unknown to Quincy. Boston had already a bathroom, a water-supply, a furnace, and gas. The superiority of Boston was evident, but a child liked it no better for that.

The magnificence of his grandfather Brooks's house in Pearl Street or South Street has long ago disappeared, but perhaps his country house at Medford may still remain to show what impressed the mind of a boy in 1845 with the idea of city splendor. The President's place at Quincy was the larger and older and far the more interesting of the two; but a boy felt at once its inferiority in fashion. It showed plainly enough its want of wealth. It smacked of colonial age, but not of Boston style or plush curtains. To the end of his life he never quite overcame the prejudice thus drawn in with his childish breath. He never could compel himself to care for nineteenth-century style. He was never able to adopt it, any more than his father or grandfather or great-grandfather had done. Not that he felt it as particularly hostile, for he reconciled himself to much that was worse; but because, for some remote reason, he was born an eighteenth-century child. The old house at Quincy was eighteenth century. What style it had was in its Queen Anne mahogany panels and its Louis Seize chairs and sofas. The panels belonged to an old colonial Vassall who built the house; the furniture had been brought back from Paris in 1789 or 1801 or 1817, along with porcelain and books and much else of old diplomatic remnants; and neither of the two eighteenth-century styles—neither English Queen Anne nor French Louis Seize—was comfortable for a boy, or for any one else. The dark mahogany had been painted white to suit daily life in winter gloom. Nothing seemed to favor, for a child's objects, the older forms. On the contrary, most boys, as well as grown-up people, preferred the new, with good reason, and the child felt himself distinctly at a disadvantage for the taste.

Nor had personal preference any share in his bias. The Brooks grandfather was as amiable and as sympathetic as the Adams grandfather. Both were born in 1767, and both died in 1848. Both were kind to children, and both belonged rather to the eighteenth than to the nineteenth centuries. The child knew no difference between them except that one was associated with winter and the other with summer; one with Boston, the other with Quincy. Even with Medford, the association was hardly easier. Once as a very young boy he was taken to pass a few days with his grandfather

Brooks under charge of his aunt, but became so violently homesick that
within twenty-four hours he was brought back in disgrace. Yet he could
not remember ever being seriously homesick again.

The attachment to Quincy was not altogether sentimental or wholly
sympathetic. Quincy was not a bed of thornless roses. Even there the
curse of Cain set its mark. There as elsewhere a cruel universe combined
to crush a child. As though three or four vigorous brothers and sisters,
with the best will, were not enough to crush any child, every one else conspired towards an education which he hated. From cradle to grave this
problem of running order through chaos, direction through space, discipline through freedom, unity through multiplicity, has always been, and
must always be, the task of education, as it is the moral of religion, philosophy, science, art, politics, and economy; but a boy's will is his life, and he
dies when it is broken, as the colt dies in harness, taking a new nature in
becoming tame. Rarely has the boy felt kindly towards his tamers. Between him and his master has always been war. Henry Adams never knew
a boy of his generation to like a master, and the task of remaining on
friendly terms with one's own family, in such a relation, was never easy.

All the more singular it seemed afterwards to him that his first serious
contact with the President should have been a struggle of will, in which
the old man almost necessarily defeated the boy, but instead of leaving, as
usual in such defeats, a lifelong sting, left rather an impression of as fair
treatment as could be expected from a natural enemy. The boy met seldom
with such restraint. He could not have been much more than six years old
at the time—seven at the utmost—and his mother had taken him to
Quincy for a long stay with the President during the summer. What became of the rest of the family he quite forgot; but he distinctly remembered standing at the house door one summer morning in a passionate
outburst of rebellion against going to school. Naturally his mother was the
immediate victim of his rage; that is what mothers are for, and boys also;
but in this case the boy had his mother at unfair disadvantage, for she was
a guest, and had no means of enforcing obedience. Henry showed a certain
tactical ability by refusing to start, and he met all efforts at compulsion by
successful, though too vehement protest. He was in fair way to win, and
was holding his own, with sufficient energy, at the bottom of the long
staircase which led up to the door of the President's library, when the door
opened, and the old man slowly came down. Putting on his hat, he took the
boy's hand without a word, and walked with him, paralyzed with awe, up
the road to the town. After the first moments of consternation at this in-

terference in a domestic dispute, the boy reflected that an old gentleman close on eighty would never trouble himself to walk near a mile on a hot summer morning over a shadeless road to take a boy to school, and that it would be strange if a lad imbued with the passion of freedom could not find a corner to dodge around, somewhere before reaching the school door. Then and always, the boy insisted that this reasoning justified his apparent submission; but the old man did not stop, and the boy saw all his strategical points turned, one after another, until he found himself seated inside the school, and obviously the centre of curious if not malevolent criticism. Not till then did the President release his hand and depart.

The point was that this act, contrary to the inalienable rights of boys, and nullifying the social compact, ought to have made him dislike his grandfather for life. He could not recall that it had this effect even for a moment. With a certain maturity of mind, the child must have recognized that the President, though a tool of tyranny, had done his disreputable work with a certain intelligence. He had shown no temper, no irritation, no personal feeling, and had made no display of force. Above all, he had held his tongue. During their long walk he had said nothing; he had uttered no syllable of revolting cant about the duty of obedience and the wickedness of resistance to law, he had shown no concern in the matter; hardly even a consciousness of the boy's existence. Probably his mind at that moment was actually troubling itself little about his grandson's iniquities, and much about the iniquities of President Polk, but the boy could scarcely at that age feel the whole satisfaction of thinking that President Polk was to be the vicarious victim of his own sins, and he gave his grandfather credit for intelligent silence. For this forbearance he felt instinctive respect. He admitted force as a form of right; he admitted even temper, under protest; but the seeds of a moral education would at that moment have fallen on the stoniest soil in Quincy, which is, as every one knows, the stoniest glacial and tidal drift known in any Puritan land.

Neither party to this momentary disagreement can have felt rancor, for during these three or four summers the old President's relations with the boy were friendly and almost intimate. Whether his older brothers and sisters were still more favored he failed to remember, but he was himself admitted to a sort of familiarity which, when in his turn he had reached old age, rather shocked him, for it must have sometimes tried the President's patience. He hung about the library; handled the books; deranged the papers; ransacked the drawers; searched the old purses and pocketbooks for foreign coins; drew the swordcane; snapped the travelling-pistols; upset everything in the corners, and penetrated the President's dressing-closet where a row of tumblers, inverted on the shelf, covered caterpillars which were supposed to become moths or butterflies, but never did. The Madam bore with fortitude the loss of the tumblers which her husband purloined for these hatcheries; but she made protest when he carried off her best cut-glass bowls to plant with acorns or peachstones that he might see the roots grow, but which, she said, he commonly forgot like the caterpillars.

At that time the President rode the hobby of tree-culture, and some fine old trees should still remain to witness it, unless they have been improved off the ground; but his was a restless mind, and although he took his hobbies seriously and would have been annoyed had his grandchild asked whether he was bored like an English duke, he probably cared more for the processes than for the results, so that his grandson was saddened by the sight and smell of peaches and pears, the best of their kind, which he brought up from the garden to rot on his shelves for seed. With the inherited virtues of his Puritan ancestors, the little boy Henry conscientiously brought up to him in his study the finest peaches he found in the garden, and ate only the less perfect. Naturally he ate more by way of compensation, but the act showed that he bore no grudge. As for his grandfather, it is even possible that he may have felt a certain self-reproach for his temporary rôle of schoolmaster—seeing that his own career did not offer proof of the worldly advantages of docile obedience—for there still exists somewhere a little volume of critically edited Nursery Rhymes with the boy's name in full written in the President's trembling hand on the fly-leaf. Of course there was also the Bible, given to each child at birth, with the proper inscription in the President's hand on the fly-leaf; while their grandfather Brooks supplied the silver mugs.

So many Bibles and silver mugs had to be supplied, that a new house, or cottage, was built to hold them. It was "on the hill," five minutes' walk above "the old house," with a far view eastward over Quincy Bay, and northward over Boston. Till his twelfth year, the child passed his summers there, and his pleasures of childhood mostly centered in it. Of education he had as yet little to complain. Country schools were not very serious. Nothing stuck to the mind except home impressions, and the sharpest were those of kindred children; but as influences that warped a mind, none compared with the mere effect of the back of the President's bald head, as he sat in his pew on Sundays, in line with that of President Quincy, who, though some ten years younger, seemed to children about the same age.

Before railways entered the New England town, every parish church showed half-a-dozen of these leading citizens, with gray hair, who sat on the main aisle in the best pews, and had sat there, or in some equivalent dignity, since the time of St. Augustine, if not since the glacial epoch. It was unusual for boys to sit behind a President grandfather, and to read over his head the tablet in memory of a President great-grandfather, who had "pledged his life, his fortune, and his sacred honor" to secure the independence of his country and so forth; but boys naturally supposed, without much reasoning, that other boys had the equivalent of President grandfathers, and that churches would always go on, with the bald-headed leading citizens on the main aisle, and Presidents or their equivalents on the walls. The Irish gardener once said to the child: "You'll be thinkin' you'll be President too!" The casualty of the remark made so strong an impression on his mind that he never forgot it. He could not remember ever to have thought on the subject; to him, that there should be a doubt of his being President was a new idea. What had been would continue to be. He doubted neither about Presidents nor about Churches, and no one suggested at that time a doubt whether a system of society which had lasted since Adam would outlast one Adams more.

The Madam was a little more remote than the President, but more decorative. She stayed much in her own room with the Dutch tiles, looking out on her garden with the box walks, and seemed a fragile creature to a boy who sometimes brought her a note or a message, and took distinct pleasure in looking at her delicate face under what seemed to him very becoming caps. He liked her refined figure; her gentle voice and manner; her vague effect of not belonging there, but to Washington or to Europe, like her furniture, and writing-desk with little glass doors above and little eighteenth-century volumes in old binding, labelled "Peregrine Pickle" or "Tom Jones" or "Hannah More." Try as she might, the Madam could never be Bostonian, and it was her cross in life, but to the boy it was her charm. Even at that age, he felt drawn to it. The Madam's life had been in truth far from Boston. She was born in London in 1775, daughter of Joshua Johnson, an American merchant, brother of Governor Thomas Johnson of Maryland; and Catherine Nuth, of an English family in London. Driven from England by the Revolutionary War, Joshua Johnson took his family to Nantes, where they remained till the peace. The girl Louisa Catherine was nearly ten years old when brought back to London, and her sense of nationality must have been confused; but the influence of the Johnsons and the services of Joshua obtained for him from President

Washington the appointment of Consul in London on the organization of
the Government in 1790. In 1794 President Washington appointed John
Quincy Adams Minister to The Hague. He was twenty-seven years old
when he returned to London, and found the Consul's house a very agreeable haunt. Louisa was then twenty.

At that time, and long afterwards, the Consul's house, far more than the
Minister's, was the centre of contact for travelling Americans, either official or other. The Legation was a shifting point, between 1785 and 1815;
but the Consulate, far down in the City, near the Tower, was convenient
and inviting; so inviting that is proved fatal to young Adams. Louisa was
charming, like a Romney portrait, but among her many charms that of being a New England woman was not one. The defect was serious. Her future mother-in-law, Abigail, a famous New England woman whose authority over her turbulent husband, the second President, was hardly so
great as that which she exercised over her son, the sixth to be, was troubled
by the fear that Louisa might not be made of stuff stern enough, or
brought up in conditions severe enough, to suit a New England climate, or
to make an efficient wife for her paragon son, and Abigail was right on
that point, as on most others where sound judgment was involved; but
sound judgment is sometimes a source of weakness rather than of force,
and John Quincy already had reason to think that his mother held sound
judgments on the subject of daughters-in-law which human nature, since
the fall of Eve, made Adams helpless to realize. Being three thousand miles
away from his mother, and equally far in love, he married Louisa in London, July 26, 1797, and took her to Berlin to be the head of the United
States Legation. During three or four exciting years, the young bride lived
in Berlin; whether she was happy or not, whether she was content or not,
whether she was socially successful or not, her descendants did not surely
know; but in any case she could by no chance have become educated there
for a life in Quincy or Boston. In 1801 the overthrow of the Federalist
Party drove her and her husband to America, and she became at last a
member of the Quincy household, but by that time her children needed
all her attention, and she remained there with occasional winters in Boston
and Washington, till 1809. Her husband was made Senator in 1803, and in
1809 was appointed Minister to Russia. She went with him to St. Petersburg, taking her baby, Charles Francis, born in 1807; but broken-hearted
at having to leave her two older boys behind. The life at St. Petersburg
was hardly gay for her; they were far too poor to shine in that extravagant
society; but she survived it, though her little girl baby did not, and in

the winter of 1814–15, alone with the boy of seven years old, crossed Europe from St. Petersburg to Paris, in her travelling-carriage, passing through the armies, and reaching Paris in the *Cent Jours* after Napoleon's return from Elba. Her husband next went to England as Minister, and she was for two years at the Court of the Regent. In 1817 her husband came home to be Secretary of State, and she lived for eight years in F Street, doing her work of entertainer for President Monroe's administration. Next she lived four miserable years in the White House. When that chapter was closed in 1829, she had earned the right to be tired and delicate, but she still had fifteen years to serve as wife of a Member of the House, after her husband went back to Congress in 1833. Then it was that the little Henry, her grandson, first remembered her, from 1843 to 1848, sitting in her panelled room, at breakfast, with her heavy silver teapot and sugar-bowl and cream-jug, which still exist somewhere as an heirloom of the modern safety-vault. By that time she was seventy years old or more, and thoroughly weary of being beaten about a stormy world. To the boy she seemed singularly peaceful, a vision of silver gray, presiding over her old President and her Queen Anne mahogany; an exotic, like her Sèvres china; an object of deference to every one, and of great affection to her son Charles; but hardly more Bostonian than she had been fifty years before, on her wedding-day, in the shadow of the Tower of London.

Such a figure was even less fitted than that of her old husband, the President, to impress on a boy's mind, the standards of the coming century. She was Louis Seize, like the furniture. The boy knew nothing of her interior life, which had been, as the venerable Abigail, long since at peace, foresaw, one of severe stress and little pure satisfaction. He never dreamed that from her might come some of those doubts and self-questionings, those hesitations, those rebellions against law and discipline, which marked more than one of her descendants; but he might even then have felt some vague instinctive suspicion that he was to inherit from her the seeds of the primal sin, the fall from grace, the curse of Abel, that he was not of pure New England stock, but half exotic. As a child of Quincy he was not a true Bostonian, but even as a child of Quincy he inherited a quarter taint of Maryland blood. Charles Francis, half Marylander by birth, had hardly seen Boston till he was ten years old, when his parents left him there at school in 1817, and he never forgot the experience. He was to be nearly as old as his mother had been in 1845, before he quite accepted Boston, or Boston quite accepted him.

A boy who began his education in these surroundings, with physical strength inferior to that of his brothers, and with a certain delicacy of mind and bone, ought rightly to have felt at home in the eighteenth century and should, in proper self-respect, have rebelled against the standards of the nineteenth. The atmosphere of his first ten years must have been very like that of his grandfather at the same age, from 1767 till 1776, barring the battle of Bunker Hill, and even as late as 1846, the battle of Bunker Hill remained actual. The tone of Boston society was colonial. The true Bostonian always knelt in self-abasement before the majesty of English standards; far from concealing it as a weakness, he was proud of it as his strength. The eighteenth century ruled society long after 1850. Perhaps the boy began to shake it off rather earlier than most of his mates.

Indeed this prehistoric stage of education ended rather abruptly with his tenth year. One winter morning he was conscious of a certain confusion in the house in Mount Vernon Street, and gathered, from such words as he could catch, that the President, who happened to be then staying there, on his way to Washington, had fallen and hurt himself. Then he heard the word paralysis. After that day he came to associate the word with the figure of his grandfather, in a tall-backed, invalid armchair, on one side of the spare bedroom fireplace, and one of his old friends, Dr. Parkman or P. P. F. Degrand, on the other side, both dozing.

The end of this first, or ancestral and Revolutionary, chapter came on February 21, 1848—and the month of February brought life and death as a family habit—when the eighteenth century, as an actual and living companion, vanished. If the scene on the floor of the House, when the old President fell, struck the still simple-minded American public with a sensation unusually dramatic, its effect on a ten-year-old boy, whose boy-life was fading away with the life of his grandfather, could not be slight. One had to pay for Revolutionary patriots; grandfathers and grandmothers; Presidents; diplomats; Queen Anne mahogany and Louis Seize chairs, as well as for Stuart portraits. Such things warp young life. Americans commonly believed that they ruined it, and perhaps the practical commonsense of the American mind judged right. Many a boy might be ruined by much less than the emotions of the funeral service in the Quincy church, with its surroundings of national respect and family pride. By another dramatic chance it happened that the clergyman of the parish, Dr. Lunt, was an unusual pulpit orator, the ideal of a somewhat austere intellectual type, such as the school of Buckminster and Channing inherited from the old Congregational clergy. His extraordinarily refined appearance, his dignity of manner, his deeply cadenced voice, his remarkable English and his fine appreciation, gave to the funeral service a character that left an overwhelming impression on the boy's mind. He was to see many great functions—funerals and festivals—in after-life, till his only thought was to see no more, but he never again witnessed anything nearly so impressive to him as the last services at Quincy over the body of one President and the ashes of another.

The effect of the Quincy service was deepened by the official ceremony which afterwards took place in Faneuil Hall, when the boy was taken to hear his uncle, Edward Everett, deliver a Eulogy. Like all Mr. Everett's orations, it was an admirable piece of oratory, such as only an admirable orator and scholar could create; too good for a ten-year-old boy to appreciate at its value; but already the boy knew that the dead President could not be in it, and had even learned why he would have been out of place there; for knowledge was beginning to come fast. The shadow of the War of 1812 still hung over State Street; the shadow of the Civil War to come had already begun to darken Faneuil Hall. No rhetoric could have reconciled Mr. Everett's audience to his subject. How could he say there, to an assemblage of Bostonians in the heart of mercantile Boston, that the only distinctive mark of all the Adamses, since old Sam Adams's father a hundred and fifty years before, had been their inherited quarrel with State Street, which had again and again broken out into riot, bloodshed, personal feuds, foreign and civil war, wholesale banishments and confiscations, until the history of Florence was hardly more turbulent than that of Boston? How could he whisper the word Hartford Convention before the men who had made it? What would have been said had he suggested the chance of Secession and Civil War?

Thus already, at ten years old, the boy found himself standing face to face with a dilemma that might have puzzled an early Christian. What was he?—where was he going? Even then he felt that something was wrong, but he concluded that it must be Boston. Quincy had always been right, for Quincy represented a moral principle—the principle of resistance to Boston. His Adams ancestors must have been right, since they were always hostile to State Street. If State Street was wrong, Quincy must be right! Turn the dilemma as he pleased, he still came back on the eighteenth century and the law of Resistance; of Truth; of Duty, and of Freedom. He was a ten-year-old priest and politician. He could under no circumstances have guessed what the next fifty years had in store, and no one could teach him; but sometimes, in his old age, he wondered—and could never decide—whether the most clear and certain knowledge would have helped him. Supposing he had seen a New York stock-list of 1900, and had studied the statistics of railways, telegraphs, coal, and steel—would he have quitted his eighteenth-century, his ancestral prejudices, his abstract ideals, his semi-clerical training, and the rest, in order to perform an expiatory pilgrimage to State Street, and ask for the fatted calf of his grandfather Brooks and a clerkship in the Suffolk Bank?

Sixty years afterwards he was still unable to make up his mind. Each course had its advantages, but the material advantages, looking back, seemed to lie wholly in State Street.

UNDERSTANDING THE TEXT

1. Keeping in mind that this is the first chapter of a lengthy autobiographical volume, what do you think Adams is trying to accomplish in it? From what point of view does he present and interpret the events of his earliest years?
2. Adams writes, "From earliest childhood the boy was accustomed to feel that, for him, life was double." Does this provide any clue to the way Adams organizes his recollections of early childhood? How many different examples of this doubleness does Adams cite in the chapter?
3. What use does the author make of the contrast between Boston and Quincy? Draw up a list of the pairs of contrasting ideas which he associates with Boston and Quincy, respectively.
4. At the end of the essay, Adams represents his future course in life as involving, in a sense, a choice between Boston and Quincy. What is the nature of the choice? What ideas would he be accepting if he went one way or the other? At this point, which of the two ways of life does he seem to prefer?
5. In view of the central contrast in the chapter, how do you interpret this sentence: "Of course there was also the Bible, given to each child at birth, with the proper inscription in the President's hand on the fly-leaf; while their grandfather Brooks supplied the silver mugs"?
6. Study closely the paragraphs in which Adams describes what summer and winter, respectively, meant to him. Discuss the way he presents the contrast. How successfully, for example, does he relate the physical details he recalls to the general ideas he wishes to convey? Does the structure of his sentences play any part in sharpening the contrast?
7. How does Henry Adams define the task of education? Does this definition have any relevance to the way he interprets his childhood?
8. In presenting his impressions of the life and character of his ex-President grandfather and his grandmother, what kinds of detail does he choose to mention?

9. Examine the first sentence in the chapter. Is there anything about its structure which reflects, and forecasts, the way the author describes, in the following pages, the influences acting on the child Henry Adams?

TOPICS FOR DISCUSSION AND WRITING

10. Do any particular places possess special meaning for you? Do you associate them, for example, with certain aspects of life, or ways of doing things, so that they have some significance beyond themselves? If so, write an essay employing descriptive detail which not only sets the place before the reader but also conveys the meaning the place has for you.

11. Think of some principles you might employ to organize an essay presenting recollections of the first ten years of your own life. Compare the various principles you might use. Which method seems best suited to the conception you have of your experiences?

12. Does Adams' definition of the task of education conform to your ideas on the subject? Does it seem to you to conform to current educational practices in schools and colleges?

13. Write an essay characterizing an older person who has had some influence in shaping your ideas or guiding your conduct. Although your essay should certainly suggest your conception of the person's general character, you will probably wish to concentrate on traits which had particular significance for you.

14. Assuming that you have not read the rest of the book from which this passage is taken, does this first chapter supply any hints as to how Adams may interpret his entire life?

The Education of Henry Adams:
A Review

LOUIS KRONENBERGER

———～———

FOUR generations after one member of the Adams family helped compose the Declaration of Independence, another sat down and wrote a book declaring it null and void. So rapidly had events come to pass that it required just a century and a quarter to demolish America's greatest act of faith with her most withering words of denial. Between John Adams and his great-grandson Henry lay the total wreck of a dream. The disaster had robbed Henry Adams not only of his illusions but equally of his usefulness; the thing that had come about was beyond Henry Adams' ability to cope with or fight against or repair; he, who had burned to participate in American life, was reduced to becoming its stern and dissident historian. Hence, to confess his own failure, and to reveal the far greater failure that had brought his own about, and to fail (as he thought) in confessing it, Adams sat down and wrote the *Education*.

The *Education* found its most responsive readers in those years following the World War when they too had reason to believe that American life had failed them; and to every American intellectual who still retained inside him vestiges of the American moralist, Adams' grim citation of a century's crimes and blunders helped explain the plight of the modern world. The demonstration seemed Euclidean enough to justify the bitterly ironic tone which overhung it: for here was Henry Adams, supremely well born, talented, eager, thoughtful, industrious, confessing that every ideal he owned had been traduced; insisting that the world of action had been impossible to enter, and the world of thought powerless to give hope.

Reprinted from *The New Republic*, March 15, 1939. Used by permission of *The New Republic*.

515

Only chaos, explosion, cataclysm loomed ahead. A sensitive person was better out of life; in it, a Henry Adams could only by turns shudder and grow brutally cynical.

The book which reached these conclusions remains an important document of American intellectual and moral inquiry, if only because not a dozen Americans of any period were intellectually and morally of a stature to produce it. It is predicated of very nearly a first-rate mind and something like a first-rate experience. If the mind fails us, it is chiefly from not being purposeful enough; if the experience, it is from being largely of one kind. Adams came to know everything within the reach of the cultivated man of the world, everything to be had of drawing rooms and libraries, colleges and clubs, churches and ruins, senates and courts; but, though such contact was capable of a thousand variations, its bounds were immovably fixed. Henry Adams was an aristocrat, and a peculiarly modern aristocrat: the tame and squeamish product of London or Boston, quite unlike his spacious Renaissance ancestor for whom privilege meant an extension, not a curtailment, of adventures.

This is palpable everywhere through the *Education;* but something else about Henry Adams is palpable in its very title. Adams self-consciously sought to channel his experiences and to convert them into education. The attitude is praiseworthy enough, but at the outset it is interesting to note what produced it. What first of all produced it, we may suppose, was his Puritan background, quivering with moral earnestness: a background which, moreover, if it served as a spur to education, served equally as a backstop; and which, if it accounts during four generations for the Adams strength, accounts no less for its want of suppleness. But the Puritan impulse coincided perfectly with something else which caused Adams to treat life as education: the nineteenth-century crusade for progress and enlightenment. The nineteenth century seemed to think that if man only knew enough and remained a "moral" animal, he could reform and stabilize the world. The belief was hardly one which Adams, as he grew older, was encouraged to share; but the atmosphere that produced it was one he never outgrew. It was a moral as well as an intellectual impulse that caused him to plunge headlong into the flood of science and philosophy that engulfed his age; it was some desperate faith in pure knowledge, which even a highly ironic temperament could not extinguish, that turned Henry Adams into a lifelong student. True enough, it was difficult for him to make something systematic and cosmic of all he studied. The result, in that line, was never much more than brilliant dilettantism; but it saved Adams, if not from disillusionment, then from disintegration.

If the *Education* were no more than a worldling's reminiscences and a student's recapitulations, all tied together with philosophical ribbons, we might praise its prose and wit and acknowledge its intellectual expressiveness of an era; but we should put it among the memorials, and not the textbooks, of American experience. But the *Education* is a grand-scale study of maladjustment, of the failure of an exceptional personality to mesh with a prodigious civilization: posing, with one gesture, the problem of the man and his times. The problem of each, by the time Adams' autobiography was made public, had grown greater and more acute; so that in the decade following Adams' death the *Education* had a significance it only partly had in his lifetime and that there is small likelihood it will ever have again.

Like most serious autobiographies, the *Education* is an attempt, not to record a man's life, but to explain it. It is the work, at bottom, of one who set out both to judge and to justify himself. This dual intention is significant, even though what Adams attempted to justify was failure. We may take the liberty of supposing that this dual intention was embodied very simply: Adams judged himself by asking a question, and justified himself by returning an answer. Why—he asks in effect—should someone who started off with every opportunity, and with faith and eagerness, have ended up with so little achieved, dissentient and in utter flight? Because, he answers, the world he had set out to serve had been seized by forces he would not accept or master; and nothing better remained than to try to understand those forces and inveigh against them.

The *Education* is, then, a perfectly *conscious* study of frustration and deflected purpose; of the failure of a superior man to find the right place, or any tolerable place, in a civilization growing ever more corrupt, rapacious, and vulgar. No one ever wrote a more deliberate apologia of his life than Henry Adams. I shall have much to say later concerning the make-up of the particular man, concerning his blunders and prejudices, his distaste for enduring his situation, his predisposition to abandon it. But all that has a psychological importance, not a philosophical one; it delimits, but does not destroy, the real meaning of his book. What gives the *Education* its lasting value, what made a generation of futilitarians clasp it to their breasts, is the validity of the predicament regardless of the shortcomings of the man. For if not Henry Adams, then another, or many others, were paralyzed by the terms of that struggle in which he was so centrally engaged.

Confronted by the greed of a banking civilization, the crookedness of boss-rule politics, the vulgarity of a parvenu culture, the cynicism of an exploit-ative ruling class, the middle-class intellectual was pretty well doomed either to suffer or succumb or escape. At the best, if his convictions had real fiber, he might die fighting the reformer's luckless battle; more likely he would accept the situation, as John Hay did, and wax fat off the spoils; or flee it and accept its more graceful counterpart elsewhere, as did Henry James; or take to excoriating it, aware that his mockery was the sign of his weakness, as Adams felt driven to do.

There appeared, in any case, to be no lasting adjustment that could be called an honest one. The superior man might, by the world's standards, succeed or fail; it hardly mattered, since he could not remain whole. No doubt he best avoided contamination by going into retirement; but then he was not fully alive, and then he had abandoned his responsibilities. If he remained in action, he might deceive himself into thinking that he was fighting the good fight by opposing specific men, by championing specific measures; but if he remained in action and refused to deceive himself, he knew he had for enemy the whole huge mass of things. And unless one was an incorrigible idealist or a convinced revolutionary, that was a task leading to dislocation and despair. Henry Adams, very early, became too pessimistic and cynical to go on being a participant. He chose, instead, a place on the sidelines, and from there set about recording the minutes of all the unsavory transactions of America's public life. The picture of such proceedings which Adams drew, or at least suggested, in the *Education* is a final one. For not only were its revelations damning, but its sources were unimpeachable. It was the indictment of a supremely placed world-ling who had listened at the most private keyholes, who had been told—or allowed to guess—the secrets of those who worked behind the scenes. Scarcely anyone else who did so little knew so much. Adams' indictment stands: the great documentary merit of the *Education* is its demonstration of what nineteenth-century America had become, and by what process, and on what terms.

The philosophical merit, which once seemed a merit so much greater, is by no means so great. For the intellectuals of the twenties, the *Education* was an epic after their own hearts. *Epic* is no idly used word; the scale and severity of the book are important. In one sense, the most misleading thing about it is its impressiveness. Written with much of the formality that Gibbon used in his *Memoirs,* and in the same third person, it comes at the reader with so magisterial an air that halfway through it he grants it the confidence reserved for an attested masterpiece. The Adams manner confers on the Adams apologia a definite extrinsic weight. There is the sense of a large mind and an imposing personality; there is the sense—unimpaired by the irony of the book—of deep purpose and high seriousness. Henry Adams, who lived his life in a minor key, took every precaution to write about it in a major one. The *Education* is a completely full-dress performance.

The 1920's could use such an authoritative approach. The 1920's could bend the knee before a master who celebrated their own misgivings and disappointments. He ennobled their dilemma. He gave dignity to their frustration. For theirs was the individualist's dilemma, and for them the idea of integrity involved the idea of withdrawal; environment, to them, defeated the artist, as participation corrupted the thinker. Their dilemma, too, sprang from personal weakness no less than from social disorder. The *Education* gave to the 1920's, not the signal to fight but the leave to withdraw, by revealing how a better man had got waylaid and misplaced, had been passed up and slurred over and left to go unsung; for surely there is something in the tone of the *Education* that suggests, as not the least of the nineteenth century's blunders, its failure to recognize the worth of Henry Adams. On its lowest level, there is an immense amount of self-pity in Adams' book. On their lowest level, there was an immense amount of self-pity in the futilitarians of the twenties. Deep called unto deep.

But at another level there was something in the *Education* to make it one of the justly pivotal books of its era. It may express futility, but its tone is not wholly negative; there is something affirmative in it. And what it affirms is a toughness of mind, a quality of searching, weighing, testing, of coming to clear-eyed conclusions about the nature of things. Above all, it sets forth a mind and morality that spurned the optimistic and opportunistic formulas, from Emerson's down, that had made of American life such a shallow, shifty, spurious thing. At least the *idea* of education which Adams, solitary and recusant, imposed upon himself, was an exemplary idea. What Adams signifies at his best is unadulterated and grown-up thinking. This was something that his pupils of the twenties, groping backward in American letters—stumbling over the confusions of the transcendentalists, the rampant Americanism that mars the democratic fervor in Whitman—could not easily find elsewhere. No wonder, then, that they thought they had found more than they actually did.

For impressive as the *Education* is, and definitive as is its mood, it somehow is not profound. It befits very few of us to condescend to

Adams on the score of his cultural background, his political knowledge, his cerebral weight; but the fact remains that it is not for his "discoveries," or his clarifications of the human struggle, that we can seek him out. Those celebrated later chapters of the *Education*—"The Dynamo and the Virgin," "A Dynamic Theory of History"—are superb intellectual exercises, but it is hard to believe that they offer a synthesis which is more than personally brilliant and picturesque. When Adams looked to the past, for example, it was originally in search of perspective. He set about contrasting twelfth-century "unity" with twentieth-century "multiplicity," and the contrast is striking. But to what end? He conceived the earlier age as the better one, but must have known that it was impossible to return to it. The structure of twelfth-century life has no application in ours; the old wheels went round from a social force that had become inoperative and spent. Yet, more and more in the manner of an escapist, Adams tried to go back; there came to be more than an aesthete's interest in his mediaeval studies, in the long twilit mystic spell of Chartres. Coldly judged, does not one pamper one's maladjustment by pining for what one cannot have?

There was nothing shallow about Adams' inquiry into human culture, either in its feeling or its facts; but it failed to produce any profound philosophy of life, even a profound skepticism. Adams knew too much, he knew (or thought he knew) too well whither things were drifting, he had—too arrogantly—a disbelief that any good could come of it, ultimately to profit from his career of "education." The philosophy he did evolve is understandable enough, and one must grant that there was a basis in experience for it. But it comes to no more than the pessimism of one who sees the world being ruined, and the cynicism of one who gives up trying to reclaim it. And in Adams there was also an uglier cynicism, of sitting back and watching the world, with a not unmalign satisfaction, go to Hell. The motif of effort and education which carefully governs Adams' autobiography tends to obscure this uglier cynicism; but from a reading of the *Letters* one knows that it was there, and one sees how, after a time, the moralist in Adams gave up being in any sense a crusader and became a merely captious and querulous censor.

A crusader in the old Adams style Henry never was at any time. In John and John Quincy Adams there was little of Hamlet and much of Coeur-de-Lion; there was the impulse, scarcely questioned, to act. Henry never had that impulse. At the very outset of his career, he thought rather of being *induced* to enter politics—thought of his dignity as soon as his duty. The silver-platter method failed, and in a way Henry would have no other. It was not simply that he was as proud as he was ambitious, or as squeamish as he was moral; it was that for a lifelong career in opposition the work was too grubby, too dispiriting, too harsh, the odds against winning were too fantastically high. The reformer who would take on so forbidding a task needed to be something of a fanatic; and after all Henry Adams was from the beginning the most sensitive of intellectuals, the most cultivated of worldlings.

It would be absurd to imagine such a man becoming a John Brown, a William Lloyd Garrison, a Debs. But it would surely not be absurd to imagine such a man becoming a Matthew Arnold. Each was born in the shadow of a name outstanding for earnestness, each was by temperament the reverse of a democrat, and each grew up to find a place waiting for him in that world where society and intellect, art and politics, meet. There may have been a decisive difference in the fact that Arnold had a living to earn, and Adams did not. But Arnold was not self-indulgent and Adams was; so that Arnold became the embattled foe of what seemed to him the powers of darkness, and Adams merely their bitter and acidulous historian. (It only counts against Adams the more that he understood the issues in a far wider sense than Arnold understood them.) There was something in Adams which, though it might have borne the arduousness of high public office, balked at the indignities of Arnold's private campaigning. By Adams' strongly developed eighteenth-century standards of worldliness, Arnold was doubtless a little plodding, a little ridiculous. He called Arnold the most honest man he knew, but he was never driven to accept the burdens of such an honesty. It was his Chesterfieldian sensibilities that largely ruined Adams; that turned him into a man who thought one way and lived another.

For he lived, during many years, in elegant and patrician retirement, choosing for his intimates the Hays, Cabot Lodges, Theodore Roosevelts for whom morally he had no respect; traveling *en prince;* entertaining *en connaisseur;* parading in his letters a calculated snobbery that sneered at Stevenson's indigent bohemianism, that instantly seized on Kipling's social second-rateness, that inveighed half to the point of mania against the Jews. He said of himself that he "should have been a Marxist," and knew, overwhelmingly, that he could never have been one. The whole story is told, I think, by Adams' reactions to English upper-class life.

With his mind he saw all too well its hypocrisy, insularity, complacence; but temperamentally the sweetest air he ever breathed was that of London dinner parties and English country houses.

The present moment is not congenial, and not disposed to be fair, to the *Education*. The book compels respect for a sense of weight behind, not in, it. It suggests tragedy; but it is not—at least on the terms it set out to be —tragic, because the author chose the less costly form of defeat, and the less noble. Impotence, to Adams, was preferable to mutilation. Psychologically—by which I mean that were Henry Adams the problem of a novelist —his life followed a convincing pattern. But in real life, an ultimate failure of character is not to be excused by being explained; nor does a lifetime of self-analysis compensate for a failure to see things through morally. If a crude capitalist era "crushed" Adams, it was as much from being enervated by the fruits of it as from being poisoned by its roots. Was Adams willing—was he ever willing—to lose just part of the world to gain his own soul? It is just possible to say Yes; but if so, Adams' reason was purely pride.

However great the merits of the *Education*, its "method" can already be seen to have failed. Culture and education are of the highest importance—according to some philosophies, the very end of living. But for Henry Adams they were clearly intended to be a means, carrying him forward to a better understanding and fulfillment of his obligations. Instead, they produced in him the indecision of a Hamlet; they became a kind of luxury, a kind of solace, and a kind of escape. It may be that Adams has taught us more in autobiography than he could have in action. It is at least certain that he has warned us more unforgettably. For it is not from confusing the mind by overloading it; it is not from dissent without protest, or opposition without strife, or humanism without humanity, that the beleaguered intellectual can save himself, or that the world he views with horror can be saved.

UNDERSTANDING THE TEXT

1. What does Kronenberger believe to be Adams' primary intention in the *Education of Henry Adams?*
2. What other possible intentions does Kronenberger discuss, and then dismiss as secondary, before arriving at what he considers the primary purpose?
3. What explanation does Kronenberger offer for the popularity of the *Education* among intellectual readers of the 1920's? What does this explanation

suggest concerning Kronenberger's opinion both of Adams and of his readers during the 1920's?

4. According to Kronenberger, what was the crux of the failure recorded in the *Education?*

5. What kinds of merit does the critic find in Adams' book? What does he consider the strong points of Adams' interpretation of his career?

6. What weaknesses in Adams' interpretation does Kronenberger note? How does he relate these deficiencies to his view of Adams' personal character?

7. In discussing the kind of person Adams was *not*, does Kronenberger give any indications as to the kind of person he thinks Adams *should* have been? In other words, does he pass any moral judgments on Adams' character?

8. Does the critic imply that, if Adams had been a different kind of person, or had taken a different attitude toward the life of his time, the *Education* might have been a more profound book?

TOPICS FOR DISCUSSION AND WRITING

9. From the sample of Adams' writing afforded in the "Quincy" chapter, comment on the accuracy and justice of Kronenberger's evaluation. Does the chapter display any of the characteristics, either literary or personal, that Kronenberger mentions?

10. Kronenberger begins his critique with a dramatic sentence summarizing his view of Adams' significance. Write a paragraph explaining the relevance of this sentence to the interpretation which follows.

11. Explaining the allusions, write brief commentaries stating the meaning of these passages: (a) "In John and John Quincy Adams there was little of Hamlet and much of Coeur-de-Lion; there was the impulse, scarcely questioned, to act." (b) "It would be absurd to imagine such a man becoming a John Brown, a William Lloyd Garrison, a Debs. But it would surely not be absurd to imagine such a man becoming a Matthew Arnold."

12. Basically, Kronenberger's interpretation of Adams rests on a premise concerning the proper relationship between the individual and society. In an essay develop and evaluate Kronenberger's ideas on this subject. You may wish to refer to the ideas of other writers represented in this book. What, for example, would acceptance of this premise lead one to say about a writer like Thoreau?

13. In this interpretation of Henry Adams, does the author state or suggest any idea similar to those developed by Parkes in his treatment of modern industrial society (pp. 469–474)?

Stranger in the Village

JAMES BALDWIN

FROM all available evidence no black man had ever set foot in this tiny Swiss village before I came. I was told before arriving that I would probably be a "sight" for the village; I took this to mean that people of my complexion were rarely seen in Switzerland, and also that city people are always something of a "sight" outside of the city. It did not occur to me—possibly because I am an American—that there could be people anywhere who had never seen a Negro.

It is a fact which cannot be explained on the basis of the inaccessibility of the village. The village is very high, but it is only four hours from Milan and three hours from Lausanne. It is true that it is virtually unknown. Few people making plans for a holiday would elect to come here. On the other hand, the villagers are able, presumably, to come and go as they please—which they do: to another town at the foot of the mountain, with a population of approximately five thousand, the nearest place to see a movie or go to the bank. In the village there is no movie house, no bank, no library, no theater; very few radios, one jeep, one station wagon; and, at the moment, one typewriter, mine, an invention which the woman next door to me here had never seen. There are about six hundred people living here, all Catholic—I conclude this from the fact that the Catholic church is open all year round, whereas the Protestant chapel, set off on a hill a little removed from the village, is open only in the summertime when the tourists arrive. There are four or five hotels, all closed now, and four or five *bistros*, of which, however, only two do any business during the winter. These two do not do a great deal, for life in the village seems to end around nine or ten o'clock. There are a few stores, butcher, baker, *épicerie*, a hardware store, and a money-changer—who cannot change travelers' checks, but must send them down to the bank—an operation which takes two or three days. There is something called the *Ballet Haus*, closed in the winter and used for God knows what, certainly not ballet, during the summer. There seems to be only one schoolhouse in the village, and this for the quite young children; I suppose this to mean that their older brothers and sisters at some point descend from these mountains in order to complete their education—possibly, again, to the town just below. The landscape is absolutely forbidding, mountains towering on all four sides, ice and snow as far as the eye can reach. In this white wilderness, men and women and children move all day, carrying washing, wood, buckets of milk or water, sometimes skiing on Sunday afternoons. All week long boys and young men are to be seen shoveling snow off the rooftops, or dragging wood down from the forest in sleds.

The village's only real attraction, which explains the tourist season, is the hot spring water. A disquietingly high proportion of these tourists are cripples, or semi-cripples, who come year after year—from other parts of Switzerland, usually—to take the waters. This lends the village, at the height of the season, a rather terrifying air of sanctity, as though it were a lesser Lourdes. There is often something beautiful, there is always something awful, in the spectacle of a person who has lost one of his faculties, a faculty he never questioned until it was gone, and who struggles to recover it. Yet people remain people, on crutches or indeed on death-beds; and wherever I passed, the first summer I was here, among the native villagers, or among the lame, a wind passed with me—of astonishment, curiosity, amusement, and outrage. That first summer I stayed two weeks and never intended to return. But I did return in the winter, to work; the village offers, obviously, no distractions whatever and has the further advantage of being extremely cheap. Now it is winter again, a year later, and I am here again. Everyone in the village knows my name, though they scarcely ever use it, knows that I come from America—though, this, apparently, they will never really believe: black men come from Africa—and everyone knows that I am the friend of the son of a woman who was born here, and that I am staying in their chalet. But I remain as much a stranger today as I was the first day I arrived, and the children shout *Neger! Neger!* as I walk along the streets.

It must be admitted that in the beginning I was far too shocked to have any real reaction. In so far as I reacted at all, I reacted by trying to be pleasant—it being a great part of the American Negro's education (long before he goes to school) that he must make people "like" him. This smile-and-the-world-smiles-with-you routine worked about as well in this situation as it had in the situation for which it was designed, which is to say that it did not work at all. No one, after all, can be liked whose human weight and complexity cannot be, or has not been, admitted. My smile was simply another unheard-of phenomenon which allowed them to see my teeth—they did not, really, see my smile and I began to think that, should I take to snarling, no one would notice any difference. All of the physical characteristics of the Negro which had caused me, in America, a very different and almost forgotten pain were nothing less than miraculous—or infernal—in the eyes of the village people. Some thought my hair was the color of tar, that it had the texture of wire, or the texture of cotton. It was jocularly suggested that I might let it all grow long and make myself a winter coat. If I sat in the sun for more than five minutes some daring creature was certain to come along and gingerly put his fingers on my hair, as though he were afraid of an electric shock, or put his hand on my hand, astonished that the color did not rub off. In all of this, in which it must be conceded there was the charm of genuine wonder and in which there was certainly no element of intentional unkindness, there was yet no suggestion that I was Human: I was simply a living wonder.

I knew that they did not mean to be unkind, and I know it now; it is necessary, nevertheless, for me to repeat this to myself each time that I walk out of the chalet. The children who shout *Neger!* have no way of knowing the echoes this sound raises in me. They are brimming with good humor and the more daring swell with pride when I stop to speak with them. Just the same, there are days when I cannot pause and smile, when I have no heart to play with them; when, indeed, I mutter sourly to myself, exactly as I muttered on the streets of a city these children have never seen, when I was no bigger than these children are now: *Your* mother was a *nigger*. Joyce is right about history being a nightmare—but it may be the nightmare from which no one *can* awaken. People are trapped in history and history is trapped in them.

There is a custom in the village—I am told it is repeated in many villages—of "buying" African natives for the purpose of converting them to Christianity. There stands in the church all year round a small box with a slot for money, decorated with a black figurine, and into this box the villagers drop their francs. During the *carnaval* which precedes Lent, two village children have their faces blackened—out of which bloodless darkness their blue eyes shine like ice—and fantastic horsehair wigs are placed on their blond heads; thus disguised, they solicit among the villagers for money for the missionaries in Africa. Between the box in the church and the blackened children, the village "bought" last year six or eight African natives. This was reported to me with pride by the wife of one of the *bistro* owners and I was careful to express astonishment and pleasure at the solicitude shown by the village for the souls of black folks. The *bistro* owner's wife beamed with a pleasure far more genuine than my own and seemed to feel that I might now breathe more easily concerning the souls of at least six of my kinsmen.

I tried not to think of these so lately baptized kinsmen, of the price paid for them, or the peculiar price they themselves would pay, and said nothing about my father, who having taken his own conversion too literally, never, at bottom, forgave the white world (which he described as heathen) for having saddled him with a Christ in whom, to judge at least from their treatment of him, they themselves no longer believed. I thought of white men arriving for the first time in an African village, strangers there, as I am a stranger here, and tried to imagine the astounded populace touching their hair and marveling at the color of their skin. But there is a great difference between being the first white man to be seen by Africans and being the first black man to be seen by whites. The white man takes the astonishment as tribute, for he arrives to conquer and to convert the natives, whose inferiority in relation to himself is not even to be questioned; whereas I, without a thought of conquest, find myself among a people whose culture controls me, has even, in a sense, created me, people who have cost me more in anguish and rage than they will ever know, who yet do not even know of my existence. The astonishment with which I might have greeted them, should they have stumbled into my African village a few hundred years ago, might have rejoiced their hearts. But the astonishment with which they greet me today can only poison mine.

And this is so despite everything I may do to feel differently, despite my friendly conversations with the *bistro* owner's wife, despite their three-year-old son who has at last become my friend, despite the *saluts* and *bonsoirs* which I exchange with people as I walk, despite the fact that I know that no individual can be taken to task for what history is doing, or has done. I say that the culture of these people controls me —but they can scarcely be held responsible for European culture. America comes out of Europe, but these people have never seen America, nor have most of them seen more of Europe than the hamlet at the foot of their mountain. Yet, they move with an authority which I shall never have, and they regard me, quite rightly, not only as a stranger in their village but as a suspect latecomer, bearing no credentials, to everything they have—however unconsciously—inherited.

For this village, even were it incomparably more remote and incredibly more primitive, is the West, the West onto which I have been so strangely grafted. These people cannot be, from the point of view of power, strangers anywhere in the world: they have made the modern world, in effect, even if they do not know it. The most illiterate among them is related, in a way that I am not, to Dante, Shakespeare, Michelangelo, Aeschylus, Da Vinci, Rembrandt, and Racine; the cathedral at Chartres says something to them which it cannot say to me, as indeed would New York's Empire State Building, should anyone here ever see it. Out of their hymns and dances come Beethoven and Bach. Go back a few centuries and they are in their full glory—but I am in Africa, watching the conquerors arrive.

The rage of the disesteemed is personally fruitless, but it is also absolutely inevitable; this rage, so generally discounted, so little understood even among the people whose daily bread it is, is one of the things that makes history. Rage can only with difficulty, and never entirely, be brought under the domination of the intelligence and is therefore not susceptible to any arguments whatever. This is a fact which ordinary representatives of the *Herrenvolk*, having never felt this rage and being unable to imagine it, quite fail to understand. Also, rage cannot be hidden, it can only be dissembled. This dissembling deludes the thoughtless, and strengthens rage, and adds, to rage, contempt. There are, no doubt, as many ways of coping with the resulting complex of tensions as there are black men in the world, but no black man can hope ever to be entirely liberated from this internal warfare—rage, dissembling, and contempt having inevitably accompanied his first realization of the power of white men. What is crucial here is that, since white men represent in the black man's world so heavy a weight, white men have for black men a reality which is far from being reciprocal; and hence all black men have toward white men an attitude which is designed, really, either to rob the white man of the jewel of his naïveté, or else to make it cost him dear.

The black man insists, by whatever means he finds at his disposal, that the white man cease to regard him as an exotic rarity and recognize him as a human being. This is a very charged and difficult moment, for there is a great deal of will power involved in the white man's naïveté. Most people are not naturally reflective any more than they are naturally malicious, and the white man prefers to keep the black man at a certain human remove because it is easier for him thus to preserve his simplicity and avoid being called to account for crimes committed by his forefathers, or his neighbors. He is inescapably aware, nevertheless, that he is in a better position in the world than black men are, nor can he quite put to death the suspicion that he is hated by black men therefore. He does not wish to be hated, neither does he wish to change places, and at this point in his uneasiness he can scarcely avoid having recourse to those legends which white men have created about black men, the most usual effect of which is that the white man finds himself enmeshed, so to speak, in his own language which describes hell, as well as the attributes which lead one to hell, as being as black as night.

Every legend, moreover, contains its residuum of truth, and the root function of language is to control the universe by describing it. It is of quite considerable significance that black men remain, in the imagination, and in overwhelming numbers in fact, beyond the disciplines of salvation; and this despite the fact that the West has been "buying" African natives for centuries. There is, I should hazard, an instantaneous necessity to be divorced from this so visibly unsaved stranger, in whose heart, moreover, one cannot guess what dreams of vengeance are being nourished; and, at the same time, there are few things on earth more attractive than the idea of the unspeakable liberty which is allowed the unredeemed. When, beneath the black mask, a human being begins to make himself felt one cannot escape a certain awful wonder as to what kind of human being it is. What one's imagination makes of other people is dictated, of course, by the laws of one's own personality and it is one of the ironies of black-white relations that, by means of what the white man imagines the black man to be, the black man is enabled to know who the white man is.

I have said, for example, that I am as much a stranger in this village today as I was the first summer I arrived, but this is not quite true. The villagers wonder less about the texture of my hair than they did then, and wonder rather more about me. And the fact that their wonder now exists on another level is reflected in their attitudes and in their eyes. There are the children who make those delightful, hilarious, sometimes astonishingly grave overtures of friendship in the unpredictable fashion of children; other children, having been taught that the devil is a black man, scream in genuine anguish as I approach. Some of the older women never pass without a friendly greeting, never pass, indeed, if it seems that they will be able to engage me in conversation; other women look down or look away or rather contemptuously smirk. Some of the men drink with me and suggest that I learn how to ski—partly, I gather, because they cannot imagine what I would look like on skis—and want to know if I am married, and ask questions about my *métier*. But some of the men have accused *le sale nègre*—behind my back—of stealing wood and there is already in the eyes of some of them that peculiar, intent, paranoiac malevolence which one sometimes surprises in the eyes of American white men when, out walking with their Sunday girl, they see a Negro male approach.

There is a dreadful abyss between the streets of this village and the streets of the city in which I was born, between the children who shout *Neger!* today and those who shouted *Nigger!* yesterday—the abyss is experience, the American experience. The syllable hurled behind me today expresses, above all, wonder; I am a stranger here. But I am not a stranger in America and the same syllable riding on the American air expresses the war my presence has occasioned in the American soul.

For this village brings home to me this fact: that there was a day, and not really a very distant day, when Americans were scarcely Americans at all but discontented Europeans, facing a great unconquered continent and strolling, say, into a marketplace and seeing black men for the first time. The shock this spectacle afforded is suggested, surely, by the promptness with which they decided that these black men were not really men but cattle. It is true that the necessity on the part of the settlers of the New World of reconciling their moral assumptions with the fact—and the necessity—of slavery enhanced immensely the charm of this idea, and it is also true that this idea expresses, with a truly American bluntness, the attitude which to varying extents all masters have had toward all slaves.

But between all former slaves and slave-owners and the drama which begins for Americans over three hundred years ago at Jamestown, there are at least two differences to be observed. The American Negro slave could not suppose, for one thing, as slaves in past epochs had supposed and often done, that he would ever be able to wrest the power from his master's hands. This was a supposition which the modern era, which was to bring about such vast changes in the aims and dimensions of power, put to death; it only begins, in unprecedented fashion, and with dreadful implications, to be resurrected today. But even had this supposition persisted with undiminished force, the American Negro slave could not have used it to lend his condition dignity, for the reason that this supposition rests on another: that the slave in exile yet remains related to his past, has some means—if only in memory—of revering and sustaining the forms of his former life, is able, in short, to maintain his identity.

This was not the case with the American Negro slave. He is unique among the black men of the world in that his past was taken from him, almost literally, at one blow. One wonders what on earth the first slave found to say to the first dark child he bore. I am told that there are Haitians able to trace their ancestry back to African kings, but any American Negro wishing to go back so far will find his journey through time abruptly arrested by the signature on the bill of sale which served as the entrance paper for his ancestor. At the time—to say nothing of the circumstances—of the enslavement of the captive black man who was to become the American Negro, there was not the remotest possibility that he would ever take power from his master's hands. There was no reason to suppose that his situation would ever change, nor was there, shortly, anything to indicate that his situation had ever been different. It was his necessity, in the words of E. Franklin Frazier, to find a "motive for living under American culture or die." The identity of the American Negro comes out of this extreme situation, and the evolution of this identity was a source of the most intolerable anxiety in the minds and the lives of his masters.

For the history of the American Negro is unique also in this: that the question of his humanity, and of his rights therefore as a human being, became a burning one for several generations of Americans, so burning a question that it ultimately became one of those used to divide the nation. It is out of this argument that the venom of the epithet *Nigger!* is derived. It is an argument which Europe has never had, and hence Europe quite sincerely fails to understand how or why the argument arose in the first place, why its effects are so frequently disastrous and always so unpredictable, why it refuses until today to be entirely settled. Europe's black possessions remained—and do remain—in Europe's colonies, at which remove they represented no threat whatever to European identity. If they posed any problem at all for the European conscience, it was a problem which remained comfortingly abstract: in effect, the black man, *as a man*, did not exist for Europe. But in America, even as a slave, he was an inescapable part of the general social fabric and no American could escape having an attitude toward him. Americans attempt until today to make an abstraction of the Negro, but the very nature of these abstractions reveals the tremendous effects the presence of the Negro has had on the American character.

When one considers the history of the Negro in America it is of the greatest importance to recognize that the moral beliefs of a person, or a people, are never really as tenuous as life—which is not moral—very often causes them to appear; these create for them a frame of reference and a necessary hope, the hope being that when life has done its worst they will be enabled to rise above themselves and to triumph over life. Life would scarcely be bearable if this hope did not exist. Again, even when the worst has been said, to betray a belief is not by any means to have put oneself beyond its power; the betrayal of a belief is not the same thing as ceasing to believe. If this were not so there would be no moral standards in the world at all. Yet one must also recognize that morality is based on ideas and that all ideas are dangerous—dangerous because ideas can only lead to action and where the action leads no man can say. And dangerous in this respect: that confronted with the impossibility of remaining faithful to one's beliefs, and the equal impossibility of becoming free of them, one can be driven to the most inhuman excesses. The ideas on which American beliefs are based are not, though Americans often seem to think so, ideas which originated in America. They came out of Europe. And the establishment of democracy on the American continent was scarcely as radical a break with the past as was the necessity, which Americans faced, of broadening this concept to include black men.

This was, literally, a hard necessity. It was impossible, for one thing, for Americans to abandon their beliefs, not only because these beliefs alone seemed able to justify the sacrifices they had endured and the blood that they had spilled, but also because these beliefs afforded them their only bulwark against a moral chaos as absolute as the physical chaos of the continent it was their destiny to conquer. But in the situation in which Americans found themselves, these beliefs threatened an idea which, whether or not one likes to think so, is the very warp and woof of the heritage of the West, the idea of white supremacy.

Americans have made themselves notorious by the shrillness and the brutality with which they have insisted on this idea, but they did not invent it; and it has escaped the world's notice that those very excesses of which Americans have been guilty imply a certain, unprecedented uneasiness over the idea's life and power, if not, indeed, the idea's validity. The idea of white supremacy rests simply on the fact that white men are the creators of civilization (the present civilization, which is the only one that matters; all previous civilizations are simply "contributions" to our own) and are therefore civilization's guardians and defenders. Thus it was impossible for Americans to accept the black man as one of themselves, for to do so was to jeopardize their status as white men. But not so to accept him was to deny his human reality, his human weight and complexity, and the strain of denying the overwhelmingly undeniable forced Americans into rationalizations so fantastic that they approached the pathological.

At the root of the American Negro problem is the necessity of the American white man to find a way of living with the Negro in order to be able to live with himself. And the history of this problem can be reduced to the means used by Americans—lynch law and law, segregation and legal acceptance, terrorization and concession—either to come to terms with this necessity, or to find a way around it, or (most usually) to find a way of doing both these things at once. The resulting spectacle, at once foolish and dreadful, led someone to make the quite accurate observation that "the Negro-in-America is a form of insanity which overtakes white men."

In this long battle, a battle by no means finished, the unforeseeable effects of which will be felt by many future generations, the white man's motive was the protection of his identity; the black man was motivated by the need to establish an identity. And despite the terrorization which the Negro in America endured and endures sporadically until today, despite the cruel and totally inescapable ambivalence of his status in his country, the battle for his identity has long ago been won. He is not a visitor to the West, but a citizen there, an American; as American as the Americans who despise him, the Americans who fear him, the Americans who love him—the Americans who became less than themselves, or rose to be greater than themselves by virtue of the fact that the challenge he represented was inescapable. He is perhaps the only black man in the world whose relationship to white men is more terrible, more subtle, and more meaningful than the relationship of bitter possessed to uncertain possessor. His survival depended, and his development depends, on his ability to turn his peculiar status in the Western world to his own advantage and, it may be, to the very great advantage of that world. It remains for him to fashion out of his experience that which will give him sustenance, and a voice.

The cathedral at Chartres, I have said, says something to the people of this village which it cannot say to me; but it is important to understand that this cathedral says something to me which it cannot say to them. Perhaps they are struck by the power of the spires, the glory of the windows; but they have known God, after all, longer than I have known him, and in a different way, and I am terrified by the slippery bottomless well to be found in the crypt, down which heretics were hurled to death, and by the obscene, inescapable gargoyles jutting out of the stone and seeming to say that God and the devil can never be divorced. I doubt that the villagers think of the devil when they face a cathedral because they have never been identified with the devil. But I must accept the status which myth, if nothing else, gives me in the West before I can hope to change the myth.

Yet, if the American Negro has arrived at his identity by virtue of the absoluteness of his estrangement from his past, American white men still nourish the illusion that there is some means of recovering the European innocence, of returning to a state in which black men do not exist. This is one of the greatest errors Americans can make. The identity they fought so hard to protect has, by virtue of that battle, undergone a change: Americans are as unlike any other white people in the world as it is possible to be. I do not think, for example, that it is too much to suggest that the American vision of the world—which allows so little reality, generally speaking, for any of the darker forces in human life, which tends until today to paint moral issues in glaring black and white—owes a great deal to the battle waged by Americans to maintain between themselves and black men a human separation which could not be bridged. It is only now beginning to be borne in on us—very faintly, it must be admitted, very slowly, and very much against our will—that this vision of the world is dangerously inaccurate, and perfectly useless. For it protects our moral high-mindedness at the terrible expense of weakening our grasp of reality. People who shut their eyes to reality simply invite their own destruction, and anyone who insists on remaining in a state of innocence long after that innocence is dead turns himself into a monster.

The time has come to realize that the interracial drama acted out on the American continent has not only created a new black man, it has created a new white man, too. No road whatever will lead Americans back to the simplicity of this European village where white men still have the luxury of looking on me as a stranger. I am not, really, a stranger any longer for any American alive. One of the things that distinguishes Americans from other people is that no other people has ever been so deeply involved in the lives of black men, and vice versa. This fact faced, with all its implications, it can be seen that the history of the American Negro problem is not merely shameful, it is also something of an achievement. For even when the worst has been said, it must also be added that the perpetual challenge posed by this problem was always, somehow, perpetually met. It is precisely this black-white experience which may prove of indispensable value to us in the world we face today. This world is white no longer, and it will never be white again.

UNDERSTANDING THE TEXT

1. The first portion of Baldwin's essay develops the author's reflections on his experience in the Swiss village. The second portion, beginning with the paragraph on p. 530 that starts "There is a dreadful abyss between the streets of this village and the streets of the city in which I was born . . . ," develops Baldwin's reflections on the relations between Negro and white in America. What common themes run through both portions of the essay? What contrasts are there between the two? How does the first section prepare the way for the second?

2. What special value, for the purposes of his argument, does Baldwin derive from the fact that the Swiss village is very small and relatively isolated, the experience of the villagers narrow?

3. What does Baldwin mean when he refers (p. 527) to the "peculiar price" the lately baptized Africans would pay?

4. What does Baldwin mean when he says (p. 527) that in the village he is among people whose culture "in a sense" created him?

5. Explain what Baldwin means when he says (p. 528) that the "rage of the disesteemed" can only be dissembled, that the dissembling strengthens rage, and that it adds, to rage, contempt.

6. ". . . the root function of language," Baldwin says, "is to control the universe by describing it" (p. 529). Analyze the passage in which this statement occurs in order to explain what Baldwin means.

7. Baldwin says that it is ironic that "by means of what the white man imagines the black man to be, the black man is enabled to know who the white man is" (p. 529). Explain the irony.

8. What, in Baldwin's view, is the essential difference between the American experience with slavery and the experience of all other slaves and slave-owners?

9. Baldwin asserts (p. 531) that the supposition that slaves may be able to wrest power from their masters rests on the further supposition that the slave remains related to his past. Explain the reasoning behind this assertion.

10. What conditions does Baldwin cite to account for the differences between European and American attitudes toward the Negro?
11. The paragraph on p. 532 beginning "When one considers the history of the Negro in America . . ." contains a number of general premises bearing on human attitudes and actions. Show how Baldwin uses these premises in analyzing the American experience with the Negro.
12. Early in the essay (p. 528) Baldwin says that the cathedral at Chartres means something to the villagers that it cannot mean to him. Later (p. 534) he says that it means something to him that it cannot mean to the villagers. What is the meaning in each case?
13. What beliefs is Baldwin referring to when he says (p. 532) that "these beliefs" threatened the idea of white supremacy?

TOPICS FOR DISCUSSION AND WRITING

14. Write a paragraph characterizing Baldwin's attitude toward the white man.
15. Write a short paper exploring the connections between Baldwin's discussion of the attitude of white Americans toward the Negro and Henry Bamford Parkes's analysis of industrialism and American ideals.
16. Using Baldwin's observations about the relations of white and Negro in America, write a paragraph supporting the thesis that the positions of both white man and Negro, as regards the problem of identity, have been radically similar.
17. Write a paragraph, based on Baldwin's essay, on the theme "People are trapped in history and history is trapped in them."

The Tyranny of Democratic Manners

MORTON J. CRONIN

I MAINTAIN that democratic manners—typified by the practice of calling the boss by his first name—have reached the point in our country where they conduce not to the preservation of personal dignity but to the abject submission of one man to another. These manners, gradually developed in colonial and post-revolutionary days, worked well in a society largely of self-sufficient farmers. But circumstances have changed, with the usual ironical result.

What happens on the job at the present time? An employee greets the boss by his first name, sits down in his presence, wears the same kind of clothes the boss wears, avoids the use of *sir*, and ostensibly comports himself in general as if he and the boss were as equal as two farmers. But of course he and the boss are not equal, and this inequality must be signalized. It must be signalized, first, because the employee is anxious to please the boss, who can advance or impede his fortunes; and, secondly, because the boss is anxious that his authority receive recognition, without which he cannot function with any confidence.

In the absence of overt and conventional methods of expressing deference, how then does the American employee acknowledge the boss's superior status? He does so by perfecting a subtle repertoire of body movements and vocal expressions. This repertoire includes the boyish grin, the deprecatory cough, the unfinished sentence, the appreciative giggle, the drooping shoulders, the head-scratch and the bottom-waggle. But there are employees, the truly gifted ones—as actors, they would adorn the Stanislavski school—who can dispense with these definable maneuvers and simply *live* the part, their whole being radiating a kind of sweet eloquence of submission.

Reprinted from *The New Republic*, January 20, 1958. Used by permission of *The New Republic*.

Now this body language, in both its definable and indefinable forms, is almost impossible to fake successfully, at least in any long-continued relationship. If it is not accompanied quite genuinely by the emotions appropriate to it, it will be contradicted and rendered sinister by involuntary movements and expressions which accord with the individual's true feelings. It is easy to execute a military salute, regardless of one's private thoughts, but the deprecatory cough—to say nothing of the Stanislavski method—requires great sincerity, else they appear villainous.

American manners, in short, decree egalitarian behavior in a hierarchical society. The result is that a subordinate, compelled to behave formally and superficially in a democratic way, is forced in making his adjustments to the facts of life to behave informally and profoundly in a hierarchical way. It should be just the opposite—the system of etiquette ought to furnish him with formal gestures of respect for his superiors and let his informal self work out its own salvation. It should be easier to render the boss what is the boss's without throwing in one's soul too.

Out of a doctrinaire devotion to palsy-walsy manners has sprung that misshapen, anomalous growth, the despotism of the nice guy. It is a truism that success on the job depends less on competence in performing one's duties than it does on ability to Get Along With People. But what is left out of this statement—it is not sporting to mention it—is that the word *People* refers to just one person—the boss. And the boss, barred from receiving any obvious obeisance, is commonly in a chronic state of insecurity—what he craves most of all is the assurance that he is really and truly the boss. The nice guy, with his fine talent for the right body language, provides this assurance better than the man who is merely efficient, is rewarded accordingly, and thus sets the pace for his clumsy fellows.

But the despotism of the nice guy reaches its fully convoluted luxuriance when, as happens, he himself is made the boss. He has not been soft-spoken, unassertive, accommodating and eager to please out of sheer masochism. However various the motives which explain his personality, ambition is one of them. Good Old Charlie likes the idea of being a boss. And if his underlings could give him a snappy salaam every day, all might be well. But Charlie would recoil from anything so Oriental in its disrespect for human dignity. All that he expects is that his subordinates will make the same sensitive, informal adjustments to his person which he used to make for the boss, a process which practically requires that they exchange their personalities for his. Only a few of them are capable of such virtuosity—Charlie's word for it is *loyalty*—but most of them do well enough to demonstrate that it is really the nice guy in authority, more than the rambunctious one, who has made America the natural habitat of the yes-man. Of course the situation is complicated by the fact that Charlie soon becomes pitifully dependent on his loyal supporters, one of whom usually emerges as a split-personality and, like a skillful wife, sweetly dominates Charlie in all things.

Everybody complains that life is too competitive, but our national imagination is so limited that the principal remedies proposed for this or any other social disease are economic remedies—better jobs, better houses, and more social security. However justified on other grounds, these remedies, beyond a certain point, just hot up this particular fire, for life becomes not less competitive but decidedly more so as one moves up the ladder. Naturally. There is more to compete for. But still the fever could be brought down a few points by a modification of manners. Once men acquire everything they need—a condition soon reached in this country—they struggle primarily for recognition. But with manners as frustratingly egalitarian as they are, who knows when he has it made? Under present circumstances the ambitious can discern no resting place short of a crushing superiority of popular fame or material wealth. Hence, the devotion of many originally fine minds to Hollywood, Broadway and the medical profession.

Consider, for instance, the folly of our disparagement of honorific titles. If a mayor were regularly addressed as *Your Honor*, and could count on this distinction after leaving office, he would be heartened in his efforts to remain honest. As it is, he must play it democratic, pooh-pooh his title, and prepare against the day when, defeated for re-election, he must face the indifference of the public at large. Mayors are commonly corrupt, judges rarely. But judges are unfailingly objects of formal homage in office, and keep their titles for life.

The sobriquets which used to attach to politicians—*Old Hickory, Tennessee Johnson, The Little Giant, The Plumed Knight*—conferred distinction. They were titles of a sort and reflected a popular disposition to honor character, individuality and superior force in public men. But now the popular taste, encouraged by gee-whiz politicians who tutoyer one another in public, is for first names and demure diminutives—*Ike, Dick, Stu, Bob, Estes* and *Foster*. What makes these familiarities characteristic of our time is precisely that they ignore what is distinctive in either the personalities or the duties of the men they designate and thus suggest that government is best which is managed by Good Joes recently graduated from a basketball team. If Woodrow Wilson were in politics today, he would probably have to submit to *Woody*—if not *Willie*—and wipe that purposeful and responsible look off his face.

But the avoidance of titles of respect is equally the fashion among highbrows. Professors in famous universities, for instance, make fun of their fellows in teachers' colleges because the latter often call one another *professor* or *doctor*, instead of plain *mister*, and are notorious for responding benignly when their students use these terms. But on this point it is the prominent professors whose perception is defective, for an examination of their total behavior reveals that they are much less democratic than those they smile at for putting on airs. Occupying positions in institutions of outstanding prestige—positions for which they have scrambled ferociously—they can afford to underemphasize their status, like wealthy men who insist that their limousines be inconspicuously black. The fact is that they maintain great distance between town and gown and also between their students and themselves.

Many of them deplore their remoteness, but without an improvement of manners there is little they can do about it. Since they discourage formal acknowledgments of their status, any meeting between them and townfolk, or even between them and their own students, imposes on both sides such a strain on their respective capacities for the appropriate body language that it is almost unbearable. The man at Lower South Central Normal suffers his students to call him professor—doctor—sir—but he can often be observed chatting loftily and genially among them, snapping his suspenders the while, undisturbed by their politely impudent questions.

But the deprecation of titles and of formal manners in general characterizes all sorts of highbrows, not just those in universities. Yet no group in America complains so clamorously that it is not sufficiently respected and appreciated. And those among them who complain most bitterly are the ones who embrace the mucker pose passionately, not only in their speech and manners but even in their dress. This furious contradiction necessitates a furious resolution. Men who will not permit their attainments to be recognized conventionally and symbolically will seek such recognition radically and violently.

But democratic manners have not only promoted unnatural relations among men in their economic and professional careers. They have also corrupted relations between men and women in their romantic and domestic lives. Here, however, the democratization of manners has been one-sided. Many suitable formalities still govern the man's behavior—he follows a woman through a door, sashays around to the gutter-side of the street, etc., etc., in all of which he pays decorous tribute to her as a woman. But our culture has relieved her almost entirely of any reciprocal gestures of conventional tribute to him as a man. She does not curtsy, nor use respectful forms of address, nor stand at his shoulder when he has his picture taken. Her grandmother practiced a sweet, conventional smile. She grins, laughs uproariously, and talks in a loud voice. For her the emphasis is now completely on body language—but, unlike that used by men with their bosses, hers is *challenging* rather than deferential.

Since he does not receive from women any standard courtesies, courtesies which, besides telling him that just being a man is a thing of some consequence, would remind him of his responsibilities, the American male gravitates in his dealings with women toward one of two roles—that of a little boy or that of a predator. Frequently he ricochets between the two. In the first role he simply abandons the effort to command respect as a male and, oddly enough, often becomes an abstract enthusiast for women, like a dull student whose every humiliation in class somehow increases his school spirit. In the role of predator he compels specific respect for himself as a man in the one decisive way that is still open. And, fortunately or unfortunately, such consolation has grown steadily more available. Women as well as men are symbolic creatures, and the radical elimination of ceremony reduces the human element in them and increases the animal part. Frustrated in her naturally human desire to express her feelings formally and stylistically, the American woman must express them directly and elementally.

But the inhuman effects of democratic manners afflict another fundamental relationship, that between parents and children. They spawn the ultimate in absurdity in those instances where parents, assuming the character of domestic politicians, encourage their youngsters to abjure the use of *mother* and *father* in favor of their parents' first names. The trouble with *mother* and *father* of course is that they suggest authority (as well as love), and thus strike an undemocratic note in the family. Often the parents' real motives, like those of tail-wagging politicians, are more complicated, for people who shun authoritative titles commonly shrink from responsibility too. But they could not persevere in this self-deception if our dedication to democratic manners did not furnish them with an exalted rationale.

Fortunately, this first-name business for parents is as yet limited. But manners generally are primitive enough in American homes, as anyone knows who accepts invitations from his friends to dine *en famille*. It is undemocratic to set up a children's table. It is also undemocratic to encourage children to listen to adult conversation. Parents and guests, consequently, listen to children's conversation. During intervals—when little mouths happen simultaneously to be stuffed up with food, for instance —the parents inevitably discuss the subject of children. Children, they tell you, are *people*. The children express themselves. The parents preen themselves. The only person who does not get a piece of this democracy is the guest. This lopsided egalitarianism even favors dogs and cats, with whom a guest must often cope with no assistance whatever from his host. They too, it seems, are *people*.

I have nearly finished. But I know that some fool—most likely, one with a Ph.D.—will read this article and forever after assert as a well-known fact that I yearn for a restoration of Tsardom, for a reinvigoration of the Hindu caste system and for a truly Chinese subjugation of women and children. So let me recapitulate, in the course of which I shall add one or two points that I forgot to mention earlier.

A sensible system of manners, sensibly formal, performs various services. Besides acting as a constant reminder of some important facts of life, it affords human beings the distinctly human satisfactions of symbolic expression. Besides making collective living possible, it provides a person, thanks to its formalities, with protective armor against collective pressures. For these formalities allow the individual to acquiesce in the social order while reserving his final judgment of it. They enable him to pledge his loyalty to men in authority without making those fine adjustments whose long-term results are the same as those of brainwashing.

Democratic manners in America are eating the heart out of American democracy. With no impressive way of saluting the system, and the position which a given official occupies in it, one must prostrate himself before the man. There is a country where such prostration is even more prostrate than in America. There the humblest citizen calls his mighty ruler *comrade*.

I suggest a prudent reform in American manners, not a revolution. If the only alternative to egalitarian manners is a nerveless society exhausted by protocol and ceremony, then this discussion is futile. But that is not the only alternative, except in the minds of latter-day Jacobins for whom the stratifications of the *ancien régime* are more real than the proletarian-izations of their own time. There are in-between solutions, attuned to reality, however they resist simple and consistent formulation, as the English know, and as America, in her own fashion, can discover. Pedantic democrats presume to speak for wisdom, creative ability and service, as against mere money in the bank. But without a rectification of manners most men would rather achieve a Cadillac than such virtues, for these virtues, unacknowledged in any regular way, do not show on a man, at least not conspicuously, whereas a Cadillac shows on anyone, conspicuously.

UNDERSTANDING THE TEXT

1. Cronin "typifies" democratic manners by the practice of calling the boss by his first name. What other aspects of American life does he consider? Why does he use calling the boss by his first name as the type of democratic manners?

2. In one paragraph summarize the central argument of Cronin's essay.

3. In his opening paragraph Cronin says that democratic manners "conduce not to the preservation of personal dignity" but to "the abject submission of one man to another." What assumption is Cronin making here about the purpose of a system of manners? Gather illustrations of the use of this assumption elsewhere in the essay.

4. Explain why, in Cronin's view, the democratic system of manners involves "throwing in one's soul too."

5. Why is it important to Cronin's argument that the "body language" (paragraph 4) should be "almost impossible to fake successfully," but must be accompanied by genuine emotions? What would happen to Cronin's argument if the body language could be made formal and conventional?

6. What is the function of the section about the "despotism of the nice guy" (pp. 538–539) in the development of Cronin's argument?

7. Explain why Cronin thinks a better system of manners would lessen the effects of competition.

8. What point are Cronin's examples of the use and non-use of honorific titles designed to illustrate? Discuss the value of his examples in helping to establish his point.

9. In the paragraph about professors in famous universities (p. 540) Cronin seems to imply that democratic manners are actually accompanied by un-

democratic behavior. Show how the same assumption is at work in his description of the professor at Lower South Central Normal. Is this assumption important elsewhere in the essay?

10. What is the essential difference between manners as between men in their economic and professional careers and manners as between men and women? Does Cronin's theory account equally well for both?

11. In his discussion of the manners of men and women (p. 541) Cronin notes that women no longer curtsy, stand at the man's shoulder when he has his picture taken, or smile sweetly and conventionally. Are these examples of merely formal "body language"? Do they contradict Cronin's point in paragraph 4, that body language must be accompanied by genuine emotions or appear villainous?

12. Throughout his essay, Cronin uses a distinction between formal or conventional behavior and informal or personal behavior. The distinction appears very prominently, for example, in the fourth and fifth paragraphs (p. 538). Find other places in the essay where this distinction is used. Give some examples of the distinction that Cronin does not include in his essay.

TOPICS FOR DISCUSSION AND WRITING

13. Make clear, in a paragraph, what a proper system of manners would be, for Cronin.

14. Cronin does not specify very precisely the reforms he would like to see in American manners. Write a paragraph giving concrete illustrations of such reforms in one segment of American life, in terms of Cronin's theory.

15. Write a one-paragraph comparison of Cronin's conception of manners and Lord Moulton's in the essay "Law and Manners" (pp. 166–169).

16. "American manners, in short, require egalitarian manners in a hierarchical society." This sentence implies a conflict between the ideal and the real nature of American society. Make clear what the conflict is, and write a paragraph comparing Cronin's view of the conflict with Parkes's.

9. Wider Horizons

Art for Art's Sake

E. M. FORSTER

*An address delivered before the American Academy
of Arts and Letters in New York, 1949*

I BELIEVE in art for art's sake. It is an unfashionable belief, and some of my statements must be of the nature of an apology. Fifty years ago I should have faced you with more confidence. A writer or a speaker who chose "Art for Art's Sake" for his theme fifty years ago could be sure of being in the swim, and could feel so confident of success that he sometimes dressed himself in esthetic costumes suitable to the occasion—in an embroidered dressing gown, perhaps, or a blue velvet suit with a Lord Fauntleroy collar; or a toga, or a kimono, and carried a poppy or a lily or a long peacock's feather in his medieval hand. Times have changed. Not thus can I present either myself or my theme today. My aim rather is to ask you quietly to reconsider for a few minutes a phrase which has been much misused and much abused, but which has, I believe, great importance for us—has, indeed, eternal importance.

Now we can easily dismiss those peacock's feathers and other affectations—they are but trifles—but I want also to dismiss a more dangerous heresy, namely the silly idea that only art matters, an idea which has somehow got mixed up with the idea of art for art's sake, and has helped to discredit it. Many things, besides art, matter. It is merely one of the things that matter, and high though the claims are that I make for it, I want to keep them in proportion. No one can spend his or her life entirely in the creation or the appreciation of masterpieces. Man lives, and ought to live, in a complex world, full of conflicting claims, and if we simplified them down into the esthetic he would be sterilised. Art for art's sake does not mean that only art matters, and I would also like to rule out such phrases as "The Life of Art," "Living for Art," and "Art's High Mission." They confuse and mislead.

What does the phrase mean? Instead of generalising, let us take a specific instance—Shakespeare's *Macbeth*, for example, and pronounce the words, "*Macbeth* for *Macbeth's* sake." What does that mean? Well, the play has several aspects—it is educational, it teaches us something about legendary Scotland, something about Jacobean England, and a good deal about human nature and its perils. We can study its origins, and study and enjoy its dramatic technique and the music of its diction. All that is true. But *Macbeth* is furthermore a world of its own, created by Shakespeare and existing in virtue of its own poetry. It is in this aspect *Macbeth* for *Macbeth's* sake, and that is what I intend by the phrase "art for art's sake." A work of art—whatever else it may be—is a self-contained entity, with a life of its own imposed on it by its creator. It has internal order. It may have external form. That is how we recognise it.

Take for another example that picture of Seurat's which I saw two years ago in Chicago—"*La Grande Jatte*." Here again there is much to study and to enjoy: the pointillism, the charming face of the seated girl, the nineteenth-century Parisian Sunday sunlight, the sense of motion in immobility. But here again there is something more; *"La Grande Jatte"* forms a world of its own, created by Seurat and existing by virtue of its own poetry: *"La Grande Jatte" pour "La Grande Jatte": l'art pour l'art.* Like *Macbeth* it has internal order and internal life.

It is to the conception of order that I would now turn. This is important to my argument, and I want to make a digression, and glance at order in daily life, before I come to order in art.

In the world of daily life, the world which we perforce inhabit, there is much talk about order, particularly from statesmen and politicians. They tend, however, to confuse order with orders, just as they confuse creation with regulations. Order, I suggest, is something evolved from within, not something imposed from without; it is an internal stability, a vital harmony, and in the social and political category, it has never existed except for the convenience of historians. Viewed realistically, the past is really a series of *dis*orders, succeeding one another by discoverable laws, no doubt, and certainly marked by an increasing growth of human inter-ference, but disorders all the same. So that, speaking as a writer, what I hope for today is a disorder which will be more favourable to artists than is the present one, and which will provide them with fuller inspirations and better material conditions. It will not last—nothing lasts—but there have been some advantageous disorders in the past—for instance, in an-cient Athens, in Renaissance Italy, eighteenth-century France, periods in China and Persia—and we may do something to accelerate the next one. But let us not again fix our hearts where true joys are not to be found. We were promised a new order after the first world war through the League of Nations. It did not come, nor have I faith in present promises, by whomsoever endorsed. The implacable offensive of Science forbids. We cannot reach social and political stability for the reason that we con-tinue to make scientific discoveries and to apply them, and thus to destroy the arrangements which were based on more elementary discoveries. If Science would discover rather than apply—if, in other words, men were more interested in knowledge than in power—mankind would be in a far safer position, the stability statesmen talk about would be a possibility, there could be a new order based on vital harmony, and the earthly mil-lennium might approach. But Science shows no signs of doing this: she gave us the internal combustion engine, and before we had digested and assimilated it with terrible pains into our social system, she harnessed the atom, and destroyed any new order that seemed to be evolving. How can man get into harmony with his surroundings when he is constantly altering them? The future of our race is, in this direction, more unpleasant than we care to admit, and it has sometimes seemed to me that its best chance lies through apathy, uninventiveness, and inertia. Universal exhaustion might promote that Change of Heart which is at present so briskly recommended from a thousand pulpits. Universal exhaustion would certainly be a new experience. The human race has never undergone it, and is still too perky to admit that it may be coming and might result in a sprouting of new growth through the decay.

I must not pursue these speculations any further—they lead me too far from my terms of reference and maybe from yours. But I do want to emphasize that order in daily life and in history, order in the social and political category, is unattainable under our present psychology.

Where is it attainable? Not in the astronomical category, where it was for many years enthroned. The heavens and the earth have become terribly alike since Einstein. No longer can we find a reassuring contrast to chaos in the night sky and look up with George Meredith to the stars, the army of unalterable law, or listen for the music of the spheres. Order is not there. In the entire universe there seem to be only two possibilities for it. The first of them—which again lies outside my terms of reference —is the divine order, the mystic harmony, which according to all religions is available for those who can contemplate it. We must admit its possibility, on the evidence of the adepts, and we must believe them when they say that it is attained, if attainable, by prayer. "O thou who changest not, abide with me," said one of its poets. "*Ordina questo amor, o tu che m'ami,*" said another: "Set love in order, thou who lovest me." The existence of a divine order, though it cannot be tested, has never been disproved.

The second possibility for order lies in the esthetic category, which is my subject here: the order which an artist can create in his own work, and to that we must now return. A work of art, we are all agreed, is a unique product. But why? It is unique not because it is clever or noble or beautiful or enlightened or original or sincere or idealistic or useful or educational—it may embody any of those qualities—but because it is the only material object in the universe which may possess internal harmony. All the others have been pressed into shape from outside, and when their mold is removed they collapse. The work of art stands up by itself, and nothing else does. It achieves something which has often been promised by society, but always delusively. Ancient Athens made a mess—but the *Antigone* stands up. Renaissance Rome made a mess—but the ceiling of the Sistine got painted. James I made a mess—but there was *Macbeth*. Louis XIV—but there was *Phèdre*. Art for art's sake? I should just think so, and more so than ever at the present time. It is the one orderly product which our muddling race has produced. It is the cry of a thousand sentinels, the echo from a thousand labyrinths; it is the lighthouse which cannot be hidden: *c'est le meilleur témoignage que nous puissions donner de notre dignité*.[1] *Antigone* for *Antigone's* sake, *Macbeth* for *Macbeth's*, "*La Grande Jatte*" *pour* "*La Grande Jatte*."

If this line of argument is correct, it follows that the artist will tend to be an outsider in the society to which he has been born, and that the nineteenth-century conception of him as a Bohemian was not inaccurate. The conception erred in three particulars: it postulated an economic system where art could be a full-time job, it introduced the fallacy that only art matters, and it overstressed idiosyncrasy and waywardness—the peacock-feather aspect—rather than order. But it is a truer conception than the one which prevails in official circles on my side of the Atlantic—I don't know about yours: the conception which treats the artist as if he were a particularly bright government advertiser and encourages him to be friendly and matey with his fellow citizens, and not to give himself airs.

Estimable is mateyness, and the man who achieves it gives many a pleasant little drink to himself and to others. But it has no traceable connection with the creative impulse, and probably acts as an inhibition on it. The artist who is seduced by mateyness may stop himself from doing the one thing which he, and he alone, can do—the making of something out of words or sounds or paint or clay or marble or steel or film which has internal harmony and presents order to a permanently disarranged planet. This seems worth doing, even at the risk of being called uppish by journalists. I have in mind an article which was published some years ago in the London *Times*, an article called "The Eclipse of the Highbrow," in which the "Average Man" was exalted, and all contemporary literature was censured if it did not toe the line, the precise position of the line being naturally known to the writer of the article. Sir Kenneth Clark, who was at that time director of our National Gallery, commented on this pernicious doctrine in a letter which cannot be too often quoted. "The poet and the artist," wrote Clark, "are important precisely because they are not average men; because in sensibility, intelligence, and power of invention they far exceed the average." These memorable words, and

[1] "It is the best testimony of our dignity that we can give."

particularly the words "power of invention," are the Bohemian's passport. Furnished with it, he slinks about society, saluted now by a brickbat and now by a penny, and accepting either of them with equanimity. He does not consider too anxiously what his relations with society may be, for he is aware of something more important than that—namely the invitation to invent, to create order, and he believes he will be better placed for doing this if he attempts detachment. So round and round he slouches, with his hat pulled over his eyes, and maybe with a louse in his beard, and—if he really wants one—with a peacock's feather in his hand.

If our present society should disintegrate—and who dare prophesy that it won't?—this old-fashioned and démodé figure will become clearer: the Bohemian, the outsider, the parasite, the rat—one of those figures which have at present no function either in a warring or a peaceful world. It may not be dignified to be a rat, but many of the ships are sinking, which is not dignified either—the officials did not build them properly. Myself, I would sooner be a swimming rat than a sinking ship—at all events I can look around me for a little longer—and I remember how one of us, a rat with particularly bright eyes called Shelley, squeaked out, "Poets are the unacknowledged legislators of the world," before he vanished into the waters of the Mediterranean.

What laws did Shelley propose to pass? None. The legislation of the artist is never formulated at the time, though it is sometimes discerned by future generations. He legislates through creating. And he creates through his sensitiveness and his power to impose form. Without form the sensitiveness vanishes. And form is as important today, when the human race is trying to ride the whirlwind, as it ever was in those less agitating days of the past, when the earth seemed solid and the stars fixed, and the discoveries of science were made slowly, slowly. Form is not tradition. It alters from generation to generation. Artists always seek a new technique, and will continue to do so as long as their work excites them. But form of some kind is imperative. It is the surface crust of the internal harmony, it is the outward evidence of order.

My remarks about society may have seemed too pessimistic, but I believe that society can only represent a fragment of the human spirit, and that another fragment can only get expressed through art. And I wanted to take this opportunity, this vantage ground, to assert not only the existence of art but its pertinacity. Looking back into the past, it seems to me that that is all there has ever been: vantage grounds for discussion and creation, little vantage grounds in the changing chaos, where bubbles have been blown and webs spun, and the desire to create order has found temporary gratification, and the sentinels have managed to utter their challenges, and the huntsmen, though lost individually, have heard each other's calls through the impenetrable wood, and the lighthouses have never ceased sweeping the thankless seas. In this pertinacity there seems to me, as I grow older, something more and more profound, something which does in fact concern people who do not care about art at all.

In conclusion, let me summarize the various categories that have laid claim to the possession of Order.

(1) The social and political category. Claim disallowed on the evidence of history and of our own experience. If man altered psychologically, order here might be attainable; not otherwise.

(2) The astronomical category. Claim allowed up to the present century, but now disallowed on the evidence of the physicists.

(3) The religious category. Claim allowed on the evidence of the mystics.

(4) The esthetic category—the subject of this article. Claim allowed on the evidence of various works of art; and on the evidence of our own creative impulses, however weak these may be, or however imperfectly they may function. Works of art, in my opinion, are the only objects in the material universe to possess internal order, and that is why, though I don't believe that only art matters, I do believe in Art for Art's Sake.

UNDERSTANDING THE TEXT

1. Why does Forster insist on distinguishing between art for art's sake and the view that only art matters? Consider the associations the term "art for art's sake" had for you before you read Forster's essay. Was he well advised to make this distinction?

2. What does Forster mean by his "terms of reference" (p. 548)?

3. How many distinct categories does Forster consider in exploring the problem of order?

4. What does Forster mean by *order?*

5. What does Forster gain by the extended metaphor of the rat? Does it seem to you a good figure for his purpose?

6. How does the sentence "But I do want to emphasize that order in daily life and in history . . . is unattainable under our present psychology" constitute a conclusion from the preceding paragraph (p. 548)?

7. Can you find out what Forster is alluding to when he describes a speaker carrying "a poppy or a lily or a long peacock feather in his medieval hand"?

TOPICS FOR DISCUSSION AND WRITING

8. In a paragraph, attack or defend the judgment that Forster's essay is an elaborate argument in a circle, in which he begins by defining what he seeks to prove.

9. Do you agree that a work of art is "the only material object in the universe which may possess internal harmony"?

10. What premise does Forster assume when he says, "If this line of argument is correct, it follows that the artist will tend to be an outlaw in the society to which he has been born . . ."?

11. This is the essay which Alistair Cooke takes as the point of departure for his "No Sympathy for Apathy" (pp. 191–195). Find the statement which Cooke takes from the essay and decide whether Forster means what Cooke says he means.

12. Compare Forster's view of science with Henry Myers' view of science, and Forster's definition of a work of art with Myers' view of literature.

13. What is Forster's view of history?

The Illusion of Security

GEORGE F. KENNAN

I

OUR TIME, this morning, is brief: the occasion pleasant. I have racked my brain to think of something to say to the members of this graduating class, at such a moment, that would not involve those bitter questions of foreign and domestic policy that have been debated at such length and at the cost of so much unpleasantness in these recent months. One alternative, of course, would be to speak of personal life. But some two decades of parenthood have finally taught me something of the reality of the gap in the generations, and of my limitations as a dispenser of wisdom and advice to younger people in personal matters. That thrusts us back on the field of public affairs, where the choice is not great.

A distinguished American recently observed, on a similar occasion, that "one of the most curious and persistent myths of democratic society is that political figures have anything important or interesting to say, especially when they are out of office."

The same, goodness knows, could be said with equal aptness of retired government officials. We are, I fear, a gloomy race. Our faith in our country is there, and undiminished, but it lies deeply imbedded within us, in troubled depths. We do not fail to greet with immense inner satisfaction those things that do seem to us to be constructive and hopeful; but by and large we follow the course of public events with a sort of anxious and paternal apprehension, like a sailor who watches a strange crew sailing his craft; and if you prod us into a reaction—as anyone does who asks us to speak at Commencement ceremonies—what you get are our anxieties, for they are so much more explicit and so much closer to our tongues than our hopes.

So this morning, at the risk of speaking of matters that have perhaps been too much spoken of already, I am going to tell of one or two things that cause me anxiety and then of a common conclusion I derive from them that might usefully be borne in mind by people just entering the status of adult citizenship.

The first of these anxieties relates to foreign affairs. As many of you may know, I have never taken an alarmist view, and do not take one now, of the nature of our conflict with Soviet power. I have never felt, and do not feel today, that another great war could possibly serve as a useful instrument for promoting the interests of either side in this unhappy conflict. In a number of reflections about the nature of our world; in the fact that war has become so obviously self-defeating and suicidal; in the growing clarity with which the last two World Wars begin now to stand out on the landscape of history as tragic, colossal follies from which no one could be said to have gained; in the tendency of time to change all things and to erode all militant faiths—in these things I have found reason for hope and good cheer, and have spent much of my time and energy in these recent years trying to persuade others to approach what we call the East-West conflict in a similar spirit.

Yet I am bound to say that in recent weeks and months I have witnessed with increasing dismay what has seemed to me to be the progressive neglect or rejection, or disappearance for one reason or another, of the more hopeful possibilities for making progress in this problem by peaceful means. Above all, I have watched with a sinking of the heart the way in which many people in our country have, as it seems to me, been pressed relentlessly into states of mind where they can see no solution to these difficulties at all, and even no end to them, except in the horrors of atomic war. This has happened in some instances because people have been impatient of partial solutions and unable to contemplate continued uncertainty. In other cases, I suspect people have been carried by the deceiving compulsions of the weapons race into conclusions that neglect all the ulterior considerations, and particularly the imponderables. In still other cases, people may have been the victims of their own brave and rash slogans. But in any event, those longer and more subtle and less obvious paths by which we might reasonably hope to make progress in this situation are ones that a great many people in our country, for one reason or another, either reject or fail to understand; and with this rejection or failure of understanding, I fear I see a deterioration in the prospects for our continuing to muddle through these difficulties in the direction of a more hopeful future.

I do not mean to blame ourselves in any exclusive way for the present trend—we do live in a world where there have been released great forces of hatred and violence and vindictiveness, and we have been confronted with a great deal more in the way of provocation than we have given, over the course of these past two decades. And I do not mean to blame any party or administration among us. But I must emphasize that today it is precisely these subjective factors—factors relating to the state of mind of many of our own people—rather than the external circumstances, that seem to constitute the most alarming component of our situation. It is such things as the lack of flexibility in outlook, the stubborn complacency about ourselves and our society, the frequent compulsion to extremism, the persistent demand for absolute solutions, the unwillingness to accept the normal long-term hazards and inconveniences of great power—it is these things in the American character that give added gravity to a situation which would in any case be grave enough, and cause me for the first time to question seriously whether we are really going to be able, with our present outlooks and approaches, to avoid the complication of our international situation to a most dangerous degree.

II

The second of the anxieties I wish to mention relates to our internal situation. It is equally well-worn and equally unstartling; but it must be mentioned nevertheless.

There has been much in our domestic life of these recent months that I am sure we should all like to forget; and I hope that we shall soon be permitted to forget a great deal of it. But there are certain overriding facts that ought not to pass too quickly out of our memories. We ought not to forget that we have witnessed in these recent months the spectacle of many millions of Americans unable to put in its place and to assess with any degree of balance and equanimity the time-honored and unexceptional phenomenon of foreign political activity, intrigue, and espionage in our midst—a phenomenon which no great power has ever been spared throughout the course of human history, and from which surely no other great power is immune today. Millions of our people have been unable to accept this normal burden of international leadership at its true worth—have been uncertain as to the value to be assigned to it, uncertain as to what weight to give it in comparison with other problems of our national life. And this uncertainty has given them a peculiar vulnerability—a vulnerability to being taken advantage of, to having their fears exploited, and to being stampeded into panicky, ridiculous, and dangerous attitudes, unworthy of their own national tradition, unworthy of themselves.

Under the sign of this weakness we have seen things that cannot fail to bring deepest concern to any thinking American. We have seen our public life debauched; the faith of our people in great and distinguished fellow citizens systematically undermined; useful and deserving men hounded thanklessly out of honorable careers of public service; the most subtle sort of damage done to our intellectual life; our scholars encouraged to be cautious and unimaginative in order to escape being "controversial," a pall of anxiety and discouragement thrown over our entire scientific community, our libraries and forums of knowledge placed on the defensive before the inroads of self-appointed snoopers and censors, a portion of our youth encouraged to fear ideas on the pretext of being defended from them.

We have seen the reputations of our great private philanthropic foundations, with their immense and unique records of contribution to the national life, recklessly attacked; ingratitude flung in the face of the entire institution of private benevolence. We have seen our people taught to distrust one another, to spy, to bear tales, to behave in a manner which is in sharpest conflict with the American tradition. We have seen our friends in other countries frustrated in their efforts to help and support us, reduced to an embarrassed and troubled silence before the calumnies of our enemies upon us, for they were no longer sure whether these calumnies did not contain some measure of truth. And all of this in the name of our protection from Communist subversion, and yet every bit of it agreeable to Communist purposes as almost nothing else could be; and all of it supported by people who then have the effrontery to come before us and to say, "Show us one innocent man who has suffered."

Now it would not be hard to name such a man; but it would be possible to name something far more important: it would be possible to name a a great people, no more innocent or less innocent than any of the other great peoples of this world, but nevertheless a people of an immense fundamental decency and good will and practical energy, a people in an unparalleled position to exercise a useful and hopeful influence in this tortured and threatened world community, a people to whom an historic opportunity had been given, to whom the hopes of the world had turned; it would be possible to name such a people and to show it now, at the moment of its greatest historic responsibility, disaffected and disoriented in some of the deepest sources of its national morale, injured in its capacity to react to the challenges history has laid upon it, reduced from its natural condition of confidence and buoyancy to a state of cynicism and fearfulness and disgust with the processes of its own public life—and all of this in the name of its protection from external subversion.

I do not mean to overrate these things. I have no doubt that in its superficial aspects all of this will pass—is probably already passing. The names, the idols, the scapegoats, the stereotypes, the abused words, and the perverted symbols—I have no doubt that these will all soon disappear, to join the records of the Know-Nothing movement and the chauvinistic hysteria of 1919 in the unhappier annals of our public life.

But I think we cannot comfort ourselves too much with this reflection. These things *have* happened. We *have* reacted this way, on this occasion. There must have been a reason for our doing so. Have we found that reason and learned from it? Are we going to be better armed to understand the next danger—to resist the next attempt by the unscrupulous to mobilize us against ourselves under the banner of our fears?

III

The causes of these phenomena have undoubtedly been many, and deep, and complex. One cannot attempt to recount them or to analyze them in the few brief moments we have at our disposal this morning. But among these possible causes there is one I should like particularly to mention as perhaps worth your attention at this time.

In the case of each of these disturbing situations I have spoken of, I wonder whether an appreciable portion of our difficulty has not been a certain philosophic error to which we twentieth-century Americans, for one reason or another, are prone. I am referring here to that peculiar form of American extremism which holds it possible that there should be such a thing as total security, and attaches overriding importance to the quest for it. A great deal of the impatience that underlies the growing despair in some quarters over the prospects for coping with world Communism by means short of large-scale violence seems to me to flow precisely from the illusion, no doubt bred by our nineteenth-century experience, that there could and should be such a thing as total military security for the United States, and that anything short of this is in the long run intolerable. And similarly, these frenzies many of us seem to have developed with respect to the problem of internal subversion—do they not reflect a belief that it should be possible for a great power to free itself completely from the entire problem of penetration and intrigue in its life by outside forces and, again, that it is intolerable that this should not be done; so intolerable, in fact, that if it *is not* done, this must be attributed to some stubborn delinquency, if not treason, in the bowels of our public establishment?

If the evil of all this were limited to the fact that it does involve a certain philosophic error, that it causes people to bark up the wrong trees and occasions an inordinate and futile sort of effort, I would not bother to speak of it this morning. But the fact is that it bears dangers worse than any of these. Shakespeare described these dangers, in his inimitable way, in the following words:—

> Take but degree away, untune that string,
> And, hark! what discord follows; . . .
> Then everything includes itself in power,
> Power into will, will into appetite,
> And appetite, a universal wolf, . . .
> Must make perforce a universal prey,
> And last eat up himself.

There is something about this quest for absolute security that is self-defeating. It is an exercise which, like every form of perfectionism, undermines and destroys its own basic purpose. The French have their wonderful proverb: *Le mieux est l'ennemi du bien*—the absolute best is the enemy of the good. Nothing truer has ever been said. A foreign policy aimed at the achievement of total security is the one thing I can think of that is entirely capable of bringing this country to a point where it will have no security at all. And a ruthless, reckless insistence on attempting to stamp out everything that could conceivably constitute a reflection of improper foreign influence in our national life, regardless of the actual damage it is doing or the cost of eliminating it, in terms of other American values, is the one thing I can think of that could reduce us all to a point where the very independence we are seeking to defend would be meaningless, for we would be doing things to ourselves as vicious and tyrannical as any that might be brought to us from outside.

This sort of extremism seems to me to hold particular danger for a democracy, because it creates a curious area between what is *held* to be possible and what *is* really possible—an area within which government can always be plausibly shown to have been most dangerously delinquent in the performance of its tasks. And this area, where government is always deficient, provides the ideal field of opportunity for every sort of demagoguery and mischief-making. It constitutes a terrible breach in the dike of our national morale, through which forces of doubt and suspicion never cease to find entry. The heart of our problem, here, lies in our assessment of the relative importance of the various dangers among which we move; and until many of our people can be brought to understand that what we have to do is not to secure a total absence of danger but to balance peril against peril and to find the tolerable degree of each, we shall not wholly emerge from these confusions.

Now I renounced, at the outset of these remarks, any intention of peddling personal advice. But perhaps I may be permitted, in conclusion, to observe that these reflections are not without their relevance to the problems of the human individual.

In this personal existence of ours, bounded as it is at both ends by suffering and uncertainty, and constantly attended by the possibility of illness and accident and tragedy, total security is likewise a myth. Here, too, an anxious perfectionism can operate to destroy those real underpinnings of existence, founded in faith, modesty, humor, and a sense of relativity, on which alone a tolerable human existence can be built. The first criterion of a healthy spirit is the ability to walk cheerfully and sensibly amid the congenital uncertainties of existence, to recognize as natural the inevitable precariousness of the human condition, to accept this without being disoriented by it, and to live effectively and usefully in its shadow.

In welcoming you, then—as it is my privilege this morning to do—into the fellowship and responsibility of maturity, let me express the hope that in each of your lives, as individuals and as citizens, *le bien* may be permitted to triumph over its ancient and implacable enemy *le mieux*. And if any of your friends come to you with the message that the problems of public life have become intolerable and require some immediate and total solution, I think you might do well to bear in mind the reply which a distinguished European statesman, Bismarck, once gave to certain of his more impatient and perfectionist contemporaries, who wanted him to solve all his country's problems right away, and entirely. "Let us leave just a few tasks," Bismarck suggested, "for our children to perform; they might be so bored in this world, if they had nothing to do."

UNDERSTANDING THE TEXT

1. This essay was originally presented as a commencement address. Identify the signs of its original context and occasion.
2. What is Kennan's purpose? What state of mind or feeling, with respect to what problems, does he wish to produce? Can you find any indications of

what Kennan takes to be the initial attitude of his audience toward these problems? Do you think he envisaged any audience beyond the graduating class?

3. What are the "one or two things" that cause Kennan anxiety in the present situation? What is the "common conclusion" he derives from them?

4. What assumptions does Kennan make about the normal conduct of foreign relations? What assumptions does he make about the extent to which governments can protect themselves against threats to their security? Does he attempt to justify these assumptions?

5. Kennan develops certain parallels between private life and public life. To what use does he put these parallels? Why is this an appropriate mode of argument on this subject and to this kind of audience?

6. What was the Know-Nothing movement? The "chauvinistic hysteria" of 1919?

7. Do you see any point in Kennan's postponement of the word "Communist" until paragraph 11 (p. 556)?

8. Identify some of the methods Kennan uses to establish an informal relation with his audience.

TOPICS FOR DISCUSSION AND WRITING

9. Do you think "no one could be said to have gained" from World Wars I and II? In what sense do you think Kennan intends this statement to be taken?

10. Kennan refers to "the peculiar form of American extremism which holds it possible that there should be such a thing as total security." Why does Kennan find this an extremist position? Do you agree?

11. Refer to Thurber's discussion of security in his essay on the psychosemanticist (pp. 252–259). Do you find any similarities between Thurber's view of security and Kennan's? Are there any similarities between the more general views of social and political relations taken by Thurber and Kennan?

12. Do you believe that security, in the sense discussed by Kennan, is an illusion?

13. If you were going to attempt a refutation of Kennan's argument, what line would you adopt and what particular points would you try to make?

The Fire Apes

LOREN C. EISELEY

〜

I

I WAS the only man in the world who saw him do it. Everybody else was hurrying. Everybody else around that hospital was busy, or flat on his back and beyond seeing. I had a smashed ankle and was using a crutch, so I couldn't hurry. That was the only reason I was on the grounds and allowed to sit on a bench. If it hadn't been for that I would have missed it. I saw what it meant, too. I had the perspective, you see, and the time to think about it. In the end I hardly knew whether to be glad or sorry, but it was a frightening experience, perhaps not so much frightening as weird because I suddenly and preternaturally saw very close to the end—the end of all of us—and it happened because of that squirrel.

The bird-feeding station stood on the lawn before my bench. Whoever had erected it was a bird-lover, not a squirrel enthusiast, that much was certain. It was on top of a section of thin pipe stuck upright in the ground, and over the end of the pipe half of a bread can had been inverted. The thin, smooth pipe and the bread can were to keep squirrels from the little wooden platform and roof where the birds congregated to feed. The feeding platform was attached just above the tin shield that protected it from the squirrels. I could see that considerable thought had gone into the production of this apparatus and that it was carefully placed so that no squirrel could spring across from a nearby tree.

In the space of the morning I watched five squirrels lope easily across the lawn and try their wits on the puzzle. It was clear that they knew the bread was there—the problem was to reach it. Five squirrels in succession clawed their way up the thin pipe only to discover they were foiled by the tin umbrella around which they could not pass. Each squirrel in turn

Reprinted from *Harper's Magazine*, September, 1949. Used by permission of the author.

slid slowly and protestingly back to earth, flinched at my distant chuckle, and went away with a careful appearance of total disinterest that preserved his dignity.

There was a sixth squirrel that came after a time, but I was bored by then, and only half watching. God knows how many things a man misses by becoming smug and assuming that matters will take their natural course. I almost drowsed enough to miss it, and if I had, I might have gone away from there still believing in the fixity of species, or the inviolability of the human plane of existence. I might even have died believing some crass anthropocentric dogma about the uniqueness of the human brain.

As it was, I had just one sleepy eye half open, and it was through that that I saw the end of humanity. It was really a very little episode, and if it hadn't been for the squirrel I wouldn't have seen it at all. The thing was: he stopped to think. He stopped right there at the bottom of the pole and looked up and I knew he was thinking. Then he went up.

He went up with a bound that swayed the thin pipe slightly and teetered the loose shield. In practically the next second he had caught the tilted rim of the shield with an outstretched paw, flicked his body on to and over it, and was sitting on the platform where only birds were supposed to be. He dined well there and daintily, and went away in due time in the neat quick fashion by which he had arrived. I clucked at him and he stopped a moment in his leisurely sweep over the grass, holding up one paw and looking at me with the small shrewd glance of the wood people. There are times now when I think it was a momentous meeting and that for just a second in that sunlit glade, the present and the future measured each other, half conscious in some strange way of their destinies. Then he was loping away with the autumn sunlight flickering on his fur, to a tree where I could not follow him. I turned away and limped back to the shadow of my bench.

"He's a smart squirrel, all right," I tried to reassure myself. "He's a super-smart squirrel, but just the same he's only a squirrel. Besides, there are monkeys that can solve better problems than that. A nice bit of natural history, an insight into a one-ounce brain at its best, but what's the significance of—"

It was just then I got it. The chill that had been slowly crawling up my back as I faced that squirrel. You have to remember what I said about perspective. I have been steeped in geological eras; my mind is filled with the osseous debris of a hundred graveyards. Up till now I have dealt with the past. I was one of the planet's undisputed masters. But that squirrel had busy fingers. He was loping away from me into the future.

The chill came with the pictures, and those pictures rose dim and vast, as though evoked from my subconscious memory by that small uplifted paw. They were not pleasant pictures. They had to do with times far off and alien. There was one, I remember, of gasping amphibian heads on the shores of marshes, with all about them the birdless silence of a land into which no vertebrate life had ever penetrated because it could not leave the water. There was another in which great brainless monsters bellowed in the steaming hollows of a fern forest, while tiny wraith-like mammals eyed them from the underbrush. There was a vast lonely stretch of air, through which occasionally skittered the ill-aimed flight of lizard-like birds. And finally there was a small gibbon-like primate teetering along through a great open parkland, upright on his two hind feet. Once he turned, and I seemed to see something familiar about him, but he passed into the shade.

There were more pictures, but always they seemed to depict great empty corridors, corridors in the sense of a planet's spaces, first empty and then filled with life. Always along those corridors as they filled, were eager watchers, watching from the leaves, watching from the grasses, watching from the woods' edge. Sometimes the watchers ventured out a little way and retreated. Sometimes they emerged and strange changes overtook the corridor.

It was somewhere there at the last on the edge of a dying city that I thought I recognized my squirrel. He was farther out of the woods now, bolder, and a bit more insolent, but he was still a squirrel. The city was dying, that was plain, but the cause was undiscernible. I saw with a slight shock that nothing seemed very important about it. It was dying slowly, in the length of centuries, and all about it the little eyes under the leaves were closing in. It was then that I understood, finally, and no longer felt particularly glad or sorry. The city was forfeit to those little shining brains at the woods' edge. I knew how long they had waited. And we, too, had been at the woods' edge in our time. We could afford to go now. Our vast intellectual corridor might stretch empty for a million years. It did not matter. My squirrel would attend to it. And if not he, then the wood rats. They were all there waiting under the leaves.

II

I suppose everyone keeps by his night light some collection of tales by which he may frighten himself back to sleep in moments of insomnia. I know that I do. And if you are like me, you have, on occasional midnights, disputed lordship of the planet with intellectual octopi, or seen mankind pushed horribly aside by giant termites. These notions may be sinister at midnight, but the truths of daylight are simpler and more terrible: mankind may perish without assistance from any of these.

The human brain was a beautiful and terrible invention. It is unique. And because it is unique there are many who believe that its achievements will never be possible of duplication in nature, that, in the words of one naturalist, "progress hangs on but a single thread. That thread is the human germ plasm." A French scholar murmurs a little uneasily "man alone in the universe is not finished." Julian Huxley defends the uniqueness of the human species with an impassioned vigor. "Among the actual inhabitants of the earth," he says, "past and present, no other lines could have been taken which would have produced speech and conceptual thought. . . . It could not have been evolved on earth except in man."

That remark is both wise, in a sense, and foolish. It is the statement of a man who has looked far into the depths of the past and seen nothing so wonderful as man. Yet it betrays also the reluctance of the human imagination as it turns toward the future—its concern with itself, its unwillingness to relinquish the stage. This genuinely profound mind is surely not unaware that an intellectual dinosaur of the dying Cretaceous might well have murmured: "The saurians alone are not finished. What possible things could improve upon us?" The Cretaceous date line would have made it a wise and Huxlian statement. It would have taken ten million years to force its serious alteration. Mr. Huxley is equally safe from refutation, so safe in fact that he sniffs contemptuously at the potential threat offered by our rowdy remaining cousins up in the family tree. "The monkeys," he says, "have quite left behind them that more generalized stage from which a conscious thinking creature could develop."

I am afraid that we are altogether too impressed by the fact that we live on the ground and that our remaining relatives, poor fellows, show a decided preference for trees. It never seems to occur to us that if they didn't stay up there we would jolly well show them what for. As for that "more generalized stage" which Mr. Huxley demands for the appearance of a thinking creature, I am quite sure that he cannot define it in a way which would seriously threaten the reputation of several existing primates.

The only way to become a "generalized stage" is to produce, in the course of time, several divergent smart descendants. No one can say that that faculty has been lost, but the whole monkey group will stay upstairs now till we are gone. And if they don't come down, there is still my squirrel, whose actions at times remind me of a certain ancient human forerunner in the Eocene. That chap wasn't recognized as "generalized" either, until somewhere along the way he began to walk on his hind feet. In the beginning, I'm not at all sure he was as smart as my squirrel.

Now I have said that Mr. Huxley is safe from refutation, geological time being what it is. If it is impossible to refute him until the passage of another sixty million years, it might be more comfortable to assume he has spoken the truth. It might have been, that is, up until last year. It was then that scientists began to scratch actively in the African bone lands. It was then that archeologists began to whisper behind their hands and exchange glances. It concerned, of course, a certain skull. That in itself was bad enough, but what ensued was worse.

He was an ape, they had said in the beginning: "A creature lacking the distinctive temporal expansions which appear to be concomitant with and necessary to articulate man is no true man." Then there had come that frightening insistence on the part of his discoverer that he had used fire and tools.

The little fellow was promptly redescribed. His type was cited in glowing terms as "intelligent, energetic, erect, and delicately proportioned little people." He was credited with speech, and spoken of respectfully as a potential human ancestor. It was more comfortable that way. Otherwise you were confronted with a spectacle like Dunsany's mysterious Abu Laheeb, that strange being squatting over its lonely fire in the marshes— the only beast in the world that made fire like man.

The mythical Abu Laheeb survived by hiding in the papyrus swamps of the upper Nile. *Australopithecus prometheus*, the ape who made fire, was not that fortunate. He disappeared. The reason why concerns Mr. Huxley's philosophy and is in some sense a refutation of it. Men say, in the books, that man is the last hope of life on the planet, the last chance, that is, for brain. In the past, however, when man was yet weak, a cousin tried to take the path he walked upon and almost succeeded. A cousin from the despised roof tree, where the eyes still watch us overhead.

To explain his failure and near success, we must go back millions of years. To explain what will come after our own extinction, we must again read backward—not for biological events which can never be repeated in exactitude, not for signs of the reappearance of forms which have had their day and will never again emerge into the light—but rather to project forward into the future those dread principles which have controlled the movement of life on this planet through untold eons of time, and which will continue to direct its destiny through the untold eons of the future. The destructiveness of man has lent a sparse and impoverished aspect to the animal life of the present day. It implies senescence and decline. Both are illusory. The great life stream awaits only its opportunity—the moment of human disappearance.

III

There are two sorts of evolutionary movement in the world of life, and one is more mysterious than the other. There are, for example, the slight differences which arise between species, the multiplicity of closely related shrubs, grasses, trees, and animals which can be observed over an acre of ground. All of these forms, plant and animal alike, may be occupying essentially the same environment or small, slightly divergent "microenvironments" within that acre. The diversity is pleasing. It leads us to comment on the infinite richness of life. Much of this burgeoning splendor is, nevertheless, without meaning so far as the grander progression of life is concerned. Some of it is the product of genetic drift which may have little importance even in terms of natural selection. It is diversity without significance, save as it represents the infinite capacities of the cell.

The real mystery, by contrast, lies on a mightier stage. It is the great symphonic movement through the world of the corridors. It is the fish who crawled ashore on his fins, the amphibian who painfully learned to walk. It is the reptile who invented the egg and thus released land vertebrates from dependence on the water. It is the saurian who flew, and who also learned to control his body temperature until he became a high-speed efficient mammalian machine whose brain did not grow torpid in the chilling night. It includes, also, a creature who came down from the trees and took his first tentative step down the long grassland corridor that was to lead him out into the magnificent vistas of conceptual thought.

The advance into those various worlds, into the air and the light out of the depths of the waters consumed millions of years of effort. It was not all an upward movement. Species by thousands died; species went into the ground; species went back to the waters; species clung to the high trees and shrieked down at their human brothers. The smaller movements we understand well—the horse from four toes to one, the age-by-age growth of horns on Triceratops or the titanotheres.

Instead it is the plunge through the forbidden zones that catches the heart with its sheer audacity. In the history of life there have been few such episodes. It is that which makes us lonely. We have entered a new corridor, the cultural corridor. There has been nothing here before us. In it we are utterly alone. In it we are appallingly unique. We look at each other and say, "It can never be done again." It is almost as though in our very bones were felt ancestral memories of the way we have come, and the feeling like magic touches us once more so that we repeat with something like terror in our voices, "It can never be done again."

Now it is one of the strange paradoxes of biology that this feeling of mystery concerning the great biological inventions which have opened the doorways of life has deepened as our knowledge has increased. Long evolutionary lines in a given environmental zone have been worked out, transition forms have been noted, and many sequences leading by imperceptible degrees from one form to another have been observed. In the beginning, Darwin and his followers assumed confidently that the major gaps which yawned between the phyla—the space, say, between the fish and the amphibian, between the reptile and the bird—would eventually be found to contain transition forms extending in the same imperceptible way from the one form to the other, even though a major life threshold had been crossed.

The lack of such transitional forms was not at first disturbing. Success in the pursuit of ancestral lines over long time-intervals led to the conclusion that these major gaps were due solely to imperfections in the geological record; that the book of Nature had, so to speak, missing pages, but that the main outlines of the story could easily be read from the pages that remained. It was not until much later that those missing pages were observed to occur with almost monotonous regularity at some dramatic transition point, involving the emergence of a new form of life and its adaptation to either an unentered corridor or a corridor offering possibilities of being intruded upon in some new way. The new type, in other words, seemed to emerge with astounding quickness, considering the generally slow evolutionary pace to be read from many of the remains which the fossil hunters were discovering in the better known strata of the earth.

This situation has led to much speculation. It has led on the part of some to a denial of the reality of evolution, on the part of others to claims for some type of "jumping evolution" in which fantastically complex mutations brought new organic forms into existence at a single step. The confusion created by this situation is perhaps nowhere better expressed than in Lecomte du Nouy's recent book, *The Road to Reason*. He says: "The general fact that paleontology only shows us a few transitional forms and still fewer really primitive forms, is also very disturbing. . . . We do not grasp the origin of any group."

It happens, however, that these widely expressed doubts are often tinged unconsciously with emotionalism. The gaps exist but isolated discoveries reveal that transitional forms are by no means non-existent. They are merely scarce. We have in growing numbers the mammal-like reptiles standing between the reptiles and the mammals. We have a strange, rare creature, Archaeopteryx, lying between the reptiles and the birds. There are other gaps which remain unclosed. These signs are, nevertheless, suggestive. More fossils will be found. Those which we possess, inadequate though they are, do not support the notion of fantastic leaps in nature.

They suggest, instead, that the march across a major barrier into a new sphere of existence is made rapidly if it is made successfully at all. A basic organic change of this nature is estimated by the brilliant modern student, G. G. Simpson, to have proceeded at a pace, in some instances, ten or fifteen times more rapid than the later recorded evolution of a given group after it has begun to exploit its new domain. The comparatively hasty crossing, hasty in a geological sense, was made by small groups of animals undergoing extreme selection pressure. As a consequence, there will never be numerous fossils. Archaeopteryx, the bird-reptile, for example, was found in 1861. It still remains a solitary specimen.

Another fact can be noted as we study these records. It is in a sense obvious, yet it has been neglected by many writers obsessed with human uniqueness or with the superiority of the mammalian line in general. It can be laid down almost as a truism. *No successful crossing into a new corridor of life can be effected if that corridor is completely dominated by prior intruders.*

This statement must be made somewhat dogmatically. Apparent exceptions can be observed, but they constitute special cases which do not affect the general principle. It could be noted, for example, that the reptiles made two separate attempts to conquer the air corridor, once by the use of membraneous wings—the giant glider Pteranodon being a popularly known example—and secondly by the evolution of true wings and feathers. Both attempts were successful for a long period, and both must have competed for a time. Eventually the Pterosaurs disappeared and left the corridor to the birds.

Two facts explain this rather unusual situation. Both forms apparently got across into the airways at approximately the same time, so that neither one had radiated and adapted sufficiently to exclude the other. In addition, the development of flowering plants with accompanying nutritious seeds in the Cretaceous period profoundly stimulated insect evolution. The nutritive possibilities in the air corridor thus increased, but increased in a direction which favored the smaller, speedier, and more effective mechanism, namely, the birds.

From the Cretaceous to the present the birds have dominated the airways, and the smaller environmental niches within the airways so effectively that no other vertebrate has successfully challenged their control. One other animal, it is true, has evolved true flight in the interim, but its position only reveals the reality of our truism. The bats, true mammals, came late to the scene. They made the crossing, but made it surreptitiously in the evening twilight. The vast majority of birds are diurnal. The bats cling to the edge of evening, and such prey as they can find there. Their numbers, in comparison with birds, are scant. Both figuratively and literally, they are creatures of the twilight, dwellers at the unwanted margin. That is why they survive.

What the bats might have been capable of under other circumstances, it is, of course, impossible to conjecture, but the tremendous energies, the unknown capacities which may be held in check while a new form of life surges endlessly against an already closed corridor, is nowhere better illustrated than in the story of the rise of the mammalian world itself. Our interpretation of that rise is apt to be distinctly colored. We think of the mammals, our own ancestral line, as a highly effective group which crowded the reptiles aside. Nothing, in actuality, could be further from the truth.

I remarked on an earlier page that the truths of daylight are often the most terrible, and that the end of the human story does not demand our extermination at the hands of some more intellectual or fantastic form of life. That statement was deliberate. The reptiles are a prime example. For 140 million years, during that period known as the Mesozoic, they were the undisputed masters of this planet. In enormous numbers they radiated into every possible geographic niche. They swam and they flew and they walked. Brainless or not, they survived a period of time far more extended than the life of man, far more extended than the whole Age of Mammals.

Now what is not very generally understood by the lay public is the fact that throughout the greater portion of this 140 million years the mammalian world was in existence. It was in existence, but it was highly inconspicuous. It was small; it hid under bushes; it concealed itself in trees. It had no giant representatives such as it developed later on after the disappearance of the reptiles. Like the bats on the edge of the bird world, it was existing on tolerance. It was marginal. To have grown larger would have been to invite the attention of the most formidable carnivores the world has ever seen—perfected killing machines with teeth like bear traps.

For a hundred million years those little mammals waited. No one would have dreamed that they, in their turn, might create monsters, and no one, above all, would have imagined that the gray and infinitely complex convolutions of the human brain were locked away in the forebrain of an insectivorous creature no larger than a rat. An observer waiting for some sign of creative emergence among those little animals in the underbrush would have grown weary as years by the million flowed away. He would have sworn that every variation in the game of life had been exploited and played out—that the reptiles were the master form—that the mammals were effective only upon an infinitely small size level.

Yet in the end, that strange end that closed the day of the Ruling Reptiles, the armored giants vanished. They vanished from the seas and the fern forests; their great gliding wings disappeared from the coastal air. Nothing living, so far as we can determine today, threatened them. The mammals were insignificant, envious eyes in the reeds—that was all. We in this remote age may murmur about climatic change or any one of a dozen vague possibilities. Sometimes we consider the notion that species may run through a lifetime, grow old and die, as does an individual organism. We do not know. But this we are unpleasantly aware of: the armored ones went in daylight. Nothing, not even their successors, thrust them aside. It would be millions of years before the shovel heads of the mammalian titanotheres grazed in the valleys that knew the thunder lizard, Triceratops.

The mammals did not destroy the great reptiles; they simply occupied, long after, an empty throne. It was only then that the long suppression of creative energy burst forth in a second marvelous efflorescence, the radiation that created the mammalian world. The story, however, has a moral that is little read: man also is the master of a corridor; there is nothing visible to compete with him. He has destroyed the great mammals and left only the little eyes under the rosebush in the garden. He is safe now to write books about his unique qualities—and he is unique, as unique as the dinosaurs. He will not be menaced from the field's edge, but the eyes are still waiting. Once they waited a hundred million years. They can do so again.

This time it will be a new corridor—the cultural corridor—that they enter, but it will not be as unique as it seems to us, writing as we do that we are the "sole representative of life in its progressive aspect and its sole trustee for any progress in the future."

Once, long ago in Africa, that cousin of whom I spoke made tools and, some think, may have experimented with the forbidden magic of fire itself. Small and timid and slight of brain, he fades back into the silences of prehistory. He made the crossing at the wrong moment, but he proved we are not so unique as we imagine, that the crossing can be made again, perhaps even from above, out of the old roof tree, where everyone sits with his tail curled safely out of reach.

It is the safety of trees or the safety of being men now. The line is sharp; there is no half-way mark as there was when the first ill-adjusted migrants stumbled into an empty world. There is no longer any room for an ape who lights fires and is not a man.

IV

Almost everything about this animal, up until recently, has been controversial except the fact that it existed. It has been called an ape. It has been called a man. It has been said to have walked upright. It has been said that this is untrue. It has been claimed that it spoke. It is said not to have spoken.

More complete specimens have lately begun to fall into the hands of the bone hunters, so that some of the questions which tormented earlier workers have been answered. Others, however, have taken their place.

The Australopithecine men-apes of South Africa are a group of small, upright-walking anthropoids who haunted the grasslands of the Vaal River area from five hundred thousand to a million years ago. They are not all alike in detail, but the whole stock is characterized by teeth of a quite human character. The great shearing canines of the existing apes are reduced to human proportions. These animals must have been omnivorous grassland wanderers, pursuing small animals, eating wild seeds, and probably robbing an occasional bird's nest. Around four feet in height, with a brain ranging at 450 to 650 cubic centimeters, their intellectual capacities, though low by human standards, were undoubtedly superior to that of any existing gorilla or chimpanzee.

They are the only grassland bipedal ape, as contrasted with primitive grassland man, of which we have any knowledge. As I pointed out earlier, they have been called apes. More lately there has been a tendency to call them men. Awkwardly enough, however, such datings as we have been able to compute for them are much too late in time to allow for their being the direct ancestors of true men. Some, at least, of the man-apes were the contemporaries, for a brief while, of primitive men.

I suppose that, if the truth were known, one reason why man is so impressed with his own uniqueness is the fact that he is alone today in the grassland corridor. In a few remote parts of Africa, a scant number of lower monkeys venture into waste spaces on the ground. The baboon is one of them. His experiment has turned in another direction. His face is doglike. He runs upon all fours.

Of that series of arboreal experimenters who ventured into the first grasslands of the planet during the Miocene epoch and who teetered diffidently from one tree clump to another, upright on their two hind feet, man alone remains. The grasslands were too open, competition too fierce as the sub-men multiplied, for the long continued survival of unlike forms. We of today see a yawning gulf between ourselves and the old forms in the trees. On the grass the others have vanished. The corridor is filled and the rifle would eliminate any wavering half-soul from the forest twilight who was so rash as to venture among us. It is too late for the crossing, too late until man has gone.

I suppose it is the illusion of uniqueness which for so long caused the student of human evolution to take a scattered series of human fossils and try to arrange them in a single line of ascent leading to modern man. It is still being tried with the new man-apes, but there are two embarrassments: their relative recency, and the diversity of their species. It is simply not possible that they are all on the main line of ascent to ourselves. That the Australopithecines have vanished while many simple arboreal relatives of ours survive is not surprising. The man-apes tried to occupy the same environmental niche as man, and as a consequence man destroyed them.

This does not mean that the Australopithecines are totally unrelated to ourselves. It does mean, however, that the old notion involving one human ancestral form and one only as taking the momentous step of climbing out of the trees and learning to walk upright—thus starting a simple and direct evolutionary movement which culminated in man of today—is a fantastic simplification of events.

Twenty million years ago the grasslands of the world were spreading. The long cooling that was to produce the Ice Age of later times had just begun. The low continents of the age of reptiles were giving way to mountain growths that swung the ancient jungles of the earlier lands far skyward, and brought drought to the inner continental basins. The grasslands spread farther and farther. Over vast areas the jungle disappeared or shrank to parkland.

We know that among the mammals of this period, many diverse orders turned to a grazing existence. Changes in their teeth tell us as much, for the high silica content of grass forces the development of a specialized grazing dentition which will resist wear. Man, of course, is not a grazer, nor were his fore-runners up in the diminishing branches.

That grassland world was, nevertheless, attractive. More and more animals were moving into it; here and there in the parklands, anthropoid apes of forms little known ventured on to the ground. A little like the archaic living gibbon, they may have scurried on their hind feet between isolated clumps of trees, snatching insects and seeds before swinging safely into the branches again. The slow changes that some of these animals were undergoing in habits and foot structure may have taken millions of years.

There must have been many of these apes on the edge of the grasslands. We need not be surprised if more than one type, over the vast Old World land mass, successfully made that crossing. The corridor was open to aggressive, lively anthropoids who were willing to hunt small animals and insects, and whose diet was unspecialized. The climate was more healthful than that of the parasite-infested jungles. A strange competition began.

It was the competition of an odd lot of animals, the apes of the grassland, uncertainly erect, but with the neurological preference for that posture already developed among the branches of the forest. It was the competition of social animals, and therefore it was the competition of groups. Out of that struggle for food, for mates, and for life, the best adapted, the most clever brained, the most successfully communicative would survive.

I say communicative because somewhere here on the grasslands in an environment infinitely more demanding and dangerous than the safe retreat of the trees, the already extensive but instinctive call range of the old tree world began to be abandoned for conceptual thought and speech. Under mysterious endocrine influences about which we know nothing, man's infancy was becoming prolonged, his brain a plastic thing upon which incipient society was beginning to mark the folkways of the group. The strangest corridor in the history of life on this planet was being entered—the cultural corridor. Its final possessors would be masters of the earth. They would write books. They would describe themselves as unique. They were not.

V

The first of those peculiar human-footed apes to which we have previously referred, was announced to an incredulous world by Professor Raymond Dart in 1924. It took over twenty years to discover more of them and to learn something of their habits. Because it was not believed, at first, that they spoke or made tools, Dart, in spite of his conviction that they were closely associated with the earlier history of the human line, referred to them as "no true men."

This year, at Makapansgat in the Central Transvaal of South Africa, Dart reported *Australopithecus prometheus*, the fire-maker. Reporters, of course, went wild. Scientists scratched their heads and looked dubiously at one another. The new fossil was reported from deposits showing evidence of the use of fire in the shape of charred bone and traces of charcoal. Though no stone weapons were discovered, there were suspicious indications that Prometheus had used the long bones of slain animals as clubs. A series of neatly fractured baboon skulls from which the brain had probably been extracted for food supplied the evidence.

A very simple tool-using capacity on the part of an animal with a 650 cubic centimeter brain capacity is acceptable. That these creatures may have been fire-users has shaken all our established notions of human culture history. The suspicion continues to be entertained in some quarters, and will continue until further reports are available, that perhaps advanced forms of men may be responsible for the fires and the broken cranial case of Prometheus himself. It is known, at least, that there are somewhat later humanly occupied caves at Makapan. It must not be forgotten, however, that it was Dr. Dart who recognized, over twenty years ago, the importance of the first Australopithecine cranium; it was conservative science that smiled and later had to eat its words.

Whether or not the human-footed apes were fire-users, we know that the animal remains with which they are associated at Makapan place them well within Early Ice Age times. Human relatives they are, but in the narrow sense, at least, they are not men. Men, low-browed, perhaps, but true men, were already in existence. The man-apes, by contrast, are a part of that ancient bipedal horde which millions of years ago came out upon the grasslands. Less massive than their divergent human brothers, they clung to the fringe of the corridor, ran before its terrors, and shared with us that dark and ancient blood from the times before man.

Perhaps at the last, late, much too late, they lit the fires that might have made them man; perhaps even—and that in itself is a weird thought, since no animal alive had done it—they watched trembling behind a bush and learned from men the secret of the fire. Perhaps already in some dim, half-human way they sensed their world was fading. Theirs were the last furred hands and theirs the last half-animal voices to be seen and heard in the cultural corridor before the pathway backward closed forever. When it opens again we shall be gone.

Sometimes at night I think one can feel even the pressure of mice waiting in the walls of old houses. All that concentrated life around us and above us, held in check, surging impatiently, ready for a new experiment, tired of us, waiting our passing, active with the busy mysteries of the cell. Sometimes one catches oneself wondering what the fire-apes were intending when they crossed the barrier, whether they were cut short in a new experiment, something smaller, more delicate, more—something, but not a human something. Something for which human beings must first be gotten out of the way. It is perhaps significant that even we ourselves feel a growing inadequacy. Perhaps that is really the secret. Perhaps we are going away.

*   *   *

Professor Eiseley has supplied the following note on the current status of research concerning "the fire-apes":

For several years after the publication of "The Fire Apes" I refused, in spite of many interested requests, to allow it to be reprinted. My reasons for this decision lay in the fact that about a year after Dr. Dart had announced his belief in the use of fire by *Australopithecus prometheus*, doubts arose in scientific quarters whether the chemical evidence used to sustain this judgment could be confirmed in the light of further research. Doubts also began to be expressed as to whether the South African man-apes were even tool-users, let alone fire-makers. Their low cranial content, not too distinct from that of the existing apes, contributed to this point of view.

While archeological argument persisted in this vein, a very early pebble tool culture of great crudity was found in scattered deposits in South Africa. It could not, however, be assigned to any particular form of man because no human or sub-human remains had been found with the artifacts. In June of 1955, however, Dr. Dart announced the discovery of fragmentary remains of *Australopithecus prometheus* from a cave along the Makapansgat River in the Transvaal. The significance of the discovery lies in the fact that the "human" remains have been secured from a stratum containing the pebble tool culture whose makers have hitherto remained unidentified.

Though this purely preliminary announcement will not end all the argument which revolves about this advancing frontier of science, it does bring the mental potentialities of this form directly before the archeologist once more and will undoubtedly force a reëxamination of our opinions as to whether the creature may or may not have used fire. If the cave site should prove to be only two hundred thousand years old, as has been suggested, it may also be questioned whether *prometheus* was a direct ancestor to modern man, or rather a collateral relative surviving after the emergence of more truly human forms elsewhere. This essay, then, has been revivified scientifically in the sense that archeological thought has described something in the nature of a circle since its publication. There will now be renewed discussion in the light of this spectacular discovery by Dr. Dart of Witwatersrand University.

LOREN C. EISELEY

21 July 1955

UNDERSTANDING THE TEXT

1. Set forth the conception of evolution which Eiseley is criticizing. On what premises does it rest? Where does Eiseley refer, directly or indirectly, to this theory?

2. Account for the division of the essay into five sections by showing what each section contributes to the problem with which the whole essay deals.

3. What does Eiseley mean by saying that "he saw the end of humanity" (p. 562)? How seriously does he expect to be taken at this point in his essay? Is there any parallel to this remark at the end of the essay? Do we take it more seriously there?

4. Why does Eiseley delay until the end of the first paragraph to name "that squirrel" as the "him" he had seen? Does he handle any other details in the first paragraph in a similar way?

5. Develop the significances of "the pictures" (p. 563) in relation to Eiseley's central theme. What did the pictures contribute to Eiseley's interpretation of the sixth squirrel's actions?

6. Does the portion of the essay dealing with the squirrels constitute an account of the actual process through which Eiseley passed in coming to his conception of evolution, or is it to be understood simply as a convenient method for setting that conception forth in an interesting and intelligible manner?

7. To what human attitudes does Eiseley attribute the conviction that man is unique? Does he present any direct attack on this conviction, or does he rest his case entirely on the superior capacity of his alternative theory to account for the facts of evolution?

8. What is the meaning of the metaphor of the *corridor?* Collect examples of Eiseley's use of this term, and show how it functions in his analysis of evolutionary problems.
9. What are "those dread principles which have controlled the movement of life on this planet" (p. 565)? Why are they *dread* principles?
10. Make clear the meanings of the following words in their contexts: *anthropocentric, dogma, osseous, wraith-like, Cretaceous, temporal, concomitant, saurian, phyla, paleontology.*

TOPICS FOR DISCUSSION AND WRITING

11. Set forth Eiseley's essential argument in one paragraph.
12. Collect examples of figurative language in the essay. Using the method of analysis which Baird applies to Darwin's *Origin of Species,* consider whether Eiseley's use of figurative language is central to his thought or merely illustrative or explanatory, and whether it arises from peculiar limitations of the available language for expressing the concepts he is developing.
13. Write an analysis of Eiseley's essay in which you make clear (a) what are the verifiable *facts* on which he bases his arguments (facts on which both he and a believer in the uniqueness of man could agree), (b) what are the *interpretations* he places on these facts, and (c) what are the *assumptions* that yield these interpretations.
14. Develop the following observation into a short paper: "God knows how many things a man misses by becoming smug and assuming that matters will take their natural course."
15. Read Julian Huxley's essay on "The Uniqueness of Man" (in *Man Stands Alone,* 1941) and write an evaluation of the conflict of views between Eiseley and Huxley.

Literature, Science, and Democracy

HENRY MYERS

AT CORNELL University, where the College of Agriculture maintains an Extension Bulletin Service which furnishes New Yorkers with pamphlets on a great variety of practical subjects, a professor of literature is often reminded that many people call *any* valuable piece of writing literature. One letter which we received recently will serve as a fair example of many. It was addressed to the Department of Literature, Cornell University, but it was clear from the contents that it was intended for the Extension Bulletin Service, which the writer obviously regarded as the center of literary activity at Cornell. "Dear Sirs," he wrote. "Will you please send me as soon as possible your latest literature on how to make sauerkraut?"

I

What is the essential difference between literature and other kinds of writing? Dictionaries still label as a colloquialism the use of the word literature to describe such current printed matter as advertising circulars, income tax directions, and college announcements, but the dictionary definition of literature as "the total of the preserved writings belonging to a given language or people" would certainly include a time-tested treatise on how to make sauerkraut, and would seem also to include old handbills or any kind of printed matter venerable enough to be called "preserved." In recent years the editors who compile anthologies for the use of students of American literature have confirmed popular usage by leaning more and more toward the broadest possible definition. A recent anthology, for example, subtitled "Selections from the Literature of the United States," includes in its offerings passages from John Smith's *Description of New*

Reprinted from *The Pacific Spectator*, Volume VIII, No. 4, Autumn, 1954. Used by permission of Mrs. Henry Myers and the editor.

England, Noah Webster's *Grammatical Institute of the English Language*, Alexander Hamilton's *Report on Manufactures*, Andrew Carnegie's *Empire of Business*, and Mr. Justice Field's concurring opinion in the Slaughterhouse cases of 1884.

In textbooks designed to show the growth of the American mind, or of American civilization, the selection of a wide variety of writings is defensible, and even desirable, but the literary critics and historians who confirm loose popular usage by including purely impersonal, factual, informative, and descriptive writings under the heading of literature make doubly necessary a reconsideration of what we mean when we speak of literature in its narrower sense as one of the humanities, in the narrower sense which includes only such writings as *Oedipus the King*, or *Hamlet*, or *Moby Dick*.

The traditional distinction between the supposedly purely aesthetic values of belles-lettres and the informational and utilitarian values of other kinds of writing is vague and misleading. Everyone understands what is meant by informational and utilitarian values, but what is meant by purely aesthetic values? If the traditional definition of belles-lettres is understood to mean that the reading of poems, plays, novels, and essays is, generally speaking, a pleasurable experience, it affirms an undeniable fact, but it seems also to imply that literature in the narrow sense is valuable only because it offers recreation, diversion, and even escape from the actualities of a practical and troubled world. In the United States amusements have always been considered a matter more of private than of public concern, and the traditional identification of belles-lettres with purely aesthetic values may explain why the federal and state governments have done so little to encourage creative artists and why, for example, Cornell's Extension Bulletin Service is cheerfully supported by the taxpayers of New York State while its program in literature is dependent upon tuition payments and income from endowments.

Inherited from aristocratic theorists, the distinction between writings that afford aesthetic pleasures and writings that serve useful purposes is misleading on both sides, and is particularly unlikely to attract the citizens of a democratic society to the serious study of literature. On one side, this traditional distinction, contrary to the evidence, implies that writings intended primarily to be informative and useful are necessarily lacking in aesthetic qualities. On the other side, and worse, the distinction implies that great literature is neither informative nor useful. Nothing could be farther from the truth.

A cookbook or a textbook may have aesthetic qualities; a mathematical or scientific demonstration may be a thing of beauty; and *King Lear*, properly read, may be as informative and as useful as a treatise on sauerkraut.

The true difference between literature and other kinds of writing is indicated by the simple, but often forgotten, fact that there are two fundamentally different views of life, two ways of looking at man and the universe, one from within, the other from the outside. These views are equally valuable and indispensable: a culture or a civilization which glorifies one view and belittles the other is out of balance and in danger.

The first view is personal and insighted. This view is more than anthropocentric; it places each individual at the center of the universe and makes it possible for him to say, as Schopenhauer said: "The world is my idea."

From the individual's own point of view, the world begins and ends with his awareness of it. As long as he clings to this point of view, and believes in its validity, man is at home in the universe. As he sees the world from his personal, insighted point of view, it is a world of values: of pleasure and pain, of joy and sorrow, of beauty and ugliness, of victory and defeat, of success and failure, of good deeds and bad deeds, of rewards and punishments, of satisfaction and remorse.

In its beginnings this personal, insighted view is the simple awareness of the individual human consciousness, but in its highest reaches it is the vision, the poetic insight, of the artist who sees other people as he sees himself, from within, and who strengthens the bonds of society by demonstrating that the inner world of one individual is in its basic conditions the same as the inner world of another.

The second view is impersonal and external: it had its beginnings in the invention of the weights, measures, scales, clocks, thermometers, and calendars which make impersonal and external description possible. In turn external, impersonal description makes possible a variety of writings, ranging from almanacs and encyclopedias through scholarly monographs on literary history and on to the chemist's periodic table and Newton's *Principia*.

When man sees himself from within and the world as his world, he is the measure of all things; when he insists upon viewing himself from the outside only, he discovers that he is no longer the measure of anything.

What, then, is the indispensable quality, the distinguishing trait, of literature? What essential characteristic distinguishes the *Oresteia* from Aristotle's *Poetics, King Lear* from the footnotes in a scholarly edition, Whitman's *Leaves of Grass* from a treatise on the care of lawns?

My genial and talented colleague at Cornell, Professor Morris Bishop, once wrote a book of light verse which carried on its cover the title, *Paramount Poems*, followed by the assertion: "If it isn't a Paramount, it isn't a Poem."

Although negative in form, this is the shortest and clearest definition of poetry that I have ever seen. In the interest of clarity I propose now to offer first a definition of literature in similar negative form. My sentence is much longer than Morris Bishop's because it is much less exclusive.

If it doesn't open up for you the inner life of at least one other human being, who may be either the author or one of his fictional creations; if it doesn't release you for a moment from your lonely island in the sea of the individual's isolation; if it doesn't inform you of some of the resources of the human spirit, of its triumphs and frustrations, or of its complexities, perversities, and incongruities; if it doesn't convince you that the inner world of the human spirit is as boundless and wonderful as the outer world of the seven seas and the starry heavens; if it doesn't indicate that the moral law is as important as the laws of thermodynamics; if it doesn't lead you toward an insighted understanding that, in spite of all outward and measurable differences, inwardly all human beings are akin—if it affects you in none of these ways, then no matter how great its other merits of diction and form and style may be, what you have been reading is not literature.

And now to turn this into positive form:

Other qualities of poetry and literary prose are important, but insight—the writer's personal view and his ability to see others as he sees himself, from within, his ability to estimate those inner values which cannot be checked by measuring rods, weights, clocks, and thermometers—is the indispensable quality, the distinguishing trait, of literature. Literature may offer more than insight, but it cannot offer less, it cannot lack insight without becoming another kind of writing. Literature without insight is a contradiction in terms.

II

If the writer's personal, insighted view of life is the essential characteristic of all literature, how shall we distinguish major literary works from minor works? How shall we distinguish *Moby Dick* from "Annabel Lee," Milton's *Paradise Lost* from his sonnet on his blindness, *Murder in the Cathedral* from "The Love Song of J. Alfred Prufrock"?

One difference is that a major work has the adequate magnitude which a minor work lacks. An epic outweighs an epigram; the story of Tom Thumb lacks tragic dimensions; and Melville was right in choosing a whale rather than a flea for the subject of his masterwork. But magnitude alone cannot explain the difference between major and minor literary works. The grandeur of the theme of Joel Barlow's *Columbiad* and the length of the poem do not add up to a great work of art; Poe's "Raven" would be a minor poem even if it contained ten thousand lines instead of one hundred.

The main difference between minor and major literary works is that the minor work introduces us only to the writer's private personal world while the major work leads us into a world which, though it is not impersonal and dehumanized as is the world seen from the outside only, is nevertheless a world common to all. The more we read of Poe's poems and tales, the more we know about the private world of Edgar Allan Poe. Shakespeare's play, in contrast, tell us very little about Shakespeare and very much about the world of human nature which we all share.

In a major literary work—in *Leaves of Grass* or in *Moby Dick*—something is added to the writer's private point of view and world.

1. The writer's insight is extended by sympathetic identification with others until he sees others as he sees himself. He then can offer us universality in addition to particularity or individuality. The very first line of the first edition of Whitman's *Leaves of Grass*—"I celebrate myself"— promises us insight into the inner life of one individual human being. If *Leaves of Grass* offered us no more than the inner world of

> Walt Whitman, a kosmos, of Manhattan the son,
> Turbulent, fleshy, sensual, eating, drinking and breeding,
> No sentimentalist, no stander above men and women or apart from them,
> No more modest than immodest.

it would still be literature. It would even be great of its kind, but the kind would be minor.

The second and third lines of *Leaves of Grass*, however, promise us more than self-revelation. "And what I assume you shall assume," Walt goes on to say. "For every atom belonging to me as good belongs to you." Throughout *Leaves of Grass*, from the opening lines to the closing lines, Whitman identifies himself with others, with an imaginative sympathy which has rarely been equaled and never surpassed. "I do not ask the wounded person how he feels," he exclaims,

> I myself become the wounded person,
> My hurts turn livid upon me as I lean on a cane and observe.
>
> I am the mash'd fireman with breast-bone broken, . . .
> I am the hounded slave, I wince at the bite of the dogs . . .
> The disdain and calmness of martyrs . . .
> All these I feel or am.

Through insight into others Whitman reaches universality: he shows us not only the particular nature of one man, Walt Whitman, but the common nature of man. He leads us into a world common to all, in which we see all men as equals and brothers who share a common fate. That is why *Leaves of Grass*, with all its blemishes in diction and form, is a major work of art while many polished and nearly flawless poems are merely minor.

2. In tragedy, which many regard as the highest form of literature, the artist offers us detachment as well as insight.

First of all, the artist in drama or fiction offers us insight. If he wishes to make his fictional personages seem real to us and capable of affecting us as intensely as living human beings affect us, he must identify himself with his creatures, live their lives for them, and see the world as they would see it. If he succeeds in doing this, he enables us in turn, as spectators and readers, to identify ourselves sympathetically with his fictional personages. Our insight depends upon the artist's insight.

To create fictional personages who seem real to us, who can affect us as living personages affect us, is a great achievement of artistic insight. The lesser artist is content to offer us no more. Satisfied with his power to engage our sympathy, he offers us no more than the happy ending of romantic fiction. He permits his Romeo to be reunited with Juliet and to live happily ever after, his Hamlet to avenge his father and rule over the kingdom, his Othello to discover his mistake in time, his Macbeth to save himself through repentance, his Captain Ahab to kill the white whale and return in triumph with an unusually large cargo of whale oil. Thus, he satisfies our desire to see those with whom we identify ourselves sympathetically turn out well and find the happiness they seek.

The minor artist can provide us with a happy ending because, as a creator of fictional personages, he enjoys a kind of omnipotence. He is lord of his little fictional universe. But he can exercise his omnipotence only at the cost of failing to satisfy our critical intelligence. Although a happy ending satisfies our sympathetic interest in fictional personages, we know at once when we see it that we have been watching events in a dream world, where the artist as creator is omnipotent, and not events in the world common to all, in which even the insighted artist must bow to necessity.

The major artist, the tragic realist who wishes to present the world common to all rather than a dream world, must temper his insight with detachment. Once he has created a fictional personage with a definite character or moral bent—a Romeo, a Hamlet, an Othello, a Captain Ahab—that character or moral bent becomes an antecedent from which certain consequences inevitably follow. The tragic realist cannot save his hero from the consequences of character, nor does he attempt to do so. He cannot rescue his hero from the universal tragic predicament of human beings, nor does he attempt to do so. The best he can do for his hero is to grant him (and us as spectators or readers) a flash of insight into the meaning of human destiny, an insight which reconciles him to his fate. At the end Captain Ahab must die, but he accepts his fate, content to be what he is. And we, as we view with insight the full unfolding of the inevitable consequences of individual character and of universal human nature, are content to be what we are, human beings who share a common fate which is both terrible and glorious.

III

Literature shows us man as he sees himself, and even when, as in tragic poetry, it shows us the world common to all, adding artistic detachment to insight, this world is still a personal world, with human values at its center.

"The world common to all": at this point we reach the question of the social function of literature. What is the source of our democratic principles? Who supports them? Let us look once more at the antithetical views of man, centering our attention on the ideas of human significance, equality, and freedom.

The first antithesis: the significance of the individual.

As he sees himself, man is the most significant of beings, the center of his universe. He is the ultimate reality; he and his values are the measures of all things.

Viewed and measured externally, however, man is a midge, an ephemeris, a shrinking mite in an expanding universe; his sense of importance in the scheme of things is, like all his opinions and values, a subjective illusion; and his claim that he is too precious to be subordinated to the will and needs of the state lacks supporting evidence.

The second antithesis: the idea of human equality.

Viewed with insight, men are equal in human worth and equal in the sense that all share a common fate. As he sees himself, each individual is supremely important, and since one supremely important individual cannot be more or less important than other supremely important individuals, all are equal in human worth—the true meaning of equality. As human beings, moreover, all are joined together in what Hawthorne once called the kinship of a common fate.

Viewed and measured from the outside, however, men are unequal in every respect: in size, shape, color, strength, wealth, social position, intelligence, and virtue. If the measurements are precise enough, it is unlikely that we shall ever find two individuals who are equal in any single respect: it is inconceivable that two men should be found equal in all measurable respects.

The third antithesis: freedom and responsibility.

As every individual knows, judging by his own feelings, and as literature testifies, man has an inner sense of freedom and responsibility. This sense is the foundation of his moral life since, if he lacked it, praise or blame for his conduct, and satisfaction or remorse on his part, would be equally pointless. This sense is also foundational to free institutions—to religion, law, education, and private enterprise as they exist in a democracy.

Judged impersonally, however, and from the outside, man is not free; his every act is seen, from this point of view, as a link in a chain of cause and effect; at best his every choice is determined by a motive, as Jonathan Edwards pointed out; at worst, his conduct is altogether determined by such impersonal and blind forces as heredity and environment.

When we consider these antithetical views of man, we discover at once the source of our democratic principles. Since the supremacy of the individual, the equality of men in human worth and rights, and the freedom and responsibility of the individual are the axioms of democracy, it is evident that American civilization rests on a foundation of insight, and that literature, with insight as its essence, is indispensable to our culture. The insighted writer meets each measurement of the external insignificance of man with an undaunted reaffirmation of man's inner view that he is at the center of things and supremely important. The great writer strengthens our self-respect and helps it to flower into respect for others by deepening our sense of equality; he reminds us that our sense of freedom and responsibility is a "stubborn fact" in our experience, and that we cannot escape from our consciences by retreating into the impersonal world of mathematics and measurement.

IV

The axioms of democracy—the doctrines of the supremacy of the individual, of the equality of men, and of man's freedom and responsibility—are derived from insight, and cannot be verified by external measurements. Unfortunately, those of us who wish to defend these axioms are handicapped by the fact that our culture is out of balance. Its respect for science is one of its glories, but its lack of respect for literature is a grave error of judgment. Why is our culture out of balance? Why do we respect objectivity only and neglect insight? Why do we regard science as a necessity and literature as a luxury?

One reason is that we are in a period of reaction against excessive claims made in the past for poetry and poetic intuition. After Immanuel Kant had apparently shown, late in the eighteenth century, that scientific reason falls into hopeless contradiction when it is applied to such questions as the existence of God and the immortality of the soul, poets were encouraged to answer transcendental questions on intuitive grounds. Wordsworth feels the presence of God in nature, and has intuitive intimations of immortality. Whitman tells us again and again that he knows he is immortal. Tennyson speaks with final confidence of

> One God, one law, one element,
> And one far-off divine event,
> To which the whole creation moves.

We respect these convictions as evidences of faith, but we have every reason to believe that the intuitions upon which the nineteenth-century poets and prophets relied cannot be empirically verified. Although literature adequately reveals the hopes and fears, and the doubts and beliefs of men concerning things beyond our present experience, literature as such cannot turn faith into certainty. Those who insist, for example, that the Bible is only great literature must look elsewhere for certainty about the supernatural; and those who accept the Bible as divinely inspired are relying on a power far beyond the natural powers of the poet. Few people today would agree with Matthew Arnold, who believed that poetry will replace theology and the poet replace the theologian. T. S. Eliot is much closer to the truth in maintaining that nothing can ever be a satisfactory substitute for something else.

The poetic insight which I have been describing as the essence of literature is altogether different from the intuition of the nineteenth-century prophet. The prophet's intuitions about the transcendental and the supernatural cannot be demonstrated, and, without the support of faith, must always remain conjectural; the poet's insights into present experience, however, may be demonstrated and may be tested by further experience and shown to be either true or false.

Most present-day critics and poets, in their reaction against the exaggerated claims made for prophetic intuition, have unfortunately gone to the other extreme. For them poetry is a purely aesthetic experience which has little or nothing to do with either meaning or morality. To go to this extreme is to throw out the baby with the bath water. Although we must reject the prophet's claim that, through intuition, he can offer us assurances about God and the hereafter, we should recognize that the poet, if he is gifted with insight, is a trustworthy observer of the life of man here and now.

A second reason for our failure to understand the nature and function of literature is the old but as yet unexploded notion that there can be only one trustworthy source of knowledge. Poets, philosophers, rhetoricians, theologians, and scientists of many varieties, exact and social, have too often been rivals rather than collaborators in the pursuit of knowledge. Each has at some time or other sought recognition as the only reliable teacher. This rivalry, which arises from the natural tendency of every man to overestimate the worth of what he knows best, or can do best, can be traced from its beginnings in Plato's attack on the poets through the attack on the philosophers by the rhetoricians, Isocrates and Quintilian, and on up to the present time. A wise man, after judiciously weighing the claims of each of the rivals, might well conclude that each has had, and still has, something valuable to contribute. Unfortunately, however, our age still honors the notion that there is only one trustworthy source of knowledge. The present-day form of this notion is a vague but widespread popular faith that statistics and other forms of external measurement will soon place poetry, metaphysics, theology, rhetoric, and ethics in a class with alchemy and astrology. Our age might well be called the Age of the Apotheosis of Objectivity.

The main reason why our culture is out of balance is, of course, that we have failed to understand the true nature and social function of literature. The burden of the problem of restoring the cultural balance falls largely on interpreters of literature—on critics, scholars, and teachers, who should, I believe, devote a little less time to purely aesthetic and technical studies, to the elucidation of puzzling texts, and to literary history, and a little more time to the heart of literature—insight.

Our generation has been so deeply impressed by the great achievements of scientists and technicians that it has forgotten the indispensable contributions of poets and artists. It is the special duty of a professor of literature to remind it that the axioms of democracy are derived from insight, and that sympathetic insight, the ability of one man to take another man's point of view, is and always will be, the only cement which can hold a free society together.

An ideal democratic culture depends upon our realization that the views of man afforded by literature and by science are complementary, not contradictory, and that only by combining these views can we hope to come close to the full truth about ourselves. In a progressive and successful democracy man must be weighed and measured by science as well as esteemed through insight.

As the poets proclaim, man has significance and dignity—that is, he has a value beyond measuring; but, as the scientists point out, he is also a relatively weak and insignificant being, who must measure his strength carefully before judging the feasibility of any enterprise. Man is a free and responsible being, but his freedom and responsibility are limited by heredity, by environment, by capacities and incapacities which we must carefully measure if we are to reward or punish him justly for his actions. All men are equal in human worth and in the kinship of a common fate, but they are unequal in every other respect, and only by careful measuring and testing can we help each individual to find the place in society in which he can do his best.

In these ways, the poet and the scientist, properly understood, are always at work, each contributing his indispensable share to the building of our society and the perfection of our democratic justice. Indeed, the poet and the scientist are not rivals but equal and trustworthy partners in the greatest of all tasks, the task of teaching man through insight to see others as he sees himself and through objectivity to see himself as others see him.

UNDERSTANDING THE TEXT

1. What is the purpose of Myers' opening paragraph? How well does it accomplish that purpose?
2. Why does Myers think the traditional distinction between the aesthetic values of belles-lettres and the informational and utilitarian values of other kinds of writing is "vague and misleading"?

3. How does he distinguish, then, between literature and other sorts of writing? Between major and minor works of literature?

4. Myers quotes Morris Bishop's statement, "If it isn't a Paramount, it isn't a Poem," and says that "this is the shortest and clearest definition of poetry that I have ever seen." How serious is he in making this statement? What does Bishop's sentence mean as a definition of poetry, in Myers' terms? How does this definition compare with the longer definition that Myers gives in the next paragraph? What does he mean when he says that his sentence is longer than Bishop's "because it is much less exclusive"?

5. Part I of the essay develops a distinction between literature and other forms of writing. Part II, building on the conception of literature set forth in I, develops a distinction between major and minor forms of literature. What does each of the remaining sections do? How are they related to Parts I and II and to each other?

6. Myers distinguishes between the intuitions of the prophet and the intuitions of the poet. On what basis? Why is it important to Myers' argument to make this distinction? He has said that the axioms of democracy, which are derived from insight, cannot be verified by external measurements. Later he says that the poet's insights "may be demonstrated and may be tested by further experience and shown to be either true or false." Is there any inconsistency between these two statements?

7. Why, in Myers' view, is literature indispensable to our culture?

TOPICS FOR DISCUSSION AND WRITING

8. Discuss this assertion: "The axioms of democracy—the doctrines of the supremacy of the individual, of the equality of men, and of man's freedom and responsibility—are derived from insight, and cannot be verified by external measurements."

9. Can you document from your own experience what Myers calls the "vague but widespread popular faith that statistics and other forms of external measurement will soon place poetry, metaphysics, theology, rhetoric, and ethics in a class with alchemy and astrology"?

10. "*King Lear*, properly read, may be as informative and useful as a treatise on sauerkraut." What do you think this means? Write a brief paper—using *King Lear* or some other work of literature with which you are familiar —in which you attempt to elaborate this assertion.

11. Tragedy, Myers says, is regarded by many as the highest form of literature. Why? Does Myers himself seem to regard it as the highest form of literature? Do you agree with this evaluation?

Prospects in the Arts and Sciences

J. ROBERT OPPENHEIMER

THE WORDS "prospects in the arts and sciences" mean two quite different things to me. One is prophecy: What will the scientists discover and the painters paint, what new forms will alter music, what parts of experience will newly yield to objective description? The other meaning is that of a view: What do we see when we look at the world today and compare it with the past? I am not a prophet; and I cannot very well speak to the first subject, though in many ways I should like to. I shall try to speak to the second, because there are some features of this view which seem to me so remarkable, so new and so arresting, that it may be worth turning our eyes to them; it may even help us to create and shape the future better, though we cannot foretell it.

In the arts and in the sciences, it would be good to be a prophet. It would be a delight to know the future. I had thought for a while of my own field of physics and of those nearest to it in the natural sciences. It would not be too hard to outline the questions which natural scientists today are asking themselves and trying to answer. What, we ask in physics, is matter, what is it made of, how does it behave when it is more and more violently atomized, when we try to pound out of the stuff around us the ingredients which only violence creates and makes manifest? What, the chemists ask, are those special features of nucleic acids and proteins which make life possible and give it its characteristic endurance and mutability? What subtle chemistry, what arrangements, what reactions and controls make the cells of living organisms differentiate so that they may perform functions as oddly diverse as transmitting information throughout our nervous systems or covering our heads with hair? What happens in the brain to make a record of the past, to hide it from consciousness, to make it accessible to recall? What are the physical features which make consciousness possible?

All history teaches us that these questions that we think the pressing ones will be transmuted before they are answered, that they will be replaced by others, and that the very process of discovery will shatter the concepts that we today use to describe our puzzlement.

It is true that there are some who profess to see in matters of culture, in matters precisely of the arts and sciences, a certain macrohistorical pattern, a grand system of laws which determines the course of civilization and gives a kind of inevitable quality to the unfolding of the future. They would, for instance, see the radical, formal experimentation which characterized the music of the last half-century as an inevitable consequence of the immense flowering and enrichment of natural science; they would see a necessary order in the fact that innovation in music precedes that in painting and that in turn in poetry, and point to this sequence in older cultures. They would attribute the formal experimentation of the arts to the dissolution, in an industrial and technical society, of authority—of secular, political authority, and of the catholic authority of the church. They are thus armed to predict the future. But this, I fear, is not my dish.

If a prospect is not a prophecy, it is a view. What does the world of the arts and sciences look like? There are two ways of looking at it: One is the view of the traveler, going by horse or foot, from village to village to town, staying in each to talk with those who live there and to gather something of the quality of its life. This is the intimate view, partial, somewhat accidental, limited by the limited life and strength and curiosity of the traveler, but intimate and human, in a human compass. The other is the vast view, showing the earth with its fields and towns and valleys as they appear to a camera carried in a high-altitude rocket. In one sense this prospect will be more complete; one will see all branches of knowledge, one will see all the arts, one will see them as part of the vastness and complication of the whole of human life on earth. But one will miss a great deal; the beauty and warmth of human life will largely be gone from that prospect.

It is in this vast high-altitude survey that one sees the general surprising quantitative features that distinguish our time. This is where the listings of science and endowments and laboratories and books published show up; this is where we learn that more people are engaged in scientific research today than ever before, that the Soviet world and the free world are running neck and neck in the training of scientists, that more books are published per capita in England than in the United States, that the social sciences are pursued actively in America, Scandinavia, and England, that there are more people who hear the great music of the past, and more music composed and more paintings painted. This is where we learn that the arts and sciences are flourishing. This great map, showing the world from afar and almost as to a stranger, would show more: It would show the immense diversity of culture and life, diversity in place and tradition for the first time clearly manifest on a world-wide scale, diversity in technique and language, separating science from science and art from art, and all of one from all of the other. This great map, world-wide, culture-wide, remote, has some odd features. There are innumerable villages. Between the villages there appear to be almost no paths discernible from this high altitude. Here and there passing near a village, sometimes through its heart, there will be a superhighway, along which windy traffic moves at enormous speed. The superhighways seem to have little connection with villages, starting anywhere, ending anywhere, and sometimes appearing almost by design to disrupt the quiet of the village. This view gives us no sense of order or of unity. To find these we must visit the villages, the quiet, busy places, the laboratories and studies and studios. We must see the paths that are barely discernible; we must understand the superhighways and their dangers.

In the natural sciences these are and have been and are likely to continue to be heroic days. Discovery follows discovery, each both raising and answering questions, each ending a long search, and each providing the new instruments for a new search. There are radical ways of thinking unfamiliar to common sense and connected with it by decades or centuries of increasingly specialized and unfamiliar experience. There are lessons of how limited, for all its variety, the common experience of man has been with regard to natural phenomena, and hints and analogies as to how limited may be his experience with man. Every new finding is a part of the instrument kit of the sciences for further investigation and for penetrating into new fields. Discoveries of knowledge fructify technology and the practical arts, and these in turn pay back refined techniques, new possibilities of observation and experiment.

In any science there is harmony between practitioners. A man may work as an individual, learning of what his colleagues do through reading or conversation; he may be working as a member of a group on problems whose technical equipment is too massive for individual effort. But whether he is a part of a team or solitary in his own study, he, as a professional, is a member of a community. His colleagues in his own branch of science will be grateful to him for the inventive or creative thoughts he has, will welcome his criticism. His world and work will be objectively communicable; and he will be quite sure that if there is error in it, that error will not long be undetected. In his own line of work he lives in a community where common understanding combines with common purpose and interest to bind men together both in freedom and in co-operation.

This experience will make him acutely aware of how limited, how inadequate, how precious is this condition of his life; for in his relations with a wider society, there will be neither the sense of community nor of objective understanding. He will sometimes find, in returning to practical undertakings, some sense of community with men who are not expert in his science, with other scientists whose work is remote from his, and with men of action and men of art. The frontiers of science are separated now by long years of study, by specialized vocabularies, arts, techniques, and knowledge from the common heritage even of a most civilized society; and anyone working at the frontier of such science is in that sense a very long way from home, a long way too from the practical arts that were its matrix and origin, as indeed they were of what we today call art.

The specialization of science is an inevitable accompaniment of progress; yet it is full of dangers, and it is cruelly wasteful, since so much that is beautiful and enlightening is cut off from most of the world. Thus it is proper to the role of the scientist that he not merely find new truth and communicate it to his fellows, but that he teach, that he try to bring the most honest and intelligible account of new knowledge to all who will try to learn. This is one reason—it is the decisive organic reason—why scientists belong in universities. It is one reason why the patronage of science by and through universities is its most proper form; for it is here, in teaching, in the association of scholars and in the friendships of teachers and taught, of men who by profession must themselves be both teachers and taught, that the narrowness of scientific life can best be moderated, and that the analogies, insights, and harmonies of scientific discovery can find their way into the wider life of man.

In the situation of the artist today there are both analogies to and differences from that of the scientist; but it is the differences which are the most striking and which raise the problems that touch most on the evil of our day. For the artist it is not enough that he communicate with others who are expert in his own art. Their fellowship, their understanding, and their appreciation may encourage him; but that is not the end of his work, nor its nature. The artist depends on a common sensibility and culture, on a common meaning of symbols, on a community of experience and common ways of describing and interpreting it. He need not write for everyone or paint or play for everyone. But his audience must be man; it must be man, and not a specialized set of experts among his fellows. Today that is very difficult. Often the artist has an aching sense of great loneliness, for the community to which he addresses himself is largely not there; the traditions and the culture, the symbols and the history, the myths and the common experience, which it is his function to illuminate, to harmonize, and to portray, have been dissolved in a changing world.

There is, it is true, an artificial audience maintained to moderate between the artist and the world for which he works: the audience of the professional critics, popularizers, and advertisers of art. But though, as does the popularizer and promoter of science, the critic fulfills a necessary present function and introduces some order and some communication between the artist and the world, he cannot add to the intimacy and the directness and the depth with which the artist addresses his fellow men.

To the artist's loneliness there is a complementary great and terrible barrenness in the lives of men. They are deprived of the illumination, the light and tenderness and insight of an intelligible interpretation, in contemporary terms, of the sorrows and wonders and gaieties and follies of man's life. This may be in part offset, and is, by the great growth of technical means for making the art of the past available. But these provide a record of past intimacies between art and life; even when they are applied to the writing and painting and composing of the day, they do not bridge the gulf between a society, too vast and too disordered, and the artist trying to give meaning and beauty to its parts.

In an important sense this world of ours is a new world, in which the unity of knowledge, the nature of human communities, the order of society, the order of ideas, the very notions of society and culture have changed and will not return to what they have been in the past. What is new is new not because it has never been there before, but because it has changed in quality. One thing that is new is the prevalence of newness, the changing scale and scope of change itself, so that the world alters as we walk in it, so that the years of man's life measure not some small growth or rearrangement or moderation of what he learned in childhood, but a great upheaval. What is new is that in one generation our knowledge of the natural world engulfs, upsets, and complements all knowledge of the natural world before. The techniques, among which and by which we live, multiply and ramify, so that the whole world is bound together by communication, blocked here and there by the immense synapses of political tyranny. The global quality of the world is new: our knowledge of and sympathy with remote and diverse peoples, our involvement with them in practical terms, and our commitment to them in terms of brotherhood. What is new in the world is the massive character of the dissolution and corruption of authority, in belief, in ritual, and in temporal order. Yet this is the world that we have come to live in. The very difficulties which it presents derive from growth in understanding, in skill, in power. To assail the changes that have unmoored us from the past is futile, and in a deep sense, I think, it is wicked. We need to recognize the change and learn what resources we have.

Again I will turn to the schools and, as their end and as their center, the universities. For the problem of the scientist is in this respect not different from that of the artist or of the historian. He needs to be a part of the community, and the community can only with loss and peril be without him. Thus it is with a sense of interest and hope that we see a growing recognition that the creative artist is a proper charge on the university, and the university a proper home for him; that a composer or a poet or a playwright or painter needs the toleration, understanding, the rather local and parochial patronage that a university can give; and that this will protect him from the tyranny of man's communication and professional promotion. For here there is an honest chance that what the artist has of insight and of beauty will take root in the community, and that some intimacy and some human bonds can mark his relations with his patrons. For a university rightly and inherently is a place where the individual man can form new syntheses, where the accidents of friendship and association can open a man's eyes to a part of science or art which he had not known before, where parts of human life, remote and perhaps superficially incompatible, can find in men their harmony and their synthesis.

These, then, in rough and far too general words, are some of the things we see as we walk through the villages of the arts and of the sciences and notice how thin are the paths that lead from one to another, and how little in terms of human understanding and pleasure the work of the villages comes to be shared outside.

The superhighways do not help. They are the mass media—from the loud-speakers in the deserts of Asia Minor and the cities of Communist

China to the organized professional theater of Broadway. They are the purveyors of art and science and culture for the millions upon millions— the promoters who represent the arts and sciences to humanity and who represent humanity to the arts and sciences; they are the means by which we are reminded of the famine in remote places or of war or trouble or change; they are the means by which this great earth and its peoples have become one to one another, the means by which the news of discovery or honor and the stories and songs of today travel and resound throughout the world. But they are also the means by which the true human community, the man knowing man, the neighbor understanding neighbor, the schoolboy learning a poem, the women dancing, the individual curiosity, the individual sense of beauty are being blown dry and issueless, the means by which the passivity of the disengaged spectator presents to the man of art and science the bleak face of unhumanity.

For the truth is that this is indeed, inevitably and increasingly, an open and, inevitably and increasingly, an eclectic world. We know too much for one man to know much, we live too variously to live as one. Our histories and traditions—the very means of interpreting life—are both bonds and barriers among us. Our knowledge separates as well as it unites; our orders disintegrate as well as bind; our art brings us together and sets us apart. The artist's loneliness, the scholar despairing because no one will any longer trouble to learn what he can teach, the narrowness of the scientist—these are unnatural insignia in this great time of change.

For what is asked of us is not easy. The openness of this world derives its character from the irreversibility of learning; what is once learned is part of human life. We cannot close our minds to discovery; we cannot stop our ears so that the voices of far-off and strange people can no longer reach them. The great cultures of the East cannot be walled off from ours by impassable seas and defects of understanding based on ignorance and unfamiliarity. Neither our integrity as men of learning nor our humanity allows that. In this open world, what is there, any man may try to learn.

This is no new problem. There has always been more to know than one man could know; there have always been modes of feeling that could not move the same heart; there have always been deeply held beliefs that could not be composed into a synthetic union. Yet never before today have the diversity, the complexity, the richness so clearly defied hierarchical order and simplification; never before have we had to understand the complementary, mutually not compatible ways of life and recognize choice between them as the only course of freedom. Never before today has the integrity of the intimate, the detailed, the true art, the integrity of craftsmanship and the preservation of the familiar, of the humorous and the beautiful stood in more massive contrast to the vastness of life, the greatness of the globe, the otherness of people, the otherness of ways, and the all-encompassing dark.

This is a world in which each of us, knowing his limitations, knowing the evils of superficiality and the terrors of fatigue, will have to cling to what is close to him, to what he knows, to what he can do, to his friends and his tradition and his love, lest he be dissolved in a universal confusion and know nothing and love nothing. It is at the same time a world in which none of us can find hieratic prescription or general sanction for any ignorance, any insensitivity, any indifference. When a friend tells us of a new discovery we may not understand, we may not be able to listen without jeopardizing the work that is ours and closer to us; but we cannot find in a book or canon—and we should not seek—grounds for hallowing our ignorance. If a man tells us that he sees differently than we, or that he finds beautiful what we find ugly, we may have to leave the room, from fatigue or trouble; but that is our weakness and our default. If we must live with a perpetual sense that the world and the men in it are greater than we and too much for us, let it be the measure of our virtue that we know this and seek no comfort. Above all, let us not proclaim that the limits of our powers correspond to some special wisdom in our choice of life, of learning, or of beauty.

This balance, this perpetual, precarious, impossible balance between the infinitely open and the intimate, this time—our twentieth century—has been long in coming; but it has come. It is, I think, for us and our children, our only way.

This is for all men. For the artist and for the scientist there is a special problem and a special hope, for in their extraordinarily different ways, in their lives that have increasingly divergent character, there is still a sensed bond, a sensed analogy. Both the man of science and the man of art live always at the edge of mystery, surrounded by it; both always, as the measure of their creation, have had to do with the harmonization of what is new with what is familiar, with the balance between novelty and synthesis, with the struggle to make partial order in total chaos. They can, in their work and in their lives, help themselves, help one another, and help all men. They can make the paths that connect the villages of arts and sciences with each other and with the world at large the multiple, varied, precious bonds of a true and world-wide community.

This cannot be an easy life. We shall have a rugged time of it to keep our minds open and to keep them deep, to keep our sense of beauty and our ability to make it, and our occasional ability to see it in places remote and strange and unfamiliar; we shall have a rugged time of it, all of us, in keeping these gardens in our villages, in keeping open the manifold, intricate, casual paths, to keep these flourishing in a great, open, windy world; but this, as I see it, is the condition of man; and in this condition we can help, because we can love, one another.

UNDERSTANDING THE TEXT

1. What distinct meanings of the word "prospect" does the author begin by indicating? For what reasons does he decide to exclude from consideration one of these meanings?

2. Since Oppenheimer has no interest in pursuing the first meaning of "prospect," why do you suppose he bothered to introduce the idea? Do his exclusion of this meaning, and the reasons he gives for excluding it, tell us anything about his general point of view in the essay?

3. When a person takes a comprehensive view (from a camera in a high-altitude rocket) of the arts and sciences, is he more likely, according to Oppenheimer, to be struck by their similarities or their differences, by their unity or their diversity?

4. What contrast does the essayist see between the behavior and attitudes of the community of scientists and the behavior and attitudes of the general human community? How does he relate this point to his advocacy of the practice of having scientists teach regularly in universities?

5. As Oppenheimer sees it, how is the artist's situation in society different from that of the scientist? What characteristics of modern society create special problems for the artist?

6. Oppenheimer asserts that the most striking feature of the contemporary world is its newness. How does he define what he means by this sense of newness? What causes does he suggest for this feeling of total change and upheaval?

7. Do the author's remarks on the mass media represent a digression from the main line of his argument?

8. What does Oppenheimer mean when he says we are living in an "open" world? What new situations and problems does he see this "openness" as creating?

TOPICS FOR DISCUSSION AND WRITING

9. As an exercise write a detailed explanation of the central analogy in Oppenheimer's essay. Point out as definitely as you can what each of the parts—the traveler on foot or by horse, the camera in the high-altitude rocket, the

villages, the pathways, the superhighways—is intended to represent in the author's discussion of the arts and sciences, and show how the parts are related.

10. In the sixth paragraph Oppenheimer refers to "a superhighway, along which windy traffic moves at enormous speed." Write a paragraph-length explanation of why the author uses the adjective "windy" to describe this traffic.

11. Oppenheimer speaks of the difficulty encountered by highly specialized scientists in communicating their insights to other people. Do you think that this difficulty exists also, in some degree, at the lower levels of scientific understanding? Write an essay, based on science instruction you have had in school and college, on any special problems of communication and understanding you have met.

12. In a succinct paper sum up the assumptions about the function of art, and the relationship between life and art, which are stated or implied in Oppenheimer's essay.

13. Aside from the patronage of colleges and universities, which Oppenheimer praises, can you think of other ways in which artists might be given the support of intimate and informed audiences?

14. If Oppenheimer's account of upheaval in the modern intellectual world is accurate, it would seem to have implications for education. What might be some of these implications? Along what directions would changes in education seem to be called for?

The Creative Mind in
Science and Art

J. BRONOWSKI

NO SCIENTIFIC theory is a collection of facts. It will not even do to call a theory true or false in the simple sense in which every fact is either so or not so. The Epicureans held that matter is made of atoms two thousand years ago and we are now tempted to say that their theory was true. But if we do so, we confuse their notion of matter with our own. John Dalton in 1808 first saw the structure of matter as we do today, and what he took from the ancients was not their theory but something richer, their image: the atom. Much of what was in Dalton's mind was as vague as the Greek notion, and quite as mistaken. But he suddenly gave life to the new facts of chemistry and the ancient theory together, by fusing them to give what neither had: a coherent picture of how matter is linked and built up from different kinds of atoms. The act of fusion is the creative act.

All science is the search for unity in hidden likenesses. The search may be on a grand scale, as in the modern theories which try to link the fields of gravitation and electro-magnetism. But we do not need to be browbeaten by the scale of science. There are discoveries to be made by snatching a small likeness from the air too, if it is bold enough. In 1932 the Japanese physicist Yukawa wrote a paper which can still give heart to a young scientist. He took as his starting point the known fact that waves of light can sometimes behave as if they were separate pellets. From this he reasoned that the forces which hold the nucleus of an atom together might sometimes also be observed as if they were solid pellets. A schoolboy can see how thin Yukawa's analogy is, and his teacher would be severe with it.

Yet Yukawa without a blush calculated the mass of the pellet he expected to see, and waited. He was right; his meson was found, and a range of other mesons, neither the existence nor the nature of which had been suspected before. The likeness had borne fruit.

The scientist looks for order in the appearances of nature by exploring such likenesses. For order does not display itself of itself; if it can be said to be there at all, it is not there for the mere looking. There is no way of pointing a finger or a camera at it; order must be discovered and, in a deep sense, it must be created. What we see, as we see it, is mere disorder.

This point has been put trenchantly in a fable by Professor Karl Popper. Suppose that someone wished to give his whole life to science. Suppose that he therefore sat down, pencil in hand, and for the next twenty, thirty, forty years recorded in notebook after notebook everything that he could observe. He may be supposed to leave out nothing: today's humidity, the racing results, the level of cosmic radiation and the stock market prices and the look of Mars, all would be there. He would have compiled the most careful record of nature that has ever been made; and, dying in the calm certainty of a life well spent, he would of course leave his notebooks to the Royal Society. Would the Royal Society thank him for the treasure of a lifetime of observation? It would not. It would refuse to open his notebooks at all, because it would know without looking that they contain only a jumble of disorderly and meaningless items.

Science finds order and meaning in our experience, and sets about this in quite a different way. It sets about it as Newton did in the story which he himself told in his old age, and of which the schoolbooks give only a caricature. In the year 1665, when Newton was twenty-two, the plague broke out in southern England, and the University of Cambridge was closed. Newton therefore spent the next eighteen months at home, removed from traditional learning, at a time when he was impatient for knowledge and, in his own phrase: "I was in the prime of my age for invention." In this eager, boyish mood, sitting one day in the garden of his widowed mother, he saw an apple fall. So far the books have the story right; we think we even know the kind of apple; tradition has it that it was a Flower of Kent. But now they miss the crux of the story. For what struck the young Newton at the sight was not the thought that the apple must be drawn to the earth by gravity; that conception was older than Newton. What struck him was the conjecture that the same force of gravity, which reaches to the top of the tree, might go on reaching out beyond the earth and its air, endlessly into space. Gravity might reach the moon: this was Newton's new thought; and it might be gravity which holds the moon in her orbit. There and then he calculated what force from the earth would hold the moon, and compared it with the known force of gravity at tree height. The forces agreed; Newton says laconically: "I found them answer pretty nearly." Yet they agreed only nearly: the likeness and the approximation go together, for no likeness is exact. In Newton's sentence modern science is full grown.

It grows from a comparison. It has seized a likeness between two unlike appearances; for the apple in the summer garden and the grave moon overhead are surely as unlike in their movements as two things can be. Newton traced in them two expressions of a single concept, gravitation: and the concept (and the unity) are in that sense his free creation. The progress of science is the discovery at each step of a new order which gives unity to what had long seemed unlike. Faraday did this when he closed the link between electricity and magnetism. Clerk Maxwell did it when he linked both with light. Einstein linked time with space, mass with energy, and the path of light past the sun with the flight of a bullet; and spent his dying years in trying to add to these likenesses another, which would find a single imaginative order between the equations of Clerk Maxwell and his own geometry of gravitation.

When Coleridge tried to define beauty, he returned always to one deep thought: beauty, he said, is "unity in variety." Science is nothing else than the search to discover unity in the wild variety of nature—or more exactly, in the variety of our experience. Poetry, painting, the arts are the same search, in Coleridge's phrase, for unity in variety. Each in its own way looks for likenesses under the variety of human experience. What is a poetic image but the seizing and the exploration of a hidden likeness, in holding together two parts of a comparison which are to give depth each to the other? When Romeo finds Juliet in the tomb, and thinks her dead, he uses in his heartbreaking speech the words:

Death that hath suckt the honey of thy breath.

The critic can only haltingly take to pieces the single shock which this image carries. The young Shakespeare admired Marlowe, and Marlowe's Faustus had said of the ghostly kiss of Helen of Troy that it sucked forth his soul. But that is a pale image; what Shakespeare has done is to fire it with the single word honey. Death is a bee at the lips of Juliet, and the bee is an insect that stings; the sting of death was a commonplace phrase when Shakespeare wrote. The sting is there, under the image; Shakespeare has packed it into the word honey; but the very word rides powerfully over its own undertones. Death is a bee that stings other people, but it comes to Juliet as if she were a flower; this is the moving thought under the instant image. The creative mind speaks in such thoughts.

The poetic image here is also, and accidentally, heightened by the tenderness which town dwellers now feel for country ways. But it need not be; there are likenesses to conjure with, and images as powerful, within the man-made world. The poems of Alexander Pope belong to this world. They are not countrified, and therefore readers today find them unemotional and often artificial. Let me then quote Pope: here he is in a formal satire face to face, towards the end of his life, with his own gifts. In eight lines he looks poignantly forward towards death and back to the laborious years which made him famous.

> Years foll'wing Years, steal something ev'ry day,
> At last they steal us from our selves away;
> In one our Frolicks, one Amusements end,
> In one a Mistress drops, in one a Friend:
> This subtle Thief of Life, this paltry Time
> What will it leave me, if it snatch my Rhime?
> If ev'ry Wheel of that unweary'd Mill
> That turn'd ten thousand Verses, now stands still.

The human mind had been compared to what the eighteenth century called a mill, that is to a machine, before; Pope's own idol Bolingbroke had compared it to a clockwork. In these lines the likeness goes deeper, for Pope is thinking of the ten thousand Verses which he had translated from Homer: what he says is sad and just at the same time, because this really had been a mechanical and at times a grinding task. Yet the clockwork is present in the image too; when the wheels stand still, time for Pope will stand still for ever; we feel that we already hear, over the horizon, the defiance of Faust which Goethe had not yet written—let the clock strike and stop, let the hand fall, and time be at an end.

> Werd ich zum Augenblicke sagen:
> Verweile doch! du bist so schön!
> Dann magst du mich in Fesseln schlagen,
> Dann will ich gern zugrunde gehn!
> Dann mag die Totenglocke schallen,
> Dann bist du deines Dienstes frei,

> Die Uhr mag stehn, der Zeiger fallen,
> Es sei die Zeit für mich vorbei!

I have quoted Pope and Goethe because their metaphor here is not poetic; it is rather a hand reaching straight into experience and arranging it with new meaning. Metaphors of this kind need not always be written in words. The most powerful of them all is simply the presence of King Lear and his Fool in the hut of a man who is shamming madness, while lightning rages outside. Or let me quote another clash of two conceptions of life, from a modern poet. In his later poems, W. B. Yeats was troubled by the feeling that in shutting himself up to write, he was missing the active pleasures of life; and yet it seemed to him certain that the man who lives for these pleasures will leave no lasting work behind him. He said this at times very simply, too:

> The intellect of man is forced to choose
> Perfection of the life, or of the work.

This problem, whether man fulfills himself in work or in play, is of course more common than Yeats allowed; and it may be more commonplace. But it is given breadth and force by the images in which Yeats pondered it.

> Get all the gold and silver that you can,
> Satisfy ambition, or animate
> The trivial days and ram them with the sun,
> And yet upon these maxims meditate:
> All women dote upon an idle man
> Although their children need a rich estate;
> No man has ever lived that had enough
> Of children's gratitude or woman's love.

The love of women, the gratitude of children: the images fix two philosophies as nothing else can. They are tools of creative thought, as coherent and as exact as the conceptual images with which science works: as time and space, or as the proton and the neutron.

The discoveries of science, the works of art are explorations—more, are explosions—of a hidden likeness. The discoverer or the artist presents in them two aspects of nature and fuses them into one. This is the act of creation, in which an original thought is born, and it is the same act in original science and original art. But it is not therefore the monopoly of the man who wrote the poem or who made the discovery. On the contrary, I believe this view of the creative act to be right because it alone gives a meaning to the act of appreciation. The poem or the discovery exists in two moments of vision: the moment of appreciation as much as that of creation; for the appreciator must see the movement, wake to the echo which was started in the creation of the work. In the moment of appreciation we live again the moment when the creator saw and held the hidden likeness. When a simile takes us aback and persuades us together, when we find a juxtaposition in a picture both odd and intriguing, when a theory is at once fresh and convincing, we do not merely nod over someone else's work. We re-enact the creative act, and we ourselves make the discovery again. At bottom, there is no unifying likeness there until we too have seized it, we too have made it for ourselves.

How slipshod by comparison is the notion that either art or science sets out to copy nature. If the task of the painter were to copy for men what they see, the critic could make only a single judgment: either that the copy is right or that it is wrong. And if science were a copy of fact, then every theory would be either right or wrong, and would be so forever. There would be nothing left for us to say but this is so or is not so. No one who has read a page by a good critic or a speculative scientist can ever again think that this barren choice of yes or no is all that the mind offers.

Reality is not an exhibit for man's inspection, labeled: "Do not touch." There are no appearances to be photographed, no experiences to be copied, in which we do not take part. We re-make nature by the act of discovery, in the poem or in the theorem. And the great poem and the deep theorem are new to every reader, and yet are his own experiences, because he himself re-creates them. They are the marks of unity in variety; and in the instant when the mind seizes this for itself, in art or in science, the heart misses a beat.

UNDERSTANDING THE TEXT

1. In what respects does Bronowski find science and art to be essentially alike?
2. What is the difference between a fact and a theory?
3. According to Bronowski, a theory is not simply true or false. Does he suggest any way in which its value or "depth" can be determined?
4. Explain what Bronowski means when he says (paragraph 3) that order must, "in a deep sense, . . . be created."
5. Why, according to Bronowski, is the story of Newton and the apple, as usually told, "only a caricature"?

6. Can you see any reason why, in discussing the similarities between creative thought in science and art, Bronowski should deal first with science and then with art, rather than proceeding in the reverse order?
7. When Bronowski says (p. 604) that the metaphors he quotes from Pope and Goethe are "not poetic," is he using the word "poetic" in the same sense in which he used it in speaking of the "poetic image" in *Romeo and Juliet?*
8. What is the relation, according to Bronowski, between the act of creation and the act of appreciation?
9. Why does Bronowski think it important to include a discussion of the act of appreciation?

TOPICS FOR DISCUSSION AND WRITING

10. Write a paragraph in which you explain and evaluate the metaphor in Bronowski's statement that the discoveries of science and the works of art are "explosions" of a hidden likeness.
11. Bronowski distinguishes between fact and theory in science. Write a paragraph making clear what it is in poetry that corresponds to these two terms.
12. The notion of finding order in our experience is prominent in Bronowski's essay. It is also prominent in Forster's "Art for Art's Sake." Write a comparison of the meanings of "order" used by the two writers.
13. Bronowski, like Oppenheimer, explores the relations between science and art. Write a paper in which you consider the differences in the ways in which the two writers define and discuss the relations between science and art.
14. Can you think of any differences between science and art that cannot be brought within the scope of the identity which Bronowski seeks to establish?

Liberty

LEARNED HAND

I HAVE chosen for the subject of my talk, "Liberty." When I say that I chose it, I am not speaking quite the truth; rather it chose itself. I was so acutely aware of the quicksands and wastes which await the explorer in that region that I tried to avoid an expedition into it. Perhaps a judge is especially aware of these; his colleagues are constantly assuring him that all he needs is to avoid license and anarchy on the one hand, and tyranny and despotism on the other; if he will only stick to that simple admonition he is sure to arrive. That is not very encouraging as a starter; but what gives the task its real difficulty is that the word is so charged with passion. About none is written a more fiery record of suffering and heroism; it is the center and the kernel of that inner life for which men will fight and die who will fight and die for anything. Furthermore, and perhaps for that reason, it has been the rallying cry of those who hold quite opposite beliefs; one can say of it after Lincoln: "Both sides pray to it and each invokes its aid against the other." Few stop to ask what they mean, and those who do soon find the answer baffling and uncertain. Why then should I venture to talk about it here tonight? Only because I could not help it. In such a world as this, so wretched and so riven, where men and women are suffering misery, mutilation, and death in the name of Liberty—whatever it may be—how can anyone be content who does not try to come to at least a tentative conclusion with himself about it? And so, although I am conscious of the small chance of success where so many have failed, I shall ask you to bear with me as I too try my luck with this Sphinx, whom like her prototype if I answer I answer at my peril.

I do not know how it is with you, but my own first spontaneous response to the word is negative; I think that I am free when I can do what I want; this tiny protoplasmal center of radiant energy demands that alien impacts shall not thwart its insistences and its self-assertions. What are these? We can start with a dictum attributed to Lawrence Henderson that they consist in the performance of our accustomed rituals. (Those of you who have read Trotter's *Instinct of the Herd* will perhaps remember analogues drawn from the accepted social observances of man's best friend, the Dog, which I forbear to quote.) Henderson's definition would be entirely satisfactory to anthropologists, who, very properly, refuse to play favorites among the conventions of mankind. It is as authentic a denial of freedom to compel a Bushman to look at his mother-in-law during the period of his wife's gestation, as it is to deny Colonel Lindbergh the privilege of assuring us of the speedy and certain collapse of Great Britain. Each has a vested right in his freedom grounded in the deepest of foundations, the current liturgies of the society to which he belongs. Since, so conceived, Liberty is negative, one freedom is as good as another; there is no objective standard except for blind partisans of the status quo whatever it may be. The rite of burying the aged alive, whatever the aged may say against it, has equal sanction with that of providing a college education for those who are not fit to receive one.

Let us then look for an objective standard. Surely we can safely begin with the satisfaction of our primitive needs. We must eat, sleep, be clothed and sheltered, and have our mates and our children. It is irrelevant that the Universe so often denies us these; we are considering hindrances by our fellows. Shall we say then that, so far as they deny us such goods, they deny our Liberty? "Do not waste our time in trivialities," you will answer, "we must of course yield these in part, and other desires scarcely less imperious; but by doing so we create civilized society so that our life shall not be 'short, brutish, and nasty.' Why go over that old stuff again? It was what Holmes meant when he said he liked to pay taxes because he felt he was buying civilization." No doubt; but if we press the inquiry a little further it gets more real. To say that we must compromise leaves all practical questions unanswered. Kant may have been right when he said that our conduct must be such that it can be made a universal rule; but that does not help us to find any particular rule; perhaps there are not any. If we declare that a freeman will yield so far, but only so far, as, having with entire detachment weighed his own good against his neighbor's, he finds the neighbor's better, that does not tell us how he is to decide which of the two is in fact the better. Of course there is the initial obstacle that entire detachment is an obvious fiction. To proceed at all we must set up some persons in our society with authority—like Plato's "Guardians" for instance, to whom we can depute the weighing of one good against another. The outlook has never been very propitious that we can find any such guardians, but for my purposes it is not important; for if we secured absolute detachment and impartiality, we should have got no further than to face the real problem.

Let me start with an example drawn from Plato's own city; not because we need doubt the answer, but because it illustrates the incommensurability of the elements that must be measured. When at times I hear, as we all do, some cultivated snob vaporing about the perfection of life in Athens, say from 480 to 430 B.C., and how it was the apex of civilization, someone is sure to interject that it was not so at all; rather that Athens was a hideous nightmare; that these supposed specimens of ultimate human perfection were shameless exploiters of a far greater number of other men whose misery, when matched against their own splendors, makes Stygian blackness to the eyes of all just and humane persons. When such a Thersites disturbs the complacency of the cultivated snob, sometimes I feel like siding with the snob—even now when the dawn of social justice has broken into bright unclouded day. I should not do so by way of challenge to the challenger's conclusion, but I should ask him to tell me the processes by which he reached it. I should say that of course I recognized that the exploitation of the weak, taken by itself, was undiluted evil; and that in its more aggravated form we need not even discuss it—for instance, the often lamented lot of those unfortunate men who were worked to death in the mines of Laurium no doubt outweighed an infinity of noble employment of leisure. I should ask him to put aside such concrete incidents disturbing to philosophic speculation and consider the issue abstractly. Supposing that an ethical or hedonistic calculus were possible, and supposing that there were no other means than the exploitation of the exploited by which the lives of the Athenian citizens could have been what they were, and supposing that these were as perfect as both he and the cultivated snob seemed to agree they were; how he could guess which way the beam would tip if one put the lives of the citizens in one scale and the good things of which they deprived their slaves in the other. I should tell him that, though I was sure of the answer, I had always been a little baffled to know how such a balance could be struck; but that, like Socrates, I was confident that he must know, since he seemed so certain. And if he, rightly angry at this offensively insincere humility, were to answer, as I suspect he might, that injustice could never be right, and that there were some things which everyone knew, among which was that oppression and justice were inherently antithetical, I should not feel that he had thoroughly illuminated all the dark places.

At any rate I know that, whatever he said, he could not tell me how to strike such a balance. While each of us can do it for himself here and now, he finds trouble even for himself when he includes his own future; and when we come to deal with a community, a community of say one hundred and thirty million persons, how can we possibly proceed? What we do in fact is to assume that all are alike; that what is a good for A is a good for B, and that A's preference—A's better—will be B's. Perhaps one cannot conduct a democracy on any other assumption; but not only is it not true in fact; but whatever its truth, it is impossible to make people believe it. They will do so in the abstract, but they fall into endless dispute in application, and the effort is apt to end either in mutual paralysis of action, or a seizure of power by a part. The resulting confusion and discord have therefore often suggested this solution: instill in all a faith that each achieves his personal and individual best by submerging himself in common aspirations, a common fate, a common self. There would be no denial of Liberty in that; nobody would feel himself under alien domination; each would realize himself in all, and all in each.

"Old stuff again," you will say, "it sounds good but you know it cannot be done; people are too different, and that is all there is to it. Once you try to make them alike you have more trouble on your hands than when you started." On the contrary I am disposed to believe that perhaps it can be done, for a time anyway, and for a very large proportion at least of a large community. Certainly I am not so sure as I used to be that it cannot be done. There are more and more signs about us that our increasingly efficient and pervasive apparatus of mass suggestion is planing off individual differences, and making us more and more facile for mass manipulation. We need not look to Russia and Germany, or to their pathetic Italian imitator; we need not leave home at all. Indeed, something of the kind was possible long before the days of the tabloid, the radio, the moving picture, and the motor car. Sparta was an instance; so was Rome for a while; and Islam in the 8th Century, Spain in the 16th, and France in the 18th. And it has always been possible to create nonpolitical groups with corporate selves. Man is a gregarious animal, extremely sensitive to authority; if it will only indoctrinate him thoroughly in his childhood and youth, he can be made to espouse any kind of orthodoxy—whether of belief or feeling. There were philosophical prophets of the Absolute Collective Self long before Hegel and Fichte. In his early manhood Plato had seen the Athenian democracy crumble from faction; he concluded that only under the Spartan model could mankind achieve that justice which was the end of society as it was of the individual. Again and again the same theme has recurred thereafter.

Now, as a practical means of realizing common purposes nothing comparable exists, as we are now learning to our cost. Lord Lothian shortly before his death—and very near, I think, to where we now are—forcibly admonished us of this. "You cannot match the power of such a people as the Germans, unless you are willing to sink your separate interests in your common cause and accept sacrifices such as they accept by means of a faith of equal fervor." Hitler is quite right in predicting the doom of democracies as he understands democracies; I wish it were more certain that he misunderstands them. A society in which each is willing to surrender only that for which he can see a personal equivalent, is not a society at all; it is a group already in process of dissolution, and no one need concern himself to stay its inevitable end; it would be a hard choice between it and a totalitarian society. No Utopia, nothing but Bedlam, will automatically emerge from a regime of unbridled individualism, be it ever so rugged.

What then, you will ask, am I really talking about? If it be true that any orthodoxy can be implanted in us, provided we are caught and schooled while young, or provided even in our later years that we are subjected to the everlasting iteration of sacred rubrics, in school, in press, in moving picture, and by radio; and if, when we have been so "conditioned," we feel authority to be no restraint but rather a means toward the realization of our deeper self; and if something of the sort is essential to survival in a robbers' world, where the strong are sure to win; if all these things be true, why should we boggle about any other Liberty; what more do we need? That other societies so organized have been predatory, does not mean that we need be predacious; our communal self can become the chalice for a more exquisite liquor of civilization than the troubled world has yet seen. In our Father's house are many mansions; we will occupy one where life shall be seemly and noble and forbearing and happy and gay; yet strong enough withal to resist any aggression.

Some day such a vision may come true; the future may have in store aeons of beatitude in which men shall find utter self-realization and utter self-expression in the utter self-surrender of the hive; I do not forget the words of the collect: "Whose service is perfect freedom." Be that as it

may, it is not on the score of its impracticability that I do not welcome
that prospect; but because I believe that its realization would suppress the
most precious part of our nature. To put it very badly, and perhaps a little
contentiously, it is man's inherent willfulness that I would preserve, and in
which I wish to set the stronghold of that Liberty I prize; that stone which
social reformers have always rejected I would make the head of the corner.

I cannot tell why to me personally such a society seems stifling; I only
know that although with Epictetus I can say: "If I were an ant, I should
play the part of an ant," in fact I am not an ant, and if I try to play the part
of an ant I know that I shall end in the care of a psychoanalyst. I will own
that when on occasion I visit my simian cousins in captivity, the spectacle
does not refresh me. Not only have they a distressing lack of reserve, but
their restlessness affects me with a homeopathic uneasiness. Kipling seems
right, and I wince that we have so many family traits in common. My
kinship with them becomes even more distasteful when I pass to the
cages of the great cats, who lie there serenely with their steady yellow
eyes, calm, self-secure, fearing nothing. Why must my cousins and I be so
agitated; why this ceaseless, errant curiosity; pausing only for an instant
and then off to something new? It is all very trying; and yet here will I
pitch my tent. James Harvey Robinson used to say that we rose from the
ape because like him we kept "monkeying around," always meddling with
everything about us. True, there is a difference, because although the ape
meddles, he forgets, and we have learned, first to meddle and remember,
and then to meddle and record. But without the meddling nothing would
have happened of all that glorious array of achievement: battleships, aeroplanes, relativity, the proton, neutron, and electron, T.N.T., poison gas,
sulfathiazole, the Fifth Symphony, *The Iliad, The Divine Comedy, Hamlet, Faust, The Critique of Pure Reason, Das Kapital,* the Constitution of
the United States, The Congress of Industrial Organizations, Huey Long,
and The New Deal. All these from just "monkeying around"!

My thesis is that any organization of society which depresses free and
spontaneous meddling is on the decline, however showy its immediate
spoils; I maintain that in such a society Liberty is gone, little as its members may know it; that the Nirvana of the individual is too high a price
for a collective Paradise. I maintain this primarily as an authentic demand
of the spirit—*animula vagula blandula . . . quae nunc abibis in loca*[1]—

---

[1] Two lines from the Emperor Hadrian's dying address to his departing soul. The
full text reads:

Animula, vagula, blandula,
Hospes comesque corporis,

and I maintain it too as practical sagacity. Because, once you get people believing that there is an authoritative well of wisdom to which they can turn for absolutes, you have dried up the springs on which they must in the end draw even for the things of this world. As soon as we cease to pry about at random, we shall come to rely upon accredited bodies of authoritative dogma; and as soon as we come to rely upon accredited bodies of authoritative dogma, not only are the days of our Liberty over, but we have lost the password that has hitherto opened to us the gates of success as well. Even in that very technology on which they so much pride themselves, the totalitarians in the end will fail; for they stand upon the shoulders of generations of free inquiry. No doubt they will try to keep their hands off materially profitable activities; but they will finally learn that you cannot put men's minds in watertight compartments; you cannot have a nation, each one of whom is half slave and half free, any more than you can have a nation in which half are wholly slave and half are wholly free. Where heterodoxy in what men prize most is a crime, fresh thinking about anything will disappear. Even the loaves and fishes will not be multiplied.

As I predicted, I have brought down a very small quarry. We started to find some positive content for liberty, and all we have discovered is that it does not follow because we are not conscious of constraint that we are not constrained. Yet little as that seems, it is not I think an altogether contemptible result, for behind it lies a faith. It is the faith that our collective fate in the end depends upon the irrepressible fertility of the individual, and the finality of what he chooses to call good. It is the faith that neither principalities, nor powers, nor things present, nor things to come, can rightfully suppress that fertility or deny that good. It is the faith in the indefectible significance of each one of us, inherited, if I understand it aright, from One who lived and died some 1900 years ago in Palestine. It is a faith not easy to live by, whose credo is full of hard sayings. If you accept it, it may cast you for the role of Prometheus, a part of whose lines, you will remember, contain a good deal about defying the Powers of this

---

Quae nunc abibis in loca.
Pallidula, rigida, nudula,
Nec, ut soles, dabis joca?

Byron translated as follows:

Ah! gentle, fleeting, wav'ring sprite,
Friend and associate of this clay!
To what unknown region borne,
Wilt thou now wing thy distant flight?
No more with wonted humour gay,
But pallid, cheerless, and forlorn.

World. Those powers are ruthless, competent, and strong; and among the properties in the play there are real lightning and a real eagle; make no mistake about that. Moreover, the audience is likely to be very small; indeed it is not improbable that there will be none at all. The only curtain calls you will get are those you give yourself. But the lead is a man's part, and perhaps some of us can fill it. Who can tell?

UNDERSTANDING THE TEXT

1. Why is it not enough for Hand's purpose to find the negative meaning of liberty outlined in paragraph 2?
2. What is Hand's final definition of liberty? Where does he give it? Is it an "objective" standard in the sense he referred to in paragraph 2? How does it differ from the negative meaning of liberty set forth at the beginning of the essay?
3. Why, even though he agrees that slave-holding in Athens was an evil, does Hand insist on discussing it at length? What does this fact tell you about the nature of Hand's purpose?
4. What situation has led to attempts to persuade the individual to submerge his individual good in the common good? Does Hand regard this as a passing and temporary phenomenon?
5. On what trait of human nature does Hand wish to base his conception of liberty? Why?
6. Characterize Justice Hand's diction and sentence structure, giving examples of his use of language from different language levels and his use of varying sentence patterns. Then try to show as many relations as you can between these stylistic traits and the aim and effect of the essay.
7. Define the meanings of the following in their contexts: *riven, prototype, liturgy, propitious, hedonistic, facile, iteration, rubric, boggle, homeopathic, sagacity, indefectible.*

TOPICS FOR DISCUSSION AND WRITING

8. Write a paragraph on Hand's list of human achievements on p. 612.
9. Summarizing his argument, Hand says, "all we have discovered is that it does not follow because we are not conscious of constraint that we are not constrained." Write a brief of Hand's argument to show the steps by which we have discovered this.
10. Write a short comparison of Hand's and Myers' views of the basic assumptions of democracy.
11. Does the essay bear any sign that it was delivered as a lecture? That it was delivered in 1941? That it was composed by a great judge?

SUPPLEMENTS

1. Writing, Reading, and Reasoning

THE PROCESSES of verbal communication and thought are closely interwoven. Without entering into the perennial argument whether thought is possible without the use of verbal symbols, we know that any piece of writing reflects the kind and quality of thinking which are characteristic of the person who wrote it. As the exercises and comments on the essays in this book have made clear, one of the cardinal tests of effective writing is its intellectual coherence, its logical consistency. Oftentimes, when we read a passage of prose, we find ourselves formulating a reaction in some such remark as "He just doesn't think straight," or, more favorably, "The ideas all hang together perfectly." Even when we remain in disagreement with the position taken by the author we are reading, we may admire the clarity of the reasoning with which he has developed and supported his point of view.

This is not to say, of course, that skill in logical manipulation is the sole quality needed by the good writer. It is entirely possible for an argument to be unassailable logically, but to be relatively ineffective in achieving the purpose for which it is designed. Sometimes, for example, a writer will set down sparely a string of statements, all of them true and all of them connected in a reasonably logical way; yet, because the writer fails to develop a successful scale of proportion for his ideas, to highlight those which need expansion, and to provide examples where they are required, the argument is much less convincing than it could have been. The error here is the substitution of a logical diagram for genuine written discourse.

Clarity of reasoning, then, does not in itself guarantee effectiveness in writing; as your study of the foregoing essays demonstrates, the total effect of a piece of prose arises from the working together of many different elements. Among these elements is the basic logical structure of the essay, or editorial, or scientific paper. Consequently, some familiarity with the principles of sound reasoning will assist the writer in sorting out his ideas and in expressing them straightforwardly. Similarly, the reader who grasps the way reasoning proceeds will be better equipped to follow, to appreciate, and to evaluate what an author is trying to tell him. In other words, while precision in reasoning should not be confused with the whole job of verbal communication, it can be regarded as an important prerequisite for success in both writing and reading.

There is nothing mysterious or out-of-this-world about the principles of clear thinking. Just as most of us managed to speak English sentences before we learned the vocabulary of grammatical analysis, so we can think about our practical problems rationally even though we may not understand, in a formal way, the specific logical processes we are using. The similarity between grammar and logic can be extended. An understanding of English grammar gives a person greater control over the resources of his language; and so a more precise and conscious knowledge of how we reason sharpens a person's ability to formulate his own ideas and to comprehend the ideas of other people. The intention of this supplement is to supply enough information about logical interrelationships to help you improve the cogency of your own prose, and to assist you in recognizing and appraising the intellectual structure of what you read.

TWO KINDS OF REASONING

Obviously, in developing an essay on any subject, the writer wants to convince the reader that he is telling the truth, that he is making accurate and sensible statements about the topic under discussion. For the writer, there are in general two kinds of "true" statements, or two avenues through which he approaches his presentation of the truth. One of these methods is direct; the other is indirect. In the direct method, which is sometimes called *induction*, the writer arrives at his statements by an immediate inspection of the actual world. This inspection of actuality may occur in a variety of ways: personal experience, reading and conversation, even statistical study.[1] Its fruit, however, is always a statement directly based on the way the writer has examined the world around him. Such statements, derived inductively, may be made concerning a wide variety of topics, and they may differ greatly in complexity. Here are a few examples, with possible sources noted: "Red-haired girls have fiery tempers" (personal experience); "All American presidents have been men" (reading of history); "Men in public life are generally motivated by a combination of ambition and avarice" (personal experience and reading). You will

[1] Note the rough-and-ready statistical induction in Hoffer's "The Role of the Undesirables," pp. 476–485.

observe, of course, that these three statements vary also in the degree in which readers would accept them as true; no one would be likely to question the second statement, while each of the other two might generate lively controversy. The three statements have in common, however, the fact that they rest fundamentally upon the writer's direct interpretation of what the world is like and how the people in it behave. In their different ways, each is a summing up of evidence drawn from some kind of experience.

The other principal method of developing a statement, which is sometimes called *deduction*, is indirect because it proceeds, not by a fresh study of actuality, but by putting together statements which are already believed to be true, and then seeing what logical consequences flow from our belief in their truth. Most of us have encountered the term "deduction" in murder mysteries; let us see how the process might operate in the exciting field of criminal detection. On the basis of his past experience, the detective accepts as true the statement that crimes committed under particular circumstances—without motive, with great brutality, with apparent unconcern about concealment—are the work of insane persons. Investigating a specific crime, the detective notes that these circumstances are present. Thereupon he turns to the assembled police officers and says, "Gentlemen, we are looking for a madman!" This final statement, the implied conclusion—this crime was committed by an insane person—was reached through a process of deduction. It follows, as we may say, as a logical consequence from the truth of two other statements. If it is true that crimes committed under circumstances A, B, and C are always the deeds of madmen, and if it is true that this specific crime was committed under circumstances A, B, C, then the detective's conclusion must in turn be a true one. On the other hand, if either of the first two statements happens to be false, our hypothetical detective may still be an excellent logician, but he will be a poor police officer.

This example suggests the way in which these two kinds of reasoning function together in everyday thought and in writing. The final statement about the crime was arrived at through deduction. The first two statements, which provided the raw material for deduction, were themselves the result of induction. The first one, the general statement about crimes committed under certain conditions, was presumably an induction from the detective's personal experience and from his knowledge of other crimes beyond his immediate experience. The second one, the statement about the specific crime under investigation, was an induction based on direct observation of the case. This interplay between induction and deduction occurs constantly in reasoning. You may recall that the generalization cited earlier—"Men in public life are generally motivated by a combination of ambition and avarice"—was introduced by Benjamin Franklin in "The Speech on the Subject of Salaries" (pp. 48–51). In Franklin's speech, this inductively derived statement becomes an important link in a chain of deductions leading to the conclusion that certain government officials should not receive salaries.[2] Or, as an exercise in practical reasoning, try coupling another induction stated earlier—"red-haired girls have fiery tempers"—with still another inductive statement—"I understand that my blind date tonight has red hair." If both these statements are believed to be true, an interesting conclusion can be deduced from them.

It is evident that the kinds of "true" statements reached through each of these processes are likely to be somewhat different. For this reason, it may be useful to speak of "truth," or at least "probability," as the result of a sound induction. Thus, the statement, "Good administrators know how to delegate authority," resting as it does on a direct study of the way men work, may be described as "true," or at least as highly probable. On the other hand, a statement produced through proper deductive reasoning may be thought of as evidencing "validity." For example, if we join with the statement already made about good administration a second statement, "Jones is a good administrator," we are able to infer that Jones knows how to delegate authority. This conclusion about Jones we recognize as "valid" —that is, as something which is implied by our acceptance of the other two statements. This distinction between truth and validity, as the end products of induction and deduction, respectively, can help us to keep clear the difference between these two basic processes of reasoning. It should be pointed out, also, that, in some sophisticated analyses of logic, the distinction between induction and deduction is drawn much less sharply than we have presented it here. For our purposes, however, in tightening the structure of what we write and in understanding the intellectual organization of what we read, it will be useful to regard induction and deduction as two different ways of developing statements about matters that interest us.

INDUCTION

Skill in using such forms of thought as induction and deduction is often closely related to ability to define clearly and to classify precisely. One of

[2] Another good example of mixed induction and deduction is Kennan, pp. 553–559.

the commonest types of induction, for example, results in a general statement about a class—of objects, or ideas, or persons. In the induction, the class as a whole is surveyed, and, on the basis of this inspection, certain characteristics common to some or all the members of the class are pointed out. In the examples given earlier, you will recall, statements were made about members of the following classes: "red-haired girls," "American presidents," and "men in public life." In fact, the complete statement arrived at by induction often involves two different classes—the class concerning which something is being said and the class to which the members of this first group are assigned by the statement itself. For instance, the descriptive remark, "Red-haired girls have fiery tempers," might be translated something like this: "Members of the class *red-haired girls* belong to the class *persons with fiery tempers.*"

Obviously, the soundness of statements derived inductively depends to a very great extent upon the writer's ability to survey thoroughly the class concerning which he wishes to say something.[3] If the class is small, and its membership is clearly defined, it will be possible to make a rather complete induction and thus to produce a generalization based on fairly exhaustive evidence. There are, for example, relatively few members of the class "presidents of the United States." Consequently, when a student writes, "No president of the United States has ever begun a term after the age of 70 years," we know that it has been possible for his inquiry to cover all the members of this small class and that, if his investigation has been reasonably careful, the generalization should be a sound one.

More frequently, however, the writer is dealing with a class which is large and perhaps vaguely defined; at any rate, all its members are not available for observation and questioning. In these cases, it is important that the writer base his general statements upon a study of members selected in such a way as to provide a reliable cross-section of the entire class. If one were writing an article about the average income of a college's alumni in the class of 1926, it might be imprudent to generalize too briskly on the basis of data supplied in answer to mailed questionnaires. Reflection suggests that alumni who voluntarily fill out questionnaires concerning income may not be typical of the entire group. Similarly, when professional poll takers risk an induction about the state of opinion within a particular political party, or among the voters of a state or the nation, they are careful to sample a representative segment of the group they are studying. Since they believe that such factors as economic status,

[3] See Marston Bates, "The Biotic Community," p. 121.

occupation, place of residence, and religion have some influence upon political tendencies, analysts of public opinion try to interview a selected group which, in terms of these crucial characteristics, resembles the population at large. Elaborate statistical precautions are taken to insure that the individuals examined are, in truth, typical of the entire class, and that the resulting induction is therefore worthy of credit.

Less pretentiously, in everything we write the same principle holds. If we are trying to establish a general interpretation of a person's character, two or three examples of typical behavior, carefully chosen to develop the point we wish to make, will be much more valuable than a dozen illustrations which bear only peripherally upon our central statement. Throughout Tocqueville's masterly analysis of nineteenth-century American life, as in the essay appearing on pages 463–466, the writer makes economical use of examples to support his generalizations; because of the aptness of the few concrete details Tocqueville includes, the reader feels no need for full documentation. On the other hand, some inductively developed statements call for a wealth of supporting details. A good example of this can be seen in Shaftesbury's sketch of Mr. Henry Hastings (pp. 136–138). Here, since the author's central point is the physical profusion of the squire's old-fashioned life, an overwhelming mass of concrete circumstances is brought forward to establish convincingly Shaftesbury's view of Mr. Hastings.

Because, as we have seen, many inductive statements are based on a scrutiny of fewer than all members of the group being studied, it is usually necessary to give the reader a clear account of the way the evidence was examined. Then, after studying such an account of procedure, the reader can make up his own mind concerning the probable truth of the statement presented to him. In reports of scientific research, for example, the investigator's description of his method of inquiry is normally an important part. Also, in framing a statement of what he has learned through induction, the careful writer keeps his language in proportion to what he has actually learned. That is, he does not leap blithely from the discovery that something is true of 55 percent of a group to the assertion that it is true of the entire group.[4]

DEDUCTION

The second principal method of reasoning—deduction—is even more directly connected than induction with the processes of definition and

[4] For examples of induction, see Wylie, pp. 184–190, and Cooke, pp. 191–195.

classification. The simplest form of deduction can be demonstrated by looking closely at the central argument of a celebrated document, the Declaration of Independence issued by representatives of the American colonies in 1776. The first part of the Declaration develops a statement which runs something like this: A ruler whose conduct evinces an intention to fasten despotism upon his people has himself severed the bonds of government, and need not be obeyed. In the long middle portion of the Declaration, with its detailed indictment of the King of Great Britain, the authors present what is, in effect, an induction leading to this statement: The King of Great Britain is a ruler whose conduct evinces an intention to fasten despotism upon his people. From these two statements there follows, logically, the conclusion: The King of Great Britain has himself severed the bonds of government, and need not be obeyed by the Americans.

What has happened in this deductive argument can best be understood by referring back to our knowledge of classification. In the first statement, the authors have asserted that the whole class of rulers who do certain things—who behave despotically—is included within the class of rulers who have lost the right to be obeyed. In the second statement, the authors place the King of Great Britain within the class of despotic rulers. Thus, through this double process of classification, the writers of the Declaration have demonstrated that the King of Great Britain belongs to the category of rulers who have lost the right to be obeyed.

When a deductive argument is presented in this simple, stripped-down form, it is called a *syllogism*. The first statement (in the Declaration, the assertion that despotic kings need not be obeyed) is known as the *major premise*. The second statement (in the Declaration, the charge that George III has behaved despotically) is the *minor premise*. The final statement (in the Declaration, the announcement that George III need not be obeyed) is the *conclusion*. Let us present a simpler example of the basic syllogistic form:

> Tall men are good basketball players. (*Major premise*)
> Herbert is a tall man. (*Minor premise*)
> Herbert is a good basketball player. (*Conclusion*)

This is an example of valid deductive reasoning, although our willingness to credit the conclusion will depend on whether we accept the major and minor premises as true.

Deductive reasoning is sometimes phrased in grammatical forms different from the categorical statements used in the examples cited up to this point. Perhaps the argument will be presented in this form:

> If tariffs are lowered, world prosperity will be insured. (*Major premise*)
> Tariffs are being lowered. (*Minor premise*)
> World prosperity will be insured. (*Conclusion*)

Or the deduction may appear in the following way:

> Either tariffs will be lowered, or a world depression will be in the offing. (*Major premise*)
> Tariffs are not being lowered. (*Minor premise*)
> A world depression is in the offing. (*Conclusion*)

It should not be thought, of course, that when we make use of deductive arguments in our writing, we always, or even usually, spell them out in the form of syllogisms. More frequently, in writing or speaking, we find it necessary and desirable to state explicitly only portions—perhaps one premise and the conclusion—of the full syllogism. A written or spoken argument based on the syllogism just presented might set forth only the minor premise and the conclusion, in this fashion: Because tariffs are not being lowered, a world depression is in the offing. In this case, the major premise—either tariffs are lowered, or a world depression is in the offing—is not expressed. Constantly, in everyday conversation, we suppress as unnecessary one of the premises underlying our statements. "He's not trustworthy; he makes frivolous jokes about serious matters," someone may say, arguing from the implicit major premise, "People who make frivolous jokes about serious matters are not trustworthy." However, although we may seldom state a syllogism in full detail, familiarity with this logical pattern and the way it operates will help us comprehend the bases of our own thinking and that of the writers whose work we are reading.[5]

Detailed treatment of the way deductive argument functions, and of the formal errors which may occur in the syllogism, would be out of place here. However, several common sources of logical error should be guarded against. One of the most persistent errors springs from the fact that the writer has given inadequate attention to the precise way his statements have set up relationships among the classes of things or ideas he is considering. Let us examine an example:

[5] For illustrations, see Tocqueville, pp. 463–466, and Kronenberger, pp. 515–522.

Cities with highly trained police forces have low crime rates. (*Major premise*)

Zenith City has a low crime rate. (*Minor premise*)

Therefore, Zenith City must have a highly trained police force. (*Conclusion*)

Now, the conclusion may or may not be true, but it does not follow from the premises; restudy of the first two statements will show why the syllogism is not valid. The major premise asserts that the class "cities with highly trained police forces" is included in the class "cities having low crime rates." The minor premise points out that Zenith City belongs to the class "cities having low crime rates." This class may comprehend many subclasses in addition to the one first mentioned, "cities with highly trained police forces"; it might include "cities remote from metropolitan centers," or "cities with high average income," and so on. So, in this syllogism, the fact that Zenith City belongs to the class "cities having low crime rates" tells us nothing, for certain, about its membership in the class "cities with highly trained police forces." Except in the world of Alice in Wonderland, statements are not automatically reversible. Even if experience has taught us that all college professors are absent-minded, this does not entitle us to assume, without further research, that all absent-minded persons are college professors. Careful attention to the grammatical form in which our statements are cast, and to what the grammar suggests concerning the relationships among individuals and classes, will do much to prevent confusion in deductive argument.

Another source of error in deduction may be the writer's tendency, in the course of an argument, to modify the terms in which he is discussing a situation. Commonly this error takes the form of beginning with a statement which covers only a portion of a particular group, and then consciously or unconsciously, in the process of arguing, broadening it to cover the entire group. Thus, a writer who asserts (1) that persons who are emotional are not entitled to vote, and (2) that many women are excessively emotional, might advance the illogical conclusion that women in general are not entitled to vote. It is never legitimate for the narrower term—in this case, "many women"—to become converted in the heat of argument to a broader term—"women in general."

The process of clear-headed deduction may also be impeded by a practice sometimes called *begging the question*. This occurs when the reasoner buries the real point of the conclusion in one of the premises, so that, as a reason for the conclusion, he advances the conclusion itself in a slightly modified form. For example, a reader or listener would hardly feel satisfied if someone arguing for the inclusion of physical activity in a program of education did so by invoking the following premise: Physical activity is good for young people. Since we can take for granted that a program of education should include things that are good for young people, this premise does not develop the argument; it simply restates the conclusion in a different way. Or, if a critic condemns contemporary poetry on the ground that literature written since 1900 is not worth reading, we are left with the feeling that not much in the way of a substantial premise has been brought forward. Thoughtful attention to the meaning of the words we are using can help us avoid this kind of substitute for real reasoning.

ANALOGY

Less common than induction and deduction, but sometimes useful to the writer, is the form of reasoning which proceeds by noting known similarities between two objects, or ideas, or situations, and then suggesting that, since they are alike in so many ways, the two things being compared must be similar in still other ways not initially known to the observer. This procedure, known as *analogy*, has been used, for example, by a number of recent writers arguing in favor of some form of world government. These writers have compared the unsettled conditions existing in the United States during the decade of the 1780's with those existing in the world following World War II; the analogy is completed by arguing that, just as the adoption of the federal constitution solved the internal problems of the United States, so dissension among the nations today can best be eased by the creation of a world government. An analogy gains force in proportion to the number of relevant resemblances which can be developed between the two things which are being compared. Even so, an analogy standing by itself without other supporting forms of reasoning is usually regarded as a relatively weak kind of proof. The noting and tracing out of analogies often serve, however, to initiate productive lines of thought in all fields of inquiry; other forms of reasoning will be necessary to arrive at firm conclusions, but the observation of analogy provides the impetus for the investigation.[6] Also, as in the essay by Sir James Jeans (pp. 197–198), analogy provides a valuable way for the writer to clarify for the reader what he is trying to convey; something relatively remote

[6] Note Marston Bates's use of Toynbee, pp. 122–123.

from the reader's experience can be made more meaningful by comparing it with something familiar to him.

Thoughtful readers will observe, and be disturbed by, carelessness in the writer's handling of induction, deduction, and analogy. The same readers will be unfavorably impressed if the writer attempts to pass off, as logical argument, certain devices which make an irrelevant appeal to the reader's emotions and prejudices. Emotional appeals have, of course, an ancient and honorable place in argument. The procedures to be enumerated here differ, however, from honest invocations of emotion in that they attempt to masquerade as rational argument, and thus may mislead the unwary reader.

Chief among these devices is the so-called *argumentum ad hominem*— which generally takes the form of trying to undermine an opponent's argument by vilifying his character. The writer addresses himself, not to the substantial issues of the case, but to the task of destroying the reader's confidence in the integrity of men who hold an opposing view. Examples need not be supplied here; they can be plucked from the air when epithets fly during a political campaign. It may be equally irrelevant logically to point out that a person with whom one agrees is the soul of honesty and gentleness; these are admirable qualities, but they do not guarantee the soundness of his arguments.

Another frequently used substitute for reasoning is the suggestion that, since a belief is accepted by a great many people, it must be correct. Fortunately it is true that soundly reasoned arguments prove acceptable to most people, but the mere fact of widespread acceptance offers in itself no certain assurance that a particular idea is true. A somewhat similar device is employed by the writer or speaker who plays up, irrelevantly and excessively, his similarity to the mass of his audience; this masquerade is intended to suggest that, since he is "one of the boys," his ideas must be sound. At the opposite extreme from this emphasis on the writer's kinship with the common man is a device which might be described as the appeal to inappropriate authority; here the fact that a man has achieved eminence in one field—physics, perhaps, or business, or education—is cited to demonstrate that his views on all subjects are entitled to unusual respect.

The common characteristic of all these special appeals is that the writer or speaker, instead of concentrating his effort on the point at issue, devotes himself to discussing the characters of the people who have espoused particular points of view. Let us stress again that it is sometimes entirely natural and legitimate for a writer to describe the kinds of persons who accept certain beliefs; this should not be confused, however, with reasoned statement.

Finally, there should be mentioned two other common errors in reasoning which originate from misleading assumptions about the way ideas or events are related. One such error acquired in ancient times the title of the *post hoc ergo propter hoc* fallacy—in other words, the mistaken belief that because an event occurs *after* another event, it must be a *consequence* of the preceding event. This is the mistake of jumping to conclusions about a causal relationship between events which follow each other in a time sequence.[7] If an atomic experiment in Nevada is followed by a hurricane along the East Coast, the thoughtless observer may assume that the nuclear explosion caused the storm. Actually, as we realize when we take time for reflection, the establishment of causal relationships between events is a complex and difficult operation; it is wise, therefore, to be wary of arguments based on the notion that things related in a time sequence are also connected causally. A somewhat similar misconception is the *genetic fallacy*—which usually takes the form of arguing that, by describing the historical origin of an idea or an institution, we thereby pass judgment logically upon its present-day worth. Tom Paine, writing as a political pamphleteer, illustrated this fallacy by arguing against the British monarchy, as an eighteenth-century institution, on the ground that the line of English kings had unsavory origins in the eleventh century. In this fallacy, as in the preceding examples included in this section, the central job of reasoning has been side-stepped in order to follow diverting but essentially irrelevant by-paths.

REASONING AND ARGUMENT

Since this is a textbook for writers and readers, we need to repeat our earlier reminder that good habits of logical analysis are important tools for the person who wishes to communicate his ideas, but that, since they are tools, they are used in widely different ways in dealing with different concrete problems. The writer who regards his ability to reason as a kind of "logic machine," and simply turns it on automatically, at the same tempo and intensity, whenever he needs to communicate is not going to

[7] Fletcher Pratt is combating this fallacy in his interpretation of the Battle of Gettysburg, pp. 207–213.

be particularly persuasive in argument. The skillful writer recognizes that sometimes the formal development of a full deductive argument will serve his purposes; the authors of the Declaration of Independence, for example, apparently felt that the legal and political situation in 1776 required them to state and defend a real syllogism. Under other circumstances, and in other forms of writing, this kind of precise deduction would be intolerably pedantic and condescending. Also, the writer constantly faces choices between possible arguments which are equally valid logically, but which may differ greatly in probable effectiveness. The student who writes a petition to the dean requesting permission to transfer from one section of a course to another might invoke any one of a number of reasons for the change. Perhaps he just naturally dislikes arising promptly for an early morning class. Or perhaps he has a job which requires his presence at the hour of the early morning class. Either one of these reasons might be incorporated into an argument which would be logically sound; the chances are, however, that the two arguments would differ considerably in persuasiveness. For full effectiveness in writing, ability to reason must be accompanied by a variety of other characteristics—sensitivity to situations and people, flexibility in using the resources of the English language, judgment in deciding which parts of a subject to emphasize—in short, all the matters illustrated by the essays in this book.

2. Taking Another Look: The Art of Revision

With Illustrations from
FRANCIS BACON
SAMUEL JOHNSON
THOMAS JEFFERSON
ABRAHAM LINCOLN
HENRY JAMES
CARL BECKER

ONE OF the earliest uses of the word "revise" in the sense of "look or read carefully over, with a view to improving or correcting," is in the Preface to the King James Version of the Bible, in 1611. Presenting their work to the public, the translators of the Bible, one of the masterpieces of English prose, said, "Neither did we disdain to revise what we had done." Like the translators of the Bible, most good writers do not disdain to revise what they have done. Some revise extensively, some do little more than touch up their work; some revise repeatedly, others are satisfied to go over their work no more than once. Habits of composition are too individual and hence too variable to be reduced to general rules. But it is safe to say that every writer, at some point in his work, takes a second look. Our most famous writings were brought to their final form not in single bursts of inspiration but by degrees, more or less slowly and painfully. The Declaration of Independence and the Gettysburg Address, for example, may seem to us incapable of any but the verbal form in which we know them, but their histories reveal the stages of rethinking and rewriting through which that perfection was achieved.

The need for revision and the amount of time a writer can afford to give to it depend, of course, not only on his talent as a writer but on the importance of what he is writing and the time at his disposal. We can assume that Jefferson spent more time in polishing his draft of the Declaration of Independence than in revising a letter to his wife. And clearly the writer who doesn't start writing until the last moments before his deadline will scarcely have time for a second look. The extensive revisions carried out by some of the writers whose work is exhibited in this supplement would probably be impossible or impracticable in the composition of a class theme. But there is much to be gained from watching craftsmen at work, even if we must limit the scale on which we apply what we learn. Bearing in mind the many differences between one writing situation and another, and between one writer's favorite methods of work and another's, we have collected in this supplement a number of examples of revision by skillful writers, in the belief that they will demonstrate the value of revision and furnish useful materials for analysis.

Revision is a continuous process. In a sense we revise as we sort out our thoughts preparatory to putting words on paper, considering this phrase and that, rejecting one and then another and finally selecting one to write down. This part of the process of writing may seem largely unconscious, but with experience we can make it more deliberate and thereby more effective. Some writers do most of their revising at this stage, composing sentences and even whole paragraphs in their minds, committing them to paper only when they are satisfied that they have evolved a finished statement. For most writers, however, it helps to have something on paper to work on, and revision in the proper sense of taking another look begins when we actually start to write. We begin a sentence, decide that it isn't headed in the right direction, scratch it out, and start over again. We finish a sentence and go back to smooth a transition or to remove a part that we decide needs a sentence to itself. We try this word and that until we get the one we want. We cross out a paragraph as unessential or put a circle around it with a note that it is to be worked in later in the paper. Most first drafts are such complicated puzzles of deletions, interlineations, and marginal notes that only the writer can make continuous sense of them. That is why most writers, at this point, make a fair or clean copy of their first draft, and after letting it cool off for a while, look at it carefully again. For most of us, revision ends when we have revised our draft, amending it as best we can, and have copied or typed it in final form to be handed in, sent to the printer, delivered as a speech, or whatever. But some writers continue to revise beyond this point. Some make changes as they read the proofs returned to them by the printer. Winston Churchill, for example, is said to put his publishers to considerable trouble and expense by making substantial changes in the proofs of his books. And many authors revise their work between one printing and the next. Several of the exhibits collected in this supplement are revisions of this sort: the author takes the occasion of a reprinting of his book to work over his text, much as if it were an unpublished draft. Thus Francis Bacon expanded his essays each time they were reprinted, and Henry James revised his novels and stories for the collected edition of his fiction.

Although revision is best thought of as a continuous process of critical inspection and amendment, the crucial stage in the process, at any rate for most writers, is the revision of the first draft. There are good technical and psychological reasons for making a special effort to revise one's work at this point. With the whole composition before him the writer can inspect the plan of organization, the coherence and subordination of the parts, the relative scale in different sections of the paper, the transitions and other devices for insuring continuity—features of the composition that are difficult or impossible to appraise in the actual process of writing. By the time the writer has made a clean copy of his first draft, some of the heat of composition has passed away; the writer is already at a distance from his material and his first thoughts, he is less involved with what he has written, and he is therefore in a better position to take an objective look at his work. Even the page, when recopied, has an appearance sufficiently different from the original to help free the writer from the enchantment of his own words. The importance of this is in the fact that when we revise we have to be both writer and audience, creator and critic, and the more of the latter the better. The chances are that the writer knows perfectly well what he means when he writes a sentence; so far as he is concerned the sentence needn't be written in any other way. But the writer's obligation is not finally to himself but to his reader. He must look at what he has written from the point of view of a reader encountering his sentences for the first time. He can't stop with "I see what I mean"; he has to ask "Will anyone else see what I mean?" To ask this question and to answer it effectively, we have to be detached, objective, critical; we have to hunt out the pitfalls of expression and meaning in which the reader may be trapped and cover them before it is too late. And to do this the writer has to be ready to make sacrifices. He may have to hack to pieces the very sentences he has sweat over the most; he may have to throw out figures of speech that seemed happy inspirations at the moment of writing; he may need to discard material that he worked hard to find; and he may have to relocate paragraphs he had a hard time placing to begin with. The attitude of mind required in revision is a mature, and adult attitude; it takes time and effort to develop. Your writing instructor, in his comments on your papers, is performing for you part of the job of the critical reader, a job you will increasingly be able to do for yourself. You will reach that point more rapidly if you make a practice of taking a second look at a copy of your first draft, when the conditions will help you to cultivate detachment and objectivity.

James Boswell tells a story about Samuel Johnson that not only testifies to the value of revision but also distinguishes its principal kinds. Johnson was famous for his prose style, especially as exhibited in his paper *The Rambler*, and he was a great believer in revision. On one occasion he remarked in company that he had not always written his college exercises twice over, and this remark prompted a young lady present to say, in the manner of admiring young ladies, "I suppose, Sir, you could not make them better." This piece of flattery touched off the following conversation:

JOHNSON: Yes, Madam, to be sure, I could make them better. Thought is better than no thought.

MISS ADAMS: Do you think, Sir, you could make your Ramblers better?

JOHNSON: Certainly I could.

BOSWELL: I'll lay a bet, Sir, you cannot.

JOHNSON: But I will, Sir, if I choose. I shall make the best of them you shall pick out, better.

BOSWELL: But you may add to them. I will not allow of that.

JOHNSON: Nay, Sir, there are three ways of making them better:—putting out, —adding,—or correcting.

Putting out, adding, correcting—these are the three sorts of revision. We can reduce, we can expand, or we can correct or amend what is already there.

1. As Boswell saw, the simplest way for a good writer to improve his work is by expanding. This is what Bacon did in revising his essays. If you compare the three versions of the essay "Of Studies" (pp. 639–641) you will notice that most of the sentences in the 1597 and 1612 versions reappear without change, or with but slight change, in the 1625 version; the differences between the versions are produced mostly by the addition of examples and the amplification of the original precepts. The great final paragraph of Lincoln's First Inaugural Address (pp. 647–649) was an addition to his original version. Most of us need more practice in "putting

out" than in "adding," but it is important to develop some facility in expansion. One of the great defects of college writing is underdevelopment —paragraphs which, having announced an intention to go somewhere, never do; skimpy sections that do not contribute their proper share to the development of the theme; paragraphs that are too thin for the scale on which other paragraphs in the composition are worked out.

A brilliant illustration of what proper expansion can do for a paragraph is afforded by the opening of President Franklin Roosevelt's First Inaugural Address, March 4, 1933. The address was delivered to a nation on the verge of panic and economic paralysis; Roosevelt caught the imagination of the country with his statement that "the only thing we have to fear is fear itself." As originally written, the speech did not contain this famous sentence; the opening paragraph was not, in fact, especially distinguished in any way:

I am certain that my fellow Americans expect that on my induction to the Presidency I will address them with a candor and a decision which the present situation of our nation impels. This is no occasion of soft speaking or for the raising of false hopes.

Roosevelt's expansion of his draft converted this negative opening into a stirring appeal:

I am certain that my fellow Americans expect that on my induction into the Presidency I will address them with a candor and a decision which the present situation of our Nation impels. This is preeminently the time to speak the truth, the whole truth, frankly and boldly. Nor need we shrink from honestly facing conditions in our country today. This great Nation will endure as it has endured, will revive and will prosper. So, first of all, let me assert my firm belief that the only thing we have to fear is fear itself—nameless, unreasoning, unjustified terror which paralyzes needed efforts to convert retreat into advance. In every dark hour of our national life a leadership of frankness and vigor has met with that understanding and support of the people themselves which is essential to victory. I am convinced that you will again give that support to leadership in these critical days.[1]

But Roosevelt was not yet done. As he waited to appear on the Capitol steps to deliver his address he thought of a new opening sentence: "This

[1] See Samuel I. Rosenman, *Working with Roosevelt*, New York, Harper & Brothers, 1952, pp. 89–91.

is a day of consecration." And as he read his speech he made a final ad-lib addition: "This is a day of national consecration."

2. "Putting out," as Johnson called it, or reduction, is probably more often necessary than expansion; it is certainly more painful for the writer. The chief reasons for cutting are to remove deadwood in our sentences, to eliminate repetition, to reduce sentences and paragraphs that are too long either for their inherent substance or for their place in the scheme of the whole composition, and to bring the whole piece within a fixed space or time limit. Here, from Matthew Arnold, is a good example of the value of putting out. The paragraph is from Arnold's essay "Democracy" as first printed in the introduction to *Popular Education in France* (1861):

> In all the remarks which I am making, I impose on myself the rule carefully to abstain from any attempt to suggest a positive application of them. I do not presume to discuss in what manner the world of facts is to adapt itself to the changed world of ideas which I have been describing. I offer general considerations,—presented, I hope, without offensiveness, as I am sure they have been formed without prejudice—considerations suggested by watching the course of men and classes in this country, to the silent reflection of thinking minds. This an isolated individual, however humble, may fairly attempt; more he cannot attempt properly; perhaps the time has not yet come for more to be attempted at all. But one breach of my rule I shall here venture to commit, by dwelling for a moment on a matter of practical institution, designed to meet new social exigencies: on the intervention of the State in public education.

This runs to 160 words; it is repetitious and wooden; the tone is offensively modest. Now see what Arnold did with it when he revised it for inclusion in his *Mixed Essays* (1879):

> In all the remarks which I have been making, I have hitherto abstained from any attempt to suggest a positive application of them. I have limited myself to simply pointing out in how changed a world of ideas we are living; I have not sought to go further, and to discuss in what particular manner the world of facts is to adapt itself to this changed world of ideas. This has been my rule so far; but from this rule I shall here venture to depart, in order to dwell for a moment on a matter of practical institution, designed to meet new social exigencies: on the intervention of the State in public education.

He has reduced the paragraph by nearly a third, eliminating two offending sentences and easing the style; both meaning and tone are more effective as a result.

Sometimes, of course, reduction is made in the interest of subtler considerations, as when Lincoln reworked the end of his First Inaugural Address (pp. 647–649) to eliminate the uncompromising sternness of his original challenge to the South. Whatever the reason, most of the writers in the exhibits that follow have worked to cast out everything not essential. Good prose, like a well-trained athlete, carries no excess poundage.

3. Johnson's third method of improvement, "correcting," is the largest category. It includes, obviously, the correction of errors of substance, as when Becker takes the philosopher Abelard out of the thirteenth century and puts him in the twelfth (p. 660), and errors of usage, real or imaginary, as when Becker changes "nothing could have been *further* from the intention of the founders" to "nothing could have been *farther* from the intention of the founders" and then changes it back, in his final text, to *further* (pp. 664–665). But correction goes beyond the elimination of errors. It includes the amendment of weak or vapid sentences. In the serialized version of his novel *The Secret Agent* Joseph Conrad permitted a character to say that certain actions were "not so effective as a person not having thought the matter over might think." Since the character speaking is not supposed to be fatuous, Conrad in the book version has him say "not so effective as a person of an ordinary mind might think." The first draft of the Gettysburg Address read in part as follows:

We are met on a great battlefield of that war. We have come to dedicate a portion of it, as a final resting place for those who died here, that the nation might live. This we may, in all propriety, do.

The last sentence is notably awkward in movement and stilted in tone, and it provides only a weak base for the paragraph that follows. Lincoln altered it to the sentence we all know: "It is altogether fitting and proper that we should do this."

Beyond the correction of errors and the elimination of weaknesses, "correction" may include almost any sort of improvement. The list is as long as grammar, logic, and rhetoric; there is room here for only a few examples. Rhythm, emphasis, and continuity may be improved, as they are when Lincoln changes "a final resting place for those who died here, that the nation might live" to "a final resting place for those who here gave their lives that that nation might live." The wording may be made more precise, as in Lincoln's alteration of "The world will little note, nor long remember what we say here; *while* it can never forget what they did here" to "*but* it can never forget what they did here." Or in his shift from "the brave men, living and dead, who struggled here, have *hallowed* it far above our poor power to add or detract" to "have *consecrated* it. . . ." Correction may produce a significant change of tone or bring out a nuance of meaning. This happens in many of Henry James's revisions; he gets such an effect, for example, in his story "Four Meetings" when he re-names the hometown of the romantic Miss Spencer, who yearns to visit Europe—when *Grimwinter* becomes *North Verona* something is added to our sense of the heroine's predicament. And we can see a similar shift in meaning when "We hold these truths to be sacred and undeniable" is changed, by Jefferson or Franklin, to "We hold these truths to be self-evident." Beyond these modes of "correction" is a further range of improvement in continuity, subordination, focus on the central theme, and adaptation to the audience.

To Johnson's three sorts of revision we may add a minor fourth. Though minor, it is something the writer has to watch out for. We often have to tidy up the area in which we have made a revision, to bring the context into line with the parts that have been changed. In the draft of his book *Modern Democracy* (Yale, 1941), Carl Becker wrote:

All human institutions, we are told, have their ideal forms laid up in heaven, and we do not need to be told that the actual institutions conform but indifferently to these ideal counterparts. It would be possible then to define democracy either in terms of the real or in terms of the ideal form—to define it as government of the people, by the politicians, for the vested interests; or to define it as the classless society in which government has conveniently withered away.

This he decided to revise, probably because "the classless society in which government has conveniently withered away" is clearly neither an ideal nor a real form of democracy, since it isn't a government at all. The last sentence he therefore revised to read

It would be possible then to define democracy either in terms of the real or in terms of the ideal form—to define it as government of the people, by the people, for the people; or to define it as government of the people, by the politicians, for whatever pressure groups can get their interests taken care of.

This revision necessitated another one. The order of the illustrative definitions, first the ideal and then the real, now reverses the order forecast by the earlier part of the sentence as originally written. So Becker makes one more change, so that the sentence reads "It would be possible then to define democracy either in terms of the ideal or in terms of the real form."

We will postpone the exhibits only long enough to illustrate all of the major sorts of revision in a sequence of eight versions of a single sentence, from Becker's "Life and Learning in the United States." Becker is explaining how, as a result of the French Revolution, the liberal and equalitarian philosophy of the eighteenth century came to be discredited. These are the stages through which a single sentence passed:

1. For the educated and governing classes, both in Europe and America, the term "revolution" was apt to recall the word "Jacobinism," and Jacobinism was apt to signify mob rule in politics and atheism in religion.

2. . . . and Jacobinism was apt to signify, *in respect to politics, mob rule, and in respect to religion, atheism.*

3. . . . and Jacobinism was apt to signify *political anarchy and religious infidelity.*

4. For the educated and governing classes, *at the opening of the nineteenth century,* both in Europe and America, the term "revolution" was apt to recall the word "Jacobinism," and Jacobinism was apt to signify political anarchy and religious infidelity.

5. *At the opening of the nineteenth century, the* educated and governing classes, both in Europe and America, *were apt to regard* the term "revolution" *as synonymous with* the word "Jacobinism," and Jacobinism was apt to signify political anarchy and religious infidelity.

6. . . . the educated and governing classes, both in Europe and America, *were in a mood* to regard the word "revolution" as synonymous with "jacobinism," and "jacobinism" *was for them the same thing as* political anarchy and religious infidelity.

7. . . . "jacobinism" was for them the same thing as *political and moral anarchy.*

8. At the opening of the nineteenth century, the educated and governing classes, both in Europe and America, were in a mood to regard the word "revolution" as synonymous with *the word* "Jacobinism," and "Jacobinism" was for them *much* the same thing as political and moral anarchy.

The examples that follow will be of greatest value if you will locate the changes each author has made and then try to reproduce the line of thought that led him to make them. We have tried to select examples of revision made for a wide variety of purposes, and you should try to distinguish as many intentions as possible, with specific reference to the details of the context. You may not agree with the writers in every instance, for revision, although it is always intended as improvement, is not invariably successful. But whether you agree with the writer or not, you will find that the attempt to retrace the writer's reasoning will give you leads for the improvement of your own writing.

$$\smile$$

I. Francis Bacon, "Of Studies"

Three versions of the essay

A. 1597 Version

Studies serve for pastimes, for ornaments, and for abilities. Their chief use for pastime is in privateness and retiring; for ornament is in discourse; and for ability is in judgment. For expert men can execute, but learned men are fittest to judge or censure.

¶ To spend too much time in them is sloth; to use them too much for ornament is affectation; to make judgment wholly by their rules is the humour of a scholar. ¶ They perfect Nature, and are perfected by experience. ¶ Crafty men contemn them, simple men admire them, wise men use them: for they teach not their own use, but that is a wisdom without them, and above them, won by observation. ¶ Read not to contradict, nor to believe, but to weigh and consider. ¶ Some books are to be tasted, others to be swallowed, and some few to be chewed and digested: that is, some books are to be read only in parts; others to be read, but cursorily; and some few to be read wholly and with diligence and attention. ¶ Reading maketh a full man, conference a ready man, and writing an exact man. And therefore if a man write little, he had need have a great memory; if he confer little, he had need have a present wit; and if he read little, he had need have much cunning, to seem to know that he doth not. ¶ Histories make men wise, poets witty; the mathemathics subtle, natural philosophy deep; moral grave, logic and rhetoric able to contend.

B. 1612 Version

Studies serve for delight, for ornament, and for ability; their chief use for delight, is in privateness and retiring; for ornament, is in discourse; and for ability, is in judgment. For expert men can execute, but learned men are fittest to judge or censure. To spend too much time in them, is sloth; to use them too much for ornament, is affectation; to make judgment wholly by their rules, is the humour of a scholar. They perfect nature, and are perfected by experience. Crafty men contemn them, simple men admire them, and wise men use them. For they teach not their own use, but that is a wisdom without them, and above them, won by observation. Read not to contradict, nor to believe, but to weigh and consider. Some books are to be tasted, others to be swallowed, and some few to be chewed and digested. That is, some books are to be read only in parts; others to be read, but not curiously; and some few to be read wholly, and with diligence and attention. Reading maketh a full man, conference a ready man, and writing an exact man. And therefore if a man write little, he had need have a great memory; if he confer little, he had need have a present wit; and if he read little, he had need have much cunning, to seem to know that he doth not. Histories make men wise, poets witty, the mathematics subtle, natural philosophy deep, morall grave, logic and rhetoric able to contend. *Abeunt studia in mores.*[1] Nay, there is no stond or impediment in the wit, but may be wrought out by fit studies: like as diseases of the body may have appropriate exercises. Bowling is good for the stone and reins; shooting for the lungs and breast; gentle walking for the stomach; riding for the head, and the like. So if a man's wit be wandering, let him study the mathematics; if his wit be not apt to distinguish, or find difference, let him study the schoolmen; if it be not apt to beat over matters and to find out resemblances, let him study lawyers' cases. So every defect of the mind may have a special receipt.

C. 1625 Version

Studies serve for delight, for ornament, and for ability. Their chief use for delight, is in privateness and retiring; for ornament, is in discourse; and for ability, is in the judgment and disposition of business. For expert men can execute, and perhaps judge of particulars, one by one; but the general counsels, and the plots and marshalling of affairs, come best from those that are learned. To spend too much time in studies is sloth; to use them too much for ornament is affectation; to make judgment wholly by their rules, is the humour of a scholar. They perfect nature, and are perfected by experience: for natural abilities are like natural plants, that need pruning by study; and studies themselves do give forth directions too much at large, except they be bounded in by experience. Crafty men contemn studies, simple men admire them, and wise men use them; for

[1] Studies pass into manners.

they teach not their own use; but that is a wisdom without them, and above them, won by observation. Read not to contradict and confute; nor to believe and take for granted; nor to find talk and discourse; but to weigh and consider. Some books are to be tasted, others to be swallowed, and some few to be chewed, and digested; that is, some books are to read only in parts; others to be read, but not curiously; and some few to be read wholly, and with diligence and attention. Some books also may be read by deputy, and extracts made of them by others; but that would be only in the less important arguments, and the meaner sort of books; else distilled books are like common distilled waters, flashy things. Reading maketh a full man; conference a ready man; and writing an exact man. And therefore, if a man write little, he had need have a great memory; if he confer little, he had need have a present wit; and if he read little, he had need have much cunning, to seem to know that he doth not. Histories make men wise; poets witty; the mathematics subtle; natural philosophy deep; moral grave; logic and rhetoric able to contend. *Abeunt studia in mores.* Nay, there is no stond or impediment in the wit, but may be wrought out by fit studies: like as diseases of the body may have appropriate exercises. Bowling is good for the stone and reins; shooting for the lungs and breast; gentle walking for the stomach; riding for the head, and the like. So if a man's wit be wandering, let him study the mathematics; for in demonstrations, if his wit be called away ever so little, he must begin again. If his wit be not apt to distinguish and find differences, let him study the schoolmen, for they are *cymini sectores.*[2] If he be not apt to beat over matters, and to call up one thing to prove and illustrate another, let him study the lawyers' cases. So every defect of the mind may have a special receipt.

II. Samuel Johnson, *The Rambler*

Passages from the original edition of 1751–52 and the
revised edition of 1756

A. 1751–52 Version

The greater part of moralists, like other writers, instead of casting their eyes abroad into the living world, and endeavoring to form from their

[2] Hairsplitters.

own observations new maxims of practice and new hints of theory, content themselves with that secondary knowledge which the perusal of books affords, and think themselves entitled to reverence and to fame by a new arrangement of an ancient system, or new illustration of established principles. (No. 129, June 11, 1751)

1756 Version

Moralists, like other writers, instead of casting their eyes abroad in the living world, and endeavoring to form maxims of practice and new hints of theory, content their curiosity with that secondary knowledge which books afford, and think themselves entitled to reverence by a new arrangement of an ancient system, or new illustration of established principles.

B. 1751–52 Version

Advice is generally offensive, not because it lays us open to regret, or convicts us of any fault which had escaped our notice, but because it shows us that we are known to others as well as to ourselves, that our artifices of hypocrisy have been detected, or that the fear of our resentment has lost its influence, and the officious monitor is persecuted with hatred, not because his accusation is considered as false, but because he assumes that superiority which we are not willing to grant him, has dared to detect what we endeavored to conceal, and to utter what his awe or his tenderness ought to have suppressed. (No. 155, September 10, 1751)

1756 Version

Advice is offensive, not because it lays us open to unexpected regret, or convicts us of any fault which had escaped our notice, but because it shows us that we are known to others as well as to ourselves: and the officious monitor is persecuted with hatred, not because his accusation is false, but because he assumes that superiority which we are not willing to grant him, and has dared to detect what we desired to conceal.

C. 1751–52 Version

The mischief of flattery is that of suppressing the influence of honest ambition, by an opinion that honor may be gained without the toil of merit; and the benefit of advice arises commonly from the discovery which it affords of the public opinion. He that could withstand conscience is frightened at infamy, and shame prevails when reason is defeated. (No. 155)

1756 Version

The mischief of flattery is, not that it persuades any man that he is what he is not, but that it suppresses the influence of honest ambition, by raising an opinion that honor may be gained without the toil of merit; and the benefit of advice arises commonly, not from any new light imparted to the mind, but from the discovery which it affords of the public suffrages. He that could withstand conscience is frightened at infamy, and shame prevails when reason is defeated.

D. 1751–52 Version

Observation will every hour furnish some instance in confirmation of Tully's precept. (No. 179, December 3, 1751)

1756 Version

Every hour furnishes some confirmation of Tully's precept.

E. 1751–52 Version

No man, surely, can think the conduct of his own life unworthy his attention, yet, among the sons of learning, many may be found, who seem to have thought of every thing rather than of themselves, and have never condescended to observe what passes daily before their eyes. Men, who while they are toiling through the intricacy of complicated systems, are insuperably embarrassed with the least perplexity in common affairs, and while they are comparing the actions, and ascertaining the characters of ancient heroes, let their days glide away without examination, and suffer vicious habits to encroach upon their minds without resistance or detection. (No. 180, December 7, 1751)

1756 Version

No man can imagine the course of his own life, or the conduct of the world around him, unworthy his attention; yet among the sons of learning many seem to have thought of every thing rather than of themselves, and to have observed every thing but what passes before their eyes: many who toil through the intricacy of complicated systems, are insuperably embarrassed with the least perplexity in common affairs; many who compare the actions and ascertain the characters of ancient heroes, let their own days glide away without examination, and suffer vicious habits to encroach upon their minds without resistance or detection.

F. 1751–52 Version

The general cause of that hostility which is perpetually exercised between one man and another is the desire of many for that which only few can possess. (No. 183, December 17, 1751)

1756 Version

The hostility perpetually exercised between one man and another is caused by the desire of many for that which only few can possess.

G. 1751–52 Version

This universal and incessant competition produces two motives to injury and malice; interest and envy, the hope of adding to our possessions what we can take from another, and the hope of alleviating the sense of our disparity by lessening another, though we gain nothing to ourselves. . . . Interest always requires some qualities not universally bestowed. The ruin of another will produce no profit to him who has not discernment to mark his advantage, courage to seize, or activity to pursue it; but the cold malignity of envy may be exerted in a torpid and quiescent state, amidst the gloom of stupidity, in the coverts of cowardice. He that falls by the attacks of interest, dies like him who is torn by hungry tigers; he may discover and resist his enemies. He that perishes in the ambushes of envy, is destroyed by unknown and invisible assailants, and dies like him who is suffocated by a poisonous vapor, without knowledge of his danger or possibility of contest. (No. 183)

1756 Version

This universal and incessant competition produces injury and malice by two motives, interest and envy; the prospect of adding to our possessions what we can take from others, and the hope of alleviating the sense of our disparity by lessening others, though we gain nothing to ourselves. . . . Interest requires some qualities not universally bestowed. The ruin of another will produce no profit to him who has not discernment to mark his advantage, courage to seize and activity to pursue it; but the cold malignity of envy may be exerted in a torpid and quiescent state, amidst the gloom of stupidity, in the coverts of cowardice. He that falls by the attacks of interest is torn by hungry tigers; he may discover and resist his enemies. He that perishes in the ambushes of envy is destroyed by unknown and invisible assailants, and dies like a man suffocated by a poisonous vapor, without knowledge of his danger, or possibility of contest.

III. The Declaration of Independence

Opening and closing paragraphs, from Thomas Jefferson's draft and from the version finally adopted by the Continental Congress

A. The Draft

When in the course of human events it becomes necessary for a people to advance from that subordination in which they have hitherto remained, & to assume among the powers of the earth the equal & independent station to which the laws of nature & of nature's god entitle them, a decent respect to the opinions of mankind requires that they should declare the causes which impel them to the change.

We hold these truths to be sacred and undeniable; that all men are created equal & independent, that from that equal creation they derive rights inherent & inalienable, among which are the preservation of life, & liberty, & the pursuit of happiness; that to secure these ends, governments are instituted among men. . . .

Final Version

When in the Course of human events, it becomes necessary for one people to dissolve the political bands which have connected them with another, and to assume among the powers of the earth, the separate and equal station to which the Laws of Nature and of Nature's God entitle them, a decent respect to the opinions of mankind requires that they should declare the causes which impel them to the separation. We hold these truths to be self-evident, that all men are created equal, that they are endowed by their Creator with certain unalienable Rights, that among these are Life, Liberty and the pursuit of Happiness. That to secure these rights, Governments are instituted among Men. . . .

B. *The Draft*

[The British people] too have been deaf to the voice of justice & of consanguinity, & when occasions have been given them, by the regular course of their laws, of removing from their councils the disturbers of our harmony, they have by their free election re-established them in power. At this very time too they are permitting their chief magistrate to send over not only soldiers of our common blood, but Scotch & foreign mercenaries to invade & deluge us in blood. These facts have given the last stab to agonizing affection, and manly spirit bids us to renounce for ever these unfeeling brethren. We must endeavour to forget our former love for them, and to hold them as we hold the rest of mankind, enemies in war, in peace friends. We might have been a free & a great people together; but a communication of grandeur & of freedom it seems is below their dignity. Be it so, since they will have it: the road to glory & happiness is open to us too; we will climb it in a separate state, and acquiesce in the necessity which pronounces our everlasting Adieu!

We therefore the representatives of the United States of America in General Congress assembled do, in the name & by authority of the good people of these states, reject and renounce all allegiance & subjection to the kings of Great Britain & all others who may hereafter claim by, through, or under them; we utterly dissolve & break off all political connection which may have heretofore subsisted between us & the people or parliament of Great Britain; and finally we do assert and declare these colonies to be free and independent states, and that as free & independent states they shall hereafter have power to levy war, conclude peace, contract alliances, establish commerce, & to do all other acts and things which independent states may of right do. And for the support of this declaration we mutually pledge to each other our lives, our fortunes, & our sacred honour.

Final Version

[The British people] too have been deaf to the voice of justice and of consanguinity. We must, therefore, acquiesce in the necessity, which denounces our Separation, and hold them, as we hold the rest of mankind, Enemies in War, in Peace Friends.

We, therefore, the Representatives of the United States of America, in General Congress, Assembled, appealing to the Supreme Judge of the world for the rectitude of our intentions, do, in the Name, and by Authority of the good People of these Colonies, solemnly publish and declare, That these united colonies are, and of Right ought to be Free and Independent States; that they are Absolved from all Allegiance to the British crown, and that all political connection between them and the State of Great Britain, is and ought to be totally dissolved; and that as Free and Independent States, they have full Power to levy War, conclude Peace, contract Alliances, establish Commerce, and to do all other Acts and Things which Independent States may of right do. And for the support of this Declaration, with a firm reliance on the protection of divine Providence, we mutually pledge to each other our Lives, our Fortunes, and our sacred Honor.

IV. Abraham Lincoln, First Inaugural Address, March 4, 1861

First edition and final text of the closing paragraphs

First Edition

My countrymen, one and all, take *time* and think *well*, upon this whole subject. Nothing valuable can be lost by taking time. Nothing worth preserving is either breaking or burning. If there be an object to *hurry* any of you, in hot haste, to a point where you would never go *deliberately*, that object will be frustrated by taking time; but no good object can be frustrated by it. Such of you as are now dissatisfied, still have the old Constitution unimpaired, and, on the sensitive point, the laws of your own framing under it; while the new administration will have no immediate power, if it would, to change either. If it were admitted that you who are dissatisfied, hold the right side in the dispute, there still is no single good reason for precipitate action. Intelligence, patriotism, Christianity, and a firm reliance on Him, who has never yet forsaken this favored land, are still competent to adjust, in the best way, all our present difficulty.

In *your* hands, my dissatisfied fellow countrymen, and not in *mine*, is the momentous issue of civil war. The government will not assail *you*, unless you *first* assail *it*. You can have no conflict, without being yourselves the aggressors. *You* have no oath registered in Heaven to destroy the government, while *I* shall have the most solemn one to "preserve, protect, and defend" it. *You* can forbear the *assault* upon it; *I* can *not* shrink from the *defense* of it. With *you*, and not with *me*, is the solemn question of "Shall it be peace, or a sword?"

NOTE: William H. Seward, Lincoln's Secretary of State, from whom he had solicited comments on the first edition of his Address, suggested the following as a closing paragraph:

I close. We are not, we must not be aliens or enemies but fellow countrymen and brethren. Although passion has strained our bonds of affection too hardly, they must not, I am sure they will not be broken. The mystic chords which, proceeding from so many battle fields and so many patriot graves, pass through all the hearts and all the hearths in this broad continent of ours, will yet again harmonize in this ancient music when breathed upon by the guardian angel of the nation.

Lincoln himself had written the following sentence on a separate slip of paper, evidently as a possible insertion in the speech:

Americans, all, we are not enemies, but friends. We have sacred ties of affection which, though strained by passion, let us hope can never be broken.

Final Text

My countrymen, one and all, think calmly and *well*, upon this whole subject. Nothing valuable can be lost by taking time. If there be an object to *hurry* any of you, in hot haste, to a step which you would never take *deliberately*, that object will be frustrated by taking time; but no good object can be frustrated by it. Such of you as are now dissatisfied, still have the old Constitution unimpaired, and, on the sensitive point, the laws of your own framing under it; while the new administration will have no immediate power, if it would, to change either. If it were admitted that you who are dissatisfied, hold the right side in the dispute, there still is no single good reason for precipitate action. Intelligence, patriotism, Christianity, and a firm reliance on Him, who has never yet forsaken this favored land, are still competent to adjust, in the best way, all our present difficulty.

In *your* hands, my dissatisfied fellow countrymen, and not in *mine*, is the momentous issue of civil war. The government will not assail *you*.

You can have no conflict, without being yourselves the aggressors. *You* have no oath registered in Heaven to destroy the government, while *I* shall have the most solemn one to "preserve, protect and defend" it.

I am loath to close. We are not enemies, but friends. We must not be enemies. Though passion may have strained, it must not break our bonds of affection. The mystic chords of memory, stretching from every battle-field, and patriot grave, to every living heart and hearthstone, all over this broad land, will yet swell the chorus of the Union, when again touched, as surely they will be, by the better angels of our nature.

~

V. Henry James, "The Passionate Pilgrim"

Three versions of one passage

1871 Version

The latent preparedness of the American mind for even the most delectable features of English life is a fact I never fairly probed to the depths. The roots of it are so deeply buried in the virgin soil of our primary culture that, without some great upheaval of experience, it would be hard to say exactly when and where and how it begins. It makes an American's enjoyment of England an emotion more fatal and sacred than his enjoyment, say, of Italy or Spain. I had seen the coffee-room of the Red Lion years ago, at home—at Saragossa, Illinois—in books, in visions, in dreams, in Dickens, in Smollett, in Boswell. It was small, and subdivided into six small compartments by a series of perpendicular screens of mahogany, something higher than a man's stature, furnished on either side with a narrow, uncushioned ledge, esteemed in ancient Britain a seat. In each of the little dining-boxes thus immutably constituted was a small table, which in crowded seasons was expected to accommodate the several agents of a fourfold British hungriness. But crowded seasons had passed away from the Red Lion forever. It was crowded only with memories and ghosts and atmosphere. . . . While I was waiting for my chop there came into the room a person whom I took to be my sole fellow-lodger. He seemed, like myself, to have submitted to proposals for dinner; the table on the other side of my partition had been prepared to receive him. He walked up to the fire, exposed his back to it, consulted his watch, and looked apparently out of the window, but really at me. He was a man of something less than middle age and more than middle stature, though indeed you would have called him neither young nor tall. He was chiefly remarkable for his exaggerated leanness. His hair, very thin on the summit of his head, was dark, short, and fine. His eye was of a pale, turbid gray, unsuited, perhaps, to his dark hair and brow, but not altogether out of harmony with his colourless, bilious complexion. His nose was aquiline and delicate; beneath it hung a thin, comely black mustache. His mouth and chin were meagre and uncertain of outline; not vulgar, perhaps, but weak. A cold, fatal, gentlemanly weakness, indeed, seemed expressed in his elegant person. His eye was restless and deprecating; his whole physiognomy, his manner of shifting his weight from foot to foot, the spiritless forward droop of his head, told of exhausted purpose, of a will relaxed. His dress was neat and careful, with an air of half-mourning. I made up my mind on three points: he was unmarried, he was ill, he was not an Englishman. (*Atlantic Monthly*, March 1871)

1885 Version

The latent preparedness of the American mind for even the most characteristic features of English life is a fact I never have got to the bottom of. The roots of it are so deeply buried in the soil of our early culture that, without some great upheaval of experience, it would be hard to say exactly when and where and how it begins. It makes an American's enjoyment of England an emotion more intimate, as the French say, than his enjoyment, for instance, of Italy or Spain. I had seen the coffee-room of the Red Lion years ago, at home—at Saragossa, Illinois—in books, in visions, in dreams, in Dickens, in Smollett, in Boswell. It was small, and subdivided into six narrow compartments by a series of perpendicular screens of mahogany, something higher than a man's stature, furnished on either side with a meagre uncushioned ledge, denominated in ancient Britain a seat. In each of these rigid receptacles was a small table, which in crowded seasons was expected to accommodate no less than four pairs of active British elbows. But crowded seasons had passed away from the Red Lion forever. It was crowded only with memories and ghosts and atmosphere. . . . While I was waiting for my chop there came into the room a person whom, after I had looked at him a moment, I supposed to be a fellow-lodger, and probably the only one. He seemed, like myself, to have submitted to proposals for dinner; the table on the other side of my partition had been prepared to receive him. He walked up to the fire, exposed his back to it, consulted his watch, and looked apparently out of the window, but really at me. He was a man of something less than middle age and more than middle stature, though indeed you would have called him neither young nor tall. He was chiefly remarkable for his exaggerated leanness. His hair, very thin on the summit of his head, was dark, short, and fine. His eye was of a pale, turbid gray, unsuited, perhaps, to his dark hair and well-drawn brows, but not altogether out of harmony with his colourless, bilious complexion. His nose was aquiline and delicate; beneath it reposed a soft, horizontal moustache. His mouth and chin were meagre and uncertain of outline; not vulgar, perhaps, but weak. A cold, fatal, gentlemanly weakness, indeed, seemed expressed in his attenuated person. His eye was restless and deprecating; his whole physiognomy, his manner of shifting his weight from foot to foot, the spiritless droop of his head, told of exhausted intentions, of a will relaxed. His dress was neat and careful, and he might have been in mourning. I made up my mind on three points: he was a bachelor, he was out of health, he was not indigenous to the soil. (*Stories Revived*, 1885)

1908 Version

The latent preparedness of the American mind even for the most characteristic features of English life was a matter I meanwhile failed to get to the bottom of. The roots of it are indeed so deeply buried in the soil of our early culture that, without some great upheaval of feeling, we are at a loss to say exactly when and where and how it begins. It makes an American's enjoyment of England an emotion more searching than anything Continental. I had seen the coffee-room of the Red Lion years ago, at home—at Saragossa, Illinois—in books, in visions, in dreams, in Dickens, in Smollett, in Boswell. It was small and subdivided into six narrow compartments by a series of perpendicular screens of mahogany, something higher than a man's stature, furnished on either side with a meagre uncushioned ledge, denominated in ancient Britain a seat. In each of these rigid receptacles was a narrow table—a table expected under stress to accommodate no less than four pairs of active British elbows. High pressure indeed had passed away from the Red Lion for ever. It now knew only that of memories and ghosts and atmosphere. . . .

While I was waiting there for my chop there came into the room a person whom, after I had looked at him a moment, I supposed to be a fellow-lodger and probably the only one. He seemed, like myself, to have submitted to proposals for dinner; the table on the other side of my partition had been prepared to receive him. He walked up to the fire, exposed his back to it, and, after consulting his watch, looked directly out of the window and indirectly at me. He was a man of something less than middle age and more than middle stature, though indeed you would have called him neither young nor tall. He was chiefly remarkable for his emphasised leanness. His hair, very thin on the summit of his head, was dark, short and fine. His eye was of a pale turbid gray, unsuited, perhaps, to his dark hair and well-drawn brows, but not altogether out of harmony with his colourless bilious complexion. His nose was aquiline and delicate; beneath it his moustache languished much rather than bristled. His mouth and chin were negative, or at the most provisional; not vulgar, doubtless, but ineffectually refined. A cold fatal gentlemanly weakness was expressed indeed in his attenuated person. His eye was restless and deprecating; his whole physiognomy, his manner of shifting his weight from foot to foot, the spiritless droop of his head, told of exhausted intentions, of a will relaxed. His dress was neat and "toned down"—he might have been in mourning. I made up my mind on three points: he was a bachelor, he was out of health, he was not indigenous to the soil. (*The Novels and Tales of Henry James*, Vol. XIII [New York: Scribner's, 1908])

VI. Henry James, "Four Meetings"

Two versions of one passage

1877 Version

Miss Caroline Spencer was not exactly a beauty, but she was a charming little figure. She must have been close upon thirty, but she was made almost like a little girl, and she had the complexion of a child. She had a very pretty head, and her hair was arranged as nearly as possible like the hair of a Greek bust, though indeed it was to be doubted if she had ever seen a Greek bust. She was "artistic," I suspected, so far as Grimwinter allowed such tendencies. She had a soft, surprised eye, and thin lips, with very pretty teeth. Round her neck she wore what ladies call, I believe, a "ruche," fastened with a very small pin in pink coral, and in her hand she carried a fan made of plaited straw and adorned with pink ribbon. She wore a scanty black silk dress. She spoke with a kind of soft precision, showing her white teeth between her narrow but tender-looking lips, and she seemed extremely pleased, even a little fluttered, at the prospect of my demonstrations. (*Scribner's*, November 1877)

1909 Version

Miss Caroline Spencer was not quite a beauty, but was none the less, in her small odd way, formed to please. Close upon thirty, by every presumption, she was made almost like a little girl and had the complexion of a child. She had also the prettiest head, on which her hair was arranged as nearly as possible like the hair of a Greek bust, though indeed it was to be doubted if she had ever seen a Greek bust. She was "artistic," I suspected, so far as the polar influences of North Verona could allow for such yearnings or could minister to them. Her eyes were perhaps just too round and too inveterately surprised, but her lips had a certain mild decision and her teeth, when she showed them, were charming. About her neck she wore what ladies call, I believe, a "ruche" fastened with a very small pin of pink coral, and in her hand she carried a fan made of plaited straw and adorned with pink ribbon. She wore a scanty black silk dress. She spoke with slow soft neatness, even without smiles showing the prettiness of her teeth, and she seemed extremely pleased, in fact quite fluttered, at the prospect of my demonstrations. (*The Novels and Tales of Henry James*, Vol. XVI [New York: Scribner's, 1909])

VII. Carl Becker, "Life and Learning in the United States"

Revised manuscript and final text

"Life and Learning in the United States" is the opening chapter of Carl Becker's *Cornell University: Founders and the Founding* (Cornell University Press, 1943). The selection given here is the first ten pages of this chapter. The final text is reprinted by permission of the Cornell University Press. The manuscript is printed through the courtesy of the Cornell University Library.

Since Becker's handwriting is frequently difficult to decipher, and since many of his corrections can be read only after close study of the manuscript itself, the editors have prepared a copy of the original manuscript. Manuscript and final text are printed on facing pages to facilitate comparison of the versions.

LIFE AND LEARNING IN THE UNITED STATES

I have often wondered what the United States would be like if it
at another time and
had been first settled by other people ~~and at an earlier time~~ --say in the
seaboard settled
thirteenth century, the eastern ~~coast~~ by Norman French, the western by
Chinese, and the two frontiers, ~~simultaneously~~ expanding east and west,
subsequently meeting on a line running roughly from New Orleans to Minneapolis through Kansas City and Omaha. It's an intriguing thought. Unfor-
prosaic   *greatest*
tunately, we must be resigned to the fact that the settlements of ~~decisive~~
importance for the future history of the United States were made chiefly
by Englishmen and in the seventeenth century.

Whether the institutions of the United States were an inheritance
from Europe or devised to meet the novel conditions of the American wilderness is much disputed. I cannot ~~answer~~ decide that dispute; but certainly the first settlers had acquired in England certain ideas about politics,
morality, and religion that must have had a decisive influence in determining the original form of the institutions they established in Virginia and
America
New England and elsewhere. Among the ideas thus brought to ~~the new world~~
were the ideas then prevailing in England about schools and universities.
might be thought
In this respect the seventeenth century ~~was~~ a bad time for the United States
to begin its institutional career. At almost no other time, certainly not
century,
~~in~~ the thirteenth could the first settlers have brought to these shores
a set of ideas more restricted or less promising for the promotion of
~~America.~~
learning in ~~the United States.~~ *the new world.*

In seventeenth century England, as in Europe generally, the prevailing idea was that schools and universities should teach nothing that would
discredit the established religion or the authority of kings and magistrates.
Francis Bacon, for example, protested against scholasticism and a slavish worship of the an-
There were, it is true, a few voices raised in protest. Milton complained *cient writers.*
that professors "take from young men the use of reason by certain charms
so
compounded of metaphysics, miracles and absurd scriptures," ~~and said~~ that
at Cambridge,
he had misspent his youth, ~~at Cambridge,~~ trying to "digest an asinine
feast of sow-thistles and brambles." And John Hall, himself a teacher at
Cambridge, maintained that the advancement of learning was thwarted by incompetent professors teaching outmoded subjects. But such voices were unheeded, and ~~scarcely un~~ what they said scarcely understood. Even Leibnitz

LIFE AND LEARNING IN THE UNITED STATES

I have often wondered what the United States would be like if it had been first settled at another time and by other people—if it had been settled, say, in the thirteenth century, the eastern seaboard by the Norman French, the western by the Chinese, with the two frontiers subsequently meeting on a line running roughly from New Orleans to Minneapolis through Kansas City and Omaha. It's an intriguing thought. Unfortunately, we must be resigned to the prosaic fact that the settlements of greatest importance for the future history of the United States were made chiefly by Englishmen, and in the seventeenth century.

Whether the institutions of the United States were inherited from Europe or newly devised to meet the novel conditions of the American wilderness is much disputed. I cannot decide that dispute; but certainly the first settlers had acquired in England certain ideas about politics, morality, and religion that must have had a decisive influence in determining the original form of the institutions they established in Virginia and New England and elsewhere. Among the ideas thus brought to America were the ideas then prevailing in England about schools and universities. In this respect the seventeenth century might be thought a bad time for the United States to begin its institutional career. At almost no other time, certainly not in the thirteenth century, could the first settlers have brought to these shores a set of ideas more restricted or less promising for the promotion of learning in the new world.

In seventeenth-century England, as in Europe generally, the prevailing idea was that schools and universities should teach nothing that would discredit the established religion or the authority of kings and magistrates. There were, it is true, some voices raised in protest. Francis Bacon protested, and with good effect, against an arid scholasticism and a slavish worship of ancient writers. Milton complained that professors "take from young men the use of reason by charms compounded of metaphysics, miracles and absurd scriptures"; the result of which was that at Cambridge he had misspent his own youth trying to digest "an asinine feast of sow-thistles and brambles." John Hall, himself a teacher at Cambridge, maintained that the advancement of learning was thwarted by incompetent teachers teaching outmoded subjects. But such voices were for the most part unheeded, and what they said was scarcely understood. Even Leib-

opposed academic freedom, and Hobbes thought the chief use of universities
was to teach subjects ~~obedience~~ *their duty* to the king. ~~Even Hartlib~~ So much was
this the prevailing idea that Hartlib, friend of Milton and Comenius and
himself a reformer, held it without being aware that he did so. "The readiest way," he said, "to reform church and commonwealth is to reform the
schools therein." No doubt; but he differed from Hobbes only in his conclusion. The premise of both was the same; namely, that teaching and learning, so far from being free, should be subordinated to political ends.

This totalitarian conception of schools and universities was brought
to the new world by the first settlers. The unexamined assumption that
made it acceptable to them was that learning is essentially dangerous; and
they were aware that, so far as schools and universities were concerned,
the danger could be met in one of two ways, either by not having any schools
or by preventing them from teaching any but familiar and accepted ideas.
William Berkeley, Governor of Virginia, preferred the first way. "Thank
God there are no ~~sch~~ free schools nor printing, and I hope we shall not
have these hundred years; for learning has brought disobedience and heresy
...into the world, and printing has divulged them....God keep us from both."
But generally speaking, in Virginia as well as in the other colonies, the
first settlers ~~were~~ less pessimistic or more courageous than Governor Berk-
eley, ~~They~~ preferred the second way. *They* believing that schools, under proper *ed the danger of learning could best be met by*
control, ~~would be very useful in meeting the danger inherent in learning~~
~~by~~ teaching the right things--the mechanic arts, the learned tongues, and
~~the~~ Christian philosophy.

In New England schools in this sense were more necessary than else-
where, because there the first settlers came, ~~as~~ *with the deliberate intention of establishing, as* Winthrop said, ~~"to estab-~~
~~lish~~ *a* due form of government both civil and ecclesiastical." What this
due form of government was, the leaders knew with great certainty, and took
care accordingly that their followers should all be like-minded men--the
"sifted wheat" for the new planting. Yet in spite of ~~their~~ *every* precautions
unlike-minded men were found among them. "Many untoward servants," says
William Bradford, "were brought over"; parents in England were glad to be
rid of children that "would necessarily follow their dissolute courses";
ship masters, making a business of transporting settlers, "to advance their

nitz opposed academic freedom, and Hobbes thought the chief use of universities was to teach subjects their duty to the king. So much was this the prevailing idea that even Hartlib, friend of Milton and Comenius, and himself a reformer, held it without being aware that he did so. "The readiest way," he said, "to reform church and commonwealth is to reform the schools therein." No doubt; but he differed from Hobbes only in his conclusion. The premise of both was the same; namely, that teaching and learning, so far from being free, should be subordinated to political ends.

This totalitarian conception of schools and universities was brought to the new world by the first settlers. The unexamined assumption that made it acceptable to them was that learning is essentially dangerous; and they were aware that, so far as schools and universities were concerned, the danger could be met in one of two ways, either by not having any schools or by preventing them from teaching any but familiar and accepted ideas. William Berkeley, Governor of Virginia, preferred the first way. "Thank God there are no free schools nor printing, and I hope we shall not have these hundred years; for learning has brought disobedience and heresy . . . into the world, and printing has divulged them. . . . God keep us from both." But generally speaking, in Virginia as well as in the other colonies, the first settlers, being either less pessimistic or more courageous than Governor Berkeley, preferred the second way. They believed that the danger inherent in learning could best be met by schools teaching, under proper control, the right things—the mechanic arts, the learned tongues, and Christian philosophy.

Schools in this sense were perhaps more necessary in New England than elsewhere, because there the first settlers came with the deliberate intention of establishing, as Winthrop said, "a due form of government both civil and ecclesiastical." What this due form of government was, the leaders knew with great certainty, and they took care accordingly that their followers should be like-minded men—the "sifted wheat" for the new planting. Yet in spite of every precaution unlike-minded men were found among them. "Many untoward servants," says William Bradford, "were brought over"; parents in England were glad to be rid of children that "would necessarily follow their dissolute courses"; ship masters, making a business of transporting settlers, "to advance their profit, cared not

profit, cared not who the persons were, so they had money to pay them";
he concludes on a plaintive note,
and so "the country became pestered with many unworthy persons, who, being come over, crept into one place or other." Even like-minded men were
believed in "soul liberty" and even went so far as to say that
apt to turn perverse. There was Roger Williams, who ~~thought~~ the land be-
soul liberty *There was*
longed to the Indians. ~~and believed in freedom of opinion;~~ that anciently
religious woman," Deborah Moodie, who cavilled at infant baptism; and Mis-
Of this profound truth the founders
tress Anne Hutchinson, who, "speaking from the mere motion of the spirit,"
~~General~~ criticised the ministers for preaching a covenant of works. Obviously,
~~Court of Mass~~
having no schools or printing would not meet the danger inherent in lear-
Day was well awake ning, since the Devil was always around to ~~teach the people~~ anyway. *lead the people into heresy*
Accordingly, noting the obvious fact that it is Accordingly, ~~it being~~ one of the chief projects of that old deluder
the General Court of Massachusetts Bay, finding that it was
satan to keep men from the knowledge of the Scriptures, as in former times
by keeping them in an unknown tongue, so in these latter times by persuad-
the General Court
ing from the use of tongues," ~~the General Court of Massachusetts Bay~~ provided for the establishment of a free school in each town in the province.
This was in 1642. In the same year Harvard College held its first Commence-
If we may go by the printed rules,
ment, graduating nine men. They had been instructed, intermittently, in
Logick, Mathematics, Physicks, Astronomy, Ethicks, Politicks, Rhetorick,
Moral Philosophy, Divinity, History, and the nature of plants; and, more
(Greek, and Latin) Hebrew)
constantly and thoroughly in those tongues in which the old deluder satan
had formerly kept the Scriptures hidden ~~Greek, Latin, Hebrew.~~ But the
chief aim, ~~without~~ apart from which all this learning was a vain thing,
was that every student should be "plainly instructed and earnestly pressed
to consider well the main end of his life and studies,...to know God and
Jesus Christ, which is eternal life." To this end every student was required "to exercise himself in reading the Scriptures twice a day"; and
"if in anything they doubt, they shall enquire as of their fellows, so
(in case of non-satisfaction) modestly of their Tutors." What the Tutors
the rules do
should do if in anything they doubted ~~is~~ not ~~said~~; but it is recorded that
in 1654 President Dunster, having doubted the doctrine of infant baptism,
was admonished on Lecture Day, and forced to resign his office.

Harvard College was founded to promote learning, but not *quite* in the
sense understood by Abelard, one of the founders of the University of Paris
twelfth
in the ~~thirteenth~~ century. Abelard said, "by doubting we are led to question

who the persons were, so they had money to pay them"; and so, the kindly governor ends on a plaintive note, "the country became pestered with many unworthy persons, who, being come over, crept into one place or other." Besides, even like-minded men were apt to turn perverse. There was Roger Williams, who believed in soul-liberty, and even went so far as to say that the land belonged to the Indians. There was that "anciently religious woman," Deborah Moodie, who cavilled at infant baptism; and Mistress Anne Hutchinson, who, "speaking from the mere motion of the spirit," criticized the ministers for preaching a covenant of works. Obviously, having no schools or printing would not meet the danger inherent in learning, since the Devil was always around to mislead the people anyway.

Of this profound truth the founders of Massachusetts Bay were well aware. Accordingly, the General Court enacted a law to the effect that, "it being one of the chief projects of that old deluder Satan to keep men from a knowledge of the Scriptures, as in former times by keeping them in an unknown tongue, so in these later times by persuading from the use of tongues," there should be established a free school in each town in the province. This was in 1642. In the same year Harvard College held its first Commencement, graduating nine men. If we may go by the printed rules of the College, these nine men had been instructed, intermittently and superficially, in Logic, Mathematics, Physics, Politics, Rhetoric, Moral Philosophy, Divinity, History, and the nature of plants; and, more constantly and thoroughly, in those tongues (Greek and Latin) in which the old deluder Satan wished to keep the Scriptures hidden. But the chief aim, apart from which all this learning was a vain thing, was that "every student should be plainly instructed and earnestly pressed to consider well the main end of his life and studies, . . . to know God and Jesus Christ, which is eternal life." To this end every student was required to "exercise himself in reading the Scriptures twice daily"; and "if in anything they doubt, they shall enquire as of their fellows, so (in case of non-satisfaction) modestly of their Tutors." What the tutors should do if in anything they doubted, the rules do not say; but it is recorded that in 1654 President Dunster, having doubted the doctrine of infant baptism, was admonished on Lecture Day, and forced to resign his office.

Harvard College was founded to promote learning, but not quite in the sense understood by Abelard, one of the founders of the University of Paris in the twelfth century. "By doubting," said Abelard, "we are led to

and by questioning we arrive at truth." At Harvard College, in the seventeenth century, doubt was evidently regarded as the chief obstacle to learning: there the rule was, by doubting we run into error, we arrive at truth
by (modestly enquiring) of the Tutors.

In spite of these precautions the splendid effort to keep the due
form of government pure and unspotted from the world was a failure. The
founders of Massachusetts Bay were intelligent and courageous men, but in
subtlety and resourcefulness they were after all no match for that old deluder satan. They were far less well

Until the eighteenth century Harvard College was rather a promise
For lack of funds than a performance. ~~there were no~~ *were few* tutor for the fifteen or twenty students to enquire modestly of, ~~until 1699,~~ *there was* and no professor *at all* until 1721. At
that time two other colleges were in existence--William and Mary, founded
in 1693, and the Collegiate College, a wandering academy that finally con-
sented, ~~about 1718,~~ *in 1716,* to settle down at New Haven, ~~and that was later, in 1745,~~ *to become, to be, in 1745,*
incorporated as Yale College *in 1745.* During the next twenty five years six other
colleges were founded--Princeton, the University of Pennsylvania, Kings
(Columbia) College, Brown, Rutgers, and Dartmouth. William and Mary, Yale,
and Princeton were modelled more or less closely upon Harvard. Kings College and the University of Pennsylvania, more especially the ~~latter were~~
latter, were, in intention at least, somewhat less restricted in their ~~pur-~~
~~poses and~~ course of study, ~~and of this something will be said presently.~~
~~But in general we may say that all of these colleges were founded for es-~~
~~sentially the same purpose--that it to say, to preserve and transmit the~~
~~learning that would safeguard what was thought to be the due form of gov-~~
~~ernment, both civil and ecclesiastical.~~
But in the eighteenth, no less than in the seventeenth century, colleges were
founded and supported by the ruling classes (a species of flexible, mixed
aristocracy composed of the families of wealth, education, and social
prestige who thought of themselves as "the better sort") to provide the
leaders of the community with a "liberal education"; and ~~they took it~~ *it was taken* for
granted that a liberal education would safeguard them against subversive
political ideas, and fortify their faith, if not
But in general it may be said that all of these colleges were established

questioning, and by questioning we arrive at truth." At Harvard College, in the seventeenth century, doubt was evidently regarded as the chief obstacle to learning. There the rule was: by doubting we run into error, we arrive at truth by enquiring, modestly, of the tutors.

Until the eighteenth century Harvard College was rather a promise than a performance. For lack of funds there were few tutors for the fifteen or twenty students to enquire modestly of; and there was no professor at all until 1721. At that time two other colleges were in existence—William and Mary, founded in 1693, and the Collegiat College, a kind of wandering academy that finally, in 1716, consented to settle down at New Haven, and that was incorporated, in 1745, as Yale College. During the next twenty-five years six other colleges were founded—Princeton, the University of Pennsylvania, King's (Columbia) College, Brown, Rutgers, and Dartmouth.

to preserve and transmit the learning that would maintain the due form
of government, both civil and ecclesiastical.

In the eighteenth century the form of government, even in New England, was rather less ecclesiastical than civil; but in the eighteenth no
less than in the seventeenth century, colleges were supported by the ruling classes (a flexible, mixed aristocracy, composed of the wealthy and
educated ~~classes~~ *people* who thought of themselves as "the better sort") to provide the leaders of the community with a liberal education; and it was tak-
en for granted that a liberal education would safeguard them against subversive ~~ideas~~ political ideas, and fortify their faith, if not in the tenets of any particular sect at least in what the prospectus of Kings College called "the Great Principles of Christianity and Morality, in which
all true Christians in each of the denominations are generally agreed."
Certainly nothing could have been ~~further~~ farther from the intention of
the founders of any of the colleges than that the most distinguished alumni of these centers of learning should become the leaders of a revolution
dedicated to the principle that all men are endowed by their Creator with
an inalienable right to overthrow any government, civil or ecclesiastical,
which did not in their opinion derive its authority from the consent of
the governed. Yet this *was* what happened; and if we ask where Jefferson, the
brace of Adamses and their confreres got these subversive ideas, the answer
is, in ~~great~~ part in college, by reading those works in the unknown tongues
in which, according to the founders of Massachusetts Bay, the old deluder
Satan had hidden the scriptures.

To establish centers of learning on the assumption that, properly
supervised, ~~they~~ no subversive ideas will be generated in them is to take
a great risk. The founders of the first American colleges took that risk.
They were intelligent and courageous men, but in subtlety and resourcefulness they were no match for ~~that~~ *the* old deluder ~~satan~~ whom they were out to
circumvent. ~~They were much less well aware than he was of the insidious~~
~~nature of doubt and the danger inherent in learning. They would have done~~
~~better, from their own point of view, to heed the warning of Governor~~
~~Berkeley, that learning brings disobedience and heresy into the world and~~
~~printing divulges them. When, therefore, they established colleges, and,~~

In the eighteenth century the due form of government had become rather more civil than ecclesiastical, and the colleges had in some measure responded to this change. But in the eighteenth no less than in the seventeenth century, the colleges were supported by the ruling classes (a flexible, mixed aristocracy, composed of the educated and wealthy families who thought of themselves as "the better sort") in order to provide the leaders of the community with a liberal education; and it was taken for granted that a liberal education would safeguard them against subversive political ideas, and fortify their faith, if not in the tenets of any particular sect, at least in what the Prospectus of King's College called "the Great Principles of Christianity and Morality in which all true Christians in each of the denominations are generally agreed." Certainly nothing was further from the intention of the founders of these institutions than that their most distinguished alumni should become the leaders of a revolution dedicated to the principle that all men are endowed by their Creator with an inalienable right to abolish any form of government, civil or ecclesiastical, which did not in their opinion derive its authority from the consent of the governed. Yet this is what came to pass; and if we ask where Jefferson, the brace of Adamses, and their confreres got these subversive ideas, the answer is that they got them in part in college, by reading works in those tongues in which, according to the founders of Massachusetts Bay, the old deluder Satan had hidden the Scriptures.

To establish centers of learning on the assumption that, properly supervised, no subversive ideas will be generated in them is to take a great risk. The founders of the first American colleges took that risk. They were intelligent and courageous men, but in subtilty and resourcefulness they were no match for the old deluder whom they were out to circumvent.

~~with a courage we can only admire, required as a condition of entrance~~
~~the ability to read~~ ~~extempore~~ ~~"Tully, or such-like classical Latine au-~~
~~thor," I suspect that the old deluder must have smiled in his hood, know-~~
~~ing that the due form of government both civil and ecclesiastical was as~~
~~good as done for.~~

Their
~~The~~ fatal error, I suspect, was to suppose that the old deluder
wished to keep men from a knowledge of the Scriptures, either by hiding
them in an unknown tongue or persuading from the use of tongues. Certain-
the old Deluder
ly ~~he~~ must have known that to read the Scriptures is to become acquainted
with various and sundry ideas, forms of government, idolatries, moralities, ~~and~~ with every species of pessimism and the most devastating doubt.
If he did indeed have anything to do with recording the Scriptures in an
unknown tongue, it must have been for another purpose than to keep them
hidden. His purpose must have been (this is only my private opinion) to
have the boys in Harvard, Yale, and Princeton exposed to Tully, and such-
so that
like classical authors, ~~where~~ they might become infected with the most ingenious ideas and plausible sophistries ever invented to bedevil the minds
of men and beguile them into disobedience and heresy.

That the old deluder had really anything to do with all this, I do
I can only ~~as a~~ refer you, as a careful historian should, to
not affirm as a fact; ~~I can only refer you, as a careful historian should,~~
an authentic ~~histori~~ official document, the Laws of Massachusetts Bay.
~~to an authentic historical document the laws of Massachusetts Bay.~~ But
it is a fact that Jefferson, the brace of Adamses and many other leaders
of the American Revolution attended Harvard, William and Mary, Yale,
the University of Pennsylvania,
Princeton, or King's College, and there learned to read and prize the classical authors. They read the Scriptures too, but they liked the pagan better than the Christian writers--preferring Demosthenes to Deuteronomy,
Cicero to Solomon and Saint Augustine, Plutarch and Livy to Eusebius or
Orosius. Reading the pagan authors, they found the content more interesting than the grammar, ~~and the content~~ no doubt because the content con-
history and
firmed them in the notion, already current in the eighteenth century, that
were both more interesting and
politics ~~was~~ more relevant than theology. The experience of ~~the~~ young
John Adams was more or less typical. Studying ~~for the ministry~~ in that
Harvard College once dominated by the Mathers, he ~~read the Scriptures but~~
the Scriptures *confessions,*
failed to find in ~~them~~ any precept "requiring...creeds, oaths, subscriptions,

Their fatal error, I suspect, was to suppose that the old deluder wished to keep men from a knowledge of the Scriptures, either by hiding them in an unknown tongue or by persuading from the use of tongues. Certainly he must have known that to read the Scriptures is to become acquainted with various and sundry ideas, forms of government, idolatries, moralities, and with every species of pessimism and the most devastating doubt. If he did indeed have anything to do with recording the Scriptures in an unknown tongue, it must have been for another purpose than to keep them hidden. His purpose must have been (this is only my private opinion) to have the boys of Harvard, Yale, and Princeton exposed to Tully, and such-like classical authors, so that they might become infected with the most ingenious ideas and plausible sophistries ever invented to bedevil the minds of men and beguile them into disobedience and heresy.

That the old deluder had really anything to do with all this I do not affirm as a fact: I only refer you, as a good historian should, to the authentic official documents. But it is a fact that Jefferson, the brace of Adamses, and many other leaders of the American Revolution attended one or other of the colleges and there learned to read and prize the classical authors. They read the Scriptures too, no doubt, but they seem to have liked the pagan better than the Christian writers—preferring Demosthenes to Deuteronomy; Cicero to Solomon and St. Augustine; Plutarch and Livy to Eusebius or Orosius. Reading the pagan authors, they found the content more interesting than the grammar, no doubt because the content confirmed them in the notion, already current in the eighteenth century, that history and politics were both more interesting and more relevant than theology. The experience of young John Adams was more or less typical. While studying in Harvard College he failed to find in the Scriptures any precept "requiring . . . creeds, confessions, oaths, subscriptions, and whole cart-loads of trumpery that we find religion en-

and whole cart-loads of trumpery that we find religion encumbered with in these days." Concluding, therefore, that "the design of Christianity was not to make...good mystery-mongers, but good men, good magistrates, and good subjects," he ~~renounced the ministry for~~ *felt drawn to* "that science by which mankind have raised themselves from the...state in which nature leaves ~~us~~ them, to the full enjoyment of the...blessings of the social union."

In ~~the~~ classical literature Adams and his confreres found an engaging, if not *an* entirely true account of what the social union was in ancient Greece and Rome, and took it as ~~a model~~ in some sense a model of what the social union should be. Reading ~~Tully and such like~~ *the* classical authors they learned to admire the ~~heroes of that time stoic and Roman~~ fortitude and civic virtues of the ~~heroes who defended~~ republican heroes of that time-- the Spartan ~~heroes who died at Thermopylae, the Athenians who stood with Spartan heroes~~ who died with Leonidas at ~~the pass~~ Thermopylae, the Athenians who stood at Marathon, ~~that~~ *the* Brutus who drove out the Tarquins, ~~the~~ Regulus ~~that~~ *who* returned to Carthage, and that other Brutus, noblest Roman of them all, who ~~in~~ from the pure and disinterested love of freedom, struck ~~Julius~~ Caesar down in the Senate house. Admiring the ancient republican heroes, it seemed to them that ~~freedom and enlightenment~~ the golden age of freedom and enlightenment ended when Caesar crossed the Rubicon, to be followed by a thousand years of despotism and superstition, ~~relieved only by the reigns of five good emperors.~~ *it seemed, so it seemed,* But in their own time the world was *obviously* emerging from this long dark age, the eternal struggle against tyranny was again the central issue, and in resisting the unwarranted measures of the British government, were they not themselves standing at Armageddon? What ~~then~~ better then could honest men do than to cultivate the ~~stoic fortitude~~ civic virtues ~~and stoic fortitude~~ of the ancient republican heroes, each in his own way becoming a latter day ~~Demosthenes~~ Brutus or Valerius Poplicola? ~~In 1774,~~ *John Adams,* elected a delegate to the first Continental Congress, ~~John~~ *seems to have* ~~Adams~~ had his eye on Demosthenes. "When Demosthenes (God forgive me for *recollecting* ~~recalling~~ his example) went ambassador from Athens to the other states of Greece to excite a confederacy against Philip, he did not go to propose a Non-Importation or Non-Consumption agreement!!!" Doubting ~~what was best~~ *whether even non-intercourse measures were sufficiently radical for a brave patriot,* ~~to do at the Continental Congress,~~ *it seems.* John Adams did not enquire modestly of cumbered with these days." Concluding, therefore, that "the design of Christianity was not to make . . . good mystery-mongers, but good men, good magistrates, and good subjects," he was drawn to "that science by which mankind have raised themselves from the . . . state in which nature leaves them, to the full enjoyment of the social union."

In classical literature Adams and his fellows found an engaging if not entirely true account of what the social union was in ancient Greece and Rome, and took it as in some sense a model of what the social union should be in modern times. Reading the classical authors they learned to admire the fortitude and civic virtues of the republican heroes of that time—the Spartans who died with Leonidas at Thermopylae, the Athenians who stood at Marathon, Brutus who drove out the Tarquins, Regulus who returned to Carthage, and that other Brutus, noblest Roman of them all, who from pure love of freedom struck Caesar down in the Senate house. Admiring the ancient republican heroes, it seemed to them that the golden age of freedom and enlightenment had ended when Caesar crossed the Rubicon, to be followed by a thousand years of despotism and superstition. But from this long Dark Age the world was in their own time emerging, the eternal struggle against tyranny was again the central issue, and in resisting the unwarranted measures of the British government were they not themselves standing at Armageddon? What better then could honest men do than to cultivate the civic virtues of the ancient republican heroes, each in his own way becoming a latter-day Valerius or Poplicola? John Adams, elected a delegate to the First Continental Congress, had his eye on Demosthenes. "When Demosthenes (God forgive me for recollecting his example) went ambassador from Athens to the other states of Greece, to excite a confederacy against Philip, he did not go to propose a Non-Importation or Non-Consumption agreement!!!" Doubting whether even non-intercourse measures, then regarded as radical, were radical enough for a true patriot, John Adams did not enquire modestly of the tutors. He *among others, and*

the tutors. He enquired, none too modestly, of Demosthenes.

So long as Adams and his compatriots were concerned only to ~~preserve~~ defend, against British legislation, the rights of British subjects, it was enough to rest their case on precedent, and fortify their courage by recalling the republican virtues of ~~ancient heroes, such as~~ Brutus and *and such like other republican ancient heroes.* Demosthenes. But resistance to British measures presently involved the colonies in war with the mother country, and war imposed upon them the hard necessity of declaring that the "colonies are and of right ought to be free and independent states." But by what right? The rights of British subjects, which were all they had hitherto claimed, ~~was~~ *were* not sufficient to justify rebellion. To justify rebellion, it was necessary for the revolutionary leaders to invoke a more inclusive principle than the rights of British subjects; and this more inclusive principle ~~could be most conveniently~~ *was* found, not in the traditional Christian story of man's origin and destiny, but in the ~~novel and~~ revolutionary doctrine of *the* natural ~~law and rights~~ *and imprescriptible rights of man.*

The American republic was thus founded on a revolutionary political philosophy, and the fact is of profound significance for the history of life and learning in the United States. Since the sixteenth century the advancement of learning had been a difficult business--carried on ~~for the most part~~ by a group of scholars mostly excluded from the universities and colleges because ~~their~~ *they accepted reason and natural law as premises in the search for knowledge, and* both their premises and their conclusions were *regarded as dangerous to morality and public authority, because they were hostile to the Christian* ~~offensive to the community.~~ But in the eighteenth century, for the first *story of man's* time since the Middle Ages, the principles ~~acceptable to the community as~~ *officially proclaimed as the origin and destiny.* ~~the~~ foundation of public authority and the good life were coming to be identified with the premises accepted by scholars as essential to the search for truth and the increase of knowledge. *Thus, as one may say,* Established political philosophy and current science made ~~one may say, as it were~~ a marriage of convenience: both accepted the doctrine of natural law as God's revelation to men; both were committed to the theory that the nature of man and the institutions best suited to him, so far from being divinely decreed and ~~dogmatically interpreted by~~ authoritatively guaranteed by church and state, could only be progressively

The American Republic was thus founded on a revolutionary ~~philosophy~~ political philosophy--a fact of profound significance for the history enquired, none too modestly, of Demosthenes.

So long as Adams and his compatriots were concerned only to defend, against British legislation, the rights of British subjects, it was enough to rest their case on precedent, and to fortify their courage by recalling the virtues of the ancient republican heroes. But resistance to British measures presently involved them in war with the mother country, and war imposed upon them the hard necessity of declaring that the colonies "are and of right ought to be free and independent states." But by what right? The rights of British subjects were not sufficient to justify rebellion. To justify rebellion it was necessary to invoke a more inclusive principle than the rights of British subjects; and this more inclusive principle was found, not in precedent, nor yet in the traditional Christian philosophy of man's origin and destiny, but in the revolutionary doctrine of the natural and impre-scriptible rights of man.

The American republic was thus founded on a revolutionary political philosophy—a fact of profound significance for the history of life and

of life and learning in the United States. Since the sixteenth century
the advancement of learning in Europe had been a difficult business. It
was carried on by a group of scholars who were mostly excluded from the
colleges and universities, and too often proscribed by governments, because the doctrine of natural law and right reason accepted by them as
the first premise in the search for truth ~~and the increase of knowledge~~
was, *ostensibly* at War with the Christian story of man's origin and destiny which
the community accepted as essential to the maintenance of morality and
public authority. But in the eighteenth century, for the first time since
the Middle Ages, the principles officially proclaimed as the foundation
of civil government and the good life were coming to be identified, and in
the American and French revolutions were identified, with the premises accepted by scholars as essential to the advancement of knowledge.

In the eighteenth century, therefore, as one may say, established
political philosophy and current science made a marriage of convenience.
Both accepted the doctrine of natural law as God's revelation to men;
both were committed to the theory that the nature of man and the institutions best suited to his happiness and welfare, so far from being divinely revealed in sacred scripture to be authoritatively interpreted and
~~enforced,~~ enforced by church and state, could only be progressively discovered by man himself through the free application of reason to experience and available knowledge. In so far as political philosophy was translated into practise, the constituted authorities were *therefore* obligated to guarantee freedom of opinion, and to regard colleges and universities as centers for the increase of knowledge ~~as well as~~ *rather than* for the preservation and
transmission of accepted ideas. In such institutions the rule would presumably be that if pupils or professors in anything doubted, they would
consult, modestly or otherwise (that was their affair), not the tutors,
not the clergy or the magistrates, or even "the Great Principles of Christianity and Morality in which all true Christians ~~are...~~are generally
agreed," but the best right reason available to intelligent and informed
men.

It is well known, however, that
~~Marriages of convenience are rarely, of course, entirely happy.~~

learning in the United States. Since the sixteenth century the advancement of learning in Europe had been a difficult business. It was carried on for the most part by scholars who were often excluded from the colleges and universities, and often proscribed by governments, because the doctrine of natural law and right reason which they accepted as the first premise in the search for truth was ostensibly at war with the Christian story of man's origin and destiny which the community accepted as the necessary foundation of morality and public authority. But in the eighteenth century, for the first time since the Middle Ages, the principles officially affirmed as the foundation of civil government were coming to be identified, and in the American and French Revolutions were identified, with the premises accepted by scholars as essential to the advancement of knowledge.

In the eighteenth century, therefore, as one may say, established political philosophy and current science made a marriage of convenience. Both accepted the doctrine of natural law as God's revelation to men; both were committed to the theory that the nature of man and the institutions best suited to his happiness and welfare, so far from being divinely revealed in sacred scripture, and to be authoritatively interpreted and enforced by church and state, could only be progressively discovered by man himself through the free application of reason to experience and available knowledge. In so far as political philosophy was translated into practice, the constituted authorities were, therefore, obligated to guarantee freedom of opinion, and to regard colleges and universities as centers for the increase of knowledge rather than merely for the preservation and transmission of familiar and accepted ideas. In such institutions the rule would then presumably be that if pupils or professors in anything doubted they would consult, modestly or not (that was their affair), not the tutors, not the clergy or the magistrates, or even the "Great Principles of Christianity and Morality in which all true Christians are generally agreed," but the best right reason available to intelligent men.

The doctrine of natural rights, however useful for justifying political separation from Great Britain, did not all at once displace the average man's faith in the Christian story of man's origin and destiny.

The liberal ideas of the eighteenth century were more prevalent among the alumni than among the administrators of colleges, and I need not say that the traditional ideas and settled habits of professors were not all at once transformed by the principles enshrined in the Declaration of Independence. Nevertheless, before and during the American Revolution we can note the beginning of such a transformation--especially in connection with Kings College, the University of Pennsylvania, and William and Mary College.

It is well known that marriages of convenience are rarely entirely happy. The doctrine of natural *law* and right reason, however useful for effecting a separation from Great Britain, did little to displace in the minds of average men the traditional faith in the Christian story of man's origin and destiny. For this reason the liberal ideas of the Enlightenment were less generally accepted, and their implications for education less well understood among the mass of the people than among the ~~leaders~~ political leaders, among the administrators than among the distinguished alumni of the colleges; and I need not say that the ingrained ideas and settled habits of professors were not all at once transformed by the doctrines enshrined in the Declaration of Independence. Nevertheless, before and during the American Revolution we can note the beginning of such a transformation--the beginning of those social and intellectual influences that were, during the course of another century, to bring about ~~a radical~~ a liberal and democratic transformation of higher education in the United States.

Marriages of convenience, as is well known, are rarely entirely happy. The doctrine of natural law and right reason, however useful for effecting a separation from Great Britain, did little to dislodge from the minds of average men faith in the traditional Christian story of man's origin and destiny. For this reason the liberal ideas of the Enlightenment were less generally accepted, and their implications for education less well understood, among the mass of the people than among the political leaders, among the administrators than among the distinguished alumni of the colleges; and I need scarcely say that ingrained habits and settled ideas of professors were not all at once transformed by the doctrines enshrined in the Declaration of Independence. Nevertheless, before and during the American Revolution we can note the beginnings of such a transformation —the beginnings of those social and intellectual influences that were, during the course of another century, to bring about a liberal and democratic transformation of higher education in the United States.

3. Biographical Notes

HENRY ADAMS (1838–1918), the great-grandson of one president and the grandson of another, was the friend and associate of most of the important statesmen of his time. He taught at Harvard, traveled widely, wrote novels (*Democracy*, 1880), history (*The United States During the Administrations of Jefferson and Madison*, 1889–1891), and biography (*John Randolph*, 1882). But he is best known for a pair of books difficult to classify: in *Mont-Saint-Michel and Chartres* (1904) he interprets the unified culture of the Middle Ages, and in *The Education of Henry Adams* (1907) he uses his own life—which he regarded as a series of failures—as an index to the centerless diversity of the modern world.

THEODORE BAIRD (1901–   ) was born in Warren, Ohio, and educated at Hobart College and Harvard. He has taught English literature at Western Reserve, Union College, and Amherst College, where he has been since 1927.

JAMES BALDWIN (1924–   ) is a talented young Negro writer. He has written two novels—*Go Tell It on the Mountain* (1953) and *Giovanni's Room* (1956); a collection of his essays was published in 1955 under the title *Notes of a Native Son*. Residence abroad has given Mr. Baldwin special opportunities to reflect on his central theme, the complex attitudes which underlie the relations of Negroes and whites.

JACQUES BARZUN (1907–   ) was born in France and came to the United States in 1919; he became a U.S. citizen in 1933. He was educated in a French *lycée* and at Columbia, where he has taught history since 1927 and where he is now Dean of the Graduate School. He has written on a wide variety of topics in the history and culture of nineteenth- and twentieth-century Europe and America. His books include *Teacher in America* (1945), *Berlioz and the Romantic Century* (1950), *The Pleasures of Music* (1951), and *God's Country and Mine* (1954).

676

MARSTON BATES (1906–   ) was born in Grand Rapids and educated at the University of Florida and at Harvard. A specialist in tropical zoölogy and ecology, Mr. Bates was a member of the staff of the International Health Division of the Rockefeller Foundation from 1937 to 1952; since 1952 he has been professor of zoölogy at the University of Michigan. In addition to *The Nature of Natural History*, Professor Bates is the author of *The Natural History of Mosquitoes* (1949), *Where Winter Never Comes: a Study of Man and Nature in the Tropics* (1952), and *The Prevalence of People* (1955).

CARL BECKER (1873–1945) was born in Iowa and educated at Cornell College and the University of Wisconsin. After teaching at Pennsylvania State College, Dartmouth, Kansas, and Minnesota, he became professor of history at Cornell University in 1917 and taught there until his death. Among his many lively and influential books on modern history and modern society are *The Heavenly City of the Eighteenth Century Philosophers* (1932), *Modern Democracy* (1941), and *How New Will the Better World Be?* (1943).

JAMES BOSWELL (1740–1795) is best known as the friend and companion of Samuel Johnson, with whom Boswell became acquainted in 1763 and whose life Boswell devoted himself to recording. The *Life of Johnson* (1791) is one of the greatest works of biography ever written. But Boswell did many other things besides his life of Johnson. The son of a Scottish judge, Boswell practiced law in Edinburgh and London, traveled widely (he wrote *An Account of Corsica*, 1768), and kept a remarkable series of diaries in which he recorded with disarming frankness the varied events of his life. These journals, discovered in recent years, are now being edited and published. Among the volumes that have appeared are *Boswell in London* and *Boswell on the Grand Tour*.

JACOB BRONOWSKI (1908–   ) has been since 1950 Director of the Coal Research Establishment of the British National Coal Board. Educated at Jesus College, Cambridge, he was Senior Lecturer at University College, Hull, from 1934 to 1942 and occupied a series of responsible research and administrative posts in the British Government from 1942 to 1950. Mr. Bronowski is especially qualified to write on the relations between poetry and science: he is both a scientist and an essayist and playwright (*The Face of Violence*, 1950); he has written an excellent popular book on science (*The Commonsense of Science*, 1951) and also two works of literary criticism (*The Poet's Defence*, 1939; *William Blake: A Man Without a Mask*, 1944).

HENRY SEIDEL CANBY (1878–   ) did his undergraduate and graduate work at Yale, where he received his Ph.D. in 1905 and where he taught English literature from 1900 to 1922. He was a founder and first editor of the *Saturday Review of Literature*, and he has been chairman of the board of judges of the Book-of-the-Month Club since 1926. Among Mr. Canby's many books are *Classic Americans* (1931), *The Age of Confidence* (1934), *Walt Whitman* (1943), and *American Memoir* (1947), an autobiography.

LORD DAVID CECIL (1902–   ) is Goldsmiths' Professor of English Literature in Oxford University and Fellow of New College. His writings have mainly concerned the culture and literature of the eighteenth and nineteenth centuries. They include a *Life of Cowper* (1929), *Early Victorian Novelists* (1934), *Two Quiet Lives* (1948), and *Lord Melbourne* (1954).

MARCHETTE CHUTE (1909–   ) has written three sound and interesting popular biographies of English writers—*Geoffrey Chaucer of England* (1946), *Shakespeare of London* (1949), and *Ben Jonson of Westminster* (1953). She was born in Minnesota and educated at the State University.

ROBERT M. COATES (1897–   ) is a graduate of Yale. He has contributed stories and art criticism for many years to the *New Yorker*, and has written a varied group of books, including *The Eater of Darkness* and *Wisteria Cottage*, novels, and *The Outlaw Years*, a history of land piracy on the Natchez Trace.

ALISTAIR COOKE (1908–   ) has been *The Manchester Guardian's* American correspondent since 1948 and has become one of the chief interpreters of the United States to the people of England. Now an American citizen, Mr. Cooke was born in England and educated at Cambridge University. He came to the United States in 1938 as commentator on American affairs for the B.B.C. *One Man's America* is a collection of his broadcast talks. He has also written a book on Douglas Fairbanks and a perceptive account of the Hiss case, *A Generation on Trial: the U.S.A. vs Alger Hiss* (1950).

ANTHONY ASHLEY COOPER, first Earl of Shaftesbury (1621–1683), was one of the most powerful figures in English politics in the seventeenth century. He at first took the king's side in the civil war, then attached himself to the supporters of the parliament, opposed the rule of Oliver Cromwell, and took a leading part in the restoration of Charles II to the throne. He held high offices, including that of lord Chancellor, but became a leader in the opposition to the king, a fomenter of the "popish plot," and a supporter of the claims to the throne of the Duke of Monmouth, Charles II's illegitimate son. He was committed to the Tower, charged and acquitted of treason, and, after planning a revolt against the government, fled to Holland, where he died.

Morton J. Cronin (1917–   ) teaches English at Los Angeles State College. He was educated at Wayne State University and the University of Minnesota; he has taught at Wayne, Oregon State College, and Minnesota. His special interest is in American literature and culture.

Loren Eiseley (1907–   ) is chairman of the Department of Anthropology at the University of Pennsylvania. He was born in Nebraska, did his undergraduate work at the University of Nebraska, and took his Ph.D. at Pennsylvania. Before joining the Pennsylvania faculty he taught at Kansas and Oberlin. Professor Eiseley is especially interested in physical anthropology and archeology. He has been a member of several anthropological expeditions to the American Southwest and is curator of the Museum of Early Man at the University of Pennsylvania. Several of his essays have been collected in *The Immense Journey* (1957); in 1958 he published a study of *Darwin's Century: Evolution and the Men Who Discovered It*.

Bergen Evans (1904–   ) is Professor of English at Northwestern University. He was educated at Miami University, Oxford, and Harvard. He has written a scholarly treatise on Robert Burton and two lively works on popular beliefs and superstitions—*The Natural History of Nonsense* and *The Spoor of Spooks*. He is well known as the Master of Ceremonies on such TV quiz shows as "The Last Word." In writing *The Dictionary of Modern American Usage* Professor Evans was joined by his sister Cornelia, who is Writing Consultant to the Department of Health, Education, and Welfare.

Otis Ferguson (1908–1943) enlisted in the Navy at the age of seventeen and served for four years before entering Clark University, where he edited the senior yearbook and won a *New Republic* college writing contest. He began free-lancing in 1933 and joined the staff of the *New Republic* in 1934. Almost all of Ferguson's work was published in the *New*

Republic, in the form of reviews and essays on books, movies, and music. At the outbreak of World War II, Ferguson entered the merchant marine and was lost at sea in 1943 when the cargo vessel on which he served was bombed at Salerno.

E. M. FORSTER (1879–   ) is one of the most distinguished of contemporary English novelists. He studied at King's College, Cambridge, where he became the friend of G. Lowes Dickinson, whose *Life* Forster wrote in 1934. Forster's novels include *A Room with a View* (1908), *Howard's End* (1910), and *A Passage to India* (1924), which is generally regarded as his greatest work. He has also written *Aspects of the Novel* (1927), two volumes of short stories, and critical essays—*Abinger Harvest* (1926) and *Two Cheers for Democracy* (1952).

BENJAMIN FRANKLIN (1706–1790) was perhaps as close to a universal genius as this country has produced. Scientist, diplomat, propagandist, statesman, journalist, publisher, inventor, humorist, and philanthropist— these are only a few of the roles in which this great man distinguished himself and benefited the world. *His Autobiography* and *Poor Richard's Almanack* are his best-known works, but they do not begin to reflect the many facets of his character and career.

DOUGLAS SOUTHALL FREEMAN (1886–1953), historian of the Confederacy, was born in Lynchburg, Virginia, and educated at Richmond College and the Johns Hopkins University, from which he received his Ph.D. in 1908. He was editor of the Richmond *News-Leader* from 1915 to 1949, and a prominent participant in civic and national affairs. His great biography of *R. E. Lee* won the Pulitzer Prize for history in 1934; his three volumes on *Lee's Lieutenants* appeared in 1942–1944; and the five volumes of his *George Washington* from 1948 to 1952.

EDWARD GIBBON (1737–1794) prepared for his lifework by living and studying abroad (he said that Westminster School and Oxford did him little good) and by serving in the Hampshire militia. His *History of the Decline and Fall of the Roman Empire*, published in six volumes between 1776 and 1788, is one of the great monuments of the human mind; it is also a wonderfully readable book. Gibbon's *Memoirs* (1796) record the events of his life with wit and urbanity.

FRANK GIBNEY (1924–   ) has been *Time* and *Life* correspondent in Japan since 1949. During World War II he served in Japan as a Navy lieutenant engaged in prisoner-of-war interrogation. His *Five Gentlemen of Japan* is therefore based on extended and varied observation of the country and its people.

L. H. GIPSON (1880–   ) was born in Colorado and graduated from the University of Idaho. A Rhodes scholar and Yale Ph.D., Professor Gipson was professor of history at Lehigh University from 1924 to 1946. His special interest is American colonial history, and his major work is his six-volume history of "The British Empire before the American Revolution."

GRAHAM GREENE (1904–   ) is an English novelist. After graduation from Oxford he was a subeditor of the London *Times* from 1926 to 1930 and wrote film reviews for the *Spectator* from 1935 to 1939. He was literary editor of the *Spectator* from 1940 to 1941 and served in the Foreign Office during World War II. His novels include *Brighton Rock*, *This Gun for Hire*, *Confidential Agent*, *The Ministry of Fear*, *The End of the Affair*, and *The Quiet American*. He has written two travel books, *Journey Without Maps*, recording a trip to Africa, and *Another Mexico*. *The Lost Childhood* is a collection of reviews and essays; several of his novels and stories have been made into movies, notably *The Fallen Idol* and *The Third Man*.

LEARNED HAND (1872–   ) is one of America's most distinguished judges. Born in Albany, New York, he prepared for the law at Harvard. After admission to the bar in 1897, he practiced until 1909, when he was appointed U.S. district judge of the Southern District of New York. In 1924 he was appointed judge of the U.S. Circuit Court, 2d Circuit, where he served until his retirement in 1951. *The Spirit of Liberty* is a collection of Justice Hand's speeches and essays.

NATHANIEL HAWTHORNE (1804–1864) is of course best known for such stories of American life as *The Scarlet Letter* and *The House of the Seven Gables*. From 1853 to 1857 Hawthorne served as American consul at Liverpool; his *English Note-Books* record his observations of the life around him during this period. *Our Old Home*, written after his return to America, incorporates much of the material of the *Note-Books* into a connected analysis of England and the English.

ERIC HOFFER (1902–   ) was born in New York, the son of a German cabinetmaker. When he was seven he became almost totally blind; his sight returned when he was sixteen. In 1922 he went to Los Angeles and for the next twenty years worked at a variety of jobs—in a box factory, as a gold prospector, in a labor camp, and at fruit picking, lettuce picking, and other sorts of migratory labor. He became a longshoreman in San Francisco in 1943. Hoffer began to write in the 1930's and in recent years has published numerous articles which reflect his wide reading and his penetrating observations of the workingman. His book *The True Believer* (1952) is a study of the psychology of mass movements in society.

WILLIAM DEAN HOWELLS (1837–1920) was one of the chief American men of letters of his time. A prolific writer of novels, short stories, plays, and criticism, Howells exerted a great influence, both through his own work and through his position as editor of the *Atlantic Monthly* from 1871 to 1881, on the rise of a new generation of realistic social novelists. Among his best-known novels are *A Modern Instance* (1882), *The Rise of Silas Lapham* (1885), and *A Hazard of New Fortunes* (1890). Howells was American consul in Venice from 1861 to 1865; *Venetian Life* is one of the by-products of that experience.

WASHINGTON IRVING (1783–1859), though trained as a lawyer, devoted his life primarily to literature. His *Knickerbocker's History of New York* (1809) established his fame, which was augmented by *The Sketch-Book* (1819–1820), containing "Rip Van Winkle" and other tales. Irving served for a time as diplomatic attaché in Spain, where he gathered material for a life of Columbus and for *The Alhambra*. Returning to America, he made a trip to the West, which he described in a lively book, *A Tour on the Prairies* (1835). The *Life of Washington*, written near the end of Irving's life, was the first scholarly study of Washington.

HENRY JAMES (1843–1916) was born in New York City, the son of Henry James, Sr., writer on social and religious subjects, and younger brother of William James, the philosopher. James lived most of his adult life in England, save for occasional visits to America, and became a British subject in 1915 to express his sympathy for the Allied cause in World War I. His many novels and short stories—of which *Daisy Miller* (1879), *The Portrait of a Lady* (1881), *What Maisie Knew* (1897), and *The Ambassadors* (1903) are representative—deal with social themes, many turning on the contact between American and European culture and values. James also wrote plays, travel books, a large amount of literary criticism, and several autobiographical volumes.

WILLIAM JAMES (1842–1910), brother of Henry James, was the founder of pragmatism and the foremost American philosopher of his time. Educated at Harvard, where he received his M.D. in 1869, James began his teaching career as an instructor in physiology at Harvard in 1872. His famous *Principles of Psychology* was published in 1890; a succession of influential works followed: *The Will to Believe* (1897), *The Varieties of Religious Experience* (1902), *Pragmatism* (1907), *A Pluralistic Universe* (1909). James exerted great influence on modern American philosophy and on American culture generally.

SIR JAMES JEANS (1877–1946) was an English physicist and astronomer. In addition to being a first-rate scientist, Jeans had an unusual gift for scientific popularization. Such books as *The Universe Around Us, The Mysterious Universe*, and *The New Background of Science* helped bridge the widening gap between modern developments in scientific theory and the knowledge and interests of laymen.

ALFRED KAZIN (1915–   ) is a New Yorker; he graduated from City College and received an M.A. from Columbia. He was literary editor of the *New Republic* in 1942–1943 and has taught at City College, Queens College, The New School, University of Minnesota, and Black Mountain College. He is now professor of English at Amherst College. His *On Native Grounds* is a study of American literature; *A Walker in the City* is an autobiography.

GEORGE KENNAN (1904–   ) was one of America's most distinguished Foreign Service officers. Mr. Kennan was born in Milwaukee; after graduating from Princeton, he entered the Foreign Service in 1927. He held diplomatic appointments in most of the capitals of Europe, was a member of the State Department Policy Planning staff, and served in 1952 as U.S. Ambassador to the Soviet Union. Now retired from the Foreign Service, he holds an appointment at the Institute for Advanced Study. He has published many articles on foreign affairs; his lectures on *American Diplomacy, 1900–1950* were published in 1951, and those on *The Realities of American Foreign Policy* in 1954. The first two volumes of his history of *Soviet-American Relations, 1917–1920* appeared in 1956–1958, and his book *Russia, the Atom and the West* in 1958.

LOUIS KRONENBERGER (1904–   ) was born in Cincinnati and studied at the University of Cincinnati. He has been editor with the publishing houses of Boni & Liveright and Alfred A. Knopf and a member of the staff of *Fortune* magazine, but his principal activity has been as a critic of the drama. Since 1938 he has been drama critic for *Time*, and he has lectured on dramatic literature at Columbia since 1950. He has written two novels, *The Grand Manner* (1929) and *Grand Right and Left* (1952); a book on eighteenth-century culture, *Kings and Desperate Men* (1942); a critical study of G. B. Shaw; and a book on English comedy, *The Thread of Laughter* (1952). *Company Manners* (1954) is an analysis of American social customs. A collection of Mr. Kronenberger's essays appeared in 1955 as *The Republic of Letters*.

ALDO LEOPOLD (1886–1948) was a forester and conservationist. Born in Iowa and educated at Yale, he occupied various positions in the U.S. Forest Service from 1909 to 1931 and was Professor of Wild Life Management at the University of Wisconsin beginning in 1933.

WILMARTH S. LEWIS (1895–   ) is a graduate of Yale, and one of the country's greatest book-collectors; he has described his experiences as a collector in *Collector's Progress*, 1951. One of his special interests is the life and works of Horace Walpole, the most prolific letter writer of the eighteenth century. Mr. Lewis is editor of the *Yale Edition of Horace Walpole's Correspondence*, of which twenty-one volumes were published between 1937 and 1955.

JAMES RUSSELL LOWELL (1819–1891), essayist, poet, and critic, succeeded Longfellow as professor of Romance languages at Harvard. His powerful and conservative influence on literary taste was exerted through his work on the *Atlantic Monthly*, of which he was the first editor, and on the *North American Review*, as well as through such writings as *The Biglow Papers*, *Among My Books*, and *My Study Windows*.

THOMAS BABINGTON MACAULAY (1800–1859) was educated at Trinity College, Cambridge. After serving in Parliament from 1830 to 1834, he went to India as a member of the supreme council from 1834 to 1838. He continued his political career, as M.P., as secretary of war, and as paymaster of the armed forces. But he is best known for his historical, critical, and biographical writings. He contributed to the *Encyclopaedia Britannica* and to the principal magazines of his day. His greatest work, *The History of England*, covering the period from the reign of James II to the death of William III (roughly 1685 to 1702), appeared in five volumes between 1849 and 1861.

DWIGHT MACDONALD (1906–   ) is one of our most independent and vigorous commentators on politics, literature, and popular culture. After graduation from Yale, he was for several years an editorial writer for

Fortune magazine, edited and wrote much of the brilliant periodical *Politics*, and, more recently, has been a regular contributor of reviews and profiles to the *New Yorker*. His books include *Henry Wallace, the Man and the Myth* (1948), *The Ford Foundation* (1956), and *Memoirs of a Revolutionist* (1957).

R. M. MacIver (1882–   ) was born in Scotland and educated at Edinburgh and Oxford. He is one of the most eminent political philosophers of our time and has taught at Aberdeen, Toronto, and Columbia, where he was Lieber Professor of Political Philosophy and Sociology from 1929 to 1950. Among his books are *Society—Its Structure and Changes* (1931), *Leviathan and the People* (1939), *The Web of Government* (1947), and *Democracy and the Economic Challenge* (1952).

James Madison (1751–1836), Virginian, was educated at the College of New Jersey (Princeton). He was a member of the Continental Congress, served in the Virginia House of Delegates, and took a leading part in the plans for the Constitutional Convention and in its deliberations. With Alexander Hamilton and John Jay he wrote *The Federalist* papers (1787–1788), eighty-five essays printed in New York newspapers and designed to persuade the voters of New York to accept the new Constitution. Later Madison served in Congress and was secretary of state under Jefferson, whom he succeeded in the presidency in 1809.

John Fletcher Moulton, Baron Moulton (1844–1921), was a British lawyer and judge. Educated at St. John's College, Cambridge, he was called to the bar in 1874. He was appointed a lord justice of appeal of 1906. During World War I he was director general of explosive supplies in the Ministry of Munitions.

Henry Myers (1906–1955) was born in Newburgh, New York, and educated at Niagara University and Cornell, where he took his Ph.D. in philosophy. He taught in the Department of English at Cornell from 1935 until his death; he lectured also at Salzburg, the University of London, and Stanford. Mr. Myers wrote widely on the theory of the drama and on American literature; in 1945 he published an inquiry into the meaning of American democracy called *Are Men Equal? Tragedy: a View of Life* (1956) is a posthumous collection of his essays.

J. Robert Oppenheimer (1904–   ) has been Director of the Institute for Advanced Study at Princeton, New Jersey, since 1947. He has played a leading role in the atomic revolution of our time. He received his undergraduate degree from Harvard and his Ph.D. in physics from Göttingen. He taught physics at California and at California Institute of Technology, and was Director of the Los Alamos Scientific Laboratory from 1943 to 1945. In this position, and as a member of the general advisory committee to the Atomic Energy Commission from 1946 to 1952, Dr. Oppenheimer had much to do with the development of the atomic bomb and with the formulation of our policy on atomic weapons.

GEORGE ORWELL is the pseudonym of Eric Blair (1903–1950), one of the most independent and original minds of our time. Orwell was born in India and, after studying at Eton, returned to Asia to serve from 1922 to 1927 in the Indian Imperial Police in Burma. This experience is the basis not only for "Shooting an Elephant" but for his novel *Burmese Days* (1934). Returning to Europe, he wrote novels (*Down and Out in Paris and London* is a record of the experiences of these years) and social comment (*The Road to Wigan Pier*) and fought in the Loyalist army in the Spanish civil war (his *Homage to Catalonia* is one of the most sensitive appraisals of that strange conflict). His brilliant satire on dictatorship, *Animal Farm*, and his terrible vision of the future in *Nineteen Eighty-four* fixed his reputation as a social commentator, and his *Dickens, Dali, and Others* and *Shooting an Elephant* demonstrated his remarkable power as a critic and essayist.

HENRY BAMFORD PARKES (1904–   ) was born in England, went to Oxford, and came to the United States in 1927, doing his graduate work in history at the University of Michigan. Since 1930 he has taught history at New York University. Besides his interpretative study, *The American Experience*, he has written *Recent America*, *The Pragmatic Test*, and *The United States of America*.

FRANCIS PARKMAN (1823–1893) even before he graduated from Harvard had formulated his plan to study the history of the American frontier. *The Oregon Trail* (1849) records his strenuous trip west to gain firsthand experience of Indian life. In spite of extremely frail health and defective eyesight Parkman executed his great design of a history of the conflict between England and France for mastery of the North American continent. The many volumes of this work, which has won for Parkman the reputation of America's greatest historian, appeared between 1865 and 1892; they include *The Jesuits in North America*, *The Old Regime in Canada*, and *Montcalm and Wolfe*.

FLETCHER PRATT (1897–1956) studied at Hobart College and the University of Paris. His many books, predominantly on historical, military, and naval subjects, include *Eleven Generals* (1949), *Preble's Boys* (1950), *E. M. Stanton* (1953), and *Battles that Changed History* (1956).

GEOFFREY SCOTT (1885–1929) was born in England and educated at Oxford. He is best known for his book *The Architecture of Humanism* (1914), dealing chiefly with the architecture of the Renaissance in Italy, and for his edition of the first six volumes of James Boswell's *Private Papers from Malahide Castle* (1928–1932).

LYTTON STRACHEY (1880–1932) was a member of a distinguished English family of civil servants and writers. After graduation from Cambridge he became a leading member of the "Bloomsbury group" of writers and intellectuals that included Virginia Woolf, Clive Bell, and E. M. Forster. His biographical writings—notably *Eminent Victorians*, *Queen Victoria*, and *Elizabeth and Essex*—were tremendously successful, setting a new style of treating the great figures of the past with wit and satire.

JONATHAN SWIFT (1667–1745) was one of the world's greatest satirists. Born and educated in Dublin, he was for many years Dean of St. Patrick's in that city and throughout his life was heavily occupied with church affairs, politics, and Ireland. *Gulliver's Travels* (1726) is the work for which he is best known to modern readers, but his voluminous works include many other essays and poems that display the brilliant writing and somber view of life so prominent in *A Modest Proposal.*

HENRY DAVID THOREAU (1817–1862) was a lifelong rebel against the restraints imposed by society and government on the free life of the individual. He refused to pay his poll tax, went to prison, and wrote a great *Essay on Civil Disobedience.* He isolated himself at Walden Pond as an experiment in doing without things: *Walden* records that experiment. He wrote vigorously on behalf of John Brown. Nature was for Thoreau the great philosophical constant and source of value; his *Journals* and such books as *A Week on the Concord and Merrimack Rivers* and *The Maine Woods* record his philosophizing observations of nature.

JAMES THURBER (1894–   ) is one of America's greatest essayists and cartoonists. After studying at Ohio State, working as a State Department code clerk, and reporting for newspapers, he joined the *New Yorker* in 1926. Most of his inimitable drawings and his humorously serious essays have appeared in that magazine. Mr. Thurber has written many books; they are all good. *The Thurber Carnival* is a selection from books published up to 1945, including cartoons from *The Seal in the Bedroom* and *Men, Women and Dogs*, and prose from *Let Your Mind Alone, My Life and Hard Times*, and *Fables for Our Time*. Among Thurber's books of the last ten years are *The Beast in Me and Other Animals, The Thurber Album, Thurber Country*, and *Alarms and Diversions*.

ALEXIS DE TOCQUEVILLE (1805–1859), French historian and government official, visited the United States in 1831–1832 to study the American penal system. Out of his observations on this visit came his great *De la Démocratie en Amérique* (1835; supplementary volumes 1840; American edition 1838). Translated into many languages and continuously referred to since its publication, Tocqueville's book is generally regarded as the best early analysis of American government and institutions and as one of the best works on this country ever written. Tocqueville also wrote a history of the French Revolution, left unfinished at his death.

ANTHONY TROLLOPE (1815–1882) was one of the most prolific and popular English novelists of the nineteenth century. Among his more than forty novels are *Barchester Towers, Orley Farm, Phineas Finn*, and *The Prime Minister*. Trollope traveled in Africa, Australia and New Zealand, and Iceland as well as in America. He was the second of his family to write a book about the United States. His mother, Frances Trollope, came to America in 1827 and established a department store in Cincinnati; the store failed and Mrs. Trollope returned to England in 1831, without money, but with materials for her *Domestic Manners of the Americans*, whose criticisms of American society evoked a stream of protest from this country after its publication in 1832. In addition to his novels and travel books, Trollope wrote an interesting *Autobiography* (1883).

MARK TWAIN is the pseudonym of Samuel Langhorne Clemens (1835–1910), who was born in Missouri, the son of a Virginian who had gone west to make his fortune. Clemens was apprenticed to a printer, worked as a newspaperman, and from 1857 to the Civil War was a Mississippi River steamboat pilot. After the brief military experience described in "The Private History of a Campaign That Failed" he went to Nevada and later to San Francisco, working for newspapers. His first considerable success was achieved with the story about "The Celebrated Frog of Calaveras County" (1865); his position as one of America's greatest writers was firmly established in a long series of works, of which the best— *Tom Sawyer, Life on the Mississippi*, and *Huckleberry Finn*—are based on the experiences of his youth.

Moses Coit Tyler (1835–1900) was Professor of English at the University of Michigan from 1867 to 1881 and Professor of American History at Cornell from 1881 until his death. His fame rests upon two pioneering and still valuable studies of the history of American literature—*History of American Literature 1607–1765* (1878) and *The Literary History of the American Revolution, 1763–1783* (1897).

Rebecca West (1892–   ), English woman of letters, was born Isabel Fairfield and took her pseudonym from the name of the heroine of Ibsen's *Rosmersholm.* She has written criticism (*Henry James*, 1916; *The Stranger Necessity*, 1928; *The Court and the Castle*, 1957); fiction (*The Return of the Soldier*, 1918; *The Thinking Reed*, 1936); a widely acclaimed travel book, *Black Lamb and Grey Falcon* (1942), recording a trip she and her husband took through Yugoslavia in 1937; and, recently, political biography and analysis (*The Meaning of Treason*, 1947; *A Train of Powder*, 1955).

E. B. White (1899–   ) graduated from Cornell in 1921 and after a brief period as a newspaperman began to contribute essays and poems to the *New Yorker*, with which he has been continuously associated. From 1938 to 1943 he wrote a monthly department called "One Man's Meat" for *Harper's Magazine* (collected in book form in 1942 and 1944). White's witty and gentle but penetrating reflections on life, expressed in a distinguished prose style, are to be found in *Every Day Is Saturday*, *Quo Vadimus, or the Case for the Bicycle*, and *The Second Tree from the Corner*. He has also written two books of poems and two books for children, young and old, *Stuart Little* and *Charlotte's Web*.

Thornton Wilder (1897–   ), novelist and playwright, graduated from Yale and received an M.A. from Princeton. He has lectured on literature at the University of Chicago and at Harvard. Among his novels are *The Bridge of San Luis Rey*, which won the Pulitzer Prize in 1927, *Heaven's My Destination*, and *The Ides of March*. His best-known plays are *Our Town* and *The Skin of Our Teeth*.

Philip Wylie (1902–   ) studied at Princeton. In his varied career as a writer he has worked on the *New Yorker*, written for Paramount and M-G-M, and been an editor for Farrar & Rinehart, publishers. He has written many books and articles, including *Finnley Wren, A Generation of Vipers*, and *An Essay on Morals*.

Index of Authors and Titles

Keast, William R   *ed.*
    The province of prose, edited by William R. Keast and Robert E. Streeter. 2d ed. New York, Harper [1959]

    692 p. 25 cm.

    1. English essays. 2. American essays.   I. Streeter, Robert E., joint ed. II. Title.

PR1363.K4   1959   824.082   58–59886 ‡

Library of Congress